P9-AGA-009

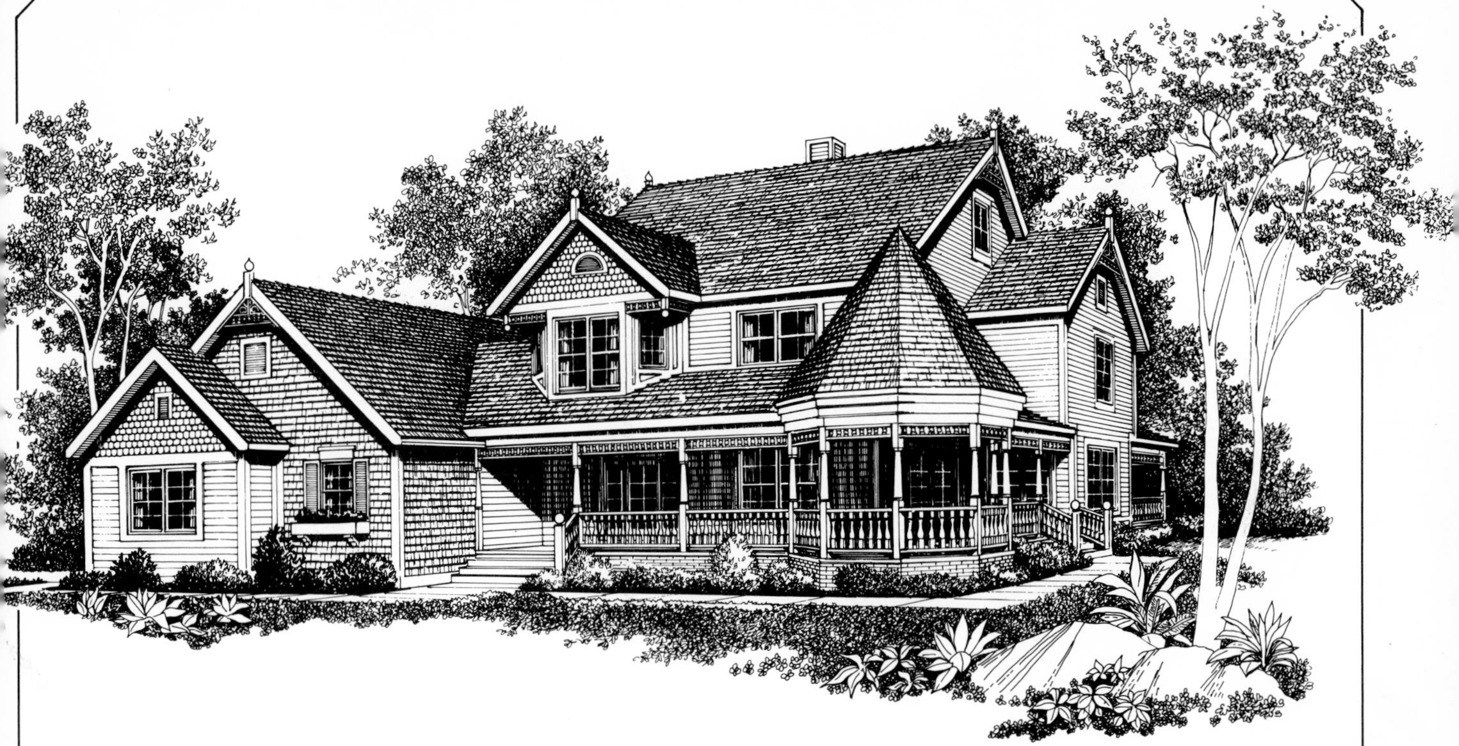

The Essential Guide To

TRADITIONAL HOMES

A Treasury of Classic Homes

- Sizes for Every Budget
- Up-To-Date Floor Plans & Modern Amenities
- Colonials, Georgians, Tudors, Victorians and many more

Table Of Contents

Published by Home Planners, Inc.
Editorial and Corporate Offices:
3275 West Ina Road, Suite 110
Tucson, Arizona 85741

Distribution Center:
29333 Lorie Lane
Wixom, Michigan 48393

Charles W. Talcott, Chairman
Rickard D. Bailey, President and Publisher
Cindy J. Coatsworth, Publications Manager
Beth Rhoades, Editor
Paul D. Fitzgerald, Book Designer

First Printing, January 1993
10 9 8 7 6 5 4 3 2 1

Printed in the United States of America

Library of Congress Catalog Card Number: 92-074616

Softcover ISBN: 1-881955-03-6
Hardcover ISBN: 1-881955-05-2

Photo Credits

On the Cover:
Front: Top and Center: Andrew D. Lautman (Design X2662, also on page 11 and Design X3309, also on pages 4 and 304).
Front: Bottom: Nick Kelsh (Design X2855, also on page 9).
Back: Andrew D. Lautman (Design X3309, also on page 4).

Pages 4 and 304: Andrew D. Lautman; Design X3309, Kathy & Mike Kalustian, owners.
Page 5: Carl Socolow; Design X2774, the home of John & Jane Deardorff.
Page 6: Laszlo Regos; Design X2683, Kellet & Saylor Builders.
Page 7: Andrew D. Lautman; Design X2889, the home of George Westmoreland.
Page 8: Jessie Walker; Design X2356.
Page 9: Nick Kelsh; Design X2855, the Elliot residence.
Page 10: Laszlo Regos; Design X2921, the home of Charles & Catherine Talcott.
Page 11: Andrew D. Lautman; Design X2662, the home of Teri Riess.
Page 12: Bill Kumph; Design X2520, the home of Kenneth & Linda Sutton.
Page 13: Laszlo Regos; Design X2563, the home of Perry & Heidi Pentiuk.

Traditional Design

Traditional homes cover a broad spectrum of styles and characteristics. Classic examples run from practical cottages to elaborate Victorians and stately Georgians. The common thread in Traditional style is a history going back to the first American settlers and beyond. The first arrivals in the New World brought architectural traditions from England, France and the Germanic states.

Most Traditional styles are derived from the English, including simple Medieval houses, Colonial, Tudor, Georgian, Cape Cod and salt box styling. Although these styles seem to vary greatly, most have certain characteristics in common, such as high-pitched roofs, large chimneys, leaded windows and masonry siding. Design X2101, on page 73, is a fine example of the English Medieval house built by 17th-Century English colonists. A common feature in the Middle Ages was the second-floor overhang.

The late 1880s brought to America the Tudor style, developed in England during the reign of the House of Tudor. Half-timbering, massive chimneys, Gothic windows, multiple exterior cladding materials and steeply pitched gables are the most discernible features of Tudor design. The sense of security and wealth inherent in Tudor design is at home from coast to coast. Examples of Tudor design can be found on pages 8, 9, 257-272, 274 and 275.

Victorian styles in a variety of versions arrived in the late 19th Century. The most frequently seen are the Queen Anne versions—two-story houses with detailed, asymmetrical facades. Characteristics common to all Victorian houses are wrap-around porches, round or octagonal wooden towers, finials at the highest points, tall chimneys, spindlework or "gingerbread" and an abundance of windows. Victorian designs appear on pages 4 and 241-256.

A special section of historical homes on pages 225-240 includes enough detail to turn almost anyone into an enthusiast of Early American architecture. This collection provides references to homes of historical significance located throughout the country.

The most renowned home in the United States, the White House, is of Georgian descent. Georgian mansions are known by their formal symmetry, substantial size, massive chimneys, bracketed cornices, central door with a pediment above and simple porches. Grand Georgian houses built of brick flourished in Williamsburg, Virginia in the 18th Century. Updated Georgian designs can be found on pages 6, 7 and 193-224.

Early Colonial houses were small boxes, usually only one room deep, supported by posts and beams. While much larger in size, most modern Colonial designs are not far removed from the basic box. Like other early designs, they include large fireplaces, as well as an overhanging upper story, casement windows, clapboards (horizontal wood siding), and heavy, utilitarian doors. Often the kitchen was a lean-to addition in the back of the home—the distinguishing mark of a salt box design. Pages 33-64 contain contemporary recreations of Colonial and salt box designs.

The Cape Cod cottage began as a simple shelter with a thoughtful design: easy to build and planned for expansion. These practical considerations made Cape Cod the most popular style in America during the early 20th Century. Cape Cod houses typically began as a basic box, one story high, with a central entry, white siding, shutters and a prominent chimney. Modern examples have grown to 1½-stories high and a less boxy shape. Pages 33-64 provide examples of Cape Cod designs of all sizes.

A long architectural history and a wide variety of design elements have been incorporated into the modern-day version of French architecture. Although similar to Georgian style in many ways, the hipped roofs of various slopes make French design easily identifiable. The Mansard roof is a two-pitched hipped version developed by the 17th-Century French architect Francois Mansart. Other style points include a symmetrical facade, brick exterior, quoins, arched windows, dormers and dentils—decorations along the cornice. Look for French designs on pages 98, 99, and 190-192.

The traditional style that seems to stand out as truly "American" is the farmhouse. Early farmhouses often resembled what many call the Dutch farmhouse, although the design is more likely derived from the Flemish. Design X2680 on page 23 is a good example of a Flemish farmhouse with a bell-shaped gambrel roof and a posted porch. The Germans, who often built in stone and brick, provided their own farmhouse interpretations, such as Design X3502 on page 27. Traditional farmhouses are simple, livable designs that commonly appear in two-story versions—all wood, with fireplaces, country kitchens and a covered front porch. See pages 5 and 17-32 for farmhouse designs of many types.

While various in their style and history, the designs in this book are all classic examples of traditional architecture. In addition to the sense of security and solid value attached to traditional style, these home plans have been designed with the livable floor plans and modern amenities demanded by today's homeowner.

Design X3309

First Floor: 1,375 square feet
Second Floor: 1,016 square feet
Total: 2,391 square feet

● Covered porches, front and back, are a fine preview to the livable nature of this Victorian. Living areas are defined in a family room with fireplace, formal living and dining rooms, and a kitchen with breakfast room. An ample laundry room, garage with storage area, and powder room round out the first floor. Three second floor bedrooms are joined by a study and two full baths.

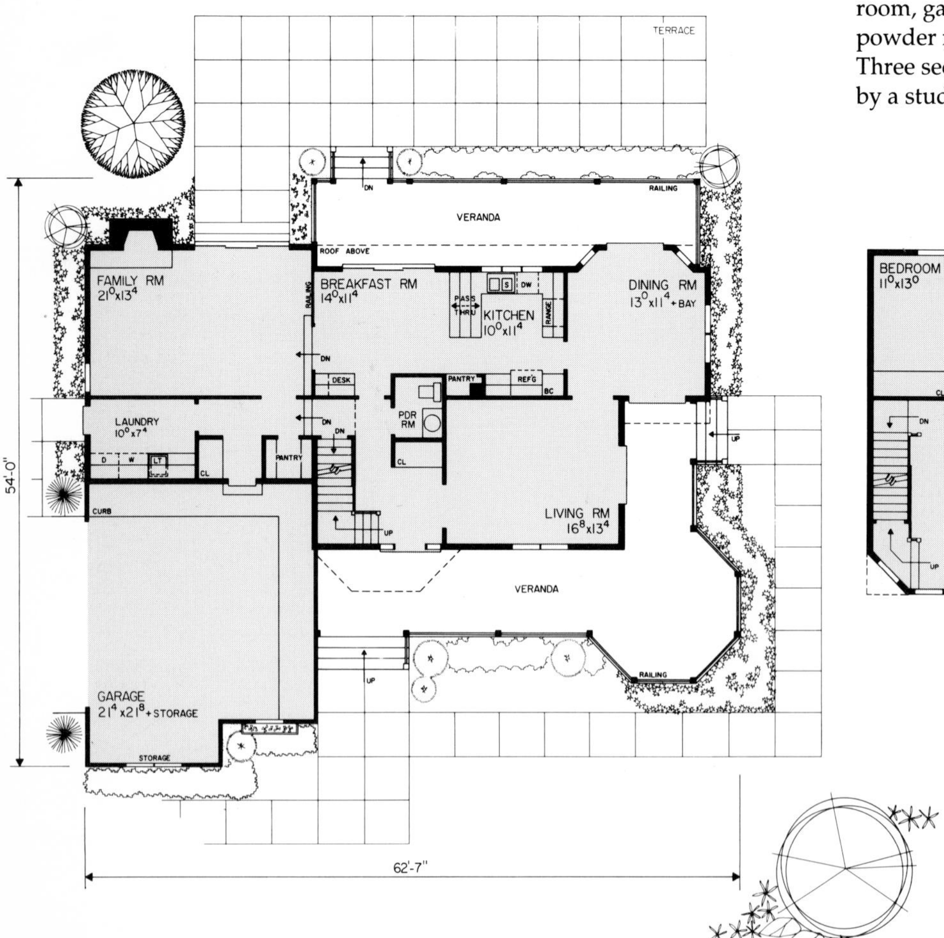

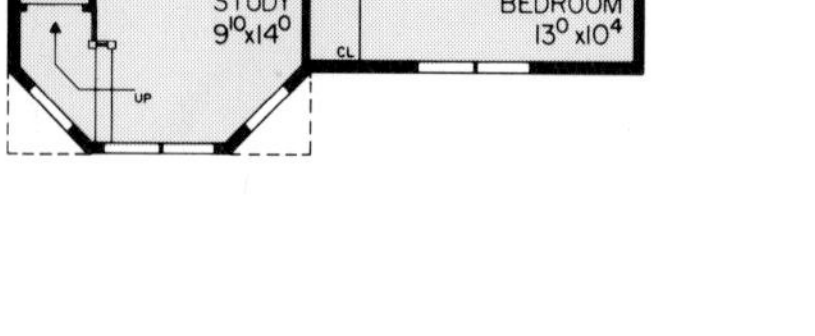

TERRACE
VERANDA
RAILING
ROOF ABOVE
FAMILY RM 21^{0}x13^{4}
BREAKFAST RM 14^{0}x11^{4}
KITCHEN 10^{0}x11^{4}
PASS THRU
DW
RANGE
DINING RM 13^{0}x11^{4}+BAY
DESK
PANTRY
REF'G
BC
LAUNDRY 10^{0}x7^{4}
D W LT
CL
PANTRY
PDR RM
CL
DN
UP
LIVING RM 16^{8}x13^{4}
CURB
VERANDA
RAILING
GARAGE 21^{4}x21^{8}+STORAGE
STORAGE
54'-0"
62'-7"

BEDROOM 11^{0}x13^{0}
SEAT
BATH
MASTER BEDROOM 13^{0}x13^{0}
WHIRLPOOL
BATH
WALK-IN CLOSET
CL
LIN
CL
DN
CL
STUDY 9^{10}x14^{0}
BEDROOM 13^{0}x10^{4}
CL
UP

Design X2774

First Floor: 1,370 square feet
Second Floor: 969 square feet
Total: 2,339 square feet

Custom Alterations? See page 301 for customizing this plan to your specifications.

● This design has something for the whole family. There is the quiet corner living room, an efficient U-shaped kitchen with pass-through to the beamed-ceiling breakfast room, sliding glass doors to the rear terrace, and a service entrance with laundry and pantry. The basement can be finished at a later time for expanded space. Upstairs are four bedrooms including a master suite with private bath.

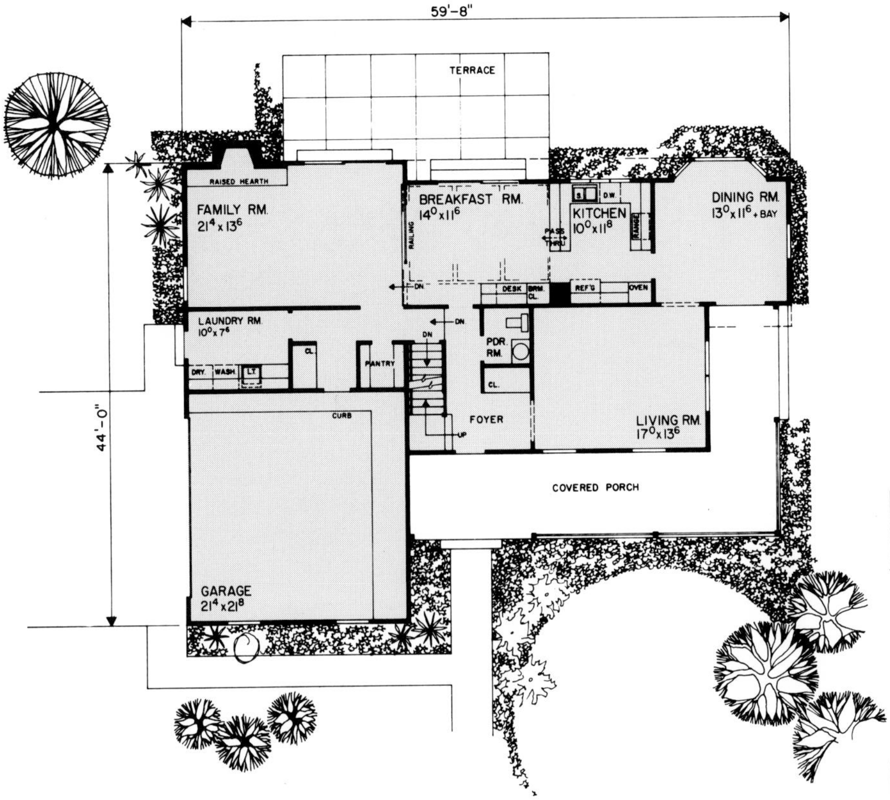

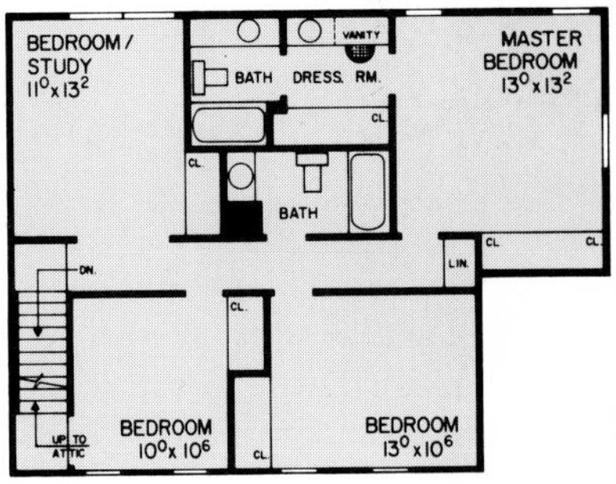

59'-8"
TERRACE
RAISED HEARTH
FAMILY RM. $21^4 \times 13^6$
BREAKFAST RM. $14^0 \times 11^6$
KITCHEN $10^0 \times 11^8$
DINING RM. $13^0 \times 11^6$ + BAY
LAUNDRY RM. $10^0 \times 7^6$
PANTRY
PDR. RM.
FOYER
LIVING RM. $17^0 \times 13^6$
COVERED PORCH
GARAGE $21^4 \times 21^8$
44'-0"

BEDROOM / STUDY $11^0 \times 13^2$
BATH
DRESS. RM.
MASTER BEDROOM $13^0 \times 13^2$
BATH
BEDROOM $10^0 \times 10^6$
BEDROOM $13^0 \times 10^6$

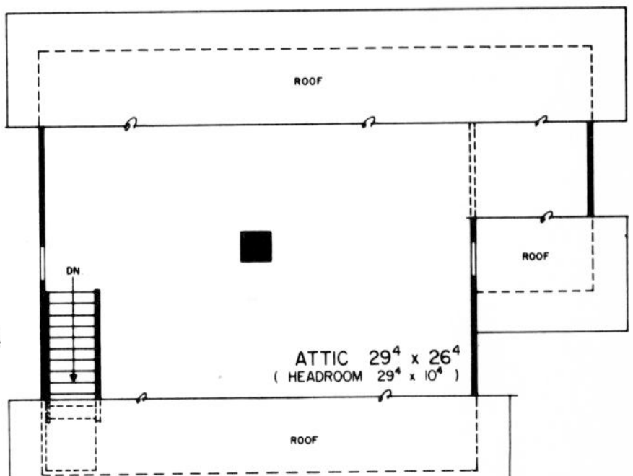

ROOF
ATTIC $29^4 \times 26^4$ (HEADROOM $29^4 \times 10^4$)
ROOF

Design X2683 First Floor: 2,126 square feet: 1,882 square feet; Total: 4,008 square feet

L **D**

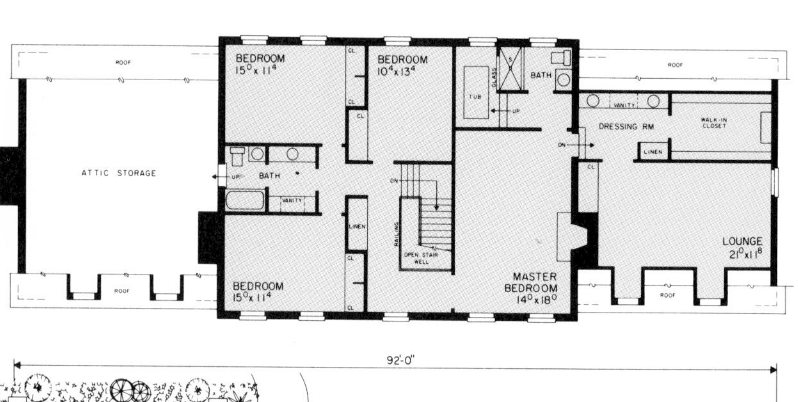

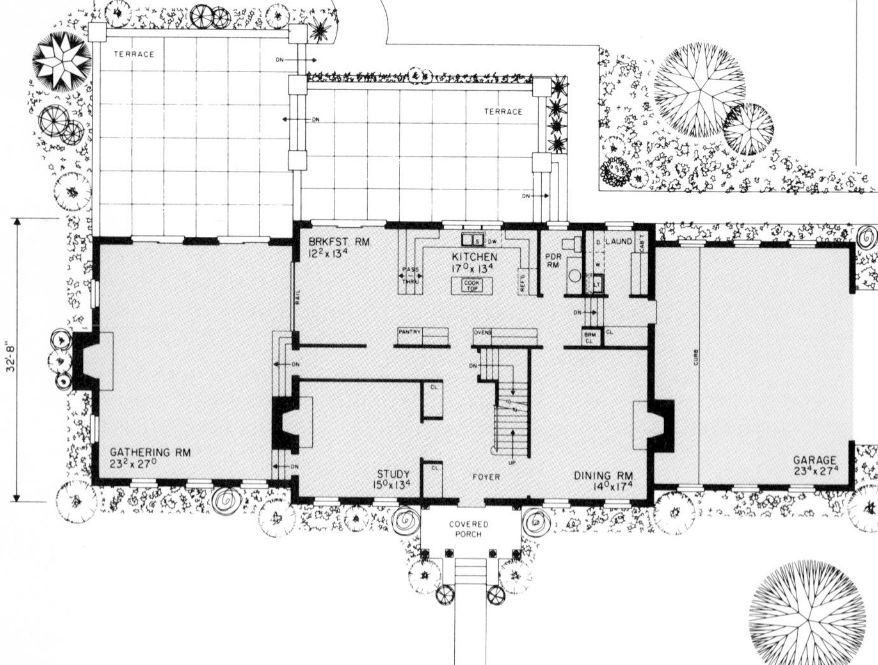

● This historical Georgian home has its roots in the 18th-Century. Dignified symmetry is a hallmark of both front and rear elevations. The full two-story center section is delightfully complimented by the 1½-story wings. Interior livability has been planned to serve today's active family. The elegant gathering room, three steps down from the rest of the house, has ample space for entertaining on a grand scale. It fills an entire wing and is dead-ended so that traffic does not pass through it. Guests and family alike will enjoy the two rooms flanking the foyer, the study and formal dining room. Each of these rooms will have a fireplace as its highlight. The breakfast room, kitchen, powder room and laundry are arranged for maximum efficiency. This area will always have that desired light and airy atmosphere with the sliding glass door and the triple window over the kitchen sink. The second floor houses the family bedrooms. Take special note of the spacious master bedroom suite. It has a deluxe bath, fireplace and sunken lounge with dressing room and walk-in closet. Surely an area to be appreciated.

Design X2889

First Floor: 2,529 square feet
Second Floor: 1,872 square feet
Total: 4,401 square feet

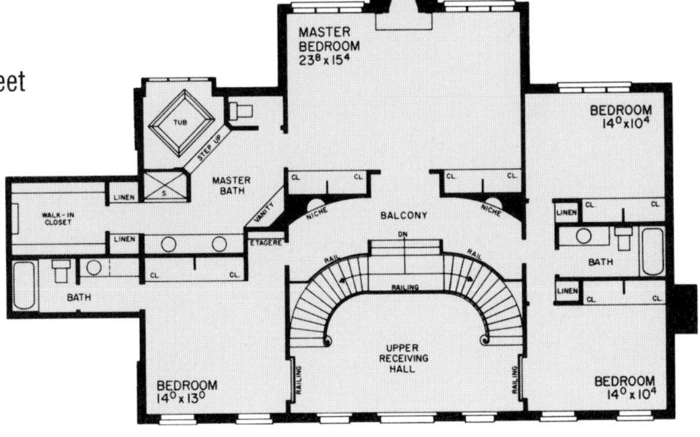

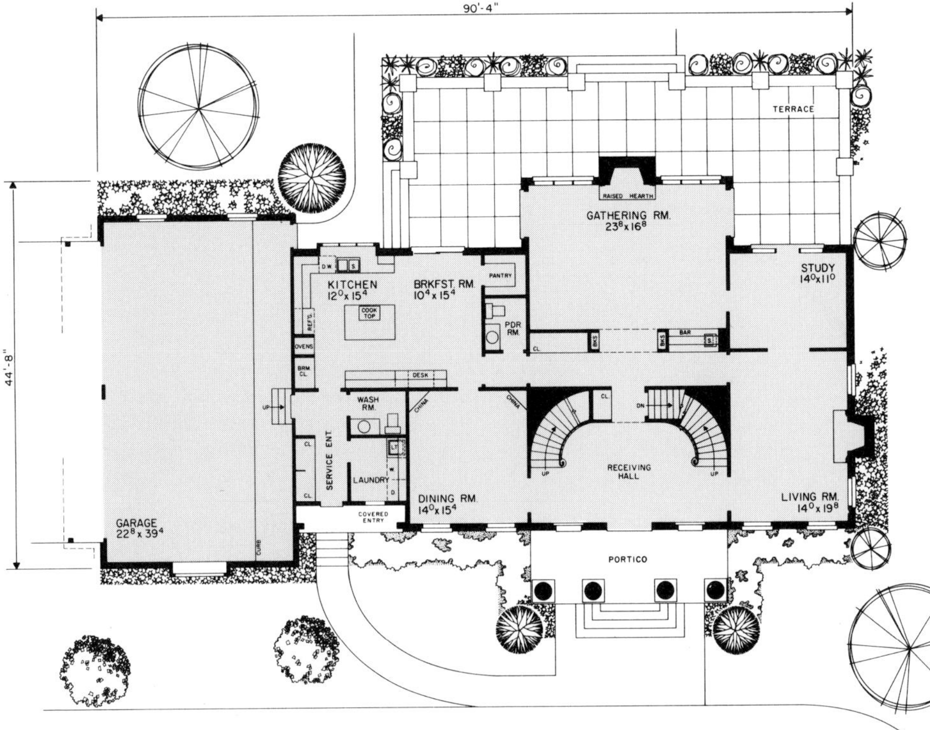

● This is truly classical Georgian design at its best. Some of the exterior highlights of this two-story include the pediment gable with cornice work and dentils, the beautifully proportioned columns, the front door detailing and the window treatment. These are just some of the features which make this design so unique and appealing. Behind the facade of this design is an equally elegant interior. Imagine greeting your guests in the large receiving hall. It is graced by two curving staircases and opens to the formal living and dining rooms. Beyond the living room is the study. It has access to the rear terrace. Those large, informal occasions for family get-togethers or entertaining will be enjoyed in the spacious gathering room. It has a centered fireplace flanked by windows on each side, access to the terrace and a wet bar. The work center is efficient: the kitchen with island cook top, breakfast room, washroom, laundry and service entrance. The second floor also is outstanding. Three family bedrooms and two full baths are joined by the feature filled master suite. If you like this basic floor plan but prefer a French exterior, see Design X2543.

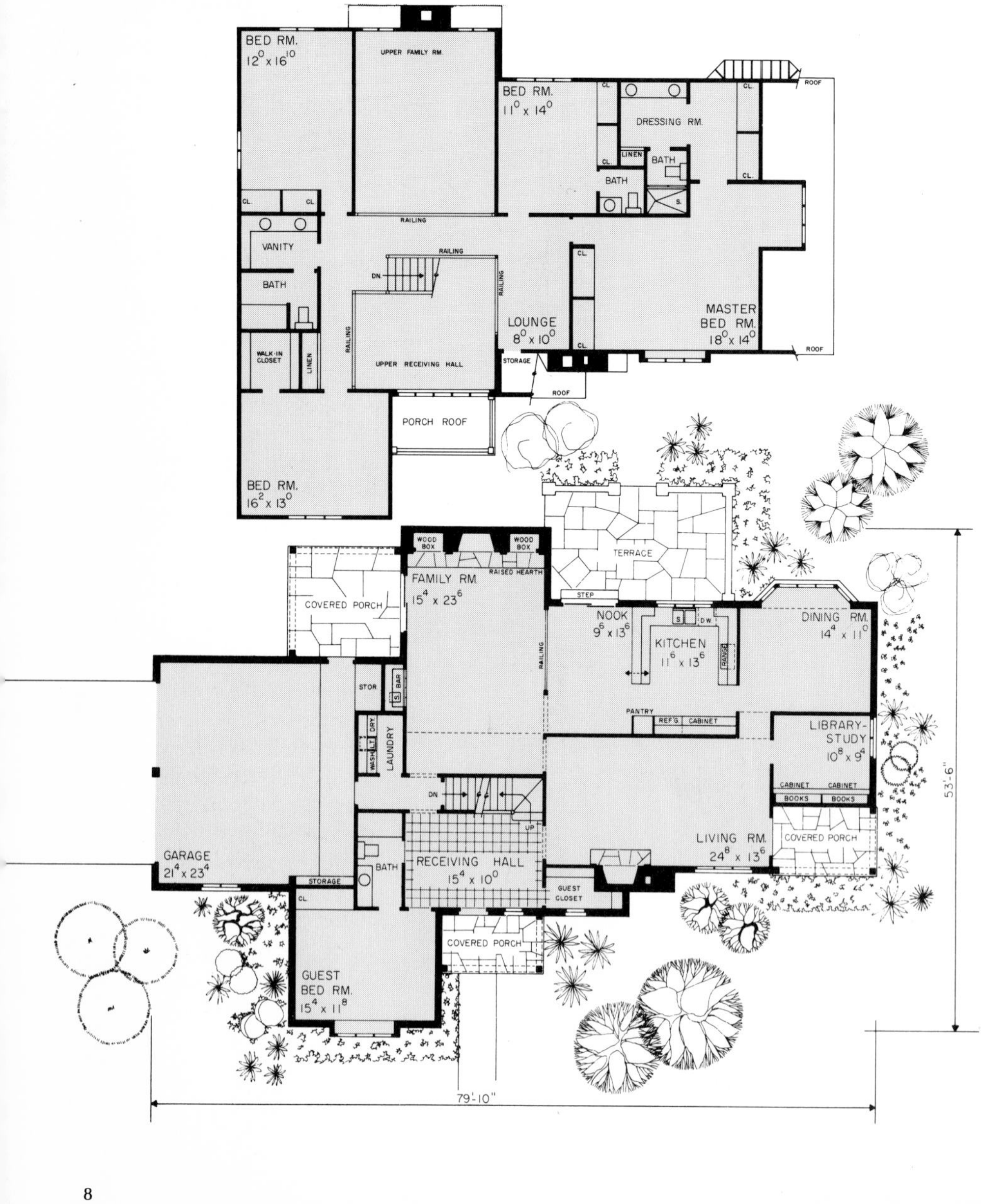

BED RM. $12^{0} \times 16^{10}$
UPPER FAMILY RM.
BED RM. $11^{0} \times 14^{0}$
DRESSING RM.
LINEN
BATH
BATH
CL.
CL.
CL.
CL.
ROOF
RAILING
VANITY
BATH
RAILING
DN
RAILING
LOUNGE $8^{0} \times 10^{0}$
MASTER BED RM. $18^{0} \times 14^{0}$
WALK-IN CLOSET
LINEN
RAILING
UPPER RECEIVING HALL
STORAGE
CL.
ROOF
ROOF
PORCH ROOF
BED RM. $16^{2} \times 13^{0}$
WOOD BOX
WOOD BOX
RAISED HEARTH
TERRACE
COVERED PORCH
FAMILY RM $15^{4} \times 23^{6}$
STEP
NOOK $9^{6} \times 13^{6}$
S. DW
KITCHEN $11^{6} \times 13^{6}$
RANGE
DINING RM. $14^{4} \times 11^{0}$
RAILING
STOR
BAR
PANTRY
REF'G. CABINET
LIBRARY-STUDY $10^{8} \times 9^{4}$
WASH
DRY
LAUNDRY
CABINET CABINET
BOOKS BOOKS
DN
UP
COVERED PORCH
LIVING RM. $24^{8} \times 13^{6}$
GARAGE $21^{4} \times 23^{4}$
BATH
RECEIVING HALL $15^{4} \times 10^{0}$
STORAGE
GUEST CLOSET
CL.
COVERED PORCH
GUEST BED RM. $15^{4} \times 11^{8}$
53'-6"
79'-10"

Design X2356

First Floor: 1,969 square feet
Second Floor: 1,702 square feet
Total: 3,671 square feet
L D

● Here is truly an exquisite Tudor adaptation. The exterior, with its interesting roof lines, window treatment, stately chimney and its appealing use of brick and stucco, could hardly be more dramatic. Inside, the drama really begins to unfold as one envisions his family's living patterns. The delightfully large receiving hall has a two story ceiling and controls the flexible traffic patterns. The living and dining rooms, with the library nearby, will cater to the formal living pursuits. The guest room offers another haven for the enjoyment of peace and quiet. Observe the adjacent full bath. Just inside the entrance from the garage is the laundry room. For the family's informal activities there are the interactions of the family room - covered porch - nook - kitchen zone. Notice the raised hearth fireplace, the wood boxes, the sliding glass doors, built-in bar and the kitchen pass-thru. Adding to the charm of the family room is its high ceiling. From the second floor hall one can look down and observe the activities below.

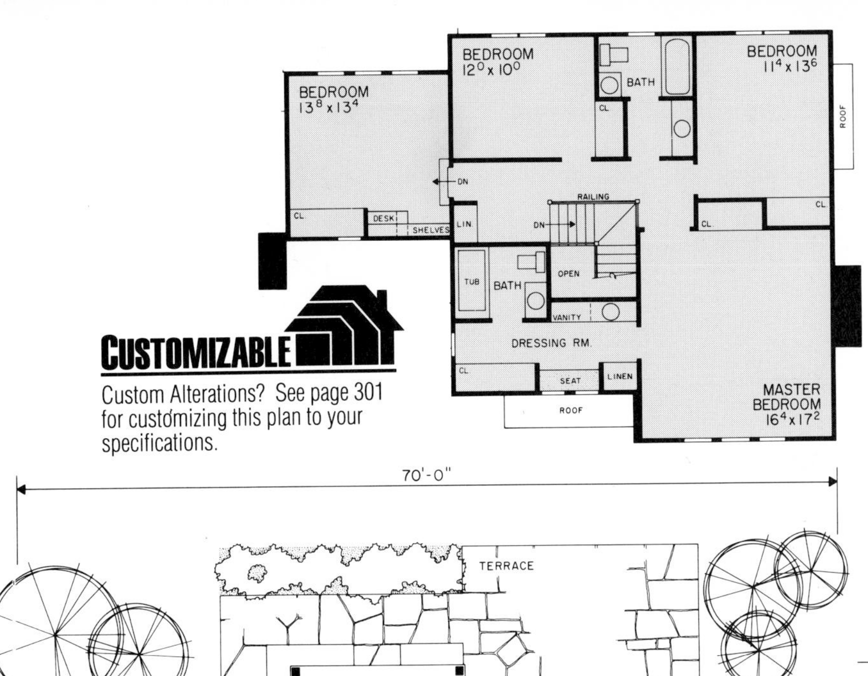

CUSTOMIZABLE

Custom Alterations? See page 301 for customizing this plan to your specifications.

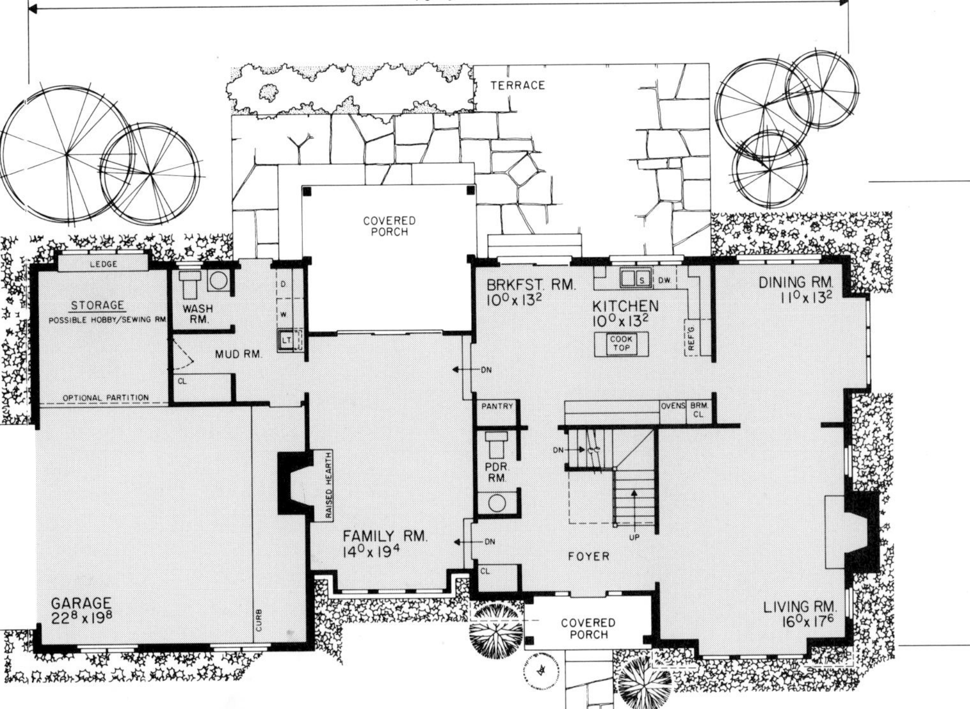

Design X2885

First Floor: 1,372 square feet
Second Floor: 1,245 square feet
Total: 2,617 square feet

L **D**

● This elegant Tudor house is perfect for the family who wants to move-up in living area, style and luxury. As you enter this home you will find a large living room with a fireplace on your right. Adjacent, the formal dining room has easy access to both the living room and the kitchen. The kitchen/ breakfast room has an open plan and access to the rear terrace. Sunken a few steps, the spacious family room is highlighted with a fireplace and access to the rear, covered porch. Note the optional planning of the garage storage area. Plan this area according to the needs of your family. Upstairs, your family will enjoy three bedrooms and a full bath, along with a spacious master bedroom suite. Truly a house that will bring many years of pleasure to your family.

Design X2921

First Floor: 3,215 square feet
Second Floor: 711 square feet
Total: 3,926 square feet

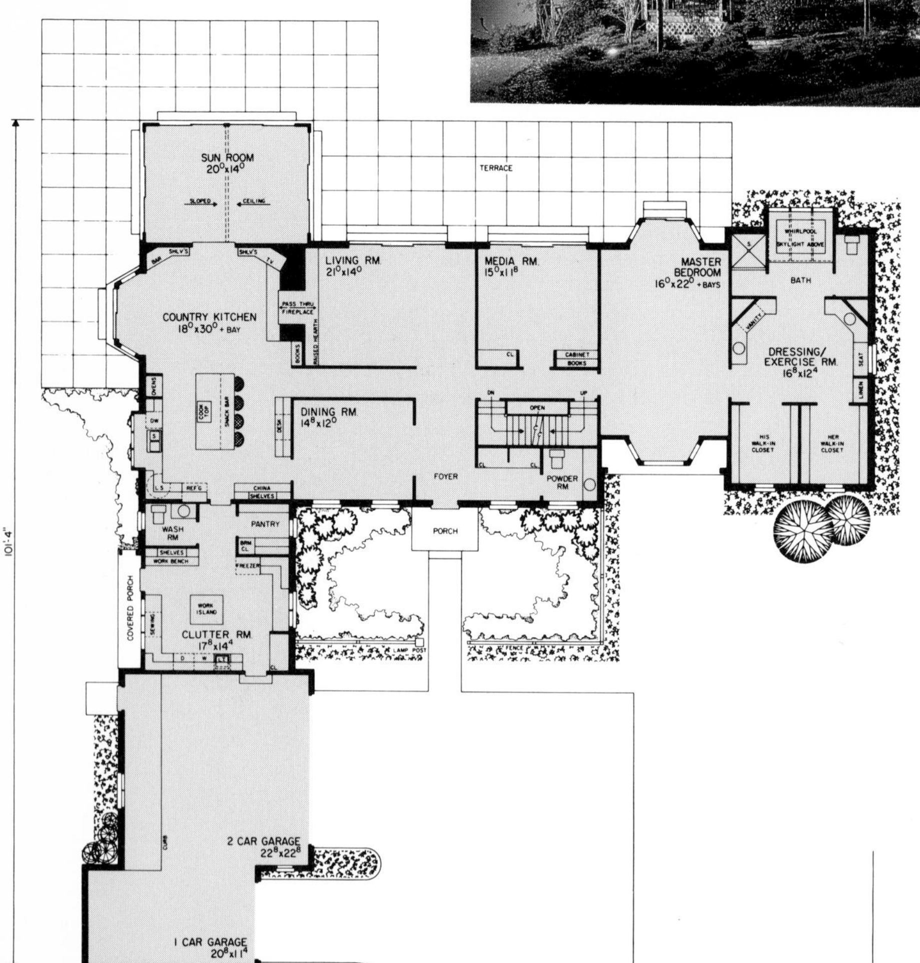

● This popular traditionally styled house features bay windows, shutters, a fanlight and a cupola on the roof. Interior planning was designed forempty-nesters whose children are grown and moved out on their own. Open planning is geared for entertaining and relaxing rather than child-rearing.

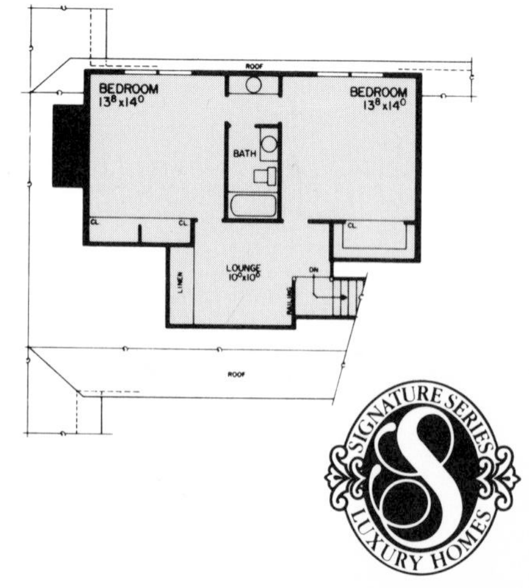

SIGNATURE SERIES LUXURY HOMES

Design X2662 First Floor: 1,735 square feet
Second Floor: 1,075 square feet; Third Floor: 746 square feet
Total: 3,556 square feet

L

● Influences from both Georgian and Federal architecture are apparent in the design of this home. The exterior is highlighted with multi-paned windows, two classic chimneys and well-proportioned dormers. The interior of this design has been planned just as carefully as the exterior, including a study, parlor, gathering room, U-shaped kitchen, formal and informal dining rooms and three fireplaces.

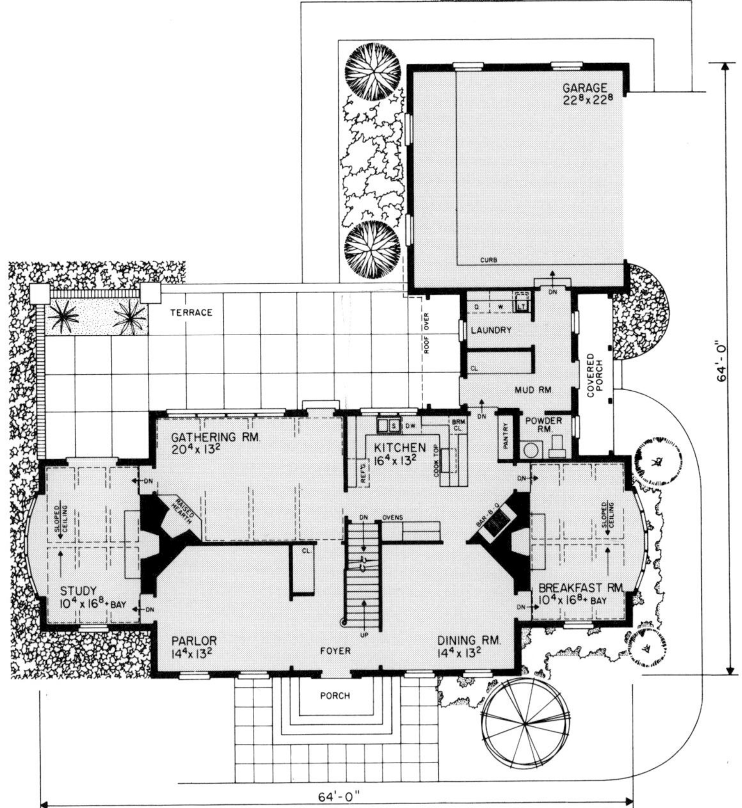

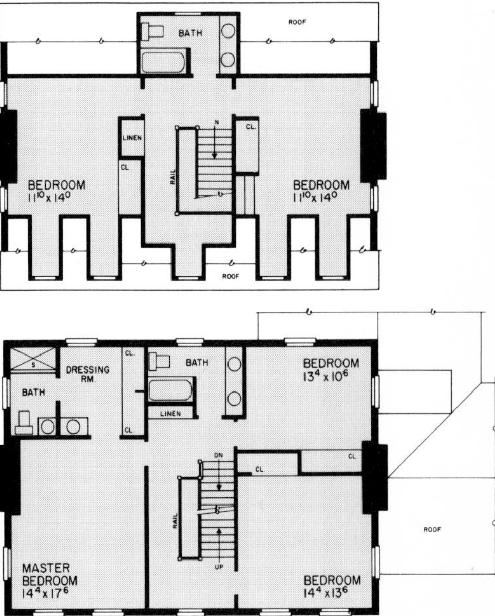

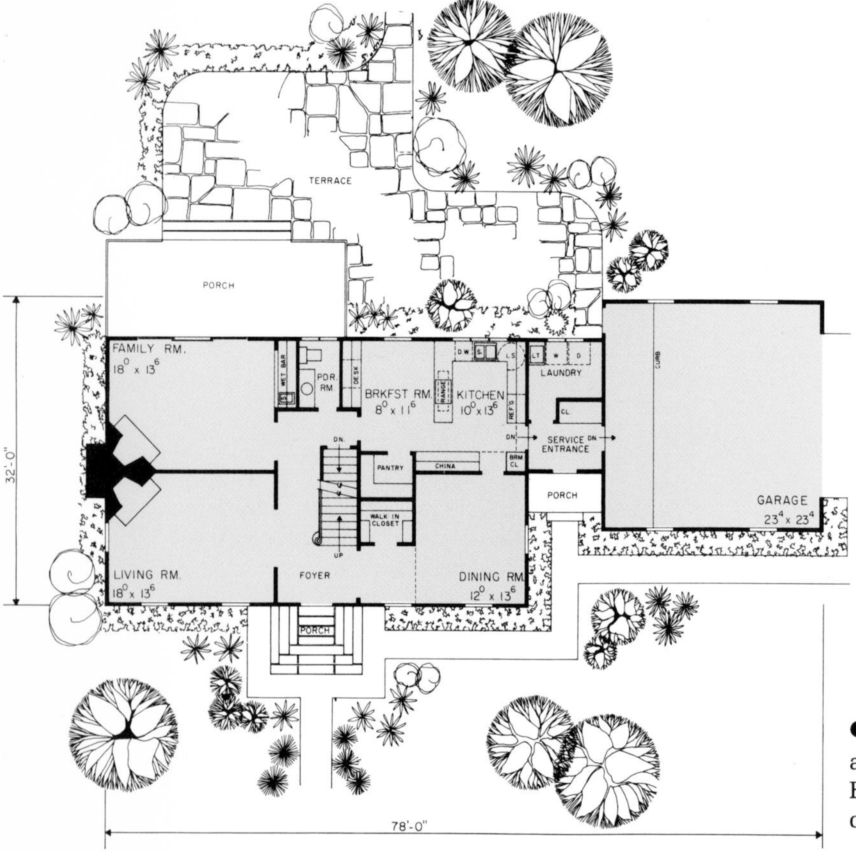

Design X2520

First Floor: 1,419 square feet
Second Floor: 1,040 square feet
Total: 2,459 square feet

L **D**

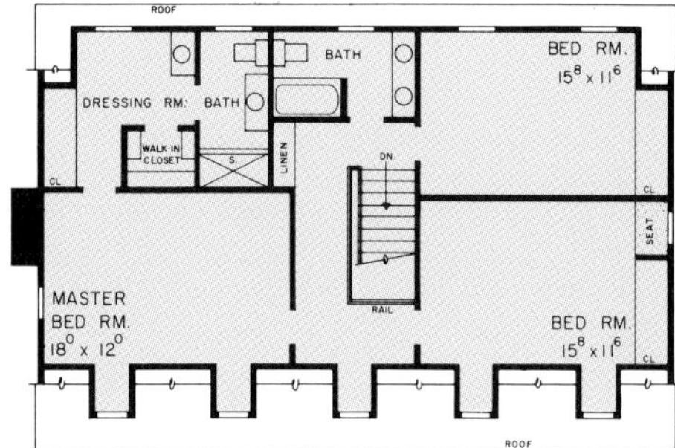

● From Tidewater Virginia comes this historic adaptation, a positive reminder of the charm of Early American architecture. Note how the center entrance opens to a fine floor plan.

Custom Alterations? See page 301 for customizing this plan to your specifications.

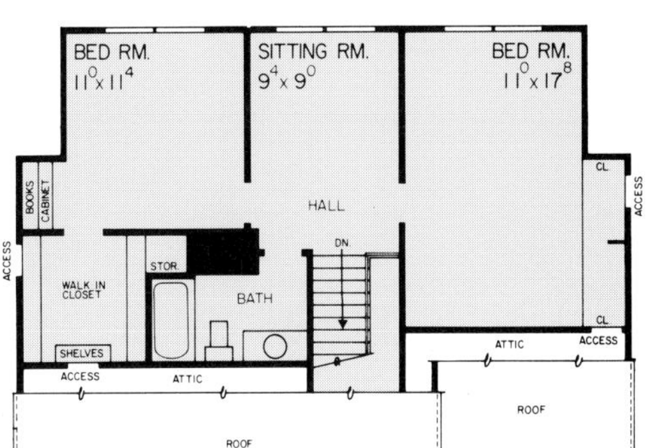

Design X2563

First Floor: 1,500 square feet
Second Floor: 690 square feet
Total: 2,190 square feet

L **D**

● You'll have all kinds of fun deciding just how your family will function in this dramatically expanded half-house. There is lots of attic storage, too. Observe three car garage.

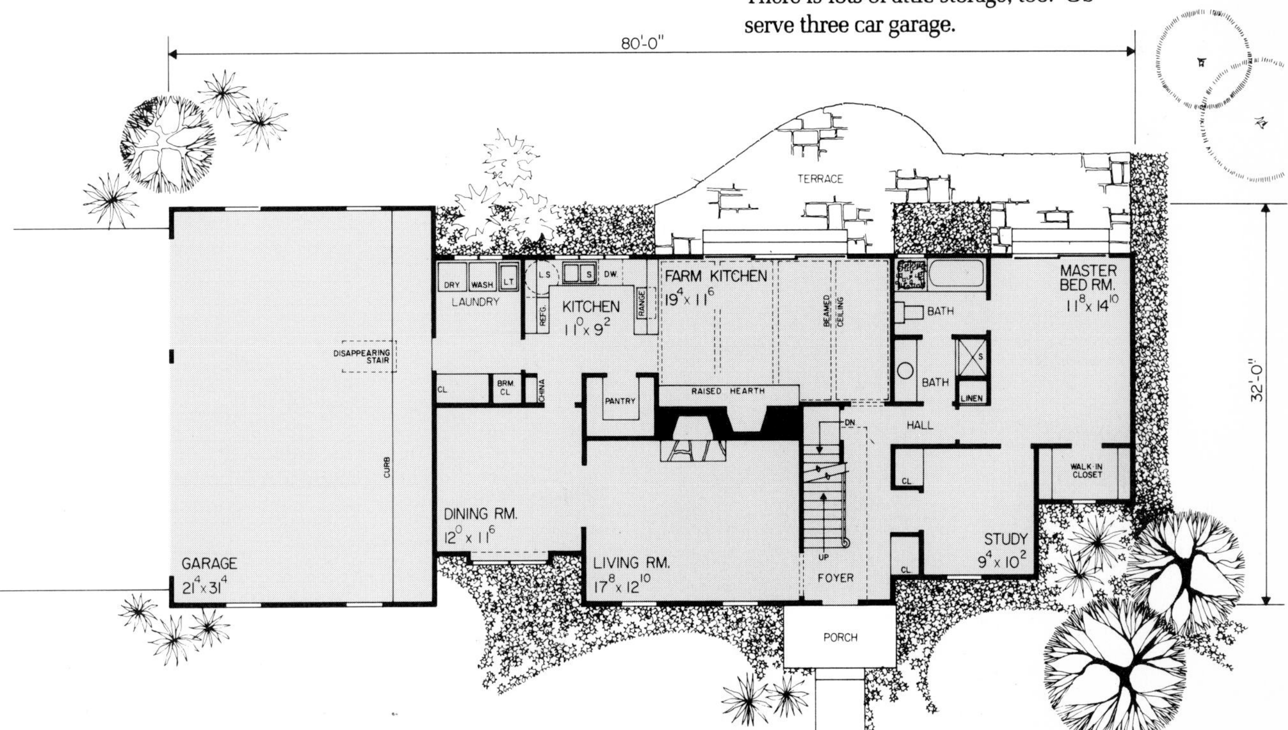

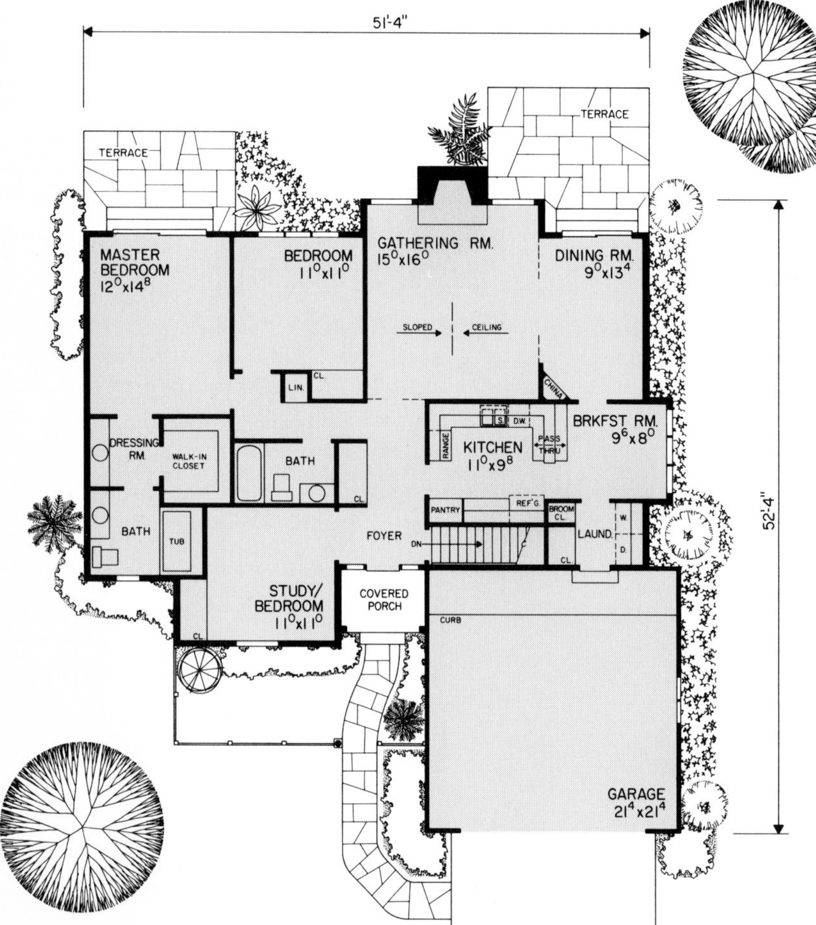

Design X2878

Square Footage: 1,521

L D

● There is a great deal of livability in this one-story design. The efficient floor plan makes optimum use of limited floor space. Ideally located, the gathering room is warmed by a fireplace. Its sloped-ceiling gives it a spacious appeal. Adjacent is the dining room which opens up to the rear terrace via sliding glass doors for dining alfresco. Ready to serve the breakfast room and dining room, there is the interior kitchen. The laundry, basement stairs and garage door are nearby. Two with an optional third bedroom are tucked away from the more active areas of the house. The master bedroom has sliding glass doors to the terrace for outdoor enjoyment. Study this cozy, clapboard cottage and imagine it as your next home.

Custom Alterations? See page 301 for customizing this plan to your specifications.

Design X3355

Square Footage: 1,387

L **D**

● Though it's only just under 1,400 total square feet, this plan offers three bedrooms (or two with study) and a sizable gathering room with fireplace and sloped ceiling. The galley kitchen provides a pass-through snack bar and has a planning desk and attached breakfast room. Besides two smaller bedrooms with a full bath, there's an extravagant master suite with large dressing area, double vanity and raised whirlpool tub.

Custom Alterations? See page 301 for customizing this plan to your specifications.

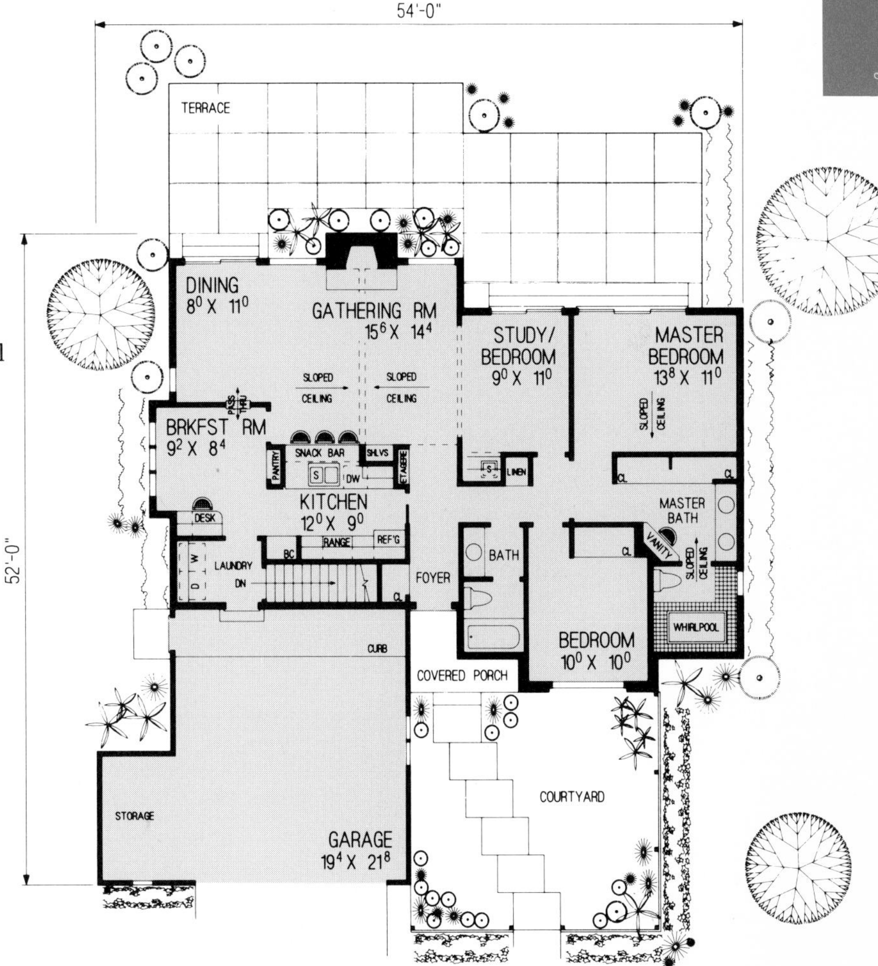

Design X2947

Square Footage: 1,830

● This charming one-story Traditional home greets visitors with a covered porch. A galley-style kitchen shares a snack bar with the spacious gathering room where a fireplace is the focal point. An ample master suite includes a luxury bath with whirlpool tub and separate dressing room. Two additional bedrooms, one that could double as a study, are located at the front of the home.

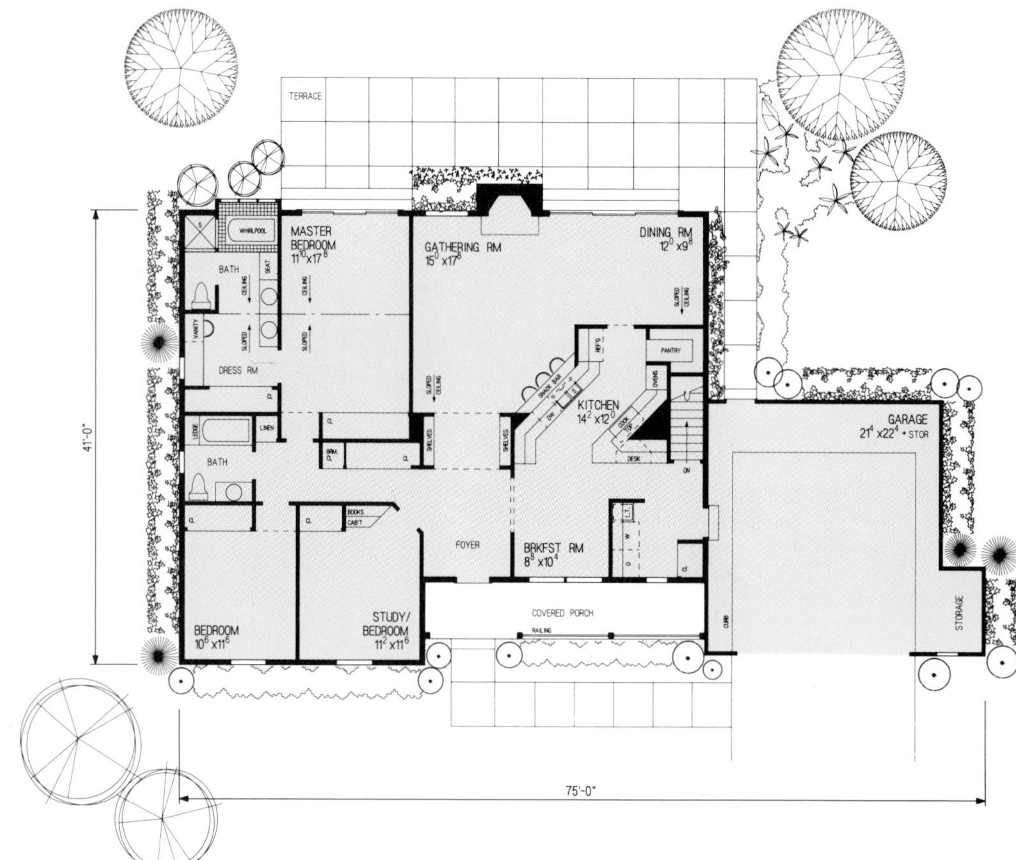

Custom Alterations? See page 301 for customizing this plan to your specifications.

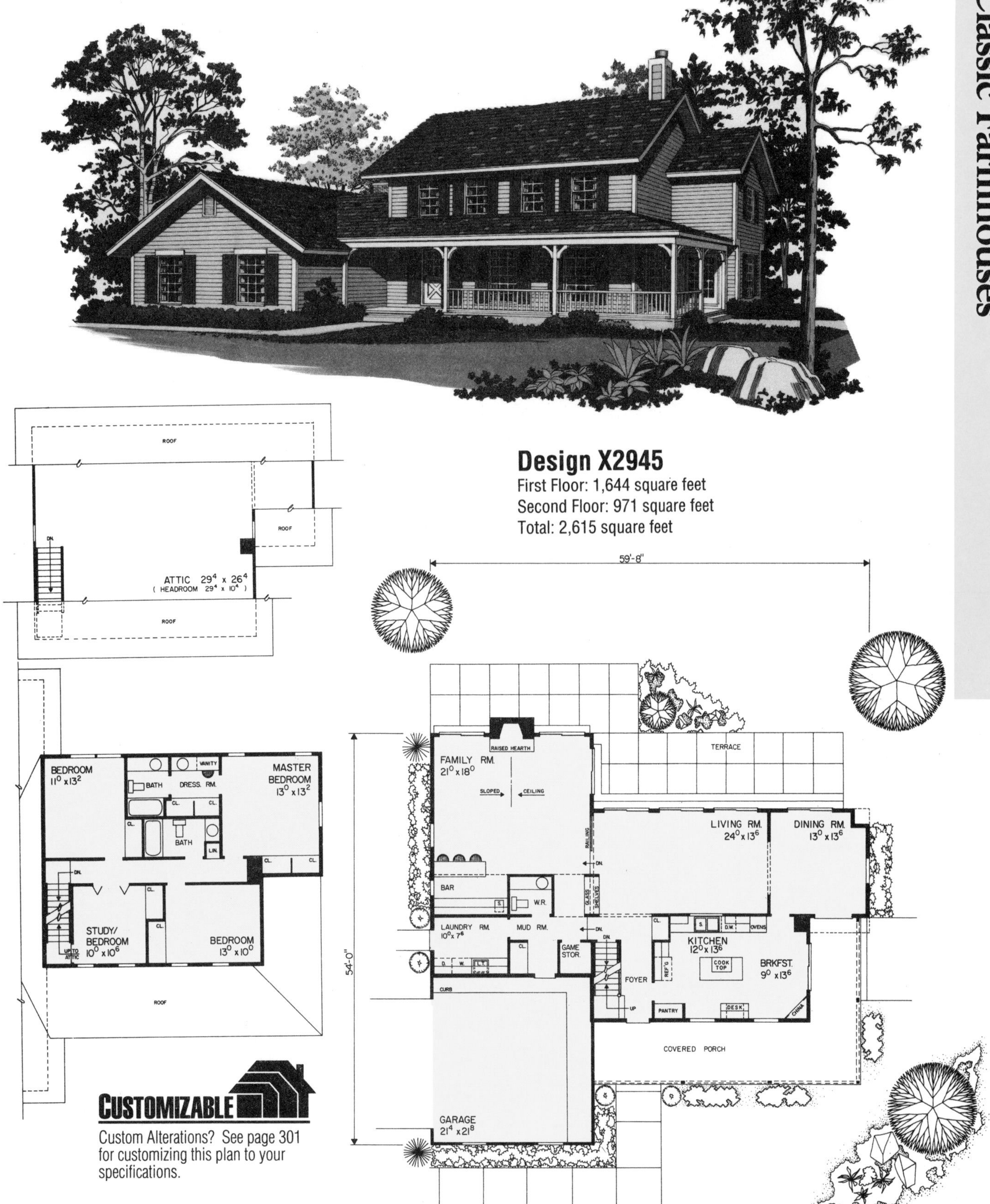

Design X2945

First Floor: 1,644 square feet
Second Floor: 971 square feet
Total: 2,615 square feet

CUSTOMIZABLE

Custom Alterations? See page 301 for customizing this plan to your specifications.

● Here is a new floor plan designed to go with the almost identical exterior of one of Home Planners' most popular houses. A masterfully affordable design, this plan manages to include all the basics - and then adds a little more. Note the wraparound covered porch, large family room with raised-hearth fireplace and wet bar, spacious kitchen with island cook top, formal dining room, rear terrace, and extra storage on the first floor. Upstairs, the plan's as flexible as they come: three or four bedrooms (the fourth could easily be a study or playroom) and lots of unfinished attic just waiting for you to transform it into living space. This could make a fine studio, sewing room, home office, or just a place for the safe, dry storage of the family's paraphernalia, Christmas decorations, etc.

Design X2776

First Floor: 1,134 square feet
Second Floor: 874 square feet
Total: 2,008 square feet

Custom Alterations? See page 301 for customizing this plan to your specifications.

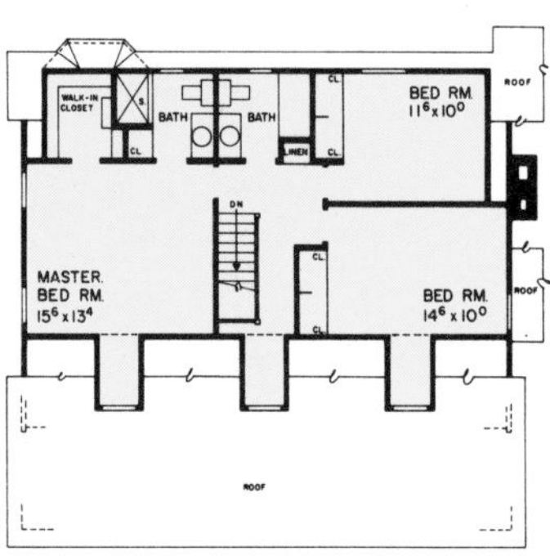

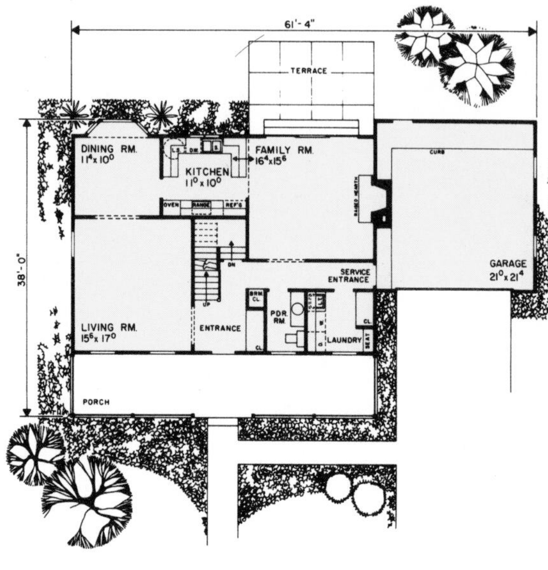

● This board-and-batten farmhouse design has all of the country charm of New England. Immediately off the front entrance is the delightful corner living room. The dining room with bay window is easily served by the U-shaped kitchen. Informal family living enjoyment resides in the family room which features a raised-hearth fireplace and sliding glass doors to the rear terrace. The second floor houses all of the sleeping facilities.

Design X2865

First Floor: 1,703 square feet
Second Floor: 1,044 square feet
Total: 2,747 square feet

● Here's a cozy traditional farmhouse with a big wraparound covered porch. Up front, flanking the entry foyer, are a living room with fireplace and formal dining room. To the rear are a study, that could be used as a guest room, and the family room with another fireplace. The kitchen/breakfast room combination is conveniently located near the service entrance off the garage. Note bedrooms with dormer windows upstairs.

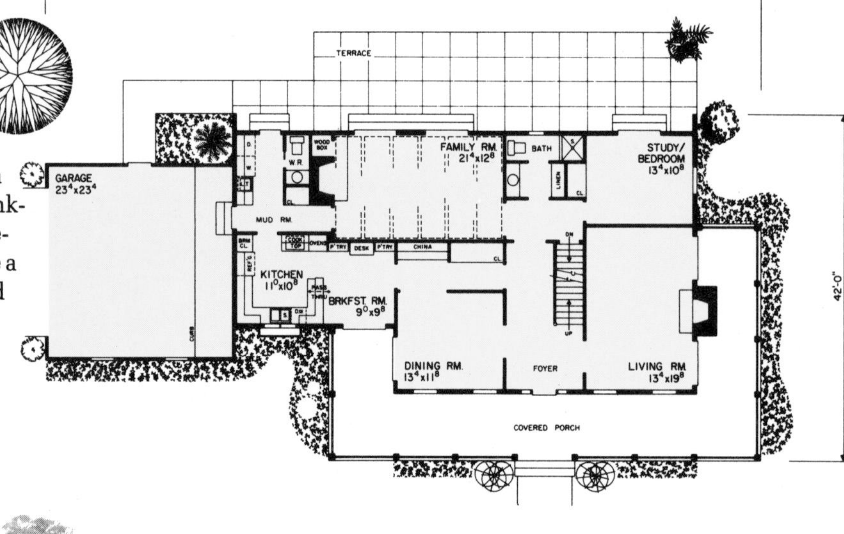

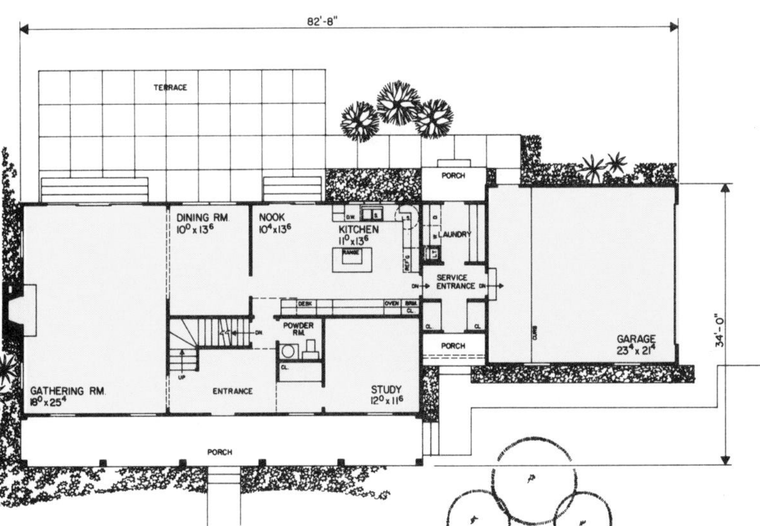

Design X2650

First Floor: 1,451 square feet
Second Floor: 1,091 square feet
Total: 2,542 square feet

L D

● The dormers and the covered porch with pillars introduce this house. Inside, the appeal is also outstanding. Note the size (18′ x 25′) of the gathering room which is open to the dining room. The kitchen/nook area is very spacious and features a cooking island, built-in desk and more. It's convenient having the laundry and the service area close to the kitchen. Make special note of the service entrance doors leading to both the front and back of the house.

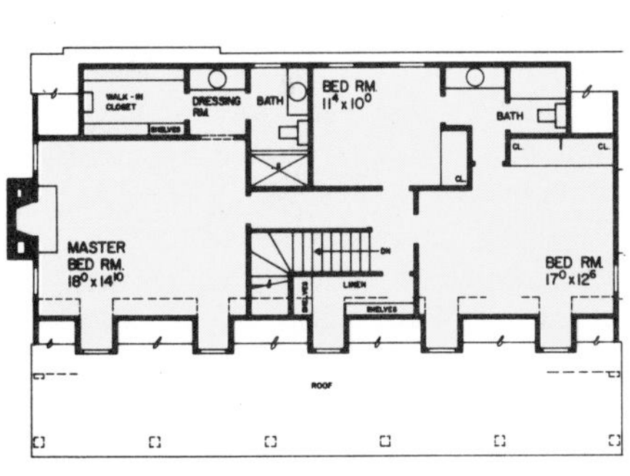

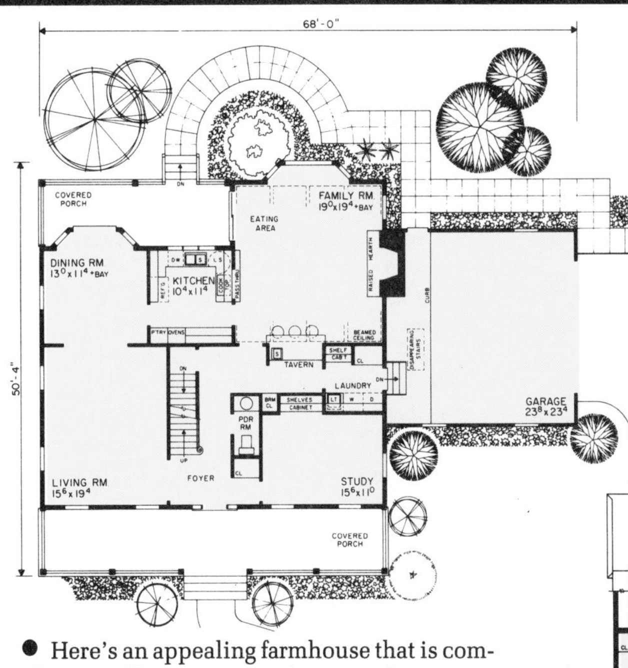

● Here's an appealing farmhouse that is complemented by an inviting front porch. Just inside is a nice-sized study to the right and a spacious living room to the left. The adjacent dining room has an attractive bay window. Just a step away is an efficient kitchen. Family activities will be enjoyed in the large family room. Upstairs you'll find a master bedroom suite featuring a bath with an oversized tub and shower and a dressing room. Also on this floor: two bedrooms, full bath and a large attic.

Design X2890

First Floor: 1,612 square feet
Second Floor: 1,356 square feet
Total: 2,968 square feet

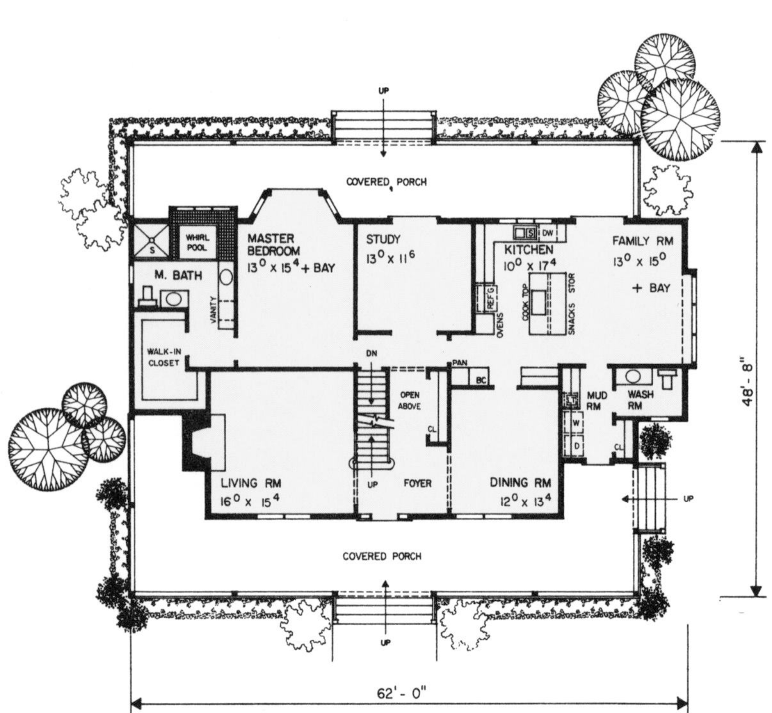

Design X3396

First Floor: 1,829 square feet
Second Floor: 947 square feet
Total: 2,776 square feet

L **D**

● Rustic charm abounds in this pleasant farmhouse rendition. Covered porches to the front and rear enclose living potential for the whole family. Flanking the entrance foyer are the living and dining rooms. To the rear is the L-shaped kitchen with island cook top and snack bar. A small family room/breakfast nook is attached. A private study is tucked away on this floor next to the master suite. On the second floor are three bedrooms and a full bath. Two of the bedrooms have charming dormer windows.

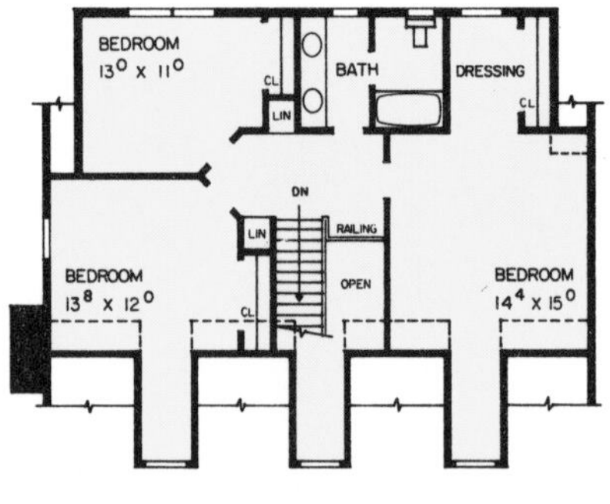

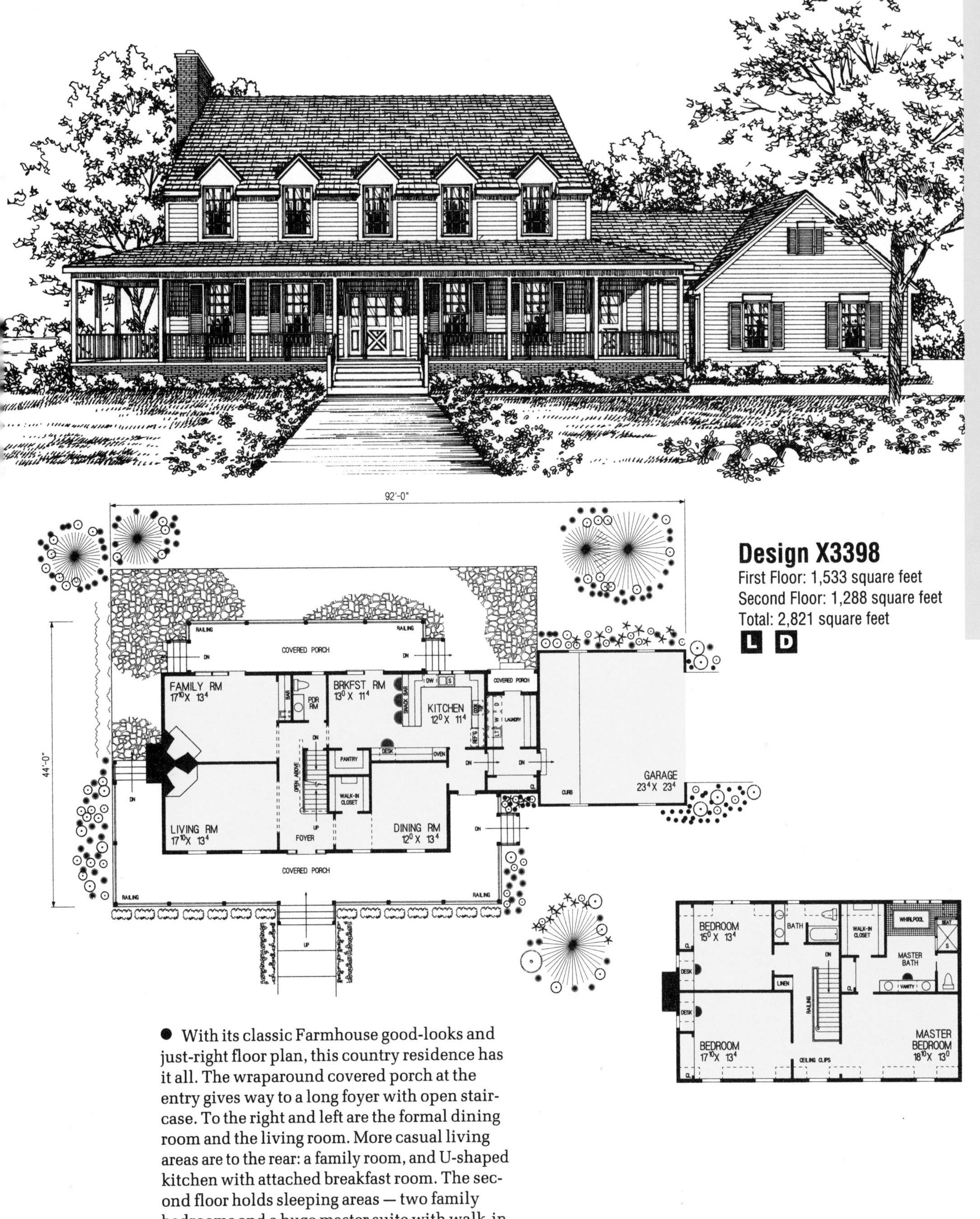

Design X3398

First Floor: 1,533 square feet
Second Floor: 1,288 square feet
Total: 2,821 square feet

L **D**

● With its classic Farmhouse good-looks and just-right floor plan, this country residence has it all. The wraparound covered porch at the entry gives way to a long foyer with open staircase. To the right and left are the formal dining room and the living room. More casual living areas are to the rear: a family room, and U-shaped kitchen with attached breakfast room. The second floor holds sleeping areas — two family bedrooms and a huge master suite with walk-in closet and pampering master bath.

Design X2988

First Floor: 1,458 square feet
Second Floor: 1,075 square feet
Third Floor: 462 square feet
Total: 2,995 square feet

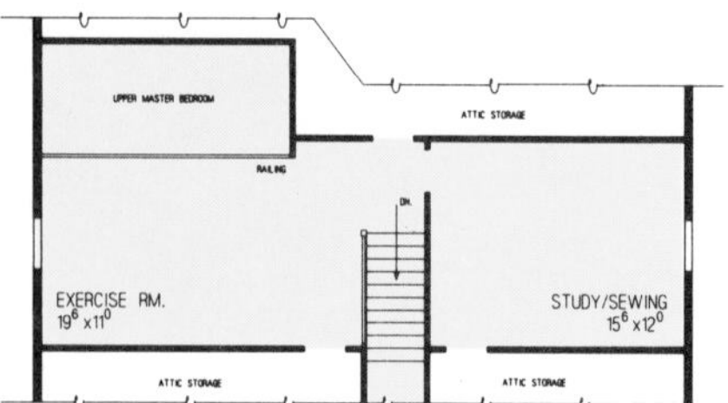

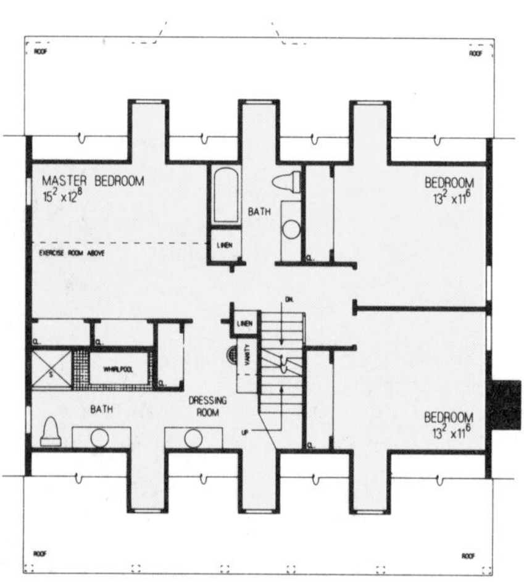

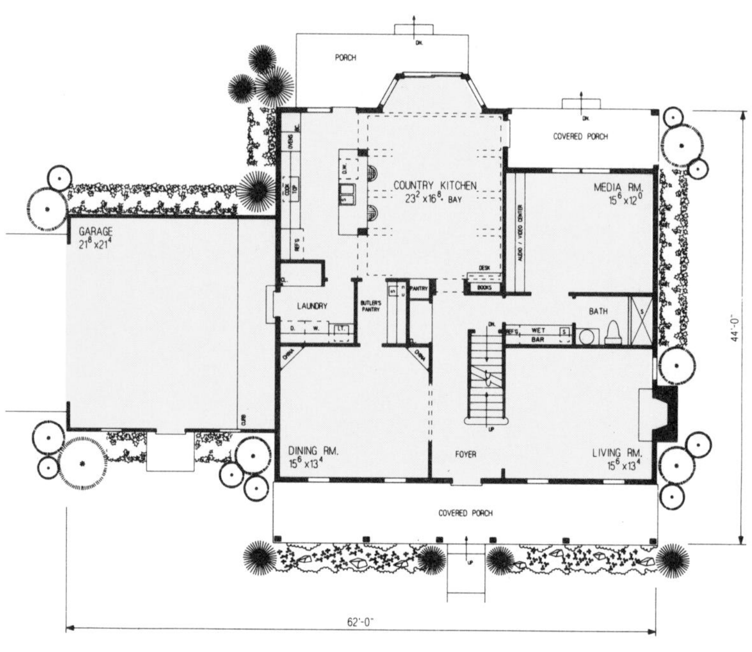

● The Joseph Guyon farmhouse, built in 1740, served as inspiration for this beautiful modern version. Three floors of living space encompass a country kitchen, living room, media room and dining room on the first floor; three bedrooms and two baths on the second floor; and an exercise room and study or sewing room on the third floor. Don't miss the covered porches front and rear, full guest bath near the media room and built-in wet bar.

Design X2680

First Floor: 1,707 square feet
Second Floor: 1,439 square feet
Total: 3,146 square feet

D

● This Early American, Dutch Colonial offers many fine features. The foyer allows easy access to all rooms on the first floor. Note the large country kitchen with beamed ceiling and fireplace. A large, formal dining room and powder room are only a few steps away. The study and the living room also have fireplaces. Two bedrooms, a full bath and the master bedroom suite are on the second floor. A fourth bedroom and bath are accessible through the master bedroom or by stairs in the service entrance.

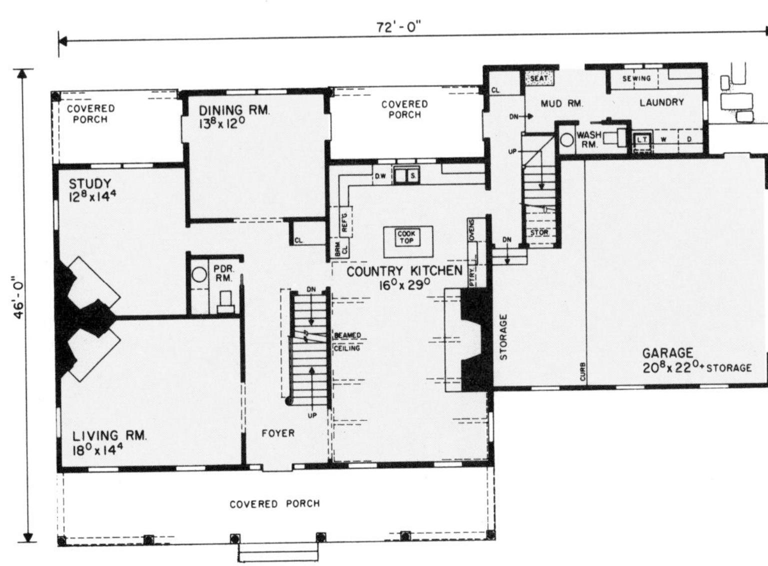

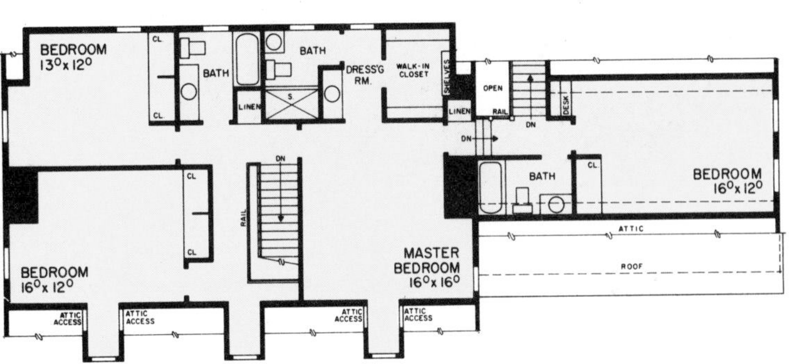

Design X2697

First Floor: 1,764 square feet
Second Floor: 1,506 square feet
Total: 3,270 square feet

● This two-story design with gambrel roof is reminiscent of the historic home of Robert Nicolson, a Williamsburg tailor and merchant. He built his house around 1751. Our updated floor plans include a large rear family room with raised-hearth fireplace and a large front living room with fireplace. A convenience kitchen offers pass-through to an informal eating area off the family room. The house includes a formal dining room as well. Upstairs are four bedrooms, including a master suite.

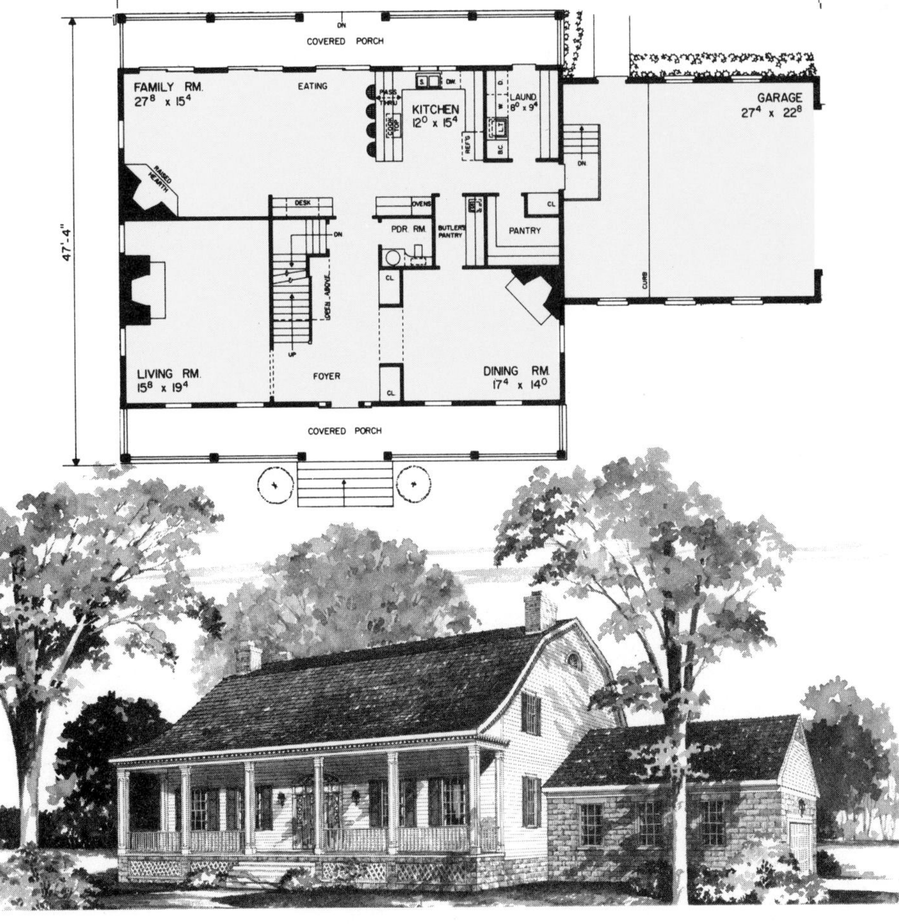

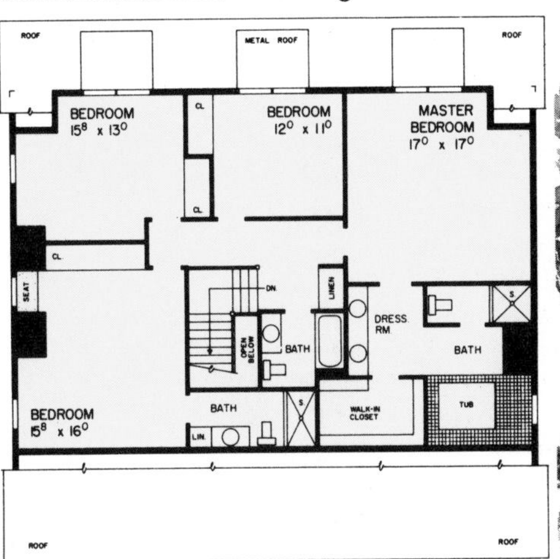

Design X3397

First Floor: 1,855 square feet
Second Floor: 1,241 square feet
Total: 3,096 square feet

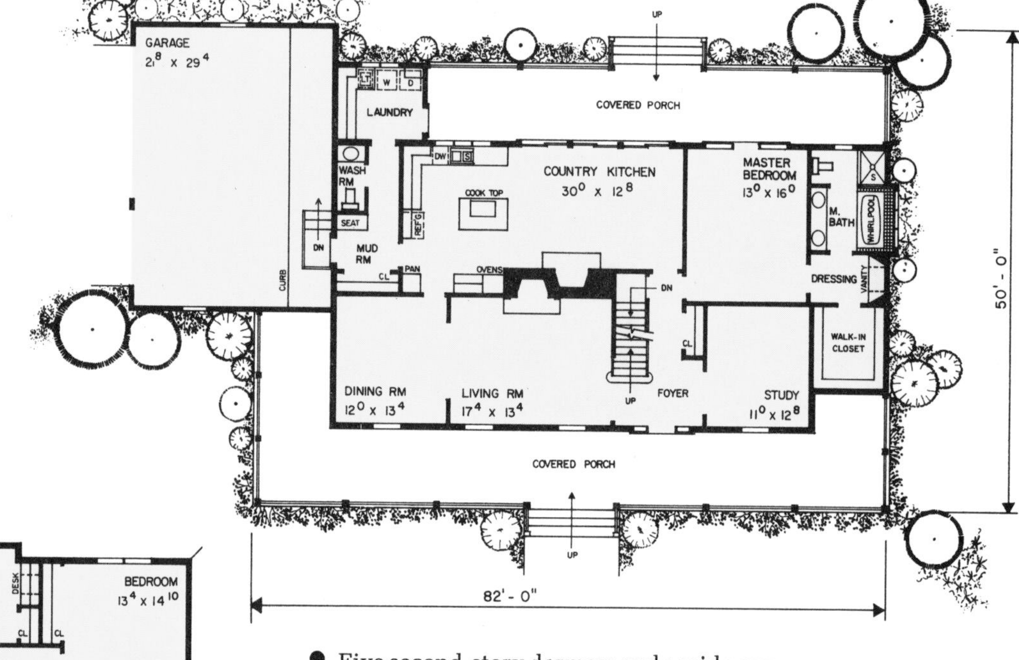

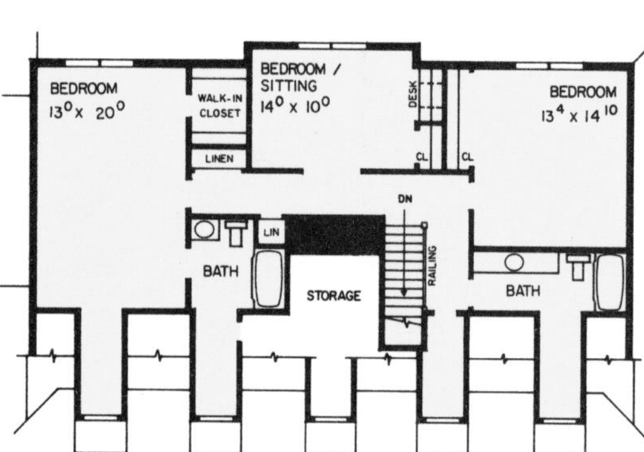

● Five second-story dormers and a wide covered front porch add to the charm of this farmhouse design. Inside, the entry foyer opens to the left to a formal living room with fireplace and attached dining room. To the right is a private study. The back of the plan is dominated by a huge country kitchen featuring an island cook top. On this floor is the master suite with a large walk-in closet. The second floor holds three bedrooms (or two and a sitting room) with two full baths.

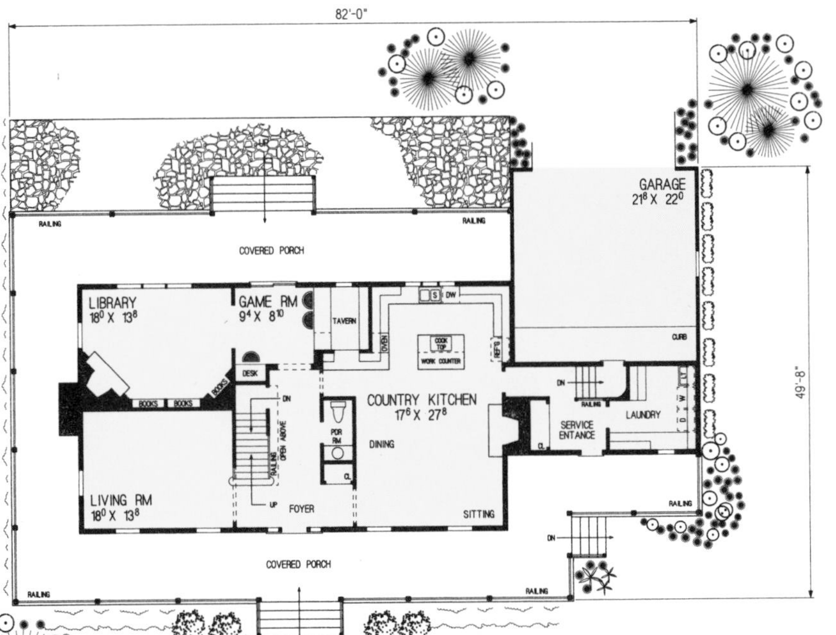

Design X3399

First Floor: 1,716 square feet
Second Floor: 2,102 square feet
Total: 3,818 square feet

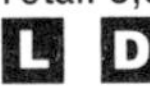

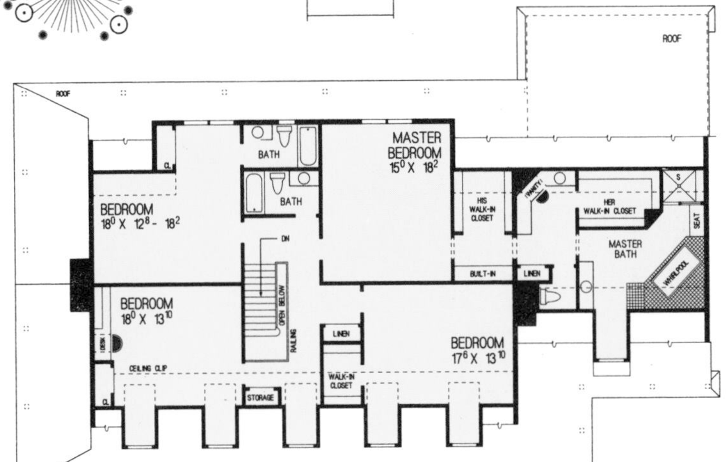

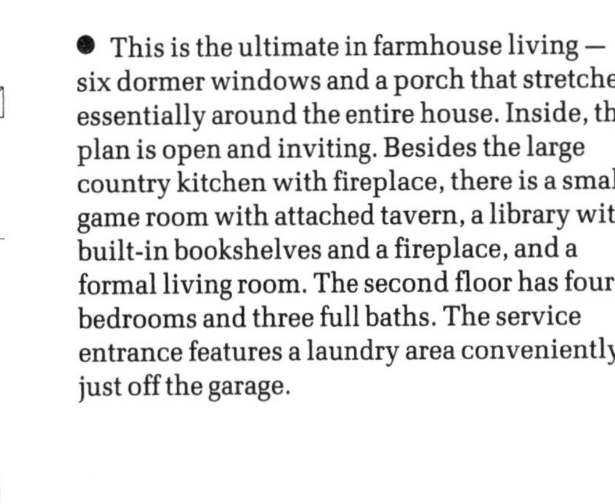

● This is the ultimate in farmhouse living — six dormer windows and a porch that stretches essentially around the entire house. Inside, the plan is open and inviting. Besides the large country kitchen with fireplace, there is a small game room with attached tavern, a library with built-in bookshelves and a fireplace, and a formal living room. The second floor has four bedrooms and three full baths. The service entrance features a laundry area conveniently just off the garage.

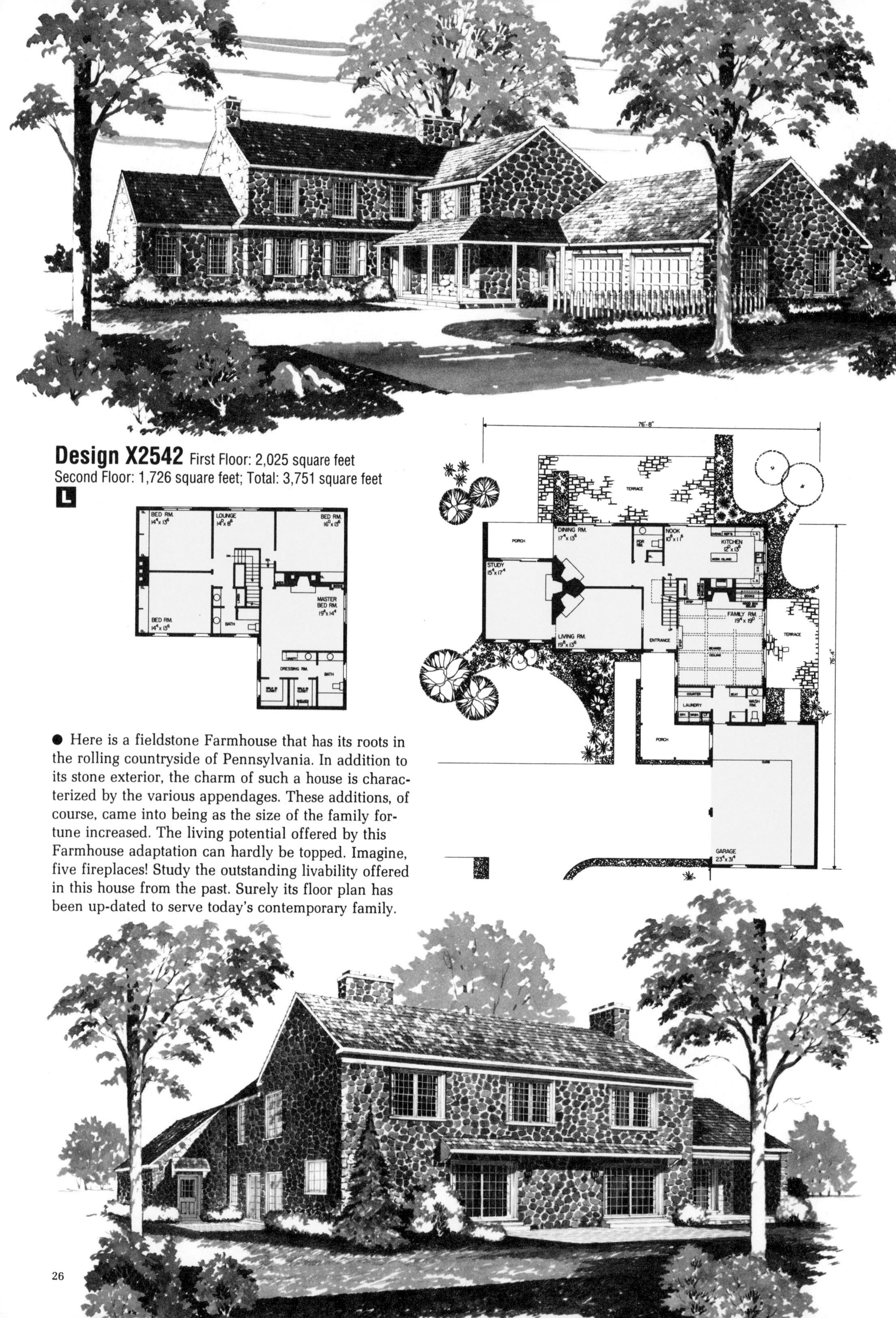

Design X2542 First Floor: 2,025 square feet

Second Floor: 1,726 square feet; Total: 3,751 square feet

L

● Here is a fieldstone Farmhouse that has its roots in the rolling countryside of Pennsylvania. In addition to its stone exterior, the charm of such a house is characterized by the various appendages. These additions, of course, came into being as the size of the family fortune increased. The living potential offered by this Farmhouse adaptation can hardly be topped. Imagine, five fireplaces! Study the outstanding livability offered in this house from the past. Surely its floor plan has been up-dated to serve today's contemporary family.

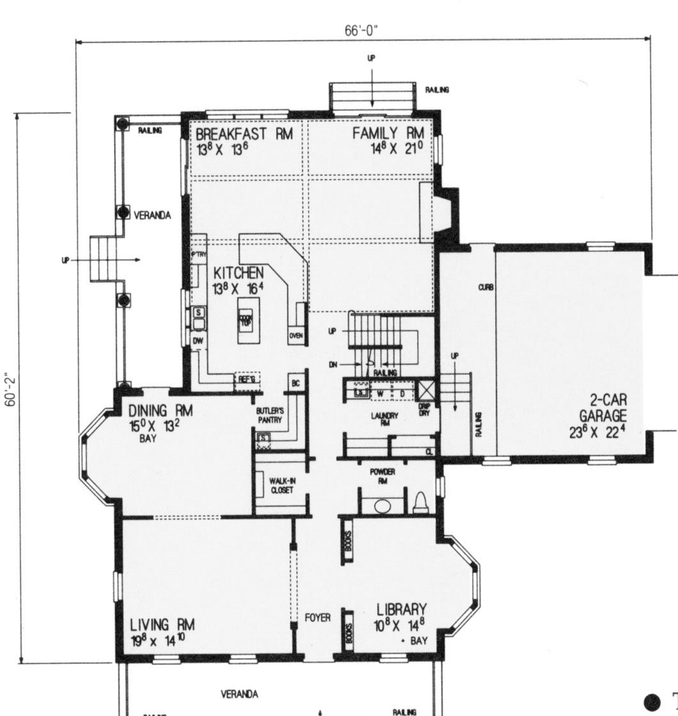

Design X3502

First Floor: 2,114 square feet
Second Floor: 2,045 square feet
Total: 4,159 square feet

● This lovely stone farmhouse is reminiscent of the solid, comfortable homes once so prevalent on homesteads throughout America. The columned front porch leads to a formal foyer with living room on the left and library on the right. The formal dining room connects directly to the living room and indirectly to the island kitchen through a butler's pantry. The family room and breakfast room have beamed ceilings and are both open to the kitchen. A covered veranda is accessed from the breakfast room and leads to a side yard. On the second floor are three bedrooms and a guest room with private bath. The master bedroom has a fireplace and a fine bath with separate shower and whirlpool tub. Two walk-in closets grace the dressing area. The two secondary bedrooms share a full bath with double vanity.

Design X2625

First Floor: 1,640 square feet
Second Floor: 1,072 square feet
Total: 2,712 square feet

● A 19th-Century Farmhouse! So it might seem. But one with contemporary features . . . like the U-shaped kitchen with a built-in desk and appliances as well as a separate dining nook. Or the 20' by 13' family room. There, a beamed ceiling and raised-hearth fireplace add traditional warmth to a modern convention.

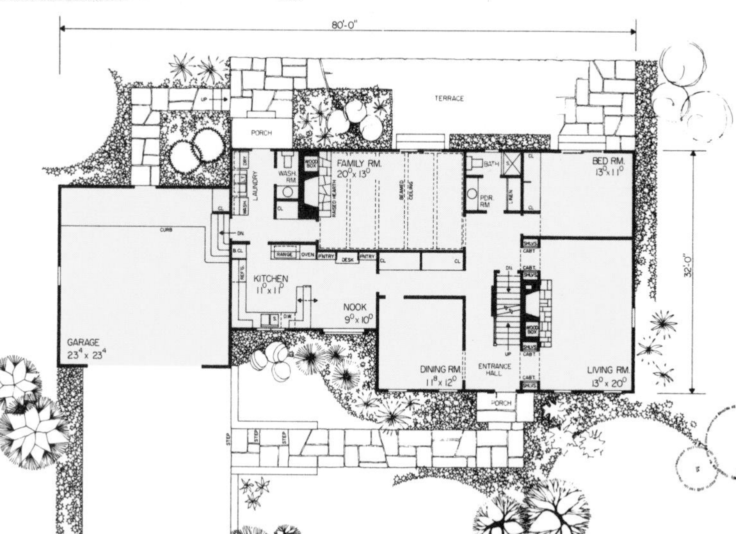

Design X2775

First Floor: 1,317 square feet
Second Floor: 952 square feet
Total: 2,269 square feet

L

● This front-porch farmhouse adaptation is characteristic of those found in the rolling hills of Pennsylvania. The interior is quite impressive. Both the formal and informal areas are outstandingly spacious. There are two eating areas: the formal dining room and the nook with sliding glass doors to a dining terrace. Many built-ins will be found in the nook/kitchen area including a desk, pantry and more. Three family bedrooms, bath and master bedroom suite are on the second floor.

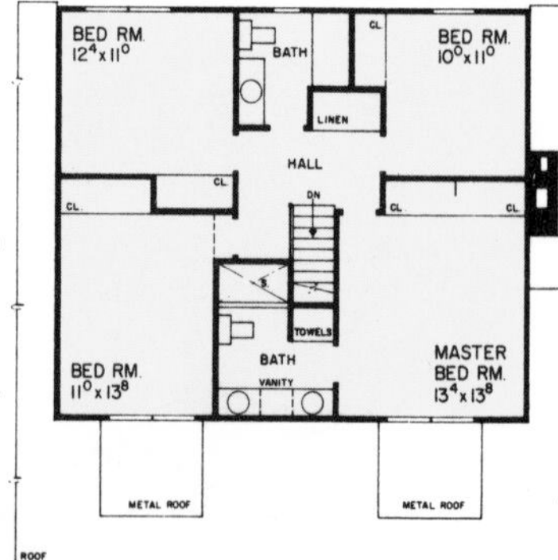

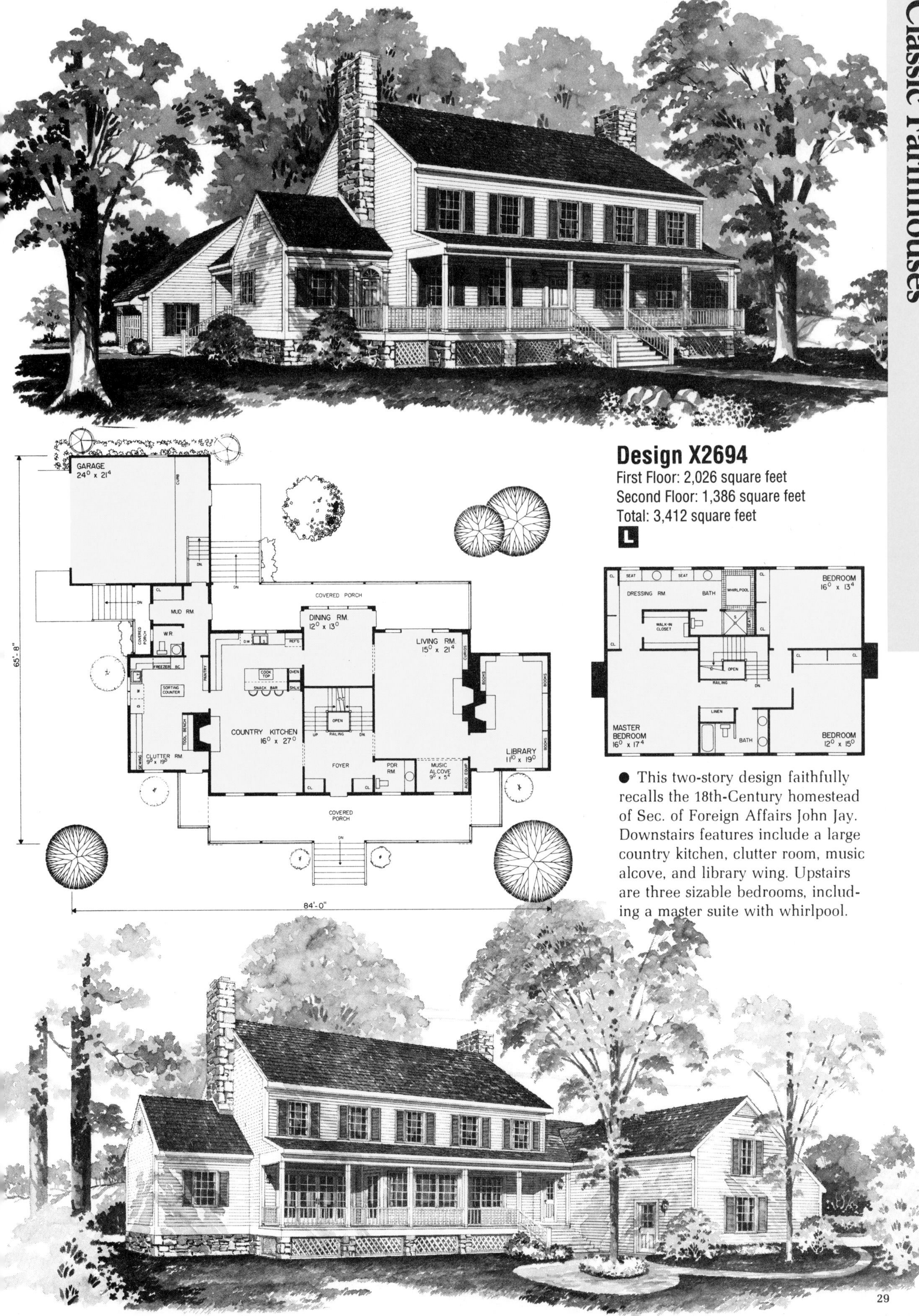

Design X2694

First Floor: 2,026 square feet
Second Floor: 1,386 square feet
Total: 3,412 square feet

● This two-story design faithfully recalls the 18th-Century homestead of Sec. of Foreign Affairs John Jay. Downstairs features include a large country kitchen, clutter room, music alcove, and library wing. Upstairs are three sizable bedrooms, including a master suite with whirlpool.

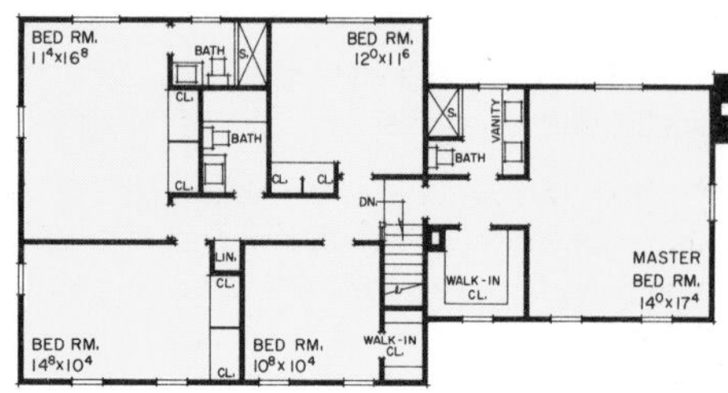

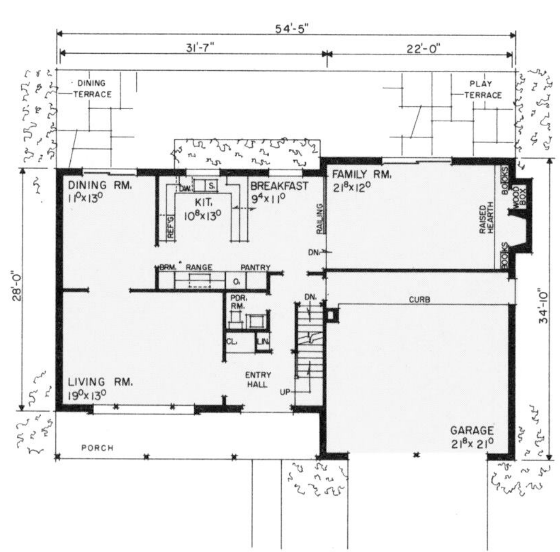

Design X1868

First Floor: 1,190 square feet
Second Floor: 1,300 square feet
Total: 2,490 square feet

● A five-bedroom Farmhouse adaptation that is truly a home for family living. The big family room will be everyone's favorite area. Note the master bedroom suite, located over the garage.

Design X2908

First Floor: 1,427 square feet
Second Floor: 1,153 square feet
Total: 2,580 square feet

L **D**

CUSTOMIZABLE

Custom Alterations? See page 301 for customizing this plan to your specifications.

● This Early American farmhouse offers plenty of modern comfort with its covered front porch with pillars and rails, double chimneys, building attachment, and four upstairs bedrooms. The first-floor attachment includes a family room with bay window. The upstairs is accessible from stairs just off the front foyer. Included is a master bedroom suite. Downstairs is a modern kitchen with breakfast room, dining room, and front living room.

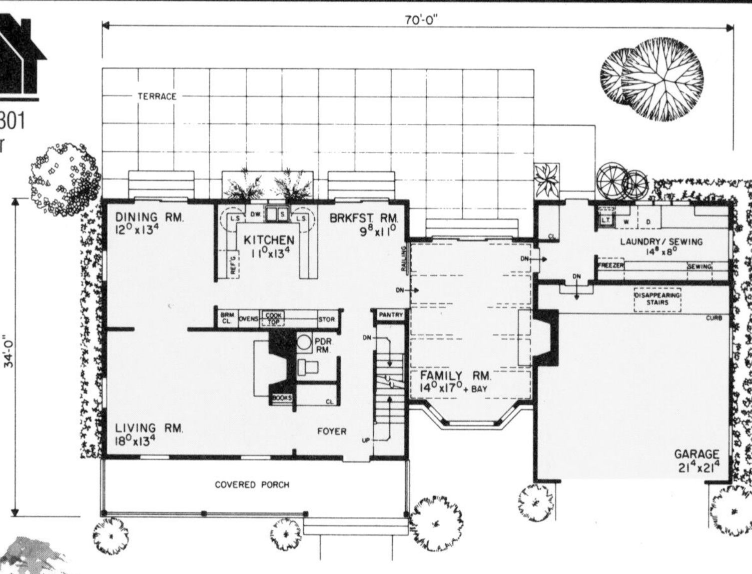

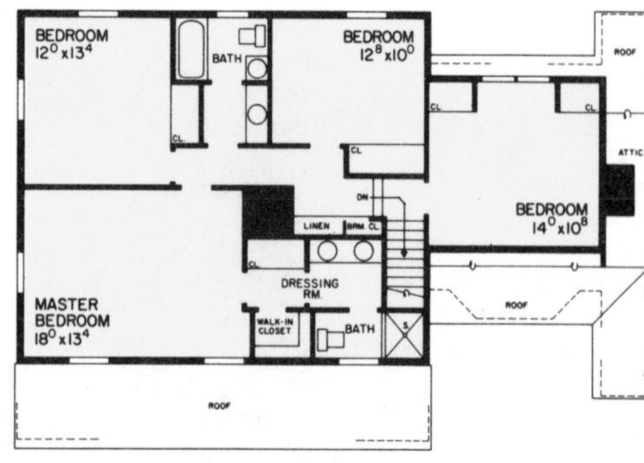

Design X2907

First Floor: 1,546 square feet
Second Floor: 1,144 square feet
Total: 2,690 square feet

● This traditional L-shaped farmhouse is charming indeed with dormer windows and covered porch supported by slender columns. A spacious country kitchen with a bay provides a convenient place for food preparation with its central work island and size. There's a formal dining room also adjacent to the kitchen. A rear family room features its own fireplace, as does a large living room in the front. All four bedrooms are isolated upstairs. Included is a large master bedroom suite with its own bath, dressing room and abundant closet space.

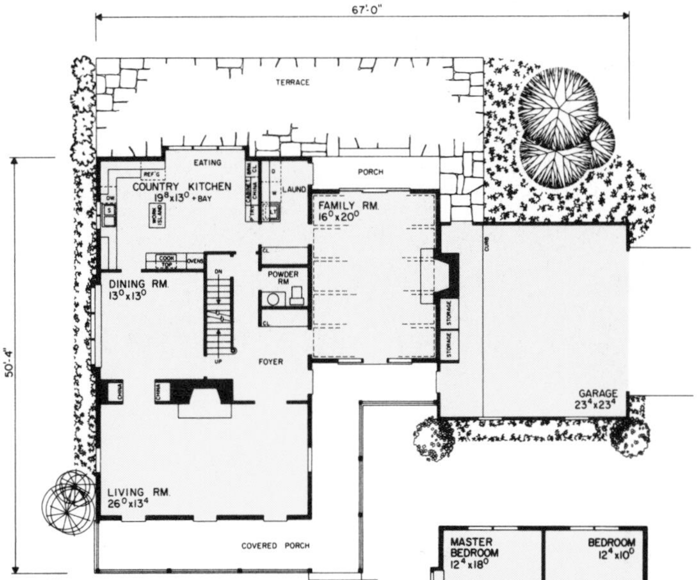

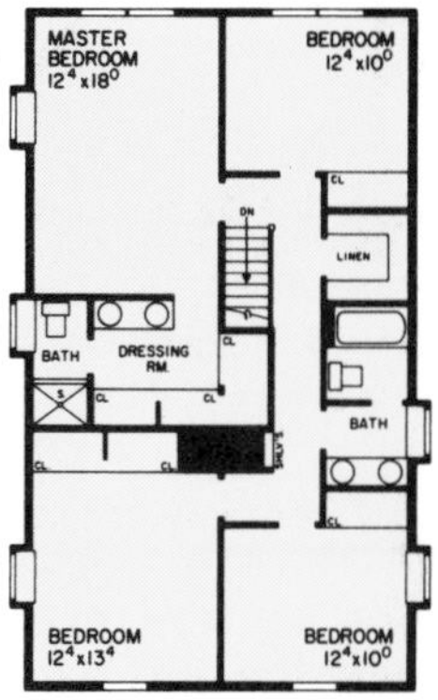

Design X2681

First Floor: 1,350 square feet
Second Floor: 1,224 square feet
Total: 2,574 square feet

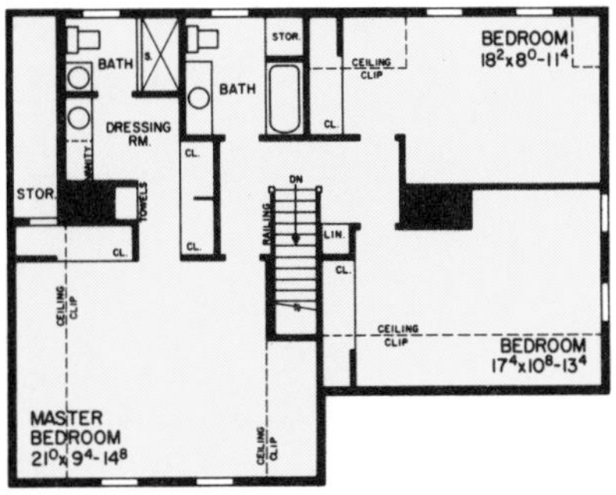

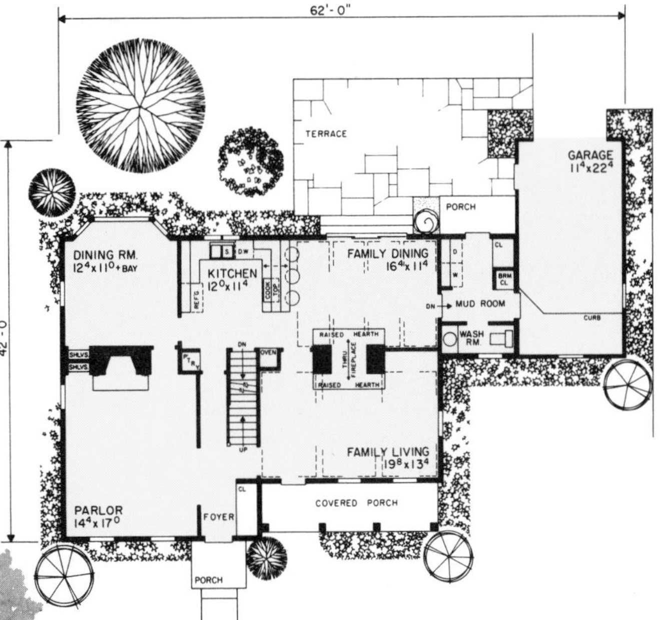

● The charm of Early America is exemplified in this delightful design. Note the three areas which are highlighted by fireplaces. The three-bedroom second floor is nicely planned. Make special note of the master bedroom's many fine features.

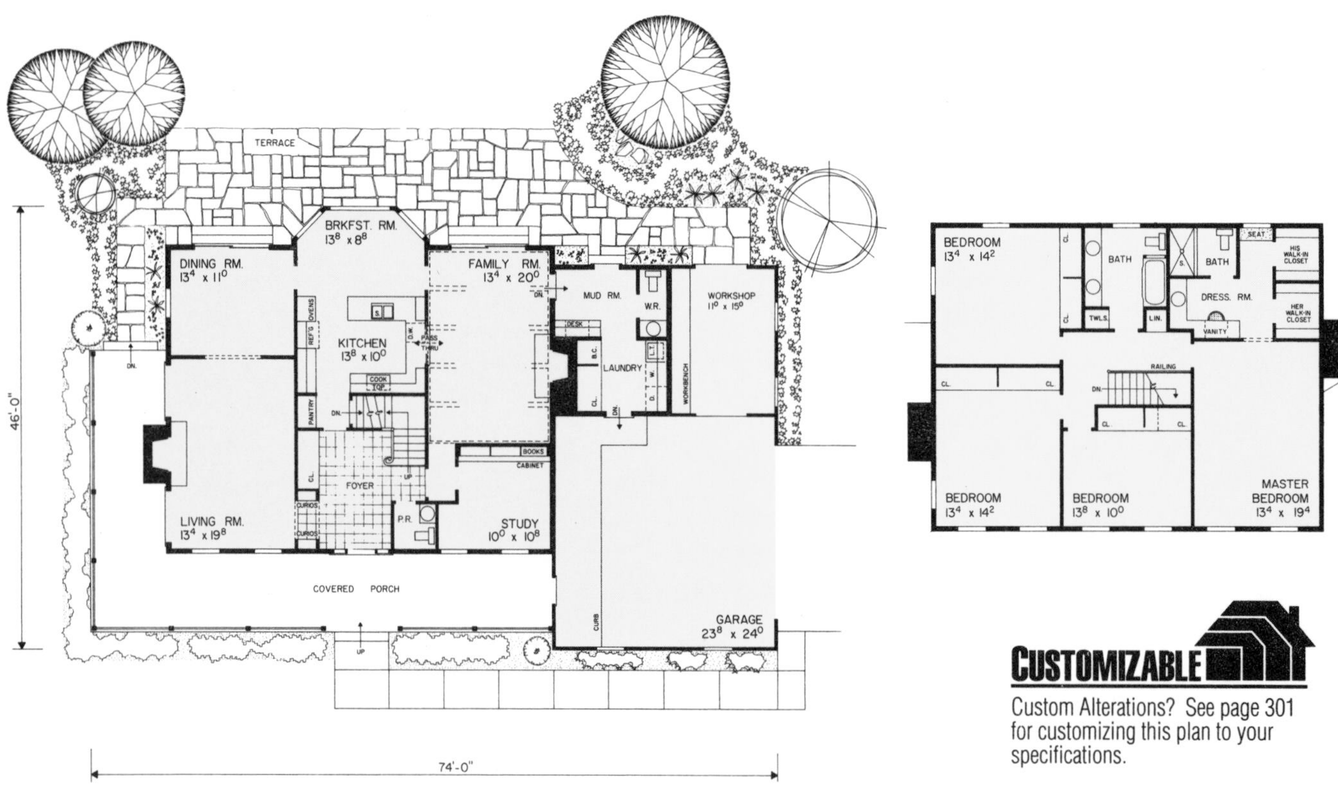

CUSTOMIZABLE

Custom Alterations? See page 301 for customizing this plan to your specifications.

Design X2946 First Floor: 1,590 square feet; Second Floor: 1,344 square feet; Total: 2,934 square feet

L **D**

● Here's a traditional design that's made for down-home hospitality, the pleasures of casual conversation, and the good grace of pleasant company. The star attractions are the large covered porch and terrace, perfectly relaxing gathering points for family and friends. Inside, though, the design is truly a hard worker; separate living room and family room, each with its own fireplace; formal dining room; large kitchen and breakfast area with bay windows; separate study; workshop with plenty of room to maneuver; mud room; and four bedrooms up, including a master suite. Not to be overlooked are the curio niches, the powder room, the built-in bookshelves, the kitchen pass-through, the pantry, the planning desk, the workbench, and the stairs to the basement.

Design X2888

Square Footage: 3,018

L

● This is an outstanding Early American design for the 20th-Century. The exterior detailing with narrow clap boards, multi-paned windows and cupola are the features of yesteryear. Interior planning, though, is for today's active family. Formal living room, informal family room plus a study are present. Every activity will have its place in this home. Picture yourself working in the kitchen. There's enough counter space for two or three helpers. Four bedrooms are in the private area. Stop and imagine your daily routine if you occupied the master bedroom. Both you and your spouse would have plenty of space and privacy. The flower porch, accessible from the master bedroom, living and dining rooms, is a very delightful "plus" feature. Study this design's every detail.

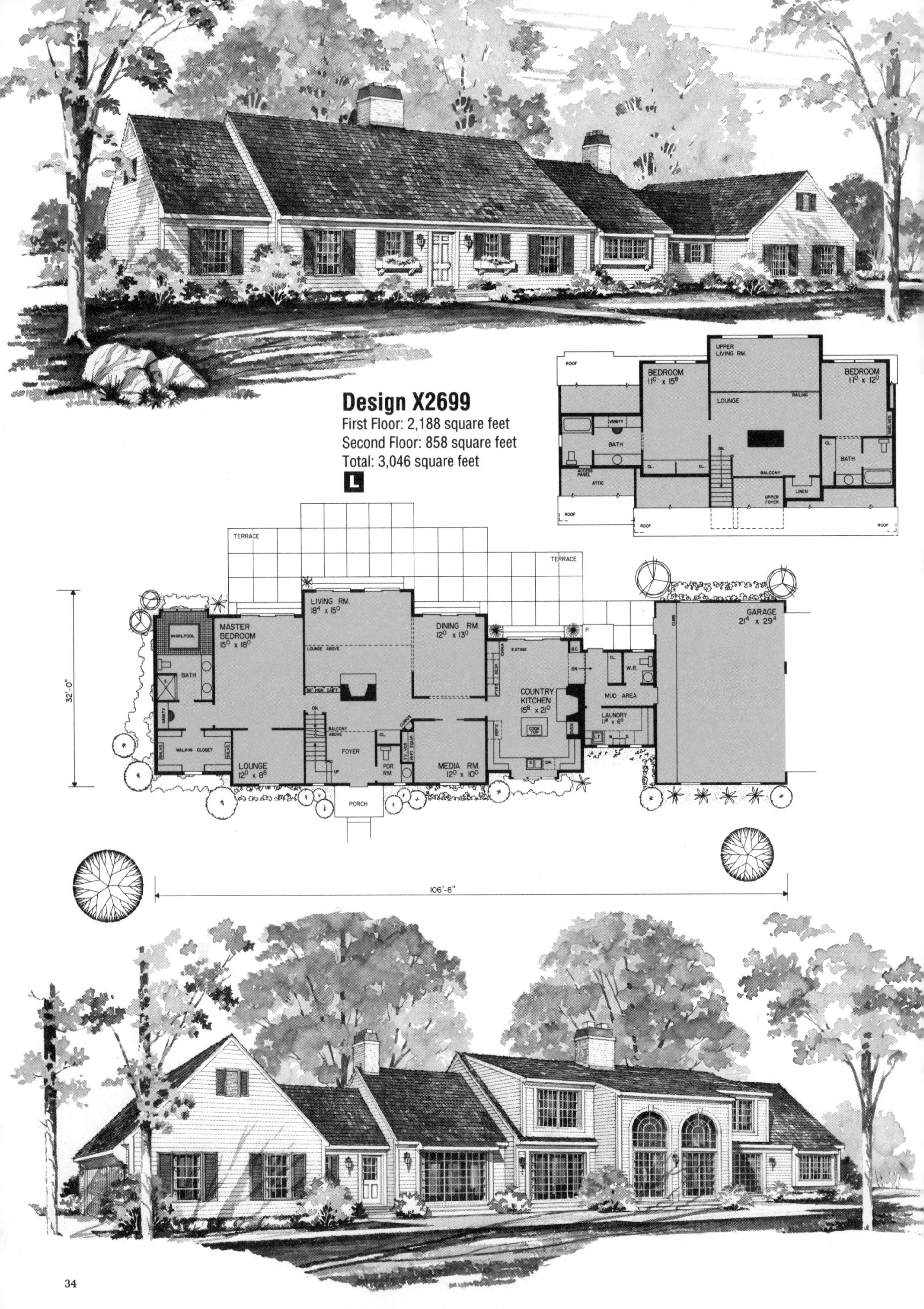

Design X2699

First Floor: 2,188 square feet
Second Floor: 858 square feet
Total: 3,046 square feet

L

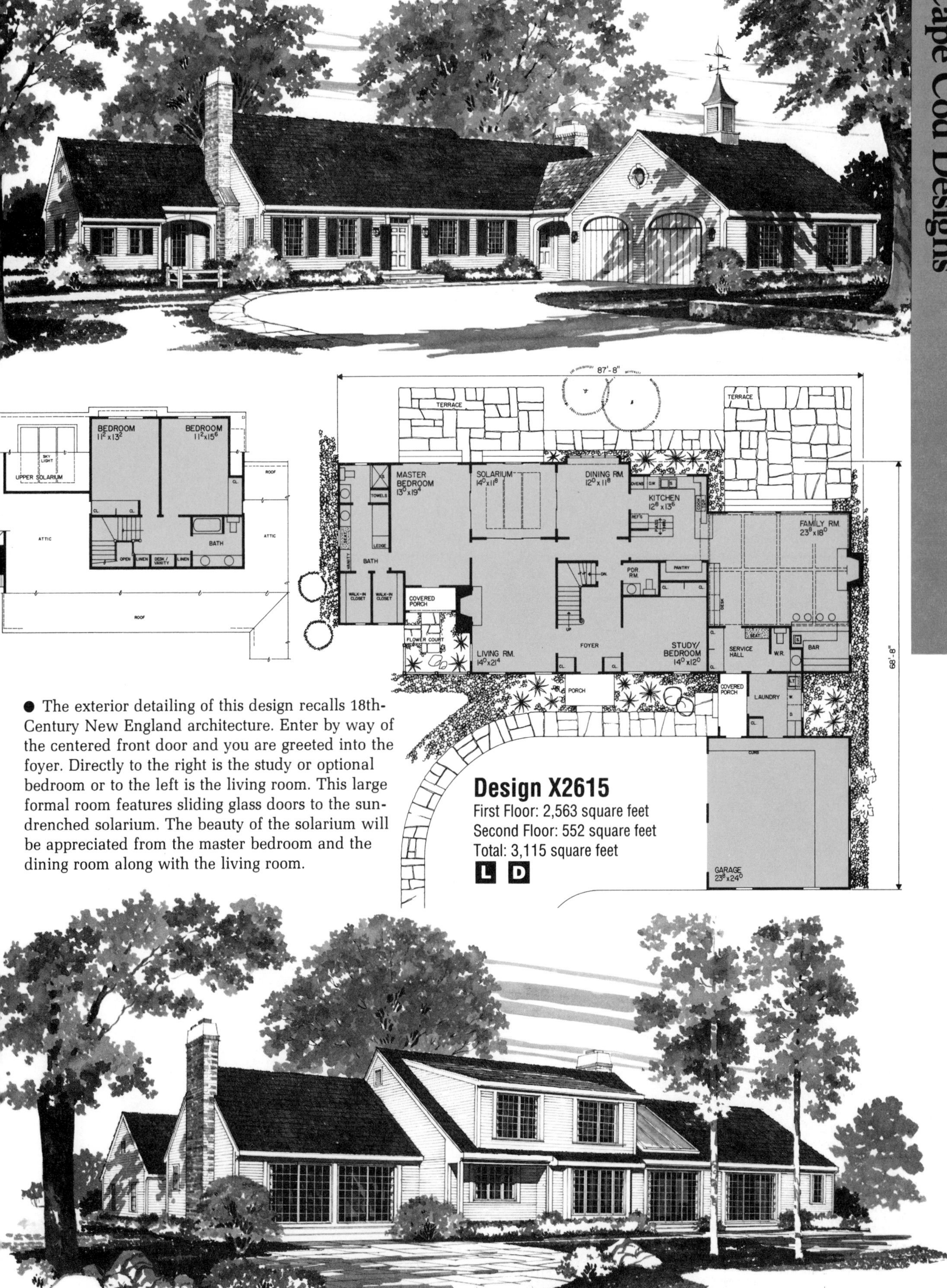

● The exterior detailing of this design recalls 18th-Century New England architecture. Enter by way of the centered front door and you are greeted into the foyer. Directly to the right is the study or optional bedroom or to the left is the living room. This large formal room features sliding glass doors to the sun-drenched solarium. The beauty of the solarium will be appreciated from the master bedroom and the dining room along with the living room.

Design X2615

First Floor: 2,563 square feet
Second Floor: 552 square feet
Total: 3,115 square feet

L **D**

Design X2995

First Floor: 2,465 square feet
Second Floor: 617 square feet
Total: 3,082 square feet

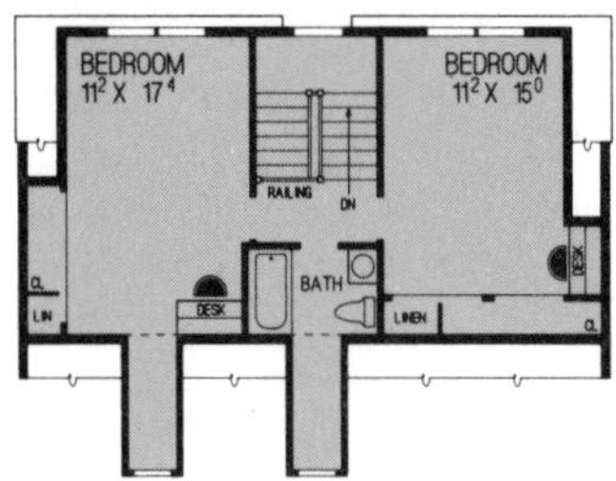

● This New England Colonial delivers beautiful proportions and great livability on 1½ levels. The main area of the house, the first floor, holds a living room, library, family room, dining room and gourmet kitchen. The master bedroom, also on this floor, features a whirlpool tub and sloped ceiling. A long rear terrace stretches the full width of the house. Two bedrooms on the second floor share a full bath; each has a built-in deck.

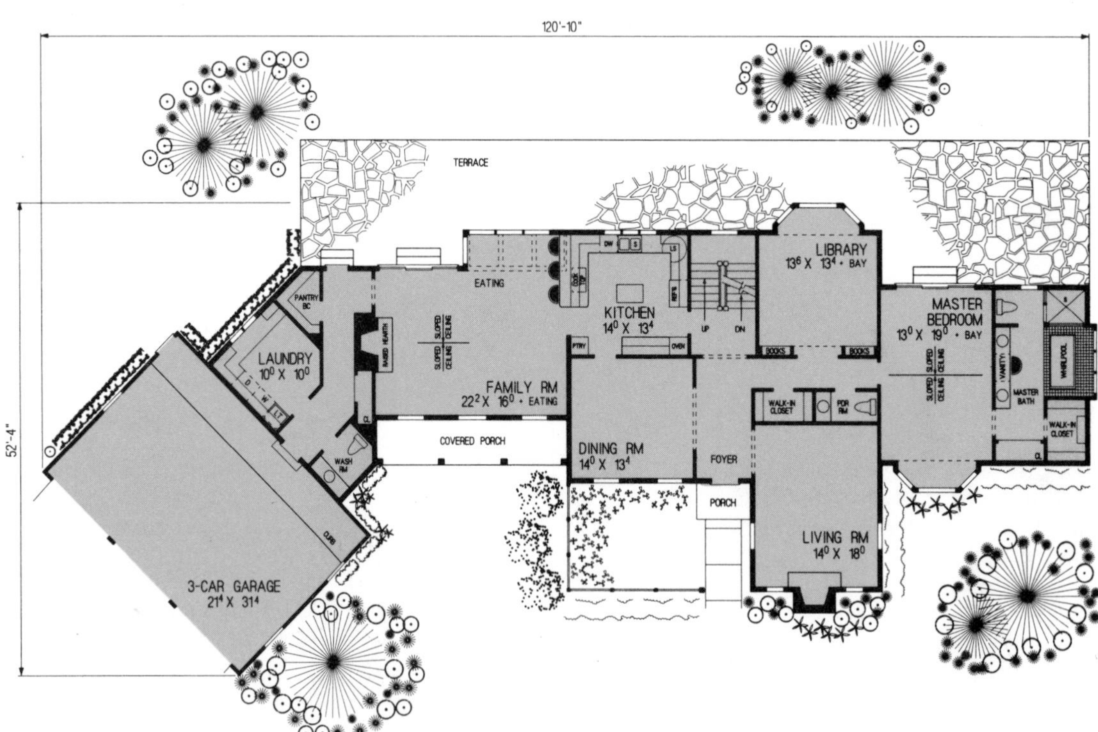

● Pleasing appearance, with an excellent floor plan. Notice how all the rooms are accessible from a hall. That's a plus for easy housekeeping. Some other extras: an exceptionally large family room which is more than 20' x 15', a gracious living room, formal dining room adjacent to the kitchen/nook area, four large bedrooms, a secluded guest suite plus a huge storage area.

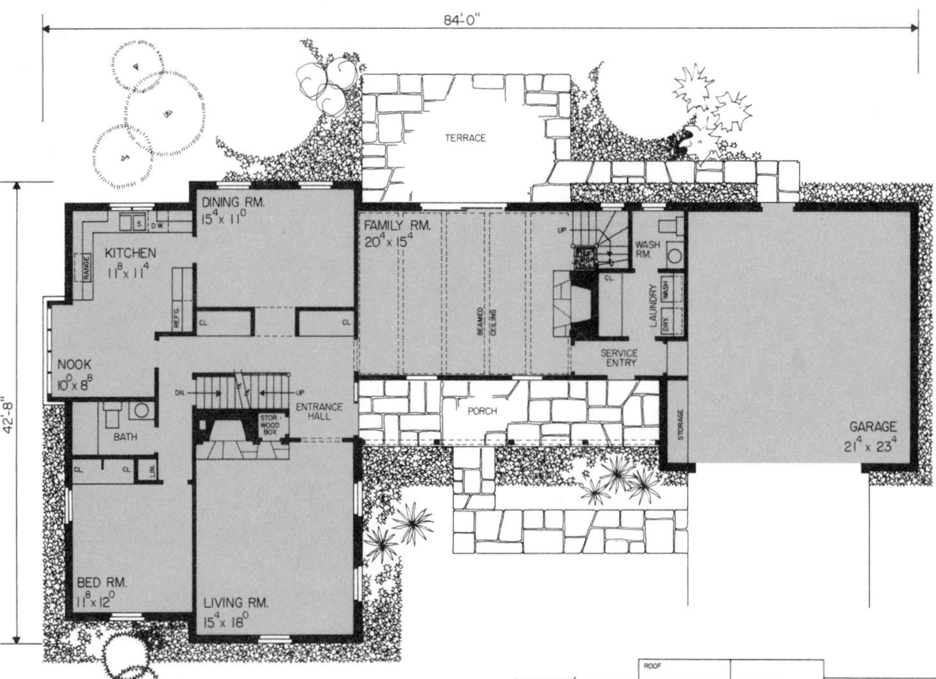

Note that the large guest suite, featuring a full bath, is only accessible by the back stairs in the family room. You could use it as a spacious library, playroom, or a hobby area. Two fireplaces (one with a built-in wood box), walk-in closets, covered front porch and rear terrace also highlight this home.

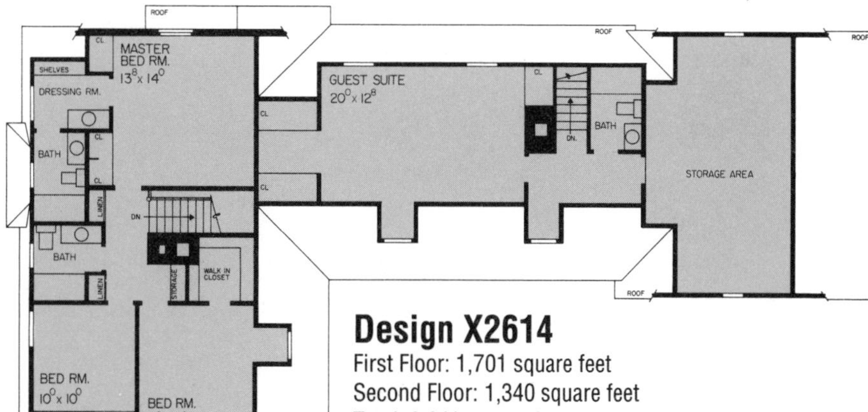

Design X2614

First Floor: 1,701 square feet
Second Floor: 1,340 square feet
Total: 3,041 square feet
D

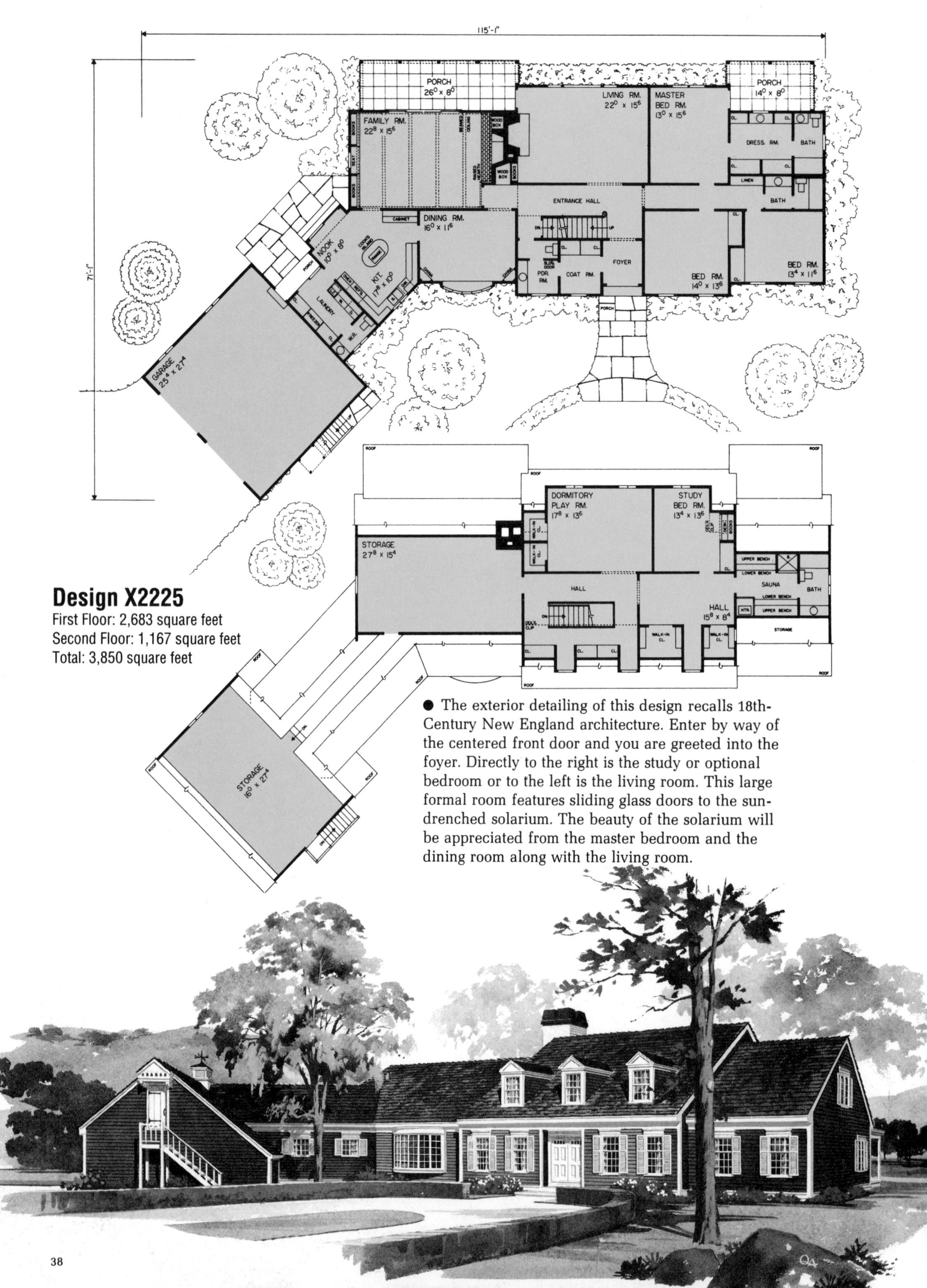

Design X2225

First Floor: 2,683 square feet
Second Floor: 1,167 square feet
Total: 3,850 square feet

● The exterior detailing of this design recalls 18th-Century New England architecture. Enter by way of the centered front door and you are greeted into the foyer. Directly to the right is the study or optional bedroom or to the left is the living room. This large formal room features sliding glass doors to the sun-drenched solarium. The beauty of the solarium will be appreciated from the master bedroom and the dining room along with the living room.

Design X1970

First Floor: 1,664 square feet
Second Floor: 1,116 square feet
Total: 2,780 square feet

D

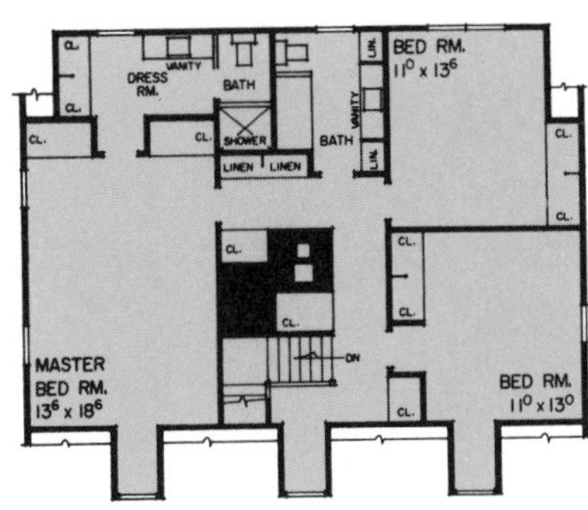

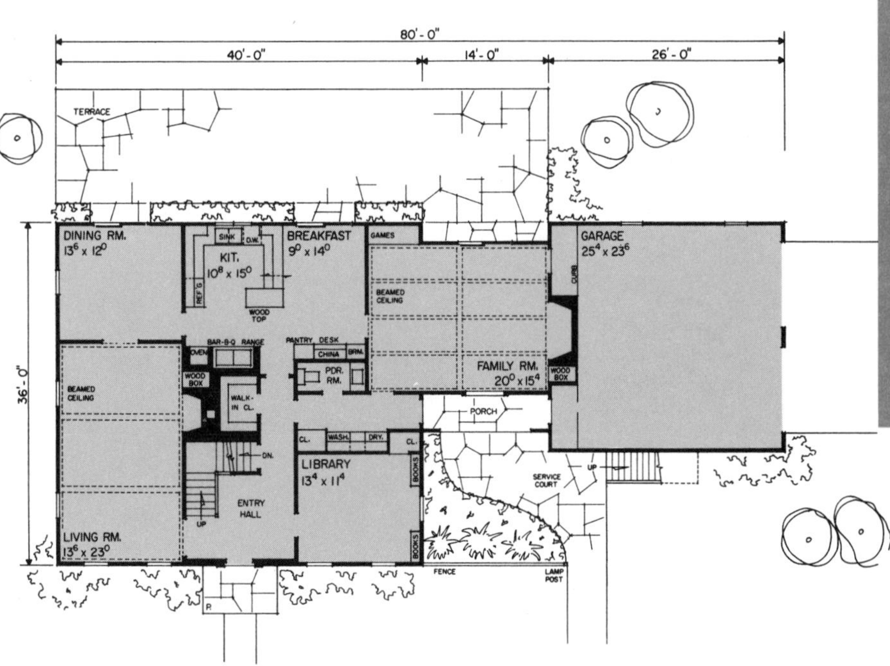

● The prototype of this Colonial house was an integral part of the 18th-Century New England landscape; the updated version is a welcome addition to any suburban scene. The main entry wing, patterned after a classic Cape Cod cottage design, is two stories high but has a pleasing groundhugging look. The steeply pitched roof, triple dormers, and a massive central chimney anchor the house firmly to its site. Entry elevation is symmetrically balanced; doorway, middle dormer, and chimney are in perfect alignment. The one story wing between the main house and the garage is a spacious, beam-ceilinged family room with splay-walled entry porch at the front elevation and sliding glass windows at the rear opening to terrace, which is the full length of the house.

● This cozy home has over 2,600 square feet of livable floor area! And the manner in which this space is put to work to function conveniently for the large family is worth studying. Imagine five bedrooms, three full baths, living, dining and family rooms. Note large kitchen.

Design X1766 First Floor: 1,638 square feet
Second Floor: 1,006; Total: 2,644 square feet

D

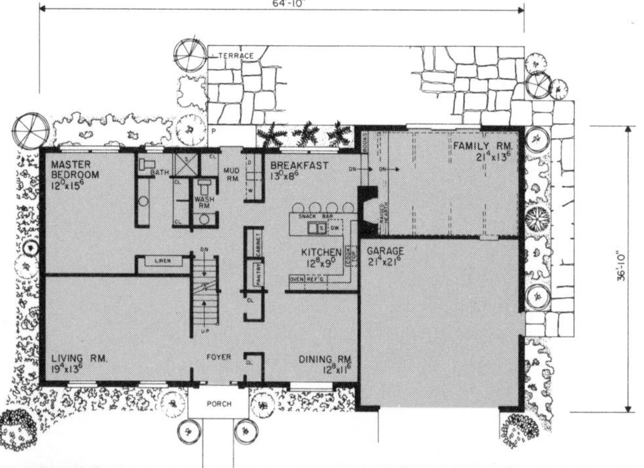

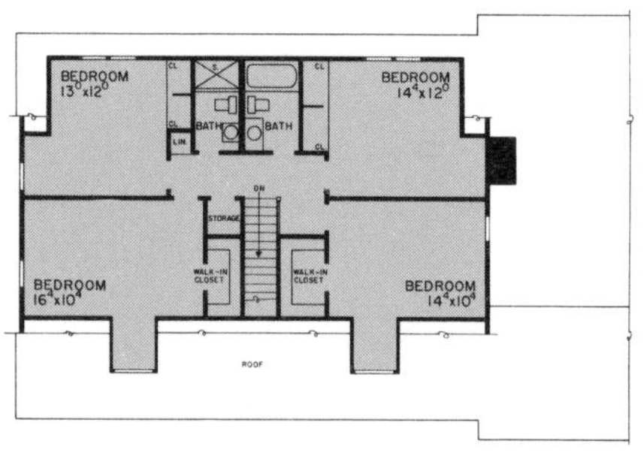

● Surely your list of favorite features will be fun to compile. It certainly will be a long one. The center entry hall helps establish excellent traffic patterns and good zoning. The formal living and dining rooms function well together, as do the kitchen and family room. Note laundry and study.

Design X2124 First Floor: 1,176 square feet
Second Floor: 922 square feet; Total: 2,098 square feet

L **D**

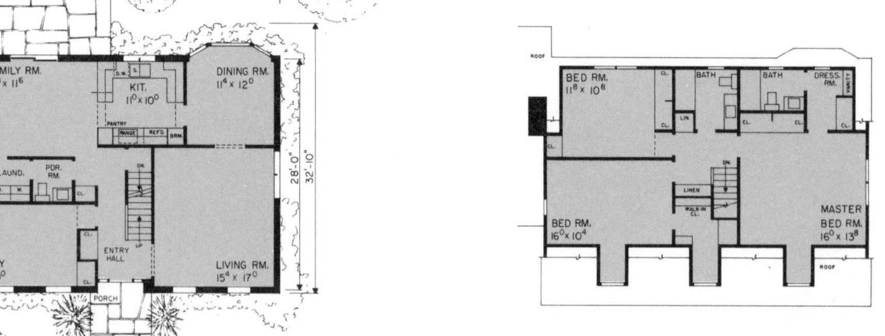

Design X1701

First Floor: 1,344 square feet
Second Floor: 948 square feet
Total: 2,292 square feet

D

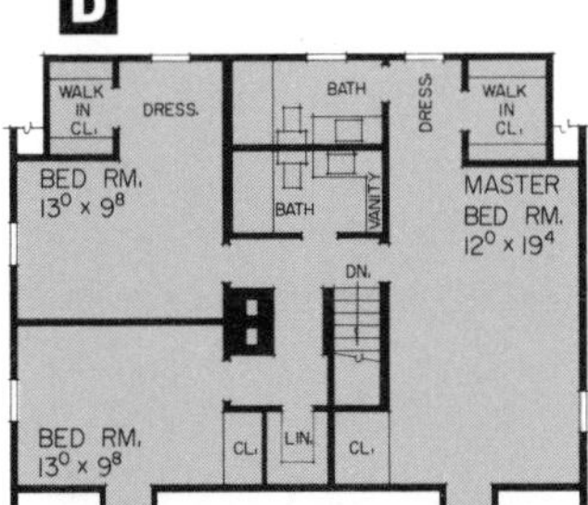

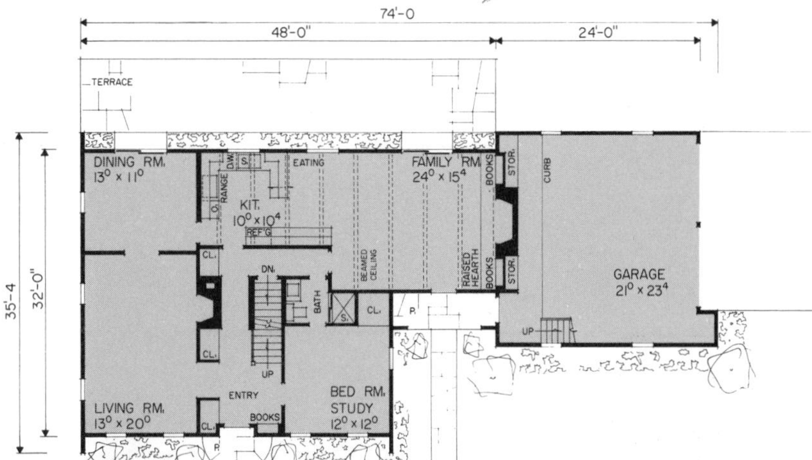

Design X1793

First Floor: 1,986 square feet; Second Floor: 944 square feet; Total: 2,930 square feet

D

● A great plan! The large family will find its living requirements satisfied admirably all throughout those active years of growing up. This would make a fine expansible house. The upstairs may be finished off as the size of the family increases and budget permits. Complete living requirements can be obtained on the first floor.

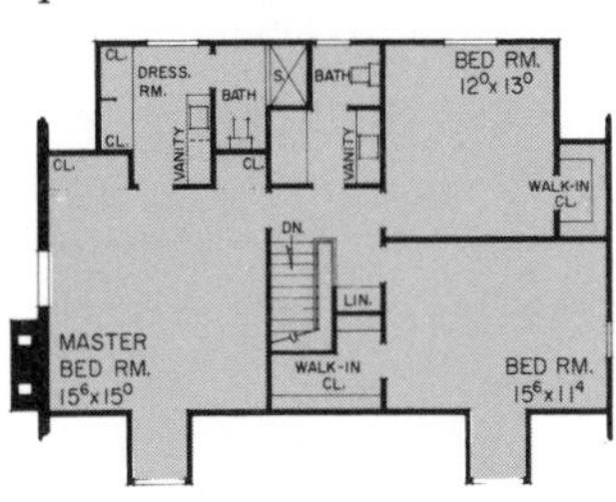

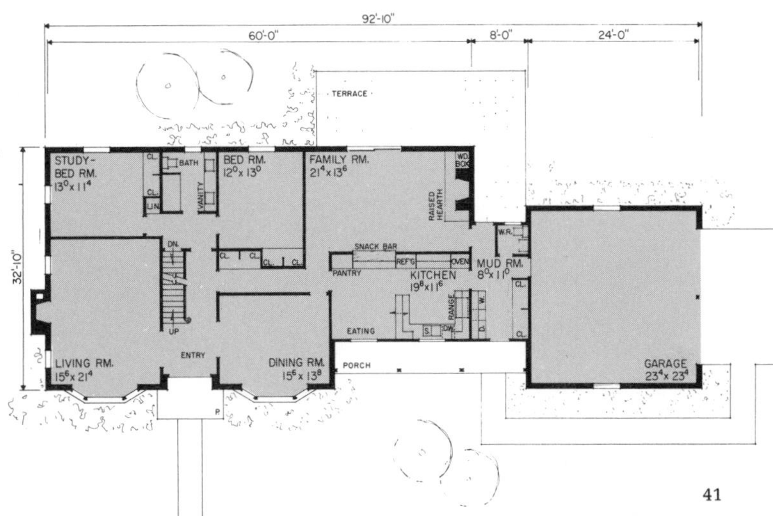

Design X1718

First Floor: 2,012 square feet
Second Floor: 589 square feet
Total: 2,601 square feet

L **D**

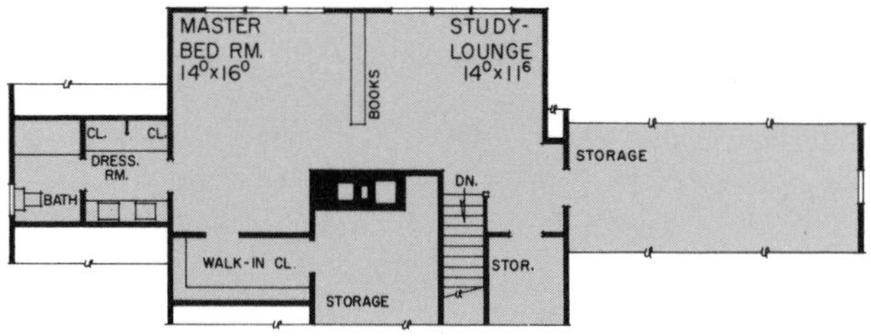

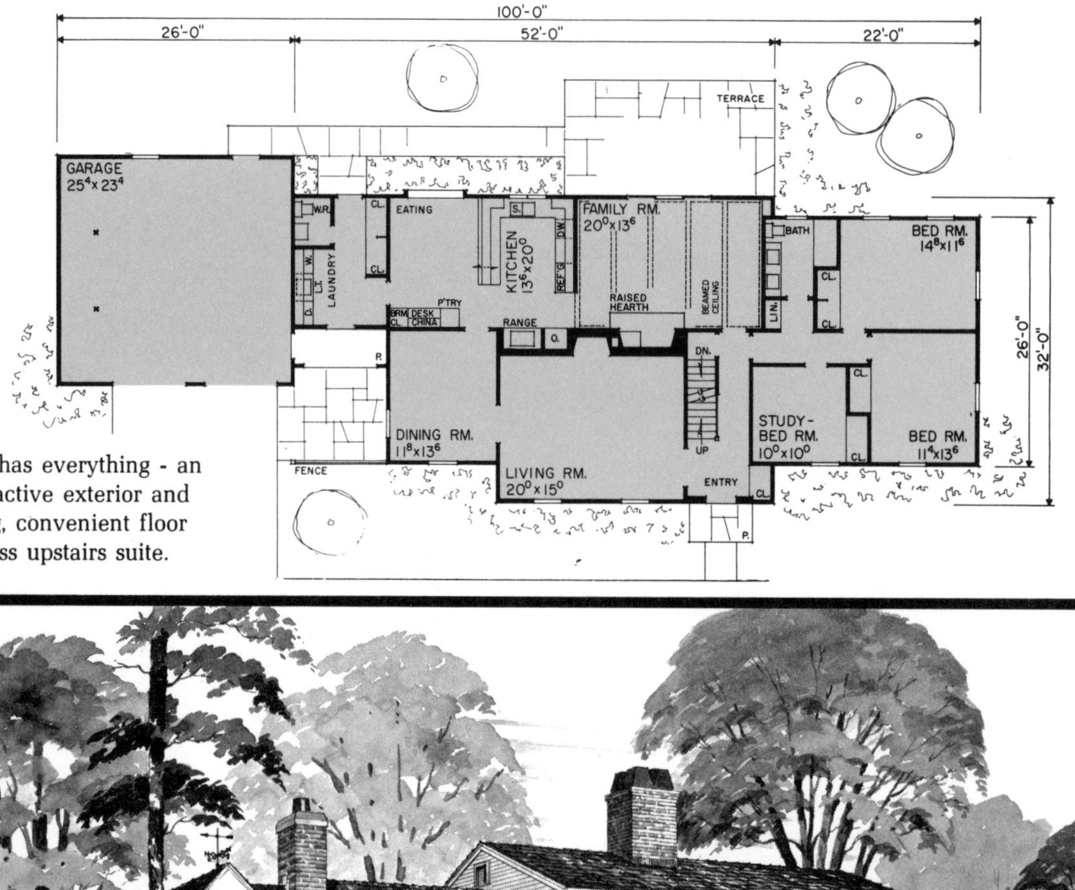

MASTER BED RM. $14^0 \times 16^0$
STUDY-LOUNGE $14^0 \times 11^6$
BOOKS
CL. CL.
DRESS. RM.
BATH
STORAGE
DN.
WALK-IN CL.
STORAGE
STOR.

100'-0"
26'-0" 52'-0" 22'-0"
TERRACE
GARAGE $25^4 \times 23^4$
W.R.
CL.
EATING
S.
D.W.
FAMILY RM. $20^0 \times 13^6$
BATH
BED RM. $14^8 \times 11^6$
W. LAUNDRY
CL.
KITCHEN $13^6 \times 20^0$
REF.
RAISED HEARTH
BEAMED CEILING
LIN.
CL.
CL.
BRM. CL. DESK CHINA P'TRY
RANGE
O.
DN.
R.
CL.
26'-0" 32'-0"
DINING RM. $11^8 \times 13^6$
UP
STUDY-BED RM. $10^0 \times 10^0$
CL.
BED RM. $11^4 \times 13^6$
FENCE
LIVING RM. $20^0 \times 15^0$
ENTRY
CL.
P.

● This house has everything - an extremely attractive exterior and a fine working, convenient floor plan. Don't miss upstairs suite.

Design X1987 First Floor: 1,632 square feet Second Floor: 980 square feet; Total: 2,612 square feet

L D

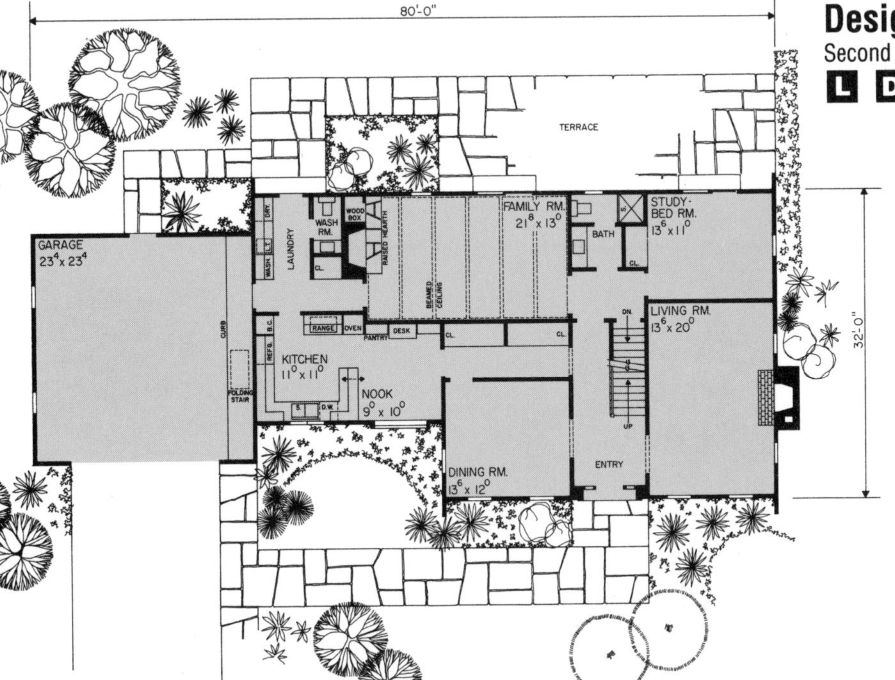

● The comforts of home will be endless and enduring when experienced and enjoyed in this Colonial adaptation. What's your favorite feature?

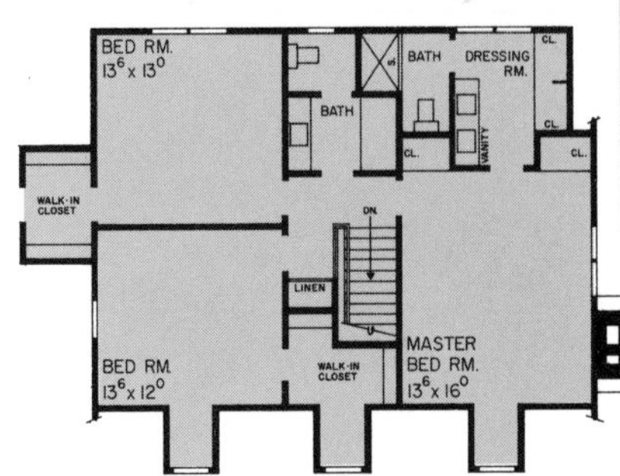

Design X2131

First Floor: 1,214 square feet
Second Floor: 1,097 square feet
Total: 2,311 square feet

L D

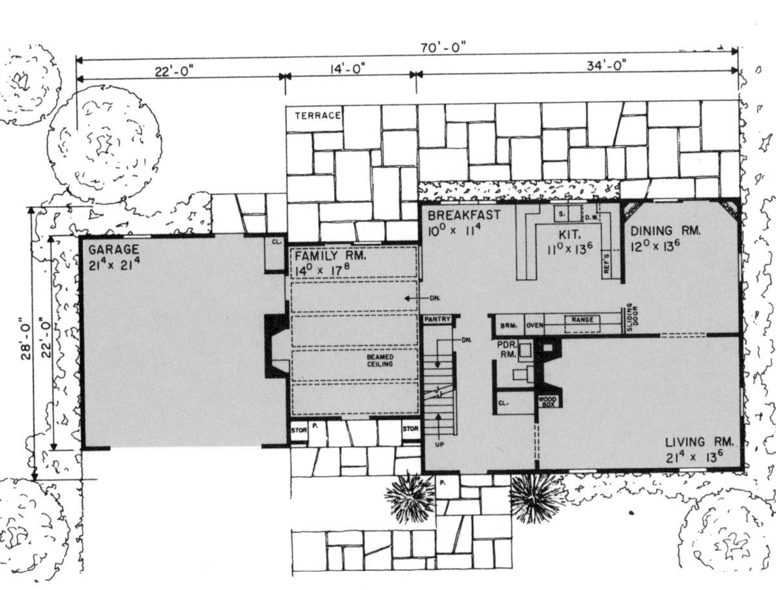

● The Gambrel-roof home is often the very embodiment of charm from the Early Colonial Period in American architechtural history. Fine proportion and excellent detailing were the hallmarks of the era.

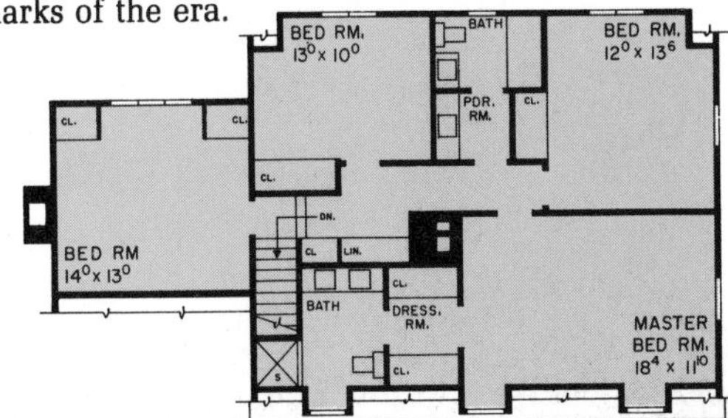

Expandable Cape Ann Cottage

Design X2983 First Floor (Basic Plan): 776 square feet
First Floor (Expanded Plan): 1,072 square feet
Second Floor (Both Plans): 652 square feet
Total: 1,428 (Basic Plan); 1,724 (Expanded Plan)

● This charming gambrel-roofed Colonial cottage is reminiscent of the simple houses built and occupied by seafarers on Cape Ann, Mass. in the 17th and 18th Centuries. However, this adaptation offers a new twist. It is designed to expand as your need and/or budget grows. Of course, building the expanded version first will deliver the bonus livability promised by the formal dining room and quiet study, plus the convenience of the attached garage.

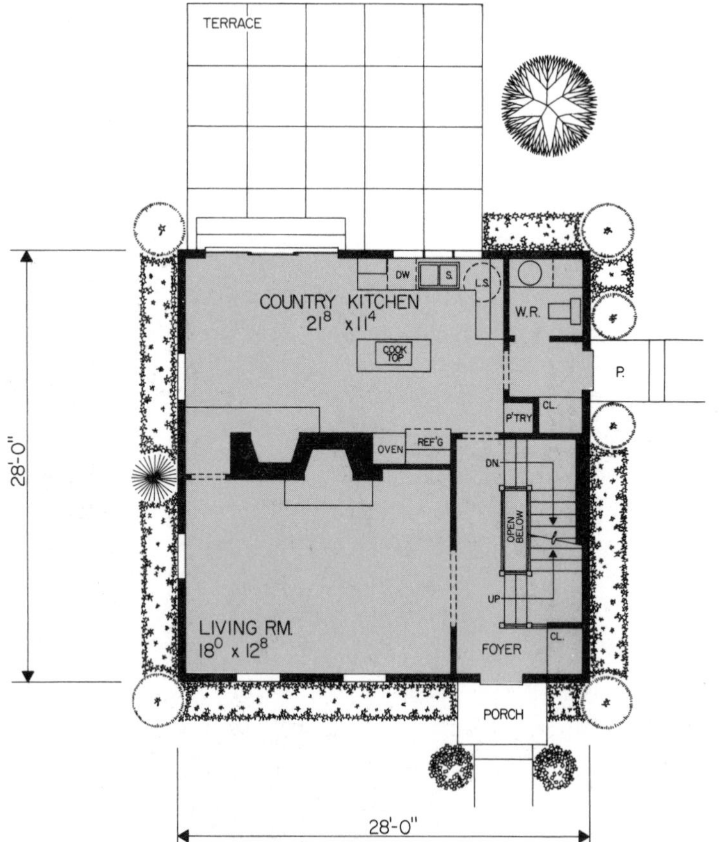

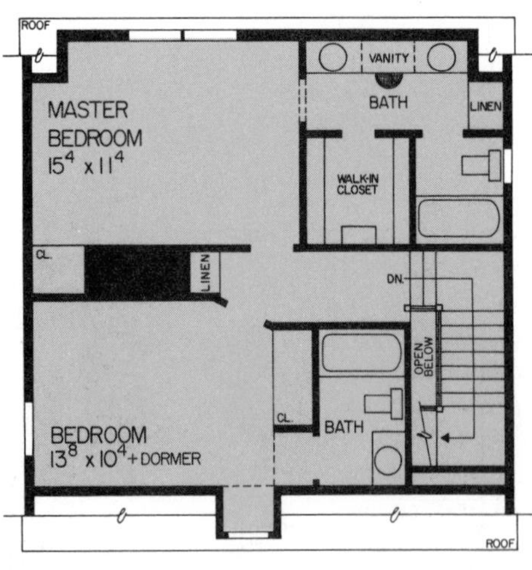

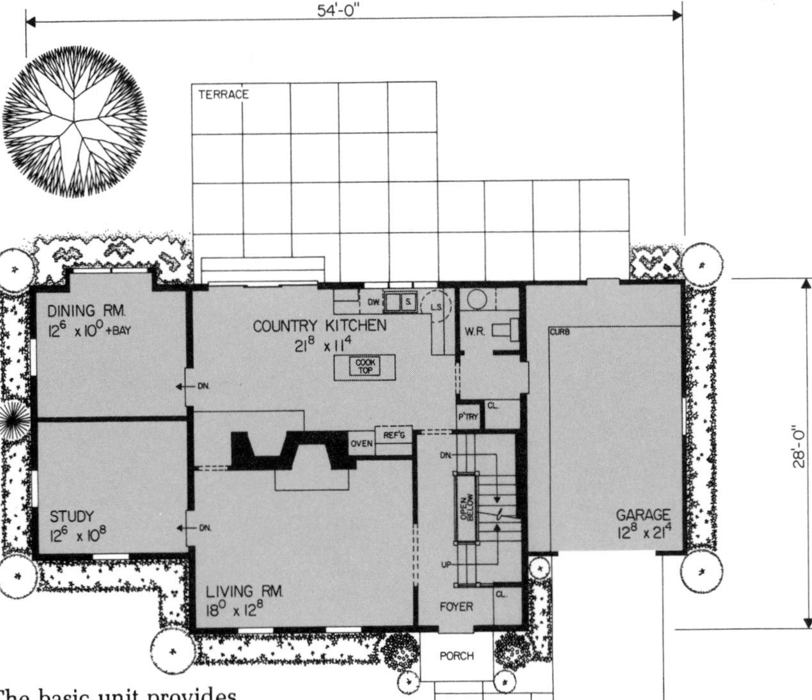

The second floor of each plan is identical. It highlights two bedrooms, and two full baths. In addition, there are two linen closets, double lavatories, built-in vanity, and walk-in wardrobe closet.

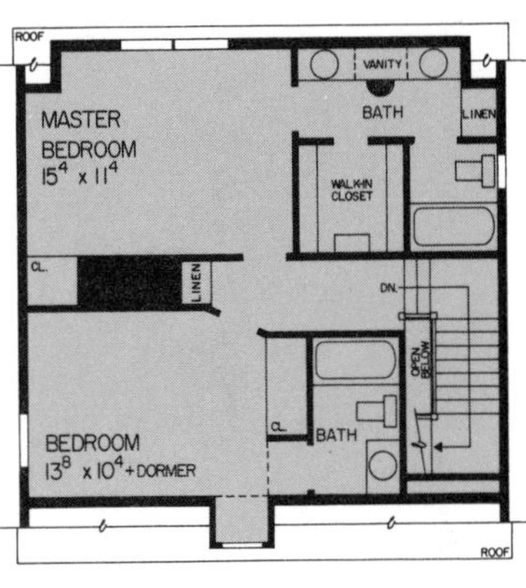

The basic unit provides fine livability potential for the small family. The country kitchen is spacious and allows for plenty of dining area. Here, the focal point is the fireplace. The efficient work center is but a few steps from the sliding glass doors to the rear terrace. The living room is of good size and also features a fireplace. The foyer routes traffic efficiently. The open stairwell leads to the basement level for the pursuit of hobbies and recreation. Don't miss the big bay window of the dining room, the pantry, or the handy wash room.

Design X1791 First Floor: 1,157 square feet

Second Floor: 875 square feet; Total: 2,032 square feet

L **D**

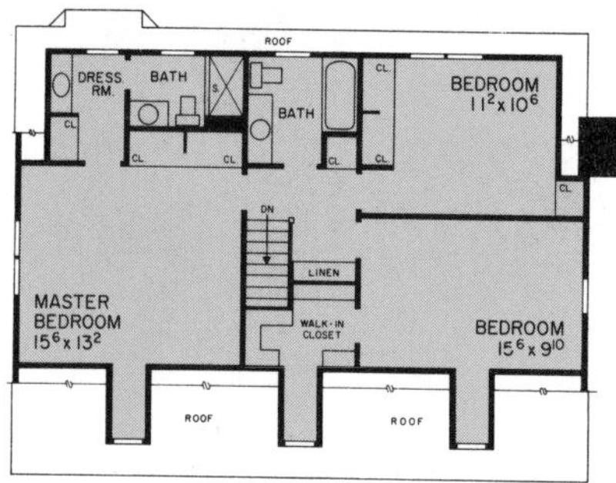

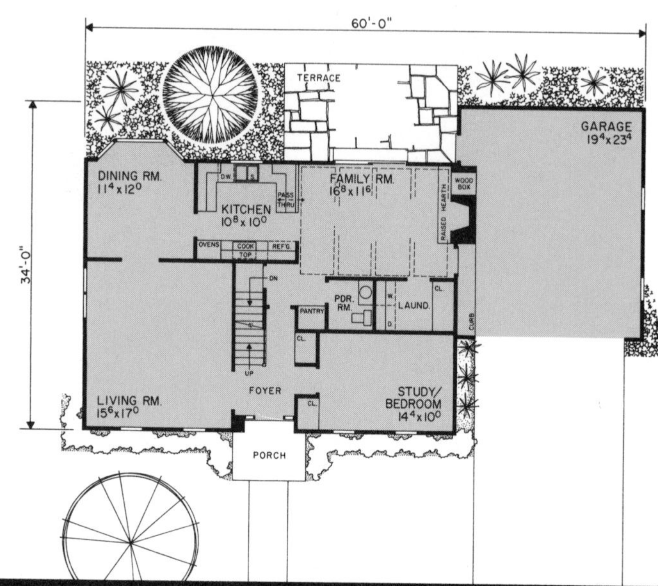

● Wherever you build this moderately sized house an aura of Cape Cod is sure to unfold. The symmetry is pleasing, indeed. The authentic center entrance seems to project a beckoning call.

Design X1870 First Floor: 1,136 square feet

Second Floor: 936 square feet; Total: 2,072 square feet

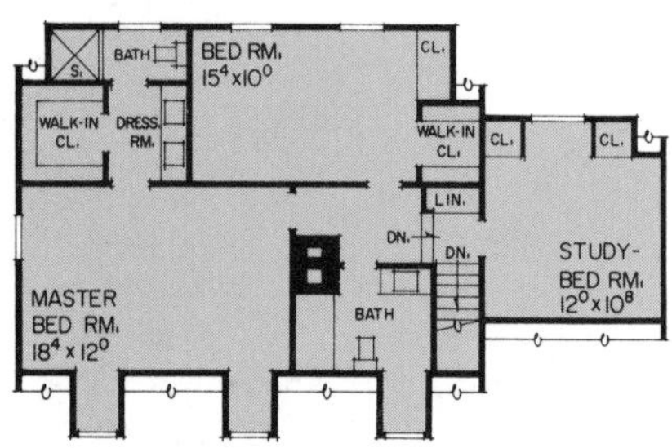

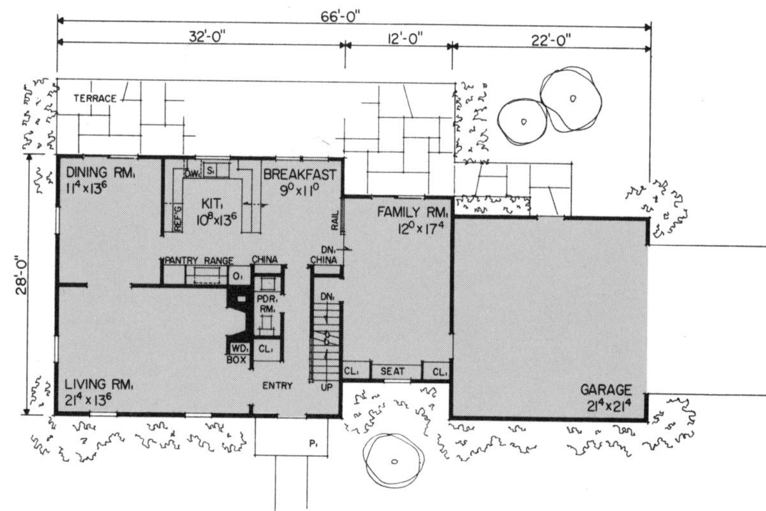

● Besides an enchanting exterior, this home has formal dining and living rooms, plus informal family and breakfast rooms. Built-ins are located in both of these informal rooms. U-shaped, the kitchen will efficiently service both of the dining areas. Study the sleeping facilities of the second floor.

Design X2396 First Floor: 1,616 square feet

Second Floor: 993 square feet; Total: 2,609 square feet

D

● Another picturesque facade right from the pages of our Colonial heritage. The authentic features are many. Don't miss the stairs to area over the garage.

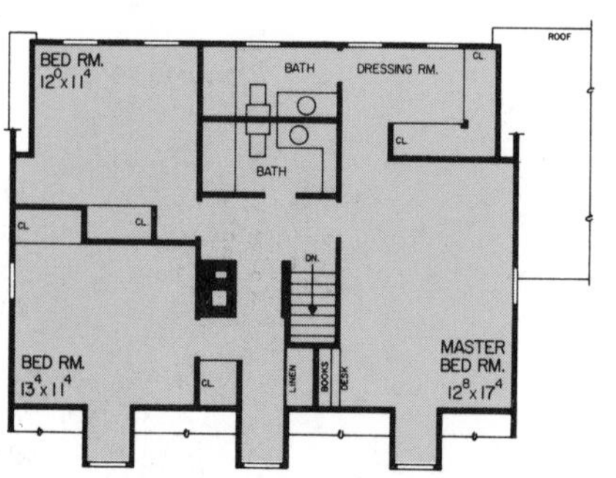

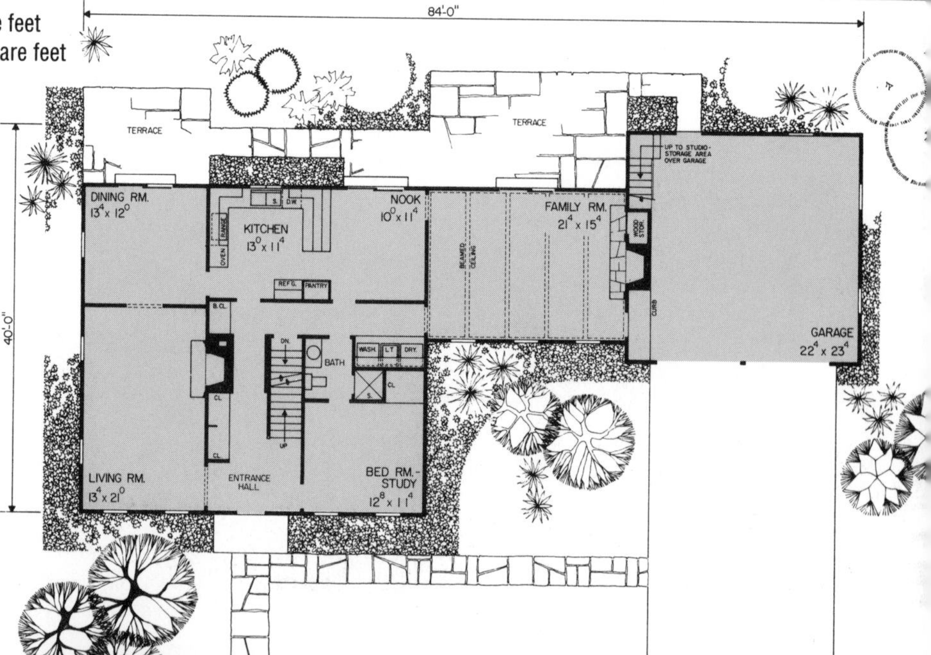

Expanding the Half-House

Design X2682

First Floor (Basic Plan): 976 square feet
First Floor (Expanded Plan): 1,230 square feet
Second Floor (Both Plans): 744 square feet
Total (Basic Plan): 1,720; Total (Expanded Plan): 1,974 square feet

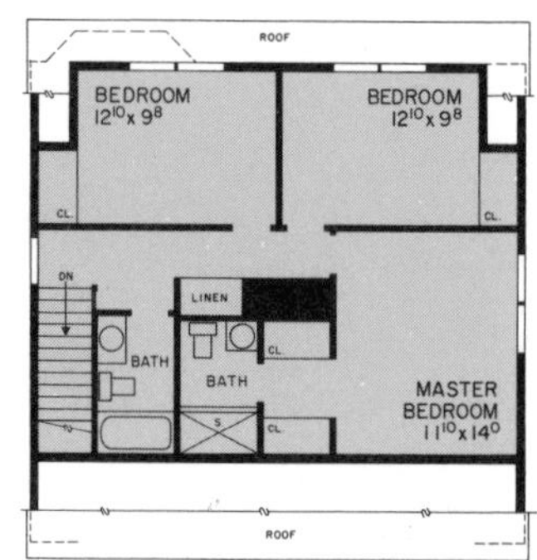

● Here is an expandable Colonial with a full measure of Cape Cod Charm. For those who wish to build the basic house, there is an abundance of low-budget livability. Twin fireplaces serve the formal living room and the informal country kitchen. Note the spaciousness of both areas. A dining room and powder room are also on the first floor of this basic plan. Upstairs three bedrooms and two full baths.

CUSTOMIZABLE

Custom Alterations? See page 301 for customizing this plan to your specifications.

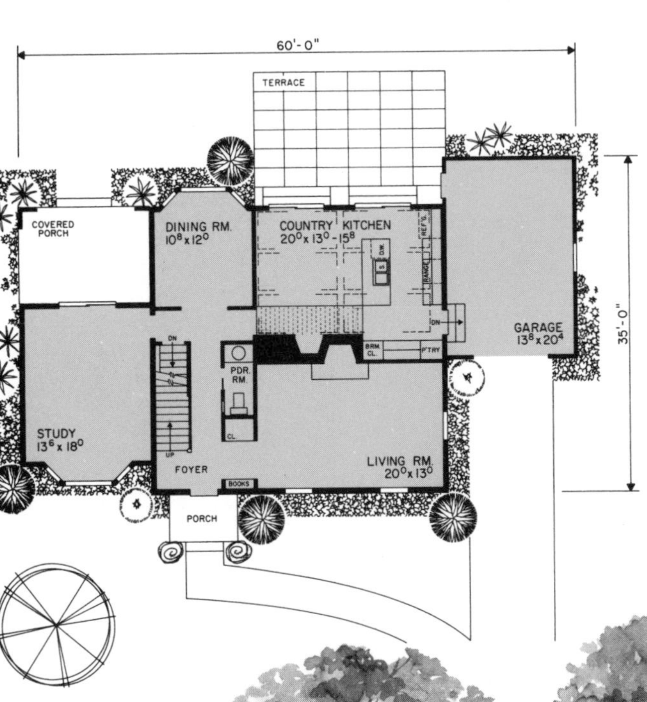

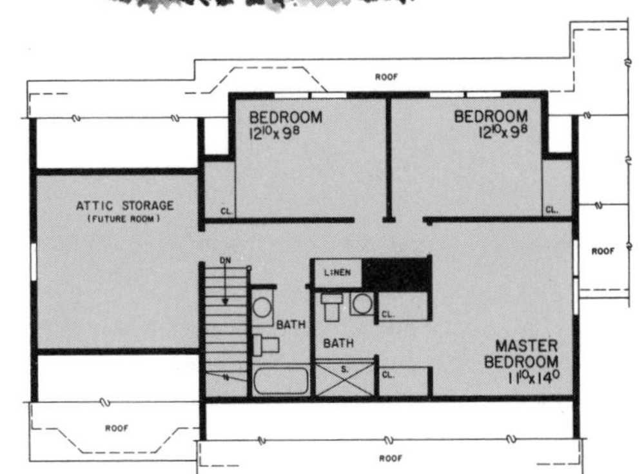

● This expanded version of the basic house on the opposite page is equally as reminiscent of Cape Cod. Common in the 17th Century was the addition of appendages to the main structure. This occurred as family size increased or finances improved. This version provides for the addition of wings to accommodate a large study and a garage. Utilizing the alcove behind the study results in a big, covered porch. Certainly a charming design whichever version you decide to build for your family.

Design X2852 First Floor: 919 square feet

Second Floor: 535 square feet; Total: 1,454 square feet

L **D**

● Compact enough for even the smallest lot, this cozy design provides comfortable living space for a small family. At the heart of the plan is a spacious country kitchen. It features a cooking island - snack bar and a dining area that opens to a house-wide rear terrace. The nearby dining room also opens to the terrace. At the front of the plan is the living room, warmed by a fireplace. Across the centered foyer is a cozy study. Two second floor bedrooms are serviced by two baths. Note the first floor powder room and storage closet located next to the side entrance. This home will be a delight.

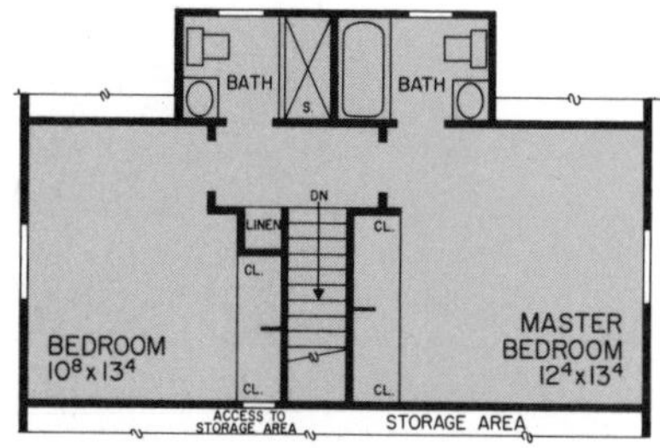

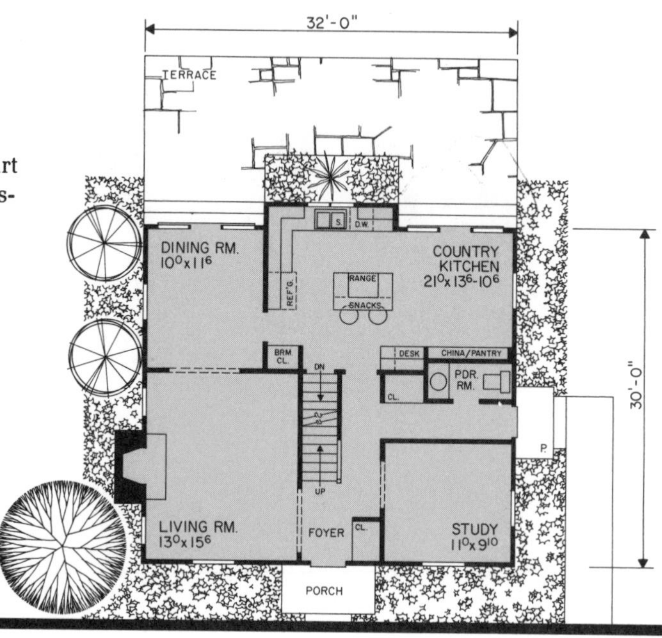

Design X2571 First Floor: 1,137 square feet

Second Floor: 795 square feet; Total: 1,932 square feet

L **D**

● Cost-efficient space! That's the bonus with this attractive Cape Cod. Start in the living room. It is spacious and inviting with full-length paned windows. In the formal dining room, a bay window adds the appropriate touch. For more living space, a delightfully appointed family room. The efficient kitchen has a snack bar for casual meals. Three bedrooms are on the second floor.

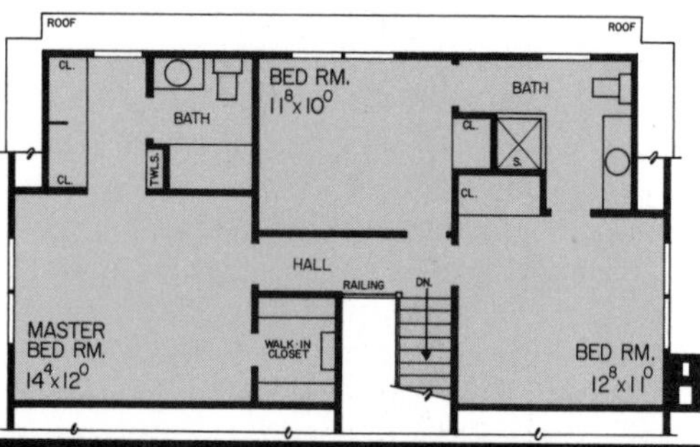

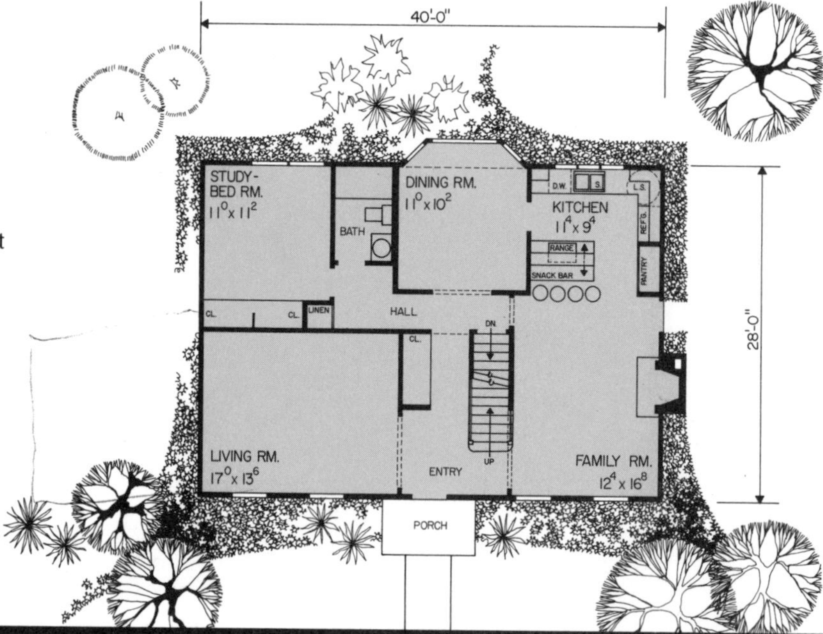

Design X3189 First Floor: 884 square feet

Second Floor: 598 square feet: Total: 1,482 square feet

D

● A large kitchen/dining area and living room are the living areas of this design. Four bedrooms, two up and two down, compose the sleeping zone. Each floor also has a full bath. A full basement and an attached garage will provide plenty of storage areas.

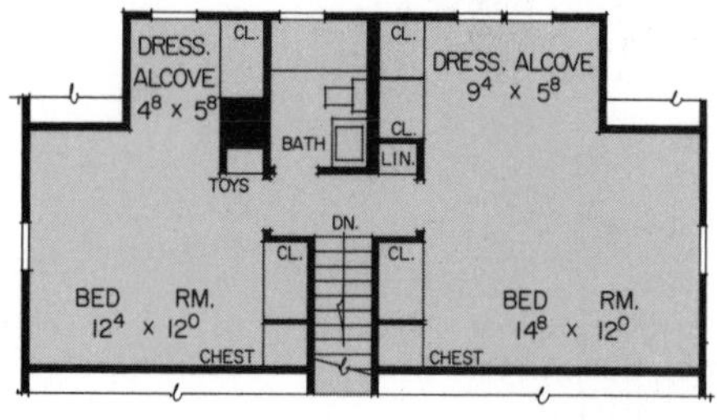

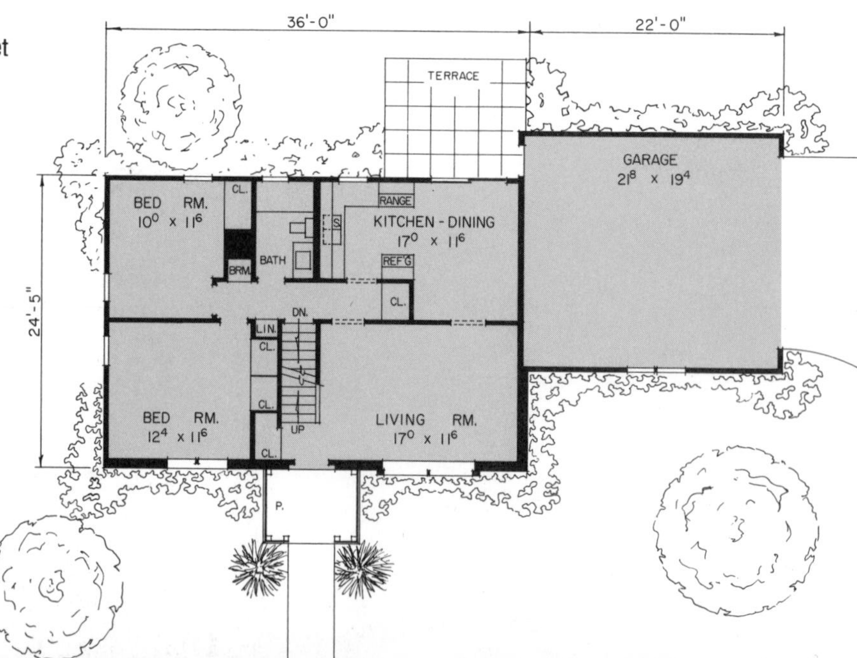

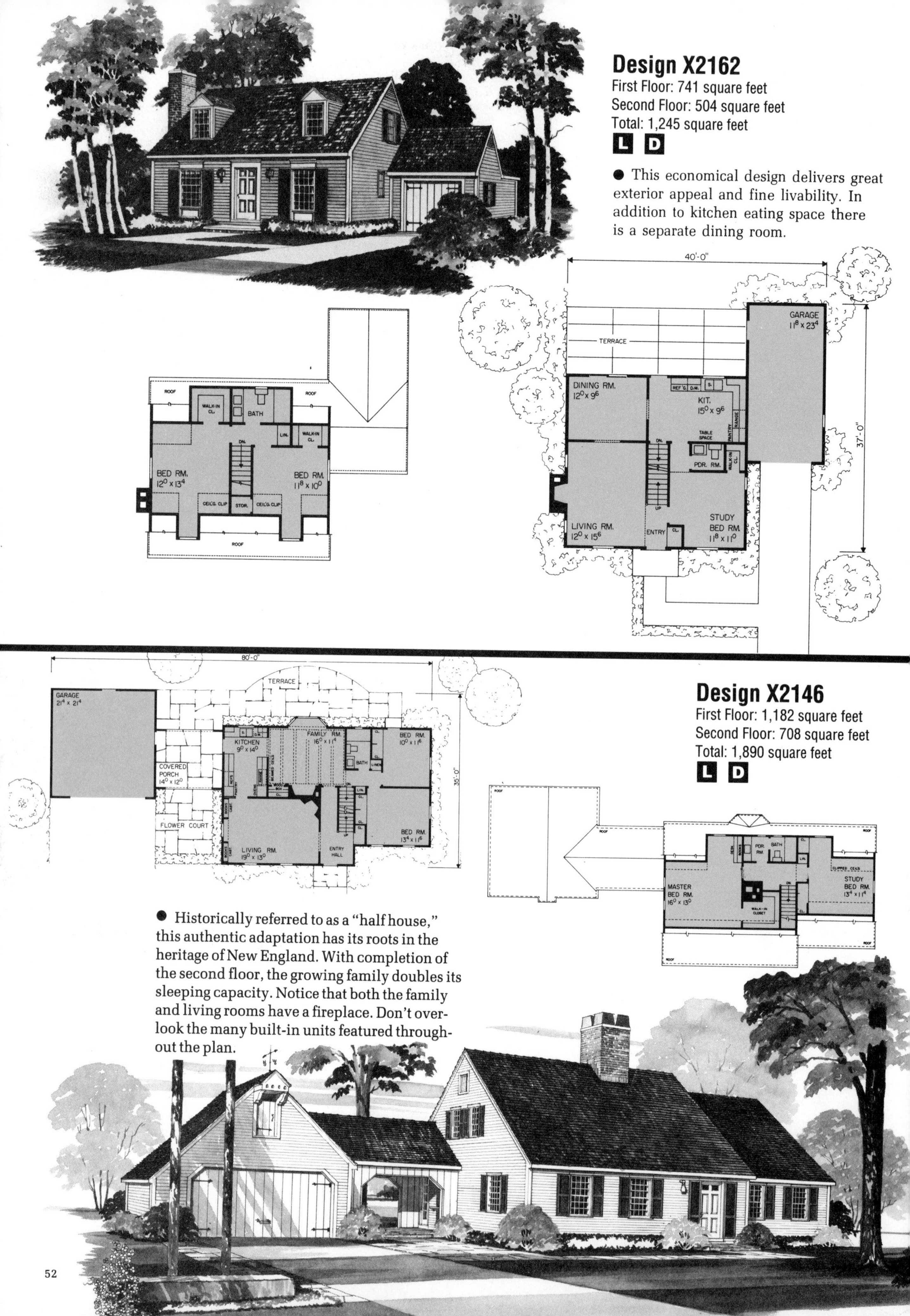

Design X2162

First Floor: 741 square feet
Second Floor: 504 square feet
Total: 1,245 square feet

L **D**

● This economical design delivers great exterior appeal and fine livability. In addition to kitchen eating space there is a separate dining room.

Design X2146

First Floor: 1,182 square feet
Second Floor: 708 square feet
Total: 1,890 square feet

L **D**

● Historically referred to as a "half house," this authentic adaptation has its roots in the heritage of New England. With completion of the second floor, the growing family doubles its sleeping capacity. Notice that both the family and living rooms have a fireplace. Don't overlook the many built-in units featured throughout the plan.

Design X1394

First Floor: 832 square feet
Second Floor: 512 square feet
Total: 1,344 square feet

L **D**

● The growing family with a restricted building budget will find this a great investment - a convenient living floor plan inside an attractively designed facade.

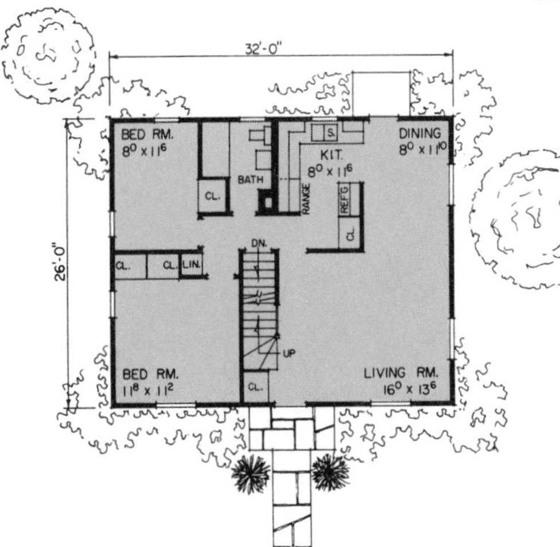

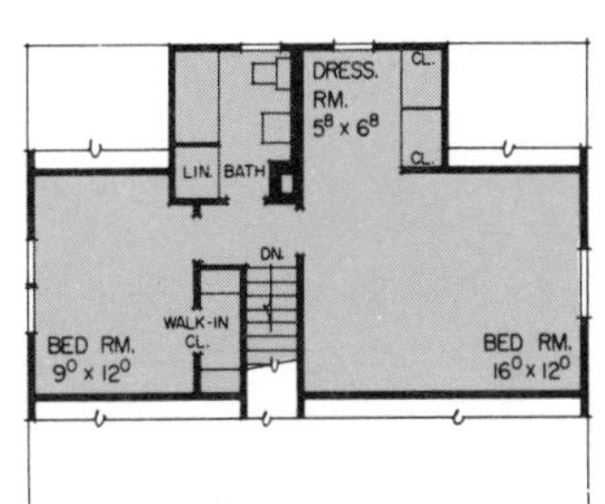

Design X2510

First Floor: 1,191 square feet
Second Floor: 533 square feet
Total: 1,724 square feet

L **D**

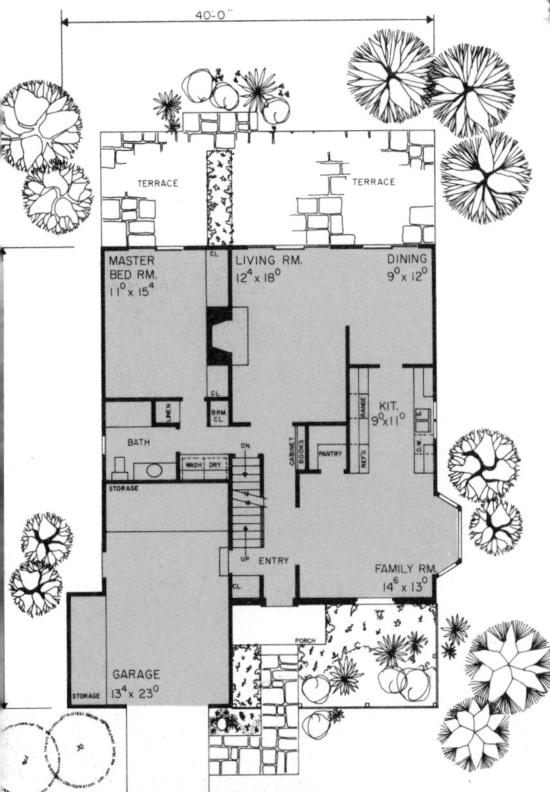

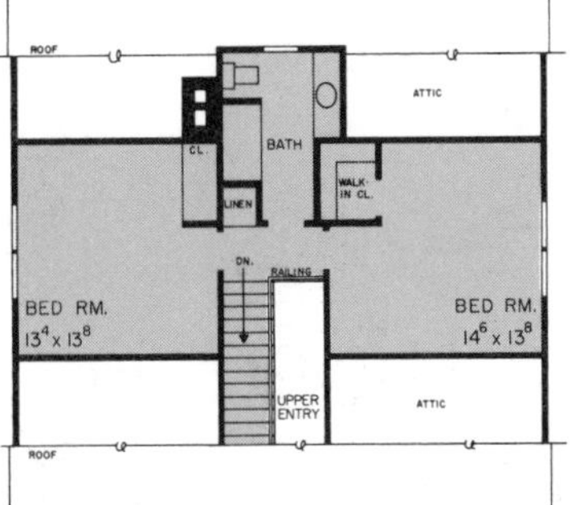

● The pleasant in-line kitchen is flanked by a separate dining room and a family room. The master bedroom is on the first floor with two more bedrooms upstairs.

Design X2657

First Floor: 1,217 square feet
Second Floor: 868 square feet
Total: 2,085 square feet

L

● Deriving its design from the traditional Cape Cod style, this facade features clapboard siding, small-paned windows and a transom-lit entrance flanked by carriage lamps. A central chimney services two fireplaces, one in the country-kitchen and the other in the formal living room which is removed from the disturbing flow of traffic. The master suite is located to the left of the upstairs landing. A full bathroom services two additional bedrooms on the second floor.

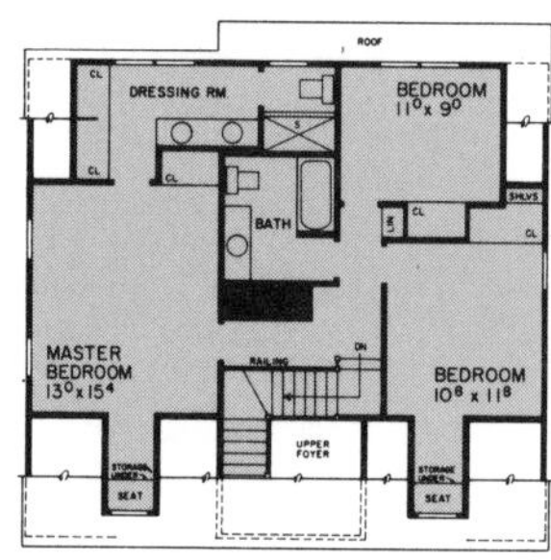

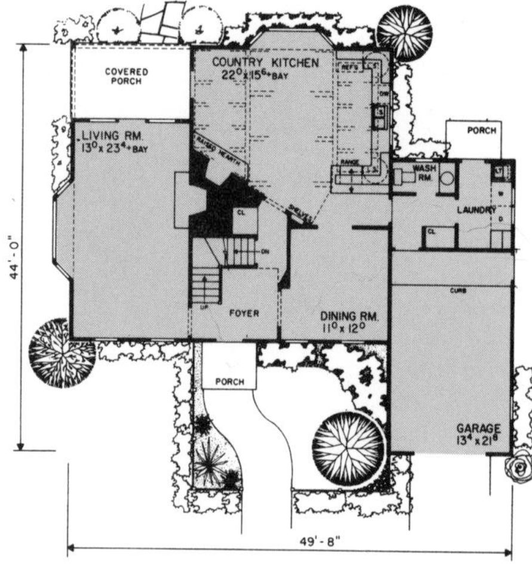

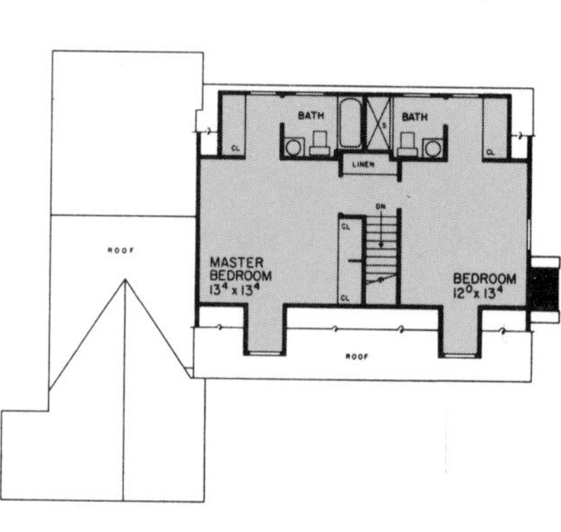

Design X2655

First Floor: 893 square feet
Second Floor: 652 square feet
Total: 1,545 square feet

L

● Wonderful things can be enclosed in small packages. Such is the case for this two-story design. The total square footage is a mere 1,545 square feet yet its features are many. Its exterior is very eye-pleasing with horizontal lines and two second-story dormers. Livability will be enjoyed in this plan. The front study is ideal for a quiet escape. Nearby is a powder room also convenient to the kitchen and breakfast room. Two bedrooms and two full baths are located on the second floor.

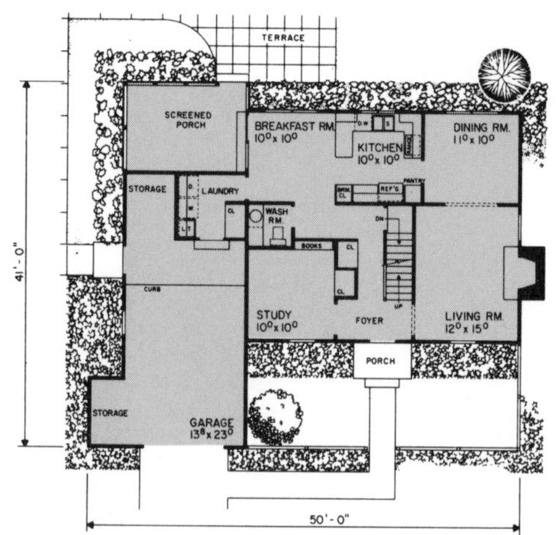

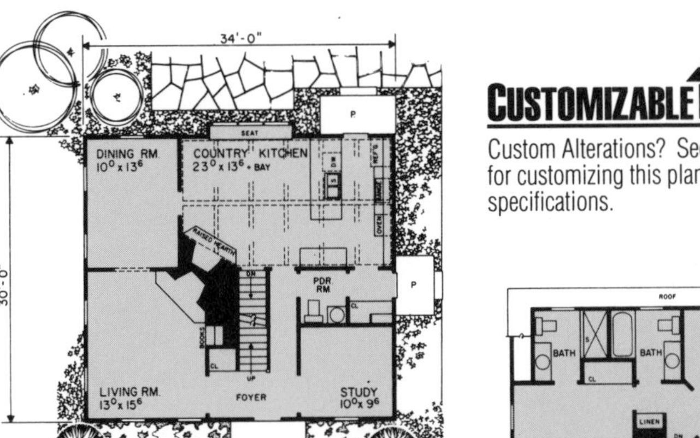

CUSTOMIZABLE

Custom Alterations? See page 301 for customizing this plan to your specifications.

Design X2661

First Floor: 1,020 square feet
Second Floor: 777 square feet
Total: 1,797 square feet

L **D**

● Any other starter house or retirement home couldn't have more charm than this design. Its compact frame houses a very livable plan. An outstanding feature of the first floor is the large country kitchen. Its fine attractions include a beamed ceiling, raised-hearth fireplace, built-in window seat and a door leading to the outdoors. A living room in the front of the plan has another fireplace which shares the single chimney. The rear dormered second floor houses the sleeping and bath facilities.

Design X2656

First Floor: 1,122 square feet
Second Floor: 884 square feet
Total: 2,006 square feet

L **D**

● This charming Cape cottage possesses a great sense of shelter through its gambrel roof. Dormers at front and rear pierce the gambrel roof to provide generous, well-lit living space on the second floor which houses three bedrooms. This design's first-floor layout is not far different from that of the Cape cottages of the 18th Century. The large kitchen and adjoining dining room recall cottage keeping rooms both in function and in location at the rear of the house.

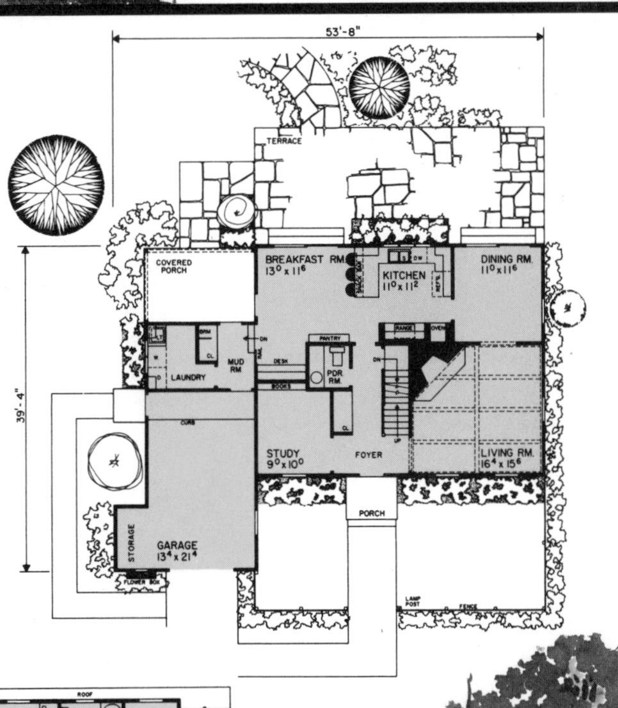

Design X2569 First Floor: 1,102 square feet
Second Floor: 764 square feet; Total: 1,866 square feet

L **D**

● What an enchanting updated version of the popular Cape Cod cottage. There are facilities for both formal and informal living pursuits. Note the spacious family area, the formal dining/living room, the first floor laundry and the efficient kitchen. The second floor houses the three bedrooms and two economically located baths.

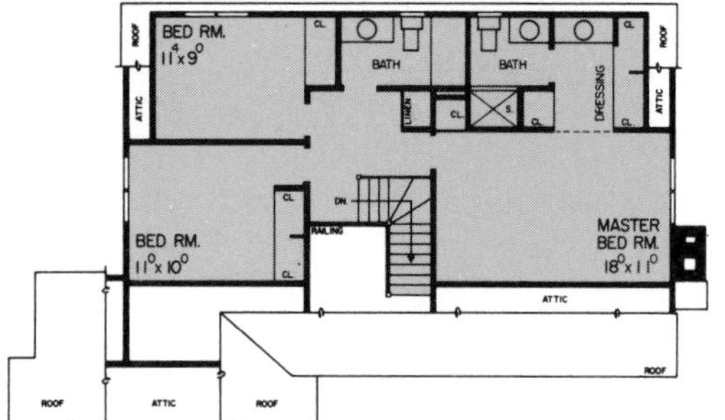

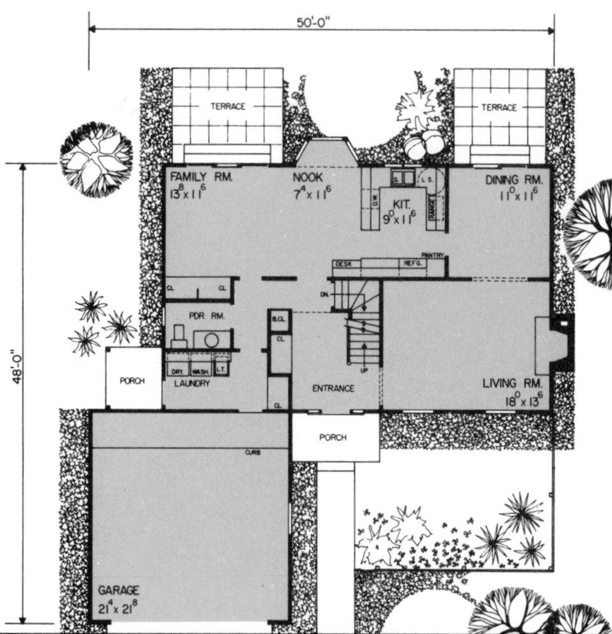

Design X2395
First Floor: 1,481 square feet
Second Floor: 861 square feet
Total: 2,342 square feet

● New England revisited. The appeal of this type of home is ageless. As for its livability, it will serve its occupants admirably for generations to come. With two bedrooms downstairs, you may want to finish off the second floor at a later date.

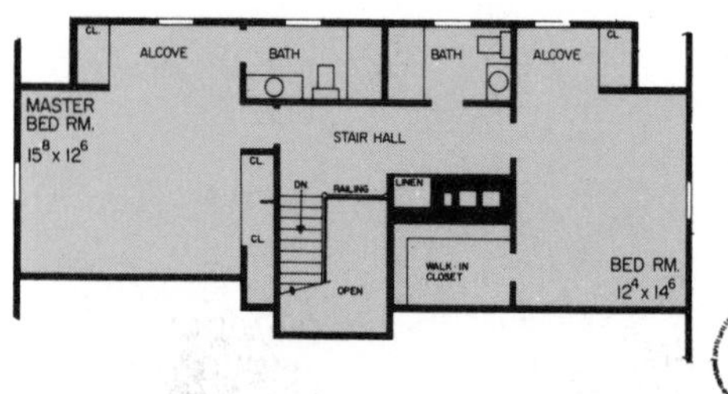

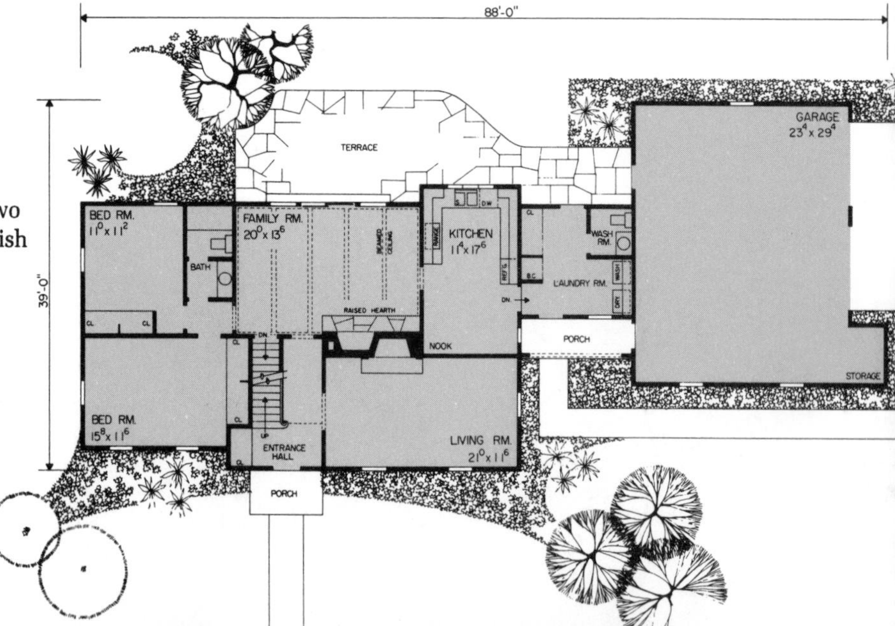

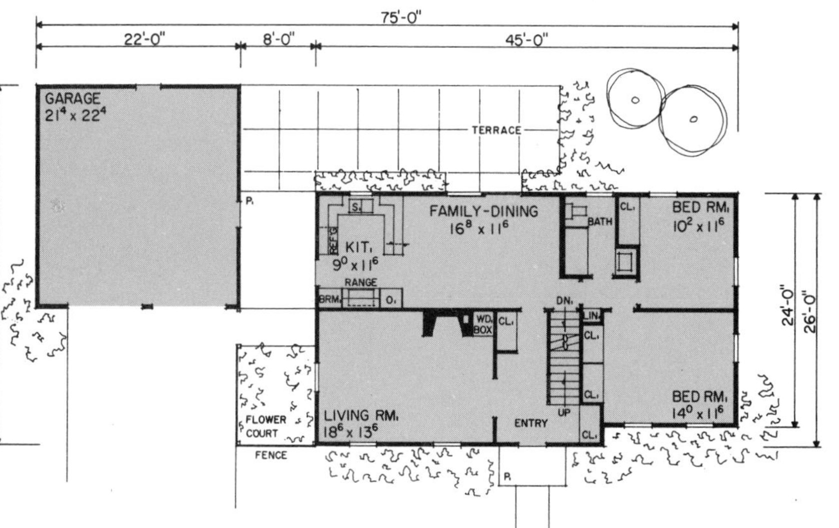

Design X3126

First Floor: 1,141 square feet
Second Floor: 630 square feet
Total: 1,771 square feet

● This New England adaptation has a lot to offer. There is the U-shaped kitchen, family-dining room, four bedrooms, two full baths, fireplace, covered porch and two-car garage. A delightful addition to any neighborhood.

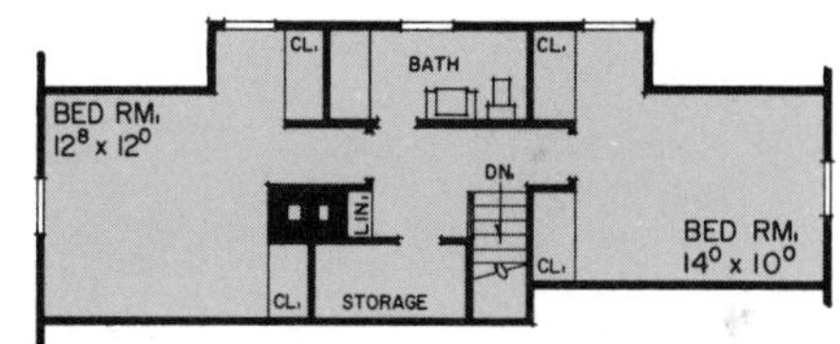

Design X3372

First Floor: 1,259 square feet
Second Floor: 942 square feet
Total: 2,201 square feet

L **D**

● Charm is the key word for this delightful plan's exterior, but don't miss the great floor plan inside. Formal living and dining rooms flank the entry foyer to the front; a family room and breakfast room with beamed ceilings are to the rear. The kitchen and service areas function well together and are near the garage and service entrance for convenience. Upstairs are the sleeping accommodations: two family bedrooms and a master suite of nice proportion.

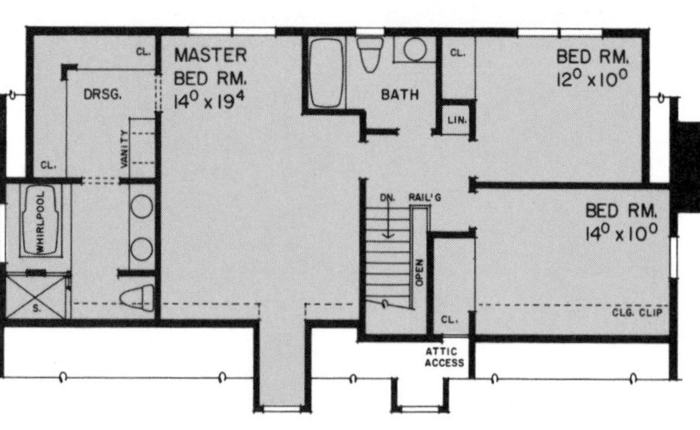

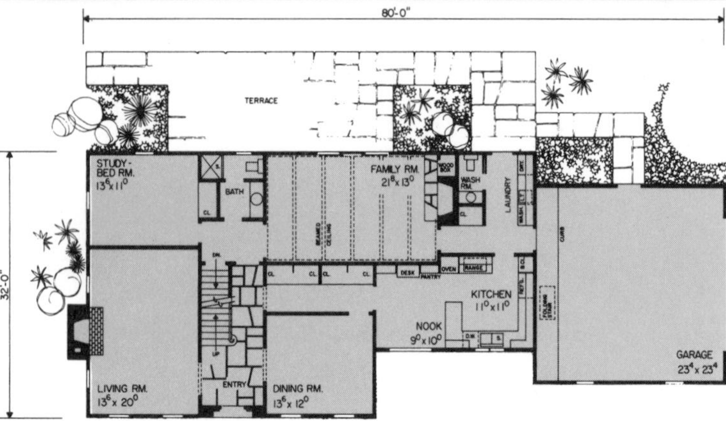

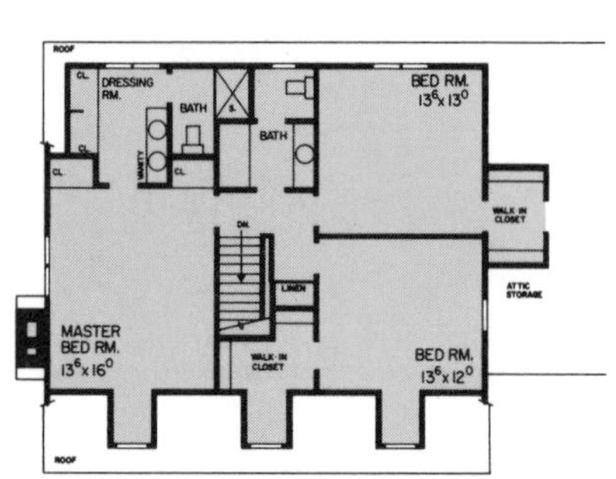

Design X2631

First Floor: 1,634 square feet
Second Floor: 1,011 square feet
Total: 2,645 square feet

L **D**

● Two fireplaces and a wealth of other amenities abound in this design. Notice how all the rooms are accessible from the main hall — keeping traffic in each room to a minimum. A large family room featuring a beamed ceiling, a fireplace with built-in wood box and double doors onto the terrace is nearby an exceptional U-shaped kitchen. Three upstairs bedrooms include a master suite with dressing room and private bath.

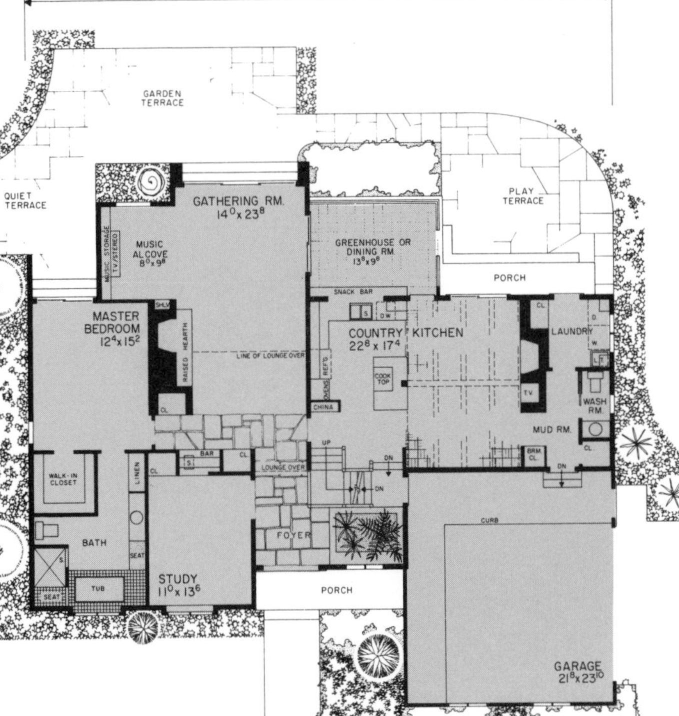

Design X2883 First Floor: 1,919 square feet
Second Floor: 895 square feet; Total: 2,814 square feet

● A country-style home is part of America's fascination with the rural past. This home's emphasis of the traditional home is in its gambrel roof, dormers and fanlight windows. Having a traditional exterior from the street view, this home has window walls and a greenhouse, which opens the house to the outdoors in a thoroughly contemporary manner. The interior meets the requirements of today's active family. Like the country houses of the past, it has a gathering room for family get-togethers or entertaining. The adjacent two-story greenhouse doubles as the dining room. There is a pass-thru snack bar to the country kitchen here. This country kitchen just might be the heart of the house with its two areas - work zone and sitting room. There are four bedrooms on the two floors - the master bedroom suite on the first floor; three more on the second floor. A lounge, overlooking the gathering room and front foyer, is also on the second floor.

Design X1902 First Floor: 1,312 square feet
Second Floor: 850 square feet; Total: 2,162 square feet

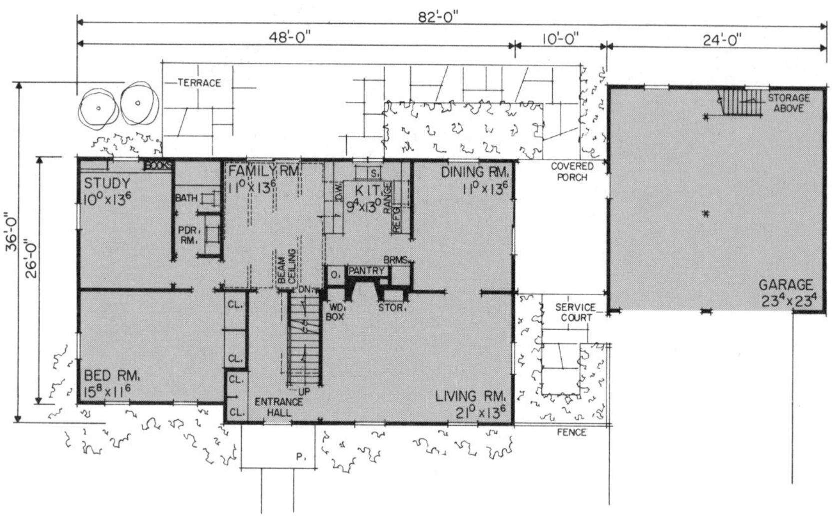

● This design has a great deal to offer the prospective home owner. The main living unit has a formal living room with fireplace and wood box, U-shaped kitchen with adjacent dining room, family room with beamed ceiling and sliding glass doors to the terrace, a study with built-in book shelves (or a second bedroom) and a bedroom. Later development of the second floor will create an additional two bedrooms and two full baths. This home offers a lot of livability and many years of enjoyable living.

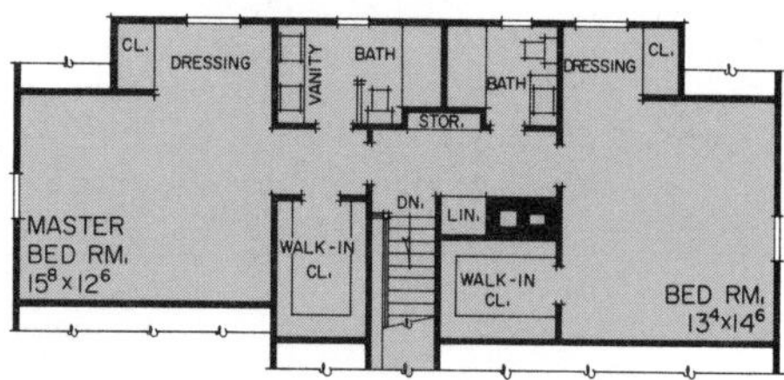

Design X1241
First Floor: 1,064 square feet
Second Floor: 898 square feet
Total: 1,962 square feet

L **D**

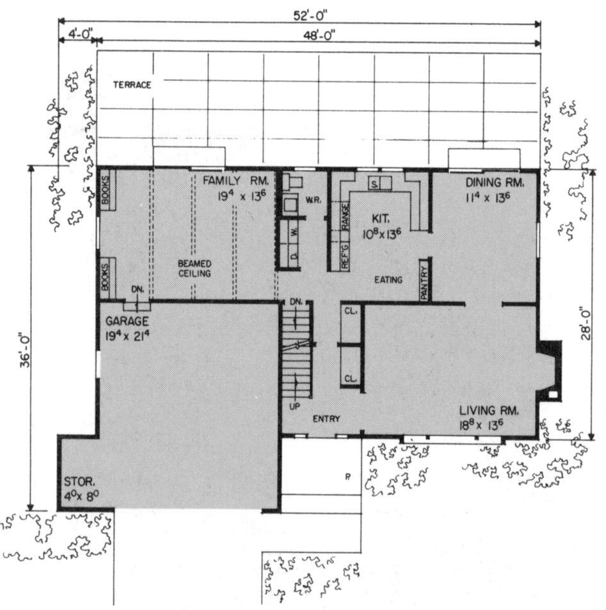

● You don't need a mansion to live graciously. What you do need is a practical floor plan which takes into consideration the varied activities of the busy family. This plan does that! This story-and-a-half design will not require a large piece of property while it returns the maximum per construction dollar. Its living potential is tremendous.

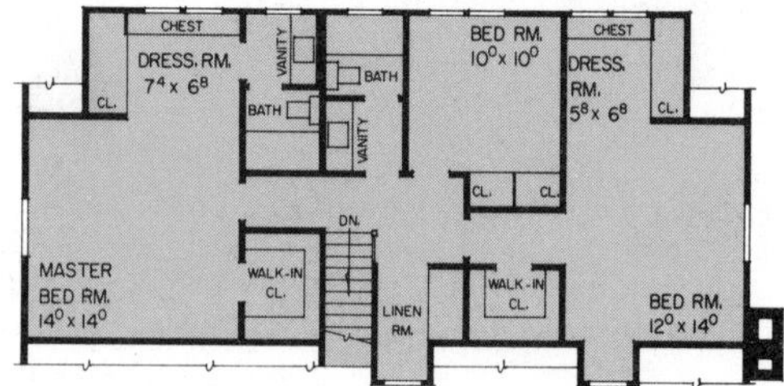

● Picturesque, indeed. This L-shaped one-and-a-half story home would attract its full share of attention even on Cape Cod. Study the excellent plan.

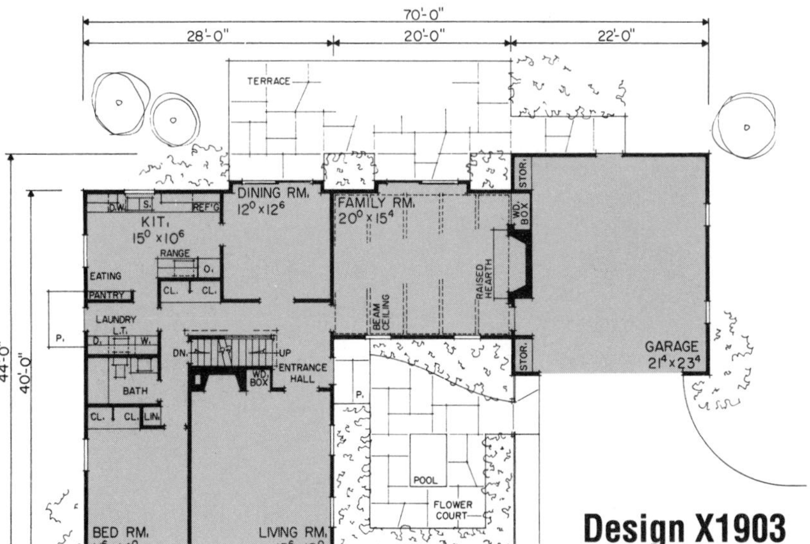

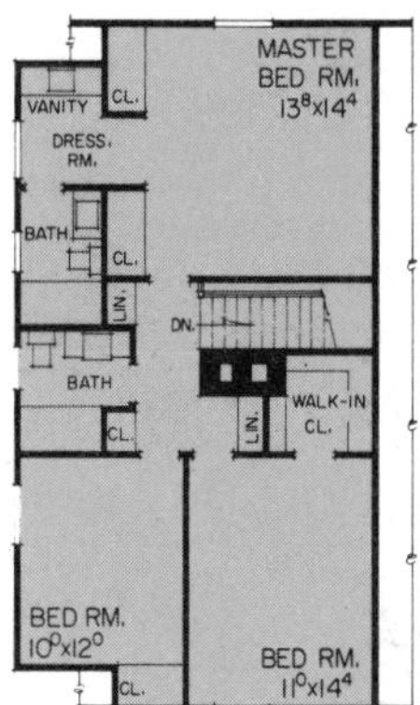

Design X1903

First Floor: 1,460 square feet
Second Floor: 854 square feet
Total: 2,314 square feet

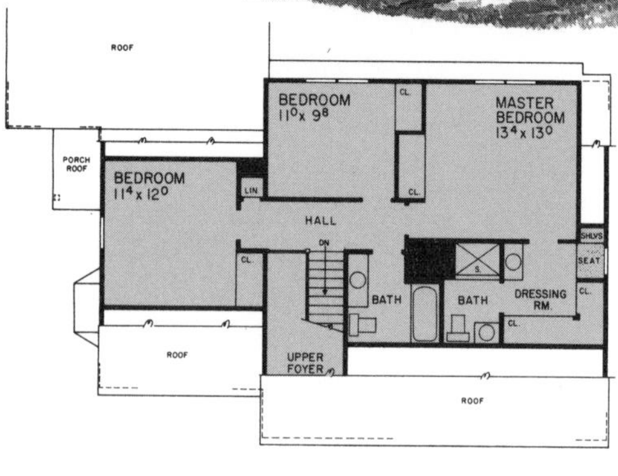

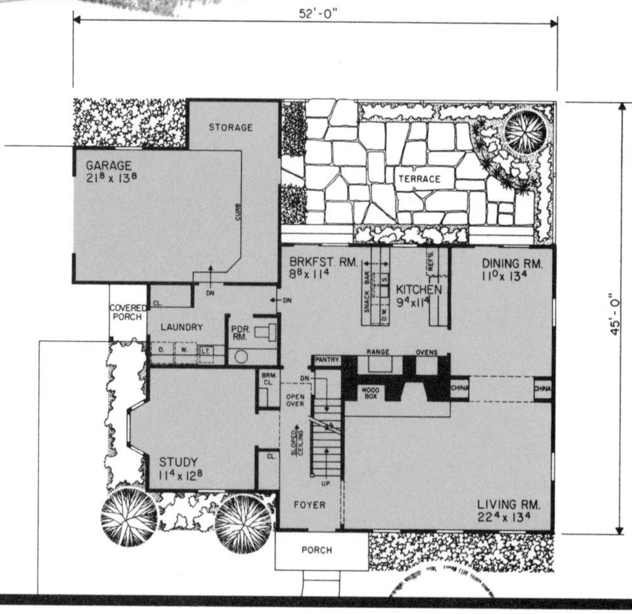

Design X2658

First Floor: 1,218 square feet
Second Floor: 764 square feet; Total: 1,982 square feet

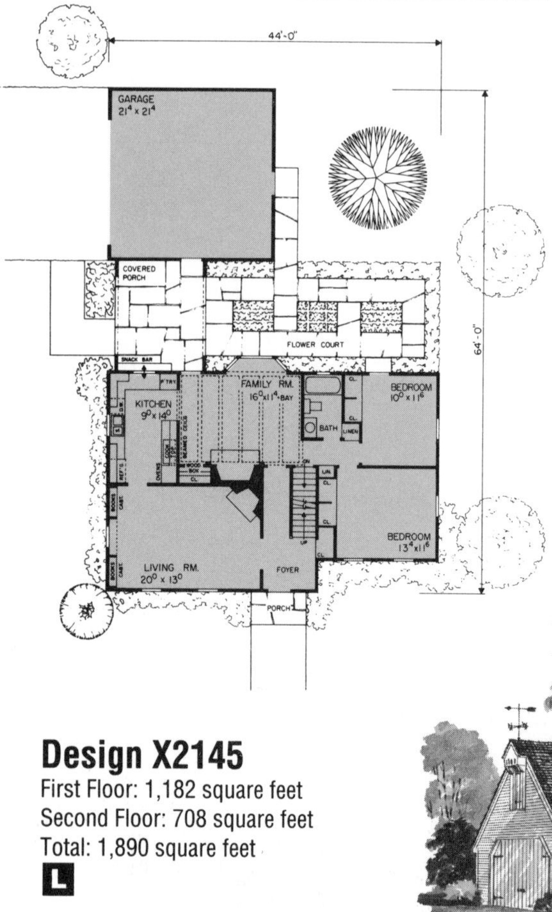

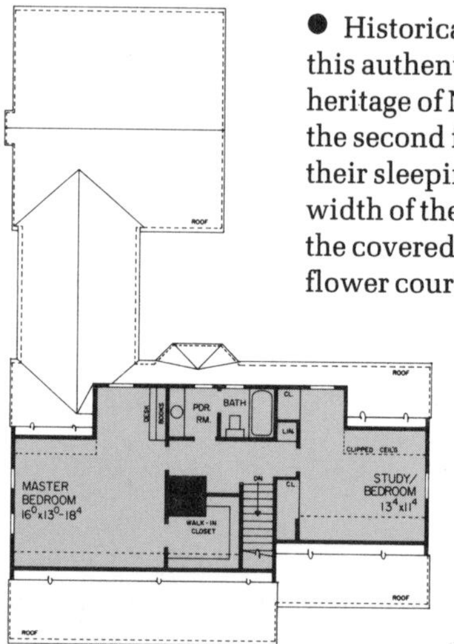

● Historically referred to as a "half house," this authentic adaptation has its roots in the heritage of New England. With completion of the second floor, the growing family doubles their sleeping capacity. Notice that the overall width of the house is only 44 feet. Take note of the covered porch leading to the garage and flower court.

Design X2145

First Floor: 1,182 square feet
Second Floor: 708 square feet
Total: 1,890 square feet

L

● Captivating as a New England village! From the weather vane atop the garage to the roofed side entry and paned windows, this home is perfectly detailed. Inside, there is a lot of living space. An exceptionally large family room which is more than 29' by 13' including a dining area. The adjoining kitchen has a laundry just steps away. Two formal rooms are in the front.

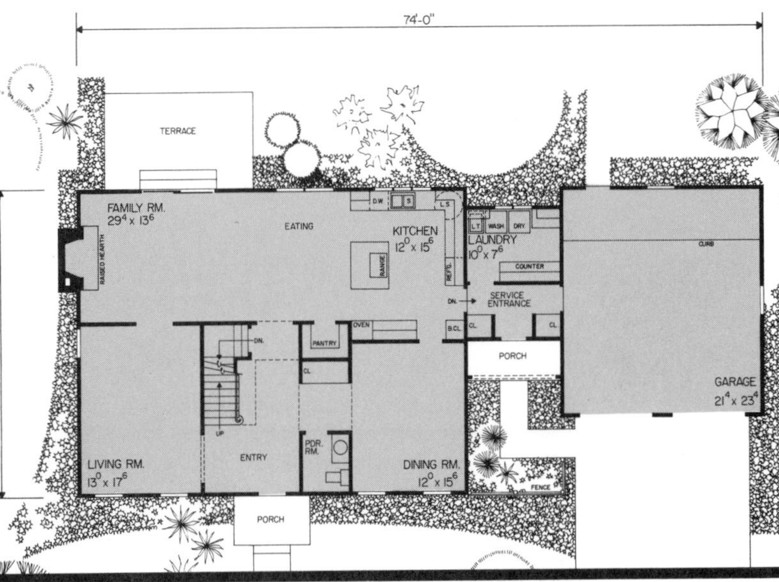

Design X2596

First Floor: 1,489 square feet
Second Floor: 982 square feet
Total: 2,471 square feet

L D

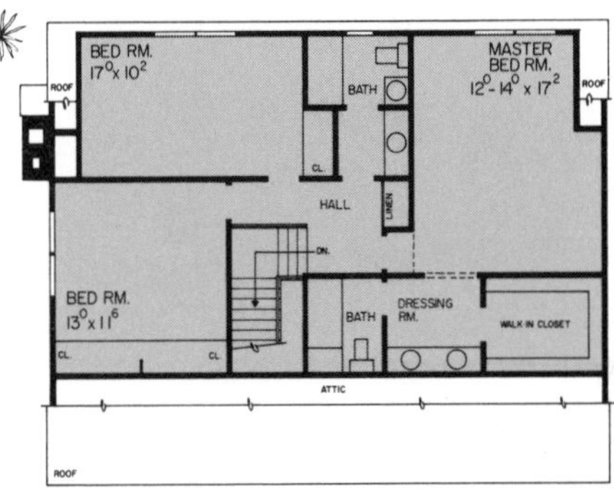

● A study of the first and second floors of this charming design will reveal that nothing has been omitted to assure convenient living. List your family's living requirements and then observe how this house will proceed to satisfy them. Features galore.

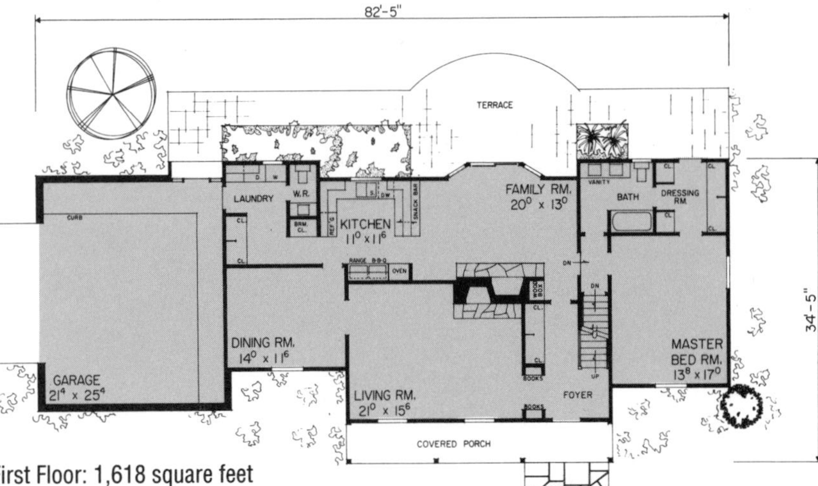

Design X1736

First Floor: 1,618 square feet
Second Floor: 952 square feet; Total: 2,570 square feet

Design X2521

First Floor: 1,272 square feet
Second Floor: 1,139 square feet
Total: 2,411 square feet

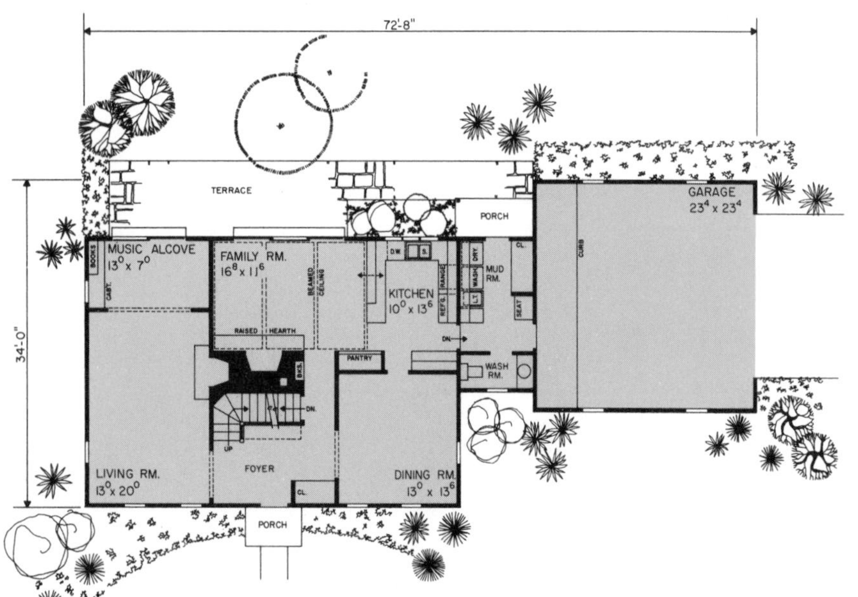

● Here is a house to remind one of the weather-beaten facades of Nantucket. The active family plan is as up-to-date as tomorrow. Along with formal and informal areas on the first floor, there is a music alcove. If a music alcove is not needed, this area would make an ideal intimate sitting area.

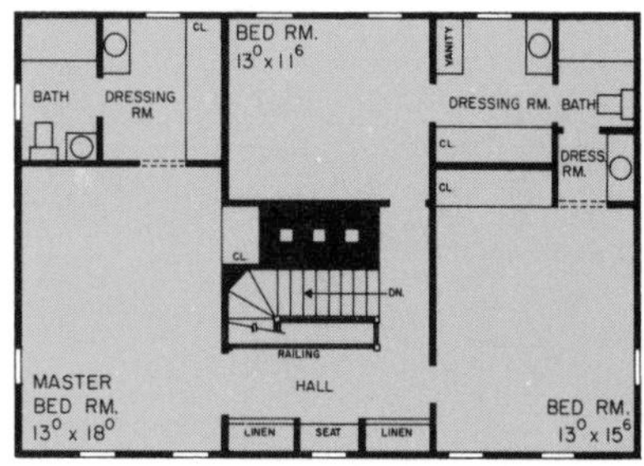

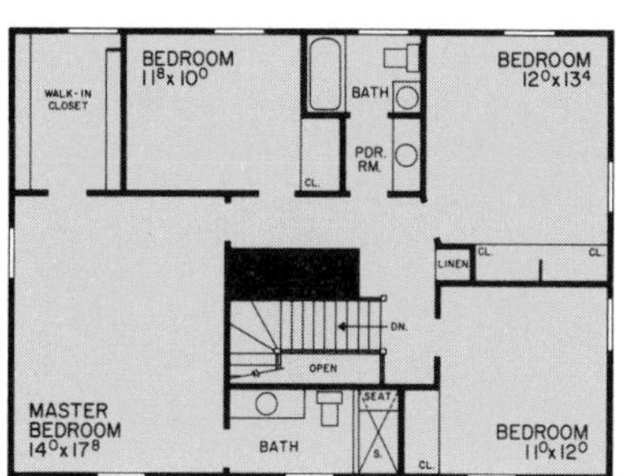

Design X2666

First Floor: 988 square feet
Second Floor: 1,147 square feet
Total: 2,135 square feet

● Charming Colonial detailing in multi-paned windows and twin coach lamps grace the exterior of this two-story. A spacious country kitchen highlights the interior. Its features include an island workcenter, fireplace, beamed ceiling, and sliding glass doors leading to the rear terrace. A washroom and a side door are only steps away. A second fireplace is in the large living room which also has sliding glass doors to the rear.

38'-0"
TERRACE
26'-0"
LIVING RM.
$13^0 x 25^4$
COUNTRY KITCHEN
$18^8 x 13^0$
D.W.
S.
L.S.
RANGE
WASH ROOM
ISLAND FOOD PREP
BEAMED CEILING
RAISED HEARTH
REFG.
BRM CL.
CL.
PORCH
DN
UP
FOYER
CL.
DINING RM.
$11^0 x 12^0$
LINE OF SECOND FLOOR
PORCH

Design X2799 First Floor: 1,196 square feet
Second Floor: 780 square feet; Total: 1,976 square feet

● This two-story traditional design's facade with its narrow clapboards, punctuated by tall multi-paned windows, appears deceptively expansive. Yet the entire length of the house, including the garage, is 66 feet.

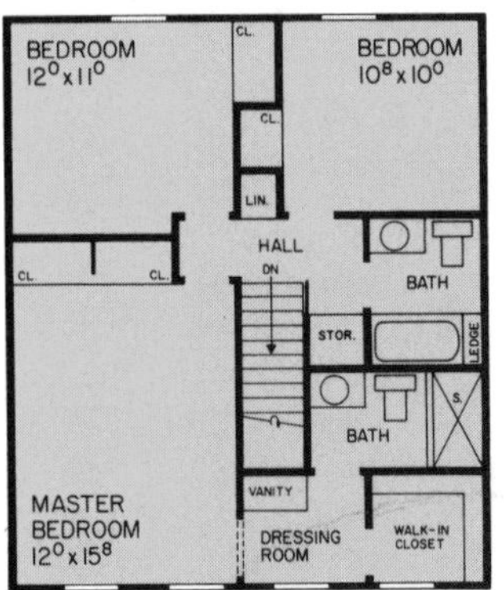

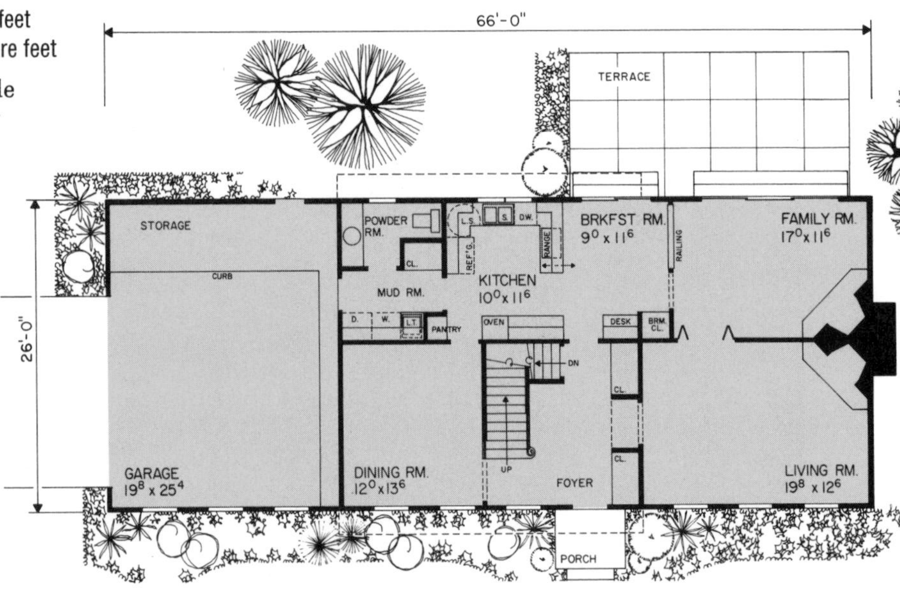

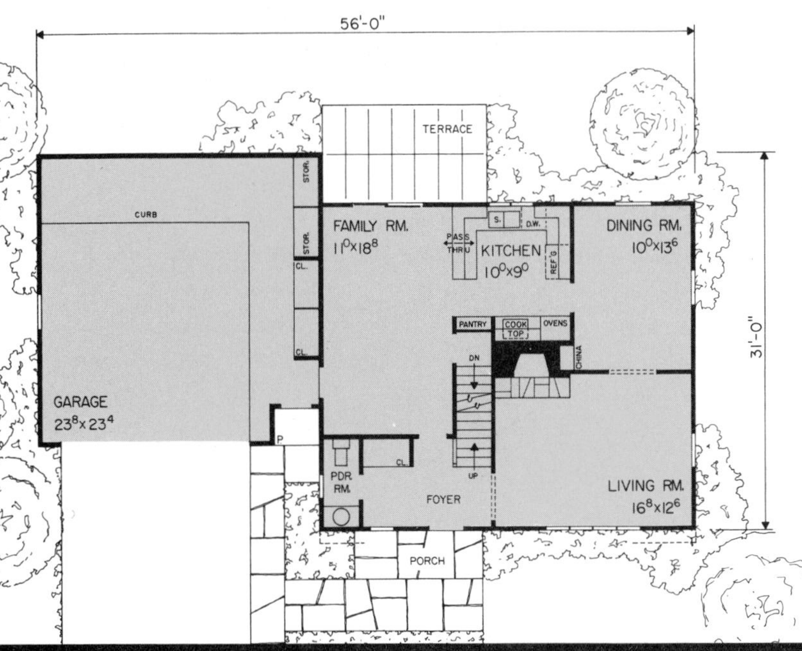

Design X1719 First Floor: 864 square feet Second Floor: 896 square feet; Total: 1,760 square feet

L D

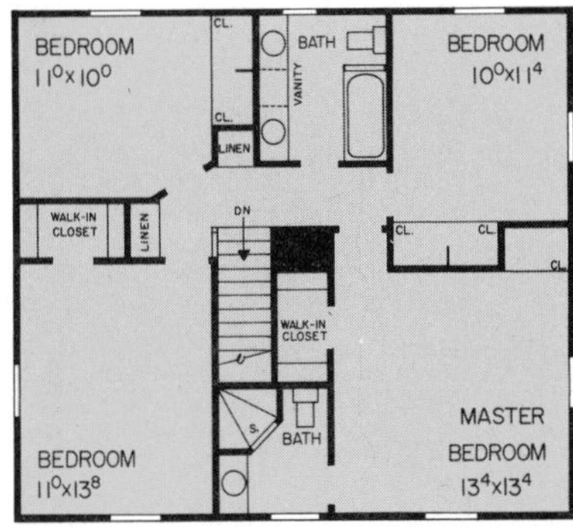

● What an appealing low-cost Colonial adaptation. Most of the livability features generally found in the largest of homes are present to cater to family needs.

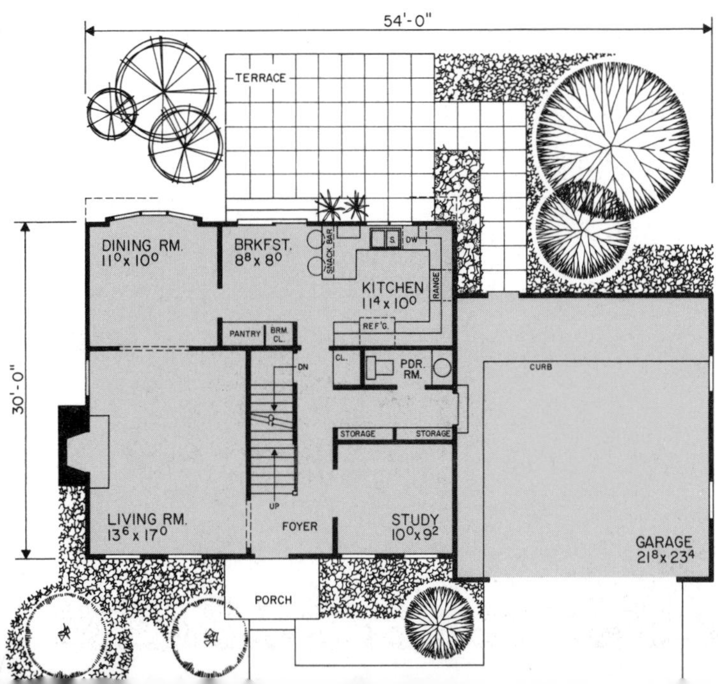

Design X2870 First Floor: 900 square feet Second Floor Left Suite: 467 square feet Second Floor Right Suite: 493 square feet; Total: 1,860 square feet

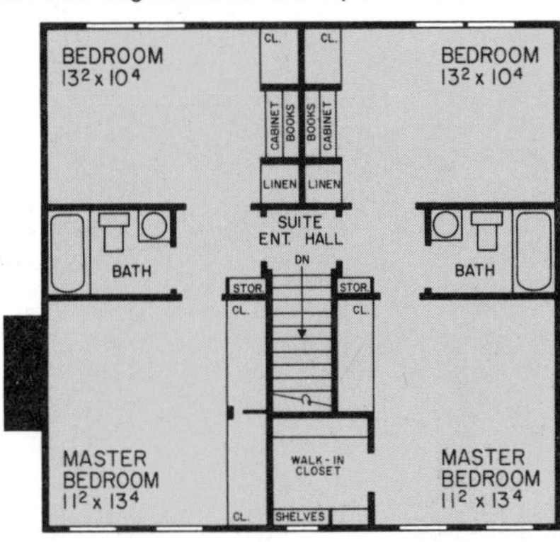

● This colonial home was designed to provide comfortable living space for two families. The first floor is the common living area, with all of the necessary living areas; the second floor has two two-bedroom-one-bath suites. Built-ins are featured in the smaller bedroom.

Design X2733 First Floor: 1,177 square feet; Second Floor: 1,003 square feet; Total: 2,180 square feet

L **D**

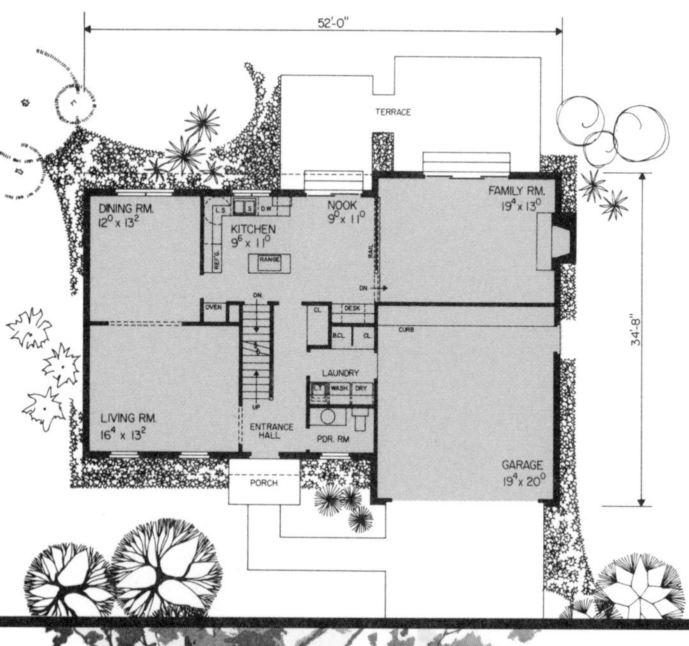

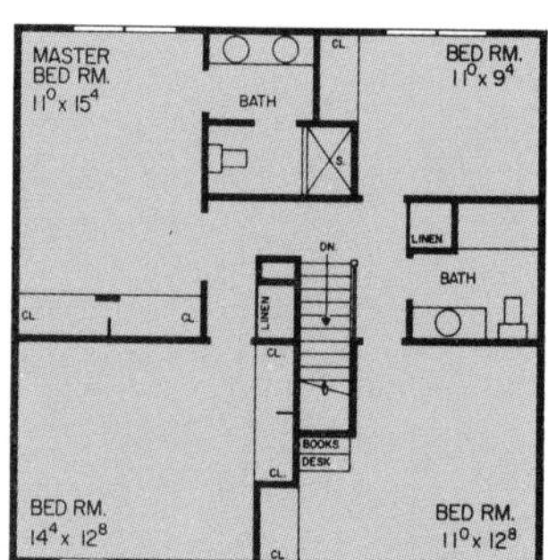

● This is definitely a four bedroom Colonial with charm galore. The kitchen features an island range and other built-ins. All will enjoy the sunken family room with fireplace, which has sliding glass doors leading to the terrace. Also a basement for recreational activities with laundry remaining on first floor for extra convenience.

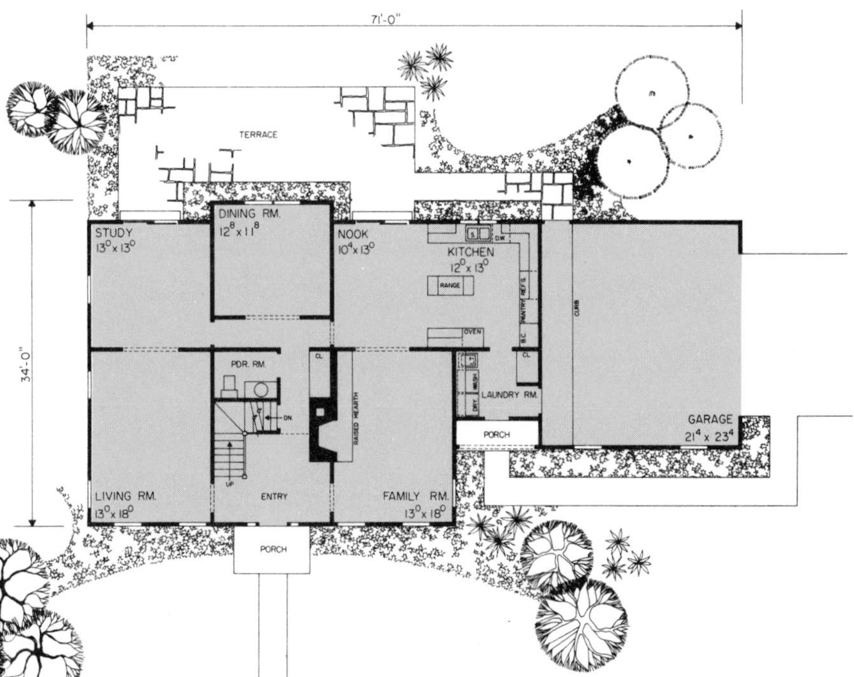

Design X2538

First Floor: 1,503 square feet
Second Floor: 1,095 square feet
Total: 2,598 square feet

L **D**

● This Salt Box is charming, indeed. The livability it has to offer to the large and growing family is great. The entry is spacious and is open to the second floor balcony. For living areas, there is the study in addition to the living and family rooms.

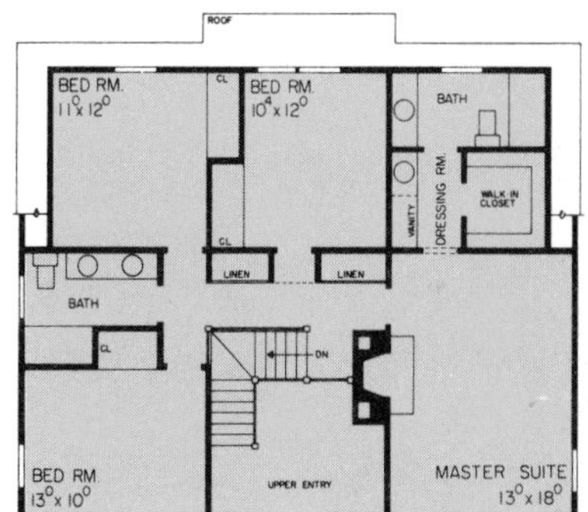

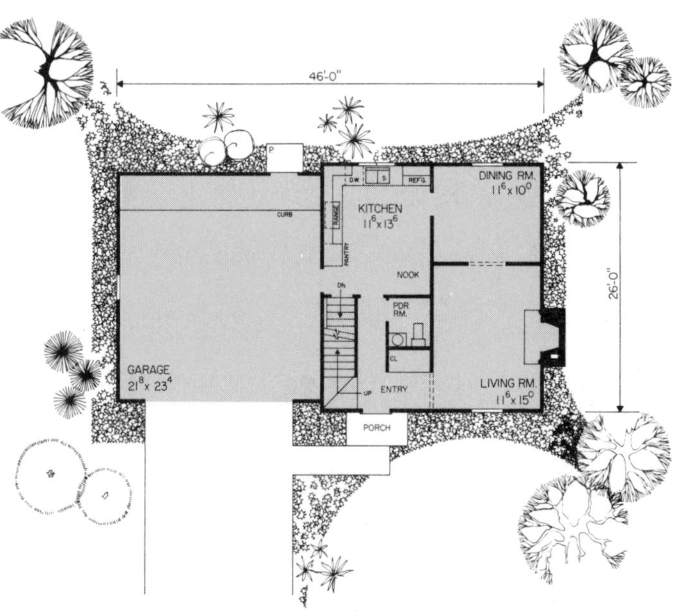

Design X2622

First Floor: 624 square feet
Second Floor: 624 square feet
Total: 1,248 square feet

L **D**

Custom Alterations? See page 301 for customizing this plan to your specifications.

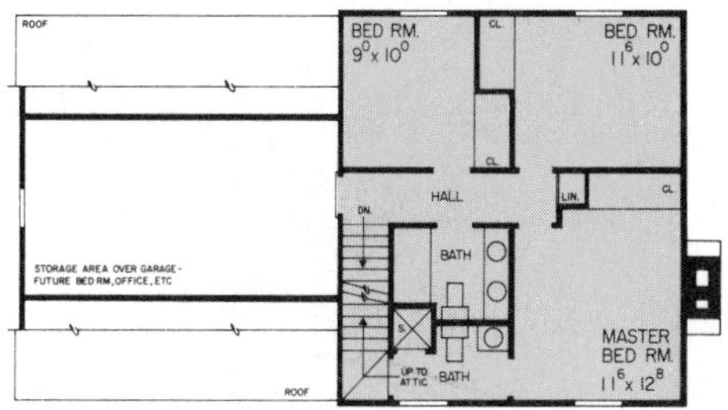

Design X2103

First Floor: 1,374 square feet
Second Floor: 1,056 square feet
Total: 2,430 square feet

D

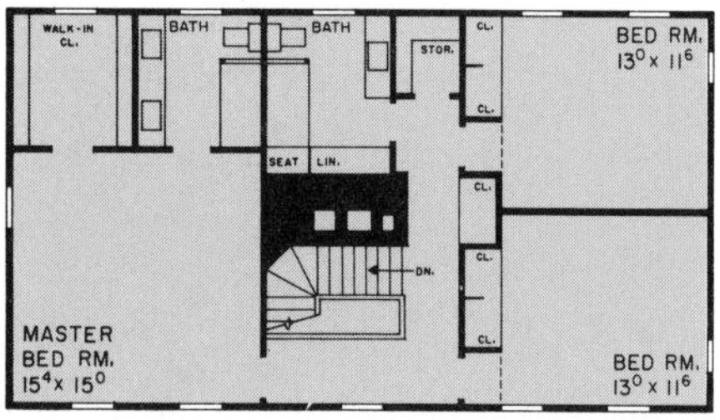

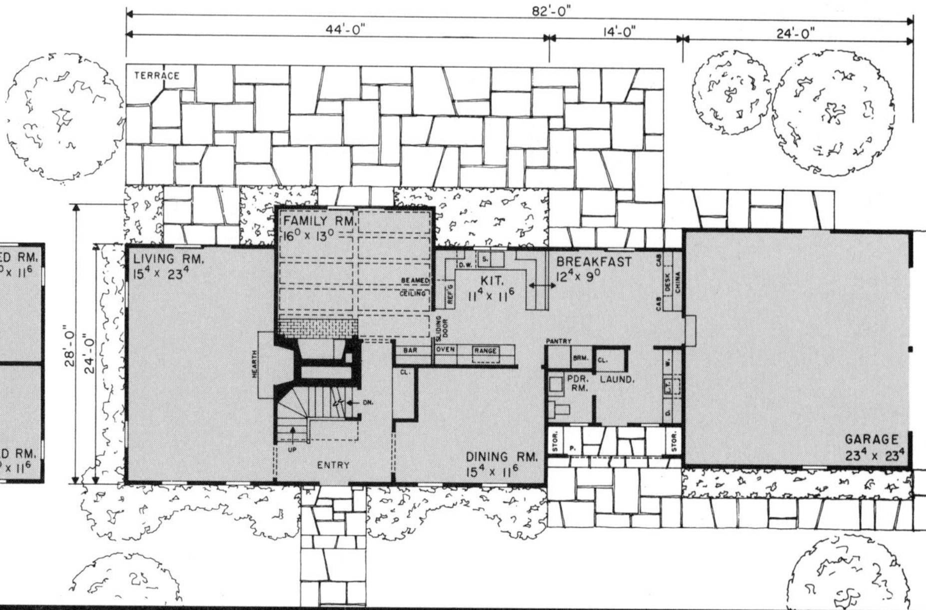

● The appeal of this Colonial home will be virtually everlasting. It will improve with age and service the growing family well. Imagine your family living here. There are four bedrooms, 2½ baths, plus plenty of first floor living space.

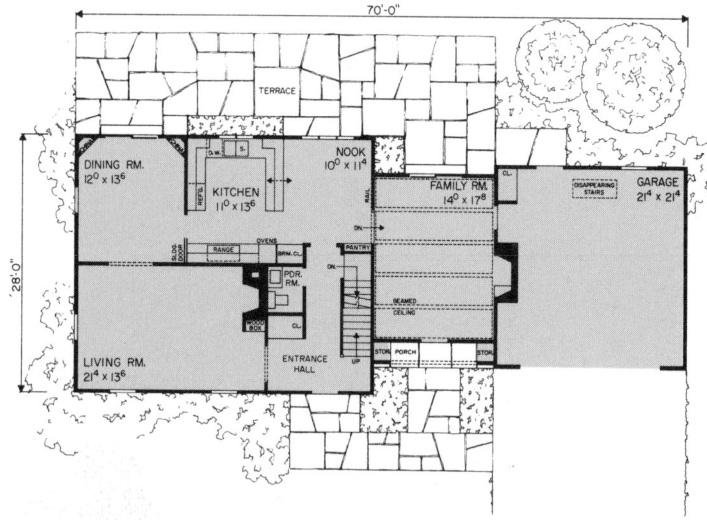

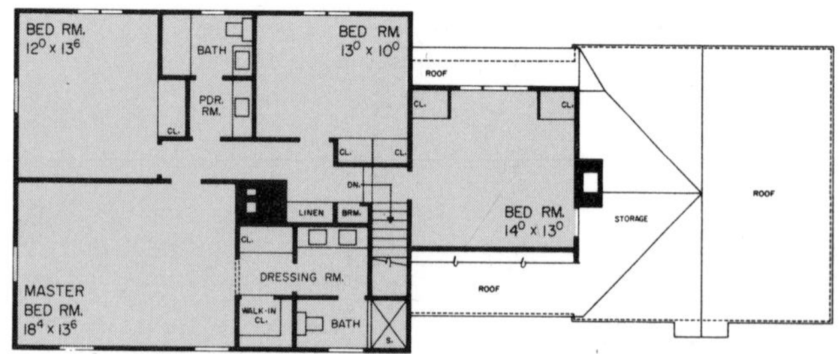

Design X2211

First Floor: 1,214 square feet
Second Floor: 1,146 square feet; Total: 2,360 square feet

Design X2731 First Floor: 1,039 square feet

Second Floor: 973 square feet; Total: 2,012 square feet

L **D**

● The multi-paned windows with shutters of this two-story highlight the exterior delightfully. Inside the livability is ideal. Formal and informal areas are sure to serve your family with ease. Note efficient U-shaped kitchen with handy first-floor laundry. Sleeping facilities on second floor.

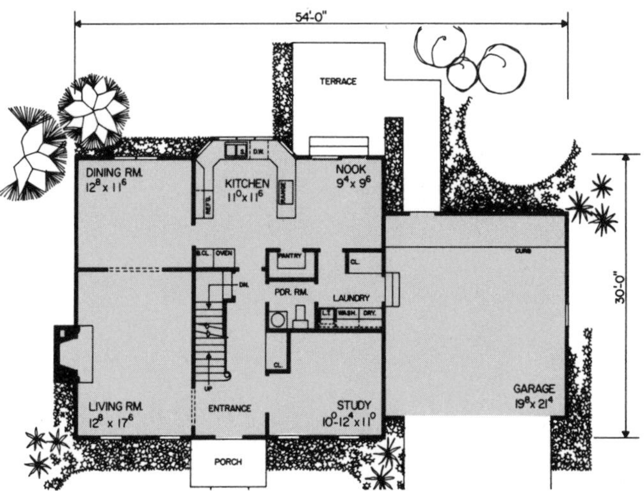

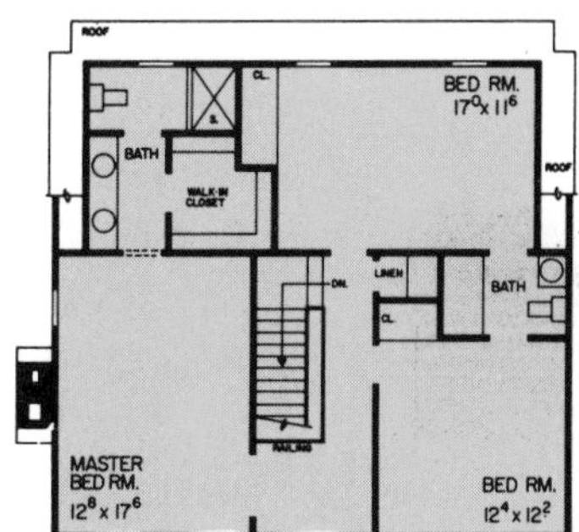

Design X2640

First Floor: 1,386 square feet
Second Floor: 1,232 square feet
Total: 2,618 square feet

D

● Here is a gracious exterior which adopts many features common to New England-style Federal homes. The symmetry and proportions are outstanding. Inside, a fine, functioning plan. Note stairs to attic for additional storage and livability.

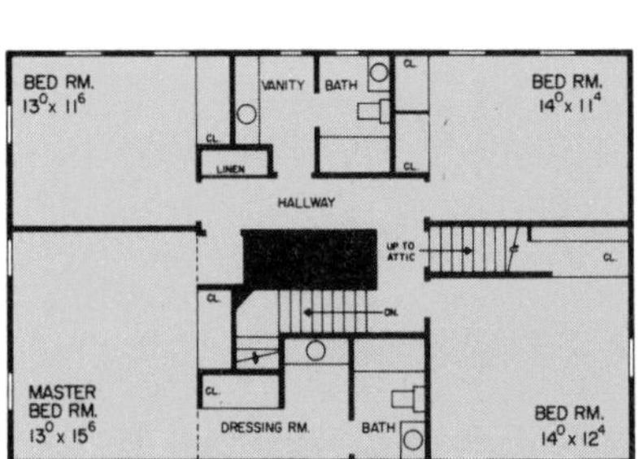

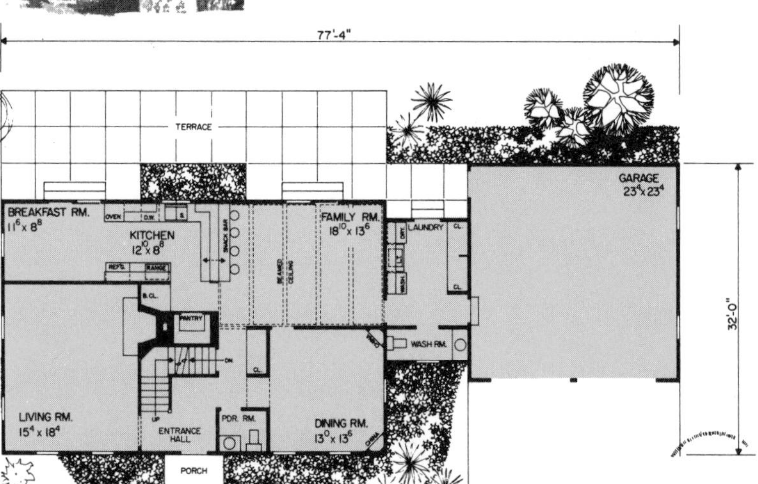

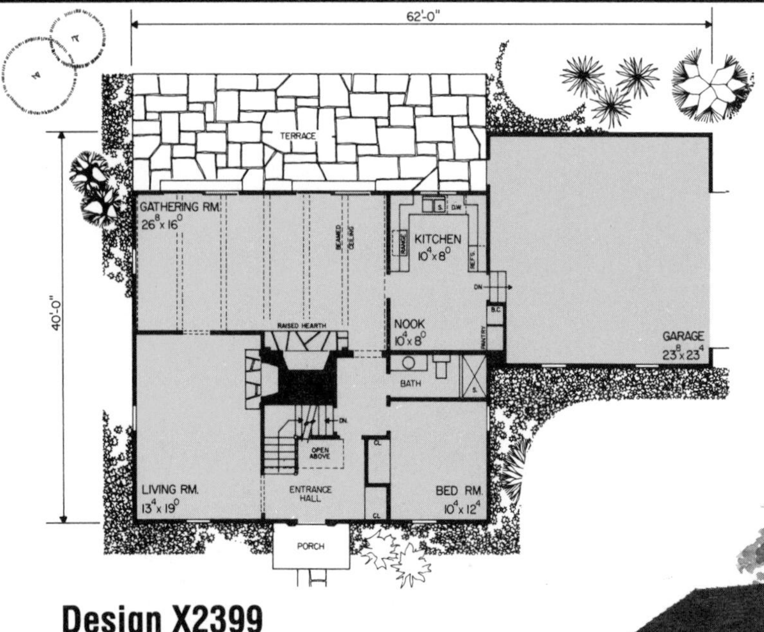

Design X2399

First Floor: 1,301 square feet
Second Floor: 839 square feet
Total: 2,140 square feet

● From Early Colonial America comes this saltbox. Narrow, horizontal siding, muntined windows, a massive central chimney, carriage lamps and a classic front entrance set the exterior character. Inside, three bedrooms, three baths and two living areas make the plan most livable.

Design X2101

First Floor: 1,338 square feet
Second Floor: 1,114 square feet
Total: 2,452 square feet

● This is a modified version of one of America's most famous Colonial dwellings, the Parson Capen of Topsfield, Mass. Dating back to the 17th-Century, the English colonists built this medieval adaptation reproducing its bracketed second floor overhang, pendant drops at the corners, massive pilastered chimney and narrow clapboards. The floor plan, of course, has been updated to cater to today's living requirements.

● A Georgian Colonial adaptation on the grand scale. The authentic front entrance is delightfully detailed. Two massive end chimneys, housing four fireplaces, are in keeping with the architecture of its day.

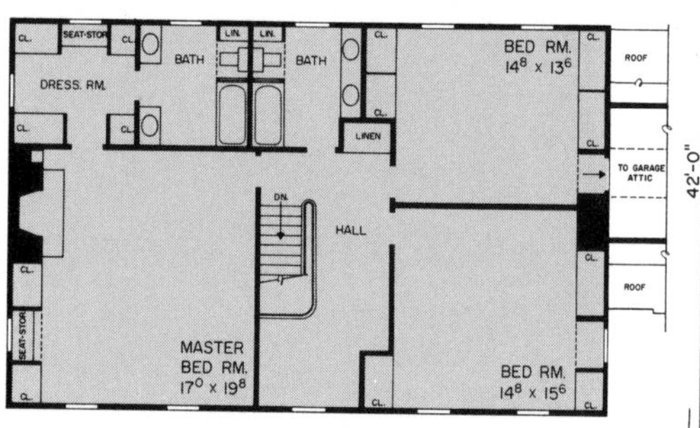

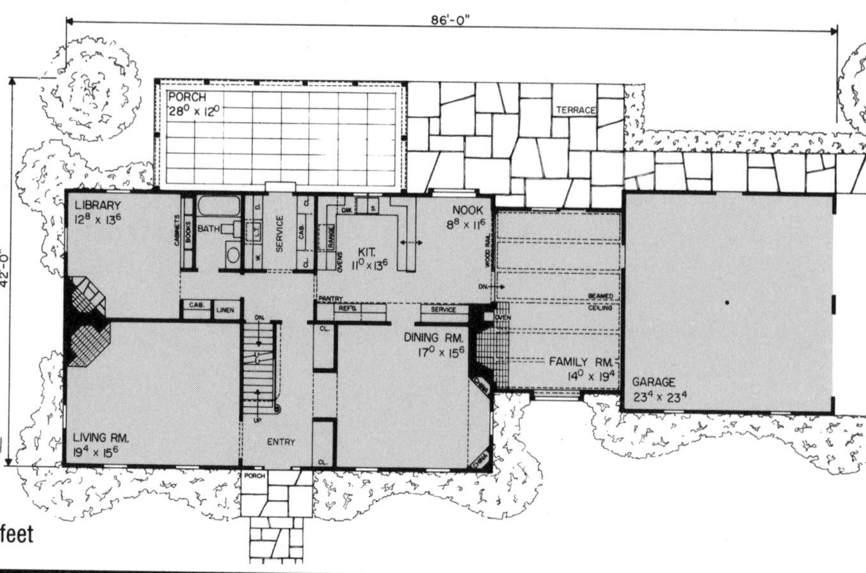

Design X2221 First Floor: 1,726 square feet Second Floor: 1,440 square feet; Total: 3,166 square feet

Design X2253 First Floor: 1,503 square feet; Second Floor; 1,291 square feet; Total: 2,794 square feet

● The overhanging second floor sets the character of this Early American design. Study the features, both inside and out.

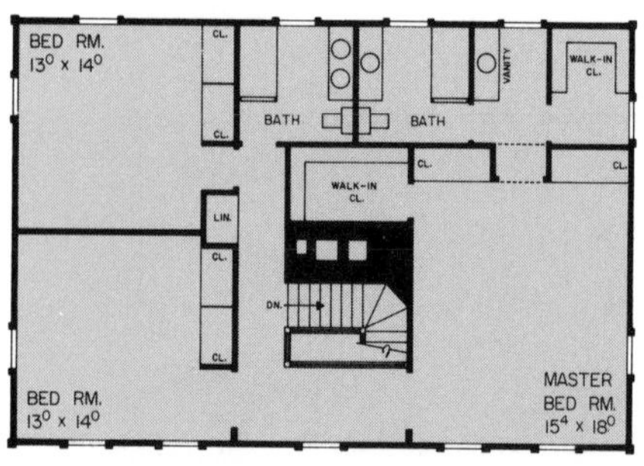

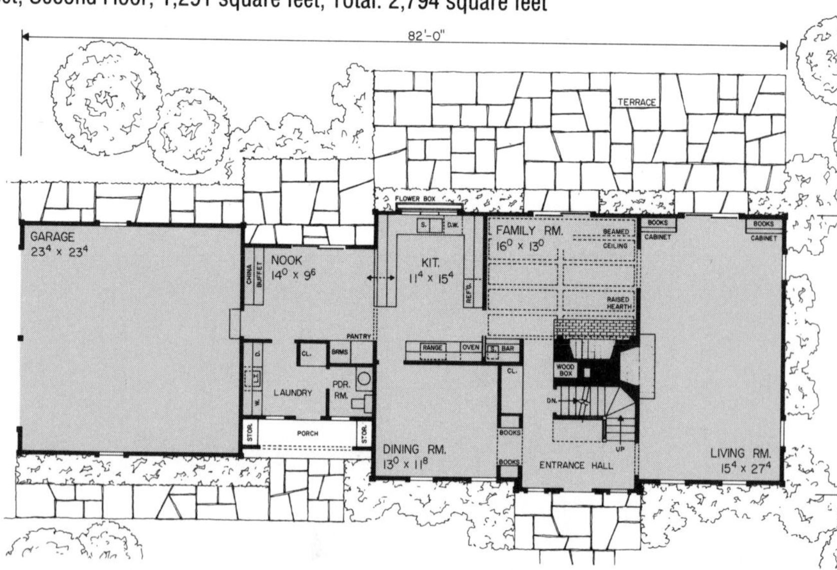

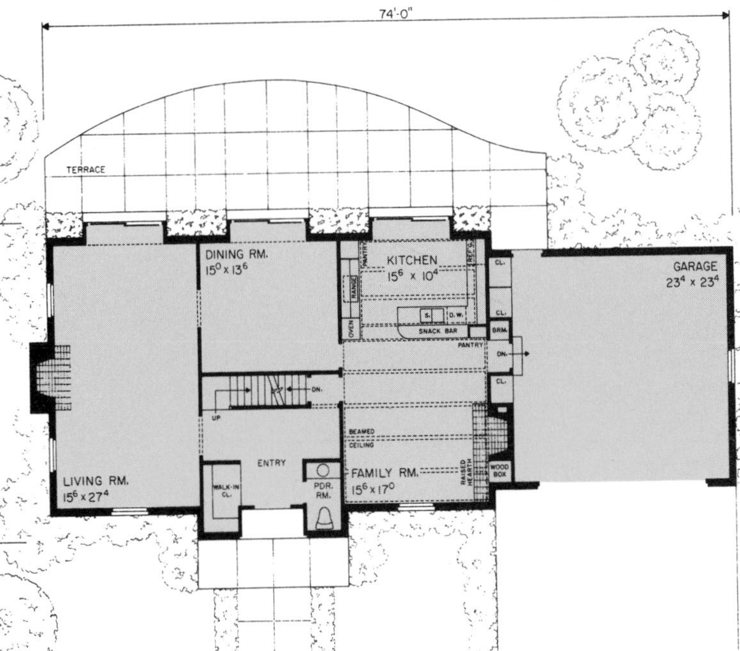

● This stately home, whose roots go back to an earlier period in American architecture, will forever retain its aura of distinction. The spacious front entry effectively separates the formal and informal living zones. Four bedrooms on second floor.

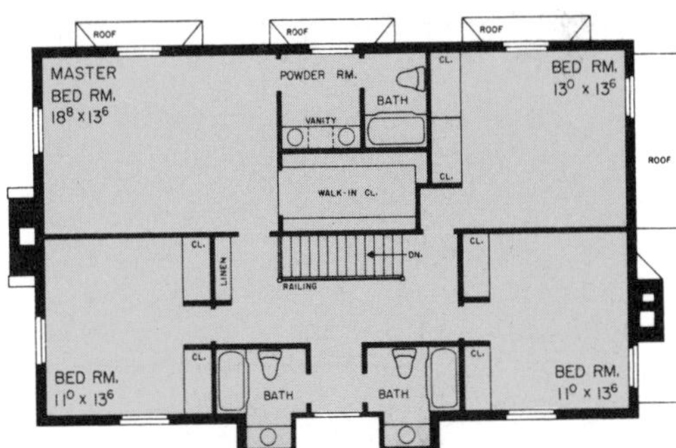

Design X2250

First Floor: 1,442 square feet
Second Floor: 1,404 square feet
Total: 2,846 square feet

Design X2687 First Floor: 1,819 square feet
Second Floor: 1,472 square feet; Total: 3,291 square feet

L **D**

● Exterior styling of this home is reminiscent of the past but its floor plan is as up-to-date as it can get. Its many unique features include: a greenhouse, 78 square feet, off the country kitchen, a media room for all the modern electronic equipment, a hobby/laundry room with a washroom and a deluxe master bath.

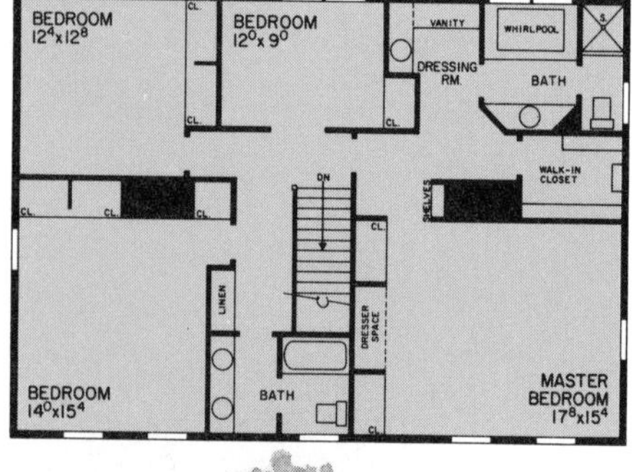

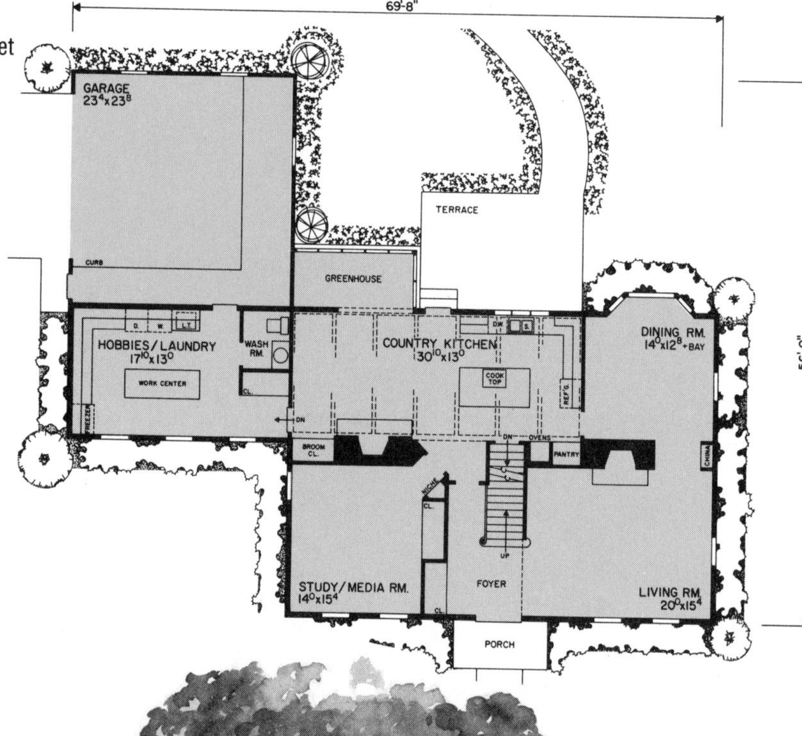

Design X2600

First Floor: 1,408 square feet
Second Floor: 1,408 square feet
Total: 2,816 square feet

● Here are two full stories of excellently planned living space. A third floor is available if the extra space is needed.

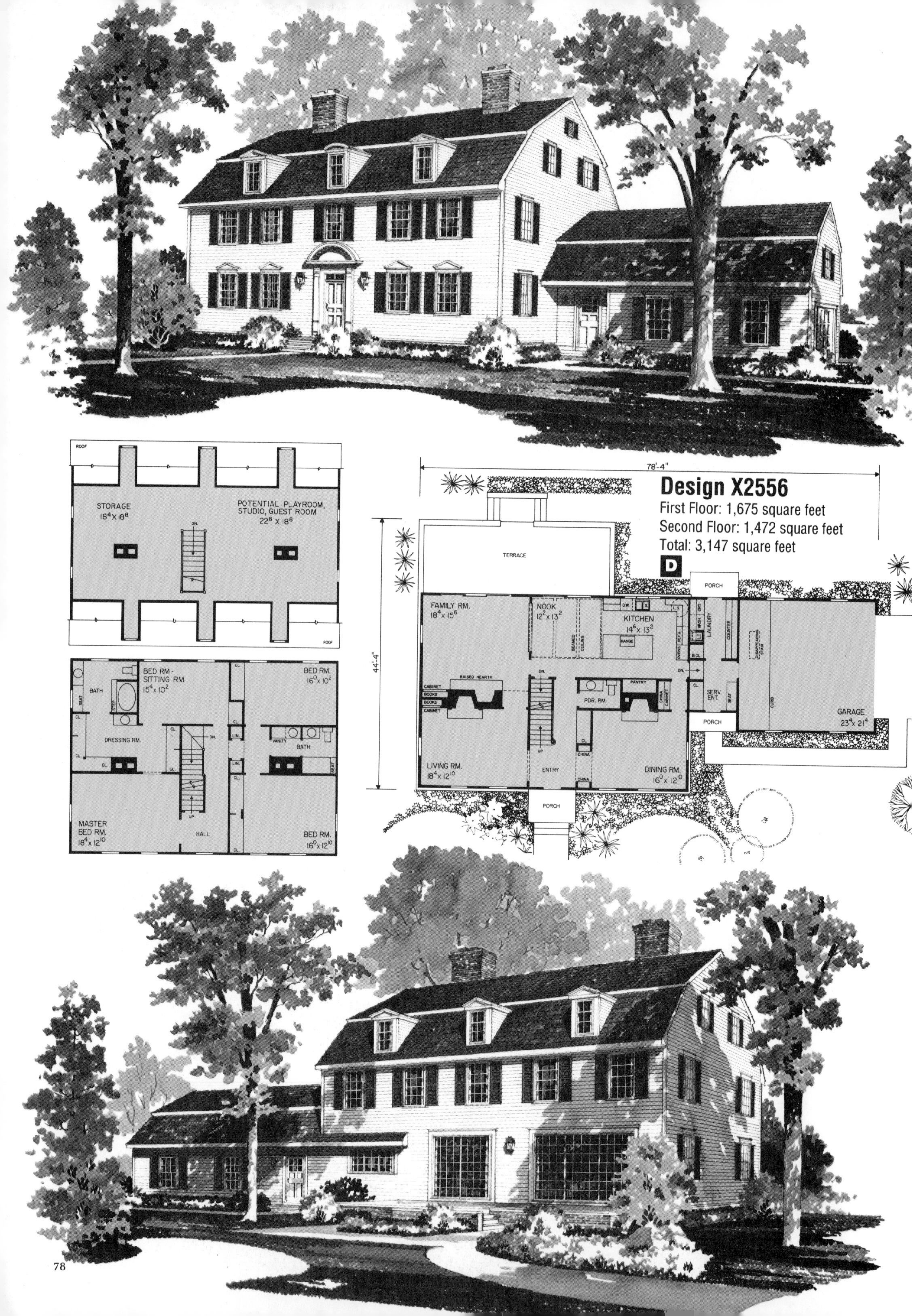

Design X2556

First Floor: 1,675 square feet
Second Floor: 1,472 square feet
Total: 3,147 square feet

D

Design X2659 First Floor: 1,023 square feet
Second Floor: 1,008 square feet; Third Floor: 476 square feet
Total: 2,507 square feet

L **D**

49'-8"
TERRACE
DINING RM. $12^0 \times 9^6$ + BAY
BREAKFAST RM. $11^6 \times 11^5$
KITCHEN $11^6 \times 11^6$
GARAGE $13^4 \times 21^4$
32'-0"
MUD ROOM
WASH RM.
LIVING RM. $14^0 \times 17^6$
FOYER
STUDY $10^8 \times 9^8$
PORCH

● The facade of this three-storied, pitch-roofed house has a symmetrical placement of windows and a restrained but elegant central entrance. The central hall, or foyer, expands midway through the house to a family kitchen. Off the foyer are two rooms, a living room with fireplace and a study. The windowed third floor attic can be used as a study and studio. Three bedrooms are housed on the second floor.

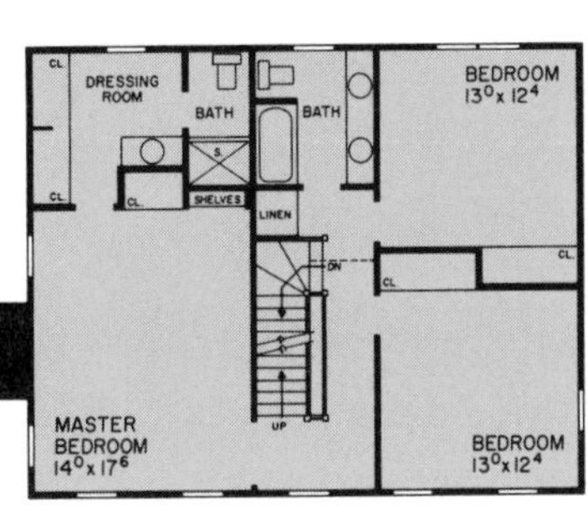

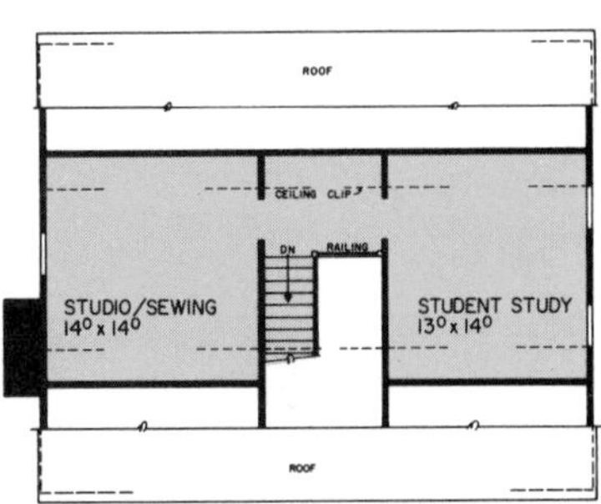

Design X3553

First Floor: 2,471 square feet
Second Floor: 1,071 square feet
Total: 3,542 square feet

L **D**

● Delightful Colonial design makes a fine statement for two-story living. The bay windows, columned front porch and charming dormers are big attractions on the exterior. Inside, a wide entry foyer directs traffic to the left to living areas and to the right to the master bedroom suite and a cozy study. The family room and living room both have fireplaces. The L-shaped kitchen is enhanced by an island cooktop and breakfast room with sliding glass doors to the rear porch. Upstairs are three secondary bedrooms and two full baths.

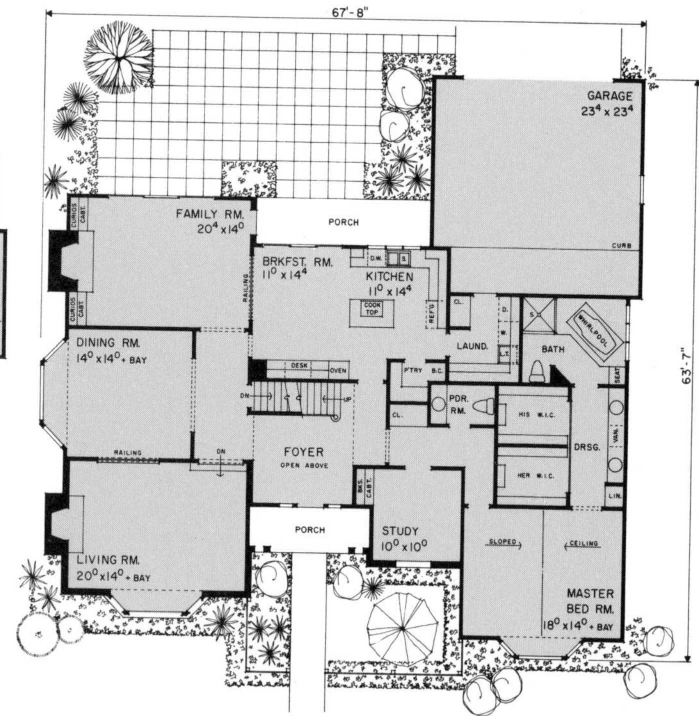

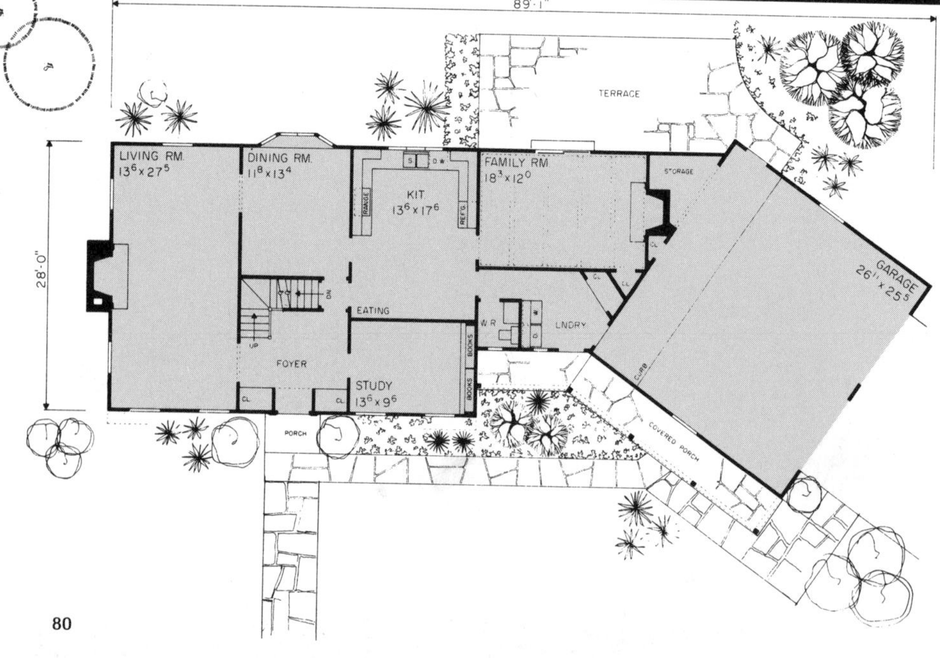

● Angular in its configuration, this inviting home offers loads of livability. There are five bedrooms, study, family room and a 27 foot long living room.

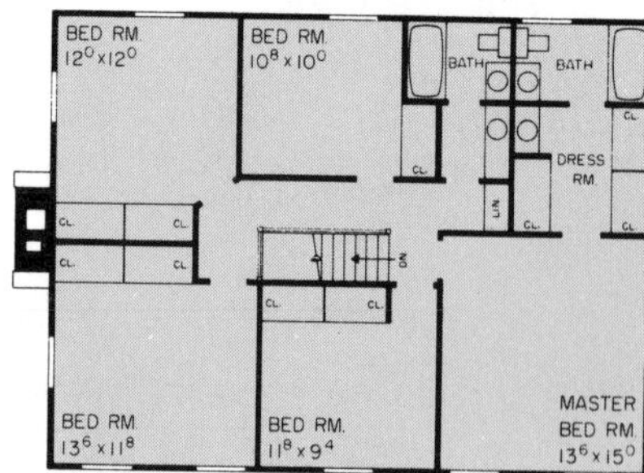

Design X2322

First Floor: 1,480 square feet
Second Floor: 1,172 square feet
Total: 2,652 square feet

D

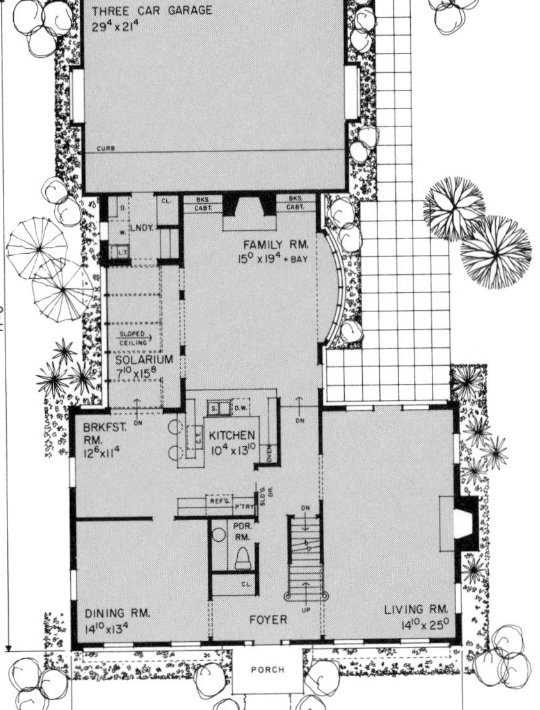

Design X3552

First Floor: 1,784 square feet
Second Floor: 1,192 square feet
Total: 2,976 square feet

● Smart exterior features mark this home as a classic: second-story pop-outs with half-round windows above multi-paned windows, charming lintels, and a combination of horizontal wood siding and brick. Its interior floor plan contains both formal and informal areas, two fireplaces, a cozy solarium and three bedrooms with a sitting room. A three-car garage provides all the space necessary for the family vehicles and plenty of additional paraphernalia.

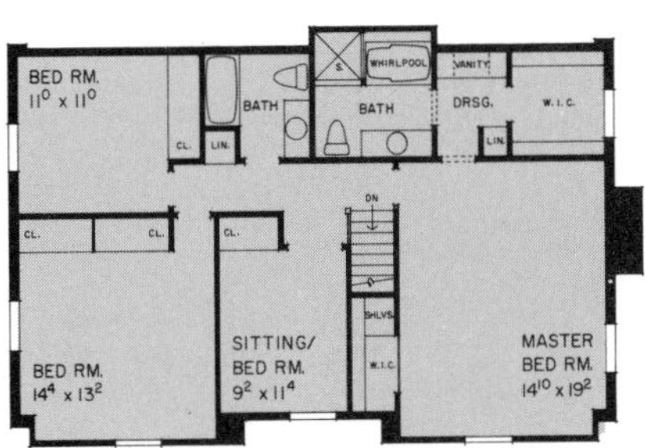

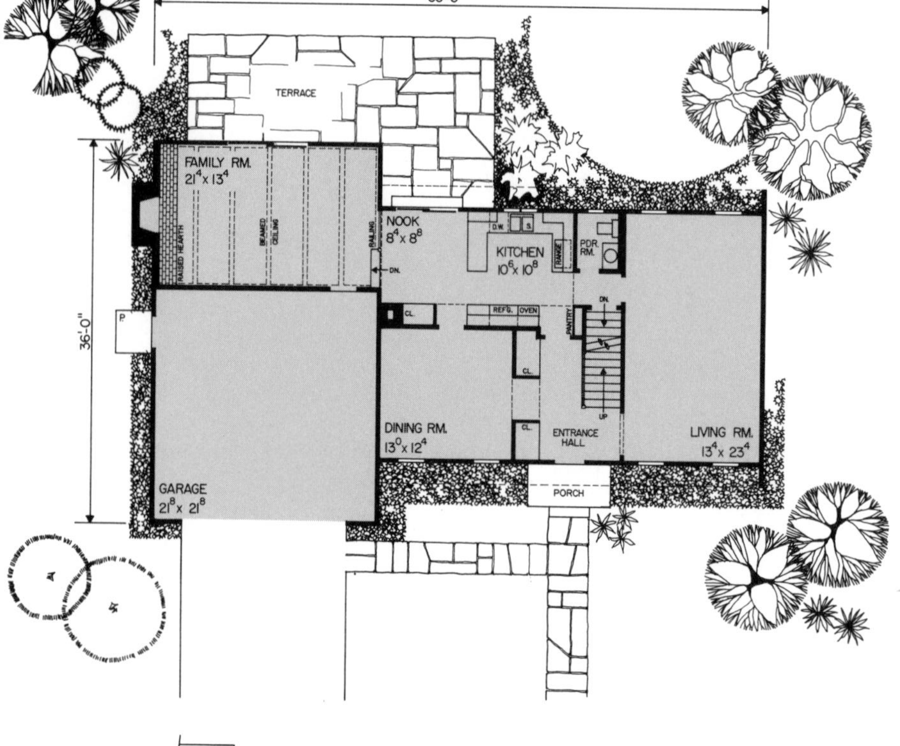

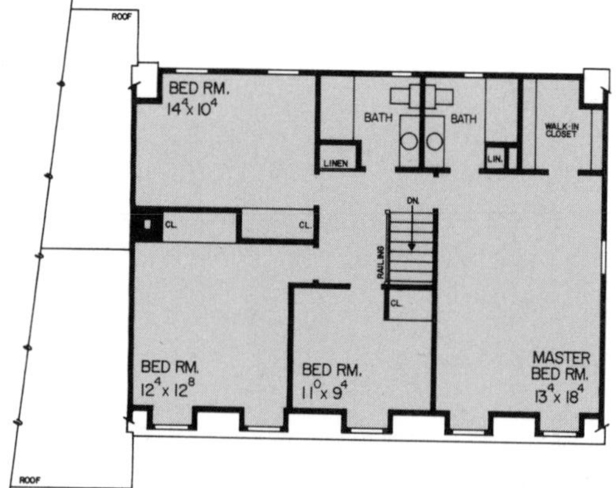

Design X2617

First Floor: 1,223 square feet
Second Floor: 1,018 square feet
Total: 2,241 square feet

● This gambrel-roof version houses a practical floor plan. Left of the front entrance hall is the formal dining room, just across the hall from the formal living room. To the rear of the plan is the comfortable beamed-ceiling family room with fireplace and terrace access. This room is sunken a few steps from the main part of the house. A handy powder room is near the front hall and also the kitchen for quick clean-ups. The breakfast nook separates the family room and kitchen. Upstairs are four bedrooms and two full baths. The master contains two dormers and a huge walk-in closet. The additional three bedrooms share a full bath.

Design X2320 First Floor: 1,856 square feet; Second Floor: 1,171 square feet; Total: 3,027 square feet

● A charming Colonial adaptation with a Gambrel roof front exterior and a Salt Box rear. The focal point of family activities will be the spacious family kitchen with its beamed ceiling and fireplace. Blueprints include details for both three and four bedroom options. In addition to the family kitchen, note the family room with beamed ceiling and fireplace. Don't miss the study with built-in bookshelves and cabinets.

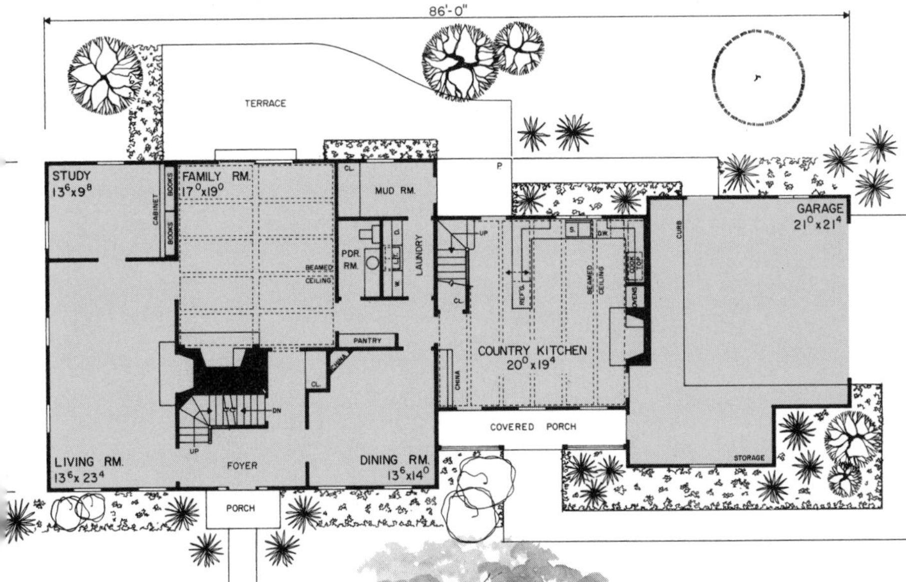

86'-0"
TERRACE
STUDY 13^{6}x9^{8}
CABINET
BOOKS
FAMILY RM. 17^{0}x19^{0}
BEAMED CEILING
MUD RM.
PDR. RM.
LAUNDRY
PANTRY
COUNTRY KITCHEN 20^{0}x19^{4}
BEAMED CEILING
CHINA
COVERED PORCH
GARAGE 21^{0}x21^{4}
CURB
STORAGE
LIVING RM. 13^{6}x23^{4}
FOYER
DINING RM. 13^{6}x14^{0}
PORCH

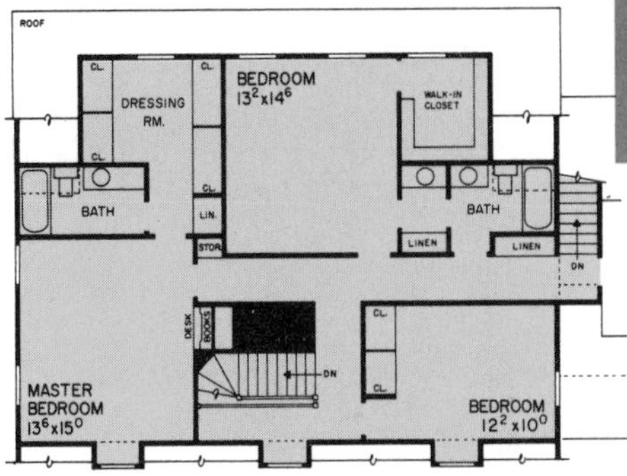

ROOF
DRESSING RM.
BEDROOM 13^{2}x14^{6}
WALK-IN CLOSET
BATH
LIN.
STOR.
BATH
LINEN
LINEN
DESK
BOOKS
MASTER BEDROOM 13^{6}x15^{0}
BEDROOM 12^{2}x10^{0}

WALK-IN CLOSET
BEDROOM 10^{6}x12^{2}
BEDROOM 10^{6}x14^{6}
BATH
BATH
LINEN
MASTER BEDROOM 13^{6}x15^{0}
BEDROOM 12^{2}x10^{0}
OPTIONAL SECOND FLOOR PLAN

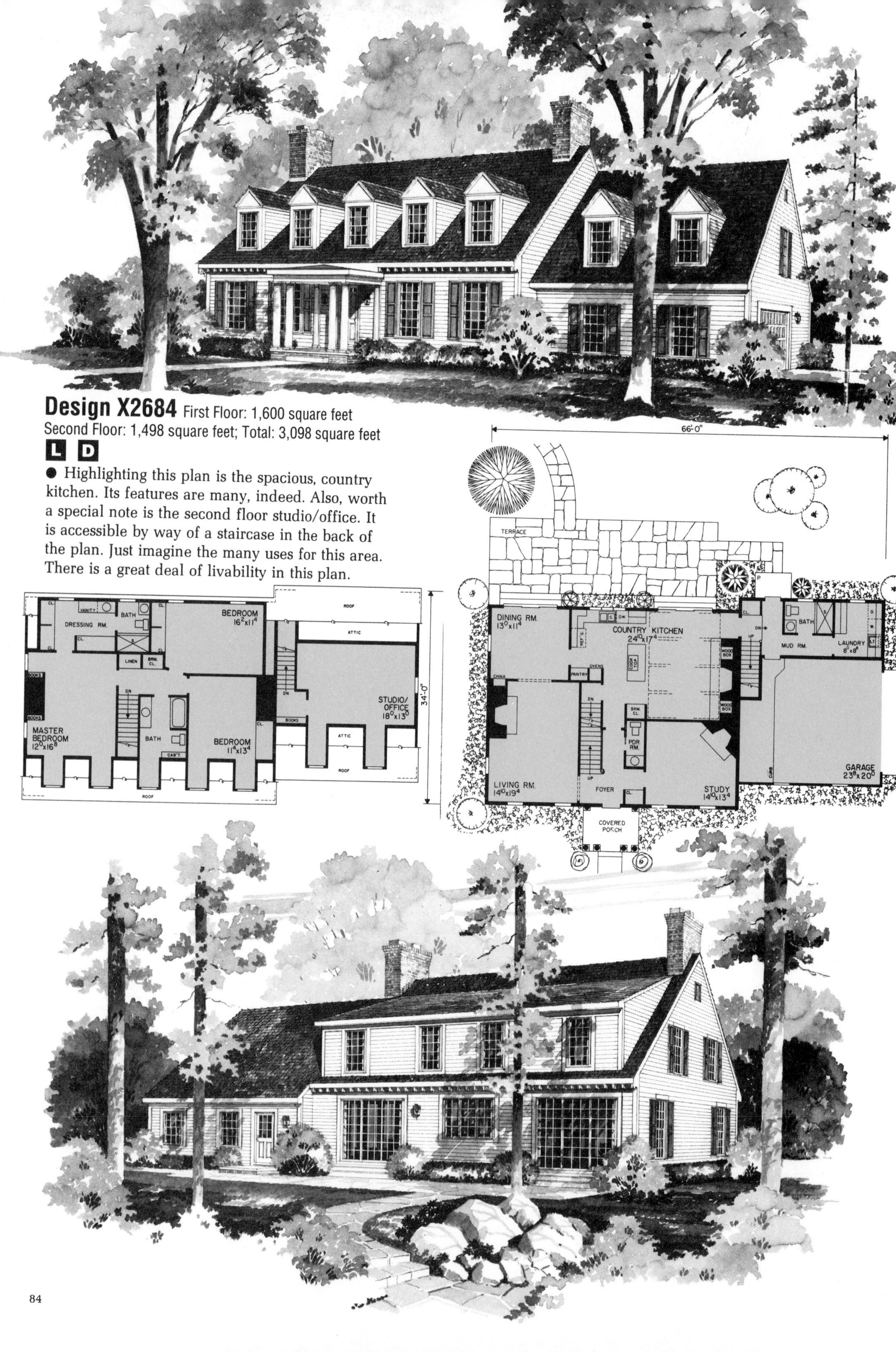

Design X2684 First Floor: 1,600 square feet
Second Floor: 1,498 square feet; Total: 3,098 square feet

L D

● Highlighting this plan is the spacious, country kitchen. Its features are many, indeed. Also, worth a special note is the second floor studio/office. It is accessible by way of a staircase in the back of the plan. Just imagine the many uses for this area. There is a great deal of livability in this plan.

Design X2610

First Floor: 1,505 square feet
Second Floor: 1,344 square feet
Total: 2,849 square feet

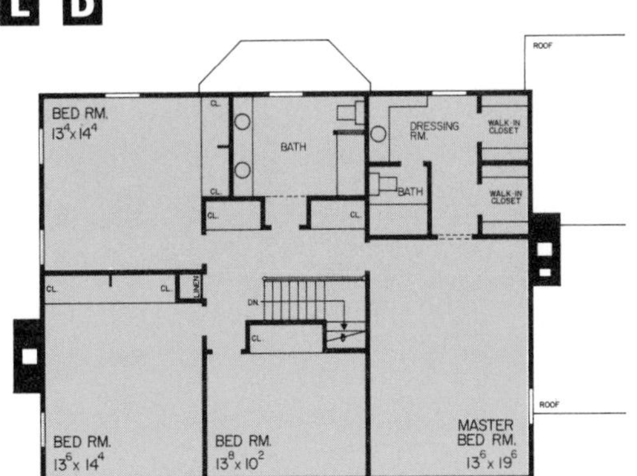

● This full two-story traditional will be worthy of note wherever built. It strongly recalls images of a New England of yesteryear. And well it might; for the window treatment is delightful. The front entrance detail is inviting. The narrow horizontal siding and the corner boards are appealing as are the two massive chimneys. The center entrance hall is large with a handy powder room nearby. The study has built-in bookshelves and offers a full measure of privacy. The interior kitchen has a pass-thru to the family room and enjoys all that natural light from the bay window of the nook. A beamed ceiling, fireplace and sliding glass doors are features of the family room. The mud room highlights a closet, laundry equipment and an extra wash room. Study the upstairs with those four bedrooms, two baths and plenty of closets. An excellent arrangement for all.

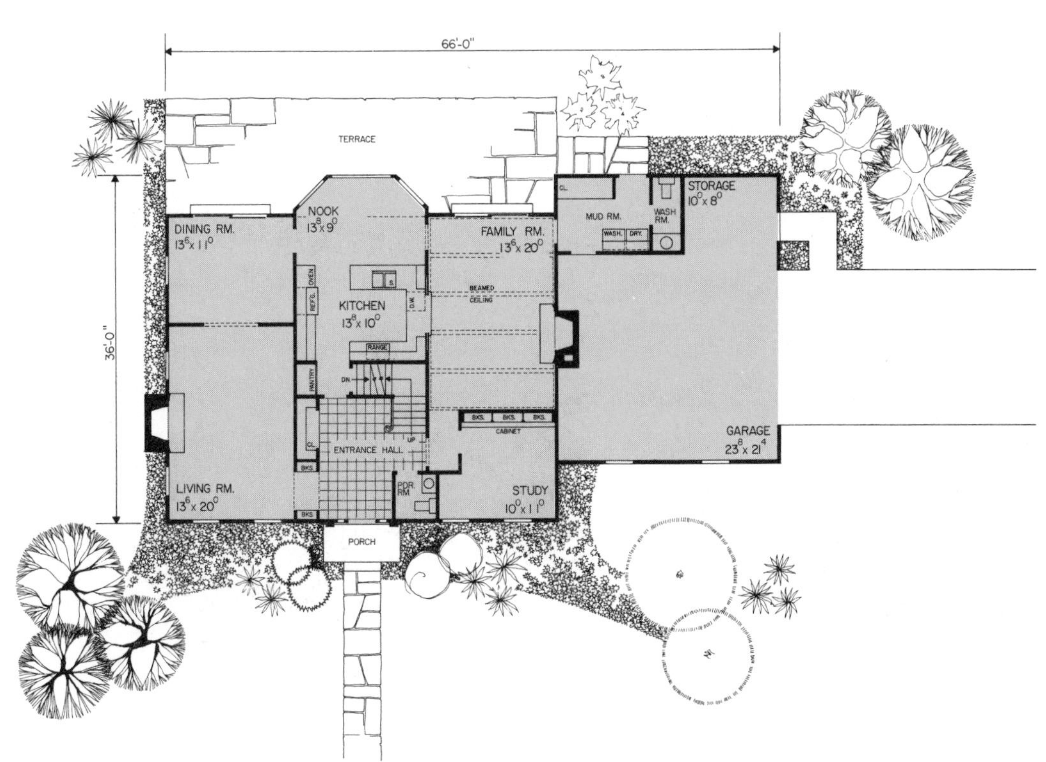

Design X3379 First Floor: 1,086 square feet
Second Floor: 902 square feet; Total: 1,988 square feet

L D

● Colonial styling is perfect in this two-story, narrow-lot plan. With the garage facing toward the front, the home is protected fromstreet noise and works well on a lot that allows very little clearance on the sides. Living areas are concentrated in the formal living and dining rooms and the media room with nearby powder room. The kitchen holds a large snack bar counter through to the breakfast room. Sliding glass doors here allow easy access to the rear terrace. The bedrooms are on the second floor and include a master with fireplace and garden whirlpool and two family bedrooms. One of the secondary bedrooms includes a large walk-in closet.

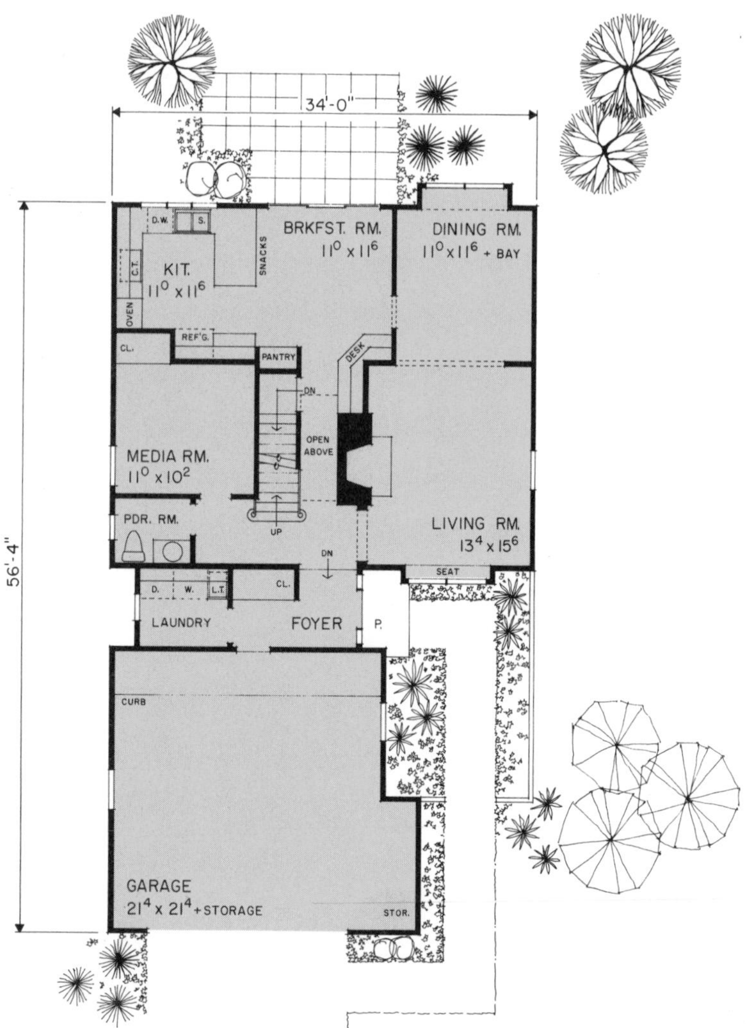

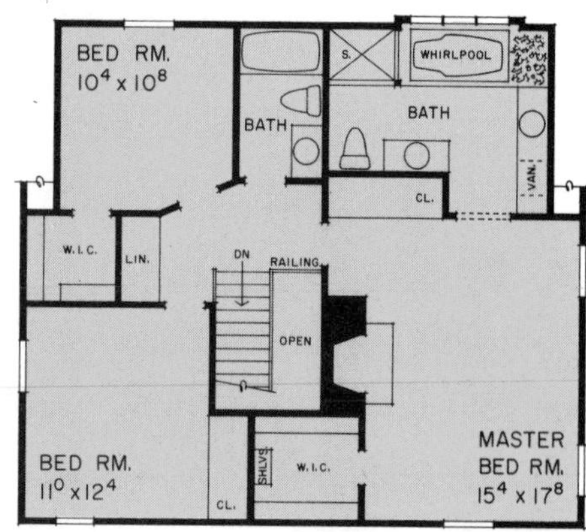

Design X3501 First Floor: 960 square feet; Second Floor: 762 square feet; Total: 1,722 square feet

● This efficient Saltbox design includes three bedrooms and two full baths plus a handy powder room on the first floor. A large living room in the front of the home features a fireplace. The rear of the home is left open, with room for a kitchen with snack bar, breakfast area with fireplace and dining room with outdoor access. If you wish, use the breakfast area as an all-purpose dining room and turn the dining room into a library or sitting room.

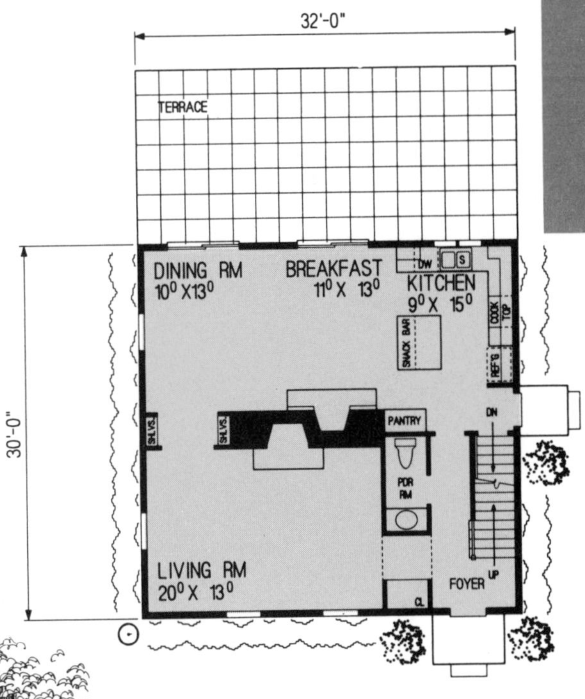

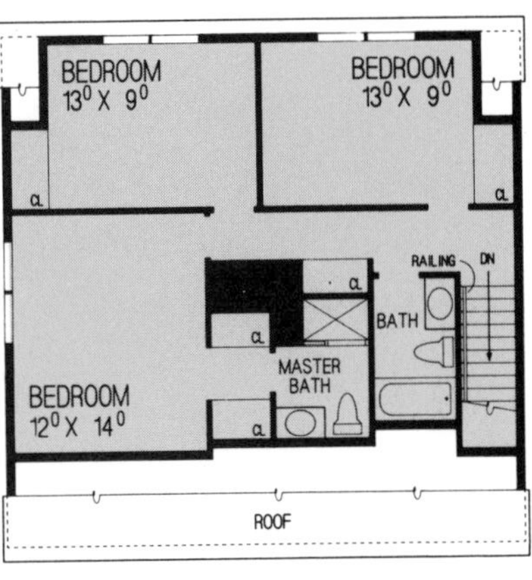

Design X2839 First Floor: 1,565 square feet; Second Floor: 1,120 square feet; Total: 2,685 square feet

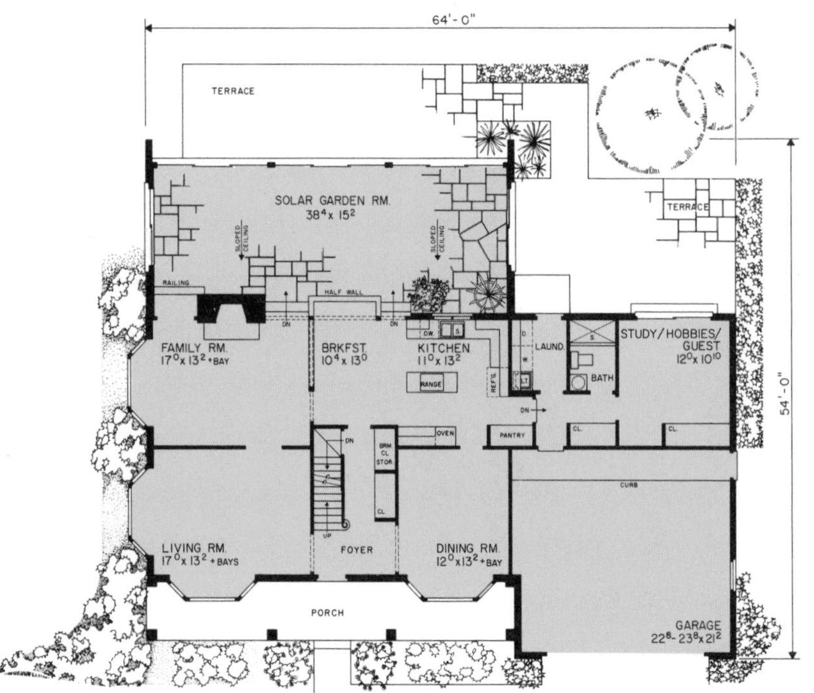

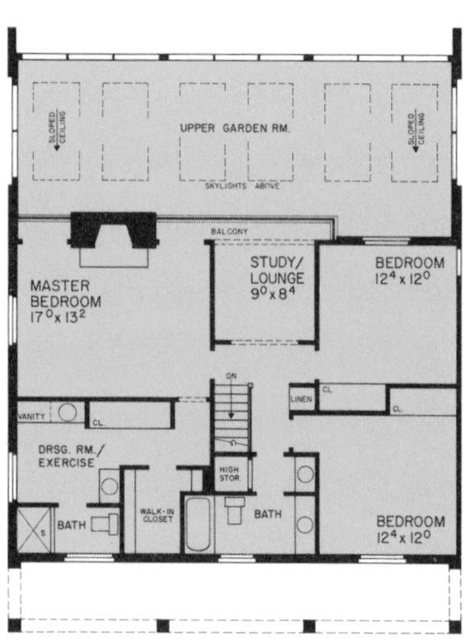

● Bay windows highlight the front and side exteriors of this three-bedroom Colonial. For energy efficiency, this design has an enclosed garden room that collects free solar energy. This area opens to the family room, breakfast room and second floor master suite. The solar garden room includes 576 sq. ft. This figure is not included in the above total.

Design X2654

First Floor: 1,152 square feet
Second Floor: 844 square feet
Total: 1,996 square feet

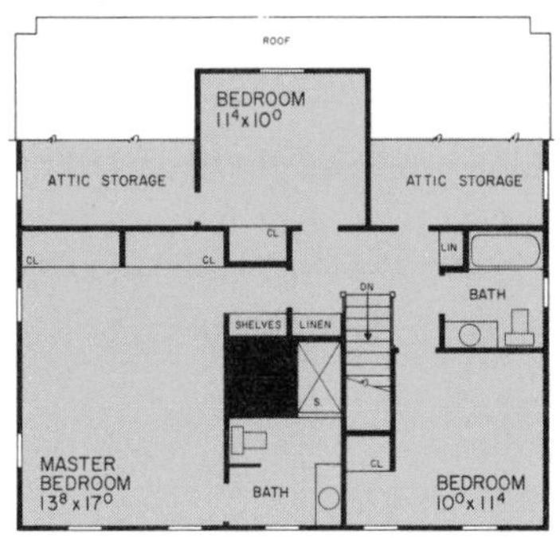

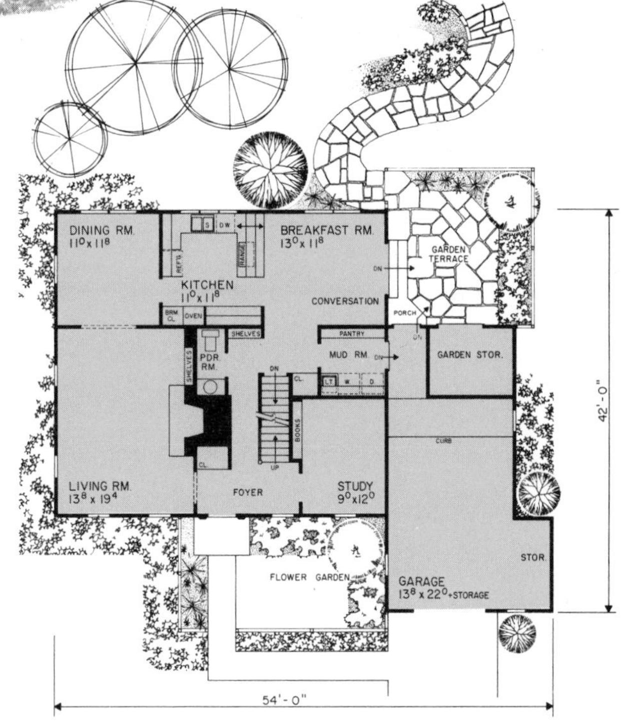

● This is certainly an authentic traditional saltbox. It features a symmetrical design with a center fireplace, a wide, paneled doorway and multi-paned, double-hung windows. Tucked behind the one-car garage is a garden shed which provides work and storage space. The breakfast room features French doors which open onto a flagstone terrace. The U-shaped kitchen has built-in counters which make efficient use of space. The upstairs plan houses three bedrooms.

Design X2649

First Floor: 1,501 square feet
Second Floor: 1,280 square feet
Total: 2,781 square feet

● This design's front exterior is highlighted by four pedimented nine-over-nine windows, five second-story eyebrow windows and a massive central chimney. Note the spacious kitchen of the interior. It is large in size and features an island range, pantry and broom closets, breakfast room with sliding glass doors to the rear porch and an adjacent laundry room which has access to the garage.

72'- 0"
TERRACE
PORCH
STUDY $10^0 \times 13^6$
CL
CHINA CABT.
DINING RM. $12^0 \times 11^6$
PDR RM.
KITCHEN $11^4 \times 13^6$
RANGE
BRKFST. RM. $10^4 \times 11^6$
CURB
32'-0"
DN
BRM. CL.
PANTRY
LAUNDRY
UP
LIVING RM. $15^4 \times 17^6$
FOYER
FAMILY RM. $13^0 \times 15^6$
GARAGE $21^4 \times 23^4$
PORCH

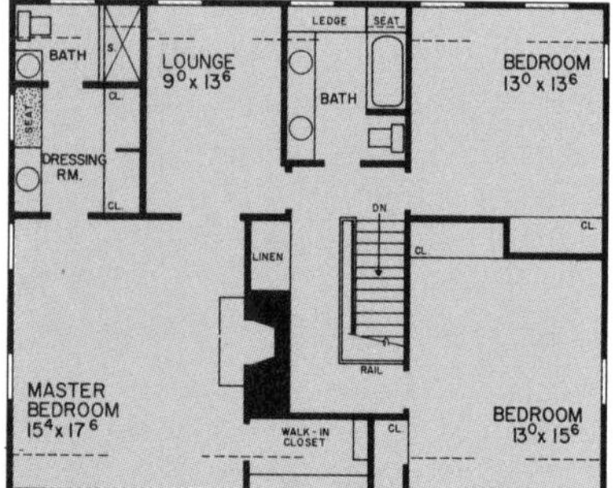

Design X2616

First Floor: 1,415 square feet
Second Floor: 1,106 square feet; Total: 2,521 square feet

● Unlike the majority of the Salt Boxes of Colonial New England, this design has a distinguishing feature: a saw-tooth-shaped side wing that shares the same rear roofline as the house to which it was appended. History is exquisitely detailed in this exterior yet its floor plan has been planned to serve today's family conveniently.

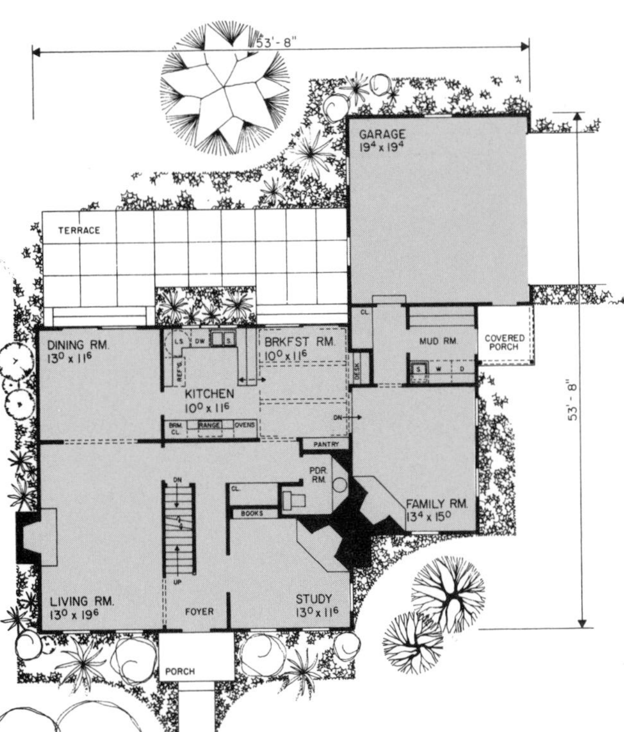

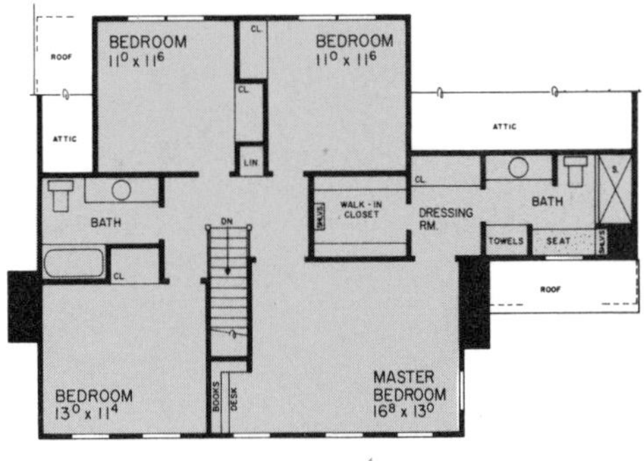

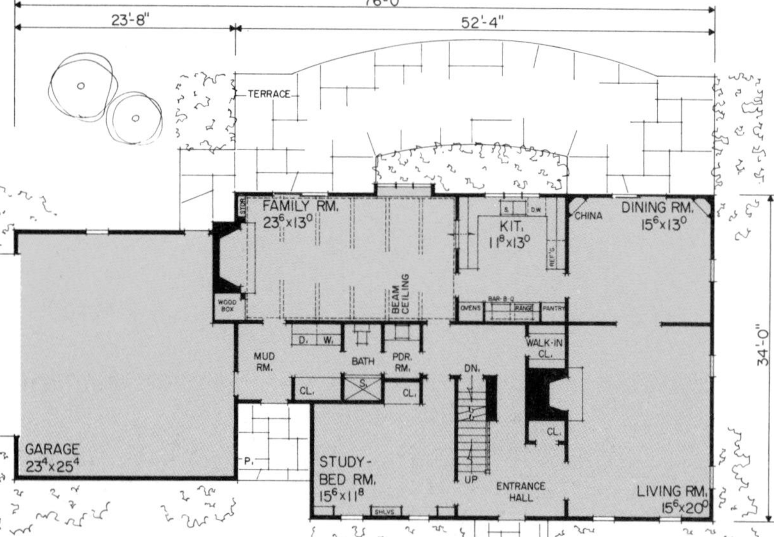

Design X1900

First Floor: 1,672 square feet
Second Floor: 1,287 square feet
Total: 2,959 square feet

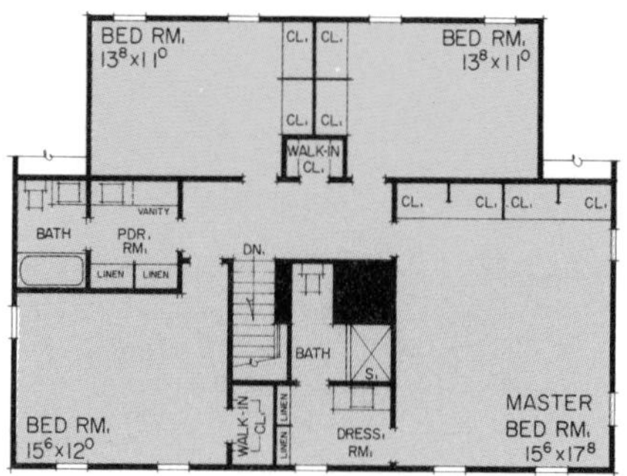

● The history of the Colonial Salt Box goes back some 200 years. This unusually authentic adaptation captures all the warmth and charm of the early days both inside as well as outside. To reflect today's living patterns, an up-dating of the floor plan was inevitable. The result is a room arrangement which will serve the active family wonderfully. Formal living and dining take place at one end of the house which is free of cross-room traffic. Informal living activities will center around the family room and expand through sliding glass doors to the terrace. The mud room area is strategically located and includes the laundry and a full bath. An extra study/bedroom supplements four bedrooms upstairs. Count the closets and the other storage areas.

Design X2623

First Floor: 1,368 square feet
Second Floor: 1,046 square feet; Total: 2,414 square feet

L D

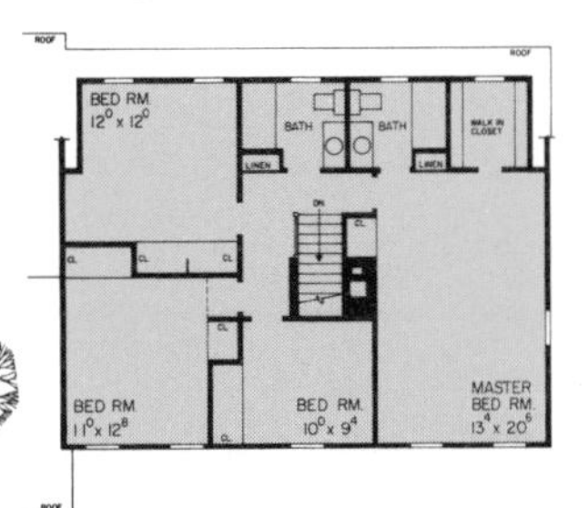

● Take note of this four bedroom saltbox design. Enter through the large entrance hall to enjoy this home. Imagine a living room 13 x 27 feet. Plus a family room. Both having a fireplace. Also, sliding glass doors in both the family room and nook leading to the rear terrace.

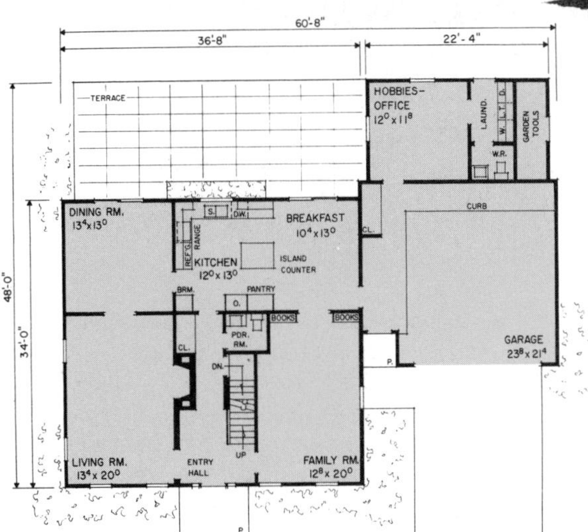

Design X1814

First Floor: 1,471 square feet
Second Floor:1,052 square feet
Total: 2,523 square feet

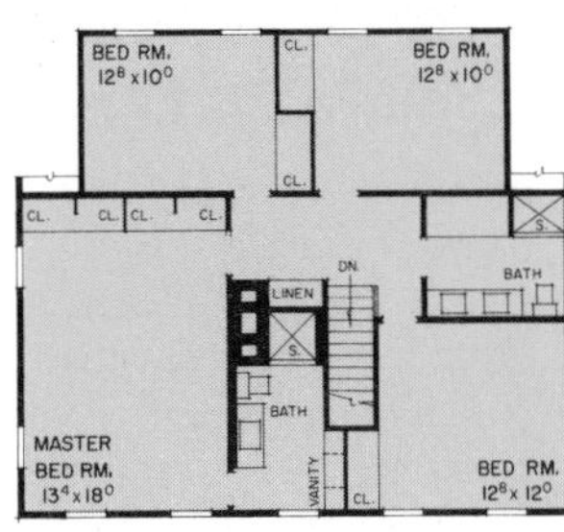

● A saltbox design that has all of the usual traditional exterior features. The interior shows what up-to-date floor planning can do inside the charm of yesteryear's exterior. A central entrance hall routes traffic directly to all major areas. The work area can be made to capture that cozy country kitchen atmosphere.

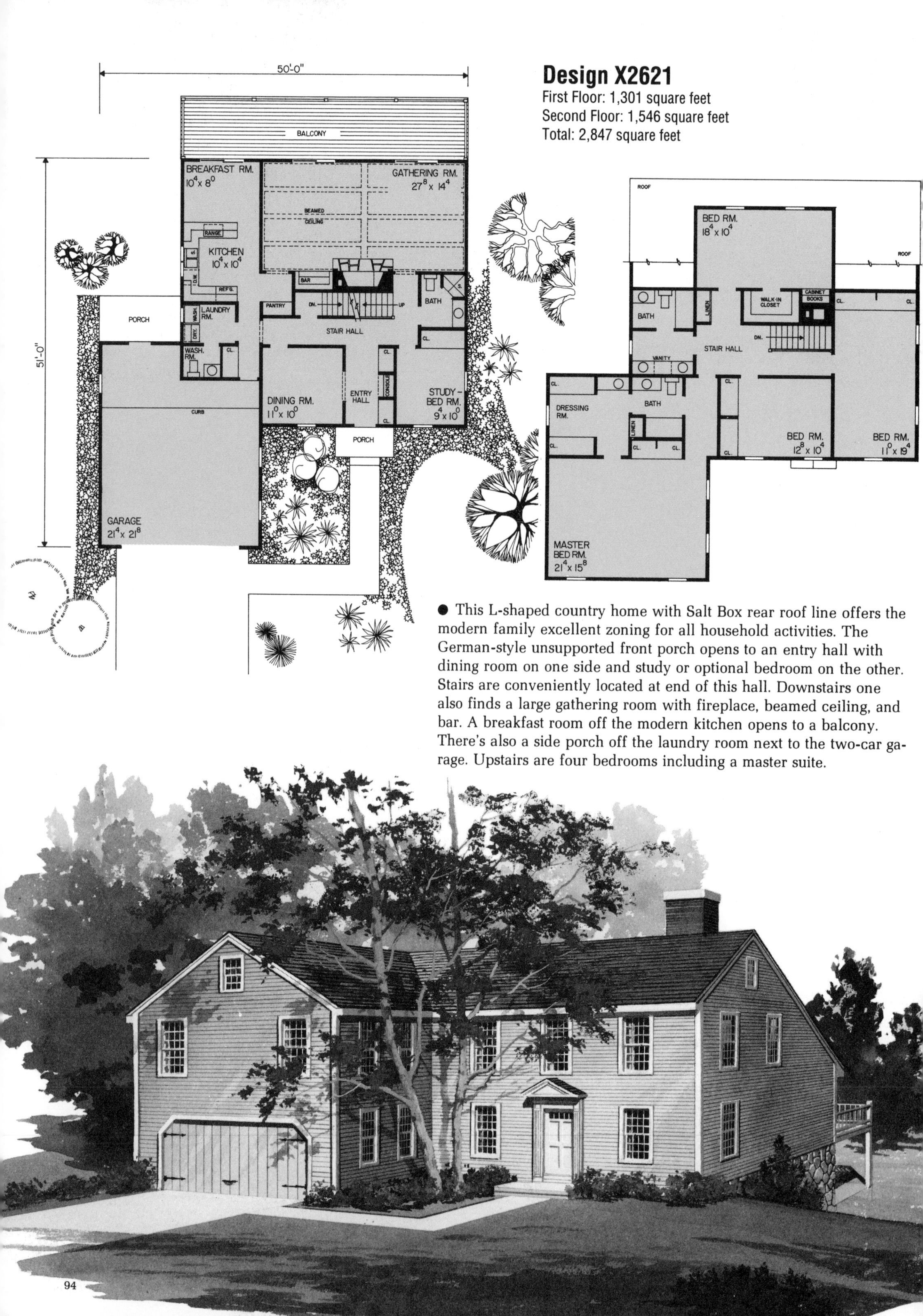

Design X2621

First Floor: 1,301 square feet
Second Floor: 1,546 square feet
Total: 2,847 square feet

● This L-shaped country home with Salt Box rear roof line offers the modern family excellent zoning for all household activities. The German-style unsupported front porch opens to an entry hall with dining room on one side and study or optional bedroom on the other. Stairs are conveniently located at end of this hall. Downstairs one also finds a large gathering room with fireplace, beamed ceiling, and bar. A breakfast room off the modern kitchen opens to a balcony. There's also a side porch off the laundry room next to the two-car garage. Upstairs are four bedrooms including a master suite.

● This Colonial has all the exterior charm of its Early American ancestry, yet its modern interior plan belies its roots. To the immediate left of the entry is a living room with music alcove and fireplace; to the right a formal dining room. In its own wing, a few steps down from the living room, is a cheery sun room. The country kitchen with island range, built-in china cabinet, and a fireplace offers plenty of space for informal eating and overlooks the rear terrace. A laundry, washroom, and garage are also found on this floor. Three bedrooms and two baths on the second floor include the master suite with whirlpool bath.

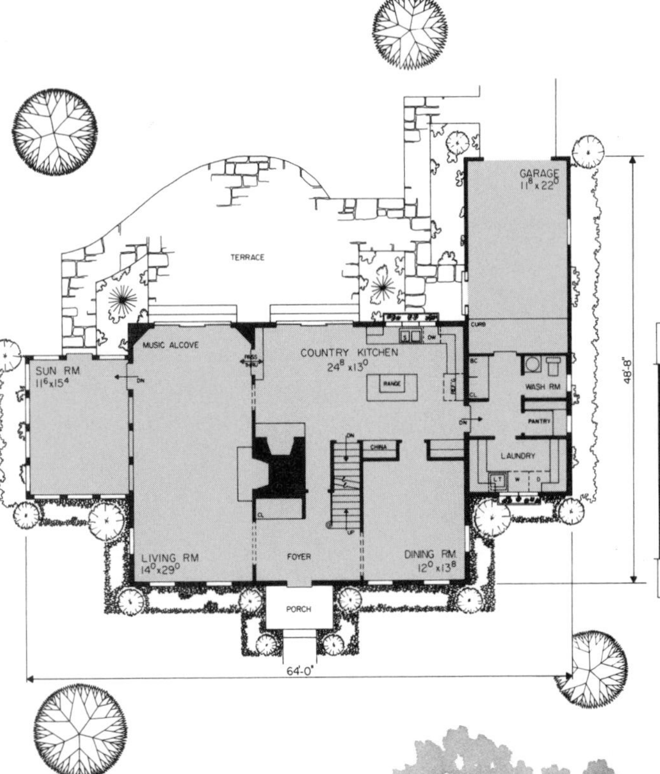

Design X2986

First Floor: 1,592 square feet
Second Floor: 1,054 square feet
Total: 2,646 square feet

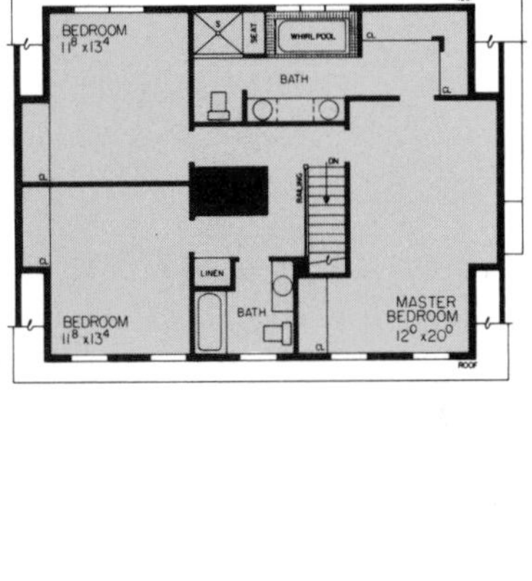

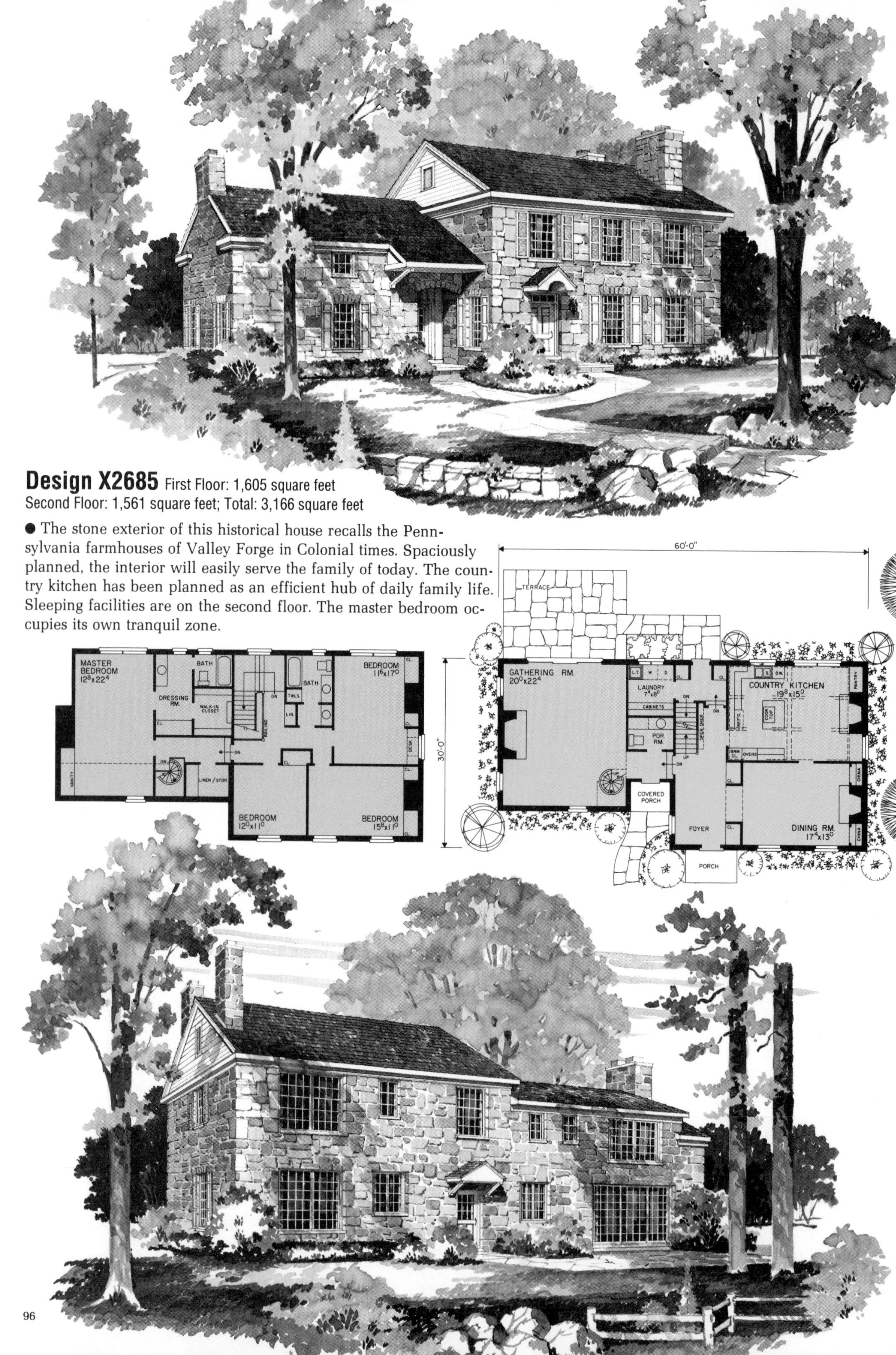

Design X2685 First Floor: 1,605 square feet

Second Floor: 1,561 square feet; Total: 3,166 square feet

● The stone exterior of this historical house recalls the Pennsylvania farmhouses of Valley Forge in Colonial times. Spaciously planned, the interior will easily serve the family of today. The country kitchen has been planned as an efficient hub of daily family life. Sleeping facilities are on the second floor. The master bedroom occupies its own tranquil zone.

Design X3349

First Floor: 2,807 square feet
Second Floor: 1,363 square feet
Total: 4,170 square feet

L D

- Grand traditional design comes to the forefront in this elegant two-story. From the dramatic front entry with curving double stairs to the less formal gathering room with fireplace and terrace access, this plan accommodates family lifestyles. Notice the split-bedroom plan with the master suite on the first floor and family bedrooms upstairs. A four-car garage handles the largest of family fleets.

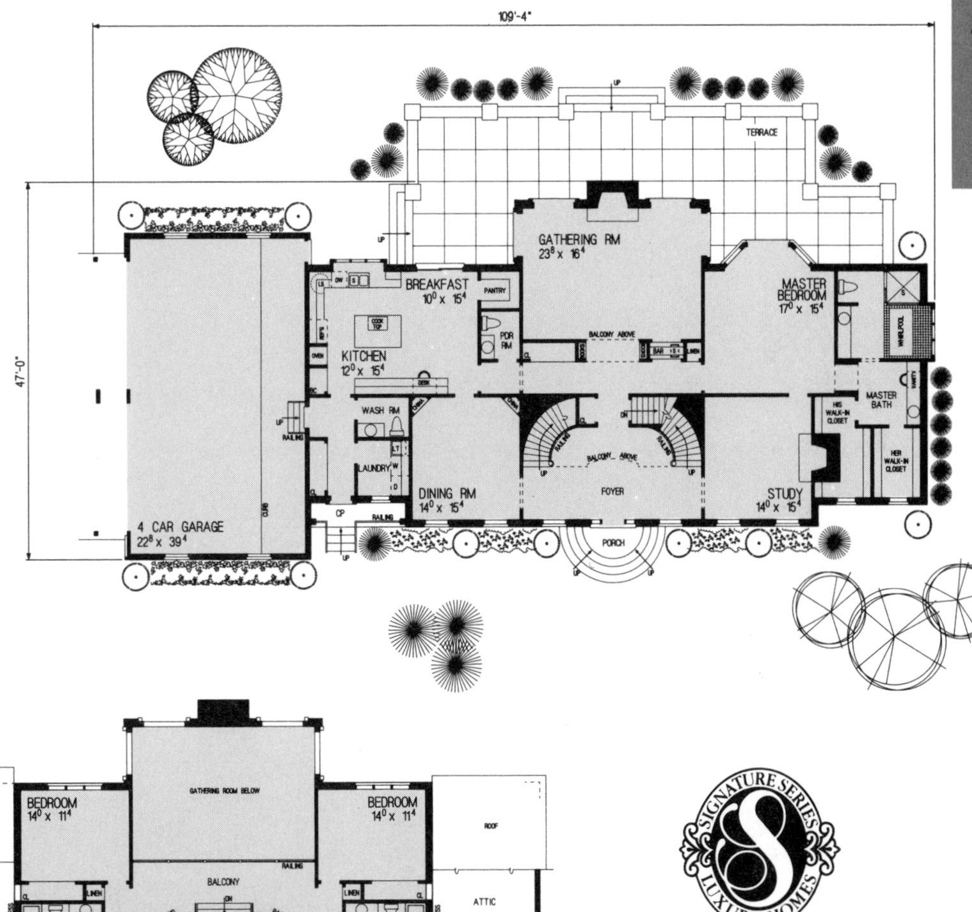

Design X2543 First Floor: 2,345 square feet

Second Floor: 1,687 square feet; Total: 4,032 square feet

L **D**

● This best-selling French adaptation is highlighted by effective window treatment, delicate cornice detailing, appealing brick quoins and excellent proportion. Inside are a gathering room, formal living and dining rooms, study, gourmet kitchen and four upstairs bedrooms.

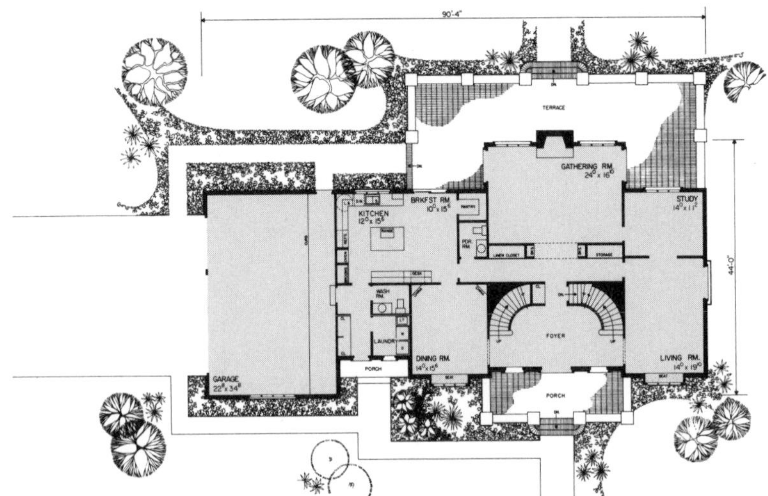

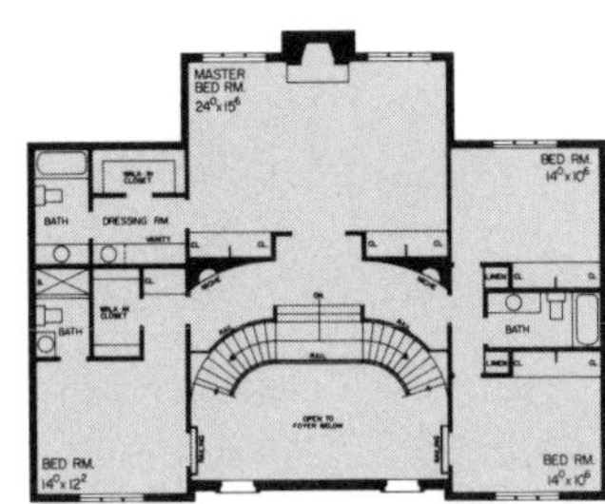

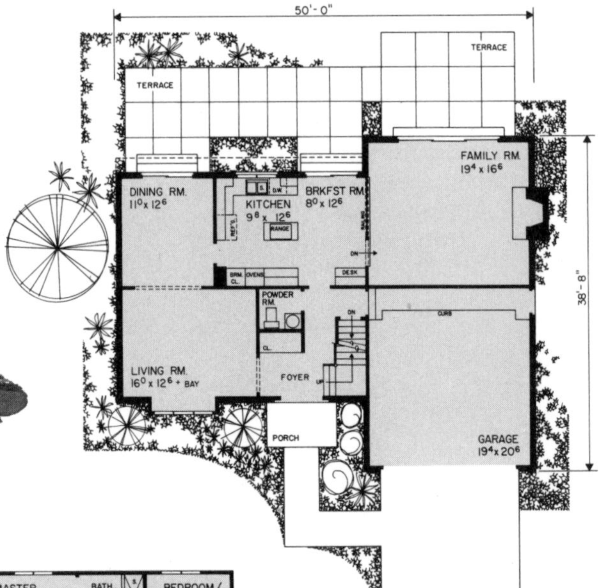

Design X2798

First Floor: 1,149 square feet

Second Floor: 850 square feet

Total: 1,999 square feet

L **D**

● A relatively narrow lot can house this two-story French design. The kitchen features an island range and an adjacent breakfast room with sliding glass doors to the rear terrace. A large, sunken family room is highlighted by a fireplace. Each of the four bedrooms will serve its occupants ideally.

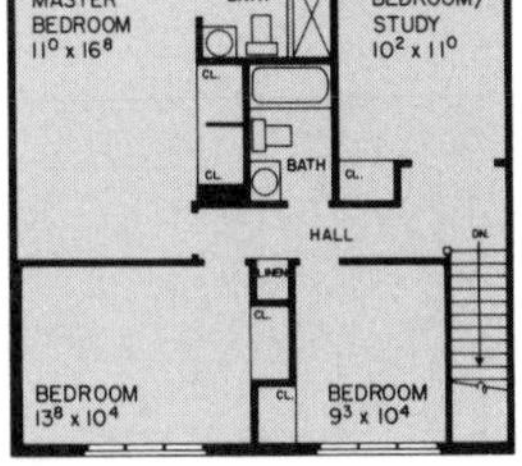

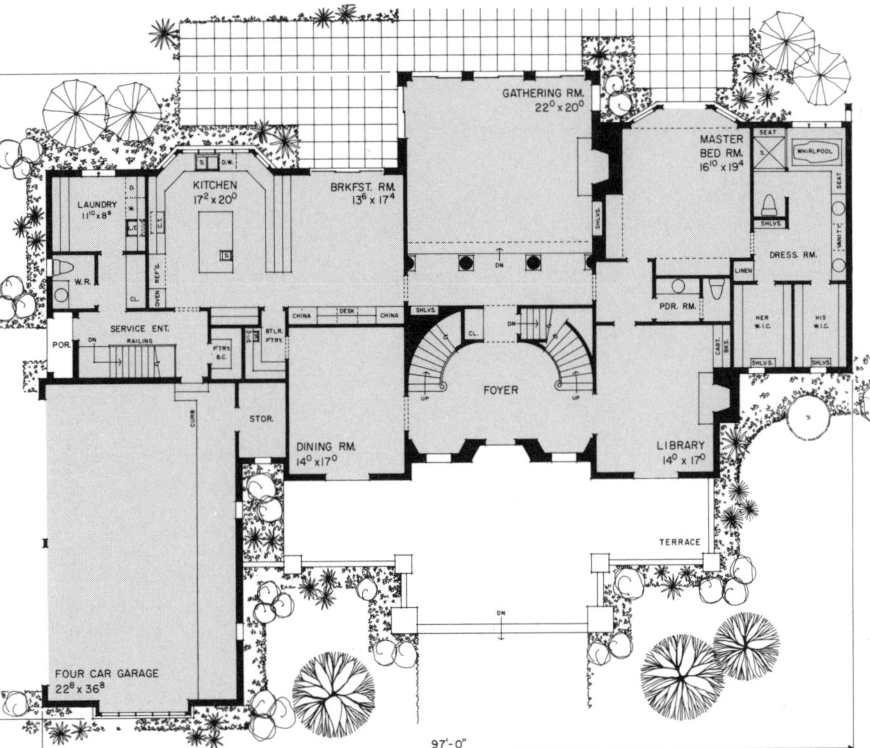

Design X3380

First Floor: 3,350 square feet
Second Floor: 1,298 square feet
Total: 4,648 square feet

● Reminiscent of a Mediterranean villa, this grand manor is a show-stopper on the outside and a comfortable residence on the inside. An elegant receiving hall boasts a double staircase and is flanked by the formal dining room and the library. A huge gathering room is found to the back. The master bedroom is found on the first floor for privacy. Upstairs are four additional bedrooms and two full baths.

Design X3381

First Floor: 2,485 square feet
Second Floor: 1,864 square feet
Total: 4,349 square feet

L **D**

● A place for everything and everything in its place. If that's your motto, this is your house. A central foyer allows access to every part of the home. To the left sits the spacious gathering room with fireplace and music alcove. Straight ahead, the open living and dining rooms offer sweeping views of the back yard. The modern kitchen and conversation area are situated to the right of the home. Near the entrance, a library with bay window and built-in bookcase is found. Look for extra amenities throughout the home: curio cabinets in the foyer, stairwell, conversation area and hall; built-in desk; walk-in closet and a second fireplace. Upstairs, the master suite features an enormous walk-in closet and a pampering bath. Another bedroom has a private bath, while the remaining two bedrooms share a bath with dual lavs.

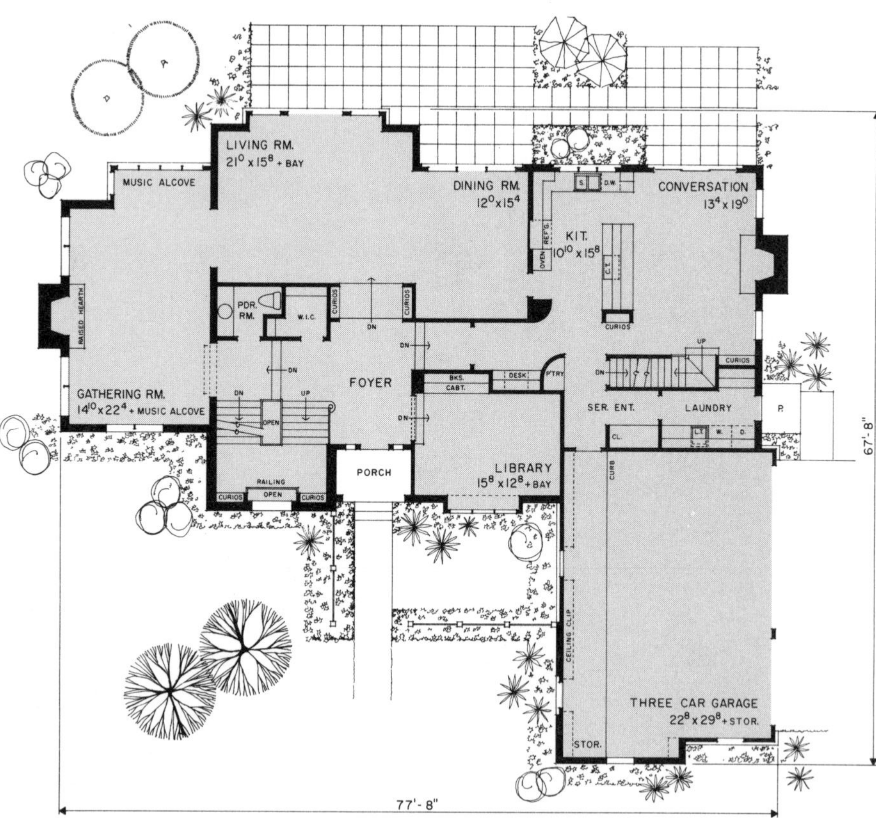

Design X3378

First Floor: 2,997 square feet
Second Floor: 1,415 square feet
Total: 4,412 square feet

● This large traditional home fits right in whether built in the busy city or a secluded rural area. Living areas on the first floor include a media room with bay window, gathering room with raised-hearth fireplace and a formal dining room. The kitchen area supplies room enough for a crowd with a snack bar and a 17-foot breakfast room with terrace access. A convenient first-floor master suite also includes terrace access, along with a sitting room and a dressing and bath area fit for a king. Two bedrooms and two full baths on the second floor are joined by a lounge and spacious bonus room. Note the three-car garage.

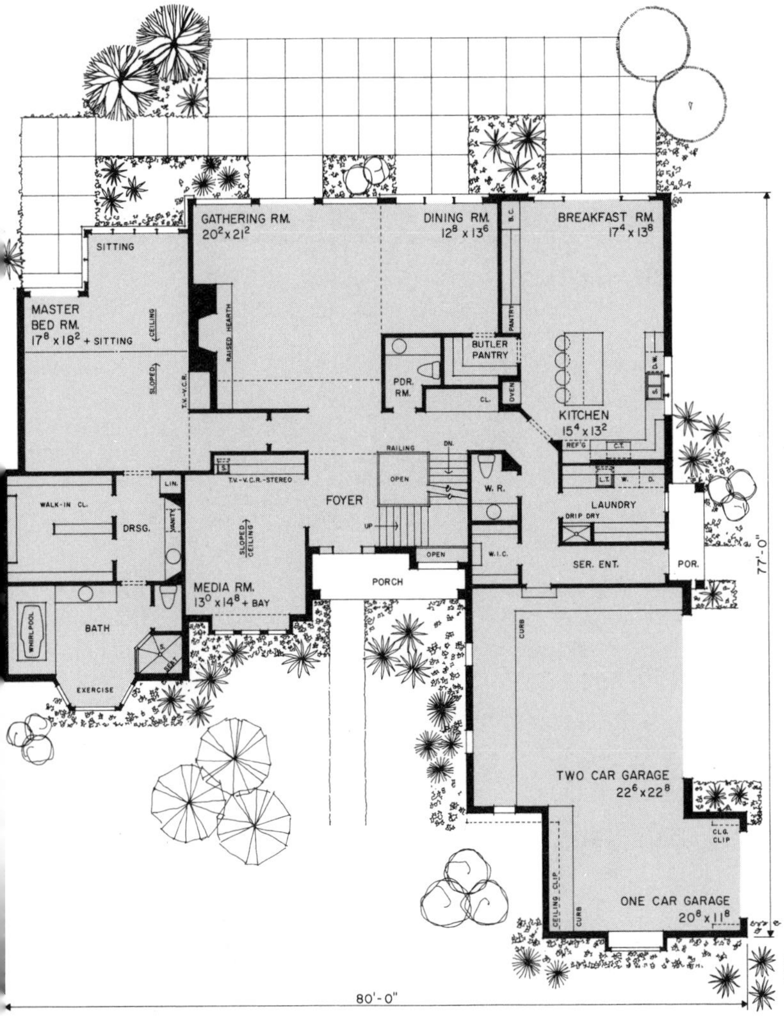

GATHERING RM. 20² x 21²
DINING RM. 12⁸ x 13⁶
BREAKFAST RM. 17⁴ x 13⁸
SITTING
MASTER BED RM. 17⁸ x 18² + SITTING
SLOPED CEILING
RAISED HEARTH
T.V.-V.C.R.
BUTLER PANTRY
PANTRY
PDR. RM.
CL.
OVEN
D.W.
KITCHEN 15⁴ x 13²
REF'G
C.T.
RAILING
DN.
OPEN
T.V.-V.C.R.-STEREO
FOYER
W. R.
L.T.
W.
D.
LAUNDRY
DRIP DRY
WALK-IN CL.
DRSG.
LIN.
VANITY
SLOPED CEILING
UP
OPEN
W.I.C.
SER. ENT.
POR.
MEDIA RM. 13⁰ x 14⁸ + BAY
PORCH
WHIRLPOOL
BATH
EXERCISE
CURB
TWO CAR GARAGE 22⁶ x 22⁸
CL. & CLIP
CEILING CLIP
CURB
ONE CAR GARAGE 20⁸ x 11⁸
77'-0"
80'-0"

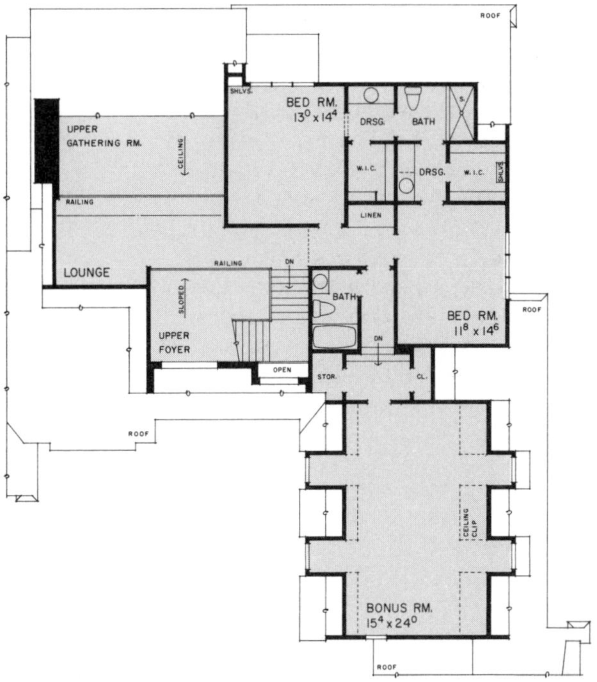

ROOF
SHLVS.
BED RM. 13⁰ x 14⁴
DRSG.
BATH
UPPER GATHERING RM.
CEILING
W.I.C.
DRSG.
W.I.C.
SHLVS.
RAILING
LINEN
LOUNGE
RAILING
DN
BATH
SLOPED
UPPER FOYER
OPEN
DN
BED RM. 11⁸ x 14⁶
ROOF
STOR.
CL.
ROOF
CEILING CLIP
BONUS RM. 15⁴ x 24⁰
ROOF

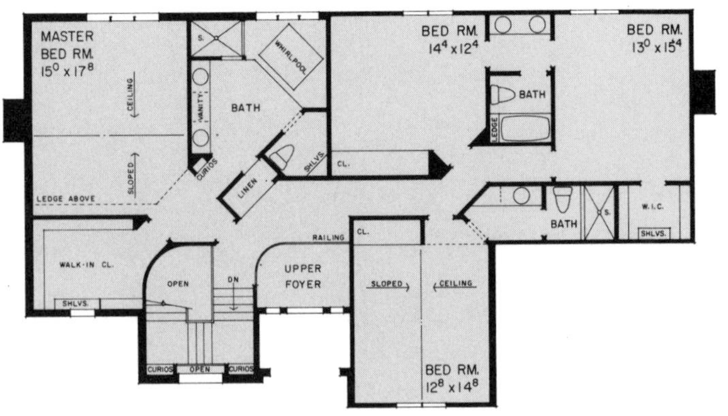

Design X3555

First Floor: 1,948 square feet
Second Floor: 1,669 square feet
Total: 3,617 square feet

L **D**

● Round-top windows add elegance to the interior and exterior of this traditional home. Large gathering areas on the first floor flow together for ease in entertaining. The sunken gathering room stretches from the front of the house to the back, with a terrace at each end and a fireplace in the middle. Another fireplace is found in the conversation area adjoining the kitchen. The formal dining room features a bay window. Sleeping areas upstairs include a master bedroom with spacious bath and walk-in closet, three family bedrooms and two full baths.

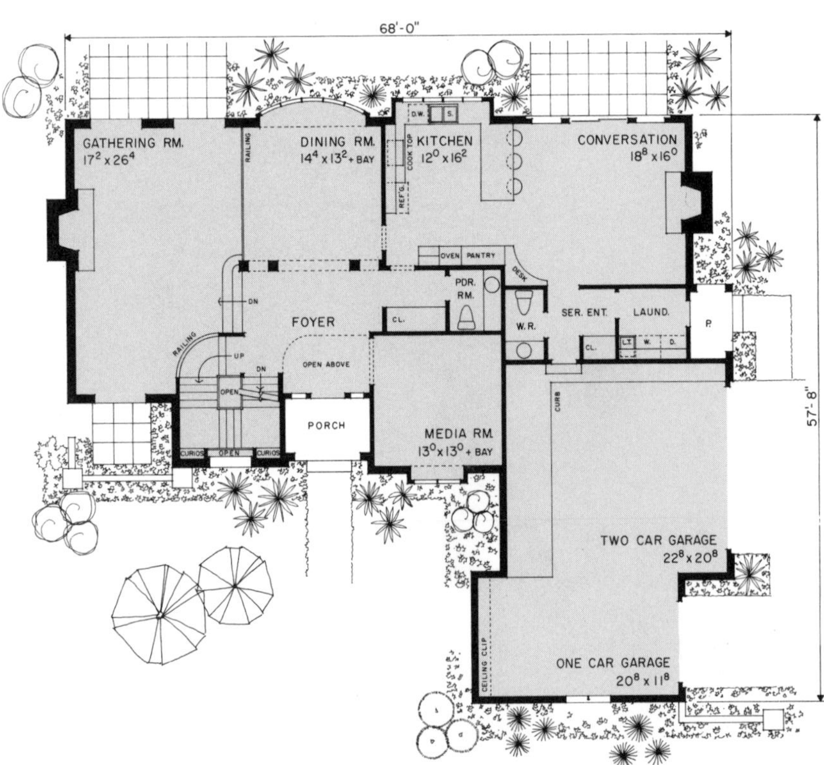

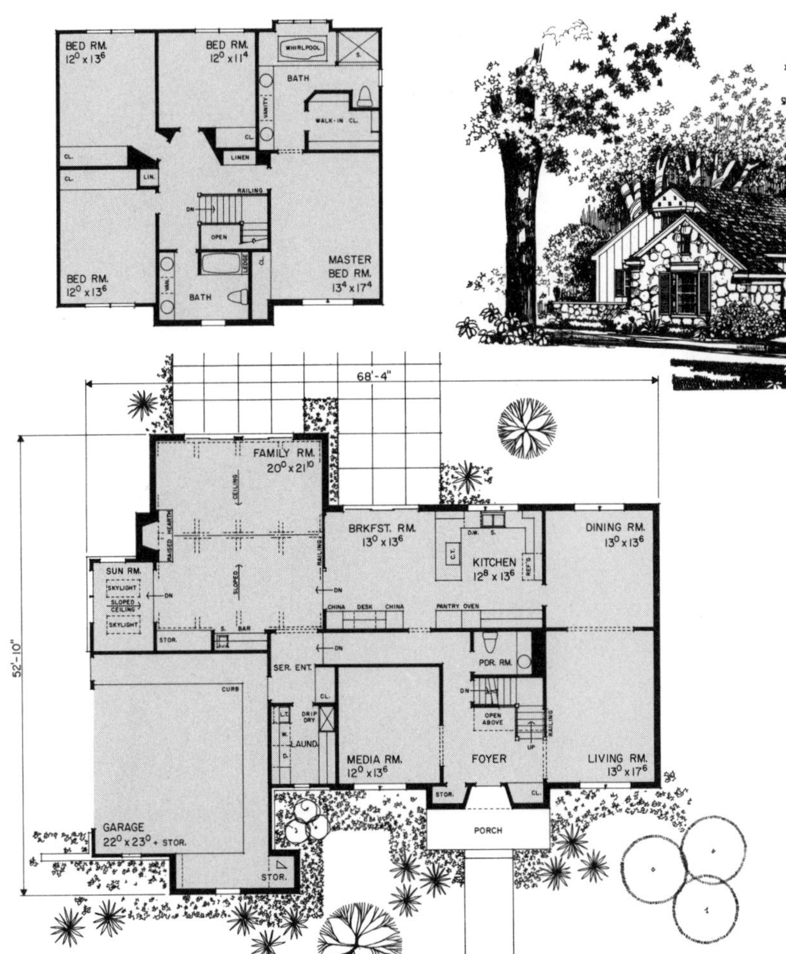

Design X3370

First Floor: 2,055 square feet
Second Floor: 1,288 square feet
Total: 3,343 square feet

L **D**

● The combination of stone and brick allow an impressive facade on this traditional two-story. The symmetrically designed interior will provide efficient traffic patterns. Note the formal living and dining areas to the right and huge family room to the rear. The U-shaped kitchen has an attached breakfast room and built-ins. There are four bedrooms on the second floor. The master features a walk-in closet, double vanity and whirlpool tub.

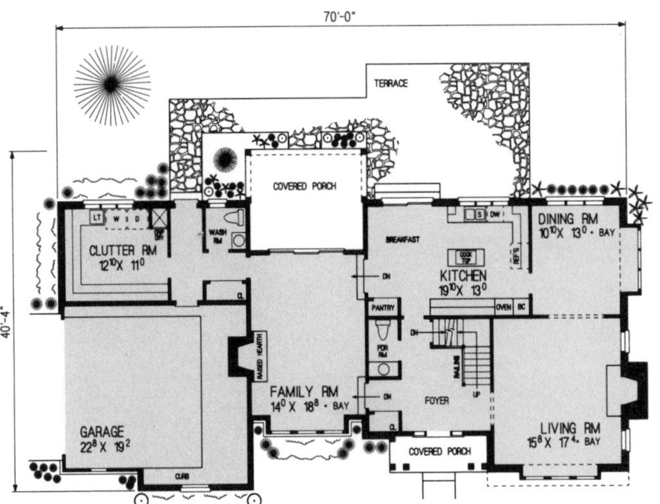

Design X3356

First Floor: 1,610 square feet
Second Floor: 1,200 square feet
Total: 2,810 square feet

L **D**

● Traditionally speaking, this home takes blue ribbons. Its family room has a raised-hearth fireplace and there's a covered porch reached through sliding glass doors for informal eating. The living room also has a fireplace and is near the boxed-windowed dining room. A clutter room off the garage could be turned into a hobby or sewing room. Three bedrooms on the second floor include a master suite with His and Hers walk-in closets and three family bedrooms.

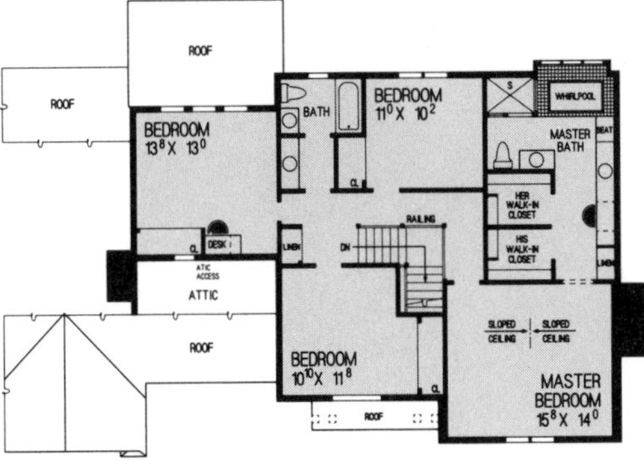

Design X2722

First Floor: 2,330 square feet
Second Floor: 921 square feet
Total: 3,251 square feet

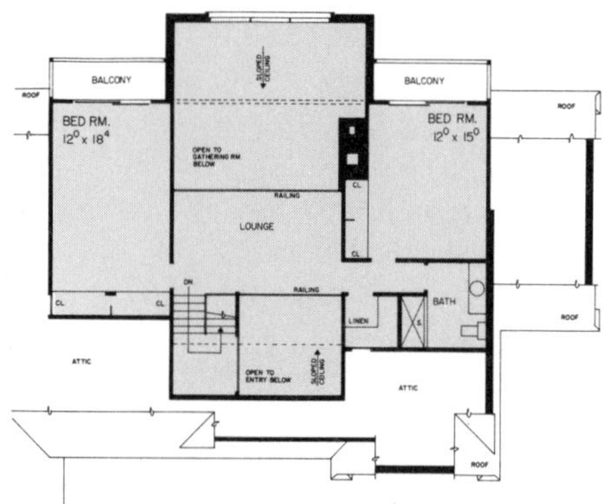

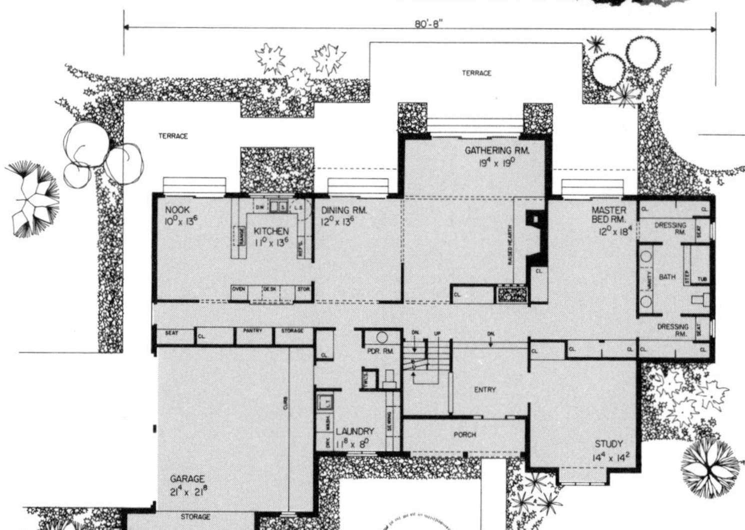

Design X3334

First Floor: 2,193 square feet
Second Floor: 831 square feet
Total: 3,024 square feet

● A traditional favorite, this home combines classic style with progressive floor planning. Four bedrooms are split — master suite and one bedroom on the first floor, two more bedrooms upstairs. The second-floor lounge overlooks a large, sunken gathering room near the formal dining area. A handy butler's pantry connects the dining room and kitchen.

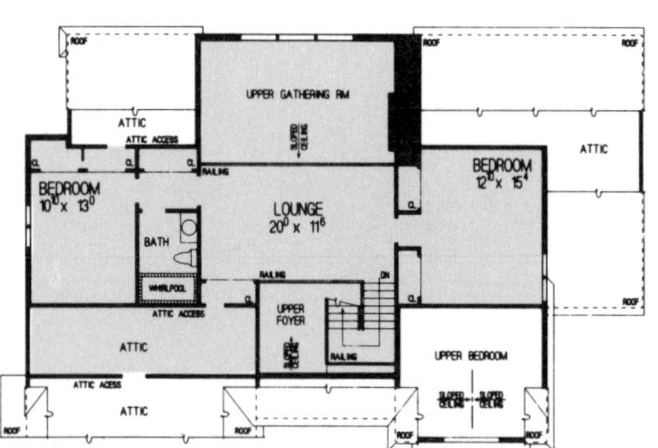

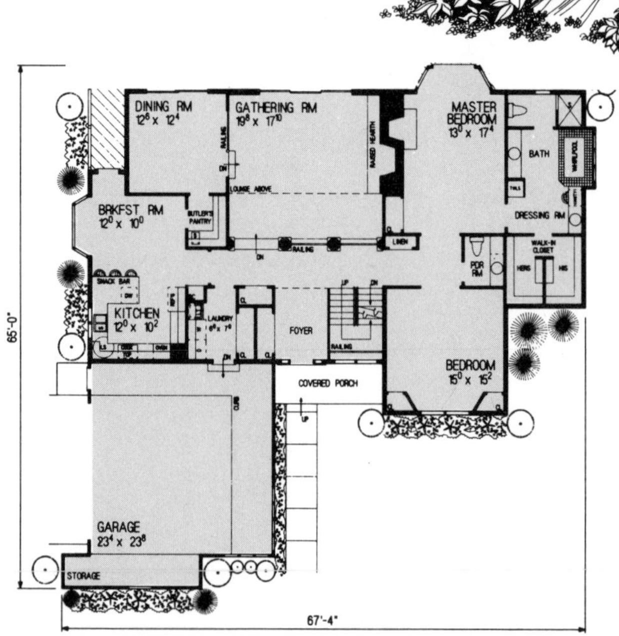

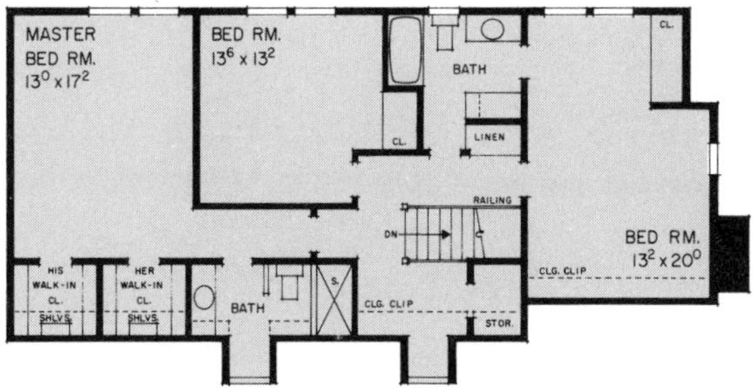

Design X3363

First Floor: 1,926 square feet
Second Floor: 1,189 square feet
Total: 3,115 square feet

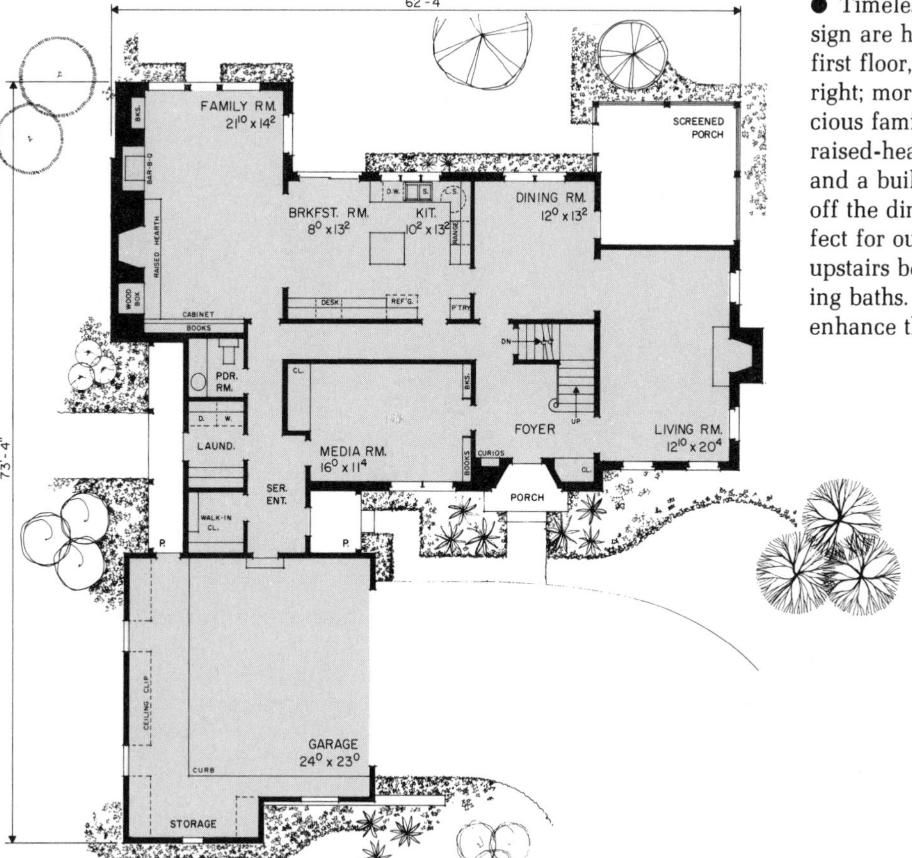

● Timeless traditional style and 1½-story design are highlights in this lovely home. On the first floor, formal living areas are found to the right; more casual living to the left. The spacious family room devotes one full wall to a raised-hearth fireplace with built-in wood box and a built-in barbecue and bookshelves. Just off the dining room is a screened porch, perfect for outdoor eating. Examine the three upstairs bedrooms and you'll find two adjoining baths. His and Hers walk-in closets enhance the master suite.

Design X2500

First Floor: 1,851 square feet
Second Floor: 762 square feet
Total: 2,613 square feet

L **D**

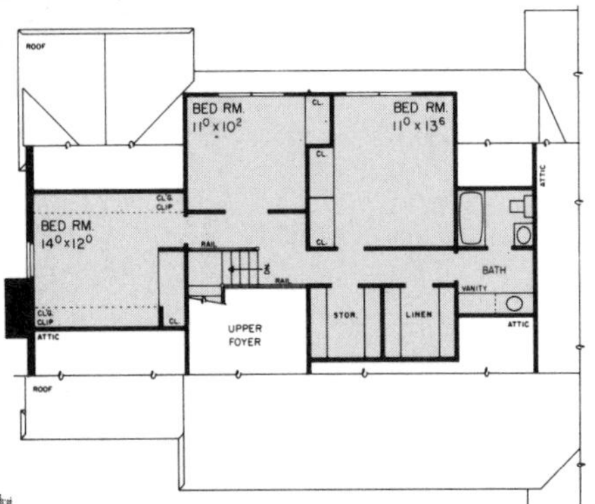

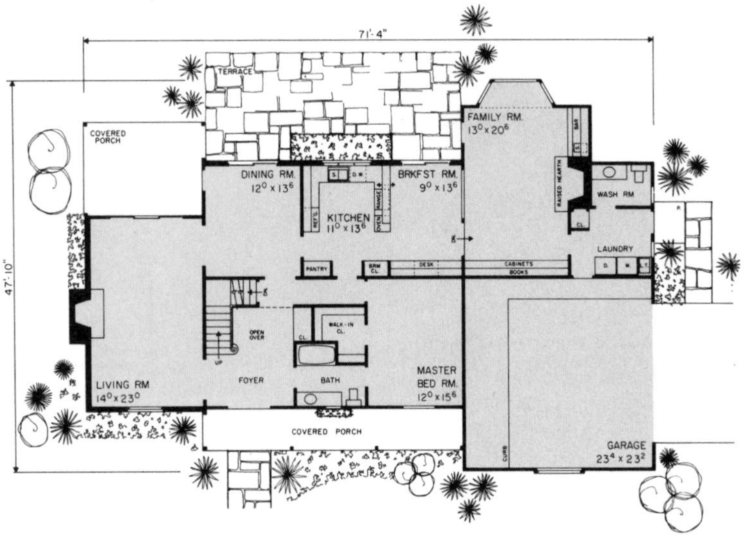

● Large families will enjoy the wonderful floor plan offered by this charming home. Don't miss the covered rear porch and the many features of the family room.

Design X2599

First Floor: 2,075 square feet
Second Floor: 1,398 square feet
Total: 3,473 square feet

D

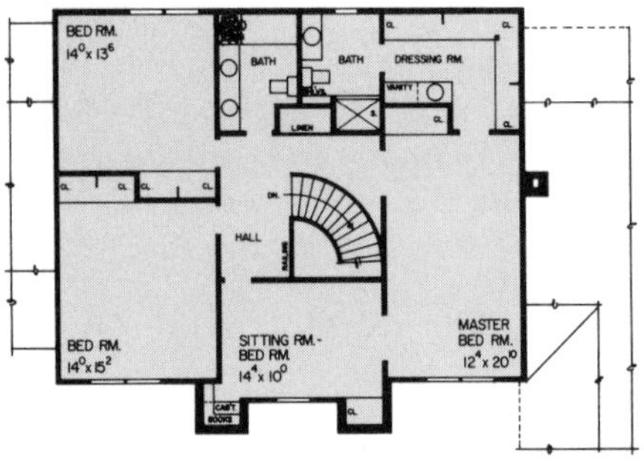

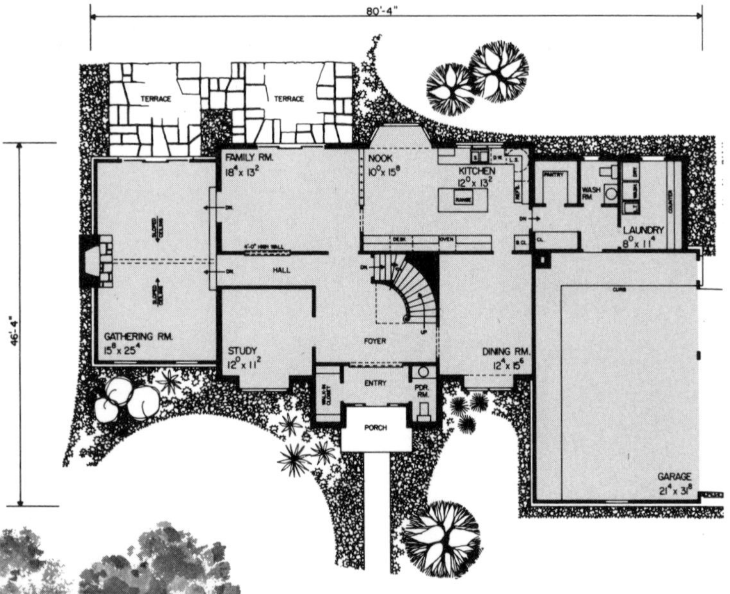

● This traditional two-story with its projecting one-story wings is delightfully proportional. The symmetrical window treatment is most appealing. Inside, there is a large foyer with curving, open staircase to the second floor. Besides a formal living room and dining room, there are a formal study and upstairs sitting room. The second floor also offers a three- or four-bedroom sleeping area. The master suite has a large dressing area with plenty of closet space.

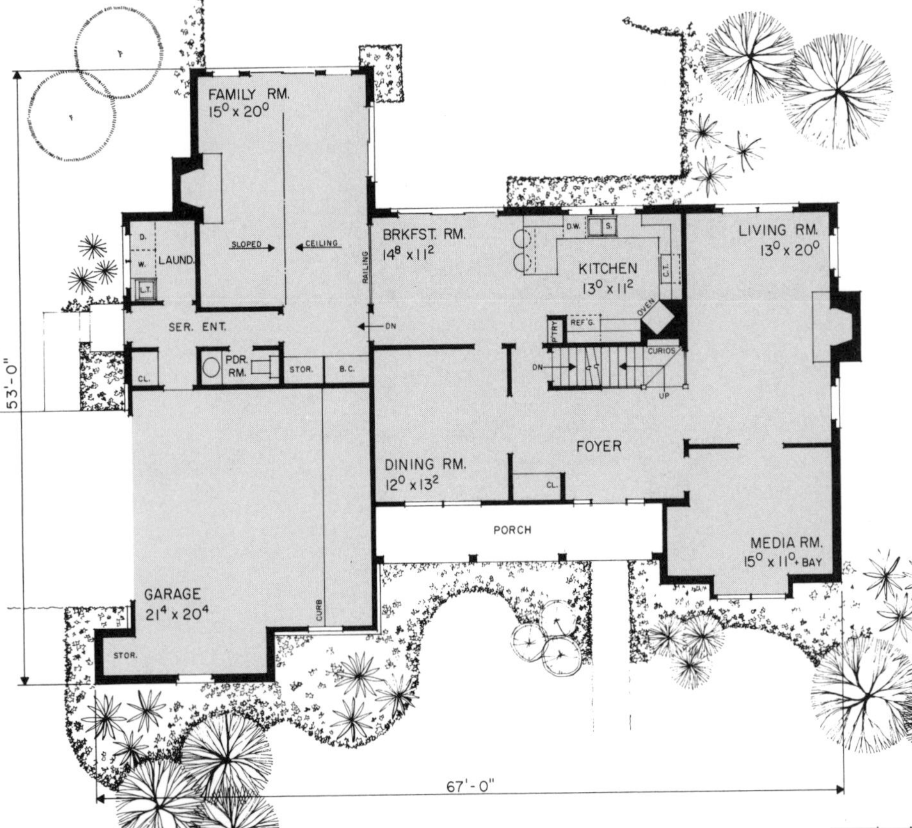

● One of the most popular home renditions is the two-story four-bedroom, and few designs of this type offer as much as the one shown here. The gracious entry opens to the right to a media room and to a living room with fireplace. On the left is a formal dining room. At the back, find the kitchen with attached breakfast room and just a step down is everyone's favorite family room. All four bedrooms are located on the second floor. The master suite features a double-size walk-in closet and bumped-out window in the bath. Three family bedrooms share a full bath.

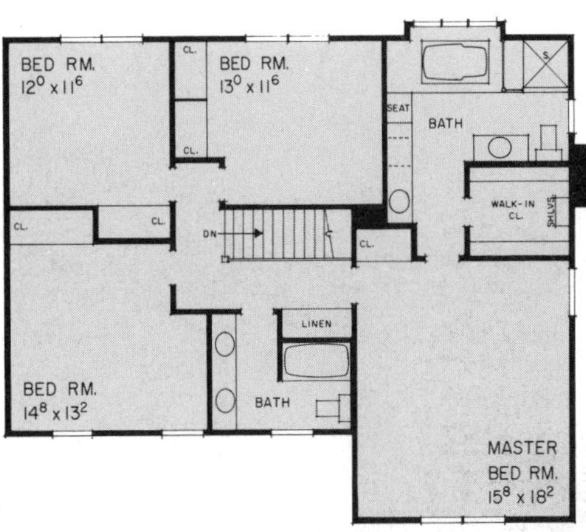

Design X3365

First Floor: 1,731 square feet
Second Floor: 1,248 square feet
Total: 2,979 square feet

Design X3353

First Floor: 2,191 square feet
Second Floor: 874 square feet
Total: 3,065 square feet

L D

● This captivating 1½-story Southern Colonial provides the best in livability. On the first floor are the living room, dining room and private media room. A country kitchen with fireplace offers casual living space. The master suite is also located on this floor and has a lavish master bath with whirlpool spa. Upstairs are two family bedrooms, each with its own bath, and a central lounge overlooking the living room.

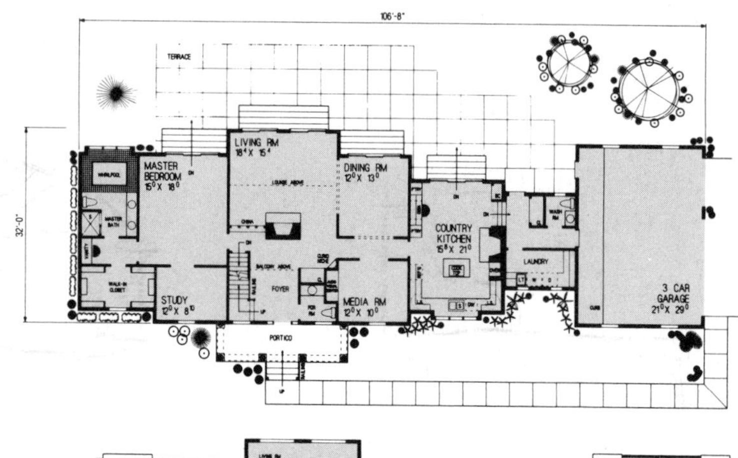

Design X2718

First Floor: 1,941 square feet
Second Floor: 791 square feet
Total: 2,732 square feet

D

● New living patterns are established in the 1½-story home. The front entry hall features an impressive open staircase to the upstairs and basement. Adjacent is the master bedroom which has a compartmented bath with both tub and stall shower. The spacious dressing room steps down into a unique, sunken conversation pit. This cozy area has a planter, built-in seat and a view of the through-fireplace opening to the gathering room. Here, the ceiling slopes to the top of the second-floor lounge which looks down into the gathering room.

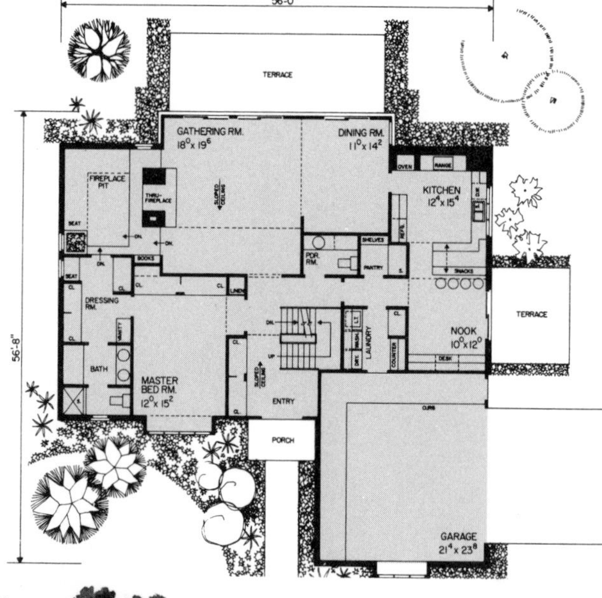

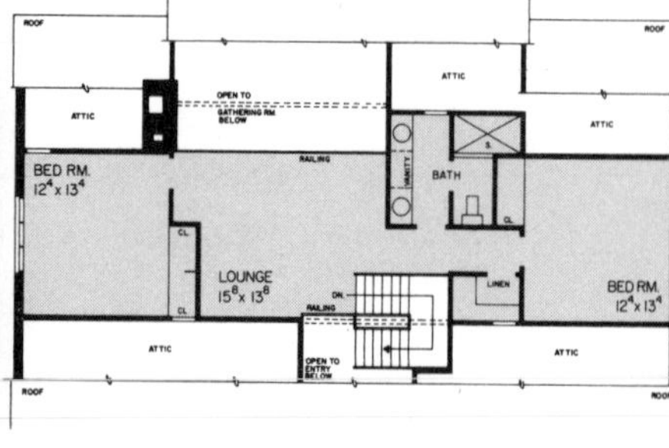

Design X3343 First Floor: 1,953 square feet
Second Floor: 895 square feet; Total: 2,848 square feet

● Beyond the simple traditional styling of this home's exterior are many of the amenities required by today's lifestyles. Among them: a huge country kitchen with fireplace, an attached greenhouse/dining area, a media room off the two-story foyer, split-bedroom planning, and a second-floor lounge. There are three bedrooms upstairs, which share a full bath.

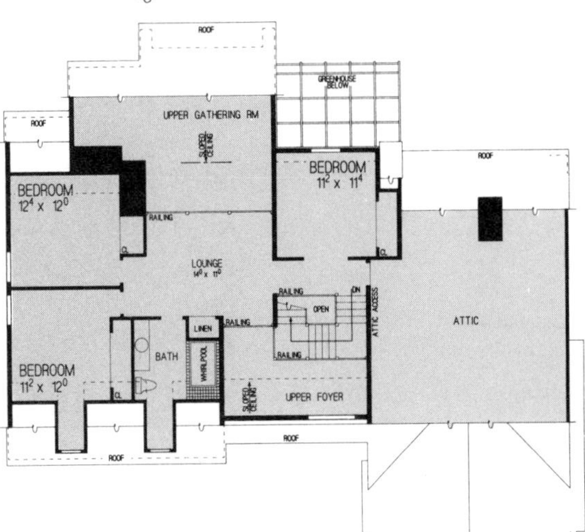

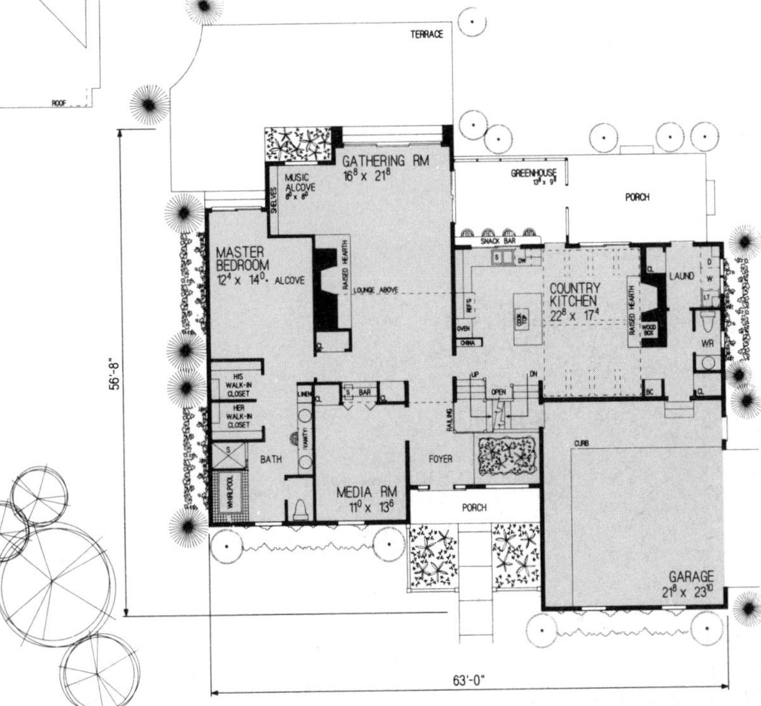

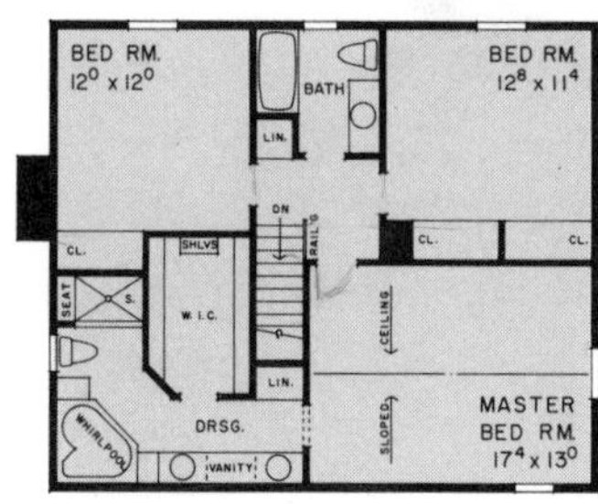

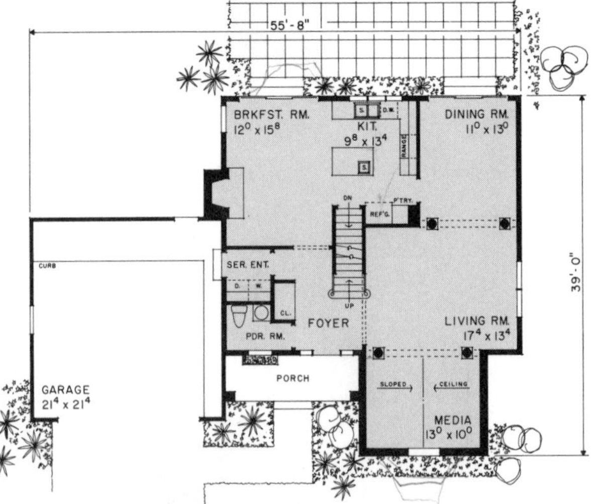

Design X3564

First Floor: 1,113 square feet
Second Floor: 928 square feet
Total: 2,041 square feet

● A quaint traditional exterior conceals a modern and elegantly designed floor plan. As you enter through the foyer, formal living areas to the right of the home include a media room with sloped ceiling, a large living room and a dining room with outdoor access; all maintain an open feeling yet are distinctly separted by columns.

Design X2285

First Floor: 1,118 square feet
Second Floor: 821 square feet
Total: 1,939 square feet

● An appealing 1½-story design for a modest budget. A flexible first-floor plan includes a family room (or dining room) with beamed-ceiling and a large living room with a fireplace. Two bedrooms on the second floor are generously sized and include plenty of closet space.

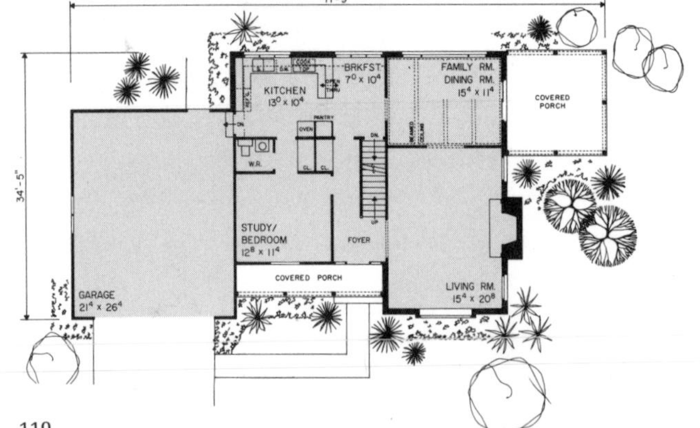

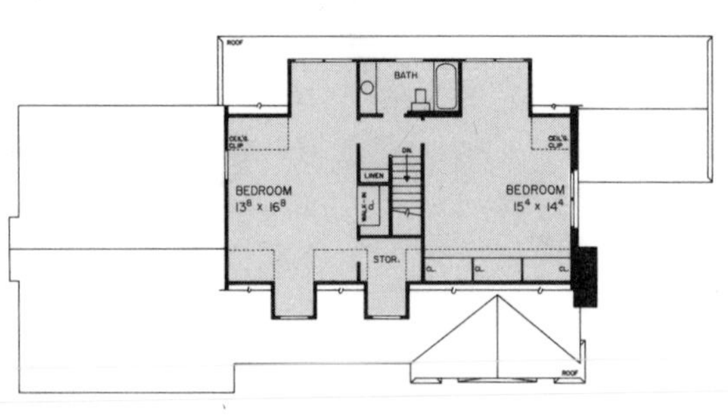

Design X2488

First Floor: 1,113 square feet
Second Floor: 543 square feet
Total: 1,656 square feet

D

● A cozy cottage for the young at heart! Whether called upon to serve the young, active family as a leisure-time retreat at the lake, or the retired couple as a quiet haven in later years, this charming design will perform well. As a year round second home, the upstairs with its two sizable bedrooms, full bath and lounge area, looking down into the gathering room below, will ideally accommodate the younger generation.

CUSTOMIZABLE

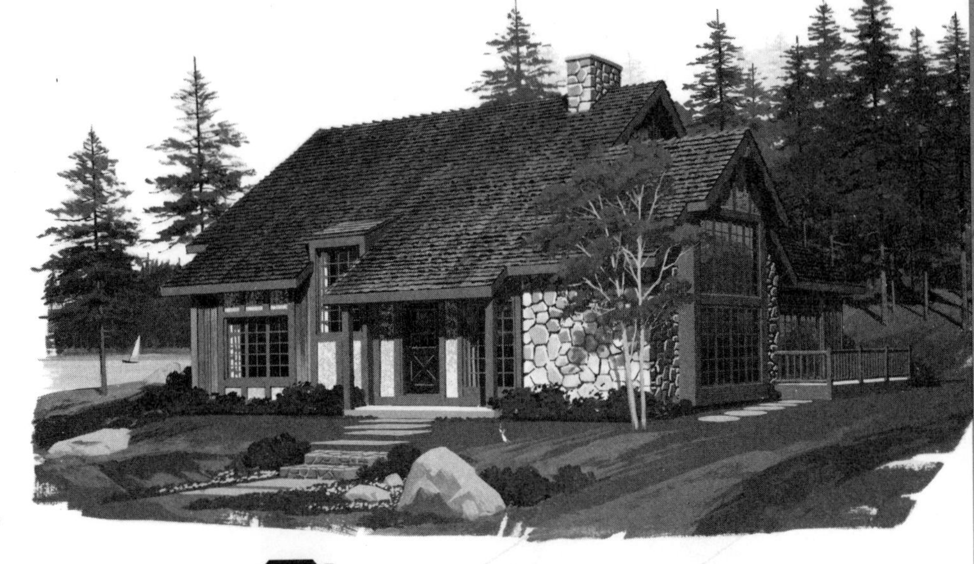

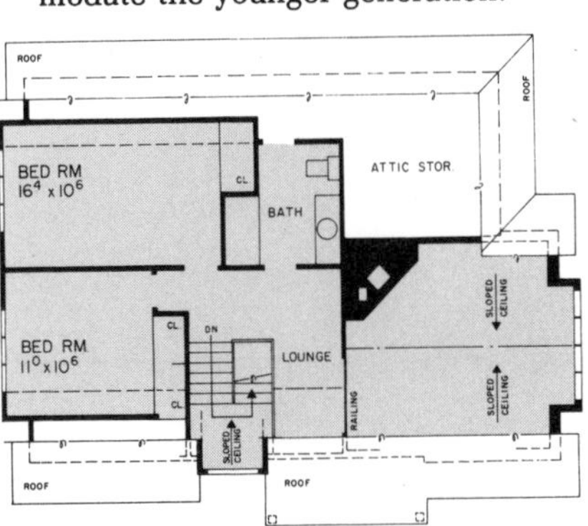

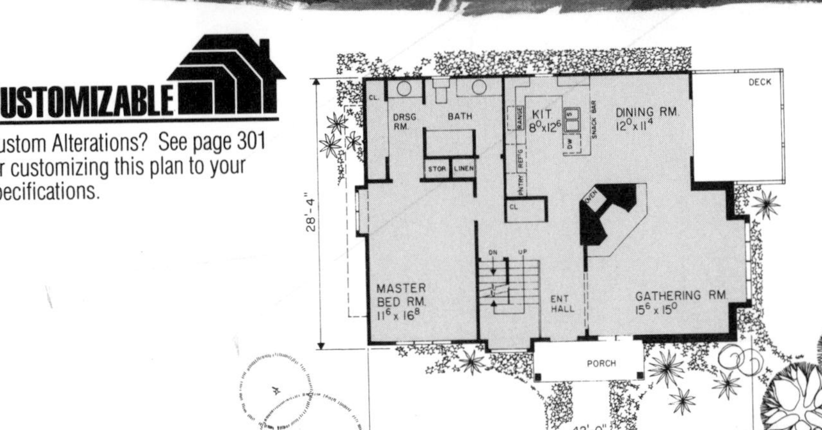

Custom Alterations? See page 301 for customizing this plan to your specifications.

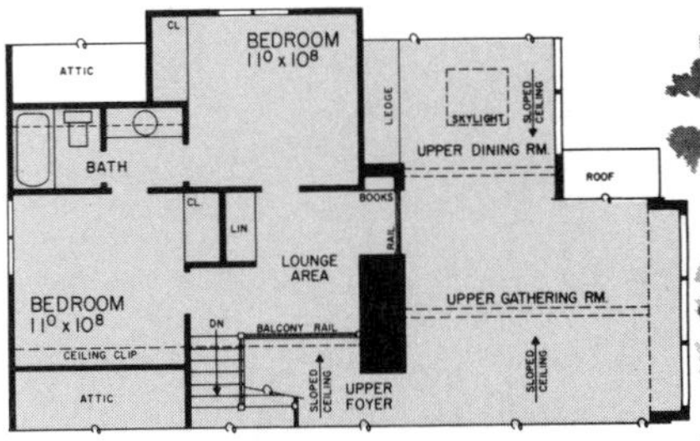

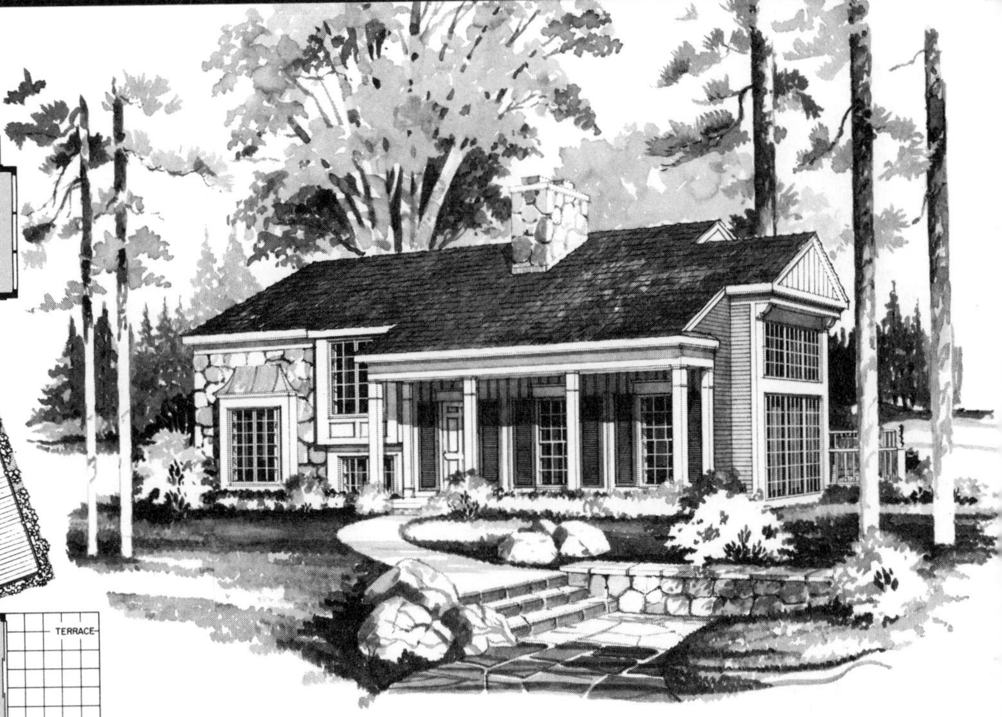

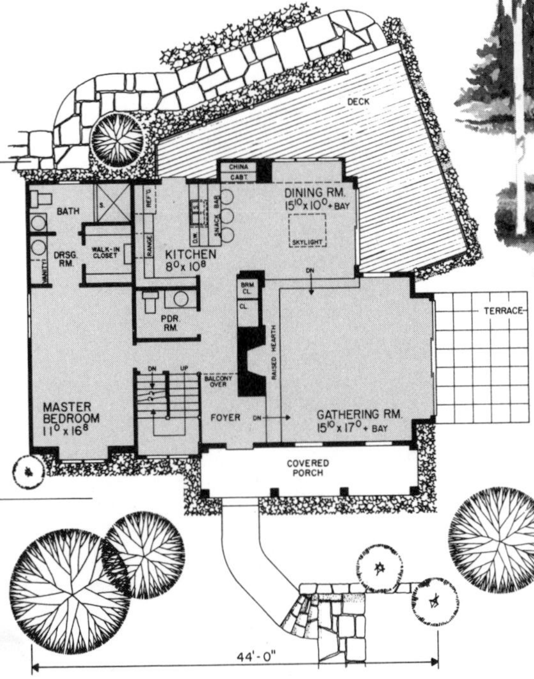

Design X2853

First Floor: 1,161 square feet
Second Floor: 475 square feet; Total: 1,636 square feet

● Natural stone, board-and-batten, multi-paned windows, overhanging eaves and the covered front porch highlight the exterior of this two-story home. Not only is the exterior well designed, but so is the interior. The sunken gathering room's ceiling is open to the second floor and is sloped for an even more dramatic appeal.

Design X1354

First Floor: 644 square feet
Second Floor: 572 square feet
Total: 1,216 square feet

L **D**

● Livability galore for the 50-foot building site. The homemaker will enjoy the U-shaped work center with the extra washroom and laundry equipment nearby.

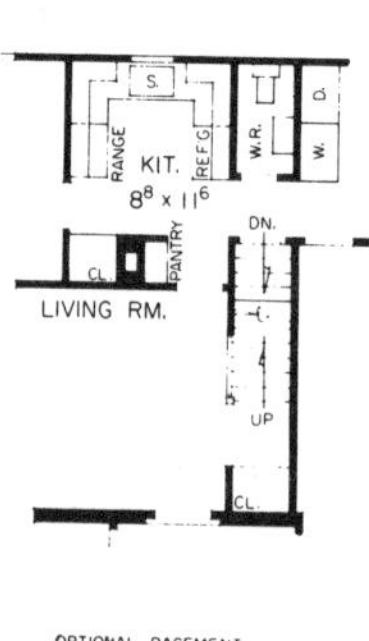

OPTIONAL BASEMENT

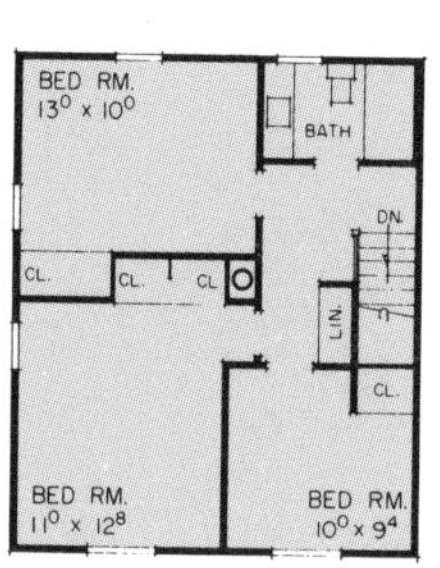

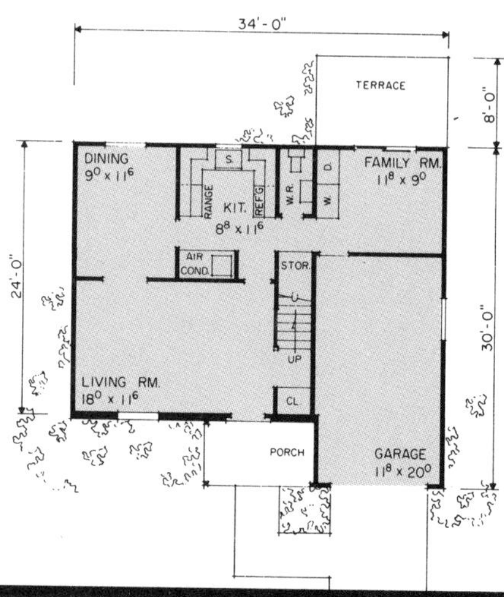

Design X1996

First Floor: 1,056 square feet
Second Floor: 1,040 square feet
Total: 2,096 square feet

L **D**

● This traditional design includes four bedrooms in just over 2,000 square feet, one a master bedroom with walk-in closet and private bath. Living areas include a family room, living room with fireplace, dining room with sliding glass doors and a breakfast room.

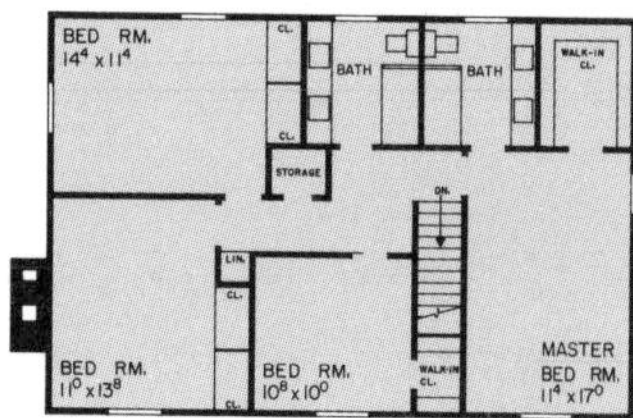

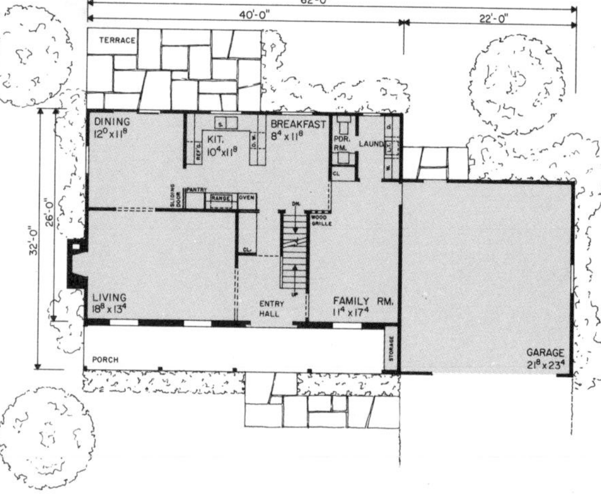

Design X1723

First Floor: 888 square feet
Second Floor: 970 square feet
Total: 1,858 square feet

● You'll not need a large parcel of property to accommodate this home. Neither will you need too large a building budget. Note fourth bedroom.

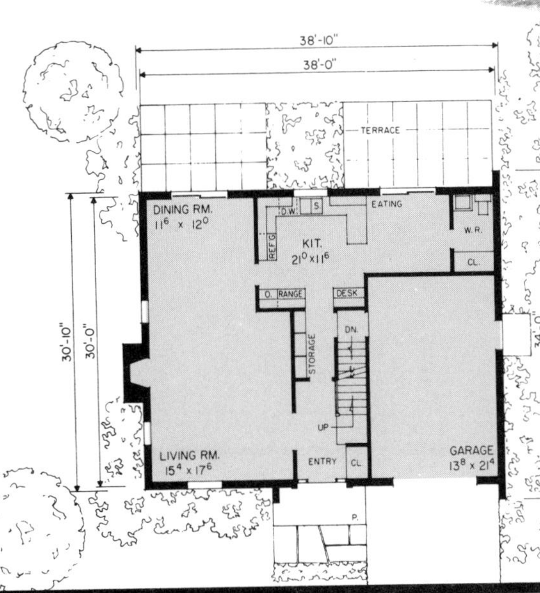

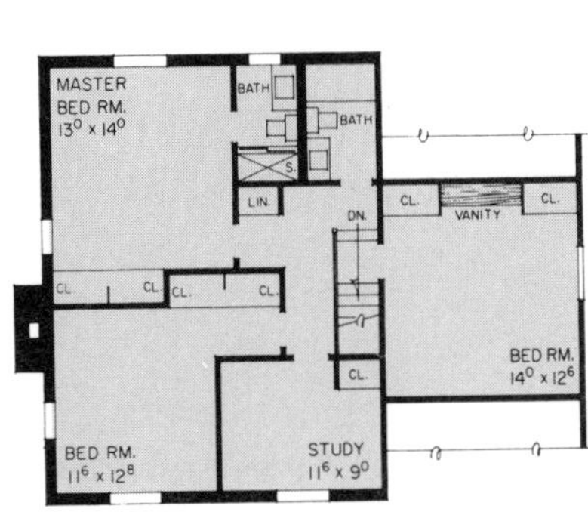

Design X1361

First Floor: 965 square feet
Second Floor: 740 square feet
Total: 1,705 square feet

L **D**

● An abundance of livability is in this charming, traditional adaptation. It will be most economical to build. Count the numerous features.

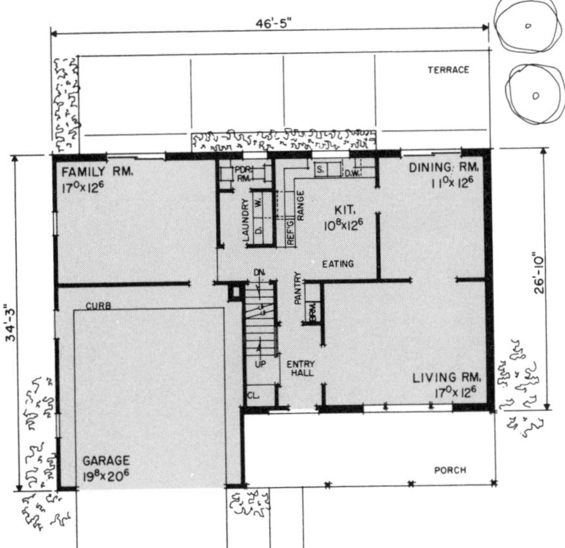

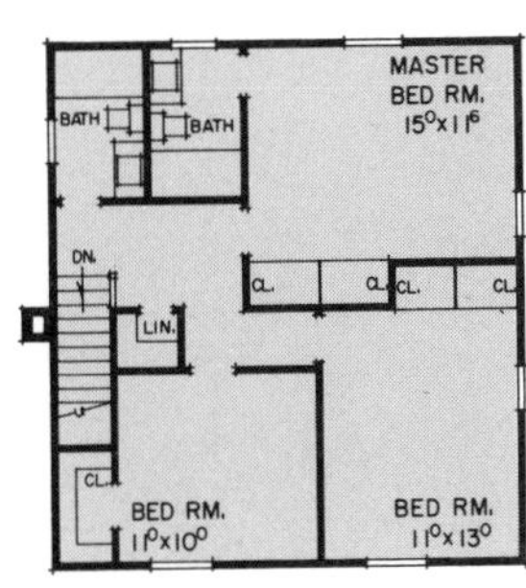

Design X1715

First Floor: 1,276 square feet
Second Floor: 1,064 square feet
Total: 2,340 square feet

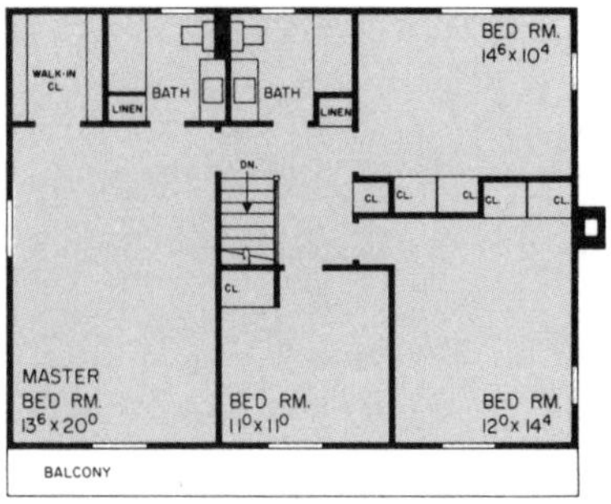

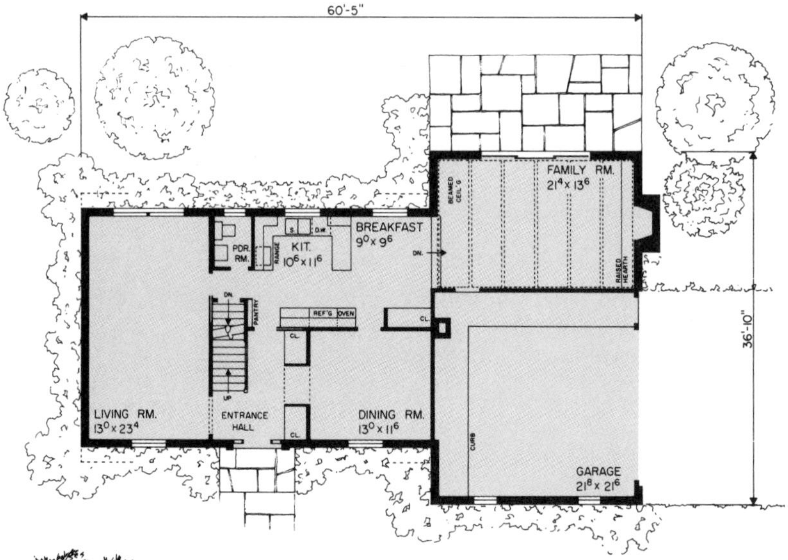

● The blueprints you order for this design show details for building each of these three appealing exteriors. Which do you like best? Whatever your choice, the interior will provide the growing family with all the facilities for fine living.

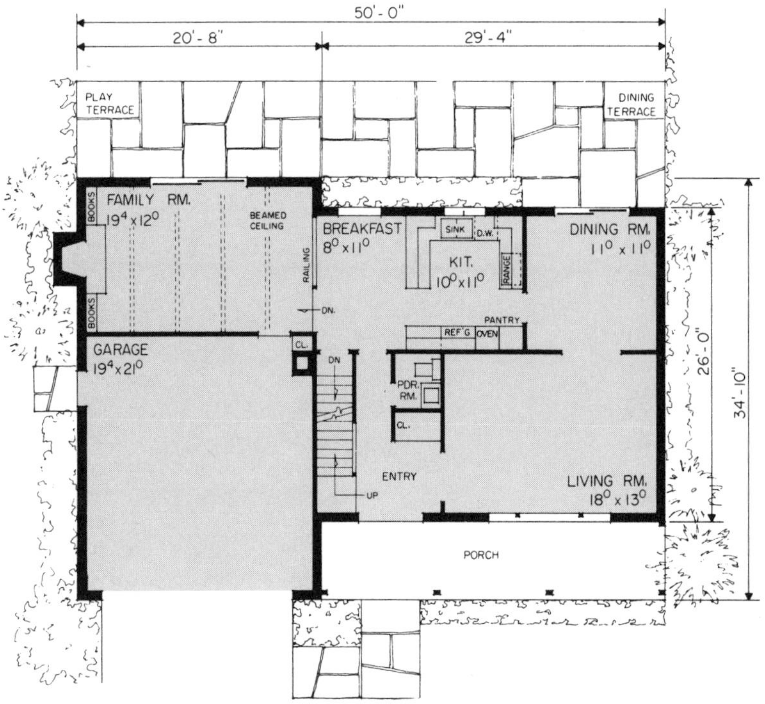

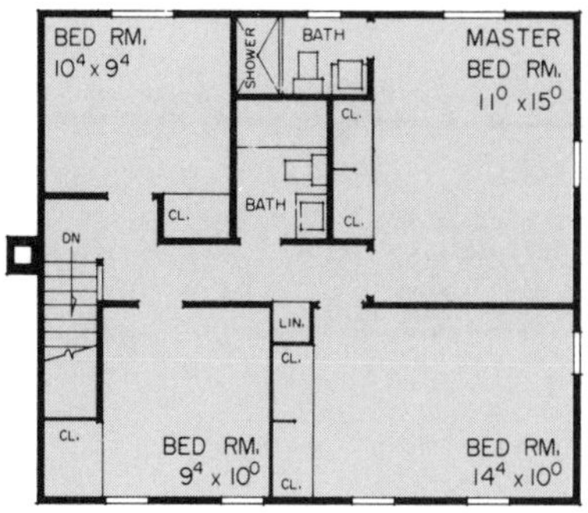

Design X1957 First Floor: 1,042 square feet; Second Floor: 780 square feet; Total: 1,822 square feet

L **D**

● When you order your blueprints for this design you will receive details for the construction of each of the three charming exteriors pictured above. Whichever the exterior you finally decide to build, the floor plan will be essentially the same except the location of the windows. This will be a fine home for the growing family. It will serve well for many years. There are four bedrooms and two full baths (one with a stall shower) upstairs.

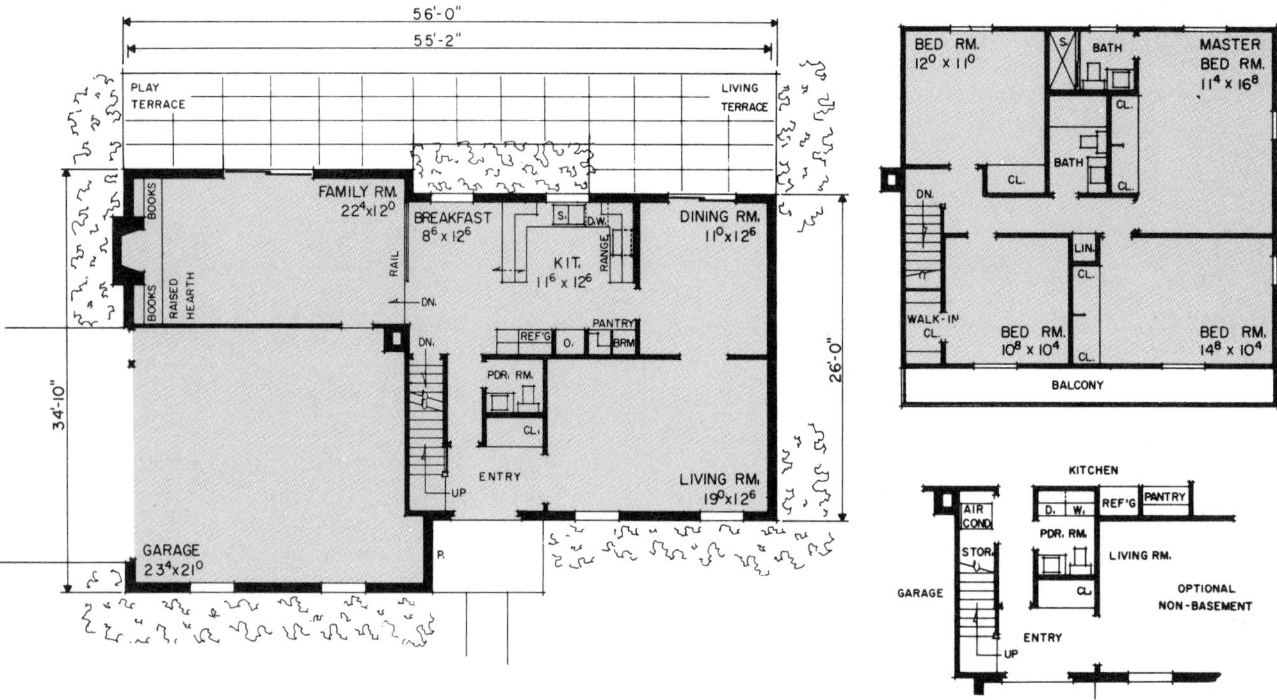

Design X1371

First Floor: 1,172 square feet; Second Floor: 896 square feet; Total: 2,068 square feet

L **D**

● If you like traditional charm and the tried-and-true living patterns of the conventional two-story idea, you'll not go wrong in selecting this design as your next home. In fact, when you order blueprints for X1371 you'll receive details for building all three optional elevations. So, you needn't decide which front exterior is your favorite right now. Any one of these will surely add a touch of class to your new neighborhood.

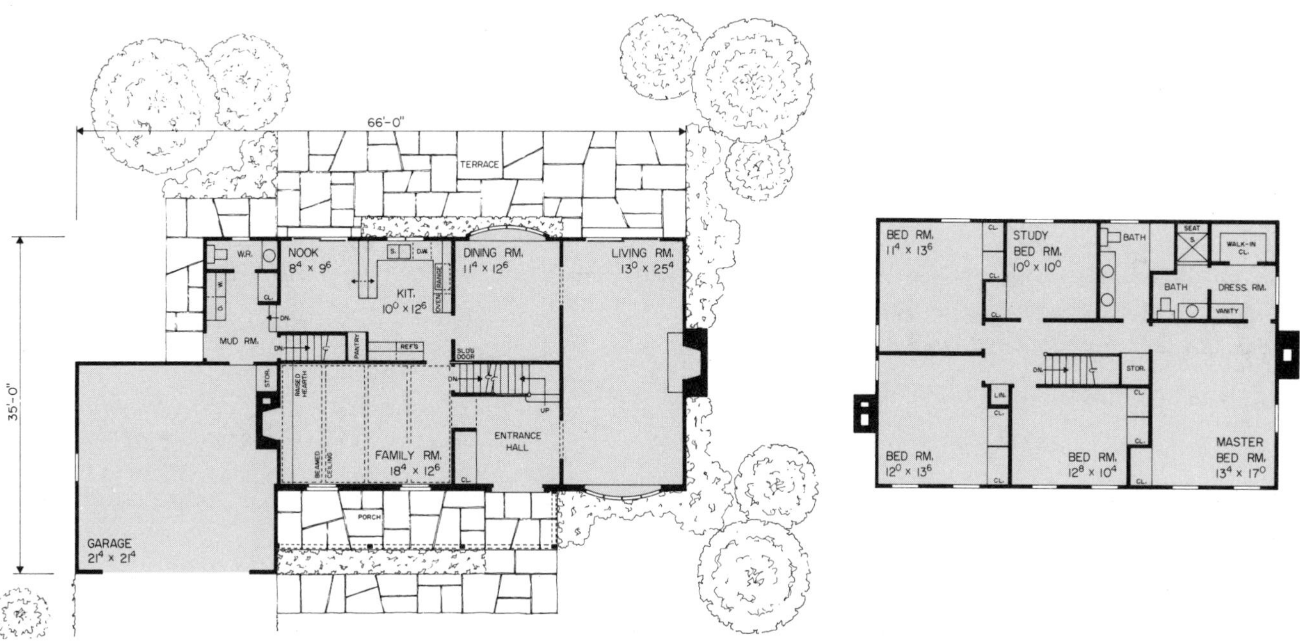

Design X2223 First Floor: 1,266 square feet; Second Floor: 1,232 square feet; Total: 2,498 square feet

L D

● The appealing double front doors of this home open wide to fine livability for the large, growing family. The spacious entrance hall is flanked by the formal, end living room and the all-purpose, beamed ceiling family room. Both rooms have a commanding fireplace. The U-shaped kitchen overlooks the rear yard and is but a step, or two, from the breakfast nook and the formal dining room. The mud room controls the flows of traffic during the inclement weather. Observe the laundry equipment and the washroom. Five bedrooms, two full baths, and plenty of closets are what make the second floor truly outstanding. There are a number of other convenient living features that make this design distinctive. How many of these can you list?

Design X2174

First Floor: 1,506 square feet
Second Floor: 1,156 square feet
Total: 2,662 square feet

L **D**

● Your building budget could hardly buy more charm, or greater livability. The appeal of the exterior is wrapped up in a myriad of design features. They include: the interesting roof lines; the effective use of brick and horizontal siding; the delightful window treatment; the covered front porch; the chimney and dove-cote detailing. The livability of the interior is represented by a long list of convenient living features. There is a formal area consisting of a living room with fireplace and dining room. The family room has a raised hearth fireplace, wood box and beamed ceiling. Also on the first floor is a kitchen, laundry and bedroom with adjacent bath. Three bedrooms, lounge and two baths upstairs plus plenty of closets and bulk storage over garage. Don't overlook the sliding glass doors, the breakfast area and the basement. An excellent plan.

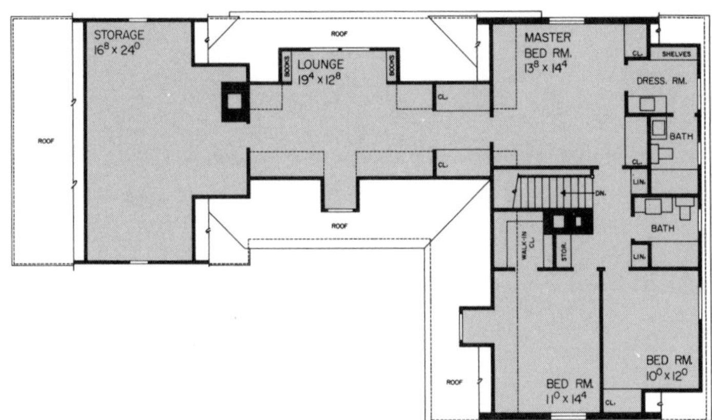

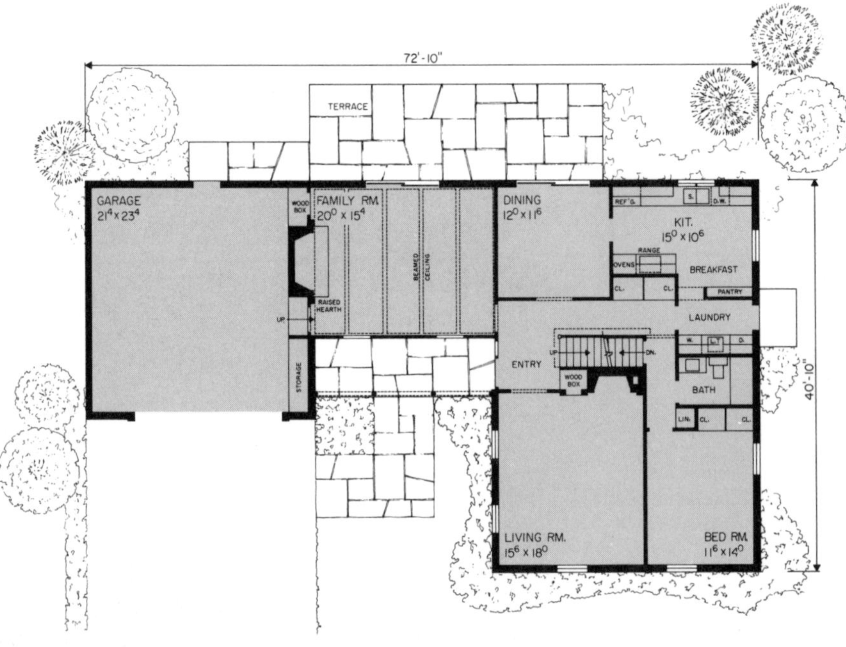

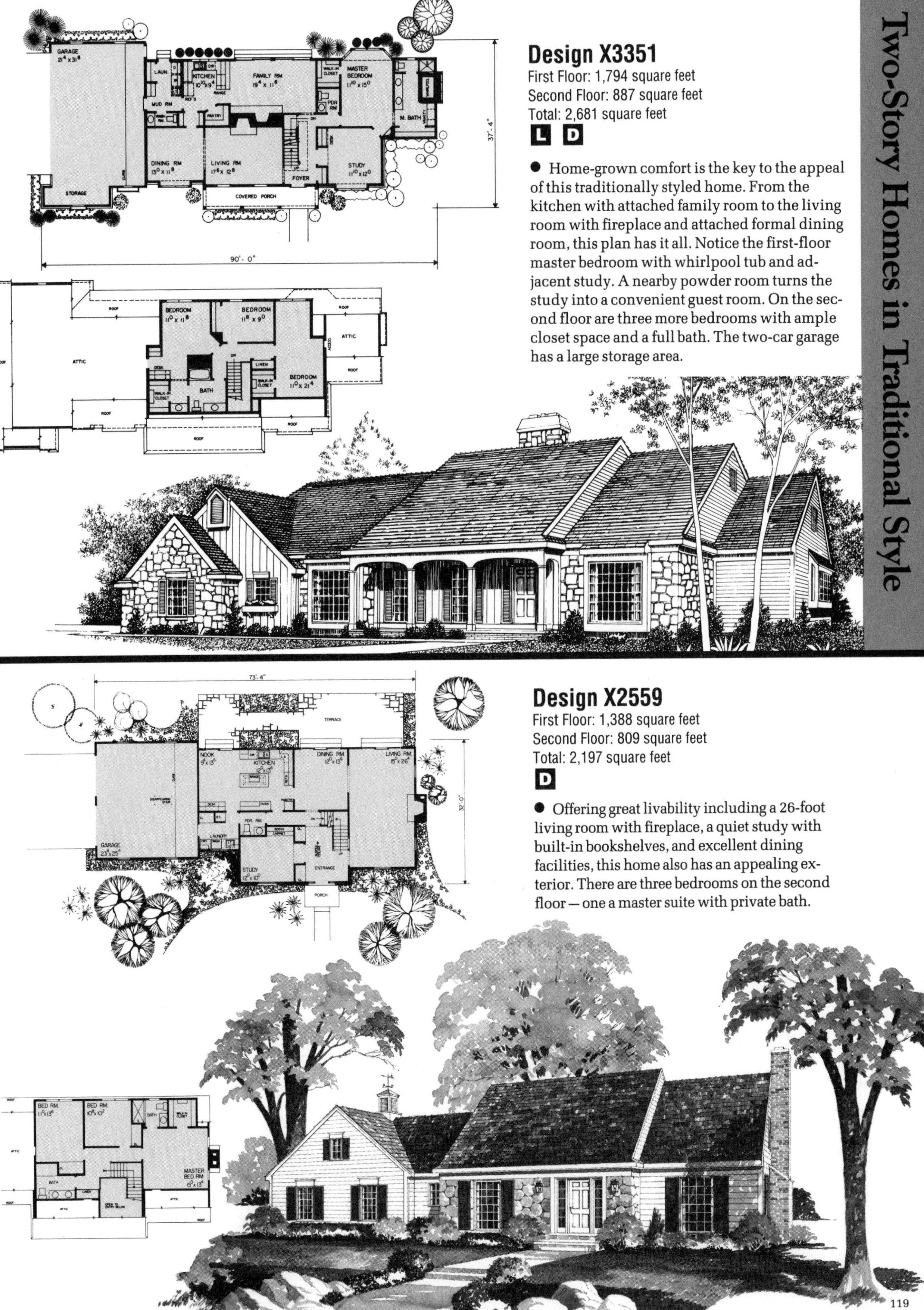

Design X3351

First Floor: 1,794 square feet
Second Floor: 887 square feet
Total: 2,681 square feet

L D

● Home-grown comfort is the key to the appeal of this traditionally styled home. From the kitchen with attached family room to the living room with fireplace and attached formal dining room, this plan has it all. Notice the first-floor master bedroom with whirlpool tub and adjacent study. A nearby powder room turns the study into a convenient guest room. On the second floor are three more bedrooms with ample closet space and a full bath. The two-car garage has a large storage area.

Design X2559

First Floor: 1,388 square feet
Second Floor: 809 square feet
Total: 2,197 square feet

D

● Offering great livability including a 26-foot living room with fireplace, a quiet study with built-in bookshelves, and excellent dining facilities, this home also has an appealing exterior. There are three bedrooms on the second floor — one a master suite with private bath.

Design X1115

First Floor: 1,440 square feet
Second Floor: 740 square feet
Total: 2,180 square feet

● A most distinctive exterior with an equally distinctive interior. A study of the plan reveals all of the elements to assure convenient living. The main living unit, the first floor, functions very efficiently. Two bedrooms and a full bath comprise the sleeping zone. The U-shaped kitchen is very efficient. The family/dining room will serve the family admirably. Adjacent to the kitchen is the laundry area, washroom and entrance from the garage. This living unit is definitely complete. Now add the second floor. Absolutely fantastic! The whole second floor is a master bedroom.

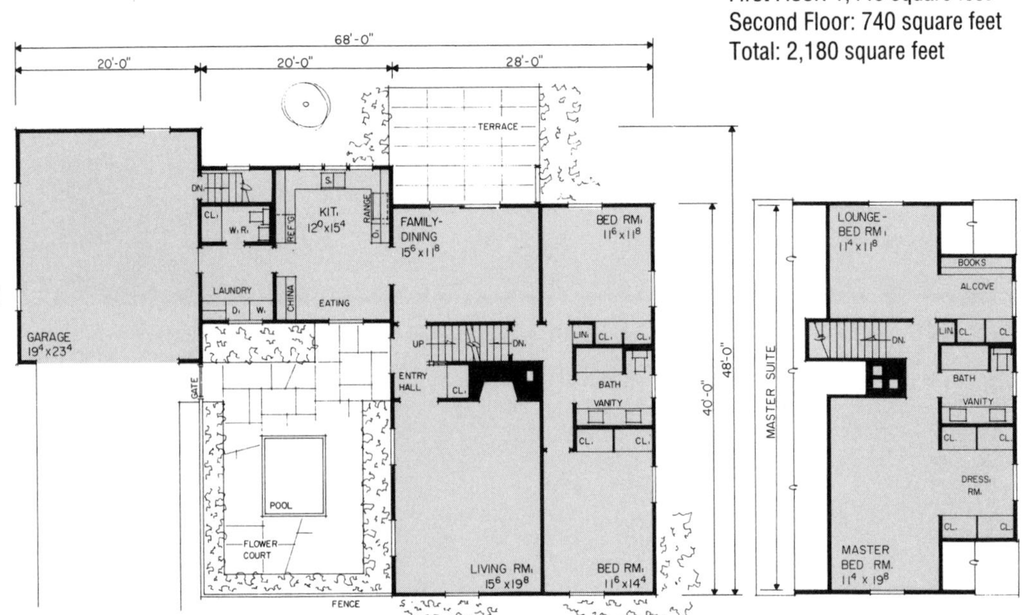

● If symmetry means anything, this pleasant house has it. The projecting wings of the sleeping zone and the garage are virtually identical. There is a world of livability to be fostered by this home.

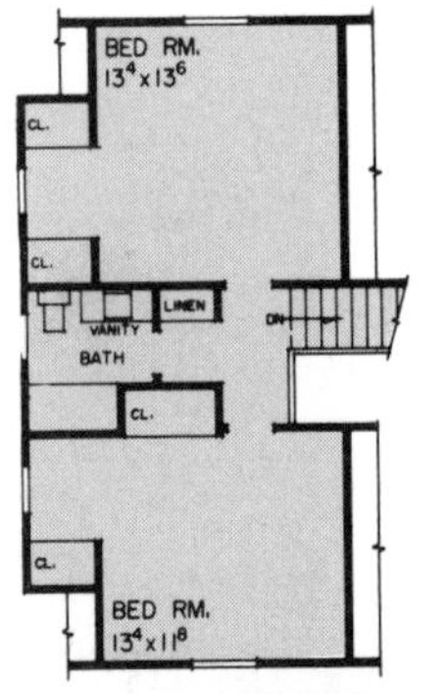

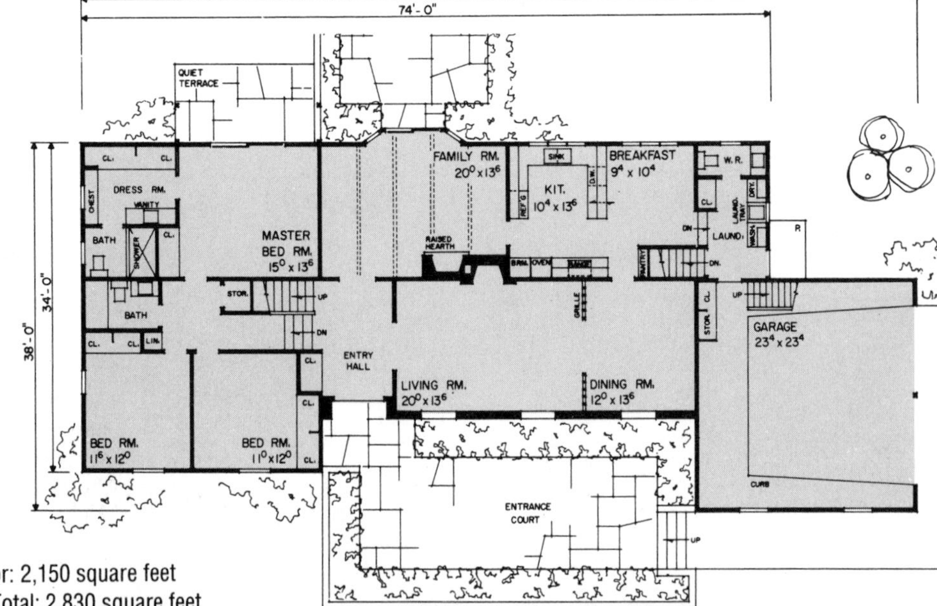

Design X1964 First Floor: 2,150 square feet
Second Floor: 680 square feet; Total: 2,830 square feet

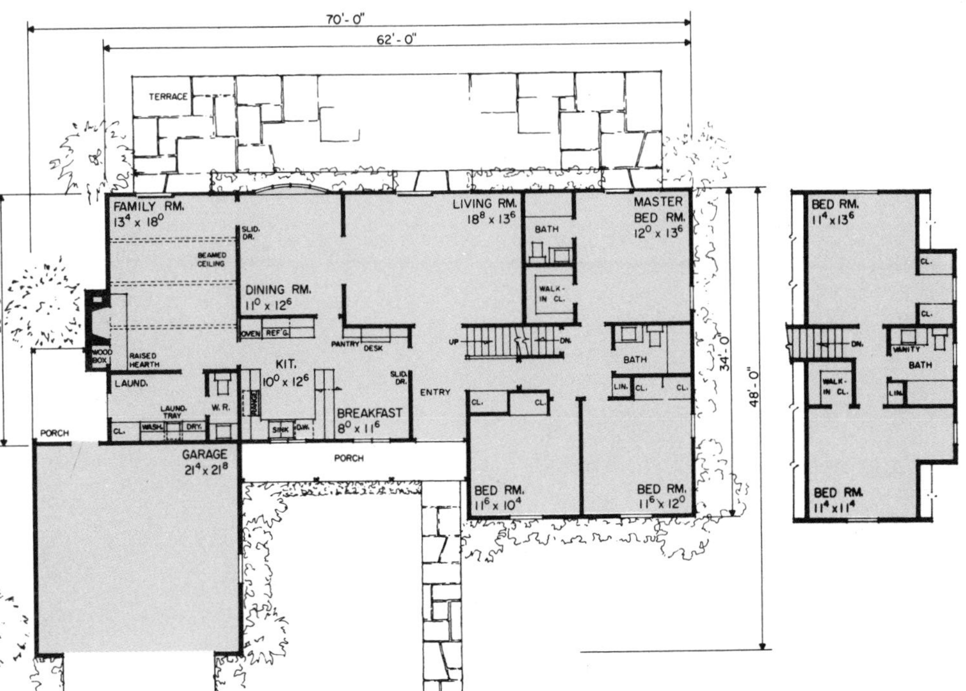

Design X1967

First Floor: 1,804 square feet
Second Floor: 496 square feet
Total: 2,300 square feet

● You'll always want that first impression your guests get of your new home to be a lasting one. There will be much that will linger in the memories of most of your visitors after their visit to this home. Of course, the impressive exterior will long be remembered. And little wonder with its distinctive projecting garage and bedroom wing, its recessed front porch, its horizontal siding and its interesting roof lines. Inside, there is much to behold. The presence of five bedrooms and three full baths will not be forgotten soon. Formal and informal areas will serve every family occasion.

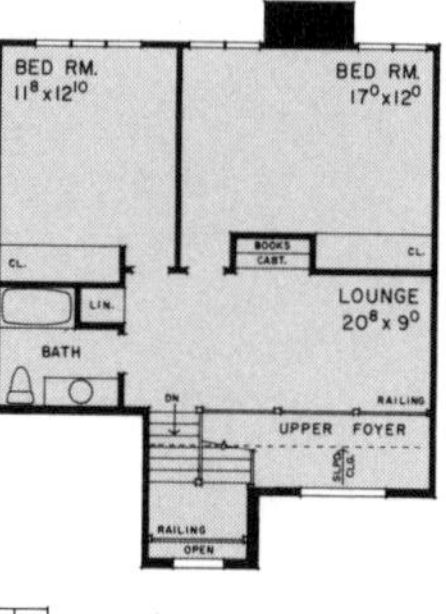

Design X3550

First Floor: 2,328 square feet
Second Floor: 712 square feet
Total: 3,040 square feet

L **D**

● A transitional 1½-story home combines the best of contemporary and traditional elements. This one uses vertical wood siding, stone and multi-paned windows to beautiful advantage. The floor plan makes great use of space with first-floor living and dining areas and a first-floor master suite. Two secondary bedrooms, a full bath and an open lounge area are found on the second floor. The garage is accessed from the island kitchen through the laundry.

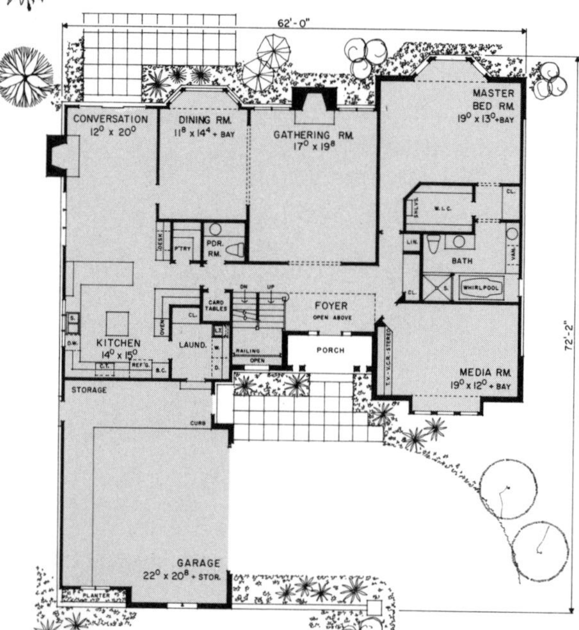

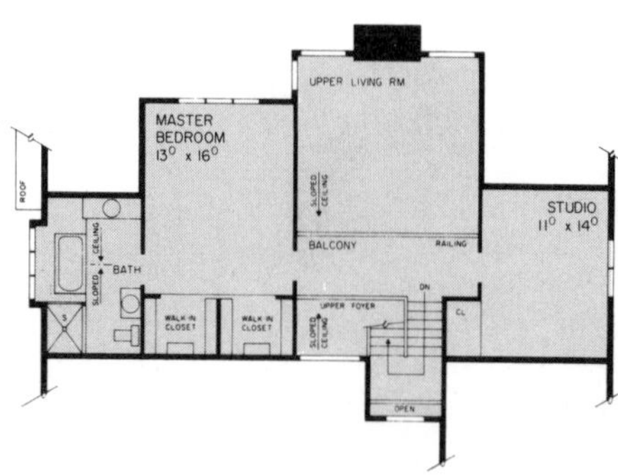

Design X2927

First Floor: 1,425 square feet
Second Floor: 704 square feet
Total: 2,129 square feet

D

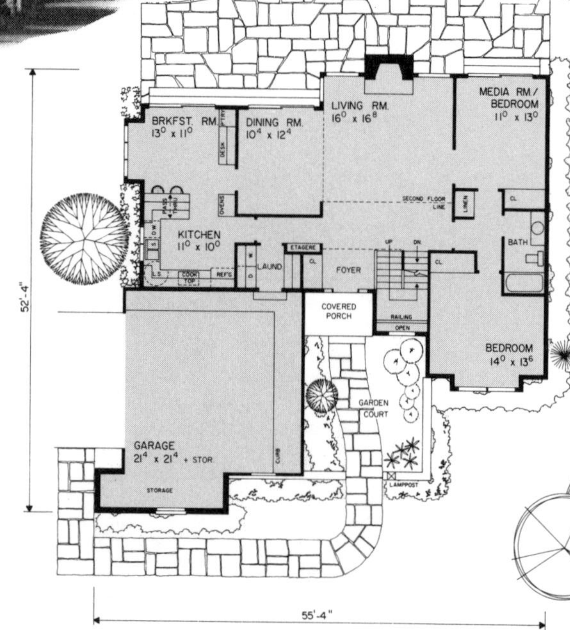

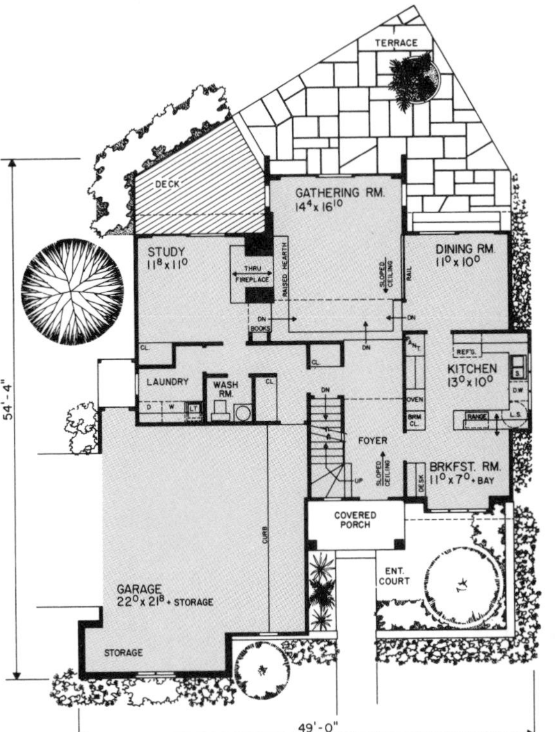

Design X2826 First Floor: 1,112 square feet
Second Floor: 881 square feet; Total: 1,993 square feet

D

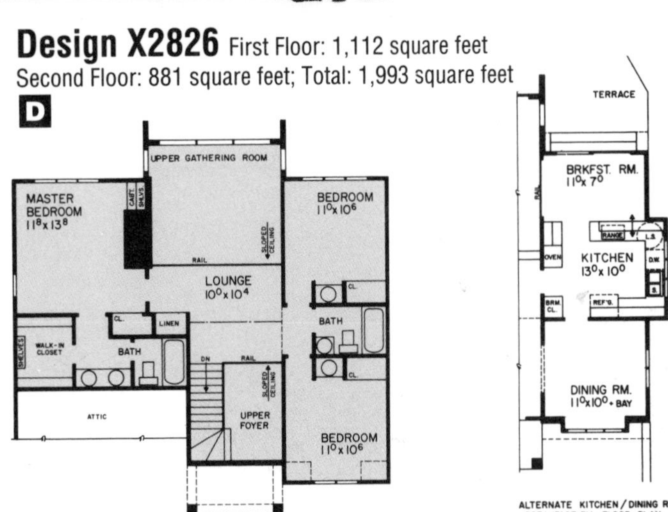

● This is an outstanding example of the type of informal, traditional-style architecture that has captured the modern imagination. The interior plan houses all of the features that people want most - a spacious gathering room, formal and informal dining areas, efficient, U-shaped kitchen, master bedroom, two children's bedrooms, second floor lounge, entrance court and rear terrace and deck. Study all areas of this plan carefully.

Design X3330

First Floor: 1,394 square feet
Second Floor: 320 square feet
Total: 1,714 square feet

● Outdoor living and open floor planning are highlights of this moderately sized plan. Amenities include a private hot tub on a wooden deck that is accessible via sliding glass doors in both bedrooms, and a two-story gathering room. An optional second-floor plan allows for a full 503 square feet of space with a balcony.

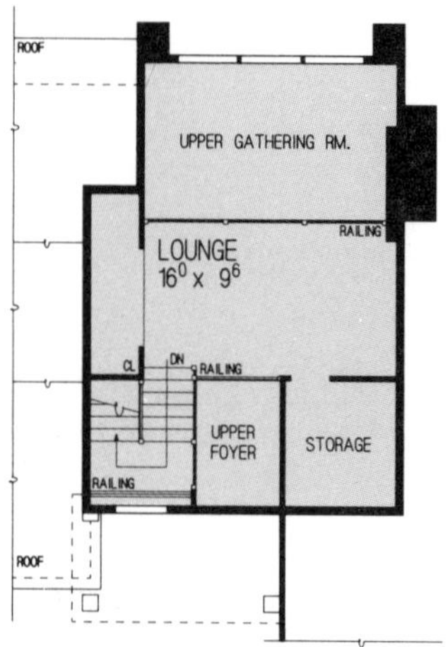

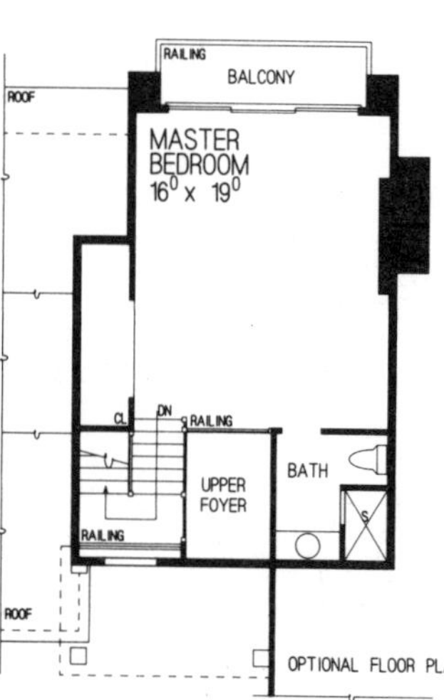

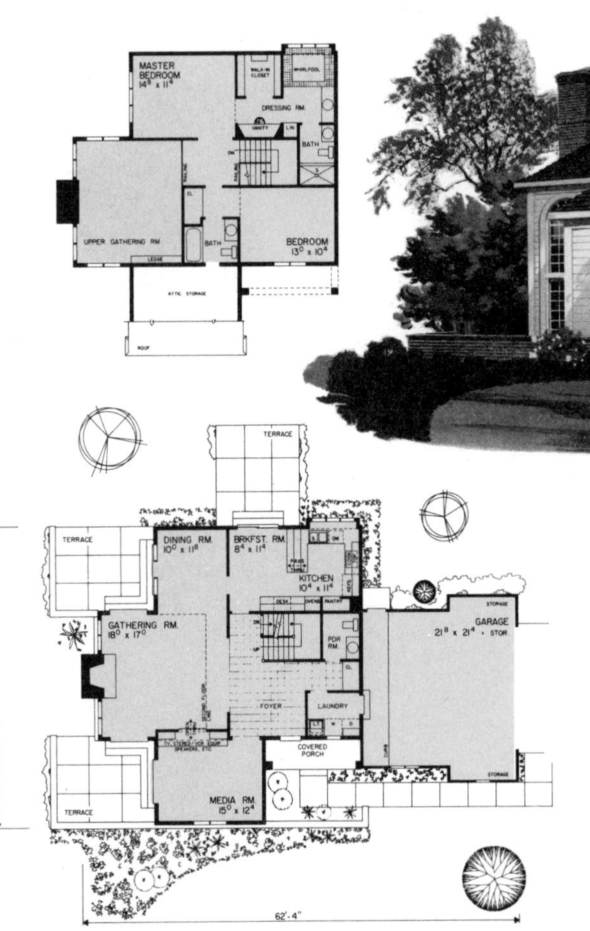

Design X2909

First Floor: 1,221 square feet
Second Floor: 767 square feet
Total: 1,988 square feet

D

● This charming traditional home with striking good looks offers the modern family many contemporary amenities. The first floor features a large gathering room with fireplace, media room for stereos and VCRs, a convenient kitchen with breakfast room, plus a dining room. The second floor includes an upper gathering room, spacious master bedroom suite and a second bedroom. Notice columns that support a covered porch and window treatments.

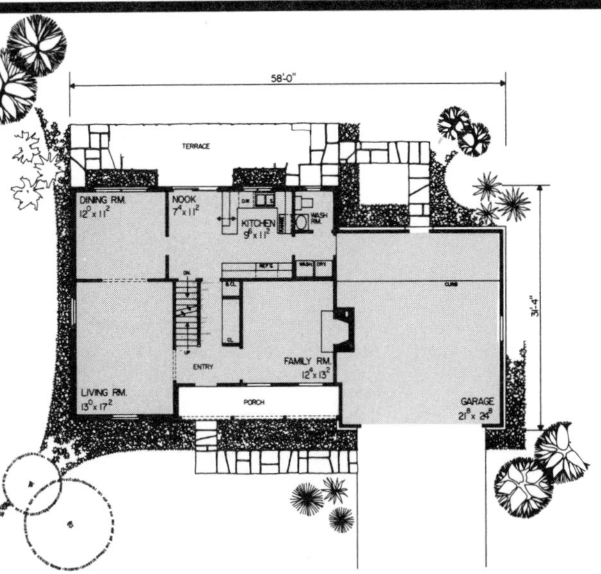

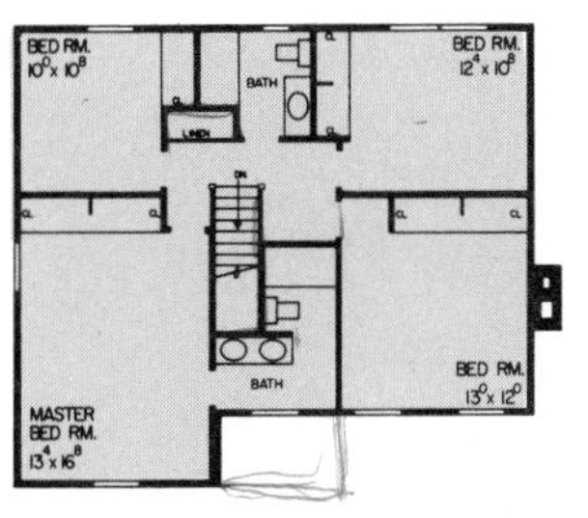

Design X2585

First Floor: 990 square feet
Second Floor: 1,011 square feet
Total: 2,001 square feet

● An elegant Colonial, this is a typical front-porch version. The exterior is highlighted with seven large-paned glass windows and pillars. After entering, go directly to the formal area of the living room and dining room or to the informal family room with fireplace. The U-shaped kitchen will serve the breakfast area and is just a step away from the washroom. Upstairs are four bedrooms and two full baths.

Design X2713

First Floor: 1,830 square feet
Second Floor: 1,056 square feet
Total: 2,886 square feet

● A country charmer—this gambrel-roofed home has detailing that delights from the first glance. A covered porch at the service entrance connects the main part of the home to the two-car garage. Behind the garage is the beamed-ceilinged family room with raised-hearth fireplace and built-in wood box. Formal entertaining is accomplished in the living and dining rooms flanking the entry. Upstairs are three bedrooms and two full baths. Note the double walk-in closets and double lavs in the master suite.

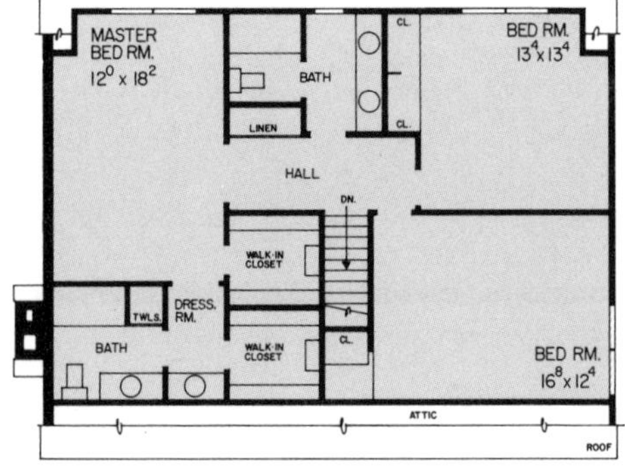

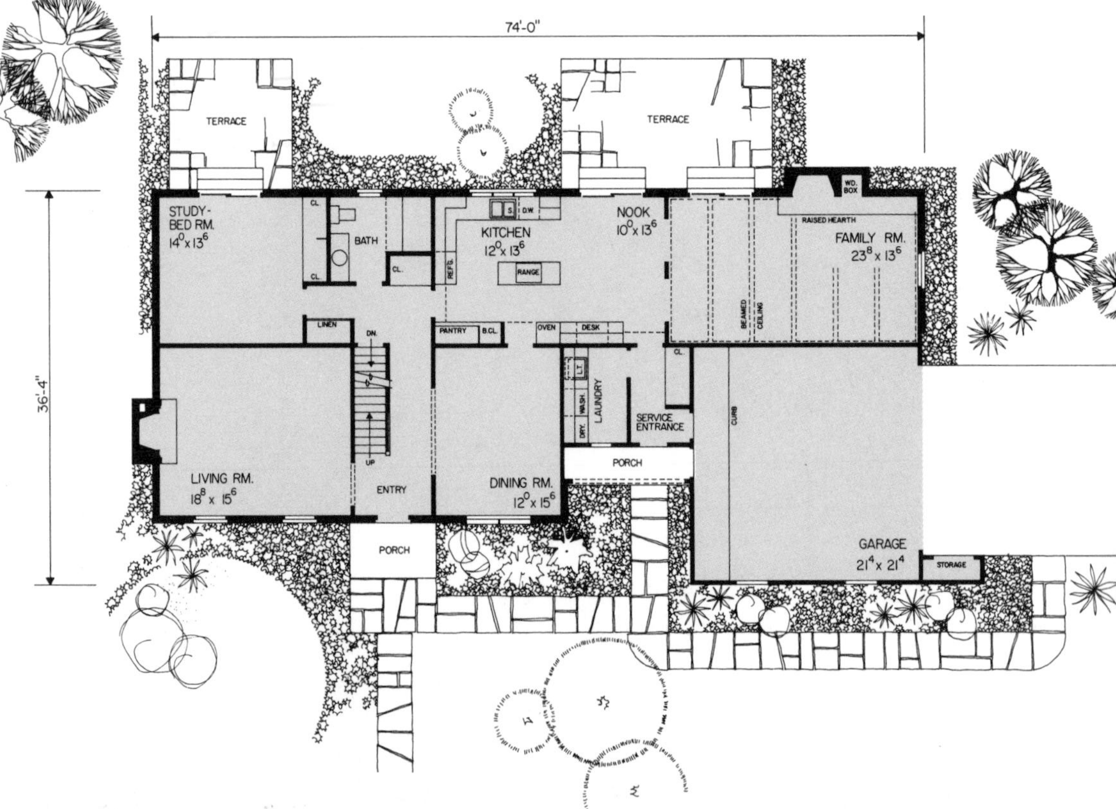

Design X2689 First Floor: 1,385 square feet
Second Floor: 982 square feet; Total: 2,367 square feet

● This cozy three-bedroom Gambrel offers charming elegance with country comfort. A large country kitchen with bay overlooks a rear terrace. There's also a separate dining room downstairs, plus a living room and screened porch. All three bedrooms are upstairs, away from the distractions of rest of the house.

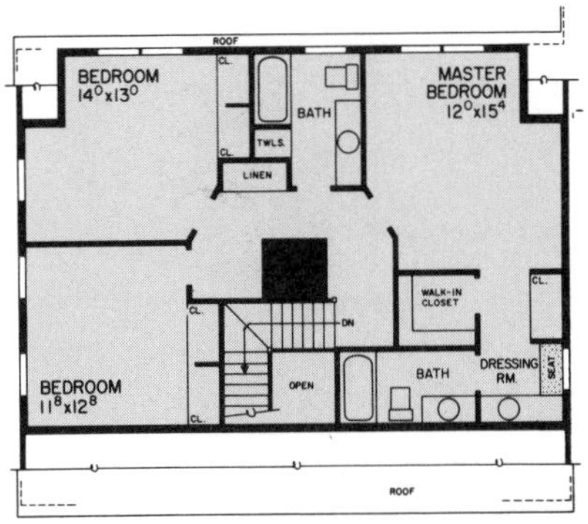

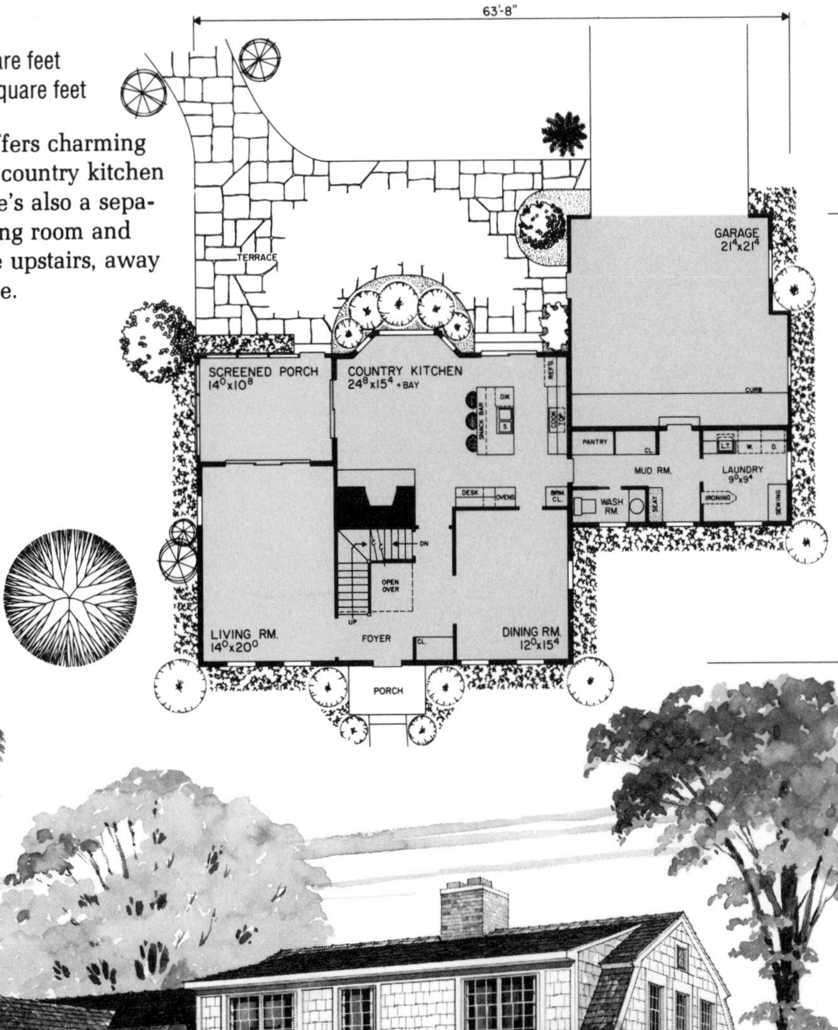

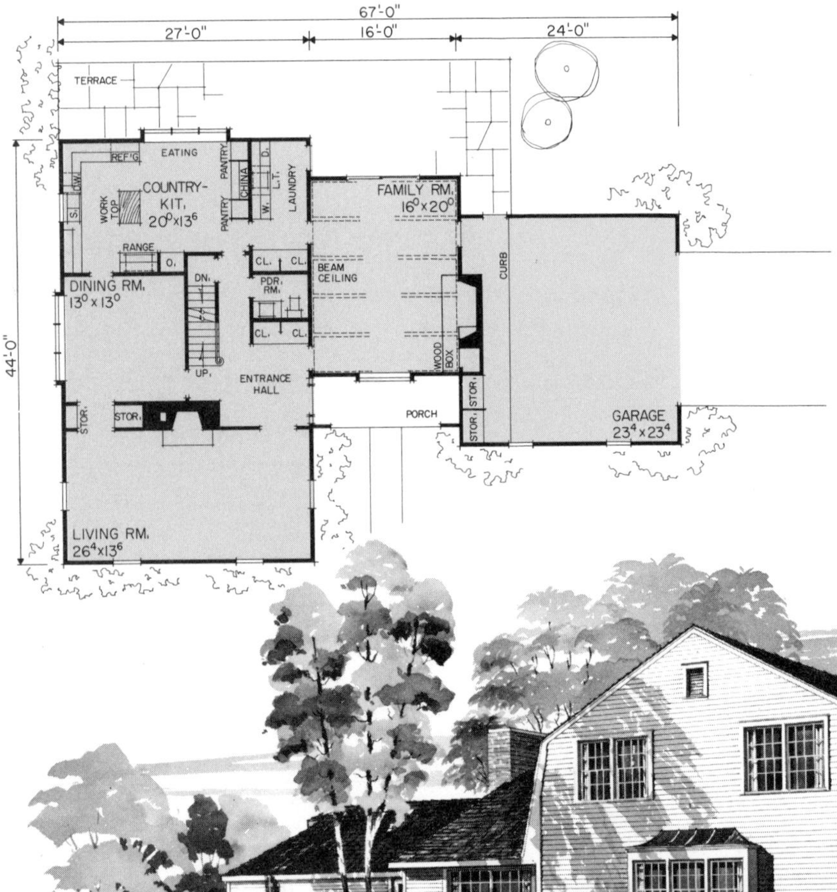

Design X1887

First Floor: 1,518 square feet
Second Floor: 1,144 square feet
Total: 2,662 square feet

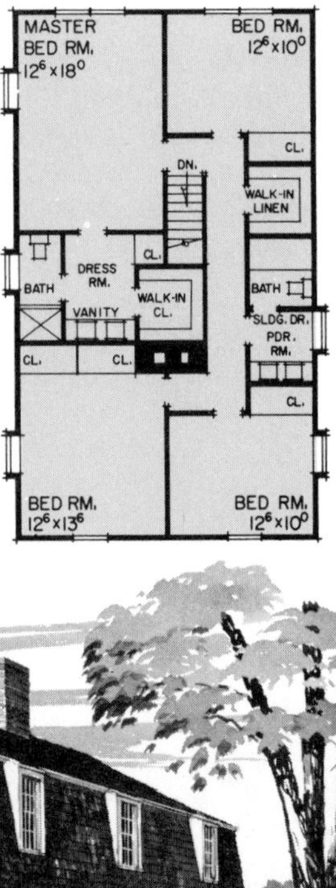

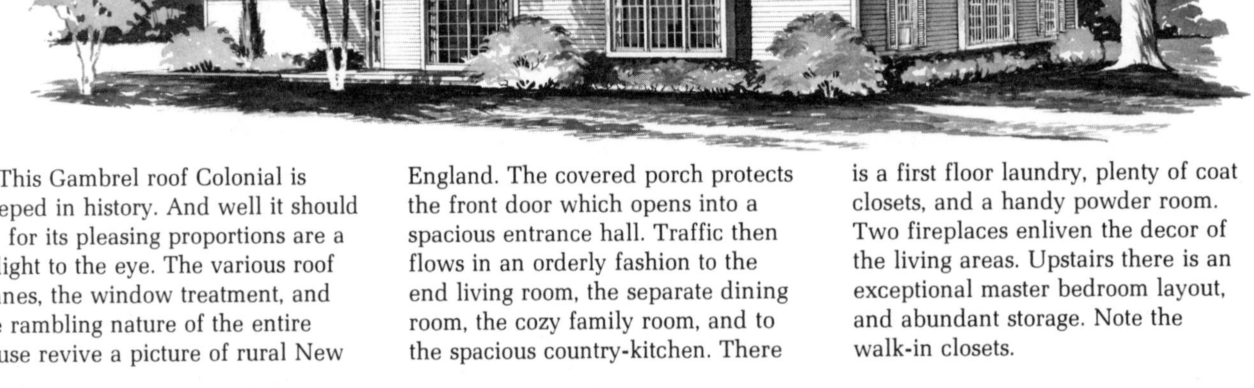

● This Gambrel roof Colonial is steeped in history. And well it should be, for its pleasing proportions are a delight to the eye. The various roof planes, the window treatment, and the rambling nature of the entire house revive a picture of rural New England. The covered porch protects the front door which opens into a spacious entrance hall. Traffic then flows in an orderly fashion to the end living room, the separate dining room, the cozy family room, and to the spacious country-kitchen. There is a first floor laundry, plenty of coat closets, and a handy powder room. Two fireplaces enliven the decor of the living areas. Upstairs there is an exceptional master bedroom layout, and abundant storage. Note the walk-in closets.

● Clapboard siding and shuttered, multi-paned windows create the delightful detailing of this two-story gambrel. Beamed ceilings and a thru-fireplace highlight the living and family rooms. The work centers, kitchen and laundry, are clustered together for greater convenience. The formal dining room is nearby to make the serving of meals easy. The second floor houses all of the sleeping facilities.

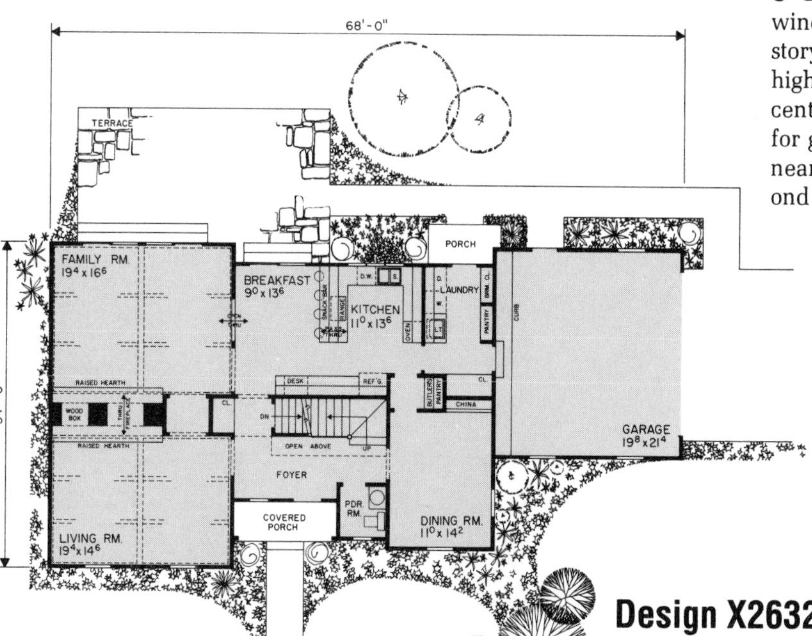

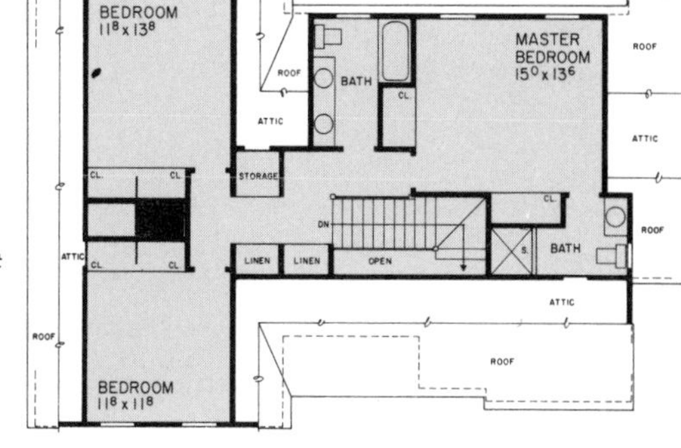

Design X2632

First Floor: 1,460 square feet
Second Floor: 912 square feet
Total: 2,372 square feet

Design X2189

First Floor: 1,134 square feet
Second Floor: 1,063 square feet
Total: 2,197 square feet

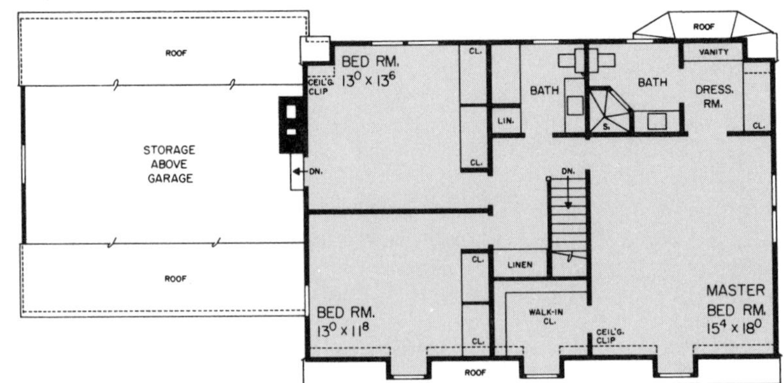

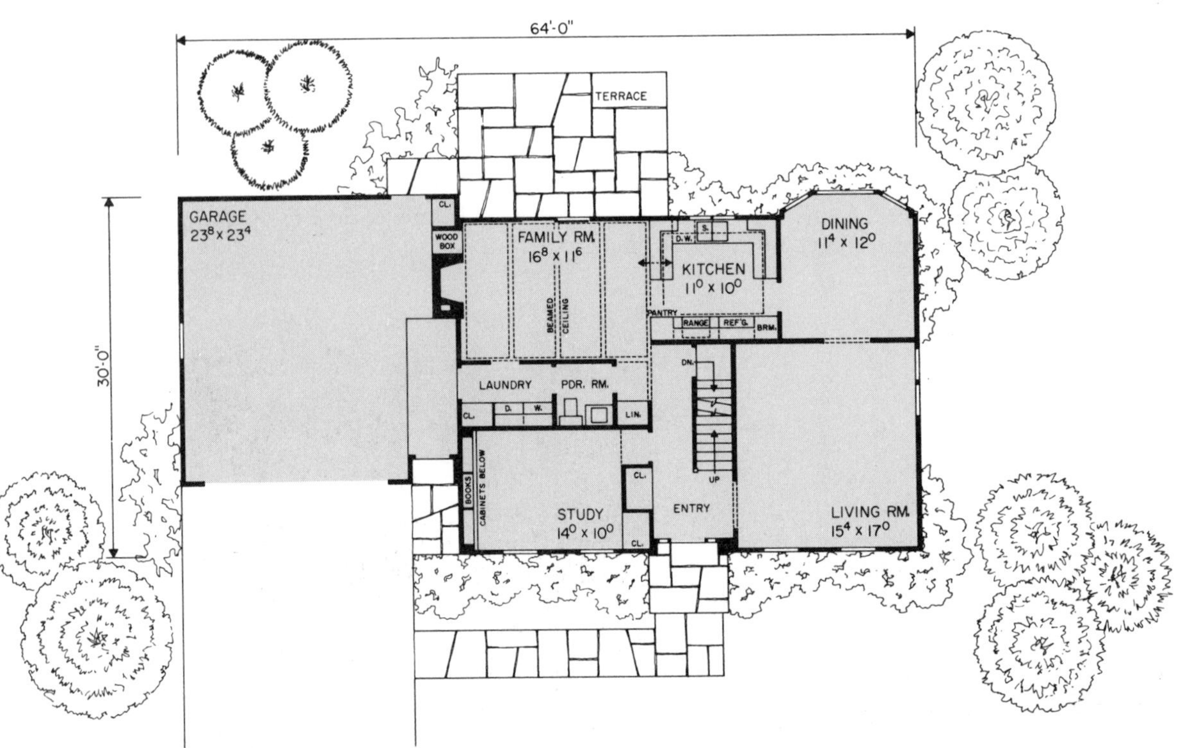

● Imagine this Colonial adaptation on your new building site! The symmetry and pleasing proportion make it a wonderful addition to the local scene. The recessed entrances add an extra measure of appeal. Inside is an abundance of features. Formal living areas include a spacious living room.

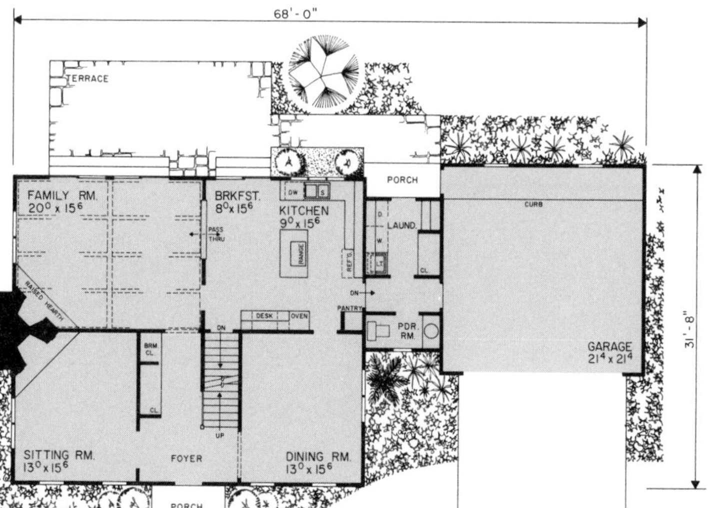

Design X2644

First Floor: 1,349 square feet
Second Floor: 836 square feet
Total: 2,185 square feet

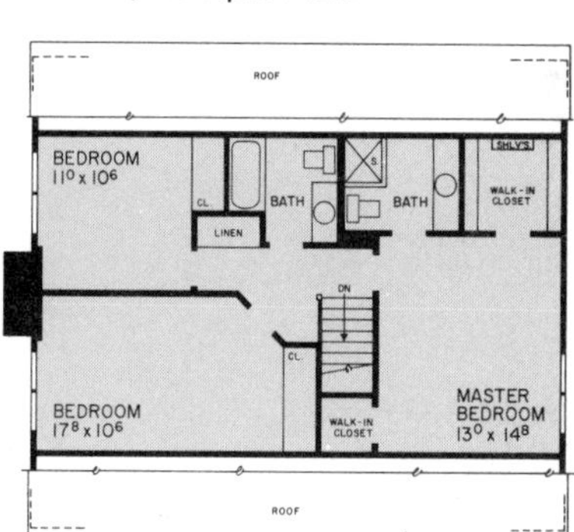

● What a delightful, compact two-story this is! This design has many fine features tucked within its framework. The bowed roofline of this house stems from late 17th-Century architecture.

Design X1986 First Floor: 896 square feet
Second Floor: 1,148 square feet; Total: 2,044 square feet

L

● This design with its distinctive Gambrel roof will spell charm wherever it may be situated - far out in the country, or on a busy thoroughfare. Compact and economical to build, it will be easy on the budget. Note the location of the family room. It is over the garage on the second floor.

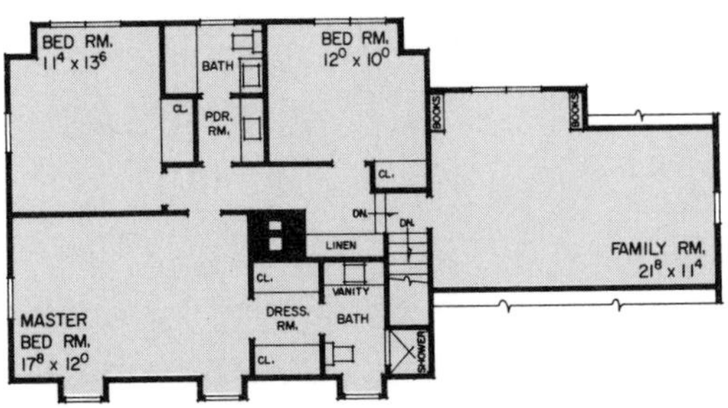

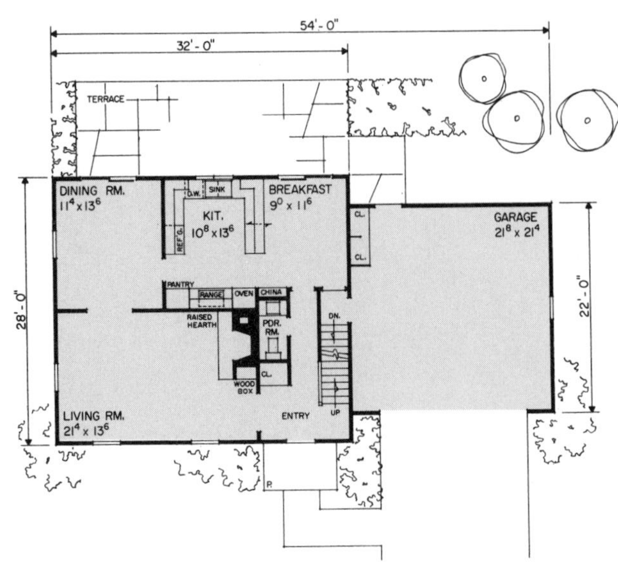

Design X1777 First Floor: 1,142 square feet
Second Floor: 1,010 square feet; Total: 2,152 square feet

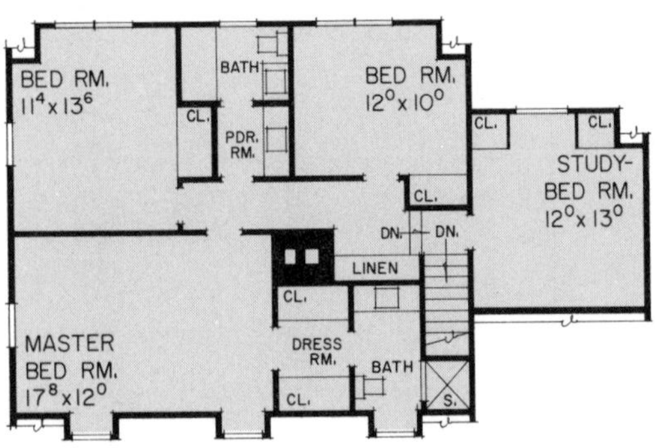

● If it's charm you are after, you'll find this design with a Gambrel roof difficult to top. Its distinctive air is enhanced by the attached family room unit and the two-car garage. The wide vertical siding delightfully contrasts with the narrow horizontal siding.

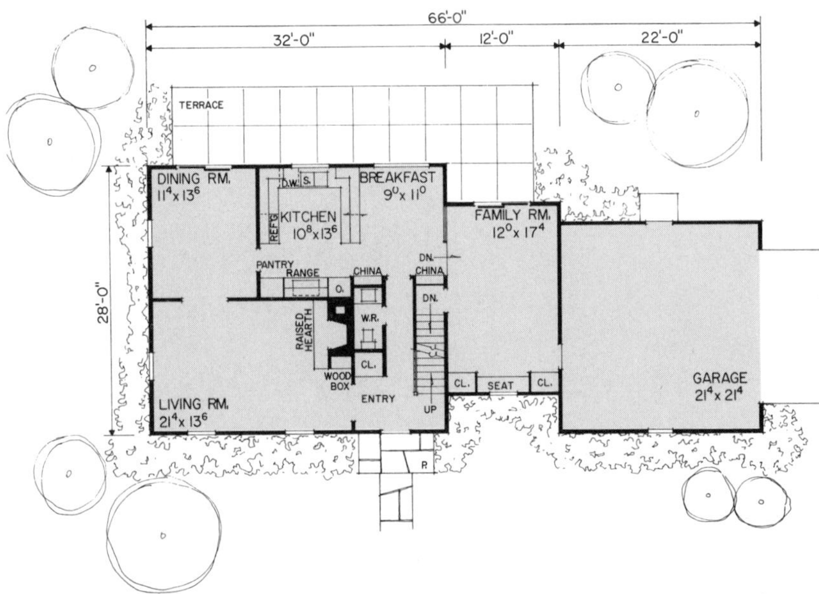

Design X2531 First Floor: 1,353 square feet
Second Floor: 1,208 square feet; Total: 2,561 square feet

● This design has its roots in the early history of New England. While its exterior is decidedly and purposely dated, the interior reflects an impressive 20th-Century floor plan. All of the elements are present to guarantee outstanding living patterns for today's large, active family.

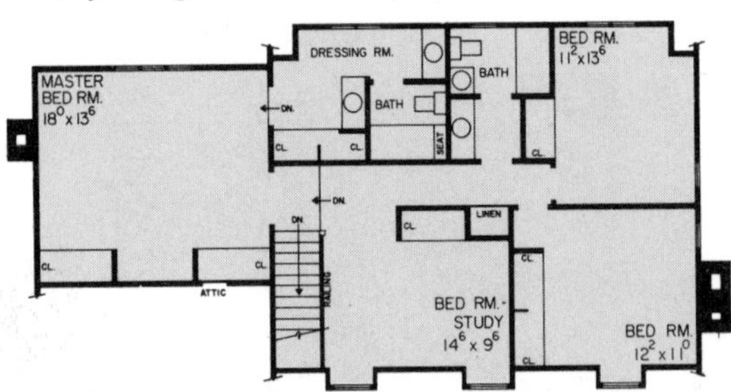

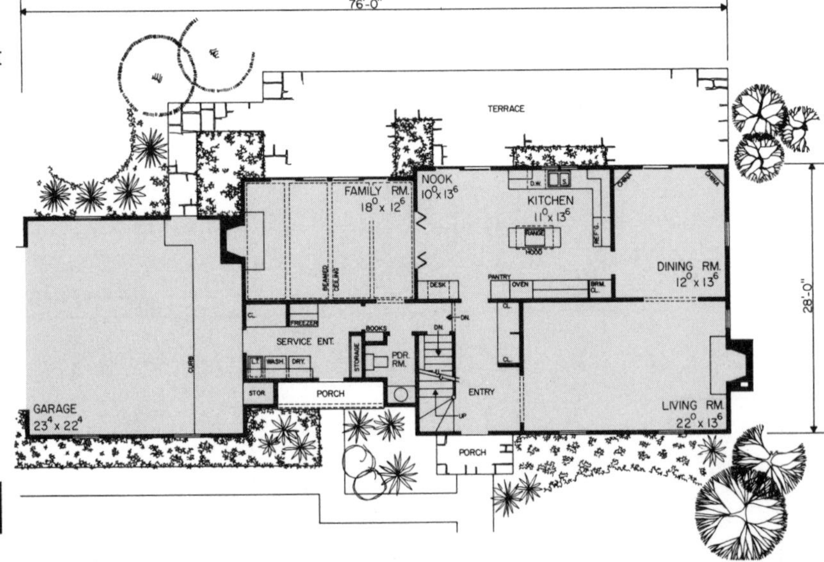

Design X1933

First Floor: 1,184 square feet
Second Floor: 884 square feet
Total: 2,068 square feet

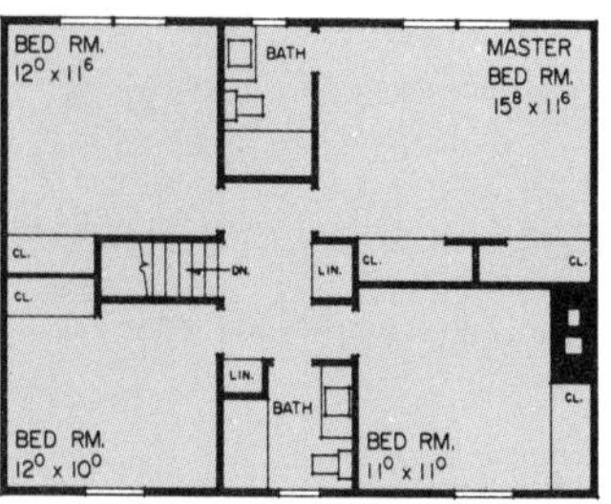

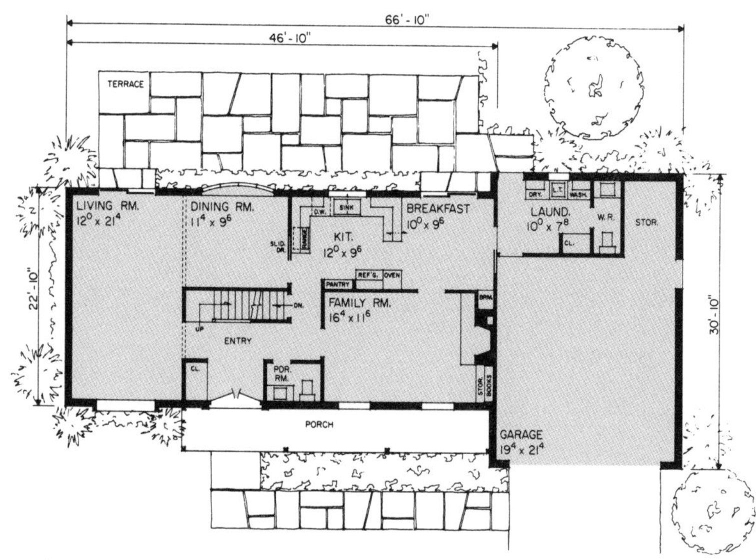

Design X2558

First Floor: 1,030 square feet
Second Floor: 840 square feet
Total: 1,870 square feet

● This relatively low-budget house is long on exterior appeal and interior livability. It has all the features to assure years of convenient living. Make a list of your favorite features.

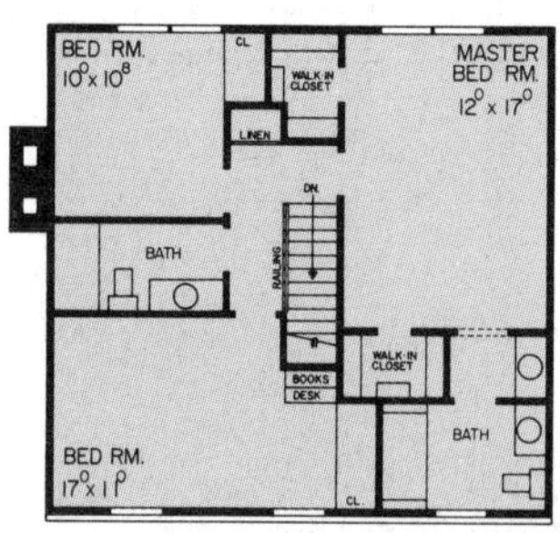

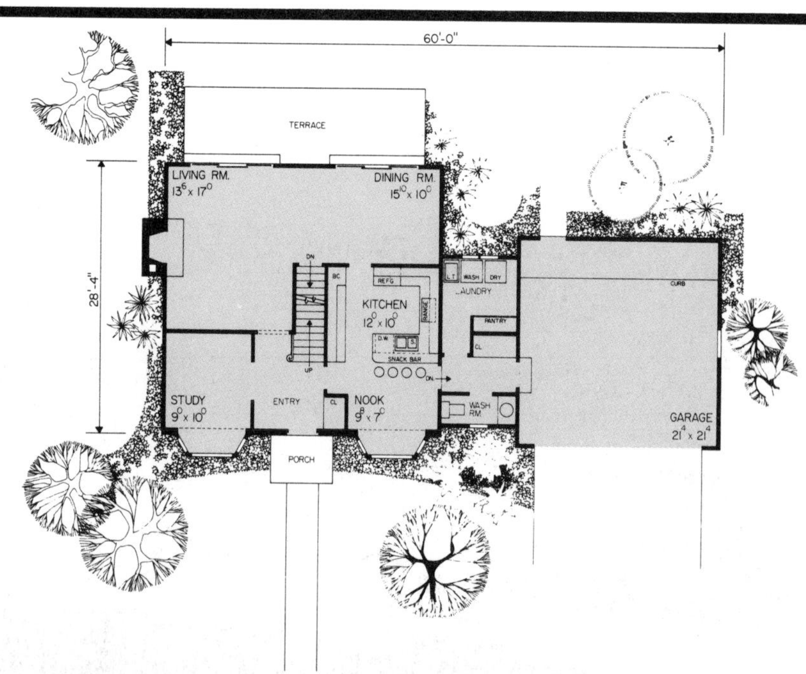

● Small house with big house features and livability. Some of the features include two full baths and extra storage upstairs; laundry, washroom and two fireplaces, each with a wood box on the first floor. Two sets of sliding glass doors lead to the terrace.

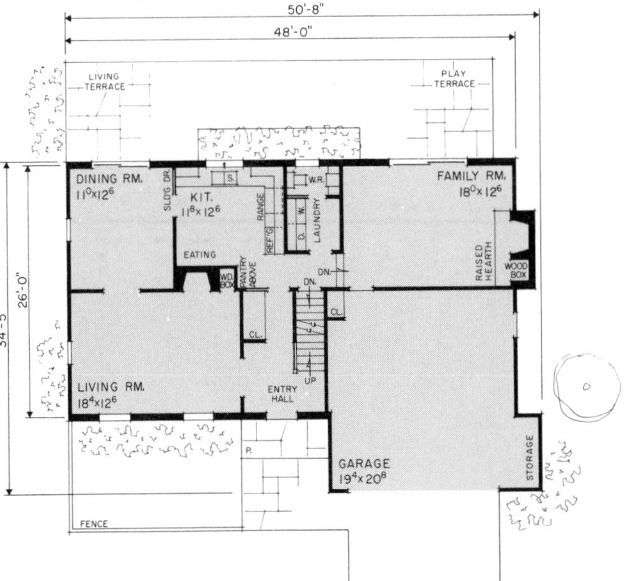

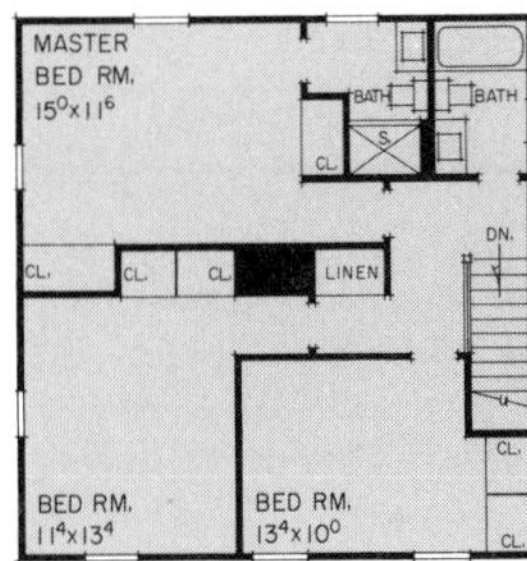

Design X1856

First Floor: 1,023 square feet
Second Floor: 784 square feet
Total: 1,807 square feet

Design X2139

First Floor: 1,581 square feet
Second Floor: 991 square feet
Total: 2,572 square feet

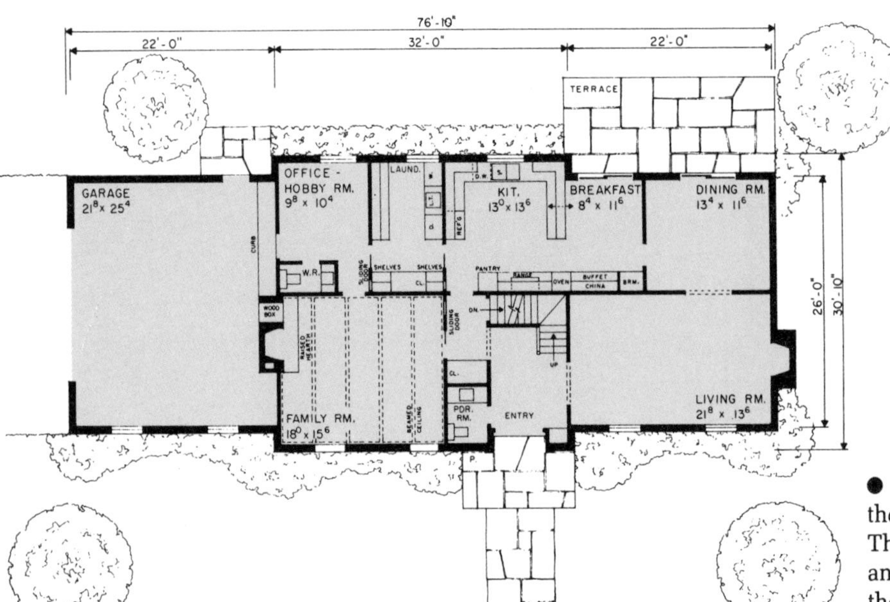

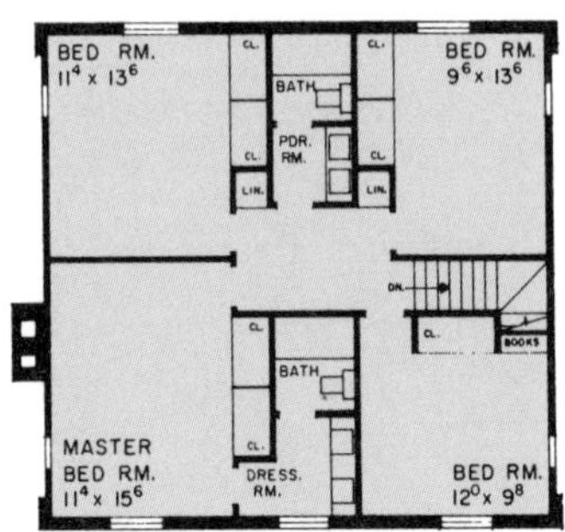

● Four bedrooms and two baths make-up the second floor of this two-story design. The first floor has all of the living areas and work center. Note the convenience of the powder room at the entry.

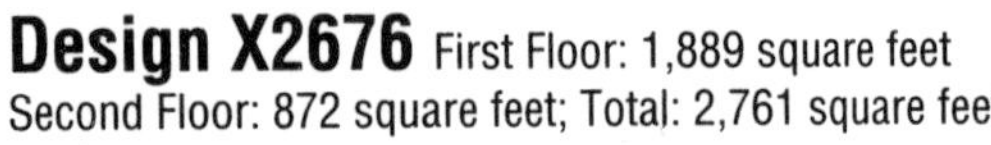

Design X2676

First Floor: 1,889 square feet
Second Floor: 872 square feet; Total: 2,761 square feet

● Here is the perfect home for those who want lots of livability. Note the easy access to each room. A luxurious master bedroom suite will provide all of the comforts you deserve. Take note of the sitting room, his/her dressing and closet areas and the raised tub. Upstairs, two nice sized bedrooms and a full bath.

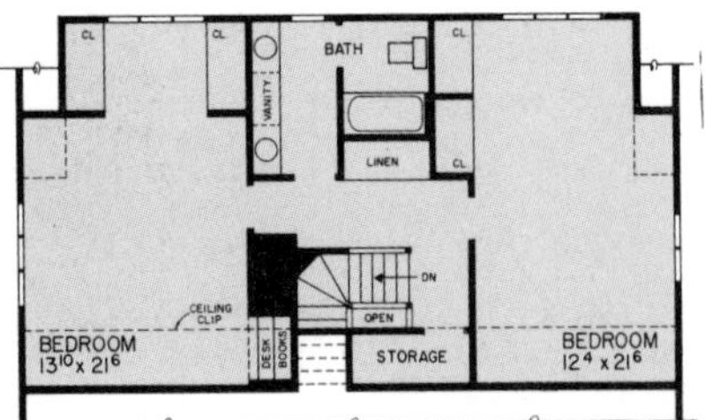

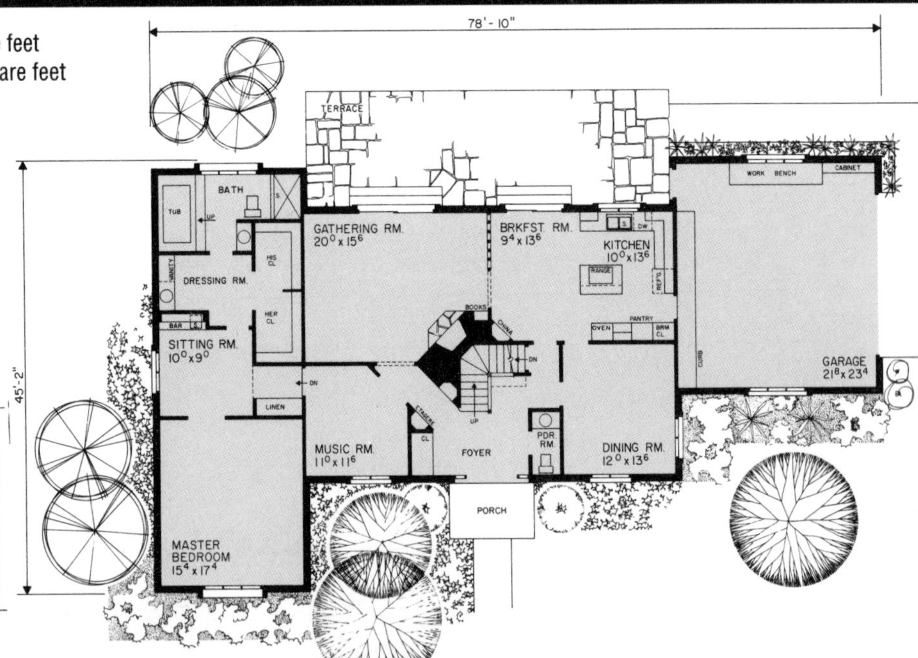

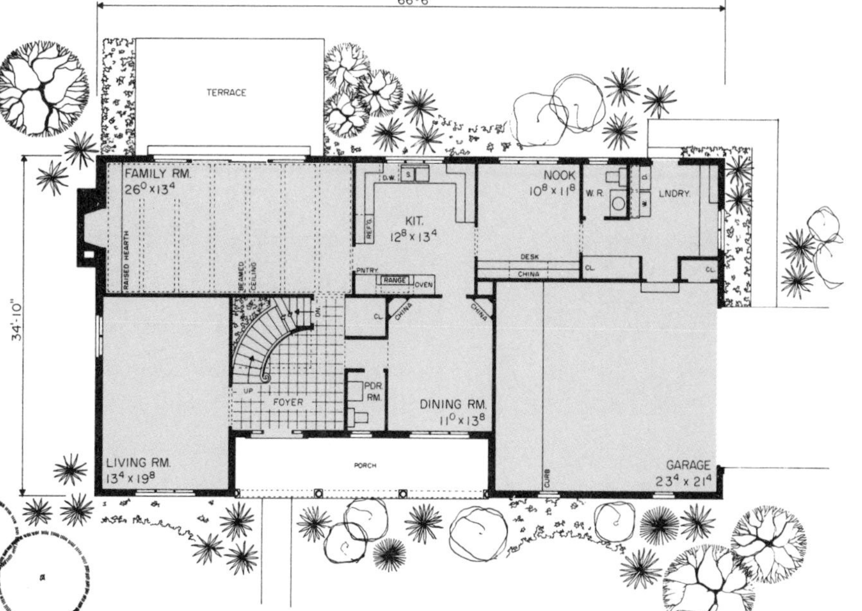

Design X2172

First Floor: 1,618 square feet
Second Floor: 1,205 square feet
Total: 2,823 square feet

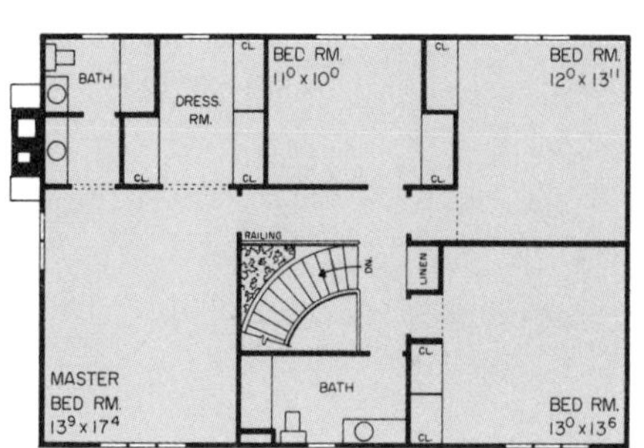

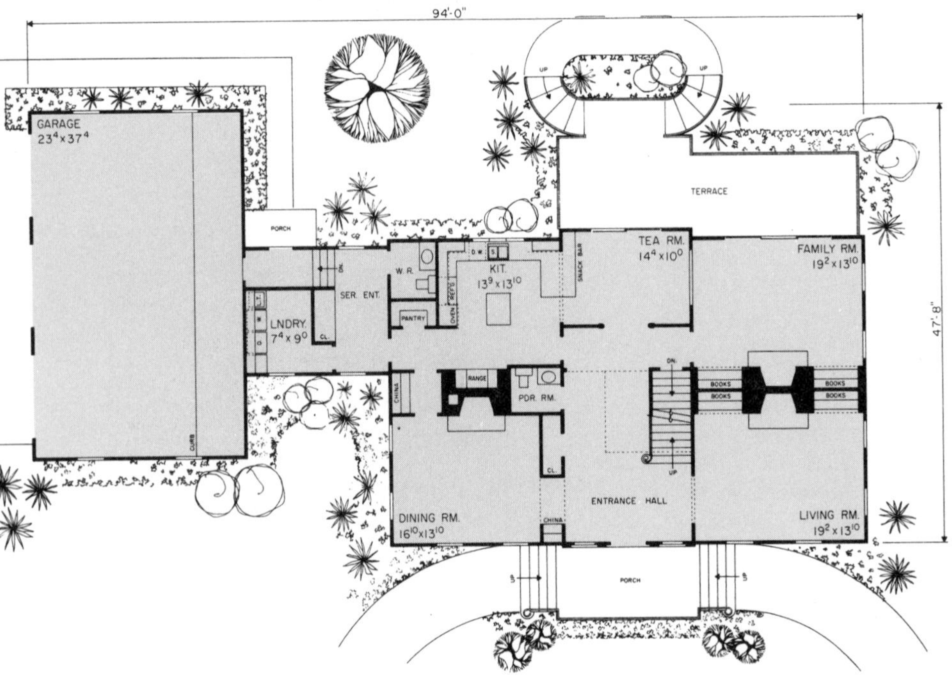

Design X2301

First Floor: 2,044 square feet
Second Floor: 1,815 square feet
Total: 3,859 square feet

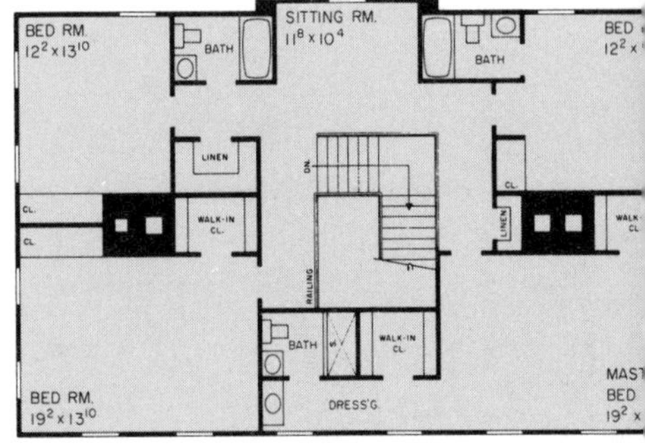

● Reminiscent of architecture with roots in the deep South, this finely detailed home is exquisite, indeed. The contemporary floor plan offers three fireplaces, built-in bookshelves in the living room and family room, and four upstairs bedrooms.

Design X2840 First Floor: 1,529 square feet; Second Floor: 1,344 square feet; Total: 2,873 square feet

● This traditional two-story design will keep you warm because it is super-insulated to shut out the cold. It is designed for cold climates and is so well insulated that it can be built facing any direction - even north. The key behind its energy efficiency is its double exterior walls separated by R-33 insulation and a raised roof truss that insures ceiling insulation will extend to the outer wall. Front and rear air locks and triple-glazed, underscaled (24" wide) windows also contribute to the energy savings. The interior floor planning has a great deal to recommend it, too. Formal and informal living areas, plus a study! The interior kitchen area will be hard to beat. It has pass-thrus to the formal dining room and the family room. All of the sleeping facilities, four bedrooms and two baths, are on the second floor. The section at right describes the technical characteristics of this super-insulated house.

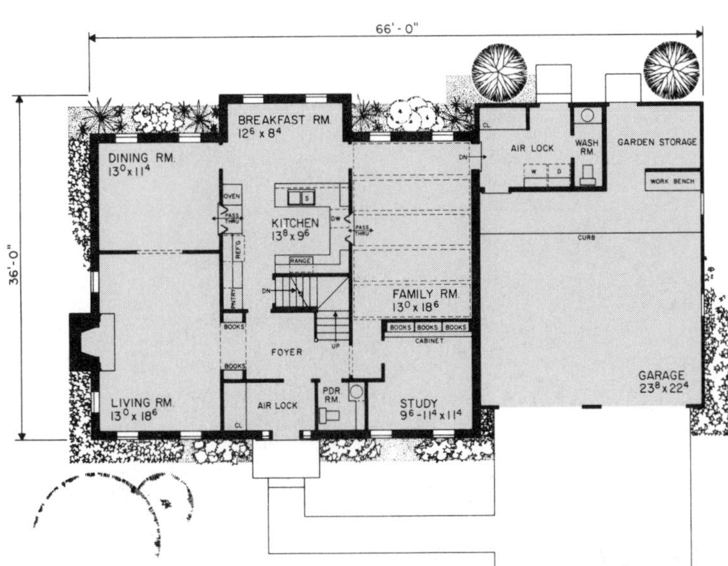

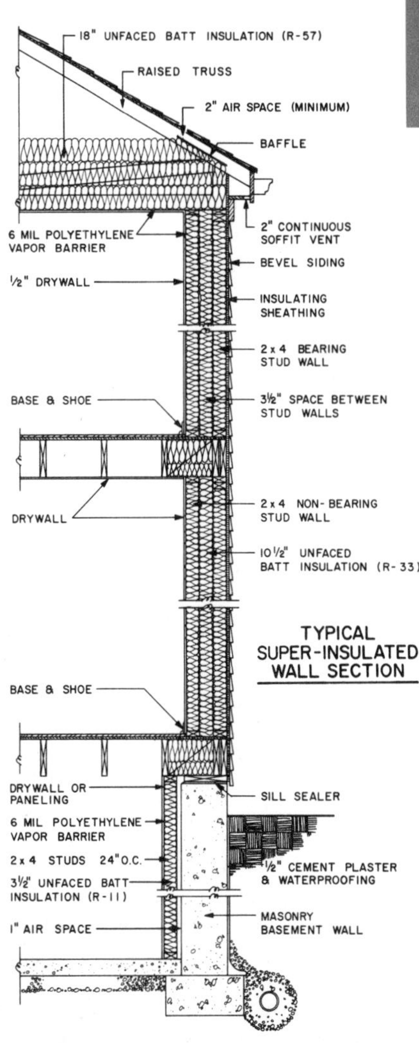

Design X1285

First Floor: 1,202 square feet
Second Floor: 896 square feet
Total: 2,098 square feet

L **D**

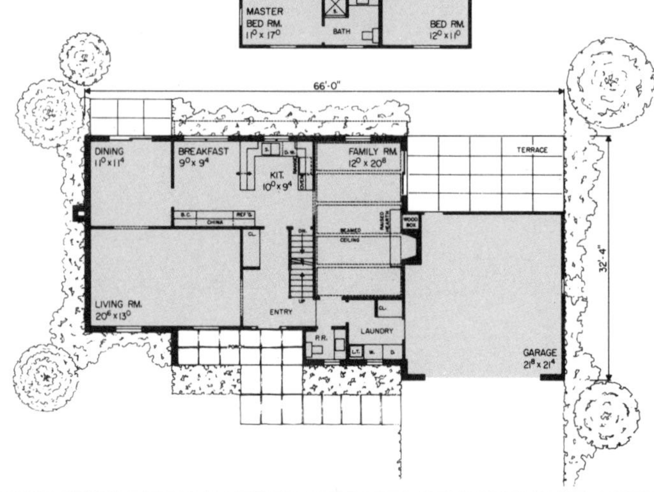

● Such a pretty traditional farmhouse design — and with so much to offer in the way of floor planning. From the front entry, turn left into a good-sized living room with attached dining room. A right turn leads to a well-placed powder room and laundry or farther back to the beamed-ceiling family room (note the fireplace with wood box here). The kitchen and adjacent breakfast room will make mealtimes a pleasure. Upstairs, four bedrooms share space with two baths.

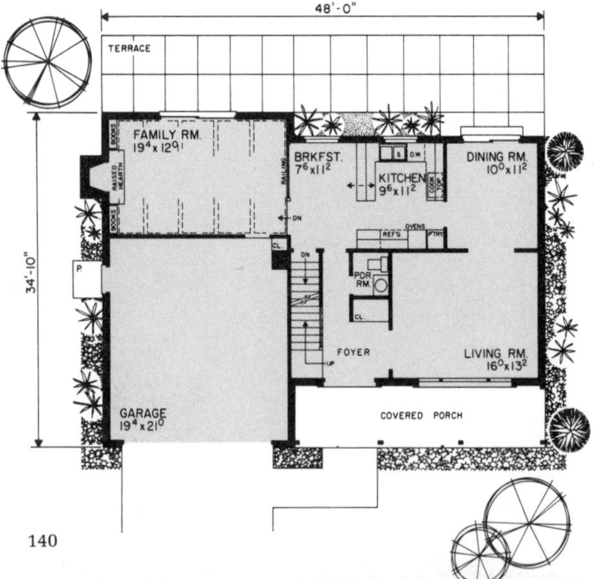

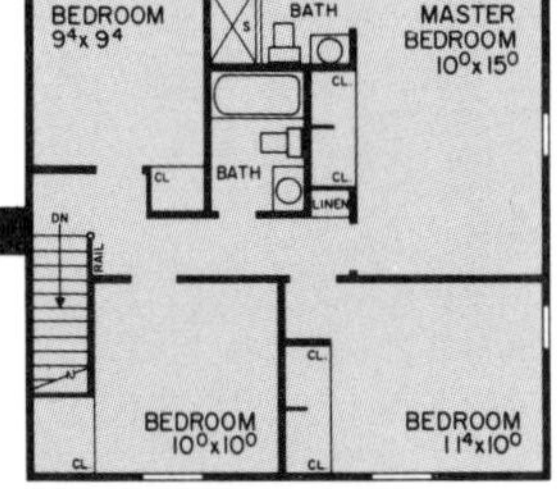

OPTIONAL 3-BEDROOM PLAN

Design X1956

First Floor: 990 square feet
Second Floor: 728 square feet
Total: 1,718 square feet

D

● The blueprints for this home include details for both the three-bedroom and the four-bedroom options. The first-floor livability does not change.

Custom Alterations? See page 301 for customizing this plan to your specifications.

Design X2540 First Floor: 1,306 square feet
Second Floor: 1,360 square feet; Total: 2,666 square feet

L **D**

● This efficient Colonial abounds in features. A spacious entry flanked by living areas. A kitchen flanked by eating areas. Upstairs, four bedrooms including a sitting room in the master suite.

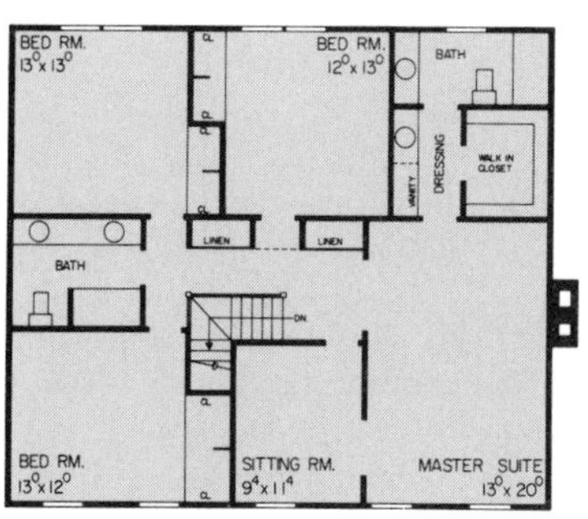

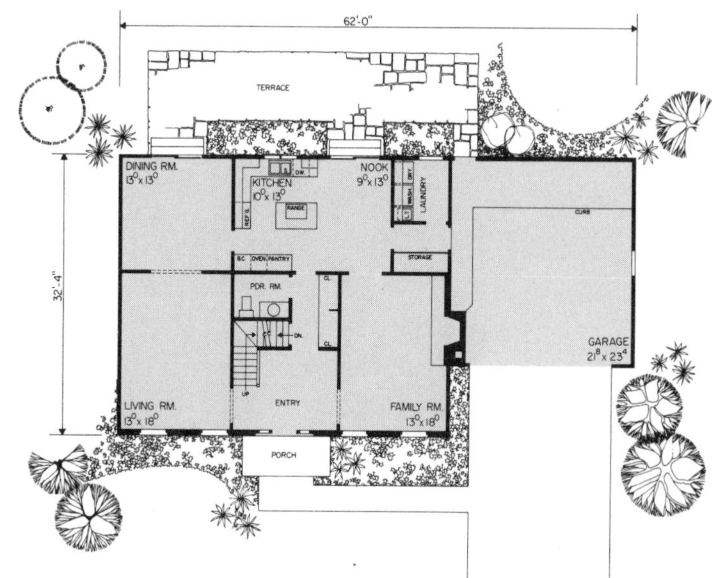

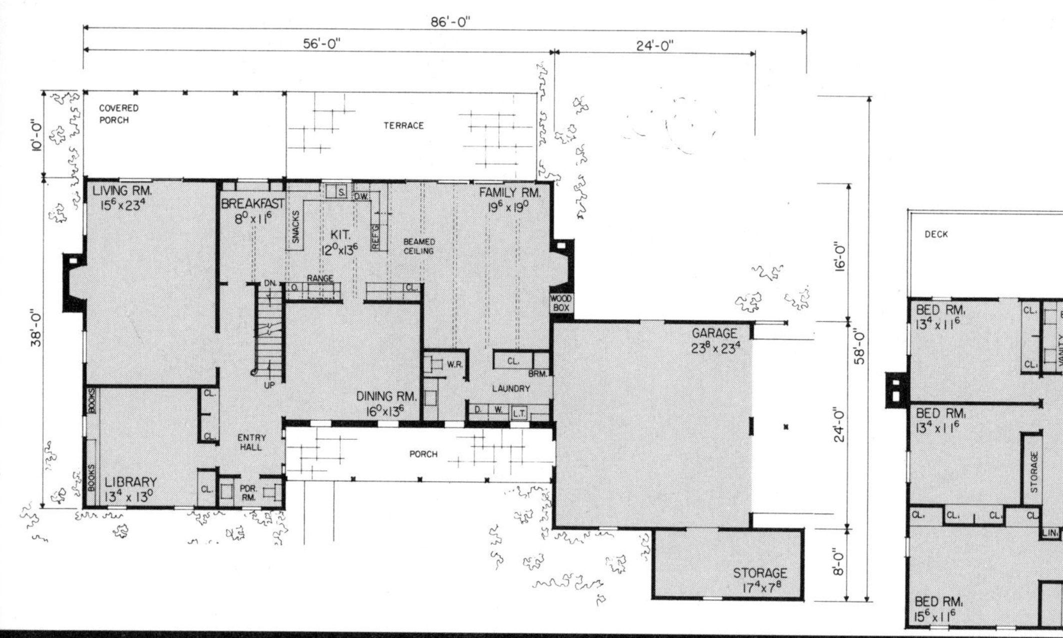

Design X1239

First Floor: 1,822 square feet
Second Floor: 1,419 square feet
Total: 3,241 square feet

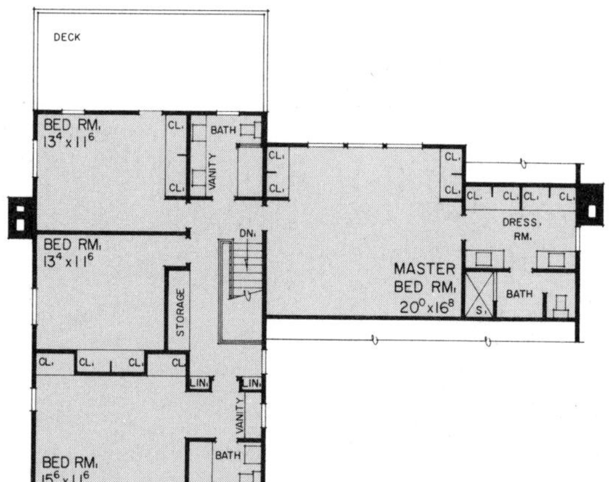

Design X1955

First Floor: 1,192 square feet
Second Floor: 1,192 square feet
Total: 2,384 square feet

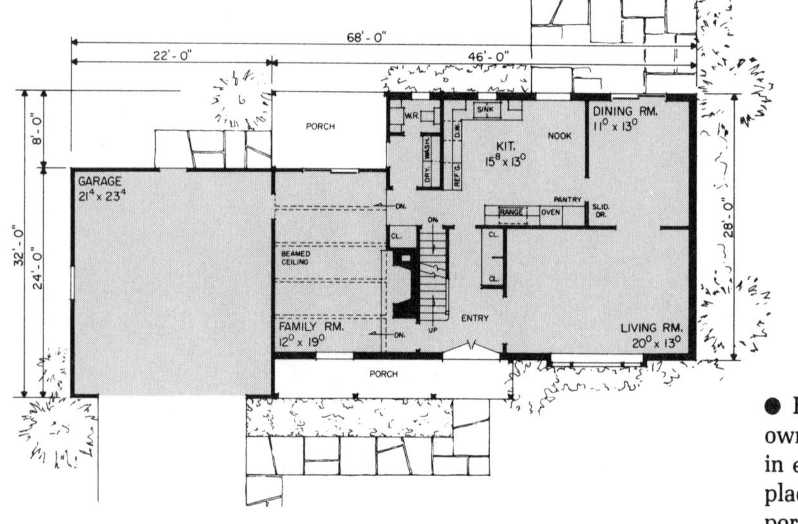

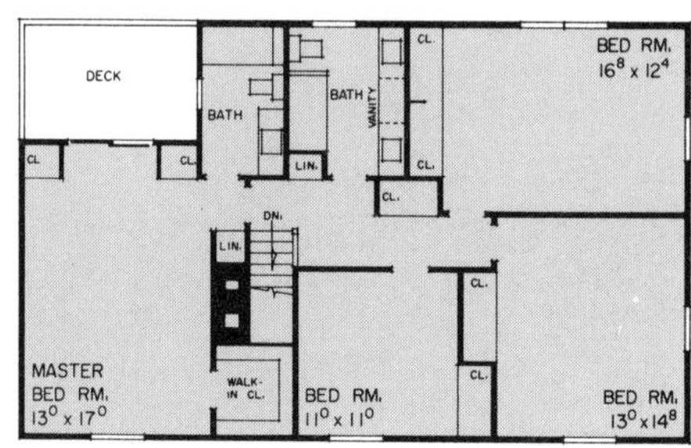

● Here is a design with all of the features a homeowner would want most in a new house. It abounds in exterior appeal and will be a neighborhood show place. Picture yourself relaxing on the front, covered porch after a hard day of work.

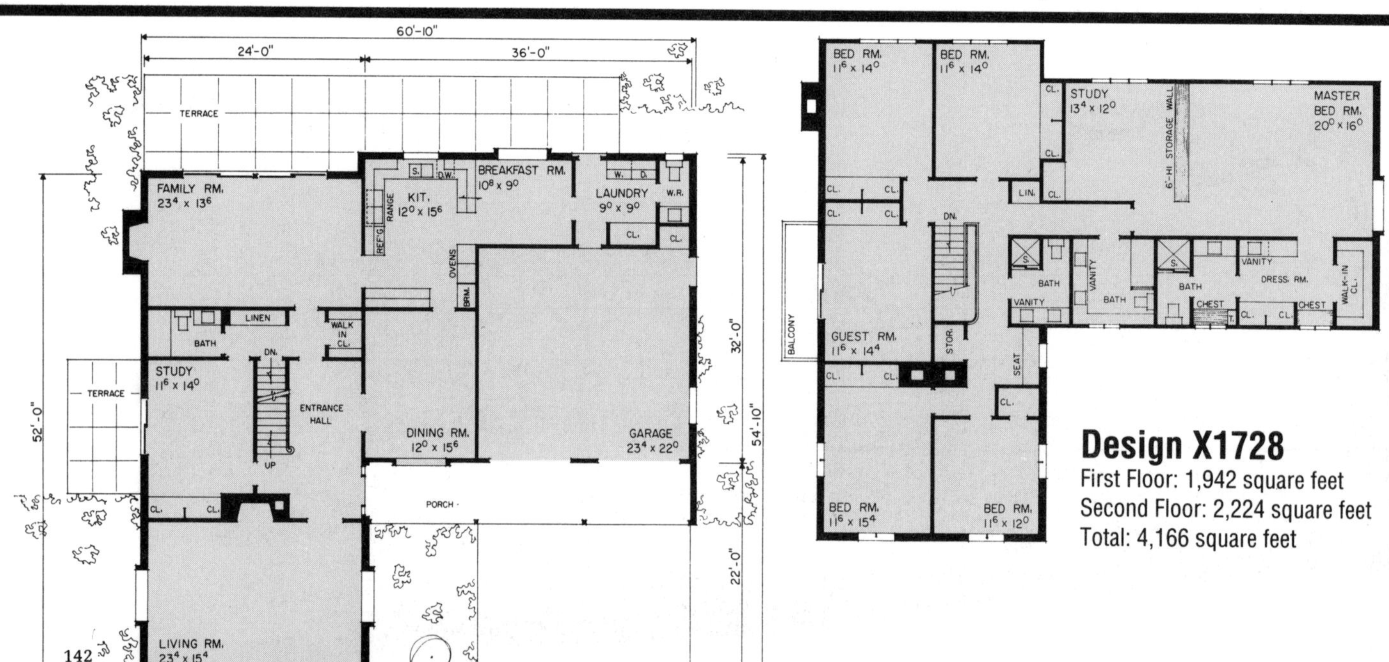

Design X1728

First Floor: 1,942 square feet
Second Floor: 2,224 square feet
Total: 4,166 square feet

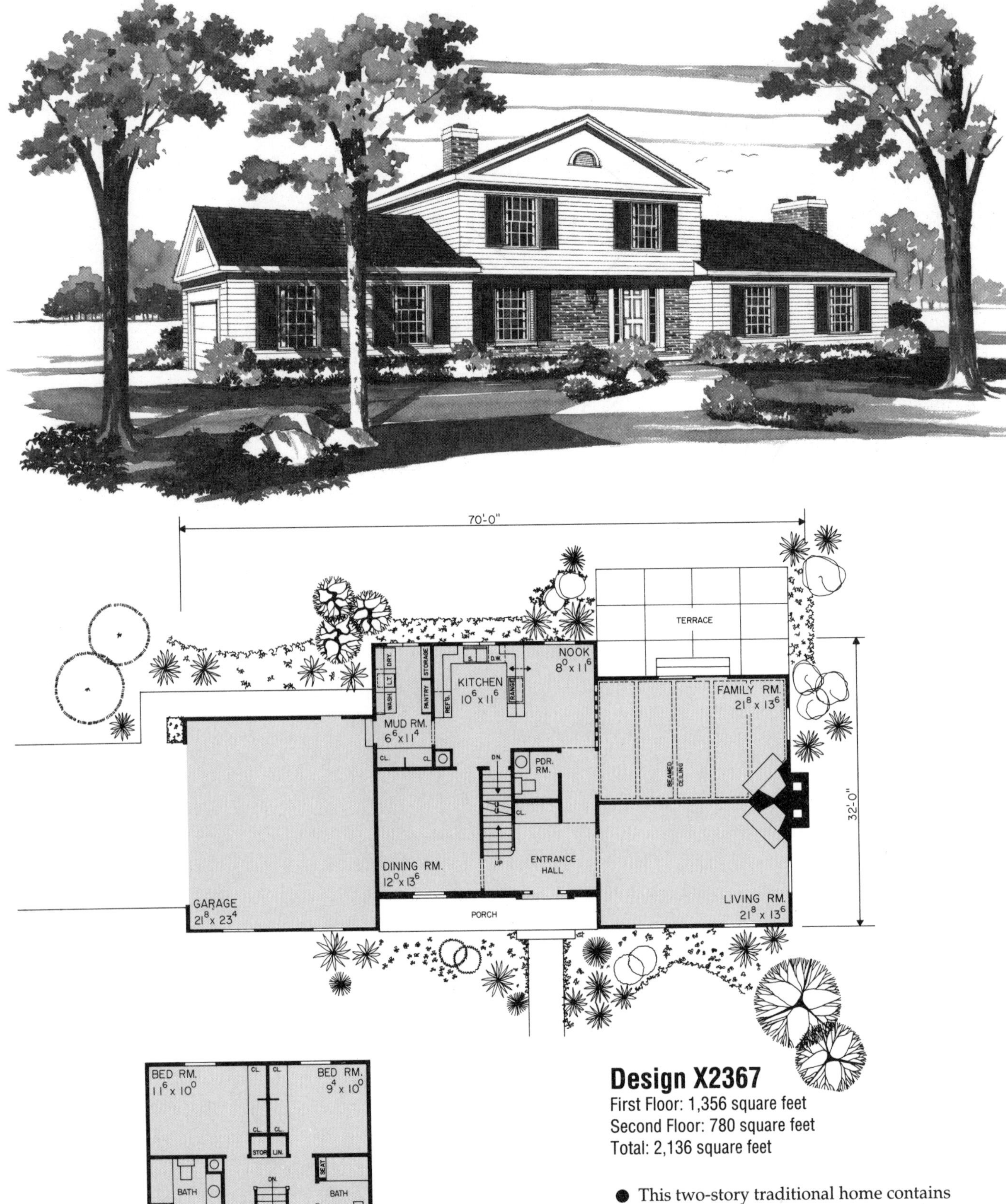

Design X2367

First Floor: 1,356 square feet
Second Floor: 780 square feet
Total: 2,136 square feet

● This two-story traditional home contains plenty of room for everyday activities. The right wing of the home consists of two expansive living areas: a family room with beamed ceiling, corner fireplace and terrace access, and a living room with corner fireplace for more formal occasions. The first floor also includes a formal dining room, kitchen with breakfast nook, and a convenient powder room. Four bedrooms and two full baths are found on the second floor.

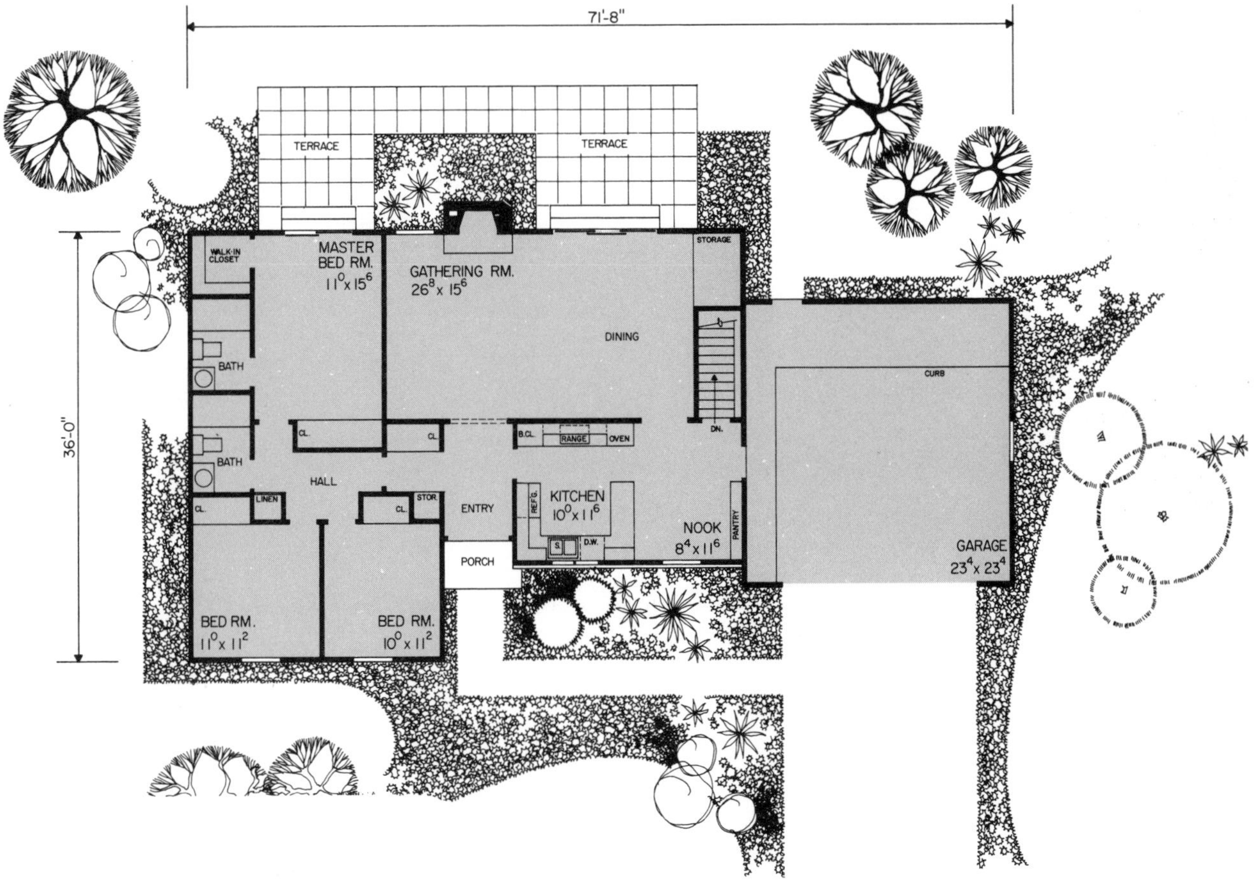

71'-8"
36'-0"
TERRACE
TERRACE
WALK-IN CLOSET
MASTER BED RM. $11^0 \times 15^6$
GATHERING RM. $26^8 \times 15^6$
STORAGE
DINING
BATH
BATH
CL.
CL.
B.CL.
RANGE
OVEN
DN.
CURB
HALL
LINEN
CL.
CL.
STOR.
ENTRY
REFG.
KITCHEN $10^0 \times 11^6$
S.
D.W.
NOOK $8^4 \times 11^6$
PANTRY
GARAGE $23^4 \times 23^4$
PORCH
BED RM. $11^0 \times 11^2$
BED RM. $10^0 \times 11^2$

Design X2597

Square Footage: 1,515

L D

● Whether it be a starter house you are after, or one in which to spend your retirement years, this pleasing frame home will provide a full measure of pride in ownership. The contrast of vertical and horizontal lines, the double front doors and the coach lamp post at the garage create an inviting exterior. Efficiently planned, the floor plan functions in an orderly manner. The 26-foot gathering room has a delightful view of the rear yard and will take care of those formal dining occasions. There are two full baths serving the three bedrooms. Additional features include: plenty of storage facilities, two sets of glass doors to the terraces, a fireplace in the gathering room, a basement and an attached two-car garage to act as a buffer against the wind.

Design X1311 Square Footage: 1,050

L **D**

● Delightful design and effective, flexible planning comes in little packages, too. This fine traditional exterior with its covered front entrance features an alternate basement plan. Note how the non-basement layout provides a family room and mud room, while the basement option shows kitchen eating and dining room. Sensible planning.

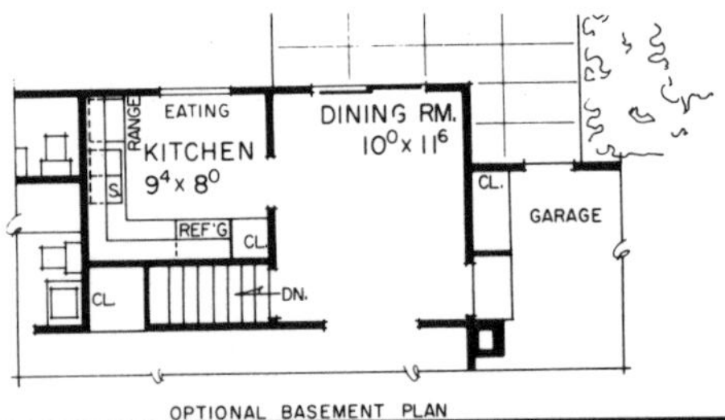

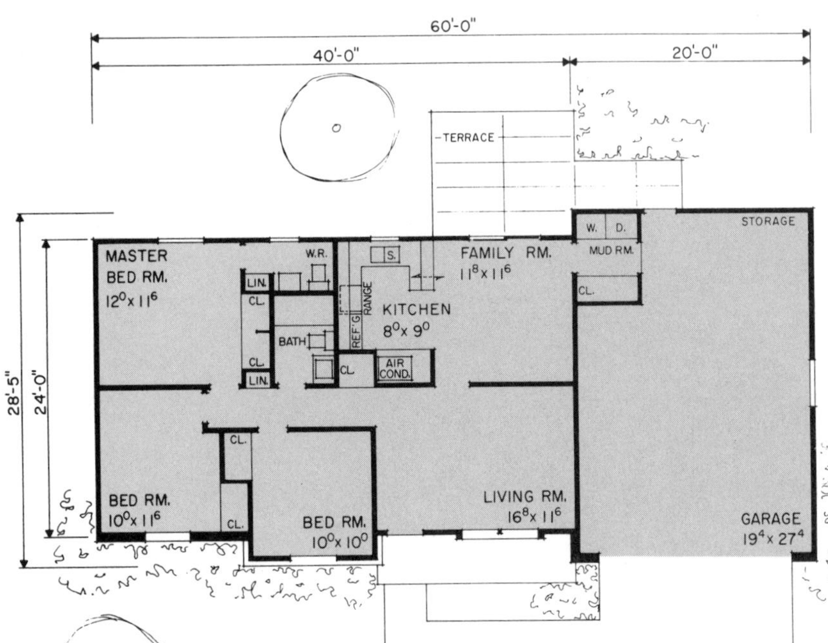

Design X1939

Square Footage: 1,387

L **D**

● A finely proportioned house with more than its full share of charm. The brick veneer exterior contrasts pleasingly with the narrow horizontal siding of the oversized attached two-car garage. Perhaps the focal point of the exterior is the recessed front entrance with its double Colonial styled doors. The secondary service entrance through the garage to the kitchen area is a handy feature. Study the plan. It features three bedrooms, two full baths, living room with fireplace, front kitchen with an eating area, formal dining room, plenty of storage potential plus a basement for additional storage or perhaps to be developed as a recreational area.

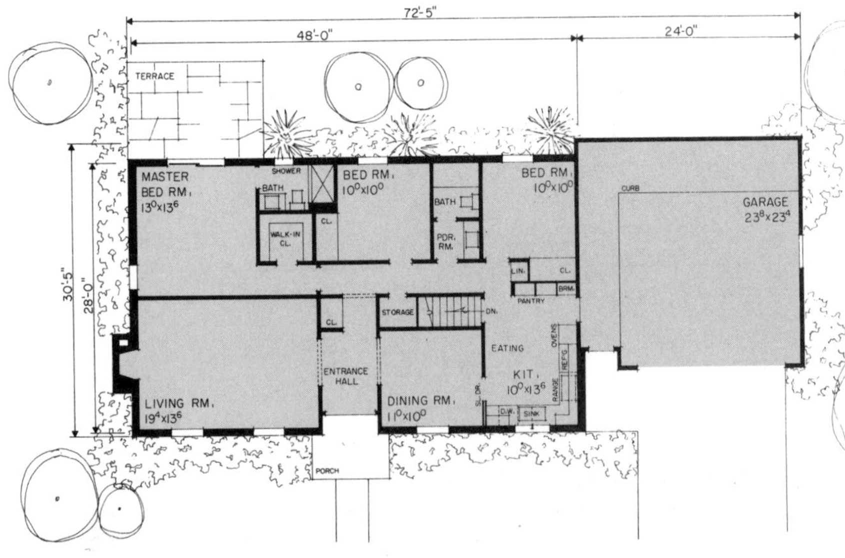

Design X1896

Square Footage: 1,690

● Complete family livability is provided by this exceptional floor plan. Further, this design has a truly delightful traditional exterior. The fine layout features a center entrance hall with storage closet in addition to the wardrobe closet. Then, there is the formal, front living room and the adjacent, separate dining room. The U-shaped kitchen has plenty of counter and cupboard space. There is even a pantry. The family room functions with the kitchen and is but a step from the outdoor terrace. The mud room has space for storage and laundry equipment. The extra wash room is nearby. The large family will find those four bedrooms and two full baths just the answer to sleeping and bath accommodations.

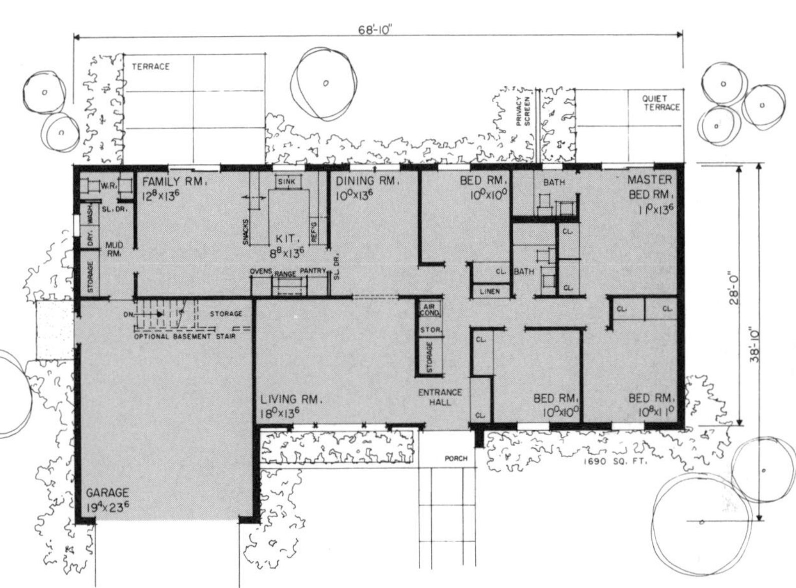

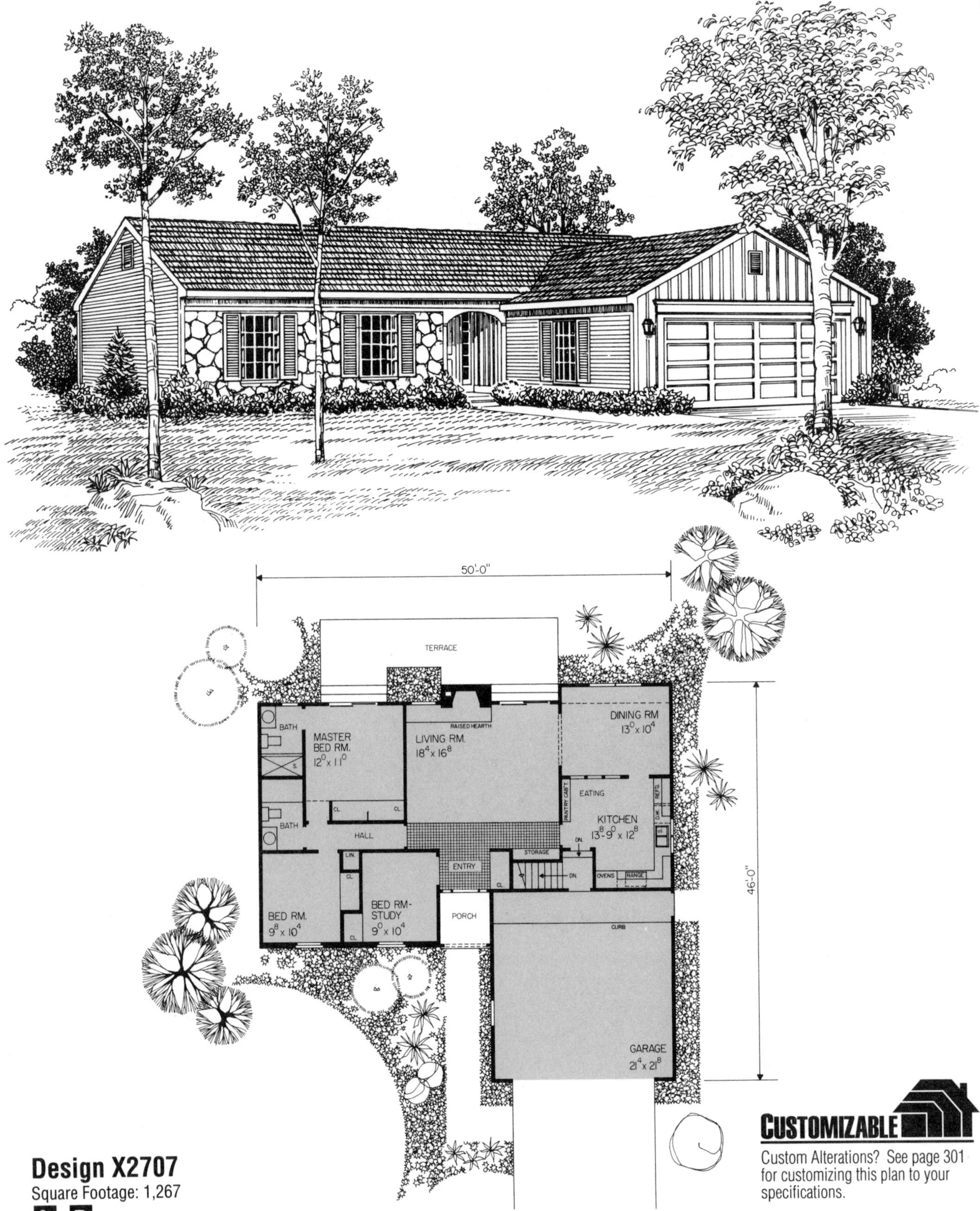

CUSTOMIZABLE

Custom Alterations? See page 301 for customizing this plan to your specifications.

Design X2707

Square Footage: 1,267

L **D**

● Here is a charming Early American adaptation that will serve as a picturesque and practical retirement home. Also, it will serve admirably those with a small family in search of an efficient, economically built home. The living area, highlighted by the raised hearth fireplace, is spacious. The kitchen features eating space and easy access to the garage and basement. The dining room is adjacent to the kitchen and views the rear yard. Then, there is the basement for recreation and hobby pursuits. The bedroom wing offers three bedrooms and two full baths. Don't miss the sliding doors to the terrace from the living room and the master bedroom. Storage units are plentiful including a pantry cabinet in the eating area of the kitchen. This plan will be efficient and livable.

Design X2505

Square Footage: 1,366

L **D**

● This design offers you a choice of three distinctively different exteriors. Which is your favorite? Blueprints show details for all three optional elevations. A study of the floor plan reveals a fine measure of livability. In less than 1,400 square feet there are features galore. An excellent return on your construction dollar. In addition to the two eating areas and the open planning of the gathering room, the indoor-outdoor relationships are of great interest. The basement may be developed for recreational activities. Be sure to note the storage potential, particularly the linen closet, the pantry, the china cabinet and the broom closet.

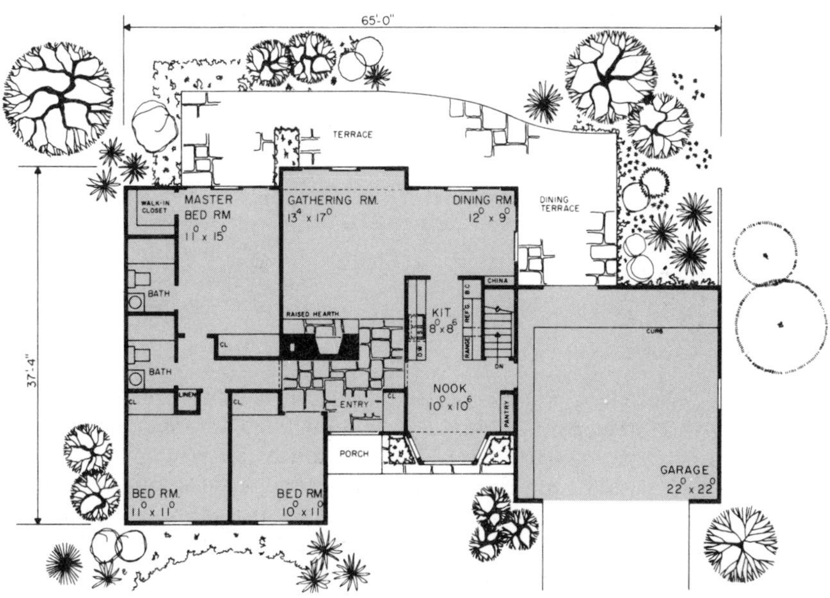

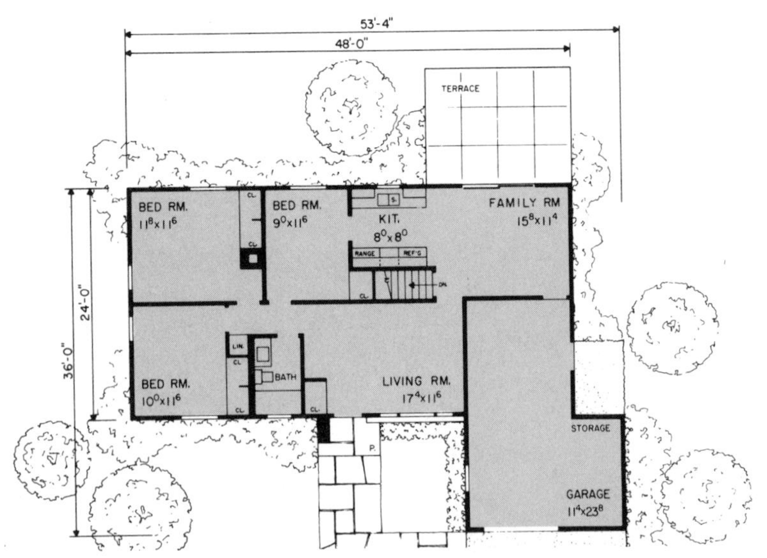

Design X1300

Square Footage: 1,008

● The projecting garage with its bulk storage area adds a full measure of design distinction. Behind the garage is a family room which functions with the kitchen.

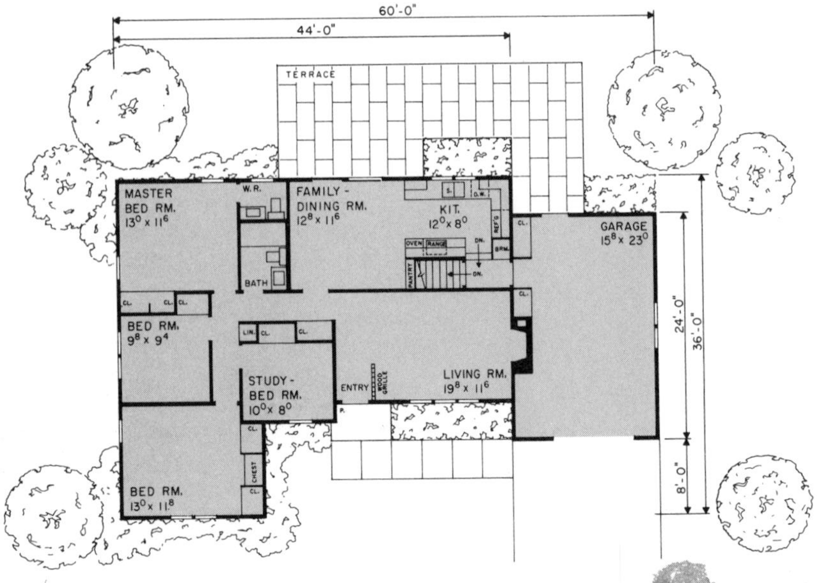

60'-0"
44'-0"
TERRACE
MASTER BED RM. $13^{0} x 11^{6}$
W.R.
FAMILY-DINING RM. $12^{8} x 11^{6}$
KIT. $12^{0} x 8^{0}$
OVEN RANGE
PANTRY
GARAGE $15^{8} x 23^{0}$
BATH
BED RM. $9^{8} x 9^{4}$
LIN.
STUDY-BED RM. $10^{0} x 8^{0}$
ENTRY
WOOD GRILLE
LIVING RM. $19^{8} x 11^{6}$
BED RM. $13^{0} x 11^{8}$
CHEST
24'-0"
36'-0"
8'-0"

● "Who could ask for anything more" is an appropriate theme for this house. It is easy on the budget with only 1,264 square feet, but it includes big-house features, such as four bedrooms, one-and-one-half baths, a fireplace, a family room and an over-sized garage, plus the convenience of more closets than the normal family would require. Don't miss the built-in chest, china cupboard and the kitchen cooking equipment.

Design X1147

Square Footage: 1,264

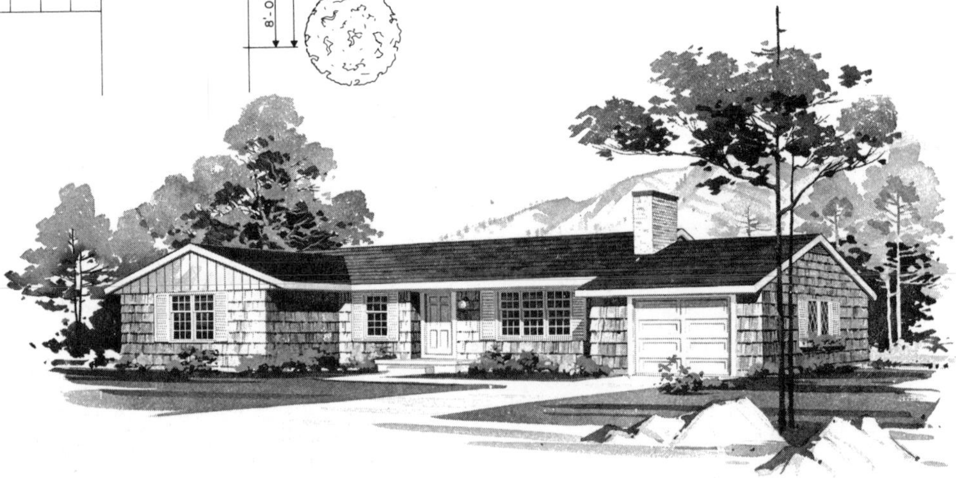

Design X1327

Square Footage: 1,392

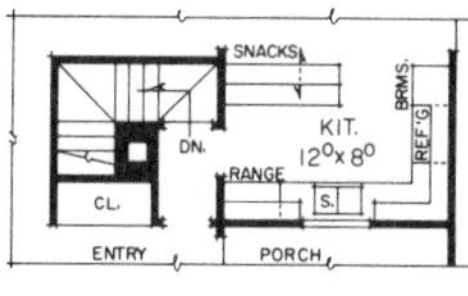

● This design overcomes the restrictions of a narrow building site. It has four bedrooms and two baths. Notice the efficient traffic patterns established between the living and family rooms and the kitchen. An optional basement plan is included with the blueprint order.

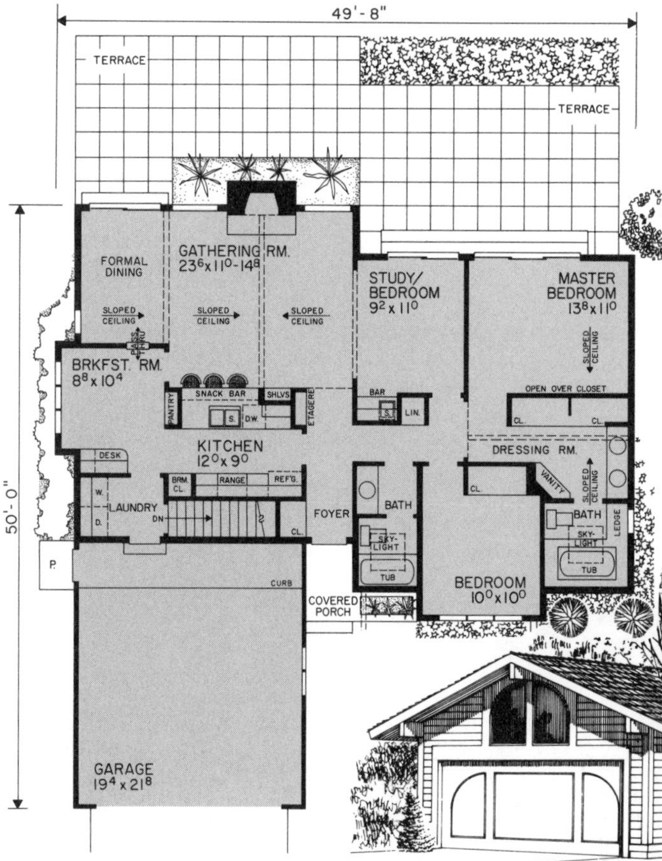

OPTIONAL BASEMENT PLAN

Design X2864

Square Footage: 1,387

L D

● Many characteristics of this design deserve mention. The entrance court and covered porch are a delightful way to enter this home. The foyer leads to an interior kitchen with breakfast room and a snack bar on the gathering room side. A study with wet bar is adjacent (it could also serve as a third bedroom). Sliding glass doors in the master bedroom area open to the rear terrace.

CUSTOMIZABLE

Custom Alterations? See page 301 for customizing this plan to your specifications.

Design X1075

Square Footage: 1,232

L **D**

● This picturesque traditional one-story home has much to offer the young family. Because of its rectangular shape and its predominantly frame exterior, construction costs will be economical. Passing through the front entrance, visitors will be surprised to find so much livability in only 1,232 square feet. Consider these features: spacious formal living and dining area; two full baths; efficient kitchen; and large, rear family room. In addition there is the full basement for further recreational facilities and bulk storage. The attached garage is extra long to accommodate the storage of garden equipment, lawn furniture, bicycles, etc.

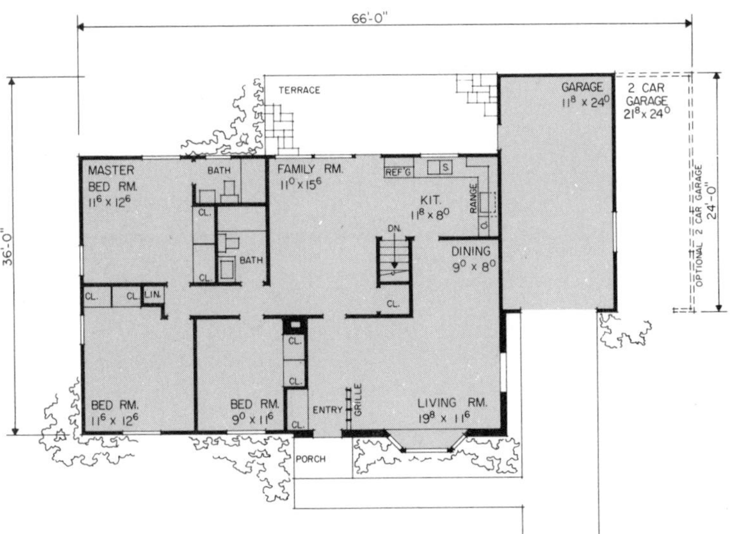

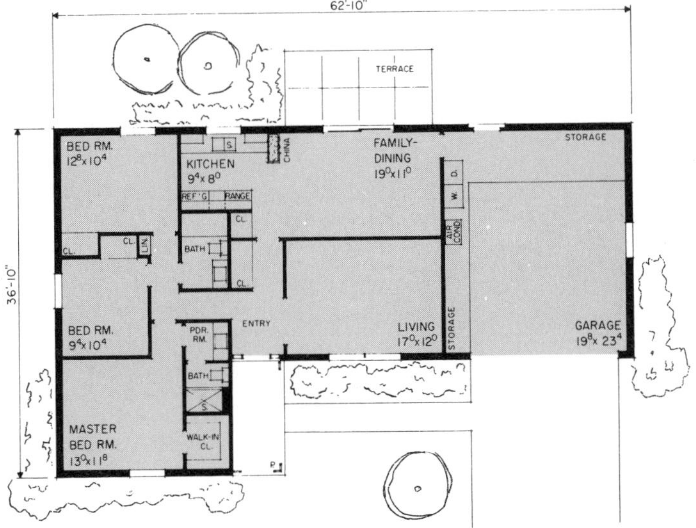

Design X1366

Square Footage: 1,280

● The extension of the main roof, along with the use of ornamental iron, vertical siding and glass side lites flanking the paneled door, all contribute to a delightful and inviting front entrance to this L-shaped design. There is much to recommend this design—from the attached two-car garage to the walk-in closet of the master bedroom. Don't overlook the compartmented master bath with its stall shower and powder room; the built-in china cabinet with an attractive planter above or the two closets right in the center of the house.

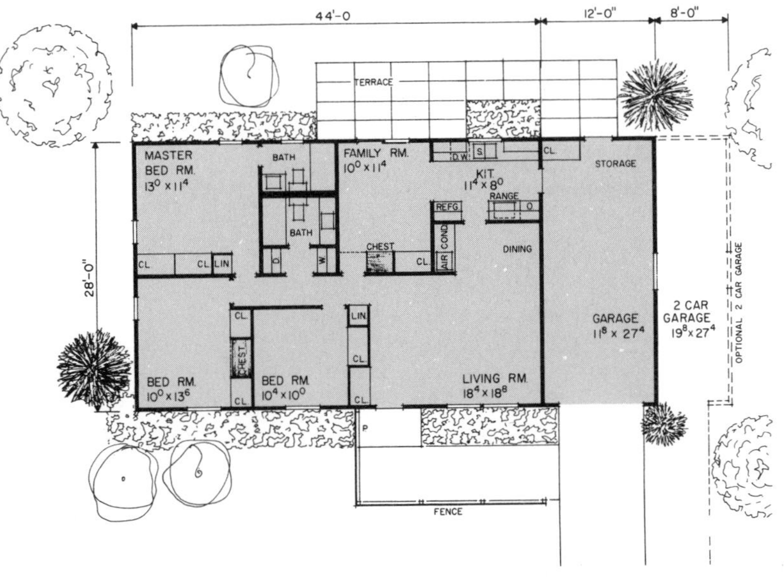

Design X1191

Square Footage: 1,232

L **D**

● A careful study of the floor plan for this cozy appearing traditional home reveals a fine combination of features which add tremendously to convenient living. For instance, observe the wardrobe and storage facilities of the bedroom area. A built-in chest in the one bedroom and also one in the family room. Then, notice the economical plumbing of the two full back-to-back baths. Postively a great money saving feature for today and in the future. Further, don't overlook the location of the washer and dryer which have cupboards above the units themselves. Observe storage facilities. Optional two-car garage is available if necessary.

Design X1305

Square Footage: 1,382

D

● Order blueprints for any one of the three exteriors shown on this page and you will receive details for building the outstanding floor plan at the right. You'll find the appeal of these exteriors difficult to beat. As for the plan, in less than 1,400 square feet there are three bedrooms, two full baths, a separate dining room, a formal living room, a fine kitchen overlooking the rear yard and an informal family room. In addition, there is the attached two-car garage. Note the location of the stairs when this plan is built with a basement. Each of the exteriors is predominantly brick—the front of Design X1305 (above) features both stone and vertical boards and battens with brick on the other three sides. Observe the double front doors of the French design, X1382 (below) and the Contemporary design, X1383 (bottom).

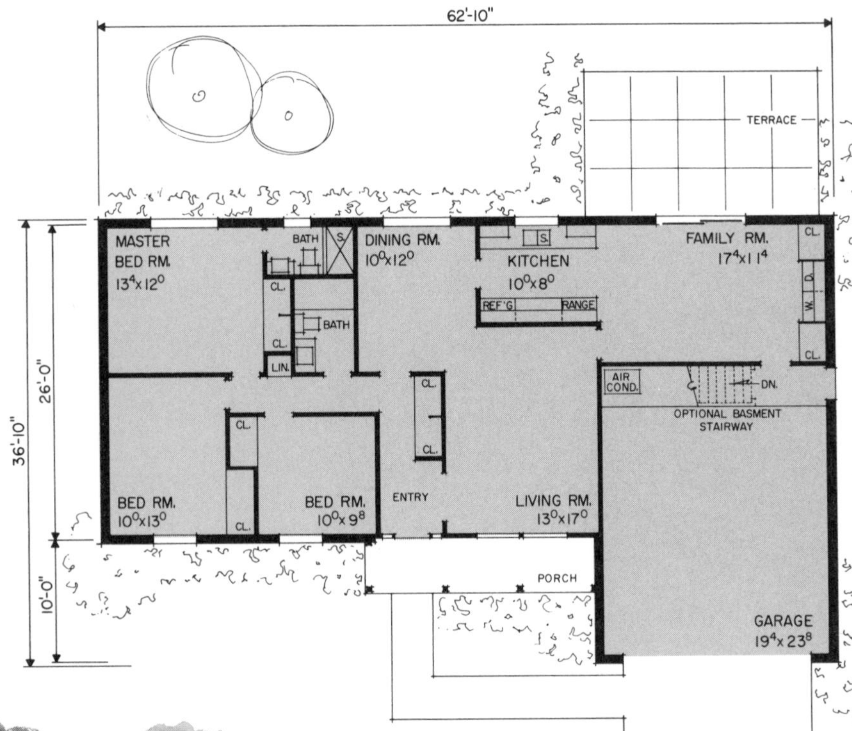

Design X1382

Square Footage: 1,382

D

Design X1383

Square Footage: 1,382

D

Design X1389

Square Footage: 1,488

D

● Your choice of exterior goes with this outstanding floor plan. If your tastes include a liking for French Provincial, Design X1389, above, will provide a lifetime of satisfaction. On the other hand, should you prefer the simple straightforward lines of contemporary design, the exterior for Design X1387, below, will be your favorite. For those who enjoy the warmth of Colonial adaptations, the charming exterior for Design X1388, bottom, will be perfect. Observe the varying design treatment of the windows, the double front doors, the garage doors and the roof lines. Don't miss other architectural details. Study each exterior and the floor plan carefully. Three charming options you won't want to miss.

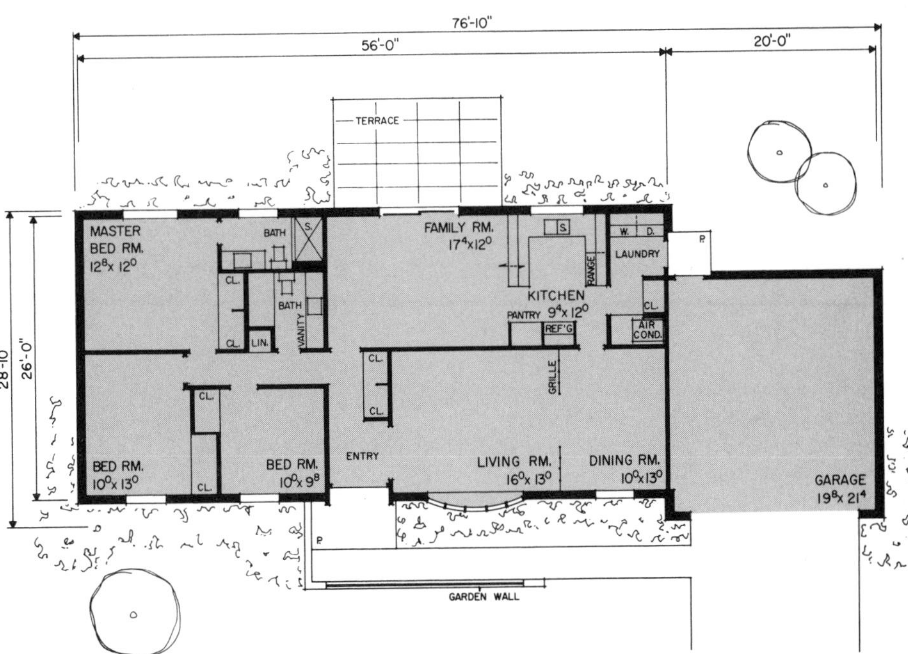

Design X1387

Square Footage: 1,488

D

Design X1388

Square Footage: 1,488

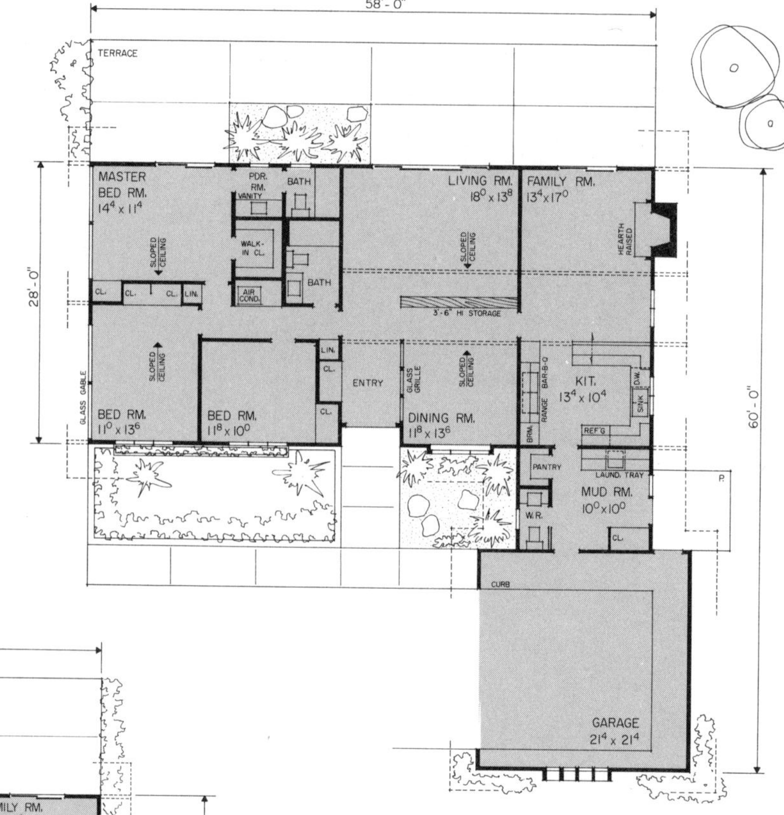

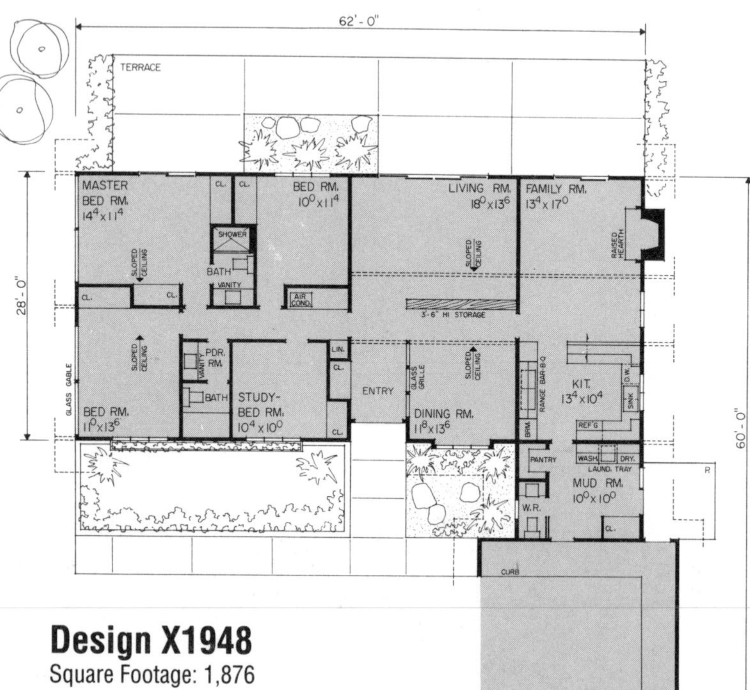

Design X1947

Square Footage: 1,764

● When it comes to housing your family, if you are among the contemporary-minded, you'll want to give this L-shaped design a second, then even a third, or fourth, look. It is available as either a three or four bedroom home. If you desire the three bedroom, 58-foot-wide design order blueprints for X1947; for the four bedroom, 62-foot-wide design, order X1948. Inside, you will note a continuation of the contemporary theme with sloping ceilings, exposed beams and a practical 42-inch-high storage divider between the living and dining rooms. Don't miss the mud room.

Design X1948

Square Footage: 1,876

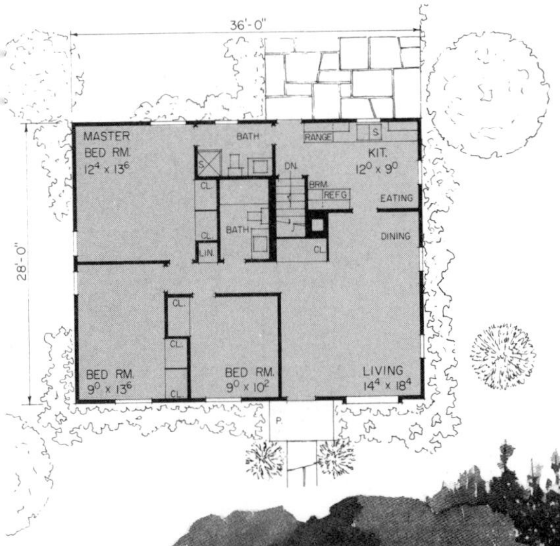

● A cozy plan, but just right for a small family or empty nesters. An ample living room/dining room area leads the way to a rear kitchen overlooking a terrace. Two full baths serve three bedrooms — one a master bedroom. Multi-paned windows with quaint shutters add a touch of charm to the design.

Design X1113

Square Footage: 1,008

L **D**

Design X1325

Square Footage: 1,942

L **D**

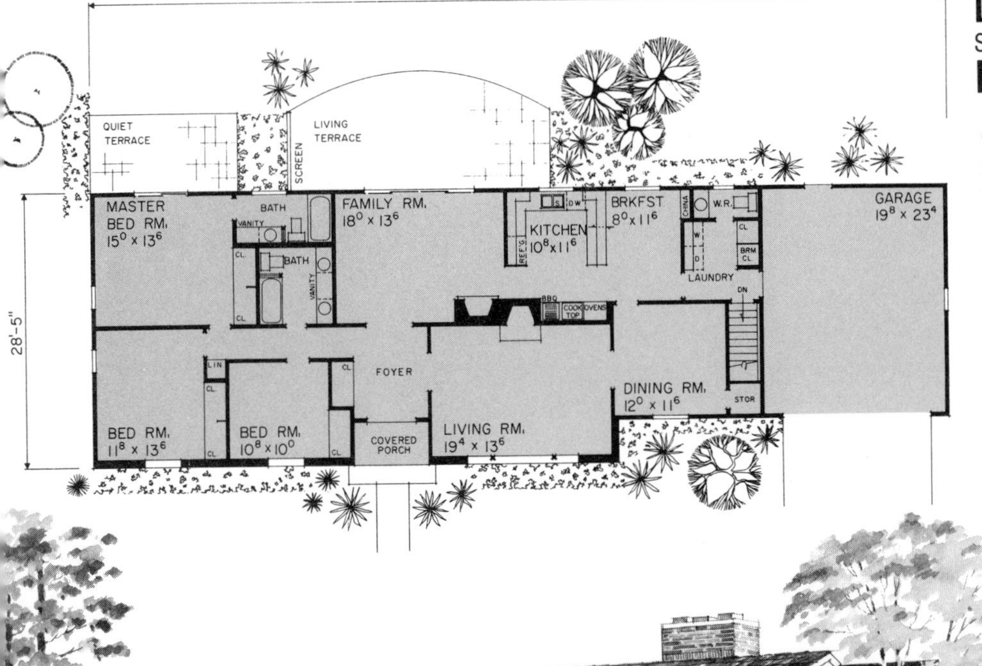

● The large front entry hall permits direct access to the formal living room, the sleeping area and the informal family room. Both of the living areas have a fireplace. When formal dining is the occasion of the evening the separate dining room is but a step from the living room. The U-shaped kitchen is strategically flanked by the family room and the breakfast areas.

Design X1938

Square Footage: 1,428

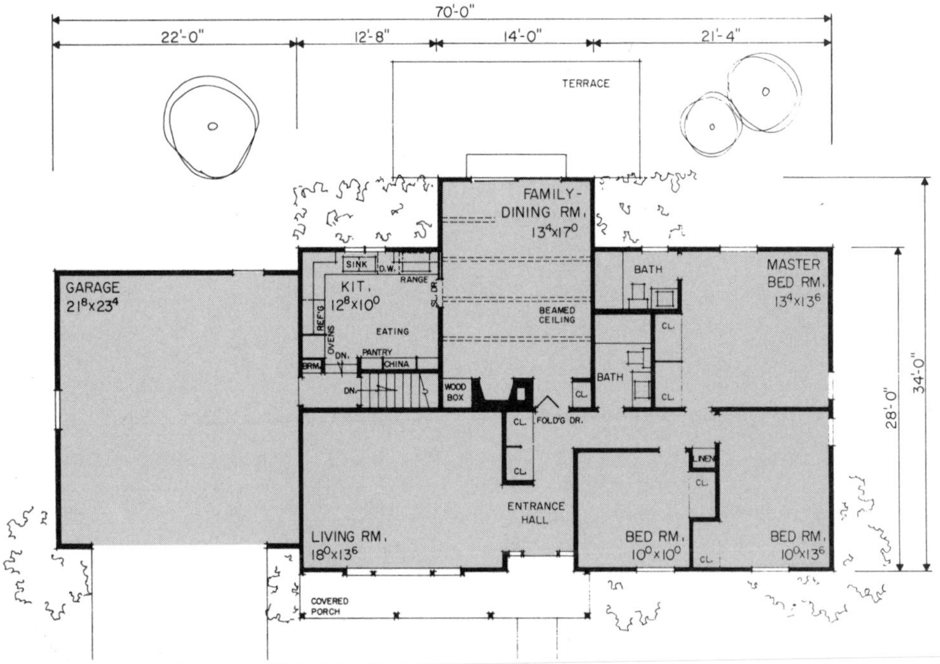

70'-0"
22'-0" 12'-8" 14'-0" 21'-4"
TERRACE
FAMILY-DINING RM. 13^{4}x17^{0}
GARAGE 21^{8}x23^{4}
SINK D.W. RANGE
KIT. 12^{8}x10^{0}
REF'G OVENS EATING
DN. PANTRY CHINA BRM.
DN. WOOD BOX
BEAMED CEILING
BATH
MASTER BED RM. 13^{4}x13^{6}
CL.
BATH
FOLD'G DR.
LINEN
ENTRANCE HALL
LIVING RM. 18^{0}x13^{6}
BED RM. 10^{0}x10^{0}
BED RM. 10^{0}x13^{6}
COVERED PORCH
28'-0" 34'-0"

● An efficient plan designed to fit each of the three delightful exteriors above. You can reserve your choice of exterior until you receive the blueprints. Each set you order contains the details for the construction of all three. Note the differences in exterior materials, window treatment, car storage facilities and roof lines. Observe the beamed ceiling, all purpose family room and the kitchen eating space. There is a lot of living in 1,428 square feet.

Design X1323

Square Footage: 1,344

L **D**

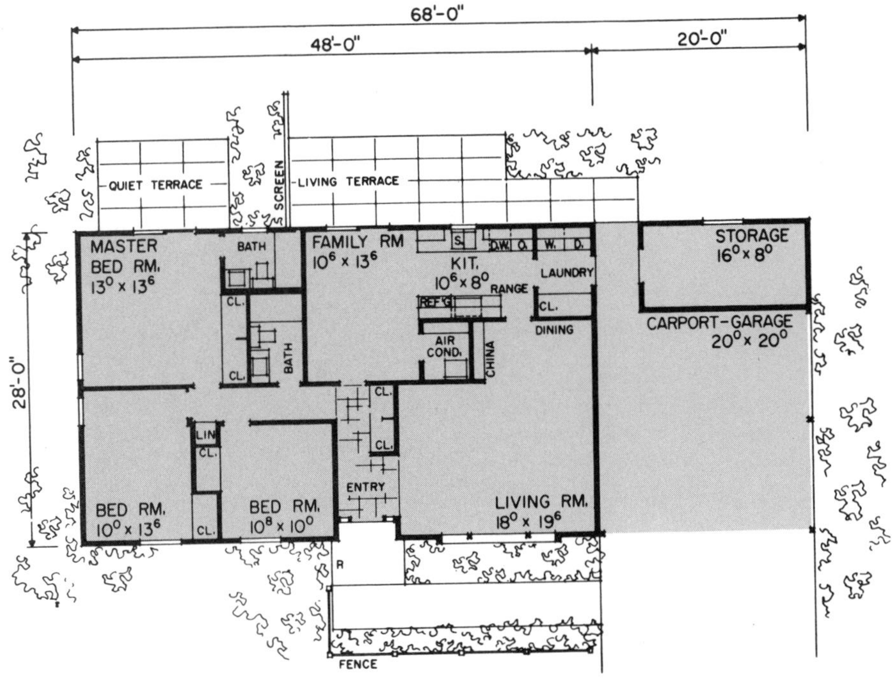

● Incorporated in the set of blueprints for this design are details for building each of the three charming, traditional exteriors. Each of the three alternate exteriors has a distinction all its own. A study of the floor plan reveals fine livability. There are two full baths, a fine family room, an efficient work center, a formal dining area, bulk storage facilities and sliding glass doors to the quiet and living terraces. The laundry is strategically located near the kitchen.

Design X2802

Square Footage: 1,729

L **D**

● The three exteriors shown at the left house the same, efficiently planned one-story floor plan shown below. Be sure to notice the design variations in the window placement and roof pitch. The Tudor design to the left is delightful. Half-timbered stucco and brick comprise the facade of this English Tudor variation of the plan. Note authentic bay window in the front bedroom.

Design X2803

Square Footage: 1,679

L **D**

● Housed in varying facades, this floor plan is very efficient. The front foyer leads to each of the living areas. The sleeping area of two, or optional three, bedrooms is ready to serve the family. Then there is the gathering room. This room is highlighted by its size, 16 x 20 feet. A contemporary mix of fieldstone and vertical wood siding characterizes this exterior. The absence of columns or posts gives a modern look to the covered porch.

Design X2804

Square Footage: 1,674

L **D**

● Stuccoed arches, multi-paned windows an a gracefully sloped roof accent the exterior of this Spanish-inspired design. Like the other two designs, the interior kitchen will efficient ly serve the dining room, covered dining porch and breakfast room with great ease. Blueprints for all three designs include detail for an optional non-basement plan.

Custom Alterations? See page 301 for customizing this plan to your specifications.

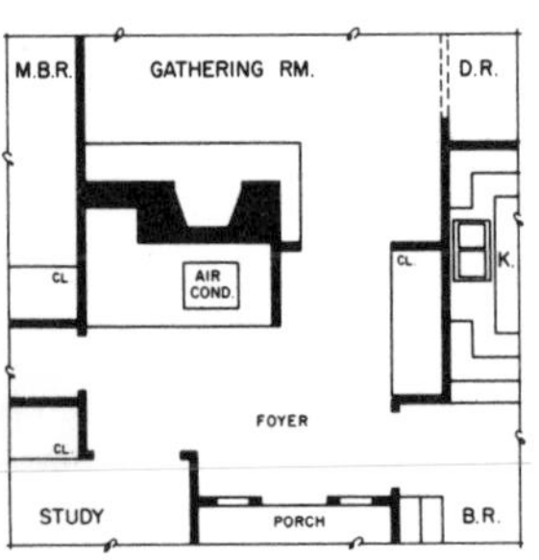

OPTIONAL NON-BASEMENT

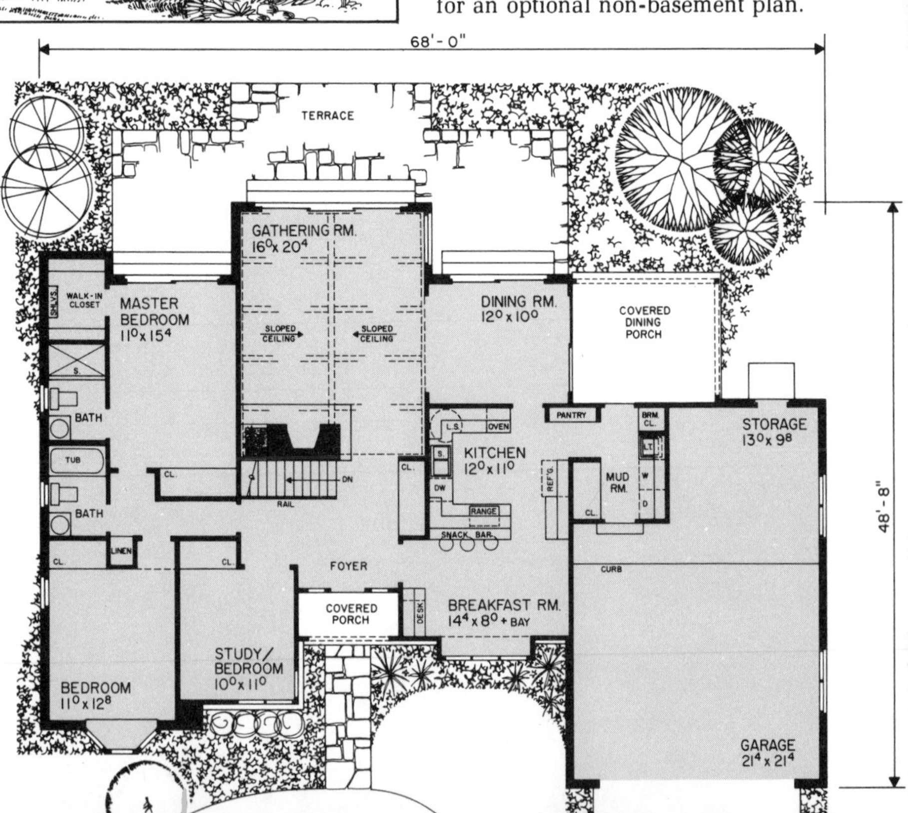

Design X2805

Square Footage: 1,547

L **D**

● Three completely different exterior facades share one compact, practical and economical floor plan. The major design variations are roof pitch, window placement and garage openings. Each design will hold its own when comparing the three exteriors. The design on the left is a romantic stone-and-shingle cottage design. This design, along with the other two designs presented here, is outstanding.

Design X2806

Square Footage: 1,584

L **D**

● This Tudor version of the plan is also very appealing. The living/dining room expands across the rear of the plan and has direct access to the covered porch. Notice the built-in planter adjacent to the open staircase leading to the basement.

Design X2807

Square Footage: 1,576

L **D**

● The contemporary version may be your choice. In addition to living/dining areas, there is a breakfast room that overlooks the covered porch. A desk, snack bar and mud room house laundry facilities and are near the U-shaped kitchen. The master bedroom has a private bath.

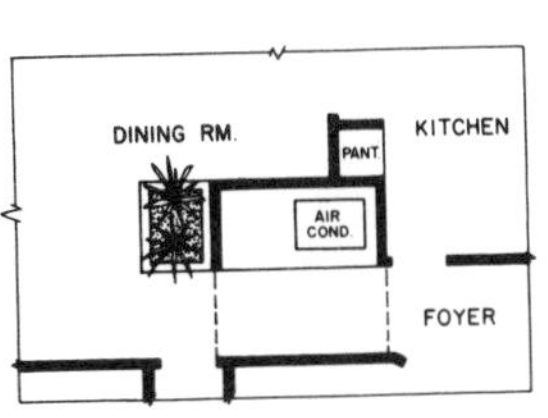

OPTIONAL NON-BASEMENT

Design X2705

Square Footage: 1,746

L D

Design X2706

Square Footage: 1,746

L D

Design X2704

Square Footage: 1,746

L D

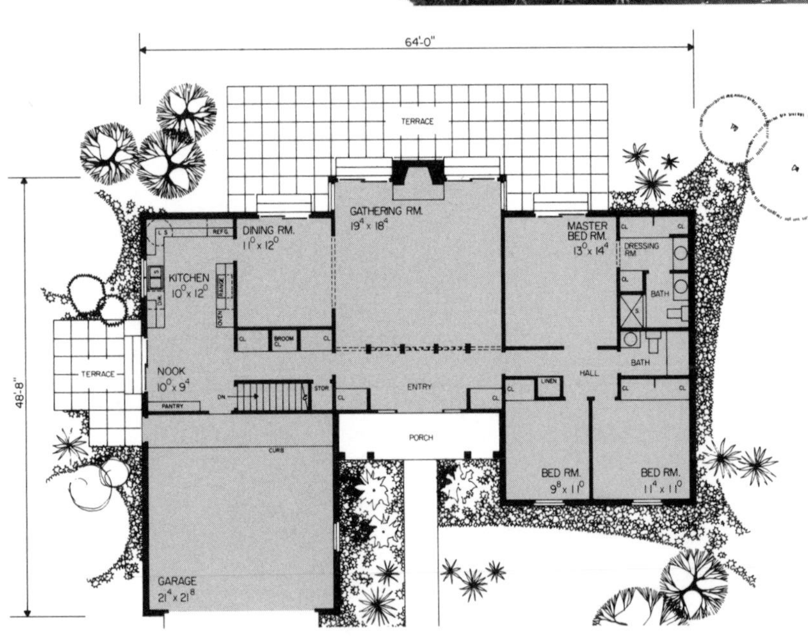

● Three different exteriors, but inside they all have the same livable plan. The gathering room is impressive in size and design with its fireplace flanked by sliding glass doors leading to the terrace. A formal dining room is nearby and leads to an L-shaped kitchen. Three bedrooms include a master suite with private dressing area and bath. For the French adaptation order X2705; for the contemporary version order X2706; and for the Colonial version order X2704.

● Here is a unique series of designs with three charming exterior adaptations—Southern Colonial, Western Ranch, French Provincial—and two distinctive floor plans. Each plan has a different design number and is less than 1,600 square feet.

● If you prefer the floor plan with a 26-foot keeping room, you should order the blueprints for Design X2611. The details for all three exteriors will be included. If you like the plan with the living room, dining room and family room, order blueprints for Design X2612 and get the details for all three exteriors.

● The two floor plans are similar in many ways. Each has a fireplace, 2½ baths, sliding glass doors to the rear terrace, a master bedroom with walk-in closet and private bath with stall shower and a basement. Two of the exteriors have covered porches. Be sure to notice the beamed ceilings and storage facilities.

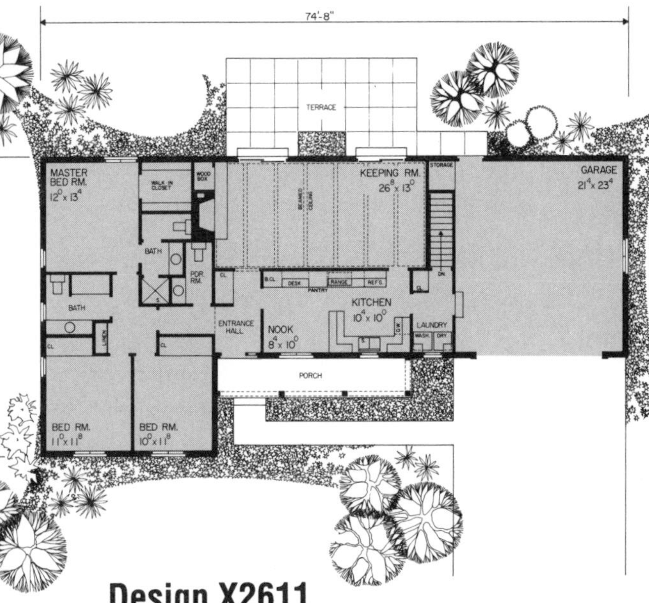

Design X2611

Square Footage: 1,557

L **D**

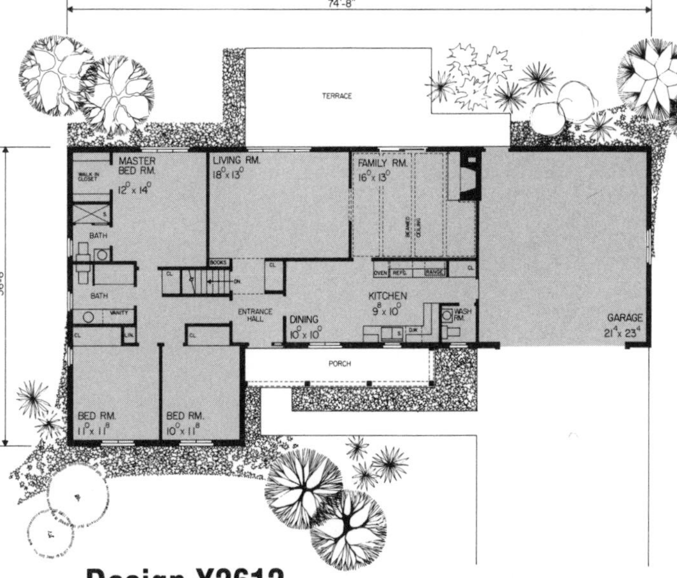

Design X2612

Square Footage: 1,571

L **D**

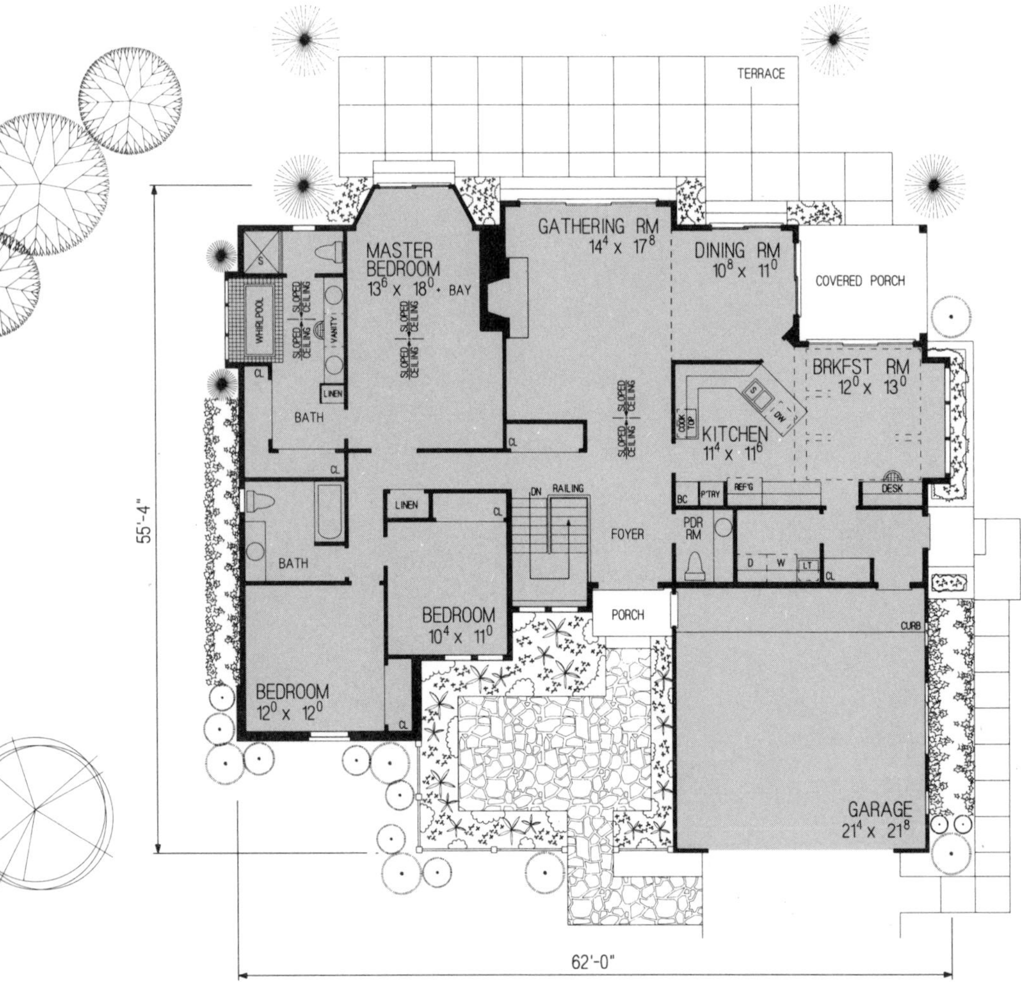

Design X3336

Square Footage: 2,022

● Compact and comfortable! This three-bedrooom home is a good consideration for a small family or empty-nester retirees. Of special note are the covered eating porch and sloped ceilings in the gathering room and master bedroom. A well-placed powder room is found at the front entry.

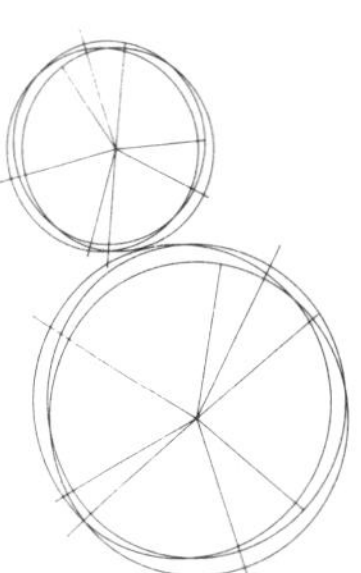

Design X3340

Square Footage: 1,611

● You may not decide to build this design simply because of its delightful covered porch. But it certainly will provide its share of enjoyment if this plan is your choice. Notice also how effectively the bedrooms are arranged out of the traffic flow of the house. One bedroom could double nicely as a TV room or study. The living room/dining area is highlighted by a fireplace, sliding glass doors to the porch, and an open staircase with built-in planter to the basement.

Design X1920

Square Footage: 1,600

L D

● This home offers a charming exterior with a truly great floor plan. The covered front porch at the entrance heralds outstanding features inside. The sleeping zone has three bedrooms and two full baths. Each of the bedrooms has its own walk-in closet. Note the efficient U-shaped kitchen with the family room and dining room to each side. There is also a laundry with wash room just off the garage. Blueprints for this design include details for both basement and non-basement construction.

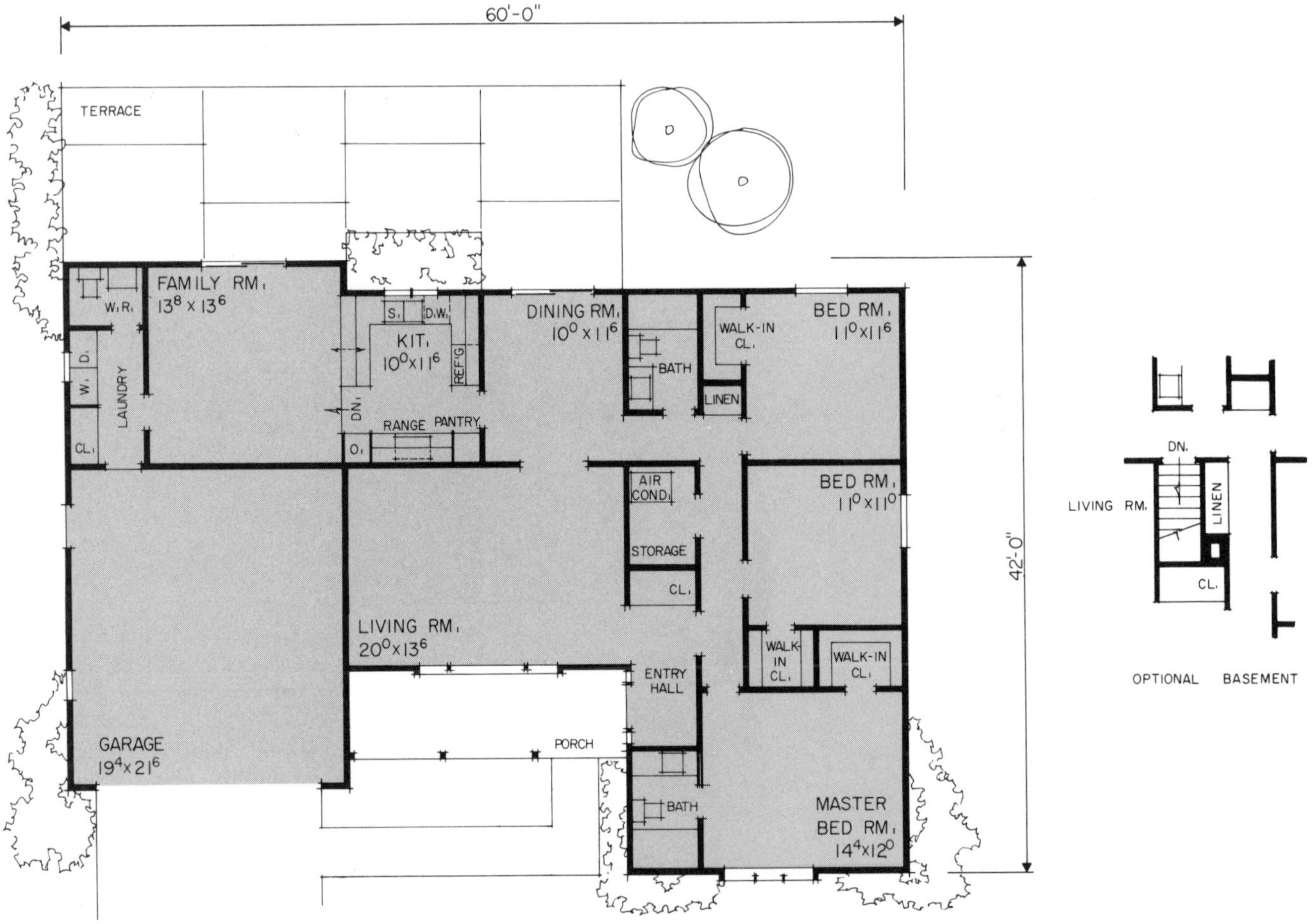

60'-0"
TERRACE
W.R.
FAMILY RM. $13^{8} \times 13^{6}$
W.
D.
LAUNDRY
CL.
S. D.W.
KIT. $10^{0} \times 11^{6}$
REFIG.
DN.
O.
RANGE PANTRY
DINING RM. $10^{0} \times 11^{6}$
BATH
WALK-IN CL.
LINEN
BED RM. $11^{0} \times 11^{6}$
AIR COND.
STORAGE
CL.
BED RM. $11^{0} \times 11^{0}$
42'-0"
LIVING RM. $20^{0} \times 13^{6}$
ENTRY HALL
WALK-IN CL.
WALK-IN CL.
PORCH
GARAGE $19^{4} \times 21^{6}$
BATH
MASTER BED RM. $14^{4} \times 12^{0}$

DN.
LIVING RM.
LINEN
CL.
OPTIONAL BASEMENT

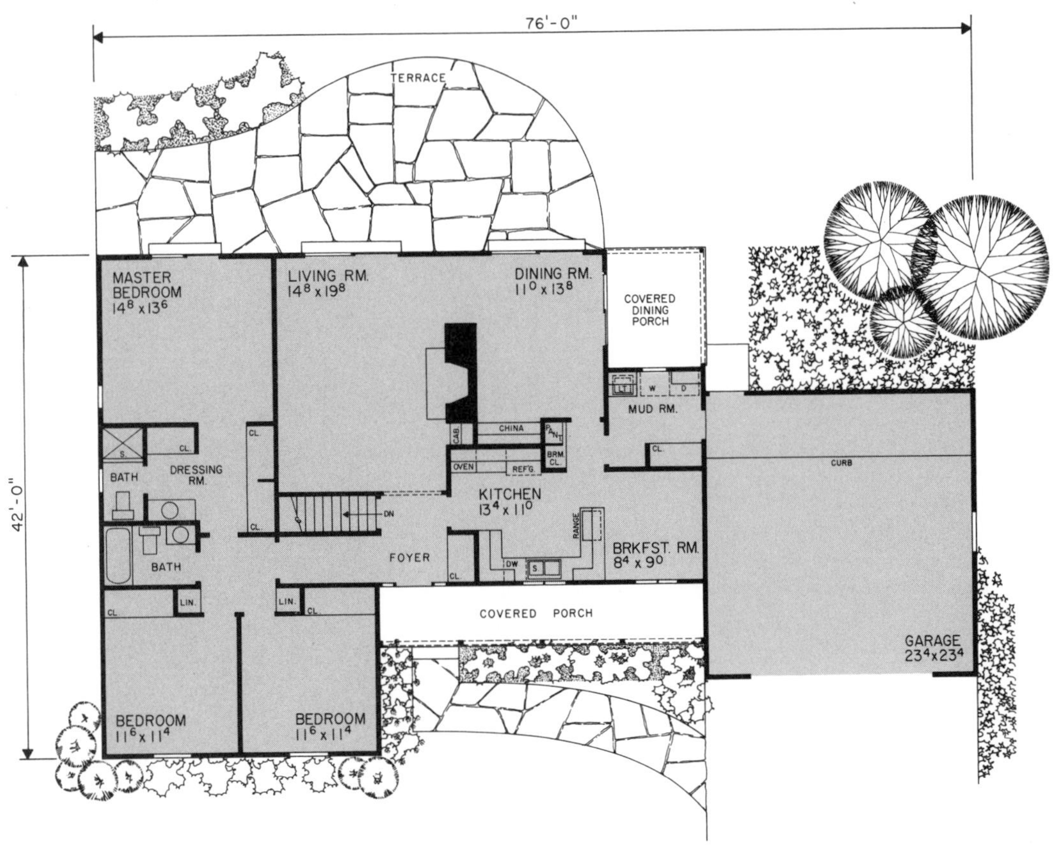

Design X2672

Square Footage: 1,717

L **D**

● The traditional appearance of this one-story is emphasized by its covered porch, multi-paned windows, narrow clapboard and vertical wood siding. Not only is the exterior eye-appealing but the interior has an efficient plan and is very livable. The front U-shaped kitchen will work with the breakfast room and mud room, which houses the laundry facilities. An access to the garage is here. Outdoor dining can be enjoyed on the covered porch adjacent to the dining room. Both of these areas, the porch and dining room, are convenient to the kitchen. Sleeping facilities consist of three bedrooms and two full baths. Note the three sets of sliding glass doors leading to the terrace.

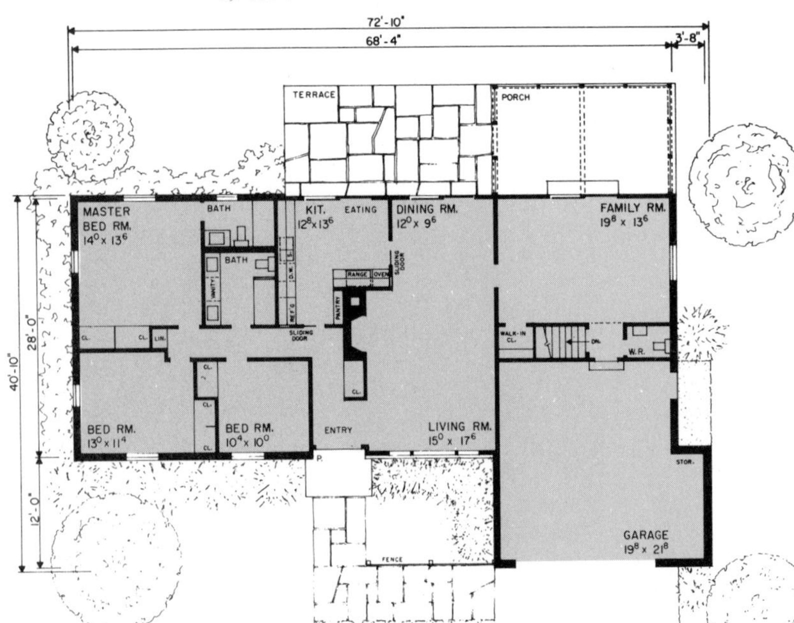

Design X1100

Square Footage: 1,752

● This modest sized, brick veneer home has a long list of things in its favor—from its appealing exterior to its feature-packed interior. All of the elements of its exterior complement each other to result in a symphony of attractive design features. The floor plan features three bedrooms, two full baths, an extra wash room, a family room, kitchen eating space, a formal dining area, two sets of sliding glass doors to the terrace and one set to the covered porch, built-in cooking equipment, a pantry and vanity with twin lavatories. Further, there is the living room fireplace, attached two-car garage with a bulk storage unit and a basement for extra storage and miscellaneous recreational activities. A fine investment.

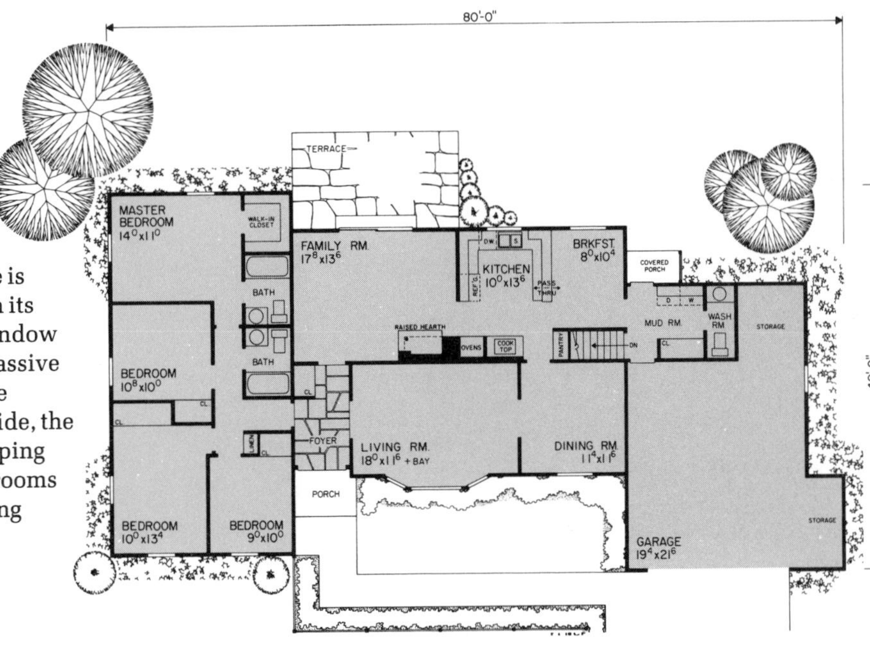

Design X1829

Square Footage: 1,800

L **D**

● All the charm of a traditional heritage is wrapped up in this U-shaped home with its narrow, horizontal siding, delightful window treatment and high-pitched roof. The massive center chimney, the bay window and the double front doors are plus features. Inside, the living potential is outstanding. The sleeping wing is self-contained and has four bedrooms and two baths. The large family and living rooms cater to divergent age groups.

Design X2360

Square Footage: 1,936

● There is no such thing as taking a fleeting glance at this charming home. Fine proportion and pleasing lines assure a long and rewarding study. Inside is a sunken living room with fireplace flanked by storage cabinets and bookshelves. The excellent kitchen is just a step from the dining room and nook.

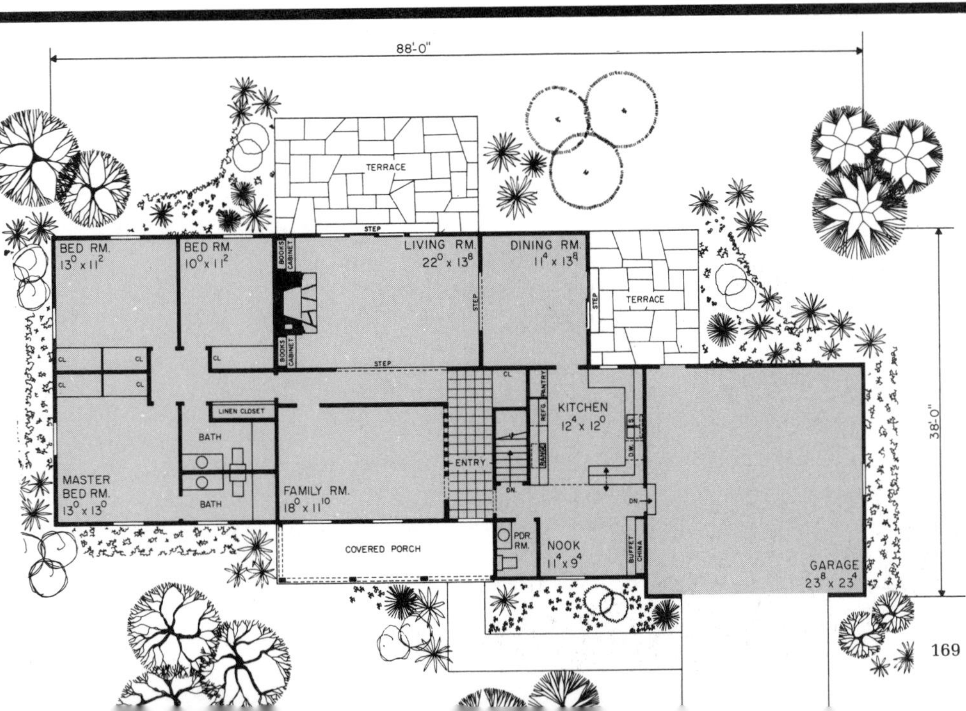

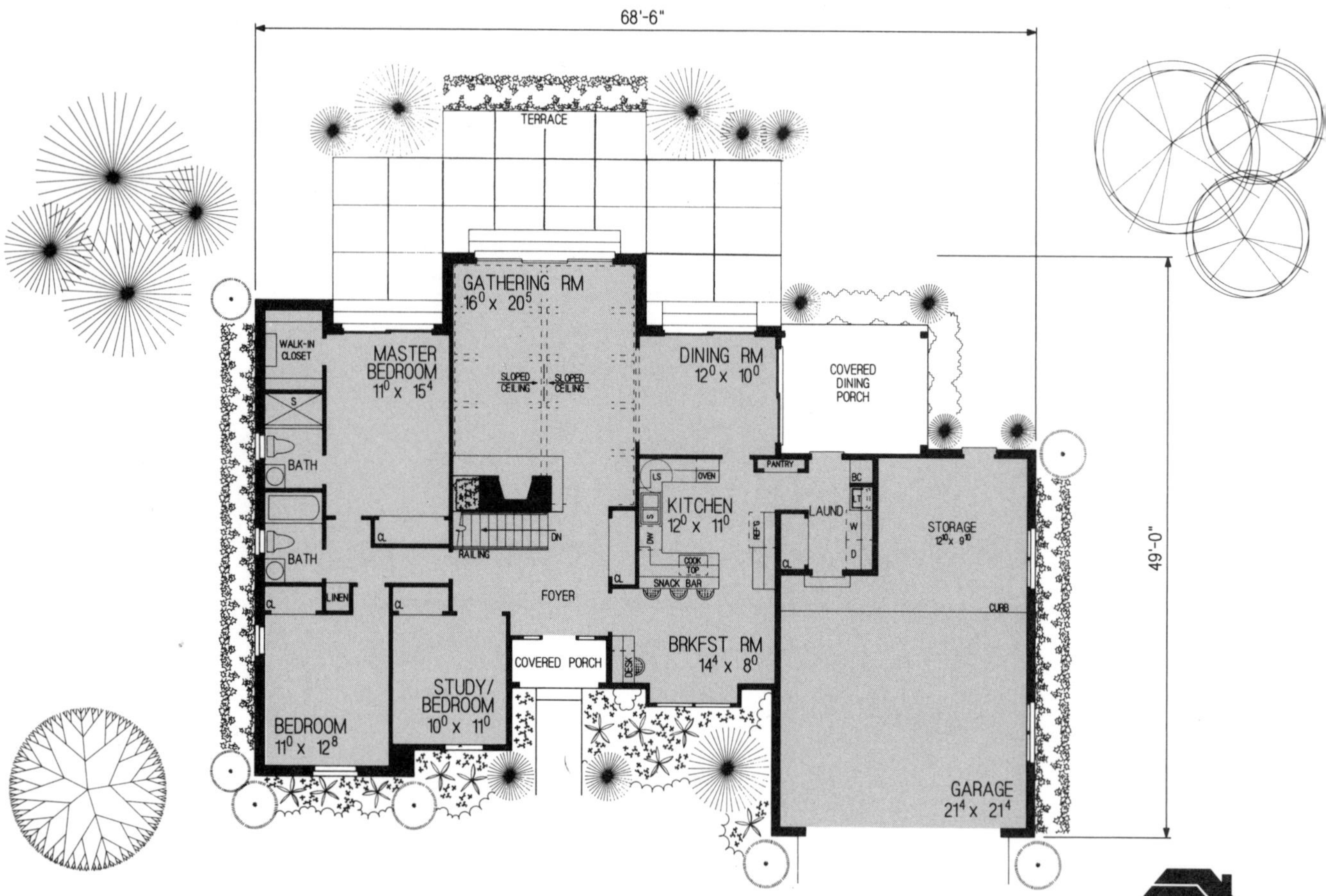

68'-6"

TERRACE

GATHERING RM
16^{0} x 20^{5}

SLOPED CEILING
SLOPED CEILING

WALK-IN CLOSET

MASTER BEDROOM
11^{0} x 15^{4}

S

BATH

BATH

CL

LINEN

RAILING

DN

DINING RM
12^{0} x 10^{0}

COVERED DINING PORCH

PANTRY

LS

OVEN

KITCHEN
12^{0} x 11^{0}

DW

COOK TOP

SNACK BAR

REF'G

LAUND

BC

W

D

STORAGE
12^{10} x 9^{10}

CURB

49'-0"

FOYER

COVERED PORCH

DESK

BRKFST RM
14^{4} x 8^{0}

BEDROOM
11^{0} x 12^{8}

STUDY/ BEDROOM
10^{0} x 11^{0}

GARAGE
21^{4} x 21^{4}

CUSTOMIZABLE

Custom Alterations? See page 301 for customizing this plan to your specifications.

Design X3345

Square Footage: 1,738

● This quaint shingled cottage offers an unexpected amount of living space in just over 1,700 square feet. The large gathering room with fireplace, dining room with covered porch, and kitchen with breakfast room handle formal parties as easily as they do the casual family get-together. Three bedrooms, one that could also serve as a study, are found in a separate wing of the house. Give special attention to the storage space in this home and the extra touches that set it apart from many homes of equal size.

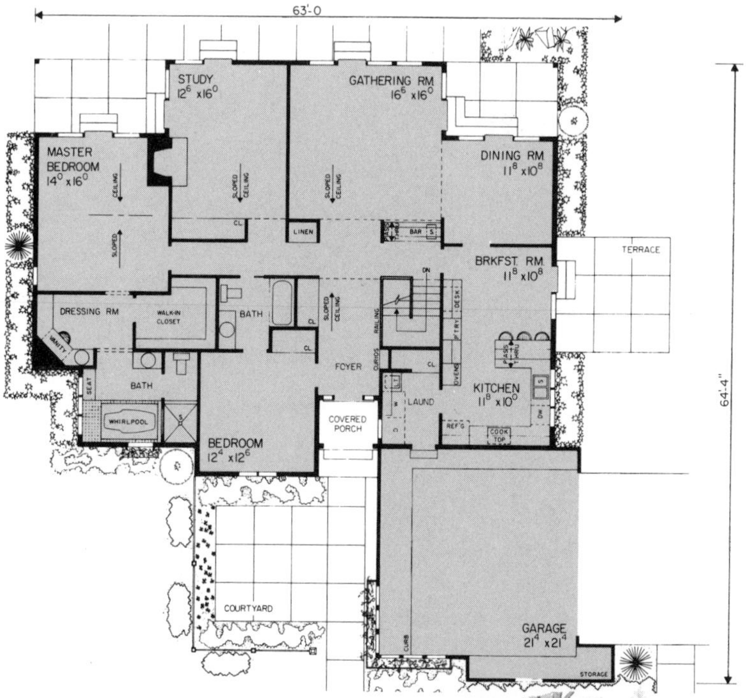

Design X2931

Square Footage: 1,998

● Little details make the difference. Consider these that make this such a charming showplace: master bedroom suite with separate dressing room, private vanities and whirlpool bath; an adjacent study with fireplace; roomy kitchen with breakfast area; spacious gathering room, rear and side terraces, attached two-car garage with storage.

CUSTOMIZABLE

Custom Alterations? See page 301 for customizing this plan to your specifications.

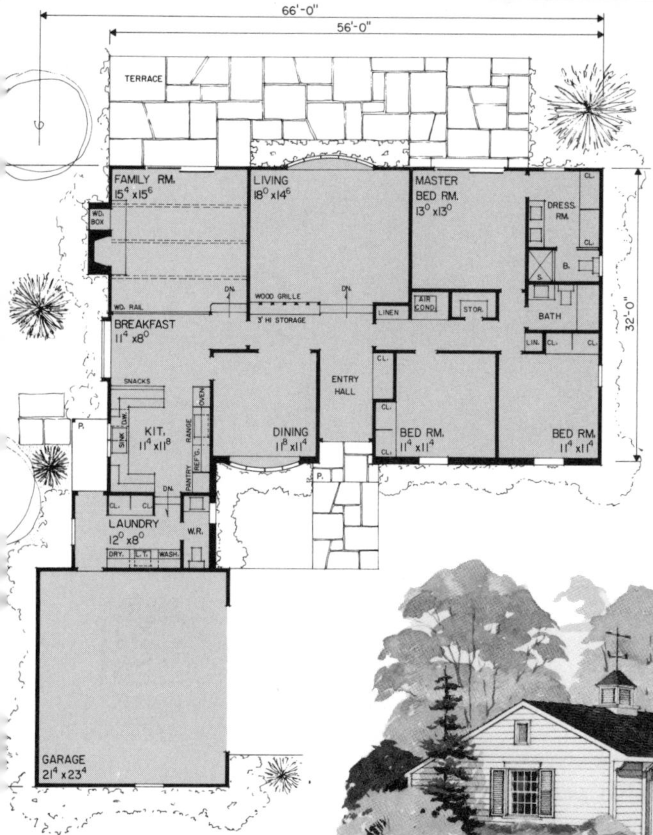

Design X1949

Square Footage: 1,992

D

● Surely a prize winner. Whether the contest be to pick the best in exterior appeal, or the finest in true livability, this L-shaped home will score at the top. The curving drive is a charming approach to the inviting front doors of the center entrance. The traditionally styled windows, the cupola, the contrasting materials of masonry and wood (or make it aluminum, if you prefer), the interesting roof lines and the excellent proportions are the exterior features which catch the eye. Inside, the highlights are, indeed, numerous. Of particular interest is the family room and the living room. Both are sunken to a depth of two steps, are free from traffic and look out upon the rear yard. That is a beamed ceiling in the family room.

Design X2603

Square Footage: 1,949

L **D**

● Surely it would be difficult to beat the appeal of this traditional one-story home. Its slightly modified U-shape with the two front facing gables, the bay window, the covered front porch and the interesting use of exterior materials all add to the exterior charm. Besides, there are three large bedrooms serviced by two full baths and three walk-in closets. The excellent kitchen is flanked by the formal dining room and the informal family room. Don't miss the pantry, the built-in oven and the pass-thru to the snack bar. The handy first floor laundry is strategically located to act as a mud room. The extra wash room is but a few steps away. The sizable living room highlights a fireplace and a picture window. Note the location of the basement stairs.

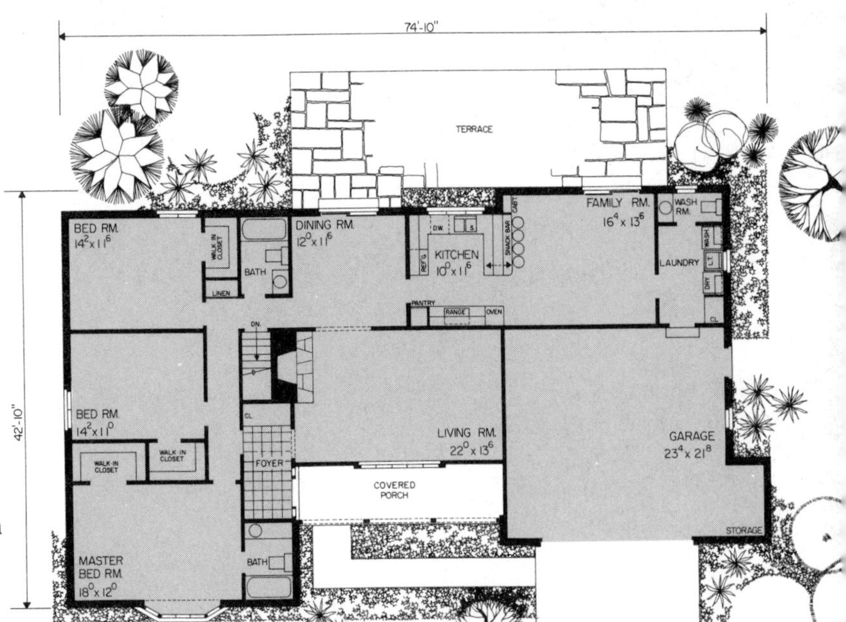

Design X1989

Square Footage: 2,282

L **D**

● High style with a plan as contemporary as today and tomorrow. There is, indeed, a feeling of coziness that emanates from the ground-hugging qualities of this picturesque home. Inside, there is livability galore. There's the sunken living room and the separate dining room to function as the family's formal living area. Then, over-looking the rear yard, there's the informal living area with its beamed ceiling family room, kitchen and adjacent breakfast room.

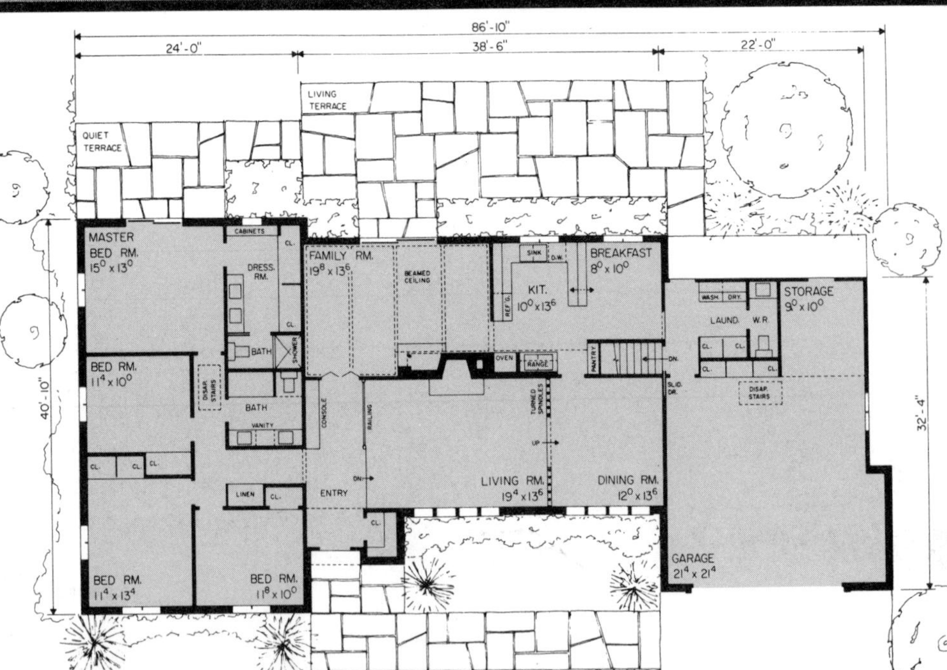

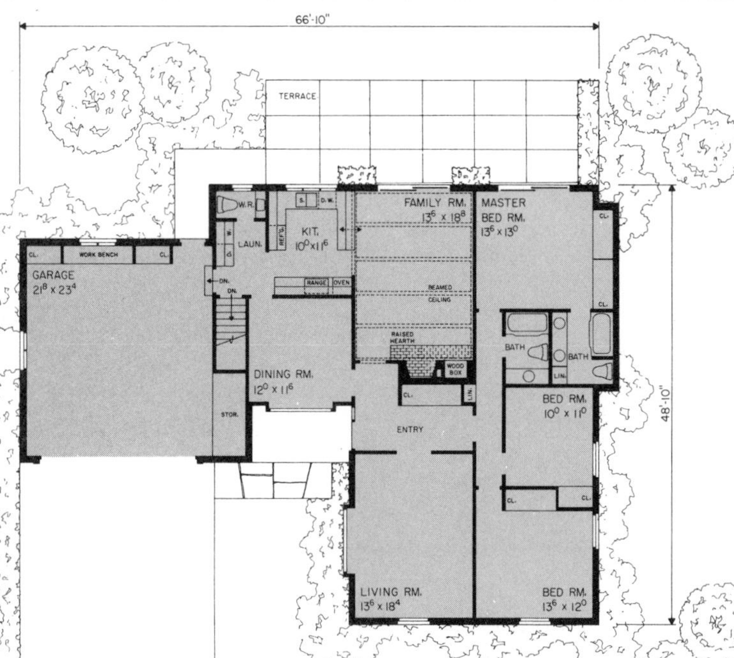

Design X2261

Square Footage: 1,825

● This distinctive L-shaped home virtually exudes traditional warmth and charm. And little wonder, for the architectural detailing is, indeed, exquisite. Notice the fine window detailing, the appealing cornice work, the attractiveness of the garage door and the massive chimney. The dovecote and the weather vane add to the design impact. The covered front porch shelters the entry which is strategically located to provide excellent traffic patterns. A service entry from the garage is conveniently located handy to the laundry, washroom, kitchen and stairs to the basement. The beamed-ceilinged family room will naturally be everyone's favorite spot for family living.

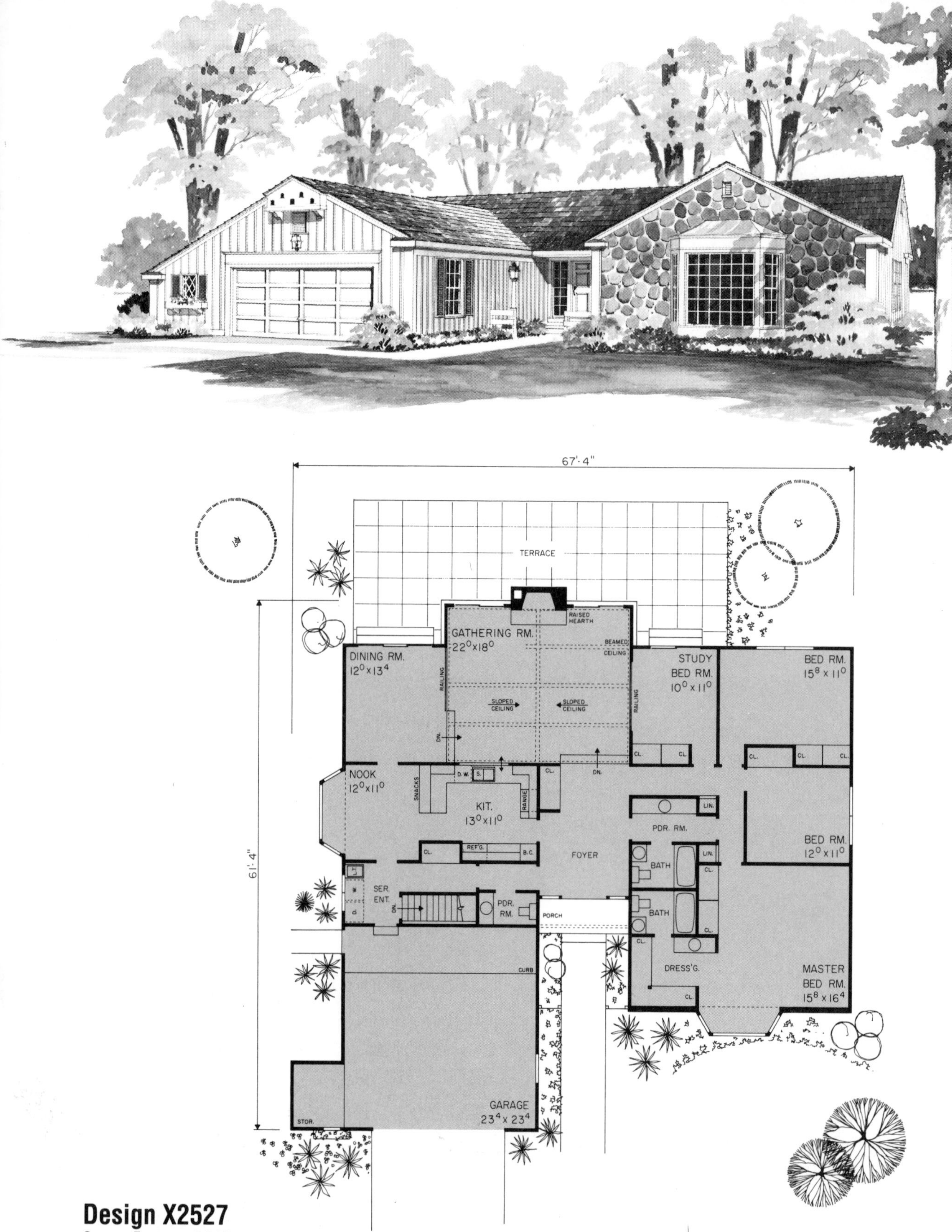

Design X2527

Square Footage: 2,392

D

● Vertical boards and battens, fieldstone, bay window, a dovecote, a gas lamp and a recessed front entrance are among the appealing exterior features of this U-shaped design. Through the double front doors, flanked by glass side lites, one enters the spacious foyer. Straight ahead is the cozy sunken gathering room with its sloping, beamed ceiling, raised hearth fireplace and two sets of sliding glass doors to the rear terrace. To the right of the foyer is the sleeping wing with its three bedrooms, study (make it the fourth bedroom if you wish) and two baths. To the left is the strategically located powder room and large kitchen with its delightful nook and bay window.

Design X2867

Square Footage: 2,388

● A live-in relative would be very comfortable in this home. This design features a self-contained suite (473 sq. ft.) consisting of a bedroom, bath, living room and kitchenette with dining area. This suite is nestled behind the garage away from the main areas of the house. The rest of this traditional, one-story house, faced with fieldstone and vertical wood siding, is also very livable. One whole wing houses the four family bedrooms and bath facilities. The center of the plan has a front, U-shaped kitchen and breakfast room. The formal dining room and large gathering room will enjoy the view, and access to, the backyard. The large, covered porch will receive much use.

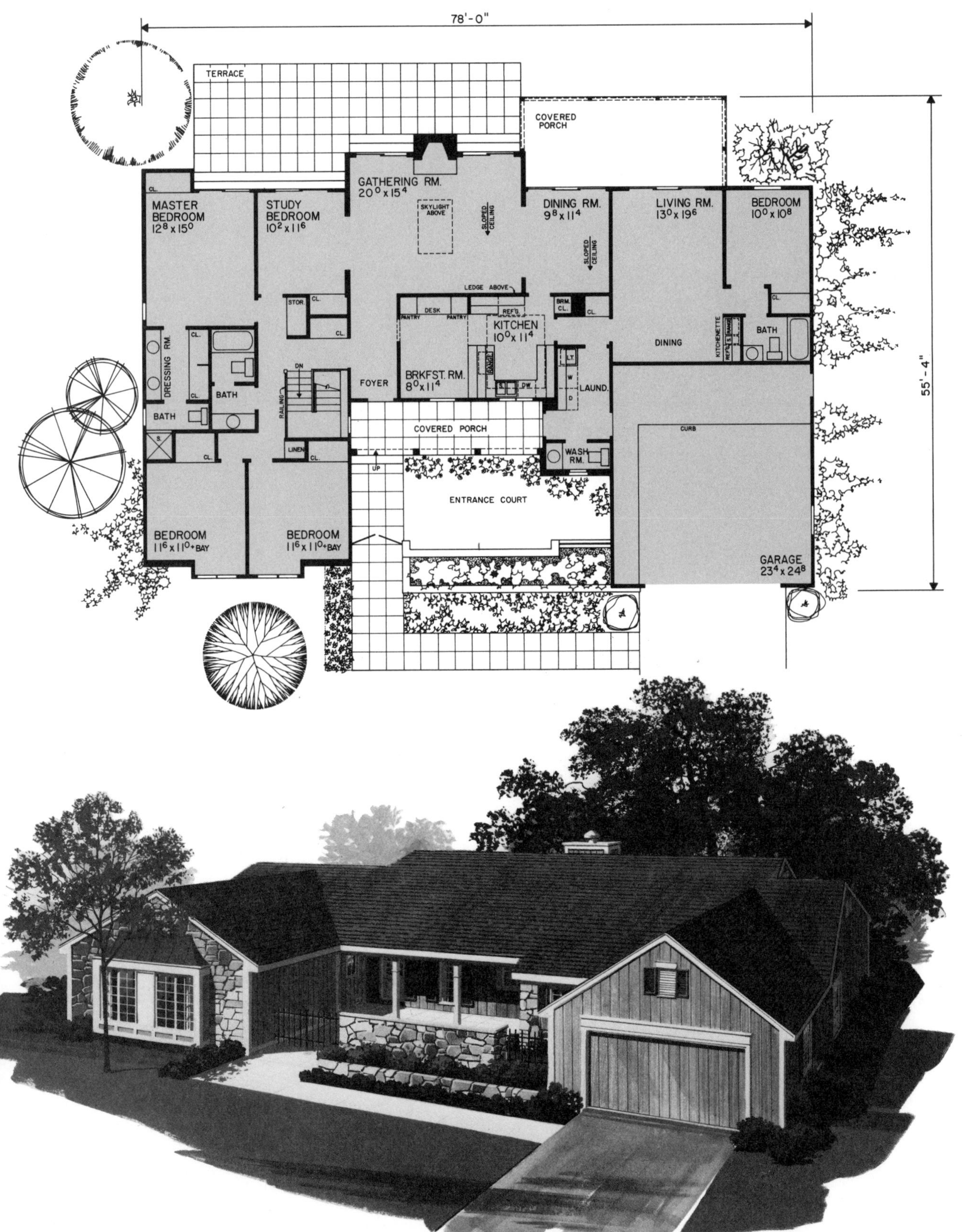

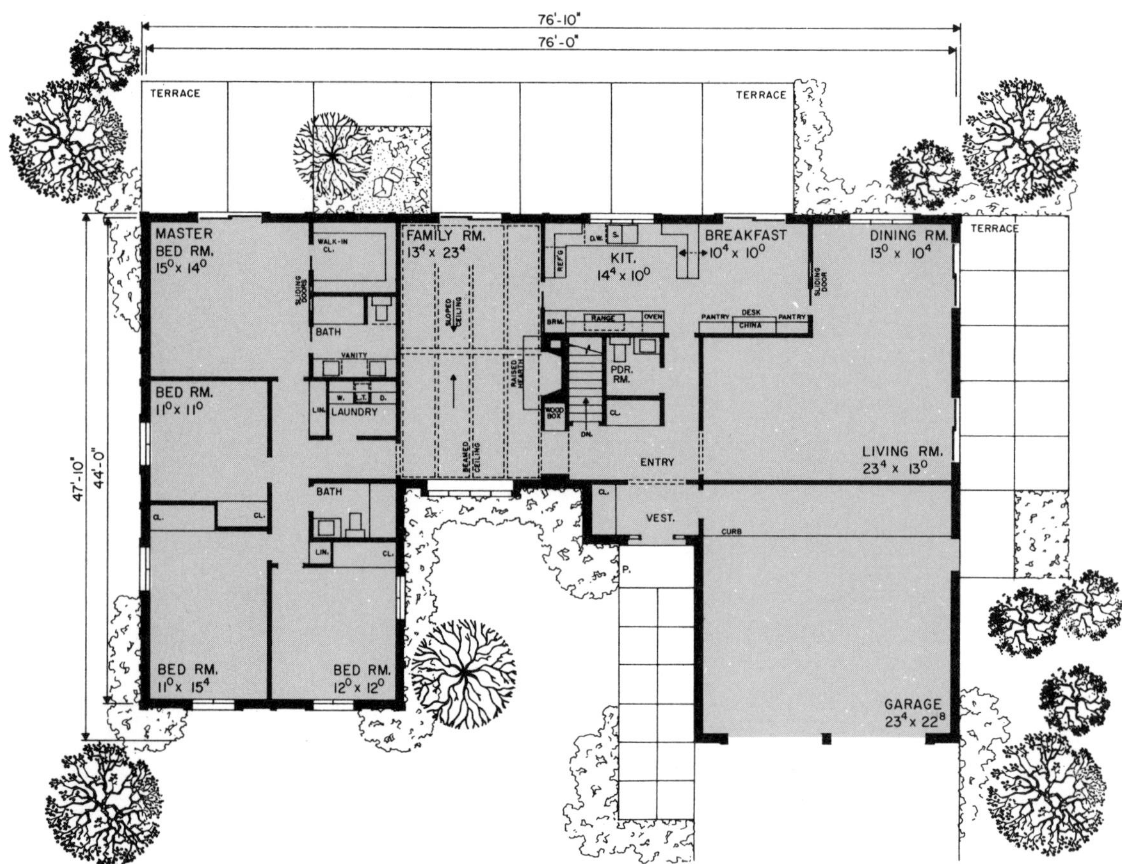

Design X2142

Square Footage: 2,450

D

● Adaptations of Old England have become increasingly popular in today's building scene. And little wonder; for many of these homes when well-designed have a very distinctive charm. Here is certainly a home which will be like no other in its neighborhood. Its very shape adds an extra measure of uniqueness. And inside, there is all the livability the exterior seems to fortell. The sleeping wing has four bedrooms, two full baths and the laundry room — just where the soiled linen originates. The location of the family room is an excellent one. It is convenient for children because their traffic usually flows between family room and bedrooms. The spacious formal living and dining area will enjoy its privacy and be great fun to furnish.

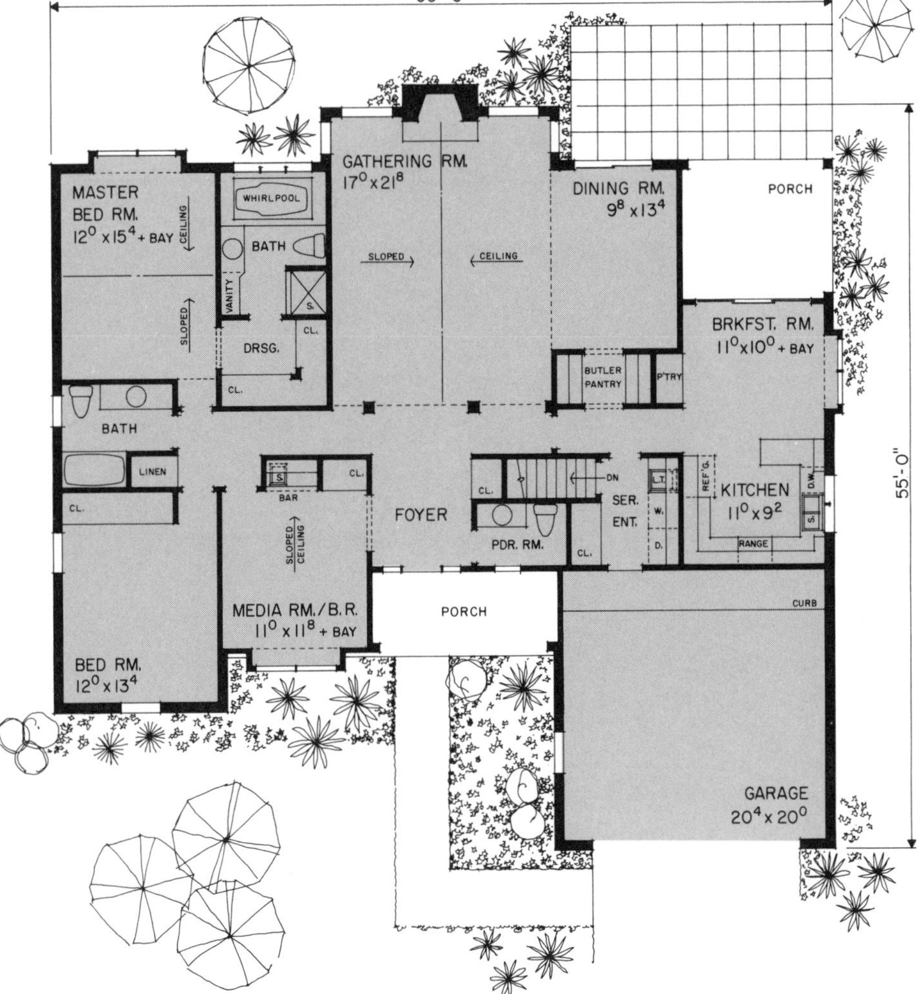

Design X3376

Square Footage: 1,999

L **D**

● Small families or empty nesters will appreciate the layout of this traditional ranch. The foyer opens to the gathering room with fireplace and sloped ceiling. The dining room is open to the gathering room for entertaining ease and contains sliding doors to a rear terrace. The breakfast room also provides access to a covered porch for dining outdoors. The media room to the left of the home offers a bay window and a wet bar, or it can double as a third bedroom.

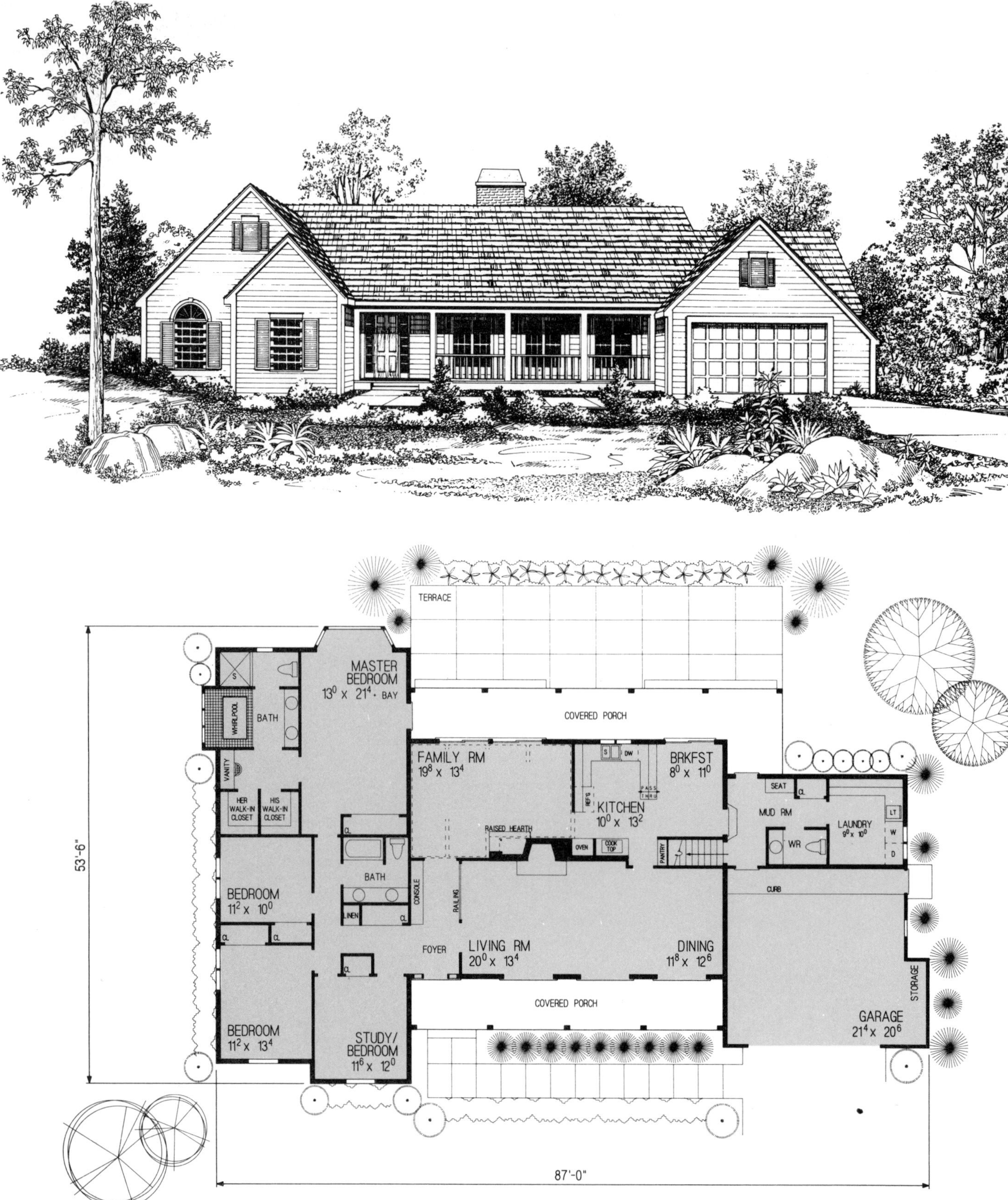

Design X3348 Square Footage: 2,549

● Covered porches front and rear will be the envy of the neighborhood when this house is built. The interior plan meets family needs perfectly in well-zoned areas: a sleeping wing with four bedrooms and two baths, a living zone with formal and informal gathering space, and a work zone with U-shaped kitchen and laundry with washroom. The two-car garage has a huge storage area.

Design X3332

Square Footage: 2,168

● Nothing completes a traditional-style home quite as well as a country kitchen with fireplace. Notice also the sloped-ceiling living room and well-appointed master suite. A handy washroom is near the laundry, just off the garage.

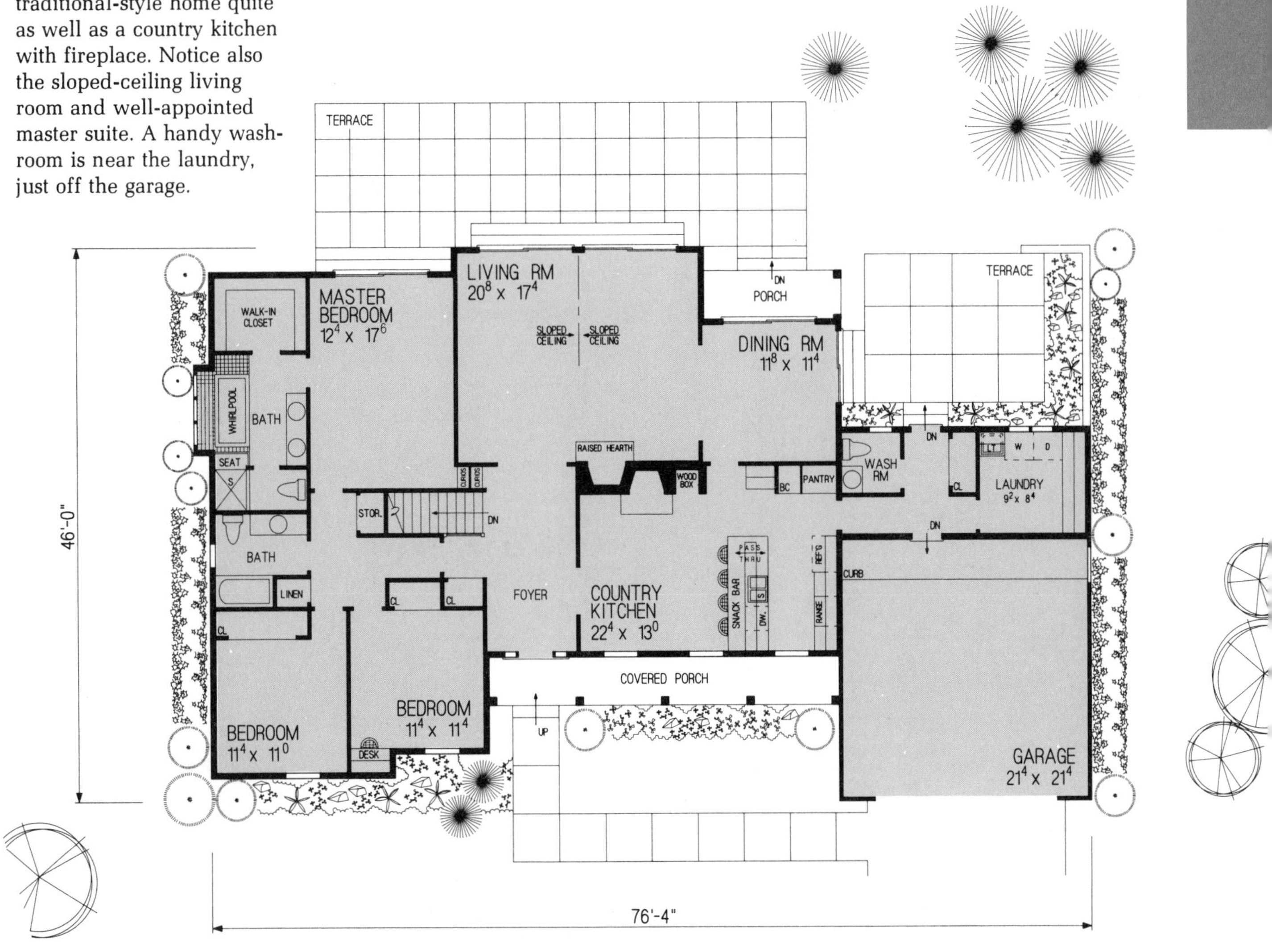

TERRACE

LIVING RM 20^8 x 17^4

SLOPED CEILING ← → SLOPED CEILING

PORCH

DN

TERRACE

MASTER BEDROOM 12^4 x 17^6

WALK-IN CLOSET

WHIRLPOOL

BATH

SEAT

S

DINING RM 11^8 x 11^4

RAISED HEARTH

WOOD BOX

CURIOS

CURIOS

STOR.

DN

BC

PANTRY

WASH RM

DN

CL

LAUNDRY 9^2 x 8^4

LT

W

D

DN

BATH

LINEN

CL

CL

CL

FOYER

COUNTRY KITCHEN 22^4 x 13^0

PASS THRU

SNACK BAR

S

DW.

REF'G

RANGE

CURB

46'-0"

COVERED PORCH

UP

BEDROOM 11^4 x 11^0

BEDROOM 11^4 x 11^4

DESK

GARAGE 21^4 x 21^4

76'-4"

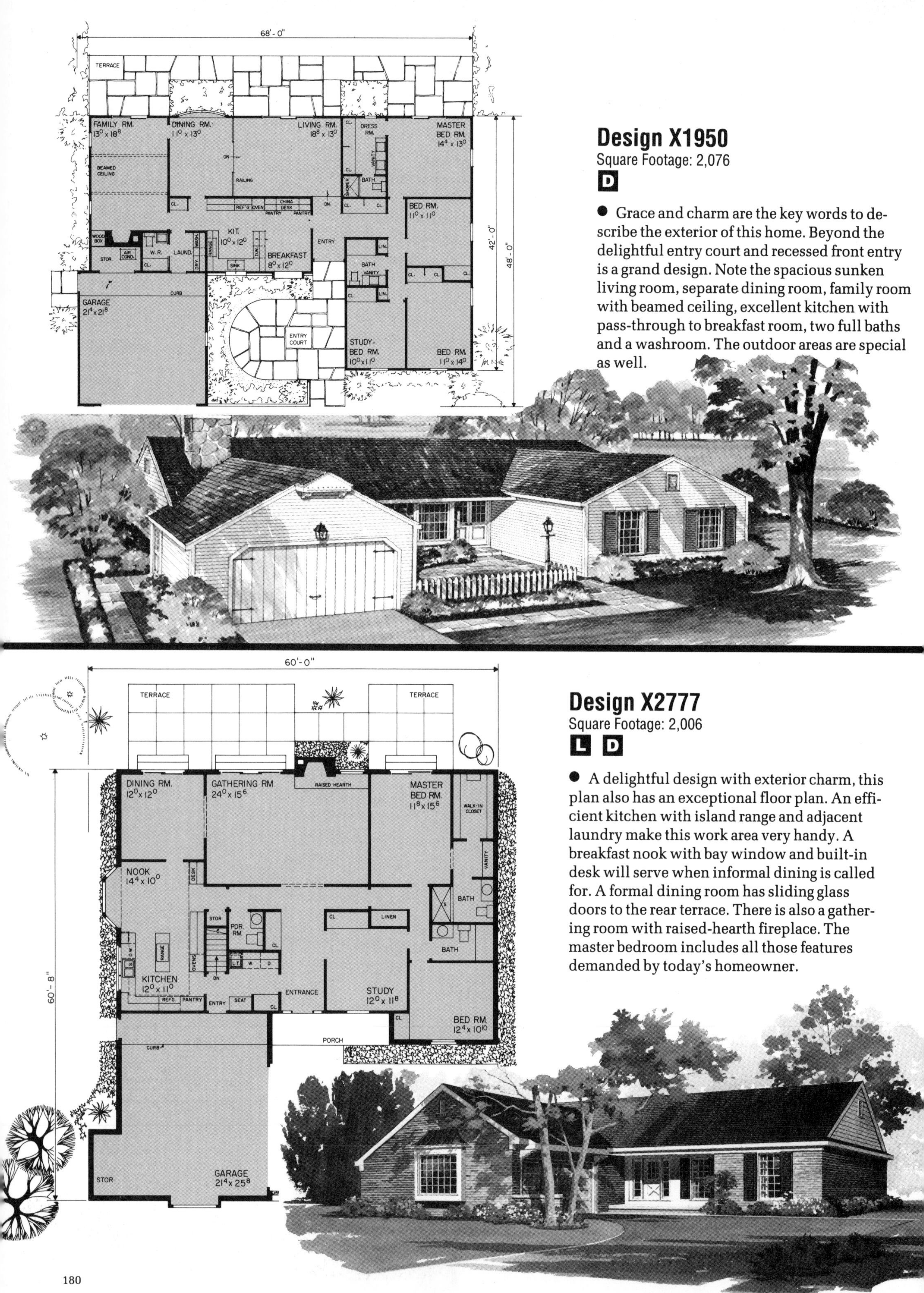

Design X1950

Square Footage: 2,076

D

● Grace and charm are the key words to describe the exterior of this home. Beyond the delightful entry court and recessed front entry is a grand design. Note the spacious sunken living room, separate dining room, family room with beamed ceiling, excellent kitchen with pass-through to breakfast room, two full baths and a washroom. The outdoor areas are special as well.

Design X2777

Square Footage: 2,006

L **D**

● A delightful design with exterior charm, this plan also has an exceptional floor plan. An efficient kitchen with island range and adjacent laundry make this work area very handy. A breakfast nook with bay window and built-in desk will serve when informal dining is called for. A formal dining room has sliding glass doors to the rear terrace. There is also a gathering room with raised-hearth fireplace. The master bedroom includes all those features demanded by today's homeowner.

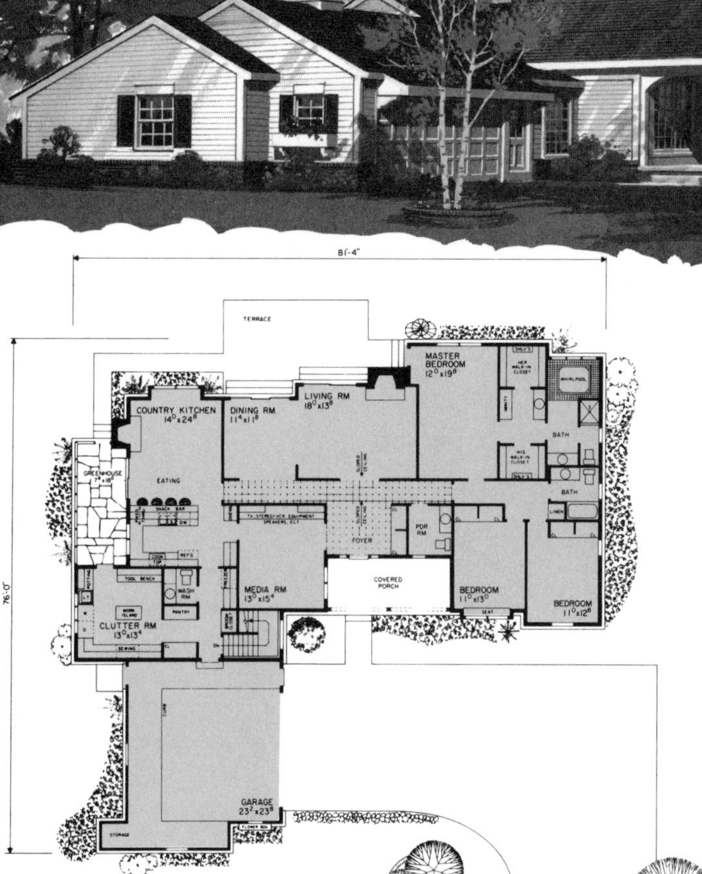

Design X2880

Living Area: 2,758 square feet
Greenhouse: 149 square feet
Total: 2,907 square feet

L **D**

● This comfortable traditional home offers plenty of modern livability. A clutter room off the two-car garage is the perfect space for a workbench, sewing and hobbies. Across the hall is a media room and nearby is the country kitchen with attached greenhouse. There are also formal dining and living rooms, a covered porch, and three bedrooms including a master suite.

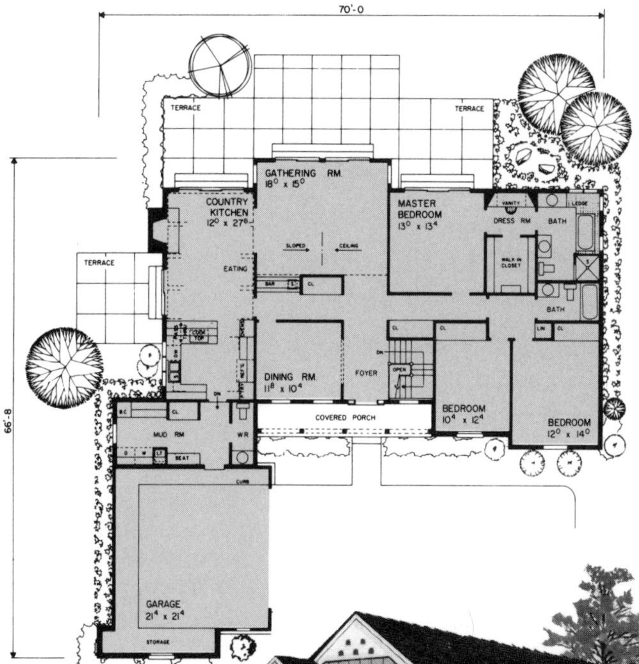

Design X2916

Square Footage: 2,129

● The covered front porch of this Early American-styled house, provides a shelter for the inviting panelled front door. Inside, the plan offers wonderful formal and informal living patterns. The country kitchen has a beamed ceiling and a fireplace. The U-shaped work center is most efficient. There are two dining areas — an informal eating space and a formal dining room. The more formal gathering room is spacious and sports a sloped ceiling and two sets of sliding glass doors to the rear terrace.

Design X2778

Square Footage: 2,761

D

● No matter what the occasion, family and friends alike will enjoy the sizable gathering room in this home. This room has a through-fireplace to the study and two sets of sliding glass doors to the large, rear terrace. Indoor/outdoor living also can be enjoyed from the dining room, study and master bedroom. There is also a covered porch accessible through sliding glass doors in the dining room and breakfast nook.

Design X1346

Square Footage: 1,644

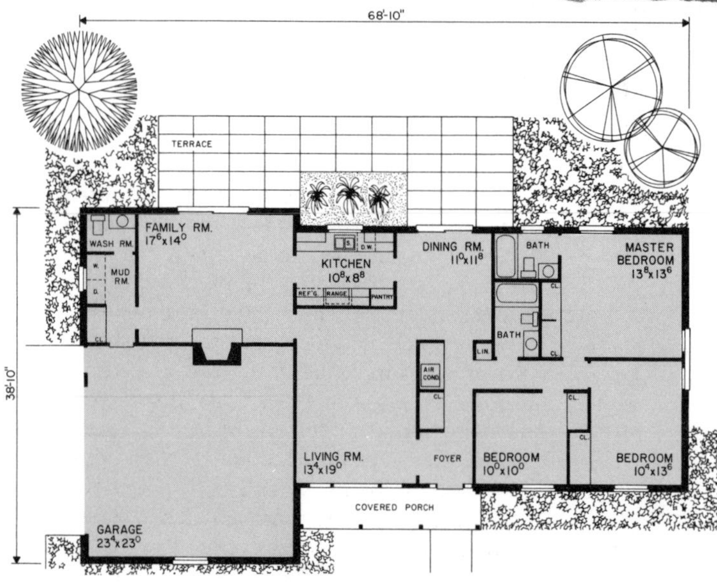

● Whether you enter through the service door of the attached garage, or through the centered front entry your appreciation of what this plan has to offer will grow. The mud room area is certainly an outstanding feature. Traffic flows from this area to the informal family room with its fireplace and access to the rear terrace.

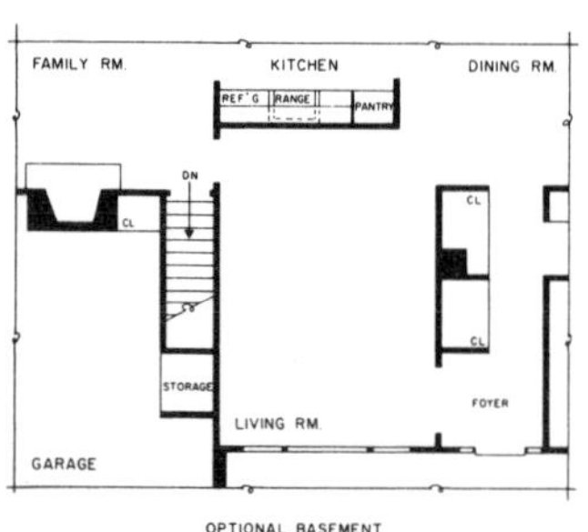

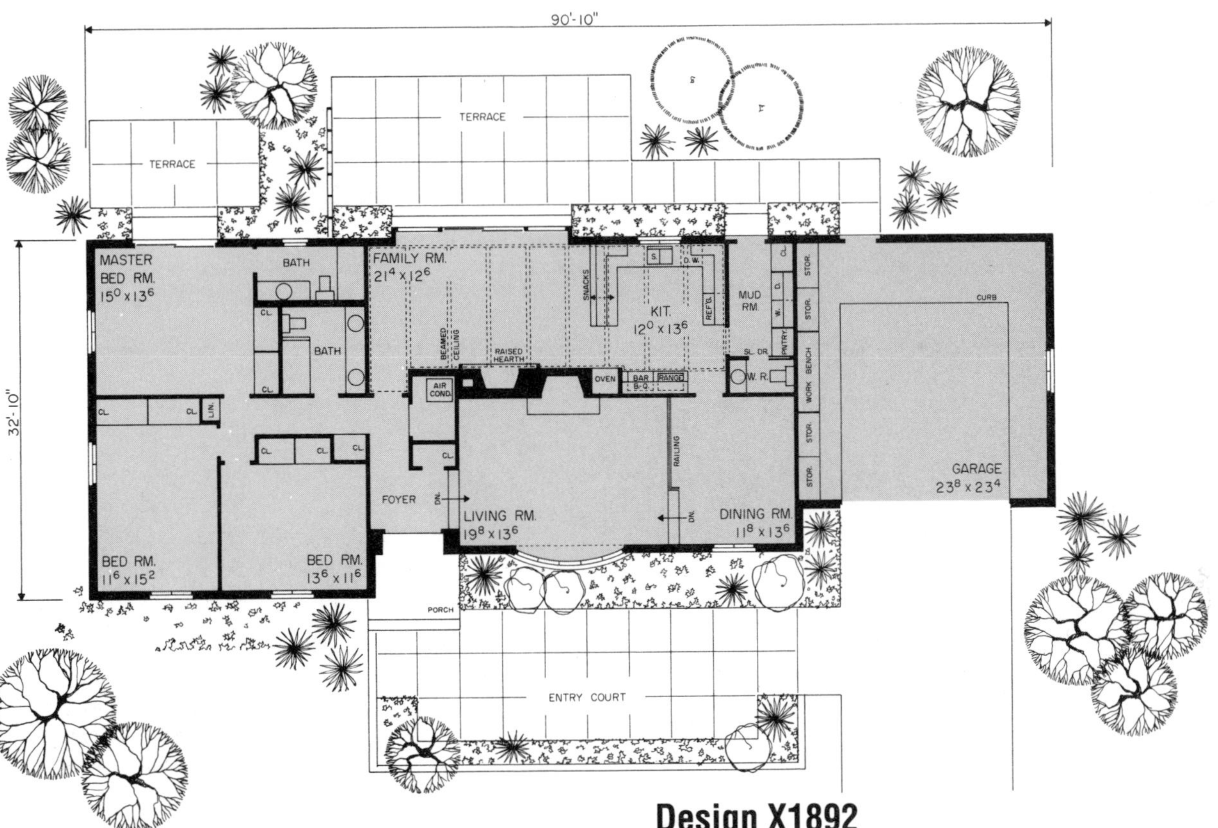

Design X1892

Square Footage: 2,036

L **D**

OPTIONAL BASEMENT

FOYER

LIVING RM.

PORCH

● The romance of French Provincial is captured here by the hip-roof masses, the charm of the window detailing, the brick quoins at the corners, the delicate dentil work at the cornices, the massive centered chimney, and the recessed double front doors. The slightly raised entry court completes the picture. The basic floor plan is a favorite of many. And little wonder, for all areas work well together, while still maintaining a fine degree of separation of functions. The highlight of the interior, perhaps, will be the sunken living room. The family room, with its beamed ceiling, will not be far behind in its popularity. The separate dining room, mud room, efficient kitchen, complete the livability.

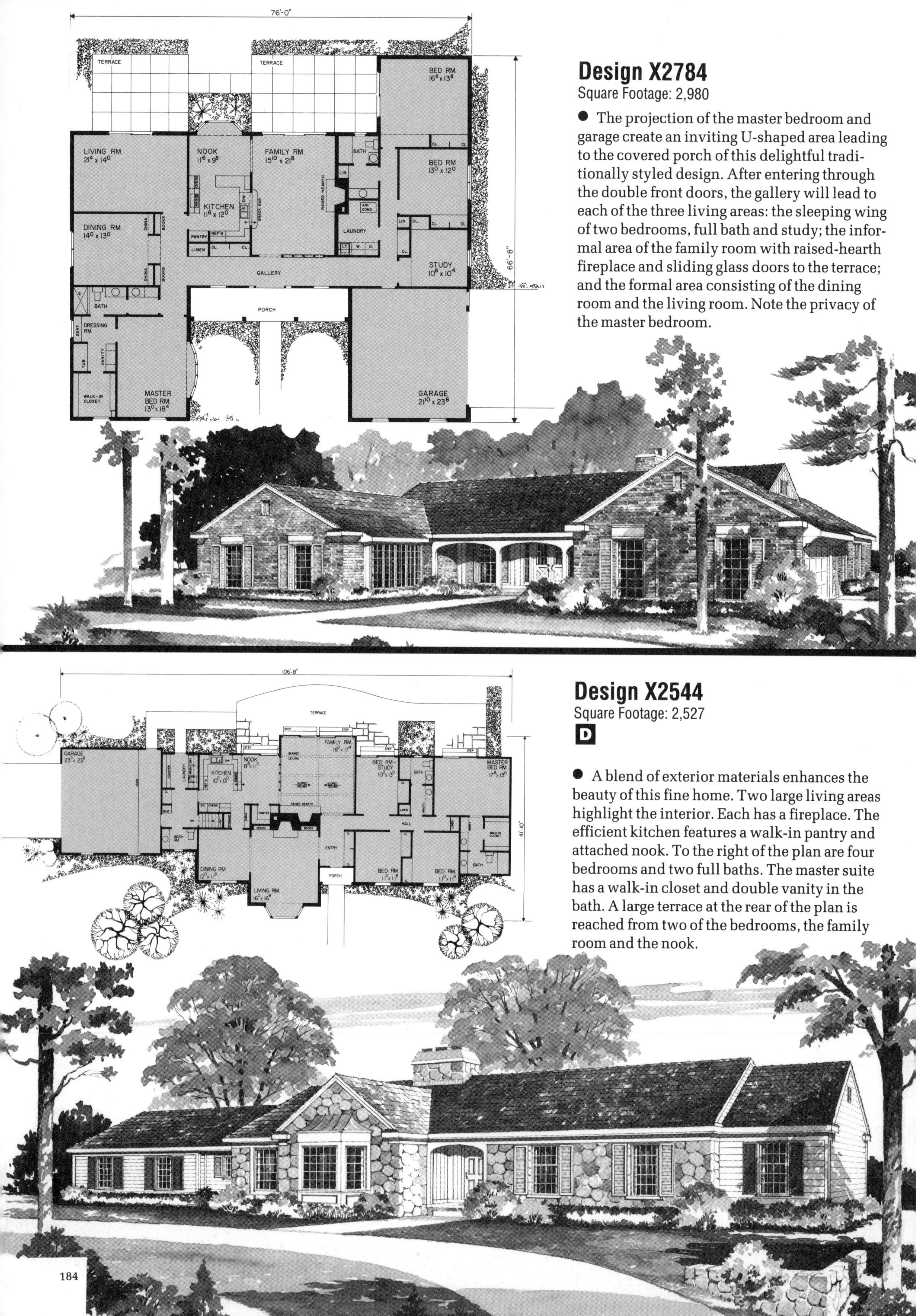

Design X2784

Square Footage: 2,980

● The projection of the master bedroom and garage create an inviting U-shaped area leading to the covered porch of this delightful traditionally styled design. After entering through the double front doors, the gallery will lead to each of the three living areas: the sleeping wing of two bedrooms, full bath and study; the informal area of the family room with raised-hearth fireplace and sliding glass doors to the terrace; and the formal area consisting of the dining room and the living room. Note the privacy of the master bedroom.

Design X2544

Square Footage: 2,527

D

● A blend of exterior materials enhances the beauty of this fine home. Two large living areas highlight the interior. Each has a fireplace. The efficient kitchen features a walk-in pantry and attached nook. To the right of the plan are four bedrooms and two full baths. The master suite has a walk-in closet and double vanity in the bath. A large terrace at the rear of the plan is reached from two of the bedrooms, the family room and the nook.

Design X2181

Square Footage: 2,612

L **D**

● It is hard to imagine a home with any more eye-appeal than this one. It is the complete picture of charm. The interior is just as outstanding. Sliding glass doors permit the large, master bedroom, quiet, living room and all-purpose family room to function directly with the outdoors. Two fireplaces, built-in china cabinets, bookshelves, complete laundry and kitchen pass-thru to breakfast room are extra features. Although the illustration of this home shows natural quarried stone, you may wish to substitute brick or even siding.

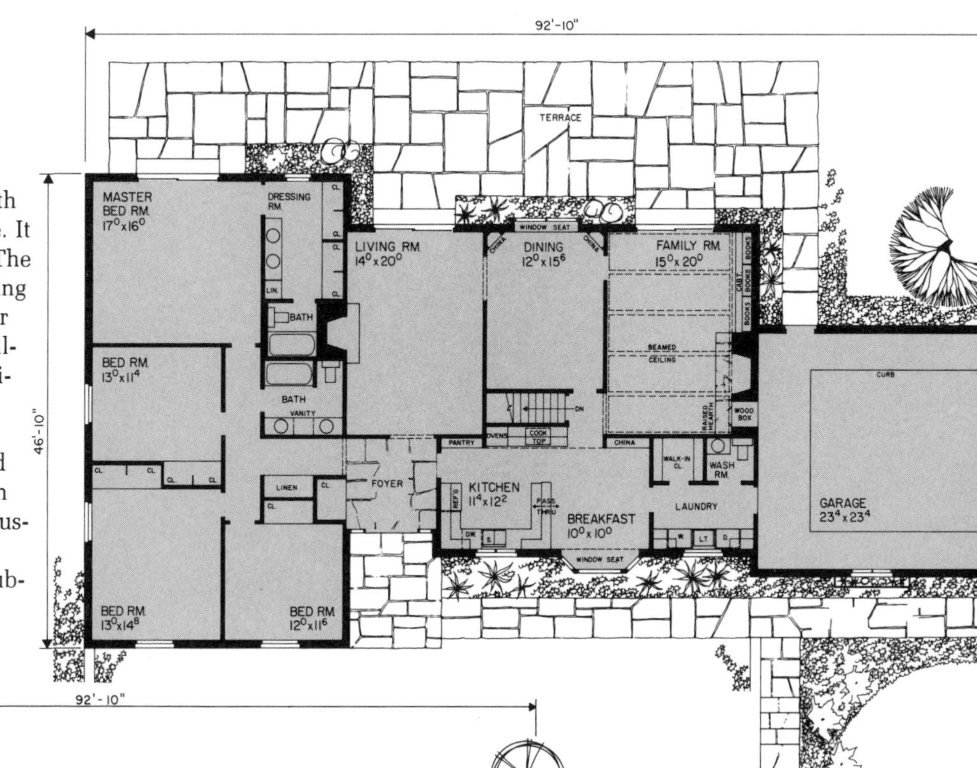

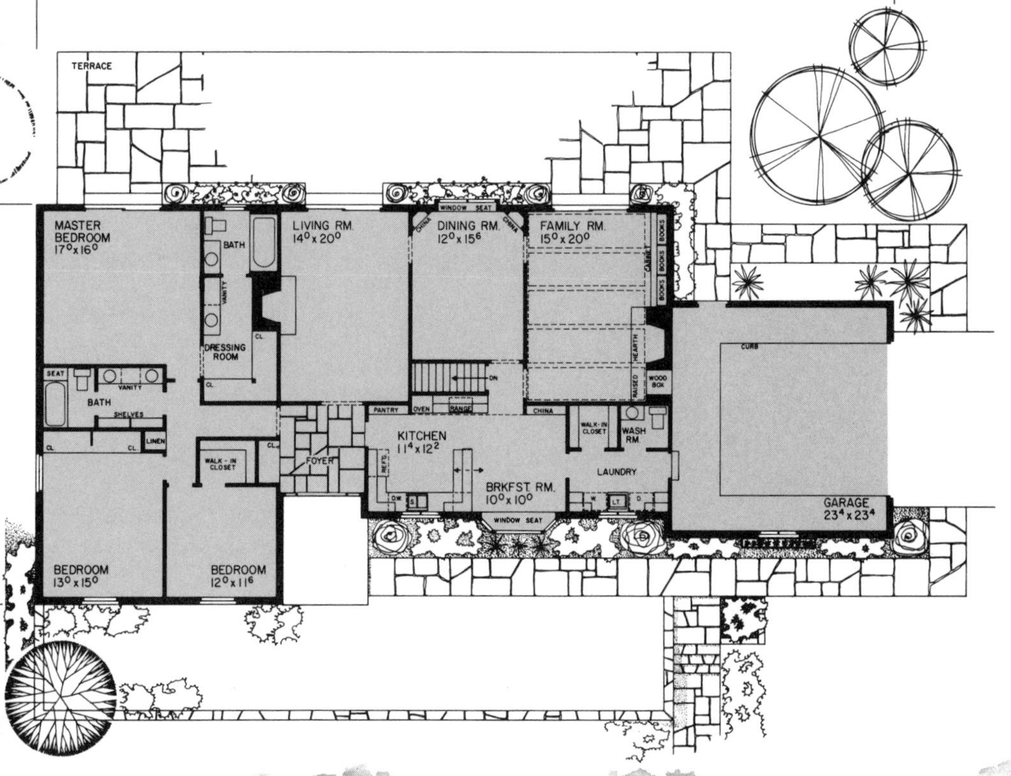

Design X2675

Square Footage: 2,478

D

● Many extra features have been designed into this delightfully traditional home. Bookshelves and cabinets are in the family room, china cabinets and a window seat are in the dining room, a second window seat is in the breakfast room, a large dressing room with vanity is in the master bedroom and the list can go on. Two fireplaces, one in each of the living areas. If you like this design, but are in need of a four bedroom home, please order Design X2181 above.

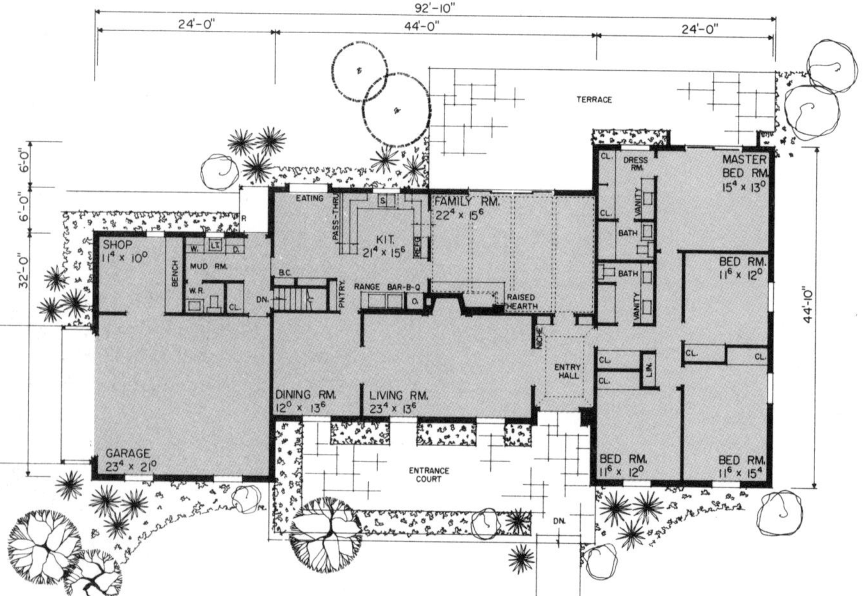

Design X1761

Square Footage: 2,548

L D

● Low, strong roof lines and solid, enduring qualities of brick give this house a permanent, here-to-stay appearance. Bedroom wing is isolated, and the baths and closets deaden noise from the rest of the house. Center fireplaces in family and living rooms make furniture arrangement easy. There are a number of extras - a workshop, an unusually large garage, and an indoor barbecue. Garage has easy access to both basement and kitchen area. There are two eating areas - a formal dining room and a breakfast nook next to the delightful kitchen.

Design X2209

Square Footage: 2,659

● Such an impressive home would, indeed, be difficult to top. And little wonder when you consider the myraid of features this one-story Colonial possesses. Consider the exquisite detailing, the fine proportions, and the symmetry of the projecting wings. The gracious and inviting double front doors are a prelude to the exceptional interior. Consider the four bedroom, two-bath sleeping wing. Formal entertaining can be enjoyed in the front living and dining rooms. For informal living there is the rear family room.

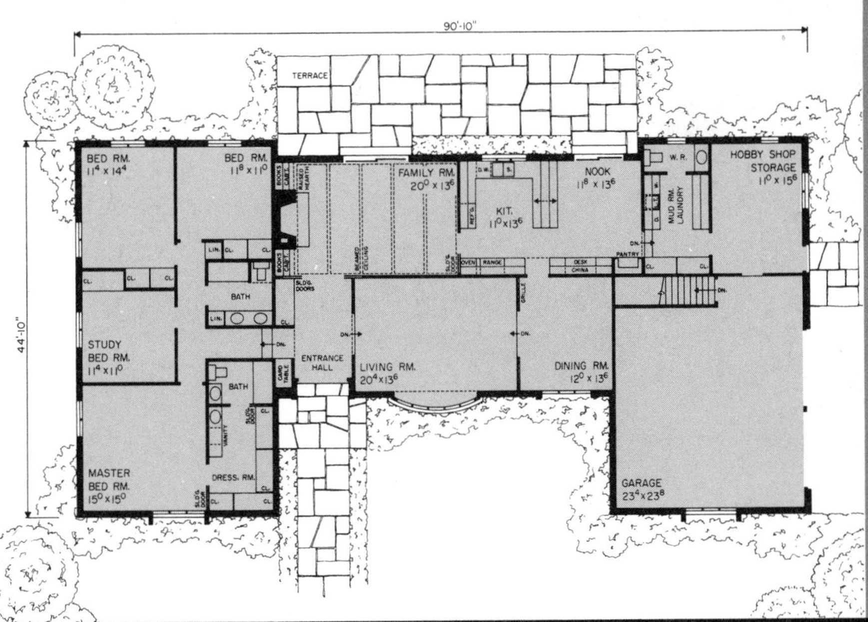

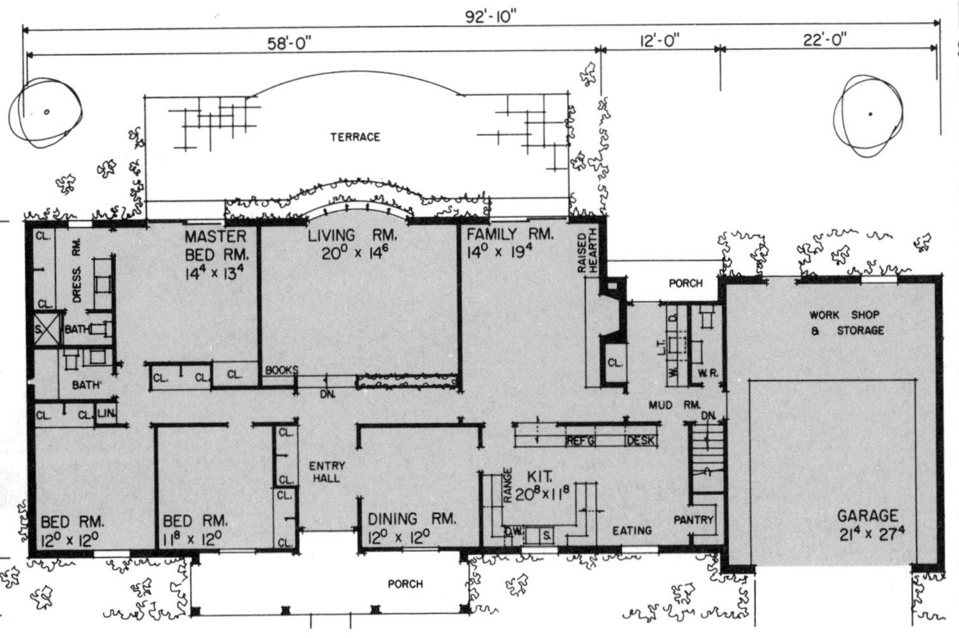

Design X1788

Square Footage: 2,218

L D

● "Charm" is one of the many words which may be used to correctly describe this fine design. In addition to its eye-appeal, it has a practical and smoothly functioning floor plan. The detail of the front entrance, highlighted by columns supporting the projecting pediment gable, is outstanding. Observe the window treatment and the double, front doors. Perhaps the focal point of the interior will be the formal living room. It is, indeed, dramatic with its bay window overlooking the backyard. Three bedrooms and two baths are in the private area.

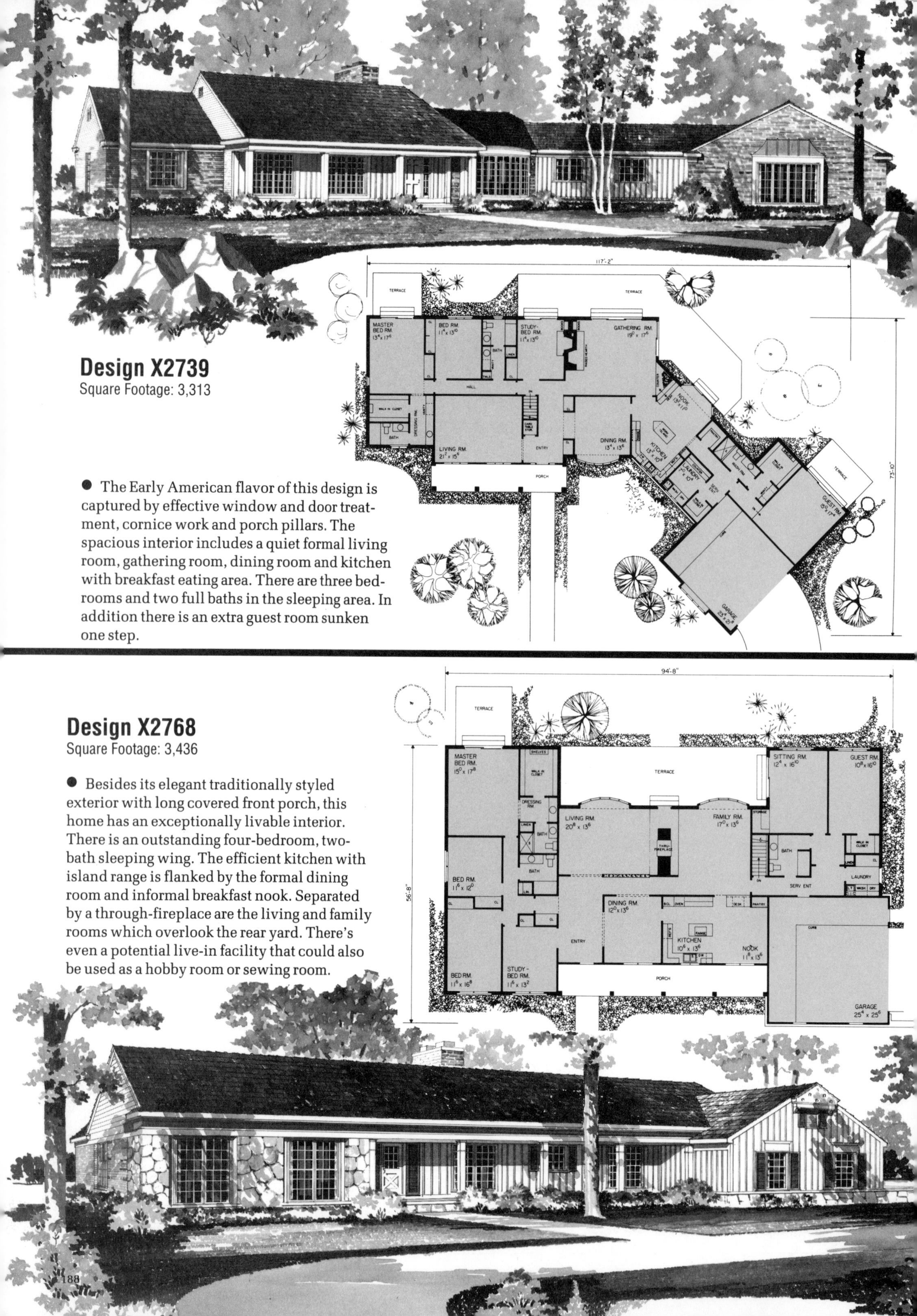

Design X2739

Square Footage: 3,313

● The Early American flavor of this design is captured by effective window and door treatment, cornice work and porch pillars. The spacious interior includes a quiet formal living room, gathering room, dining room and kitchen with breakfast eating area. There are three bedrooms and two full baths in the sleeping area. In addition there is an extra guest room sunken one step.

Design X2768

Square Footage: 3,436

● Besides its elegant traditionally styled exterior with long covered front porch, this home has an exceptionally livable interior. There is an outstanding four-bedroom, two-bath sleeping wing. The efficient kitchen with island range is flanked by the formal dining room and informal breakfast nook. Separated by a through-fireplace are the living and family rooms which overlook the rear yard. There's even a potential live-in facility that could also be used as a hobby room or sewing room.

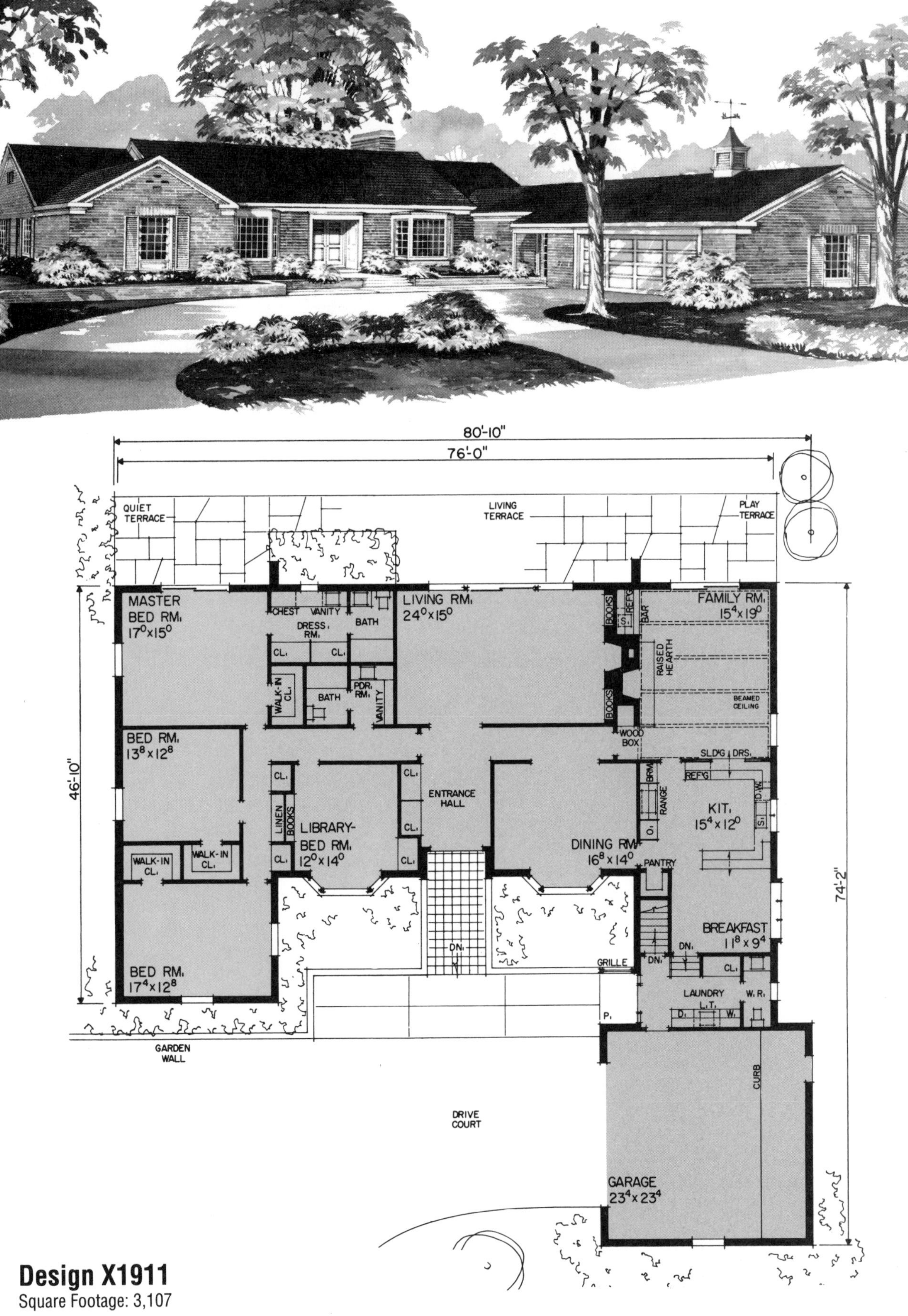

Design X1911

Square Footage: 3,107

● For luxurious, country-estate living, it is difficult to beat this impressive traditional design. The floor plan includes plenty of space, excellent room arrangements, fine traffic circulation, and an abundance of convenient living features. It may be used as a three or four-bedroom home.

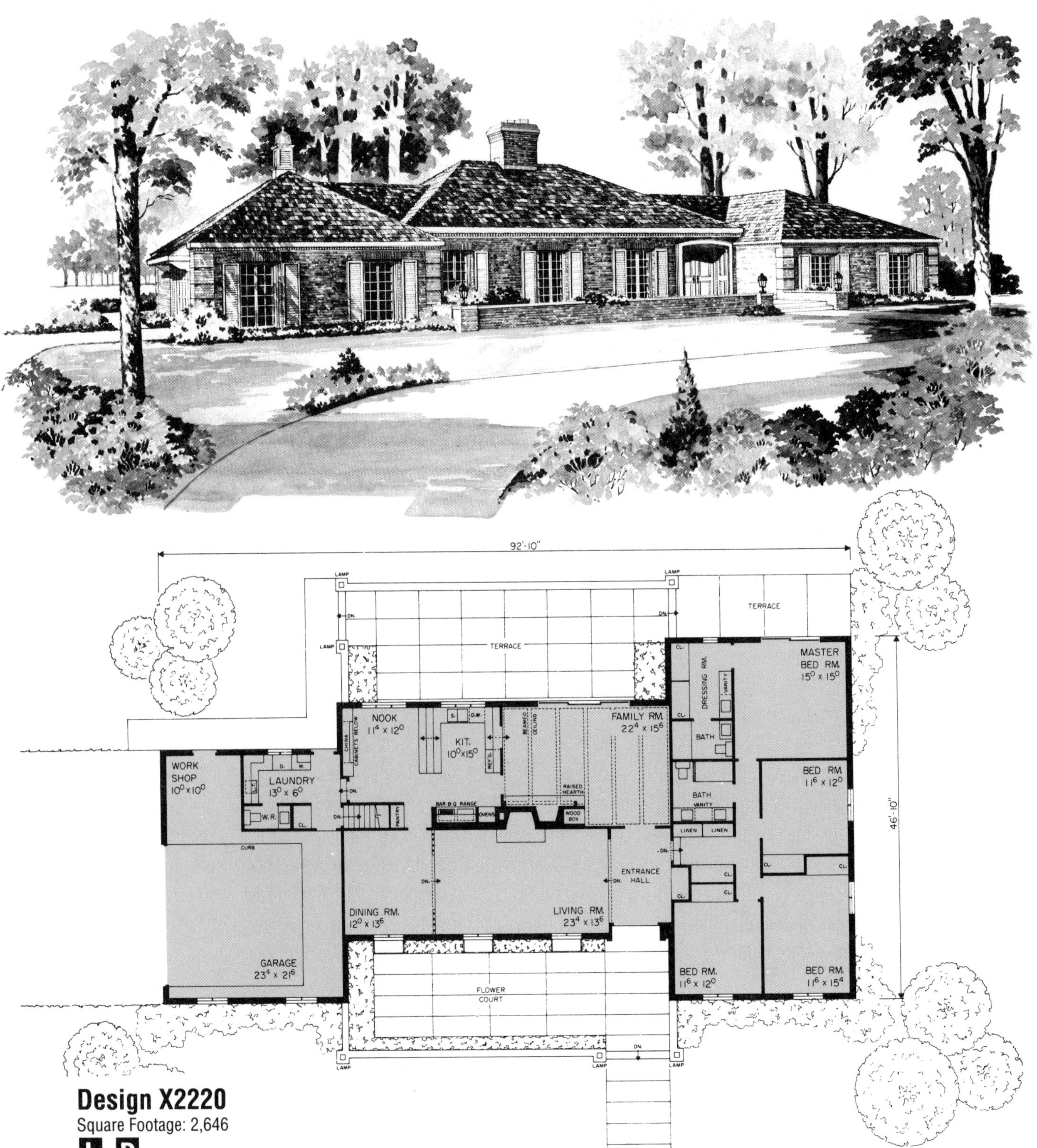

Design X2220

Square Footage: 2,646

L **D**

● The gracious formality of this home is reminiscent of a popularly accepted French styling. The hip-roof, the brick quoins, the cornice details, the arched window heads, the distinctive shutters, the recessed double front door and the massive center chimney, and the delightful flower court are all features which set the dramatic appeal of this home. This floor plan is a favorite of many. The four bedroom, two bath sleeping wing is a zone by itself. Further, the formal living and dining rooms are ideally located. For entertaining they function well together and look out upon the pleasant flower court. Overlooking the raised living terrace at the rear are the family and breakfast rooms and work center. Don't miss the laundry, extra wash room and work shop in garage.

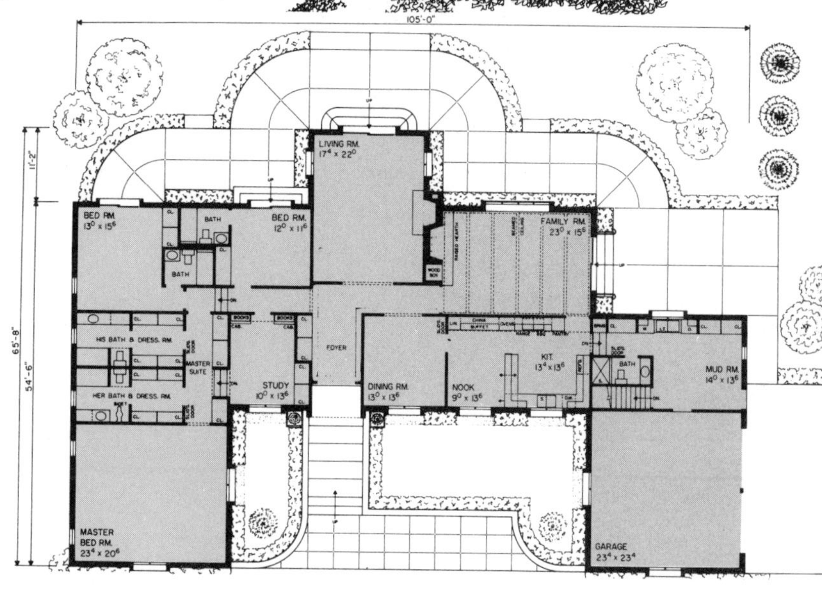

Design X2212

Square Footage: 3,577

L

● From the graceful, curving drive court to the formal living room, this expansive, hospitable French country home welcomes the visitor. Note the spacious terrace area and the many amenities.

Design X2779

Square Footage: 3,225

L **D**

● This French design is surely impressive. The exterior is highlighted with a hip roof, paned-glass windows, brick privacy wall and double front doors. The inside is just as appealing. Note the unique placement of rooms and features: formal dining room with butler's pantry, sizable parlor, gathering room with fireplace and sliding glass doors, and an adjacent study. The U-shaped kitchen has an island range, snack bar, breakfast nook and pantry.

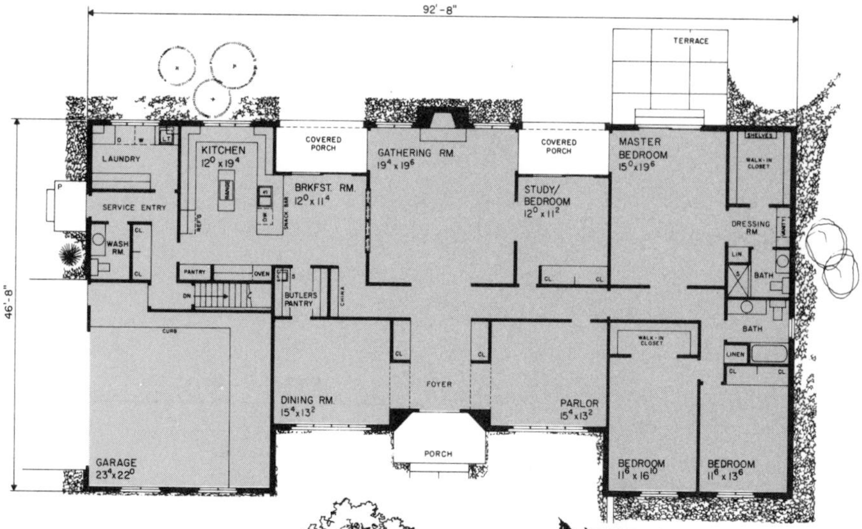

● The elegance of pleasing proportion and delightful detailing has seldom been better exemplified than by this classic French country manor adaptation. Approaching the house across the drive court, the majesty of this multi-roofed structure is breathtaking, indeed. An outstanding feature is the maid's suite. It is located above the garage and is easily reached by use of the covered porch connecting the laundry room's service entrance to the garage. If desired, it would make an excellent studio, quiet retreat or even a game room.

Design X1993

First Floor: 2,658 square feet
Master Suite: 840 square feet
Maid's Suite: 376 square feet
Total: 3,874 square feet

L

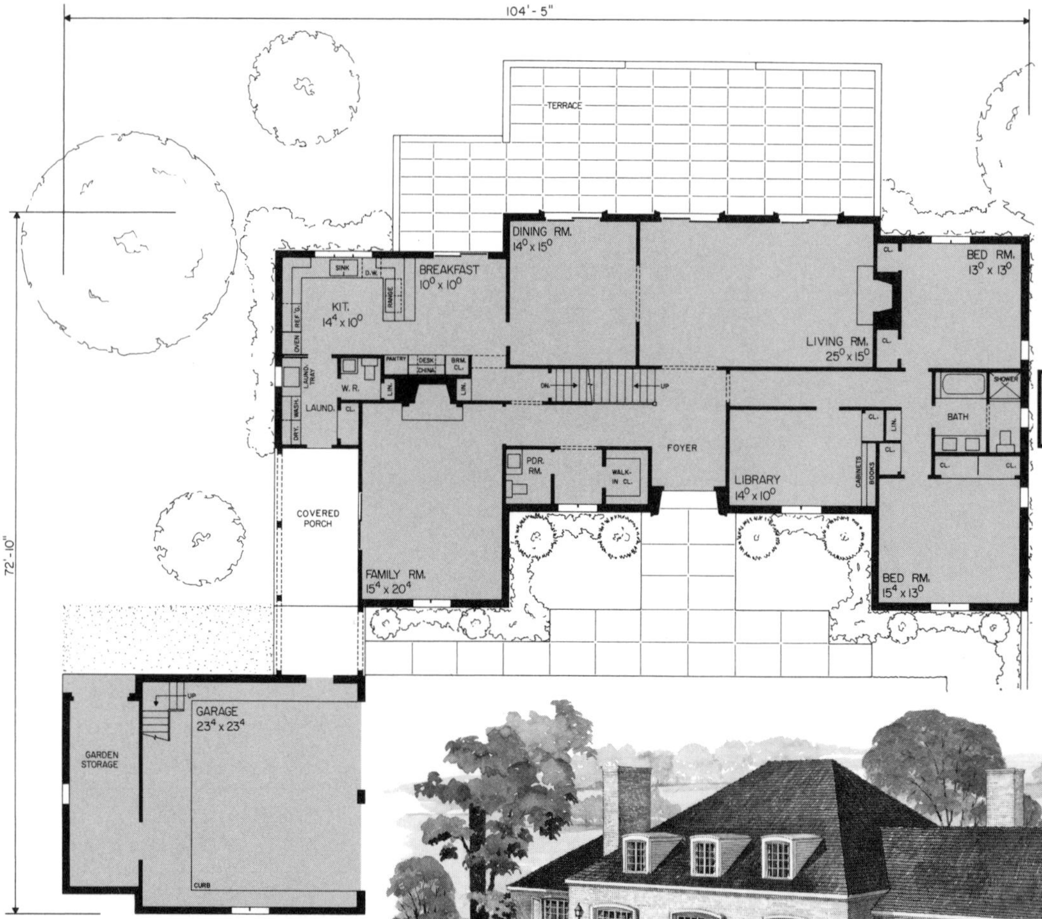

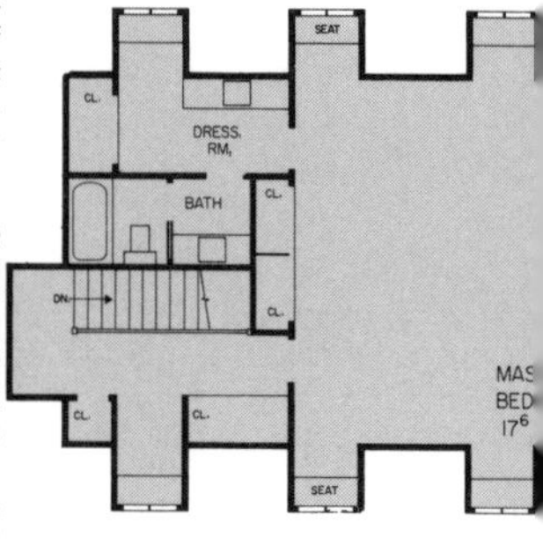

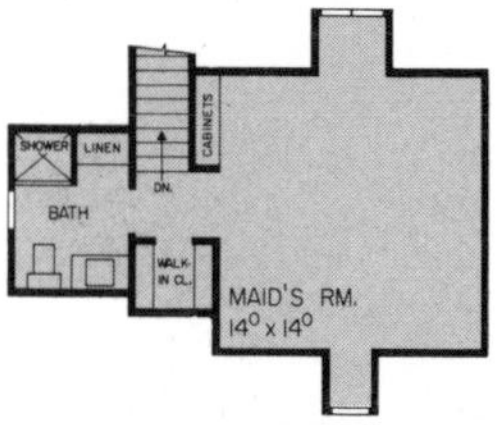

Design X2668 First Floor: 1,206 square feet
Second Floor: 1,254 square feet; Total: 2,460 square feet
L

● This elegant exterior houses a very livable plan. Every bit of space has been put to good use. The front country kitchen is a good place to begin. It is efficiently planned with its island cook top, built-ins and pass-thru to the dining room. The large great room will be the center of all family activities. Quiet times can be enjoyed in the front library. Study the second floor sleeping areas.

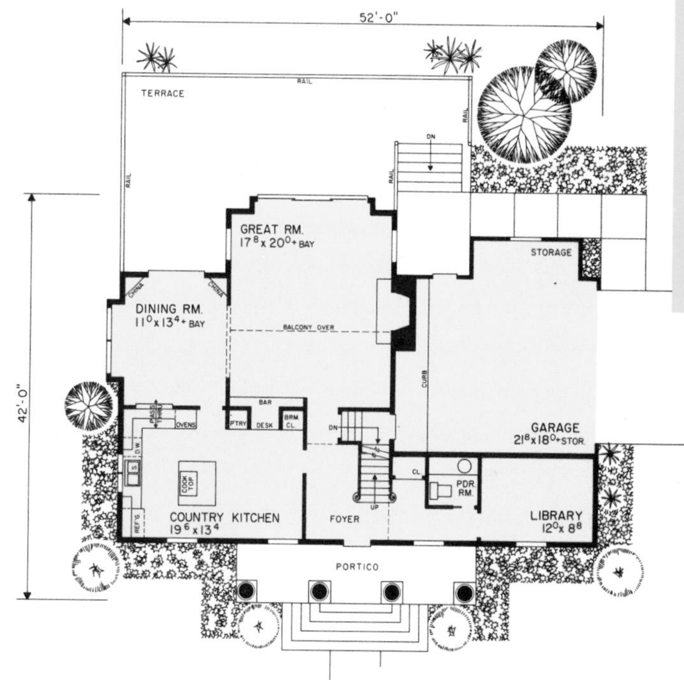

● A Southern Colonial adaptation under 2,000 square feet. The two projecting, one-story wings are devoted to the living room and garage. The two-story portion houses three bedrooms, 2½ baths, study, laundry, dining room and kitchen with eating area.

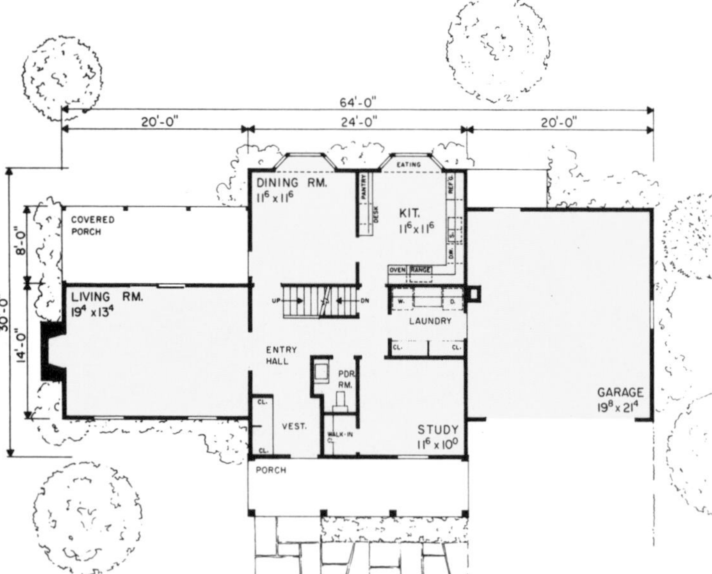

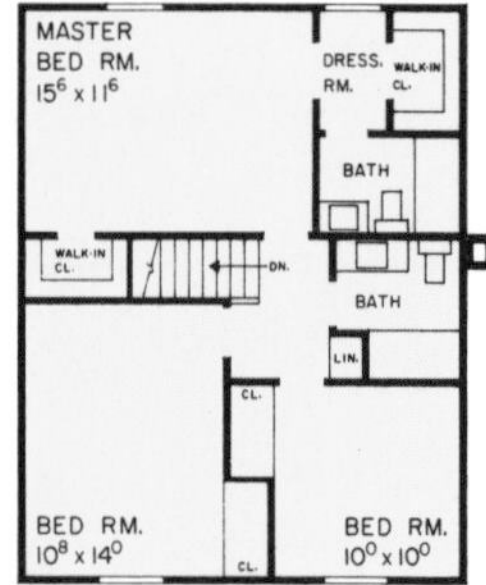

Design X2107

First Floor: 1,020 square feet
Second Floor: 720 square feet
Total: 1,740 square feet

Design X2700 First Floor: 1,640 square feet; Second Floor: 1,129 square feet; Total: 2,769 square feet

● Southern Colonial grace and much more. Inside, an elegant gathering room with sloped ceiling and a raised-hearth fireplace is more than 21′ by 23′ large. The formal living room features full-length paned windows while the formal dining room includes a large bay window. The contemporary kitchen has an adjacent breakfast room with another bay window. Around the corner, a first floor laundry offers more modern conveniences. Four large bedrooms include a master suite with two walk-in closets and private bath. This home is eminently suited to a family with traditional tastes.

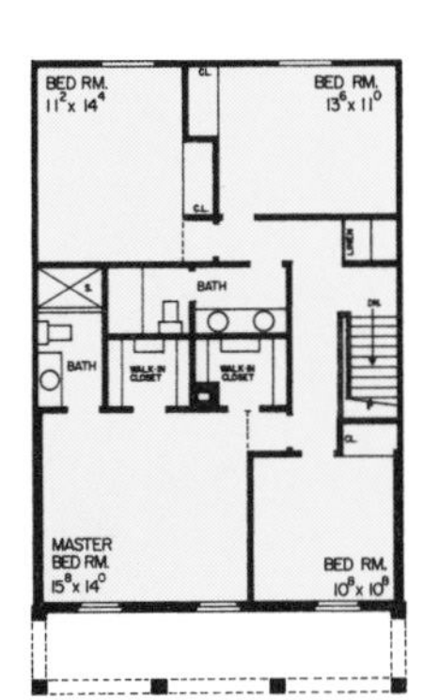

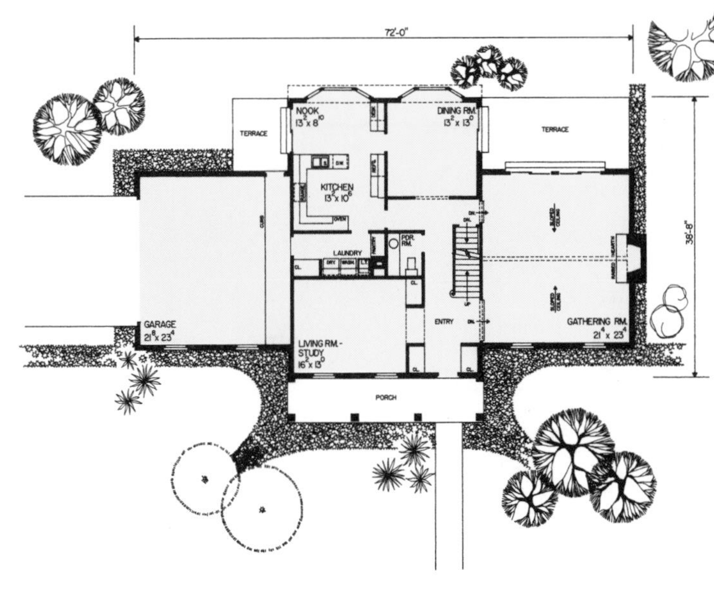

Design X1208
First Floor: 1,170 square feet
Second Floor: 768 square feet
Total: 1,938 square feet

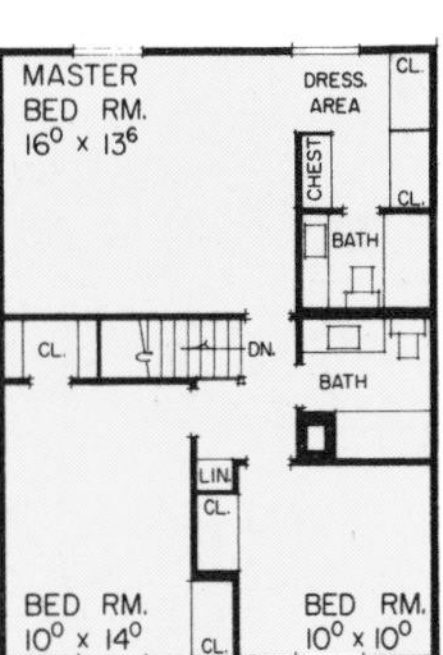

● This Colonial four-bedroom features the livable kind of plan you're looking for. A formal living room extends from the front foyer and leads to the formal dining area and nearby kitchen. A sunken family room has a raised-hearth fireplace. Three family bedrooms share a bath and are joined by the master bedroom with its own full bath.

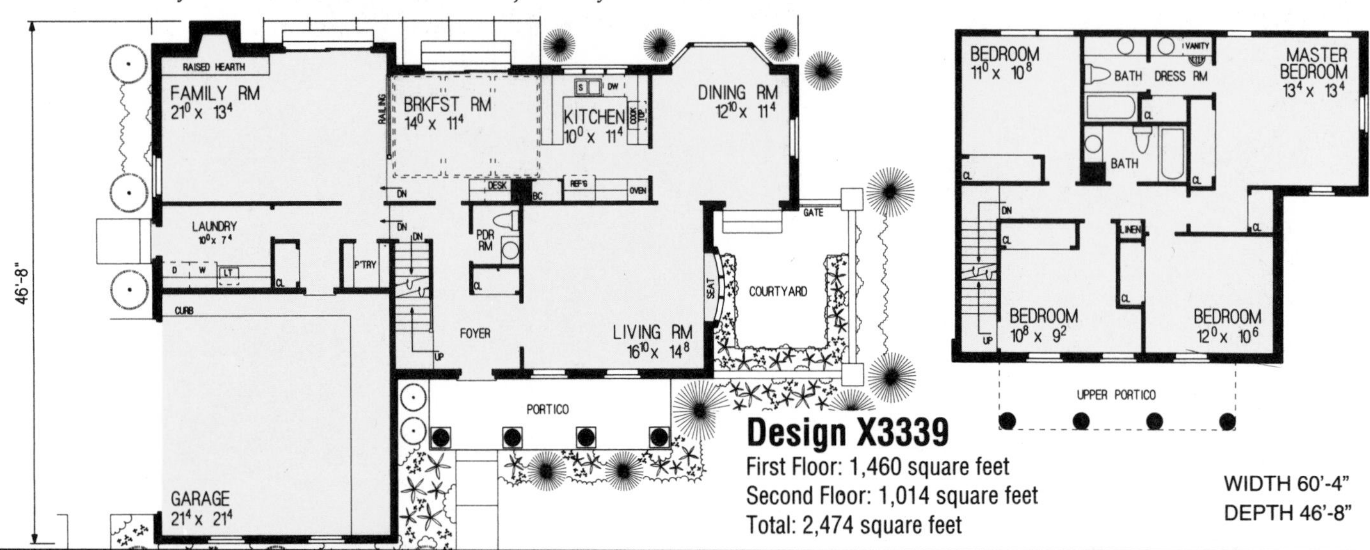

Design X3339

First Floor: 1,460 square feet
Second Floor: 1,014 square feet
Total: 2,474 square feet

WIDTH 60'-4"
DEPTH 46'-8"

Design X2524

First Floor: 994 square feet
Second Floor: 994 square feet; Total: 1,988 square feet

D

● This small two-story, with a modest investment, will result in an impressive exterior and an outstanding interior which will provide exceptional livability. Your list of features will be long and surely impressive.

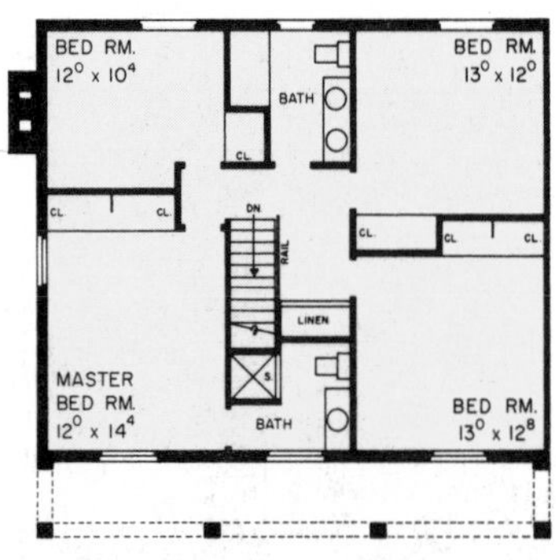

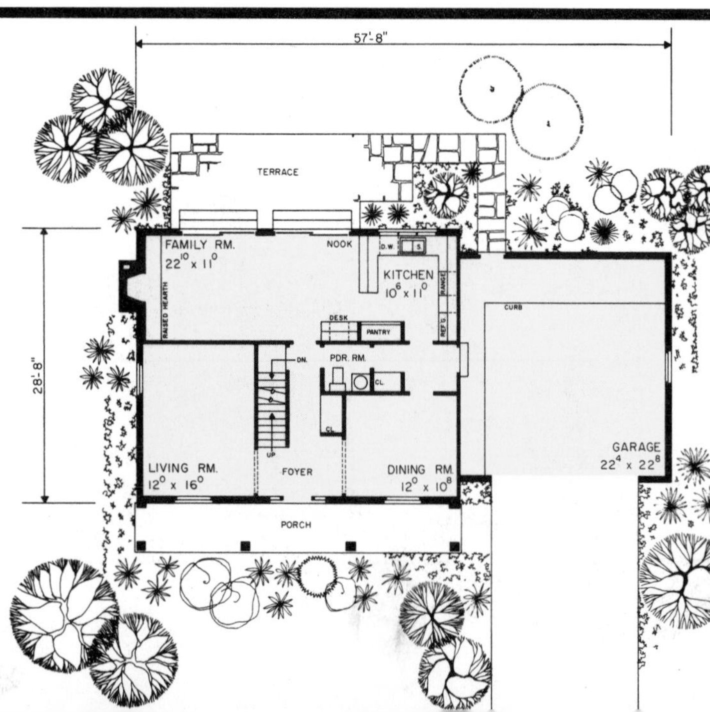

Design X2627 First Floor: 845 square feet
Second Floor: 896 square feet; Total: 1,741 square feet

● This charming, economically built, home with its stately two-story porch columns is reminiscent of the South. The efficient interior features bonus space over garage and in the third-floor attic which may be developed into another livable room. The U-shaped kitchen offers many built-ins and is conveniently located to serve the nook and the dining room with ease. Sliding glass doors in both these eating areas lead to the terrace.

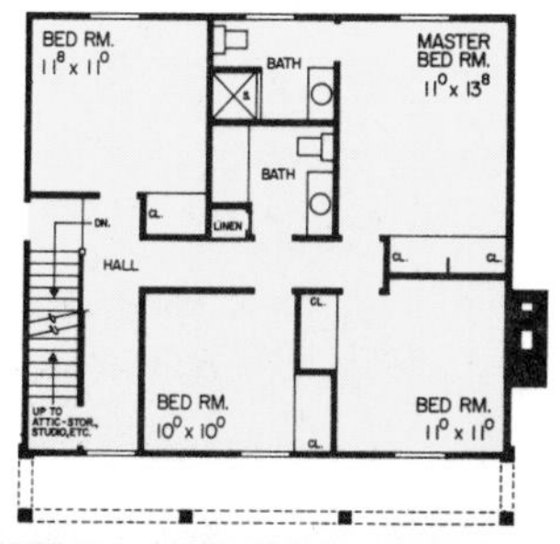

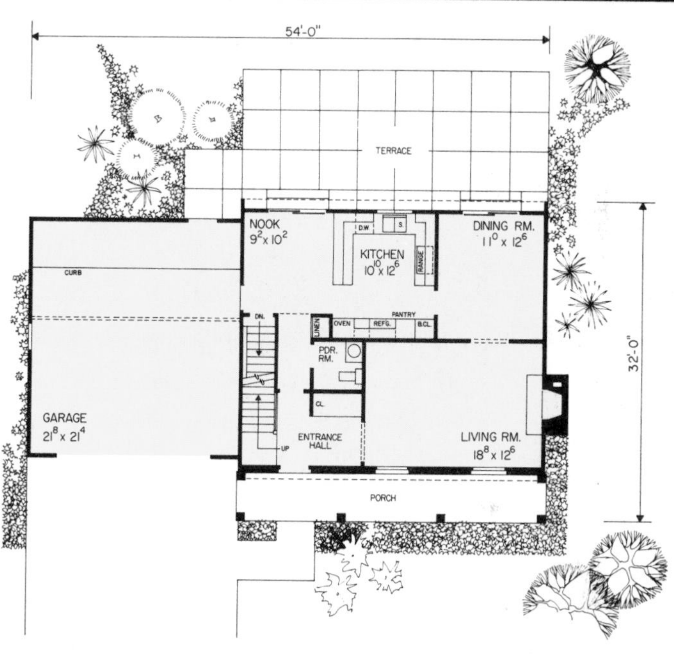

Design X2663

First Floor: 1,344 square feet
Second Floor: 947 square feet
Total: 2,291 square feet

● Reminiscent of the past, this home reflects the Greek Revival heritage. This is demonstrated in its front and rear porticoes with graceful columns. While the exterior comes from yesteryear, the floor plan is designed to serve today's active family. Notice for instance the huge gathering room that stretches from the front to the rear of the house. Three bedrooms are on the second floor.

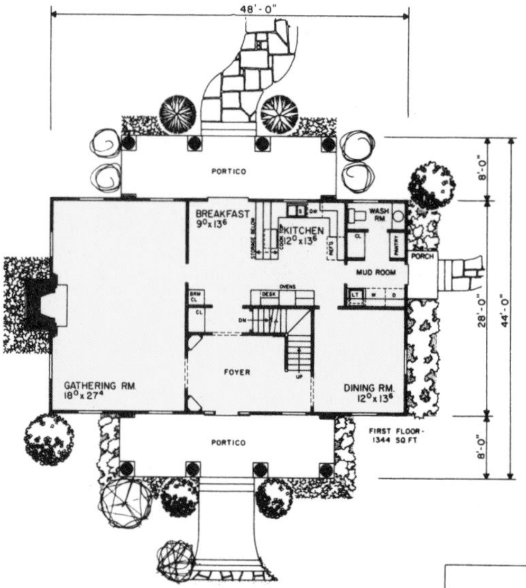

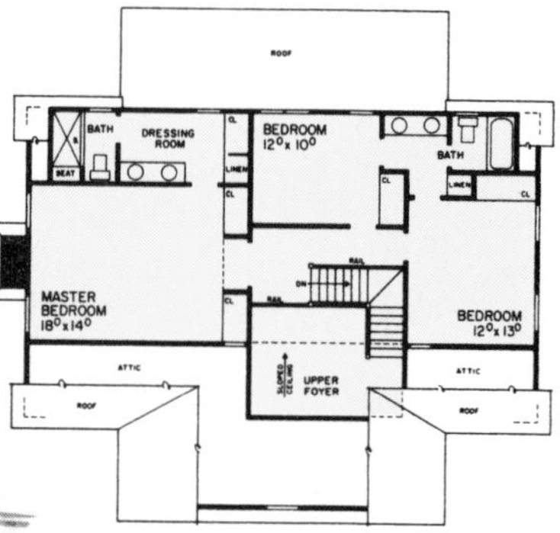

Design X2686

First Floor: 1,683 square feet
Second Floor: 1,541 square feet
Total: 3,224 square feet

L **D**

● This design has its roots in the South and is referred to as a raised cottage. This adaptation has front and rear covered porches whose columns reflect a modified Greek Revival style. Flanking the center foyer are the formal living room with the library behind and the country kitchen to the right.

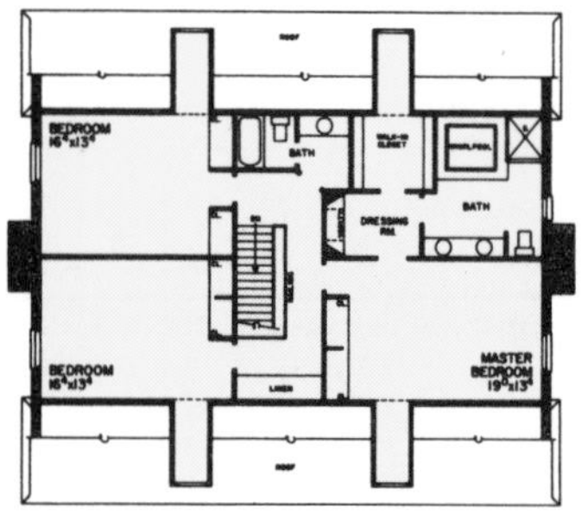

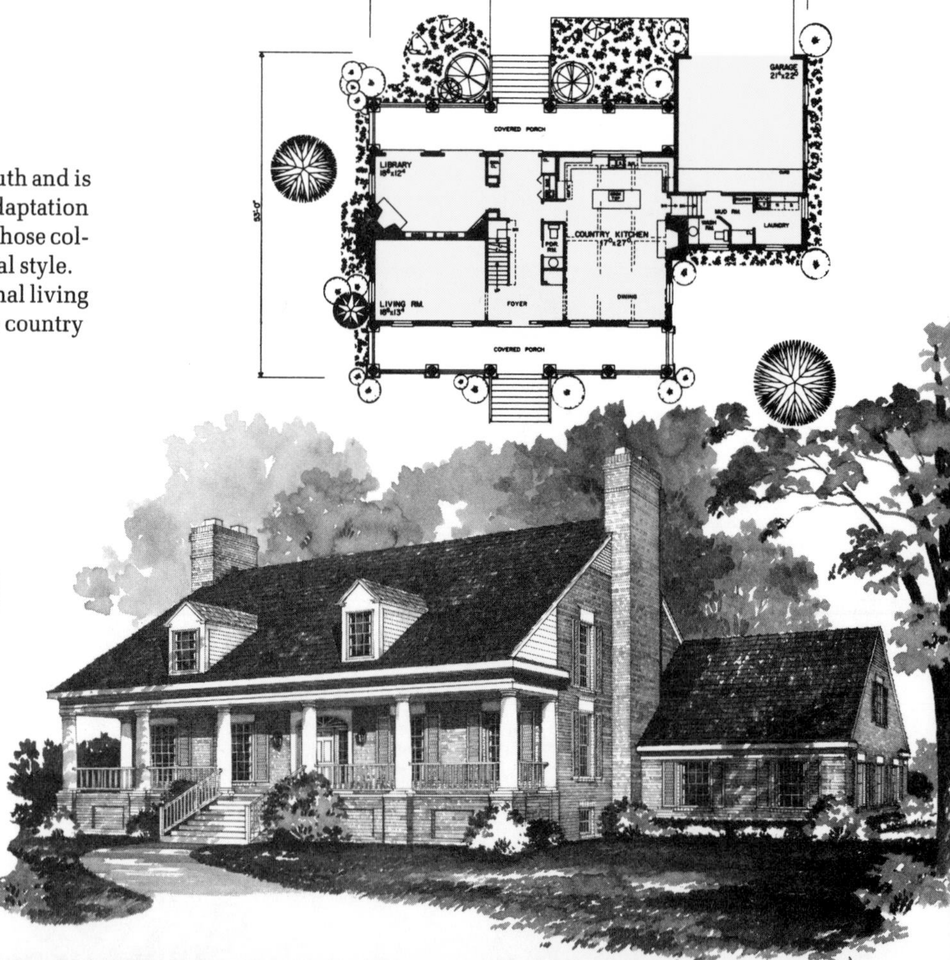

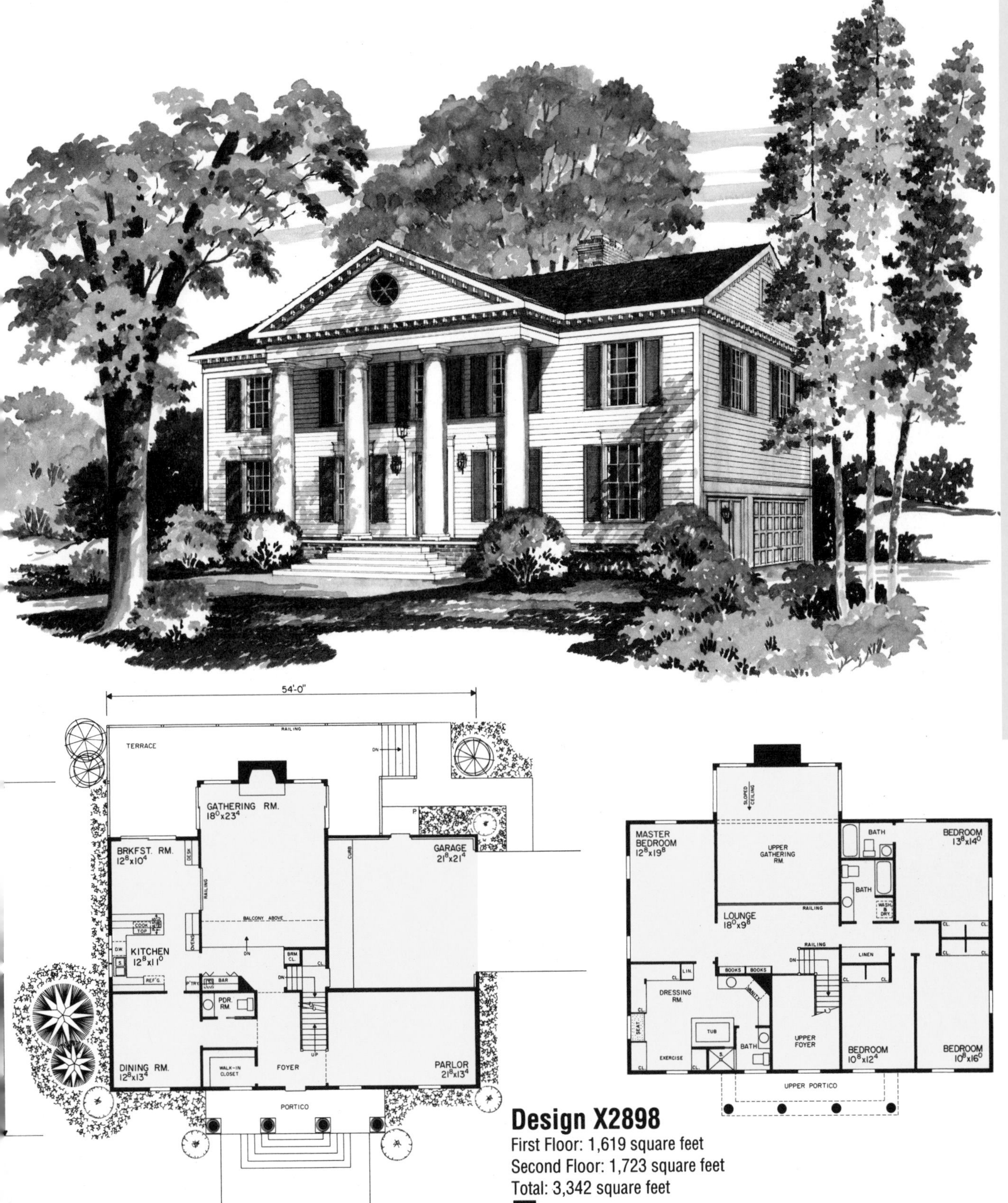

Design X2898

First Floor: 1,619 square feet
Second Floor: 1,723 square feet
Total: 3,342 square feet

D

● Four soaring Doric columns highlight the exterior of this Greek Revival dwelling. The elevation reflects a balanced design that incorporates four bedrooms and a two-car garage in one central unit. The stylish heart of this dwelling is a two-story gathering room. A balcony lounge on the second floor offers a quiet aerie overlooking this living area. Both of these areas will have sunlight streaming through the high windows. A second living area is the parlor. It could serve as the formal area whereas the gathering room could be considered informal. Entrance to all of these areas will be through the foyer. It has an adjacent powder room and spacious walk-in closet. The U-shaped kitchen will conveniently serve the breakfast and dining rooms. Second floor livability is outstanding. Study all of the features in the master bedroom: dressing room, tub and shower, large vanity and exercise area. Three more bedrooms, another has a private bath which would make it an ideal guest room.

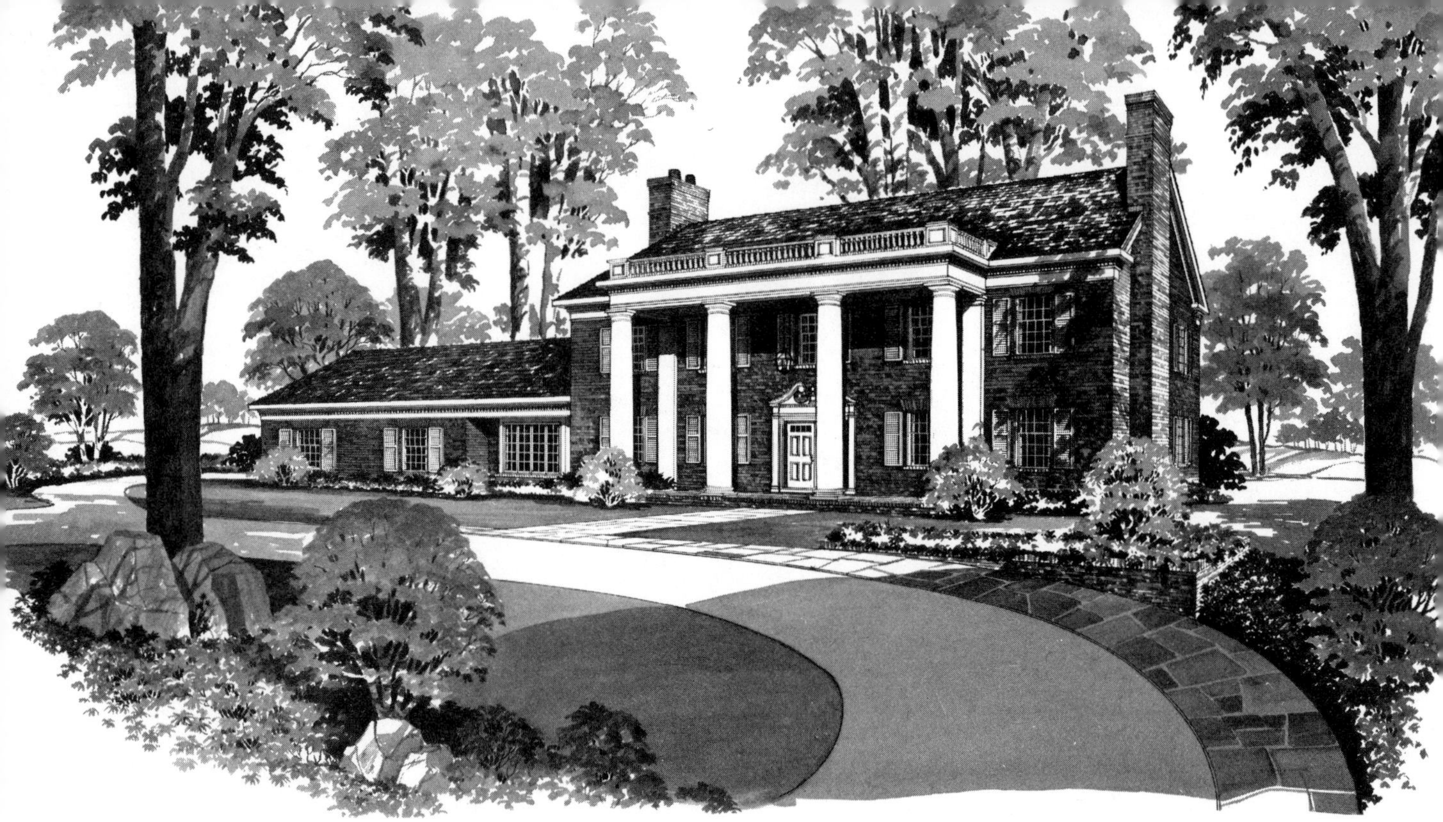

Design X2230

First Floor: 2,288 square feet
Second Floor: 1,863 square feet
Total: 4,151 square feet

● The gracefulness and appeal of this southern adaptation will be everlasting. The imposing two-story portico is truly dramatic. Notice the authentic detailing of the tapered Doric columns, the balustraded roof deck, the denticulated cornice, the front entrance and the shuttered windows. The architecture of the rear is no less appealing with its formal symmetry and smaller Doric portico. The impressive exterior of this two-story houses a total of 4,151 square feet. The spacious, formal front entrance hall provides a fitting introduction to the scale and elegance of the interior.

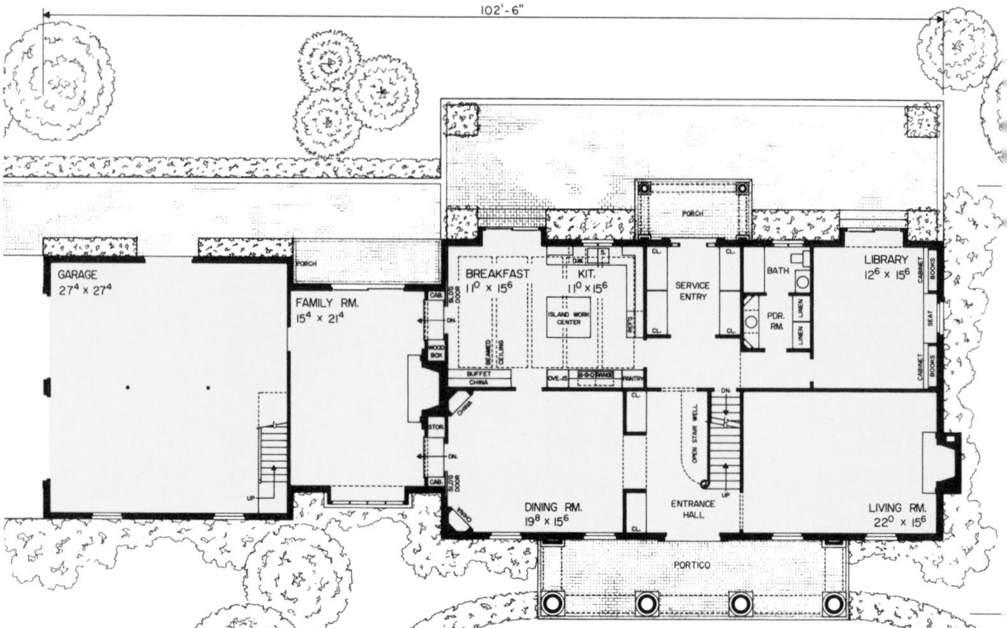
102'-6"
PORCH
GARAGE 27^4 x 27^4
PORCH
FAMILY RM. 15^4 x 21^4
BREAKFAST 11^0 x 15^6
KIT. 11^0 x 15^6
ISLAND WORK CENTER
SERVICE ENTRY
BATH
PDR. RM.
LIBRARY 12^6 x 15^6
BUFFET CHINA
DINING RM. 19^8 x 15^6
OPEN STAIR WELL
ENTRANCE HALL
LIVING RM. 22^0 x 15^6
PORTICO

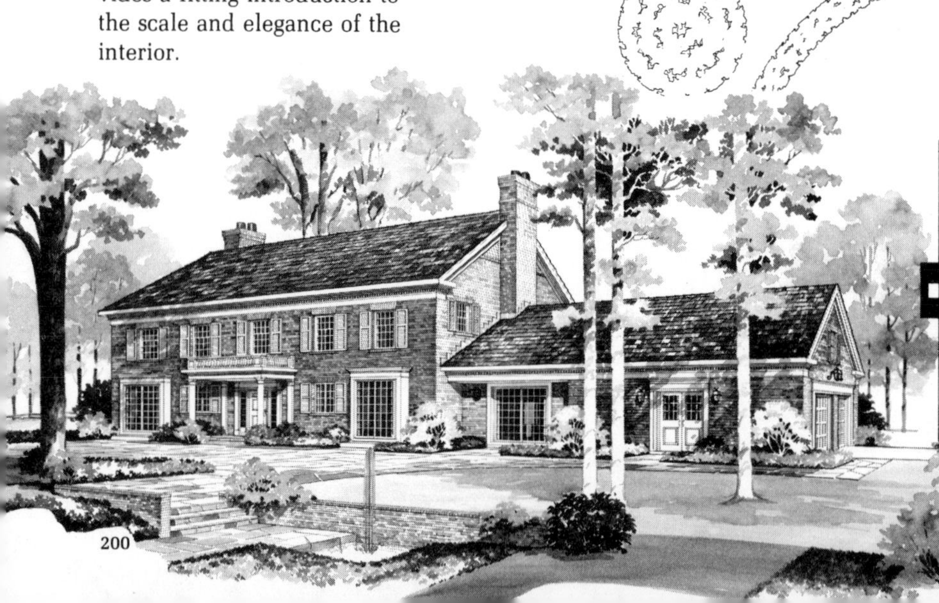

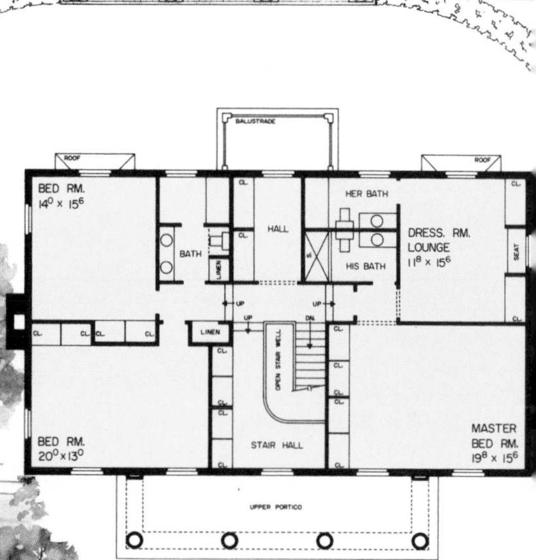
BALUSTRADE
ROOF
ROOF
BED RM. 14^0 x 15^6
BATH
HALL
HER BATH
HIS BATH
DRESS. RM. LOUNGE 11^8 x 15^6
LINEN
OPEN STAIR WELL
BED RM. 20^0 x 13^0
STAIR HALL
MASTER BED RM. 19^8 x 15^6
UPPER PORTICO

Design X2673

First Floor: 1,895 square feet
Second Floor: 1,661 square feet
Total: 3,556 square feet

● A two-story pillared entrance portico and tall multi-paned windows, flanking the double front doors, together accentuate the facade of this Southern Colonial design. This brick home is stately and classic in its exterior appeal. The three-car garage opens to the side so it does not disturb the street view. This is definitely a charming home that will stand strong for many years into the future. Not only is the exterior something to talk about, but so is the interior. Enter into the extremely spacious foyer and begin to discover what this home has to offer in the way of livability. Front, living and dining rooms are at each end of this foyer. The living room is complimented by a music room, or close it off and make it a bedroom. A full bath is nearby. The formal dining room will be easily served by the kitchen as will the breakfast room and snack bar. The family room is spacious and features a built-in wet bar which can be closed off by doors. An open, staircase leads to the second floor, four bedroom sleeping area.

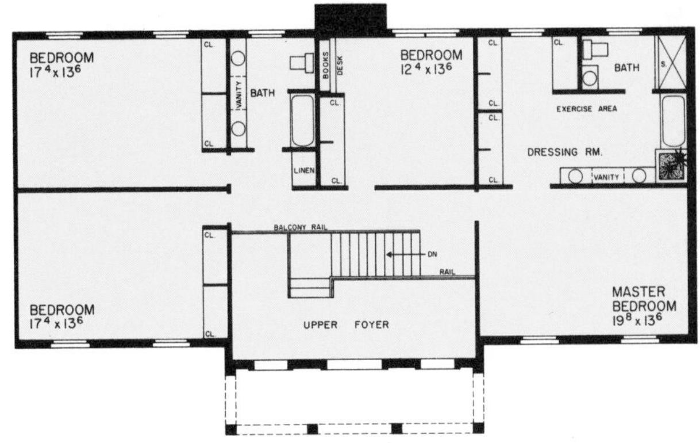

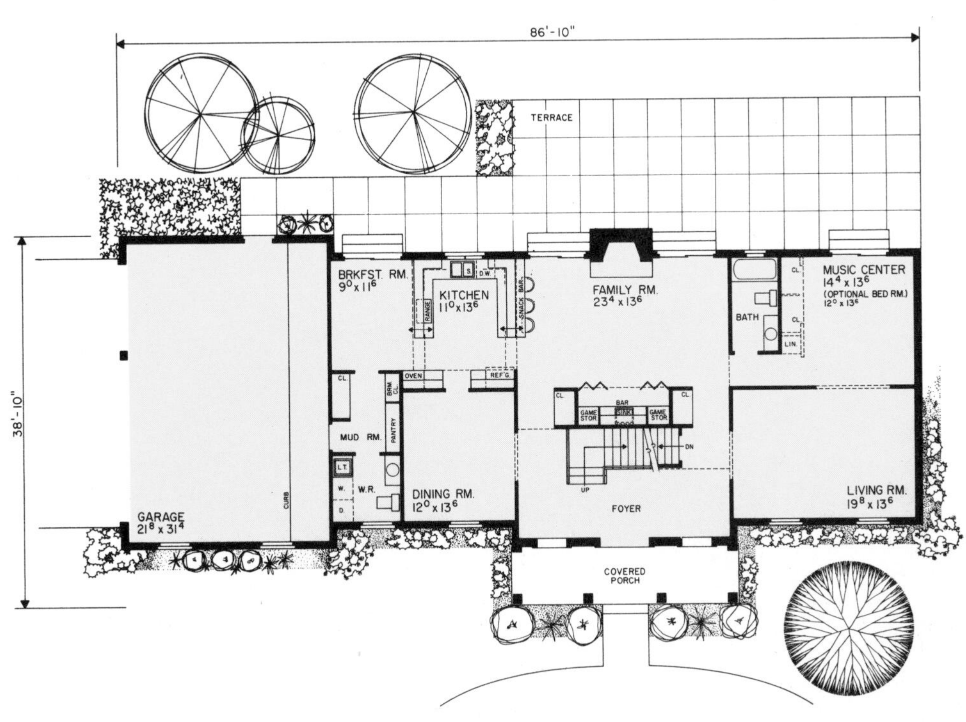

Design X3333

First Floor: 1,584 square feet
Second Floor: 1,344 square feet
Total: 2,928 square feet

● This Southern Colonial adaptation boasts an up-to-date floor plan which caters to the needs of today's families. The entrance hall is flanked by formal and informal living areas, a separate formal dining room and an informal snack bar. A curving open stairway leads to the upstairs. Here four large bedrooms are found. The master bath has an impressive whirlpool plus a stall shower. A second bath with twin lavatories serves the family bedrooms.

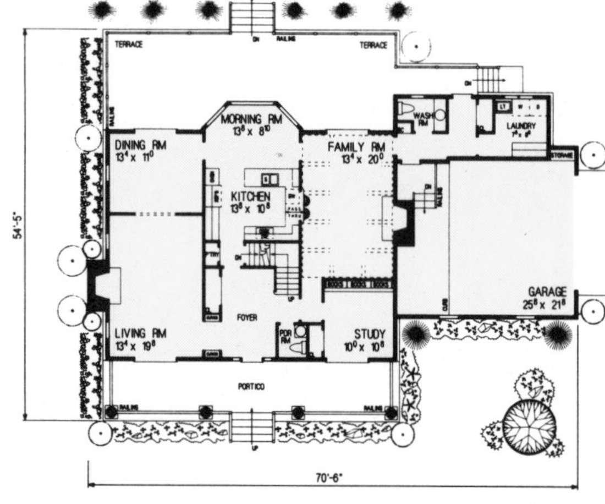

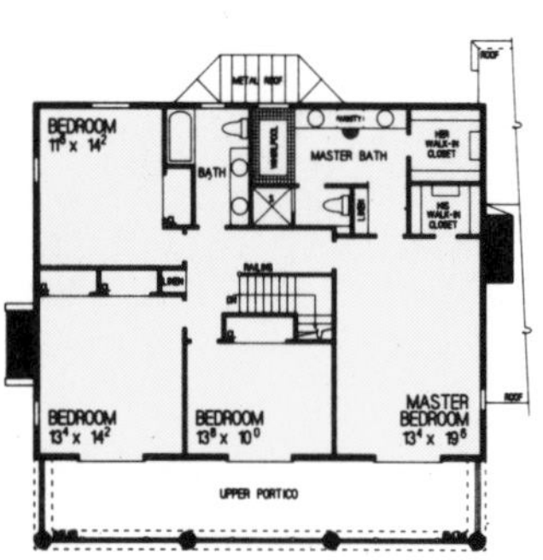

Design X2924

First Floor: 1,520 square feet
Second Floor: 1,352 square feet
Total: 2,872 square feet

● Southern Colonial architecture makes a delightful statement here. Rarely are such livable and workable designs available. There are formal and informal living areas, a separate formal dining room and an informal snack bar. A curving stairway leads to the upstairs. Here three large bedrooms are found. The master bath has an impressive whirlpool plus a stall shower. A second bath with twin lavatories serves the two family bedrooms. The master bedroom has its own fireplace.

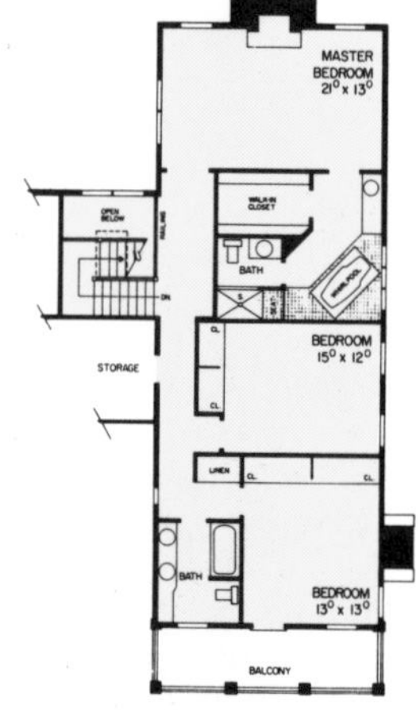

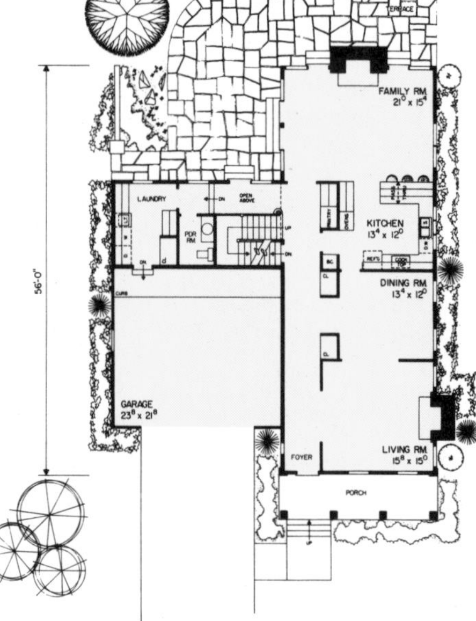

● The exterior of this full two-story is highlighted by the covered porch and balcony. Many enjoyable hours will be spent at these outdoor areas. The interior is highlighted by a spacious country kitchen. Be sure to notice its island cook-top, fireplace and the beamed ceiling. A built-in bar is in the family room.

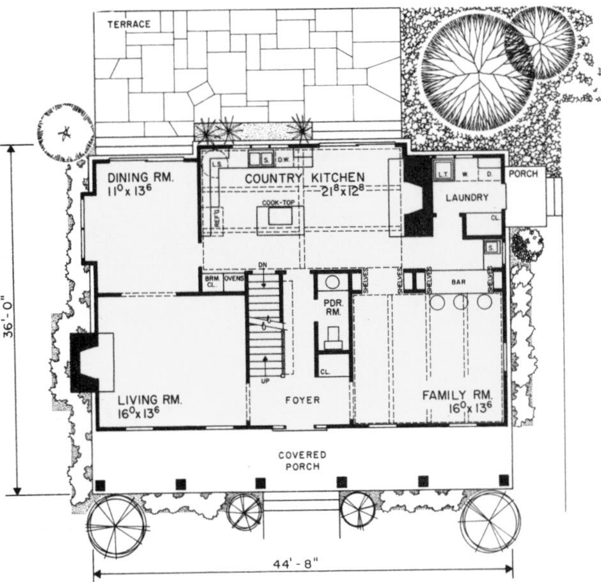

Design X2664 First Floor: 1,308 square feet
Second Floor: 1,262 square feet; Total: 2,570 square feet
D

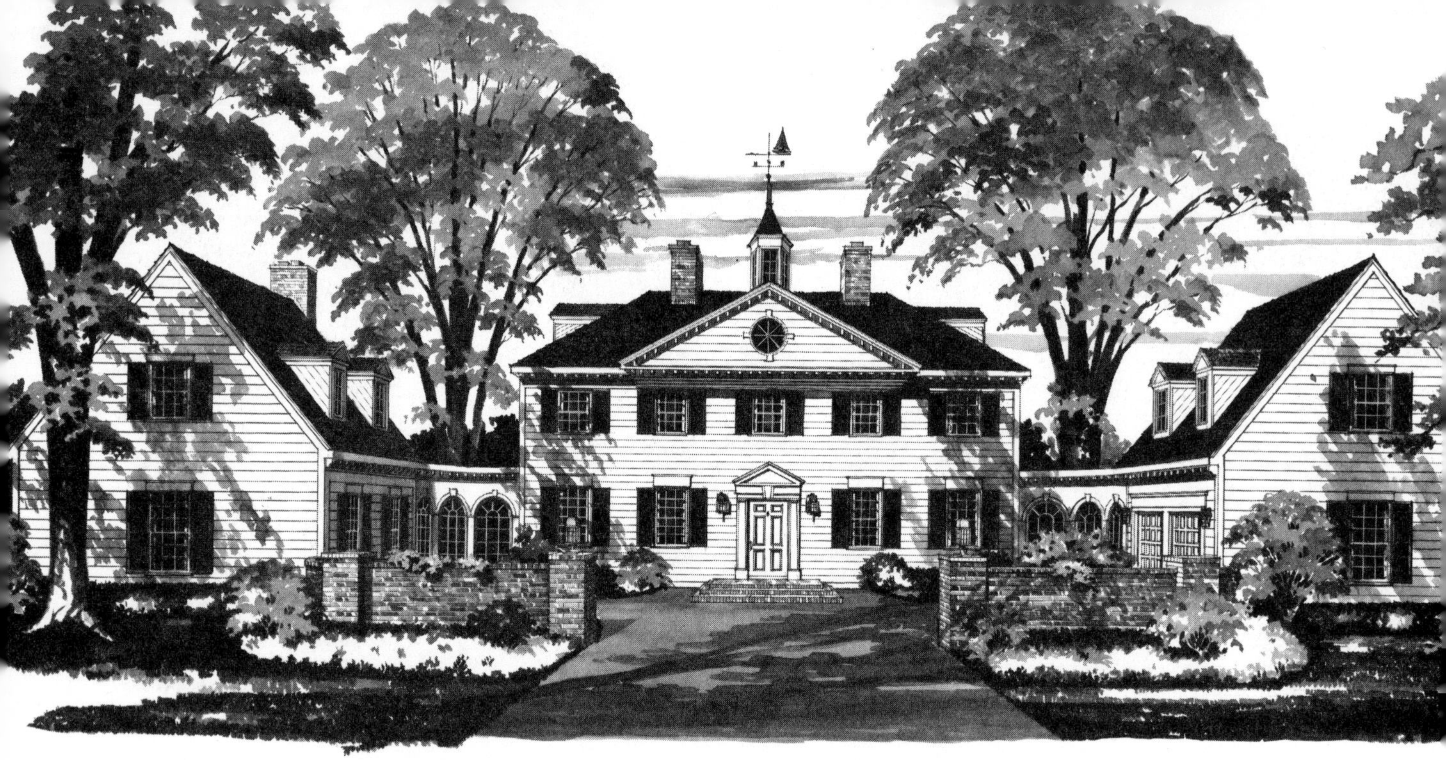

A Mount Vernon Reminiscence

● This magnificent manor's streetview illustrates a centralized mansion connected by curving galleries to matching wings. What a grand presentation this home will make! The origin of this house dates back to 1787 and George Washington's stately Mount Vernon. The underlying aesthetics for this design come from the rational balancing of porticoes, fenestration and chimneys. The rear elevation of this home also deserves mention. Six two-story columns, along with four sets of French doors, highlight this view. Study all of the intricate detailing that is featured all around these exteriors. The flanking wings create a large formal courtyard where guests of today can park their cars. This home, designed from architecture of the past, is efficient and compact enough to fit many suburban lots. Its interior has been well planned and is ready to serve a family of any size.

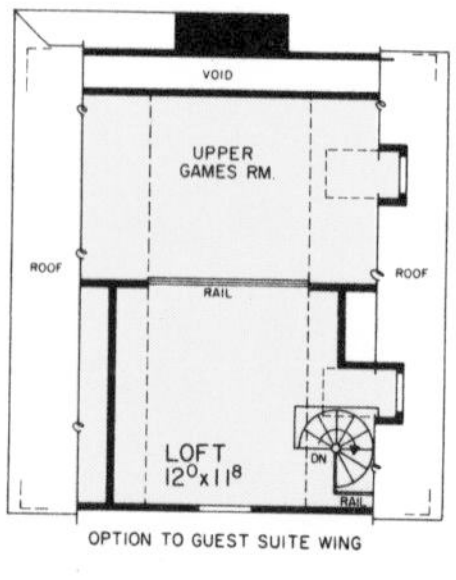

OPTION TO GUEST SUITE WING

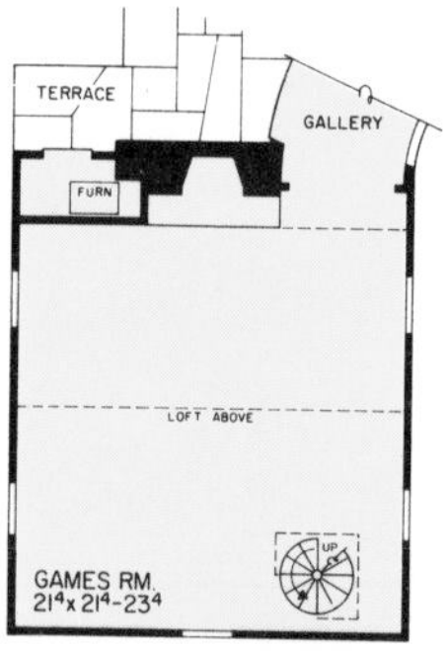

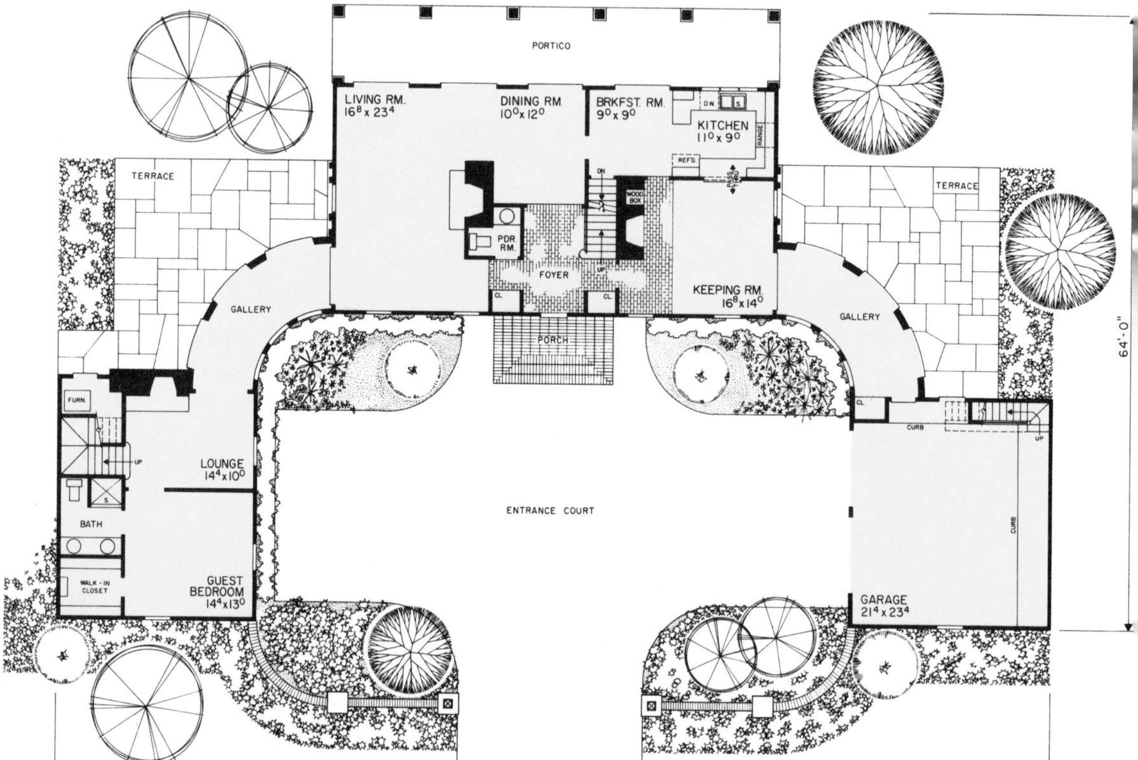

Design X2665 First Floor: 1,152 square feet; Second Floor: 1,152 square feet
Total: 2,304 square feet (Excludes Guest Suite and Galleries)

● The main, two-story section of this home houses the living areas. First - there is the large, tiled foyer with two closets and powder room. Then there is the living room which is the entire width of the house. This room has a fireplace and leads into the formal dining room. Three sets of double French doors lead to the rear portico from this formal area. The kitchen and breakfast room will function together. There is a pass-thru from the kitchen to the keeping room. All of the sleeping facilities, four bedrooms, are on the second floor. The gallery on the right leads to the garage; the one on the left, to a lounge and guest suite with studio above. The square footage quoted above does not include the guest suite or gallery areas. The first floor of the guest suite contains 688 sq. ft.; the second floor studio, 306 sq. ft. The optional plan shows a game room with a loft above having 162 sq. ft.

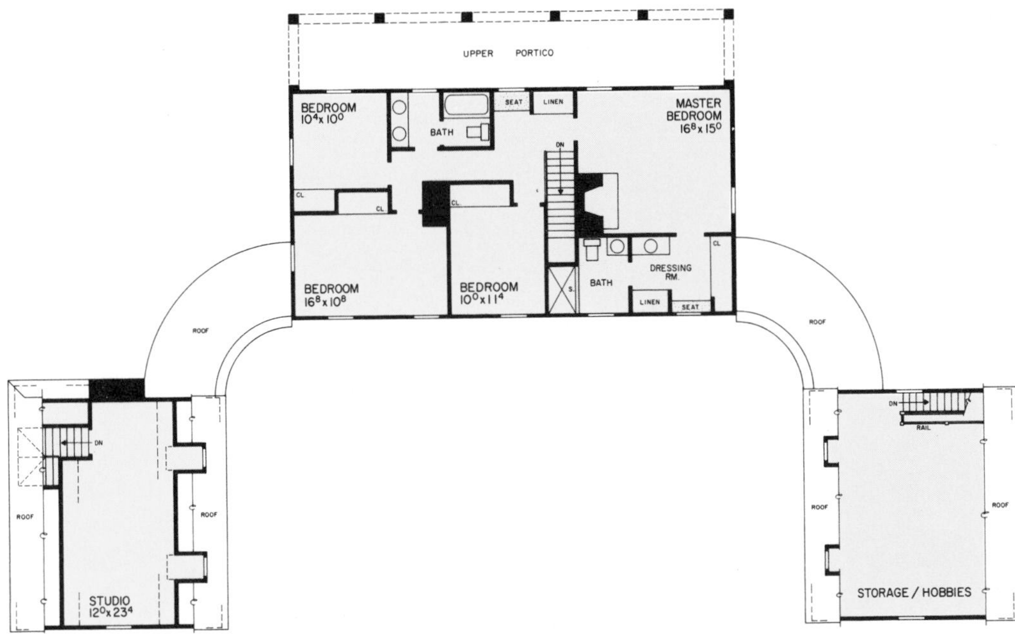

Design X3337

First Floor: 2,167 square feet
Second Floor: 1,992 square feet
Total: 4,159 square feet

● The elegant facade of this design with its columned portico, fanlights, and dormers houses an amenity-filled interior. The gathering room, study and dining room, each with fireplace, provide plenty of room for relaxing and entertaining. A large work area contains a kitchen with breakfast room and snack bar, laundry room and pantry. The four-bedroom upstairs includes a master suite with a sumptuous bath and an exercise room.

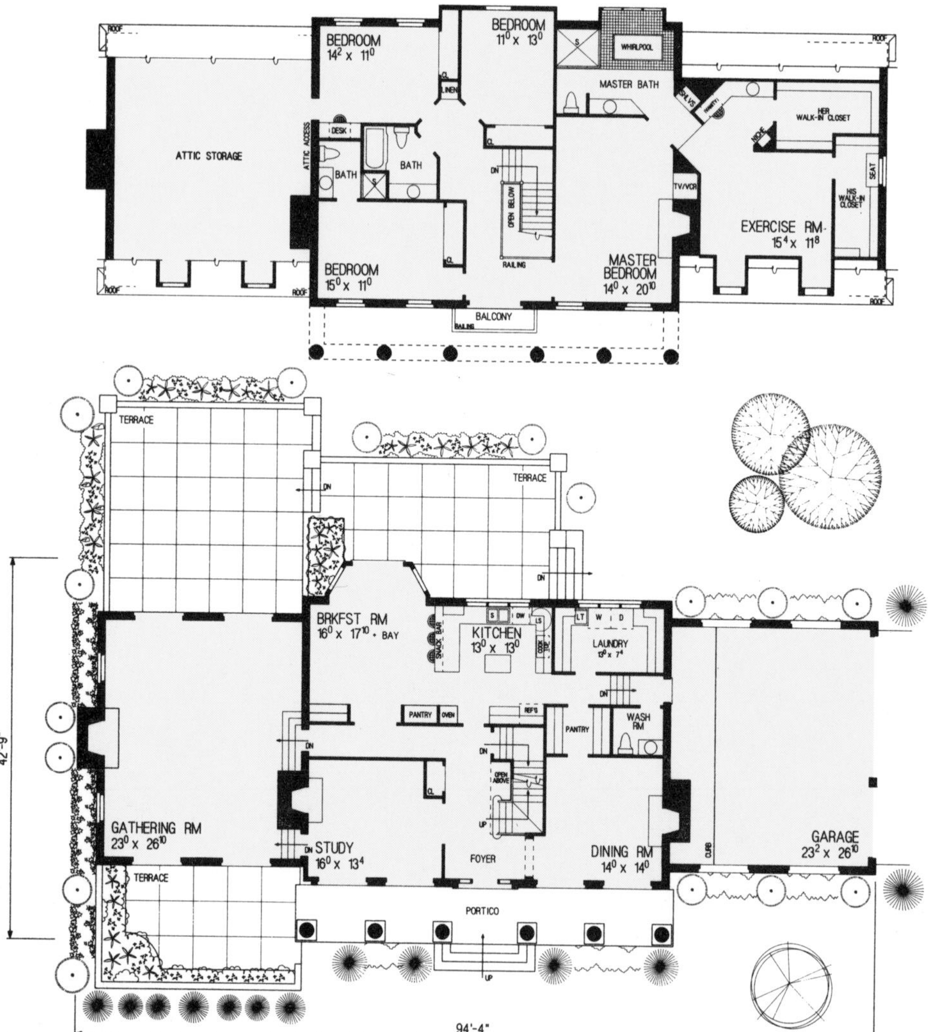

Design X3303

First Floor: 2,563 square feet
Second Floor: 1,496 square feet
Total: 4,059 square feet

● With its stately columns and one-story wings, this design is a fine representation of 18th Century adaptations. Formal living and dining areas flank the entry foyer at the front of the home. Look for a fireplace in the living room, china cabinet built-ins in the dining room. More casual living dominates the back section in a family room and kitchen/breakfast room combination that features access to the rear terrace and plenty of space for cooking and informal dining. The left wing garage is connected to the main structure by a service entrance adjacent to the laundry. The right wing contains the private master suite. Four second floor bedrooms share two full baths and each has its own walk-in closet.

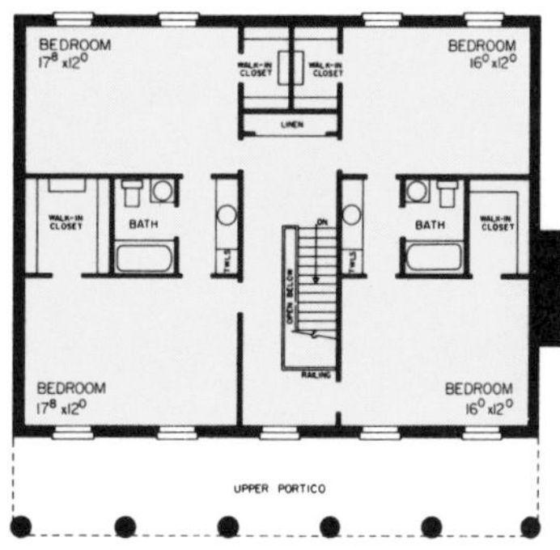

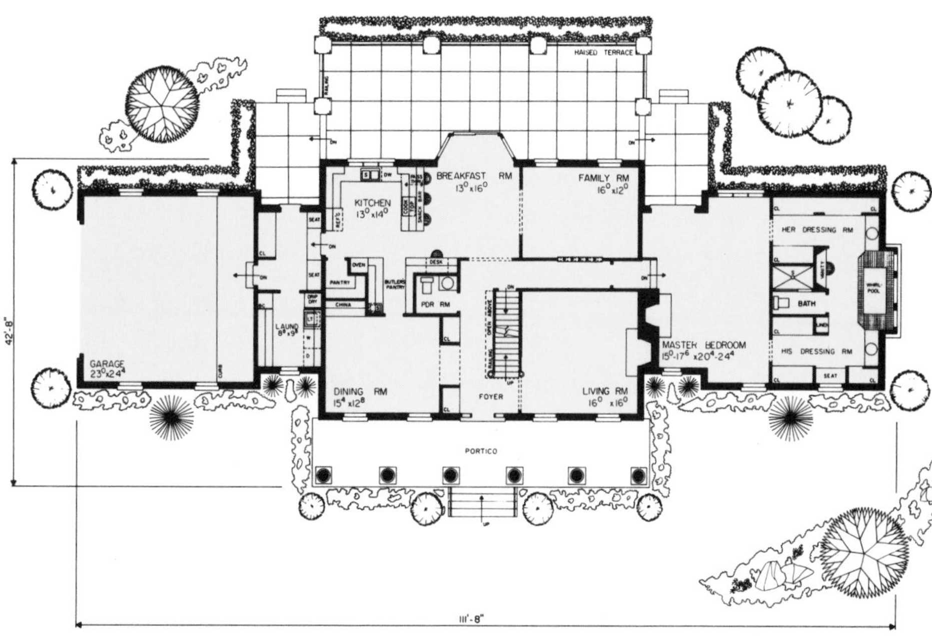

Design X3320

First Floor: 2,337 square feet
Second Floor: 1,232 square feet
Total: 3,569 square feet

● What a grand impression this home makes! A spacious two-story foyer with circular staircase greets visitors and leads to the dining room, media room and two-story gathering room with fireplace. The well-equipped kitchen includes a snack bar for informal meals. A luxurious master suite downstairs and four bedrooms upstairs complete this impressive plan.

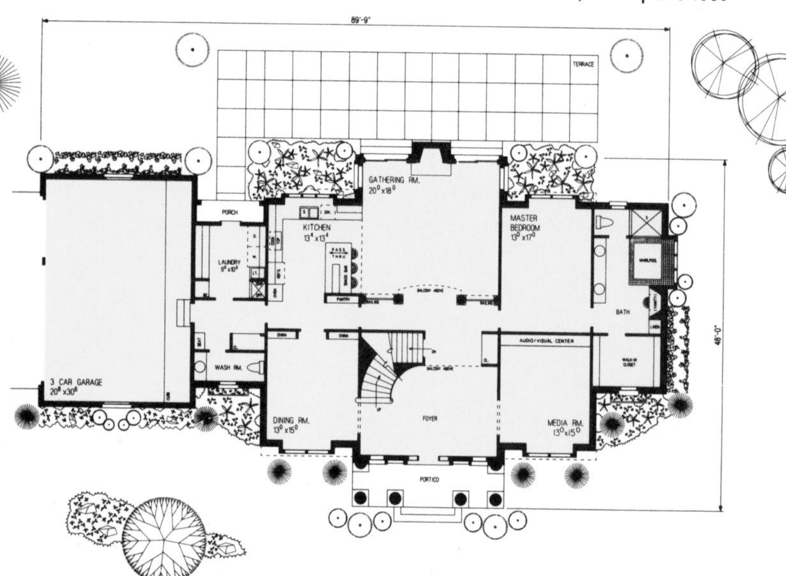

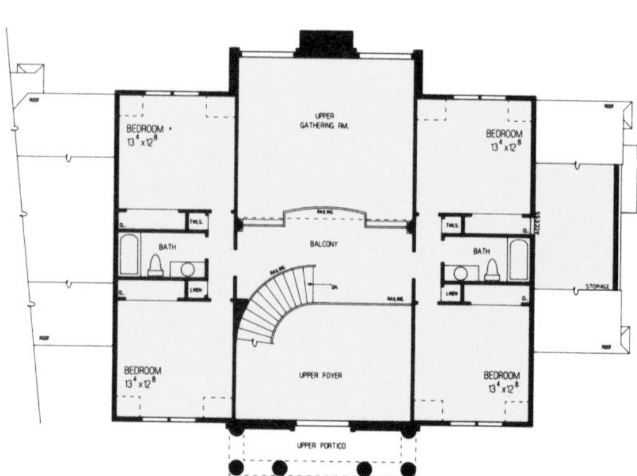

Design X2133 First Floor: 3,024 square feet; Second Floor: 826 square feet; Total: 3,850 square feet

L **D**

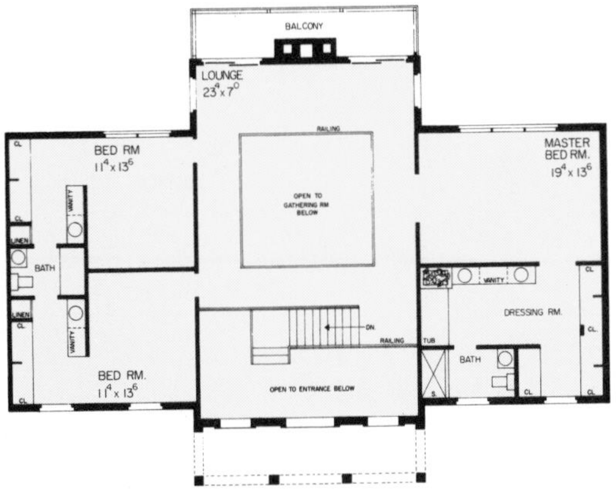

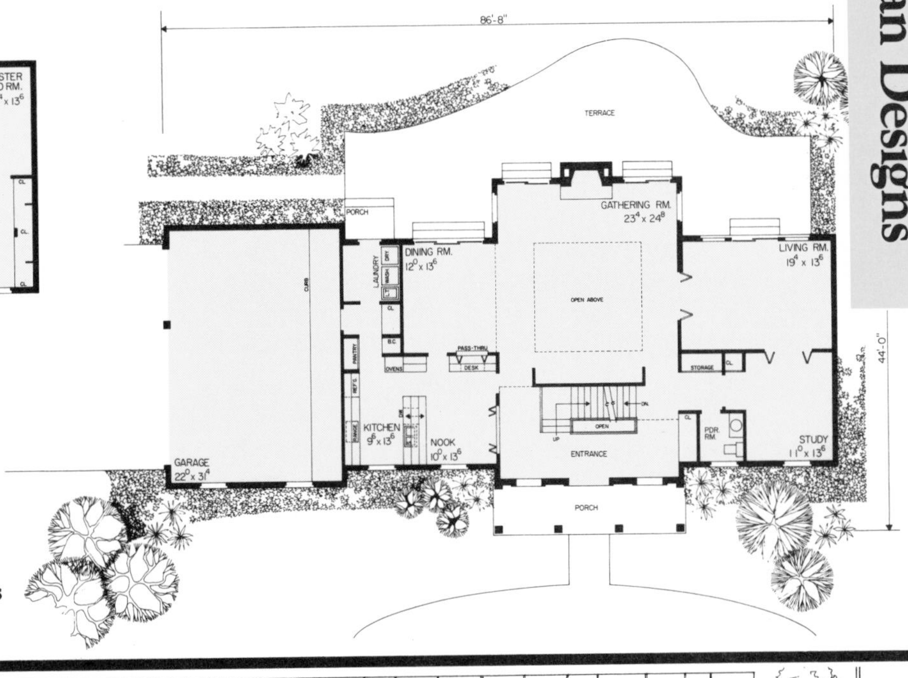

Design X2553

First Floor: 2,065 square feet
Second Floor: 1,612 square feet
Total: 3,677 square feet

● A stately Southern Colonial that could hardly be more impressive, or offer more pleasurable livability. The massive columns and the pediment gable are dramatic.

● A country-estate home which will command all the attention it truly deserves. Inside, three are 3,024 square feet on the first floor. In addition, there is a two-bedroom second floor should its development be necessary. Whether called upon to function as one or 1½-story home it will provide a lifetime of gracious living.

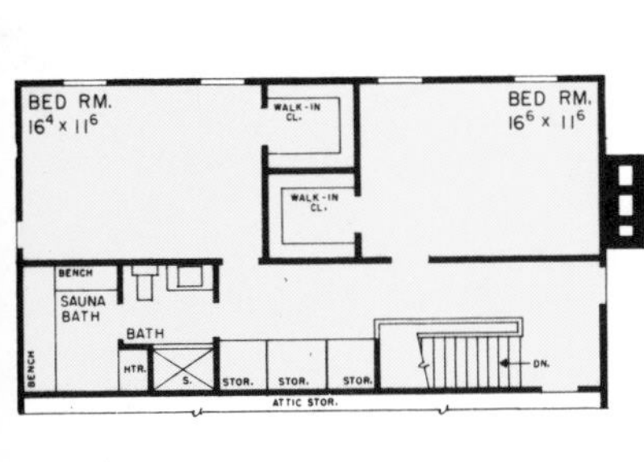

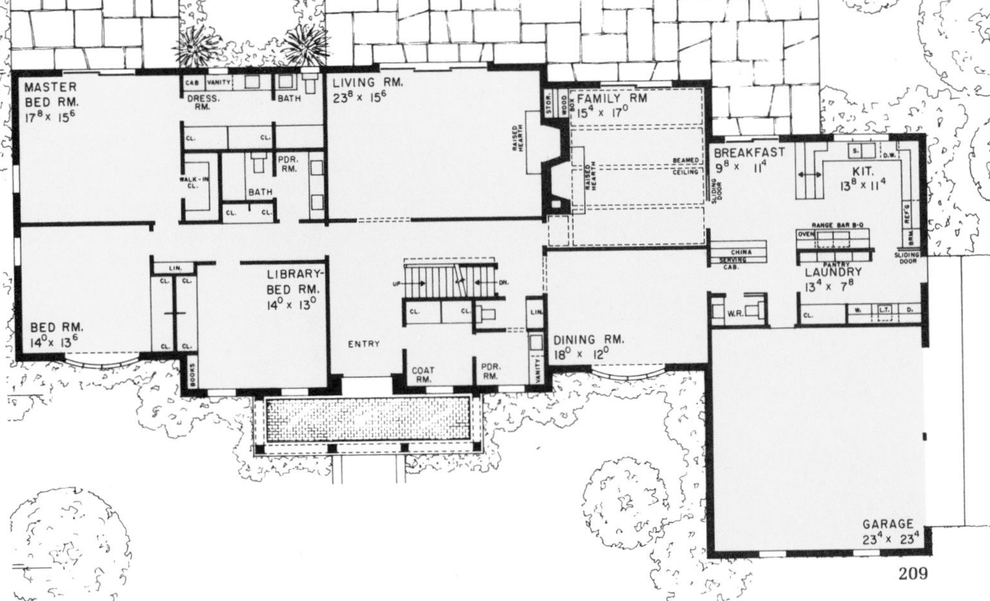

Design X2984

First Floor: 3,116 square feet
Second Floor: 1,997 square feet
Total: 5,113 square feet

● An echo of Whitehall, built in 1765 in Anne Arundel County, Maryland, resounds in this home. Its classic symmetry and columned facade herald a grand interior. There's no lack of space whether entertaining formally or just enjoying a family get-together, and all are kept cozy with fireplaces in the gathering room, study, and family room. An island kitchen with attached breakfast room handily serves the nearby dining room. Four second floor bedrooms include a large master suite with another fireplace, a whirlpool, and His and Hers closets in the bath. Three more full baths are found on this floor.

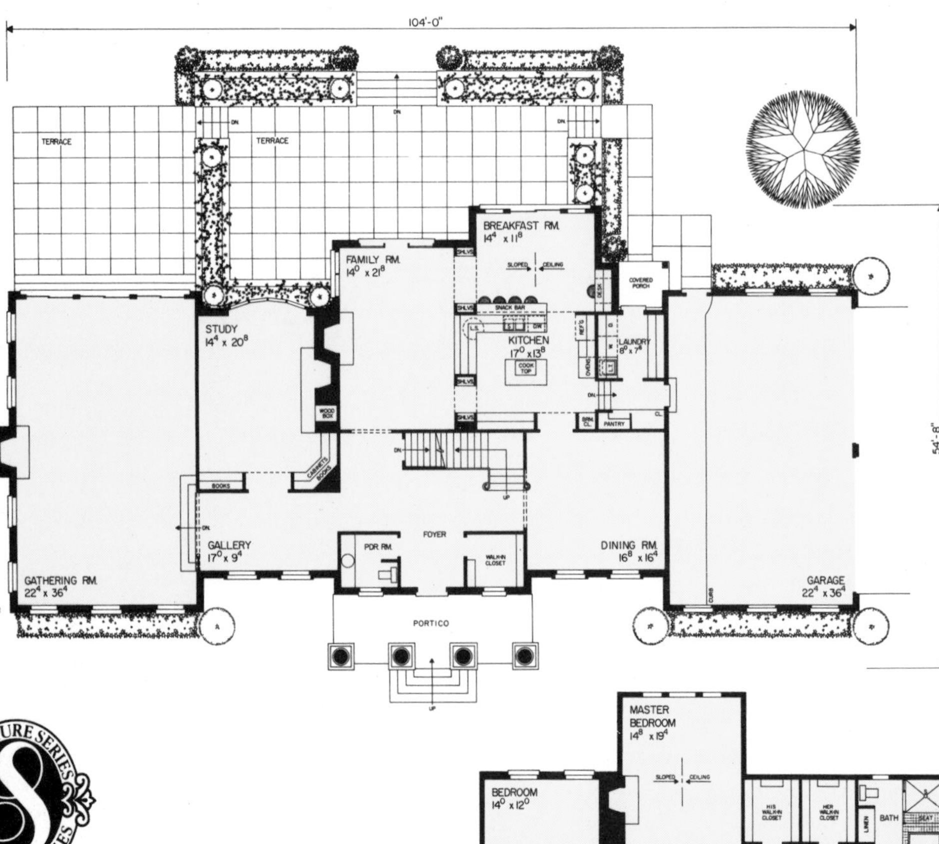

SIGNATURE SERIES LUXURY HOMES

Design X2977 First Floor: 4,104 square feet; Second Floor: 979 square feet; Total: 5,083 square feet

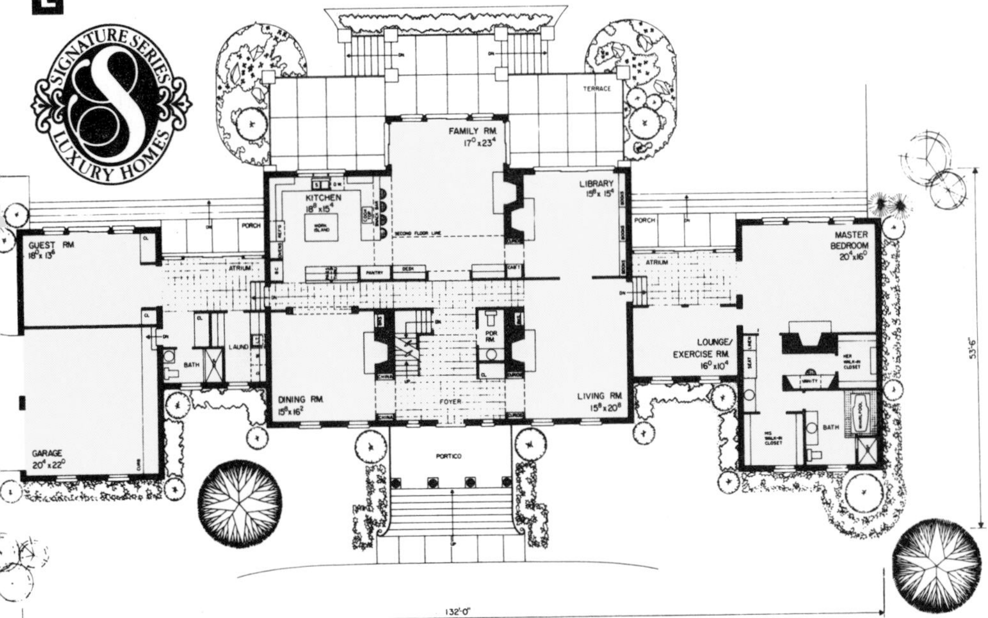

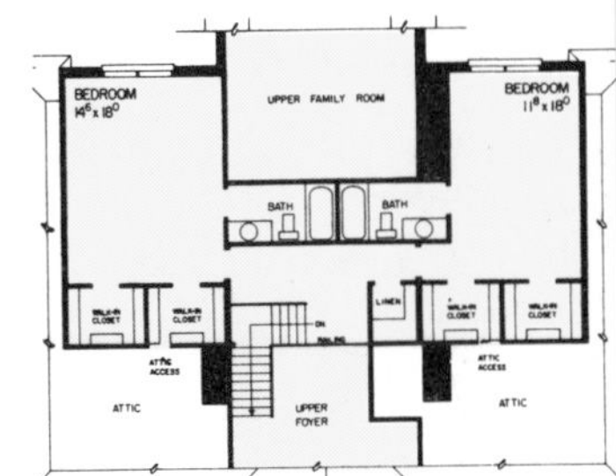

● Both front and rear facades of this elegant brick manor depict classic Georgian symmetry. A columned, Greek entry opens to an impressive two-story foyer. Fireplaces, built-in shelves, and cabinets highlight each of the four main gathering areas: living room, dining room, family room, and library.

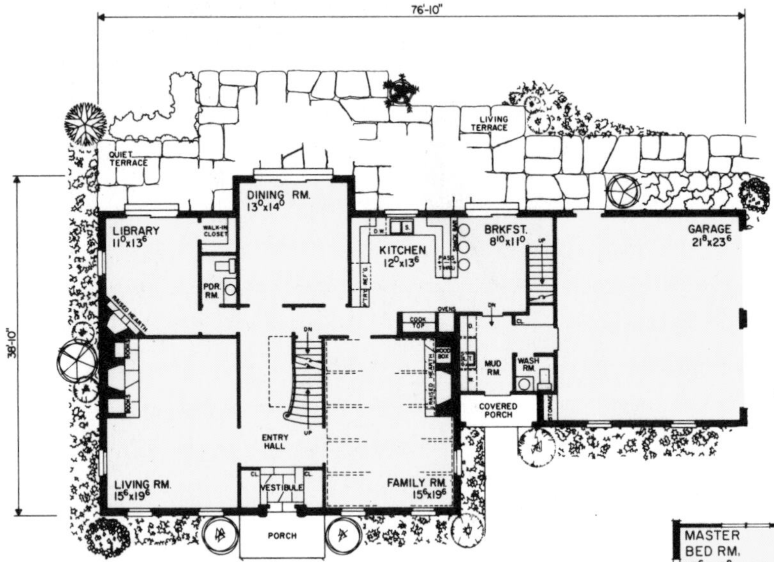

Design X1858

First Floor: 1,794 square feet
Second Floor: 1,474 square feet
Studio: 424 square feet
Total: 3,692 square feet

D

● From the delightful spacious front entry hall, to the studio or maid's room over the garage, this home is unique: four fireplaces, three full baths, two extra washrooms, a family room plus a quiet library. Note the separate set of stairs to the studio or maid's room. The kitchen is well-planned and strategically located between dining room and breakfast room.

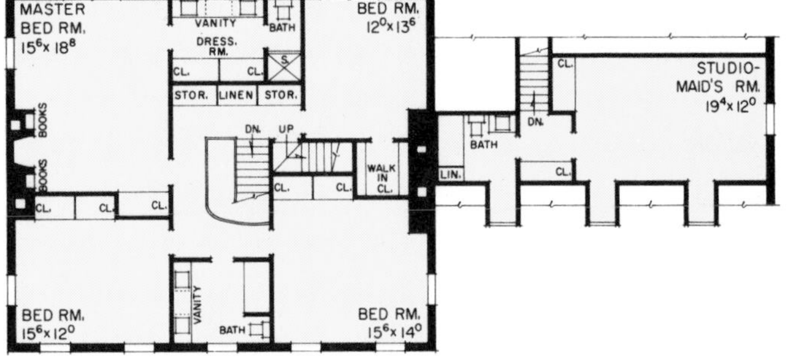

Design X2633

First Floor: 1,338 square feet
Second Floor: 1,200 square feet
Third Floor: 506 square feet
Total: 3,044 square feet

● This pleasing Georgian features a front porch with a roof supported by 12" diameter wooden columns. Sliding glass doors link the terrace and family room, providing an indoor/outdoor area for entertaining. The floor plan has been designed to serve the family efficiently. The stairway in the foyer leads to four second-floor bedrooms. The third floor is windowed and can be used as a studio and study.

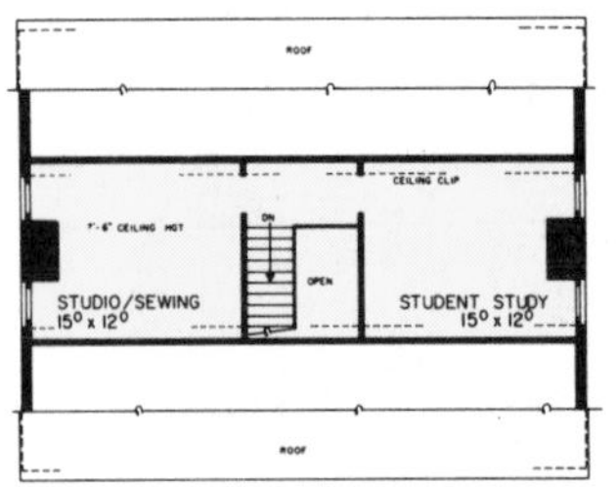

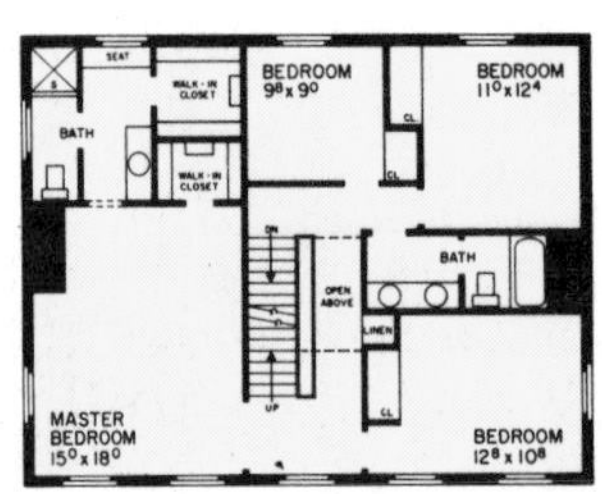

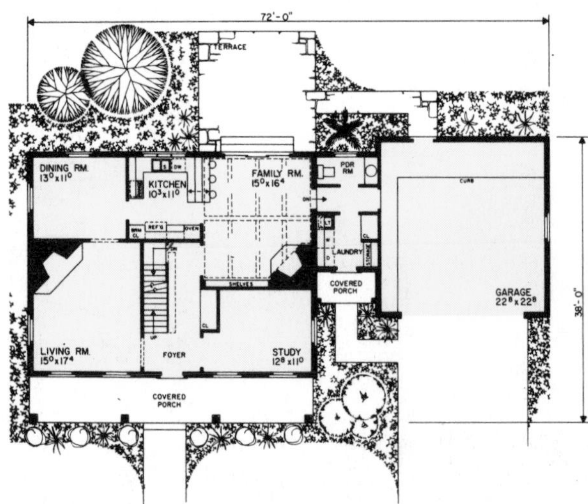

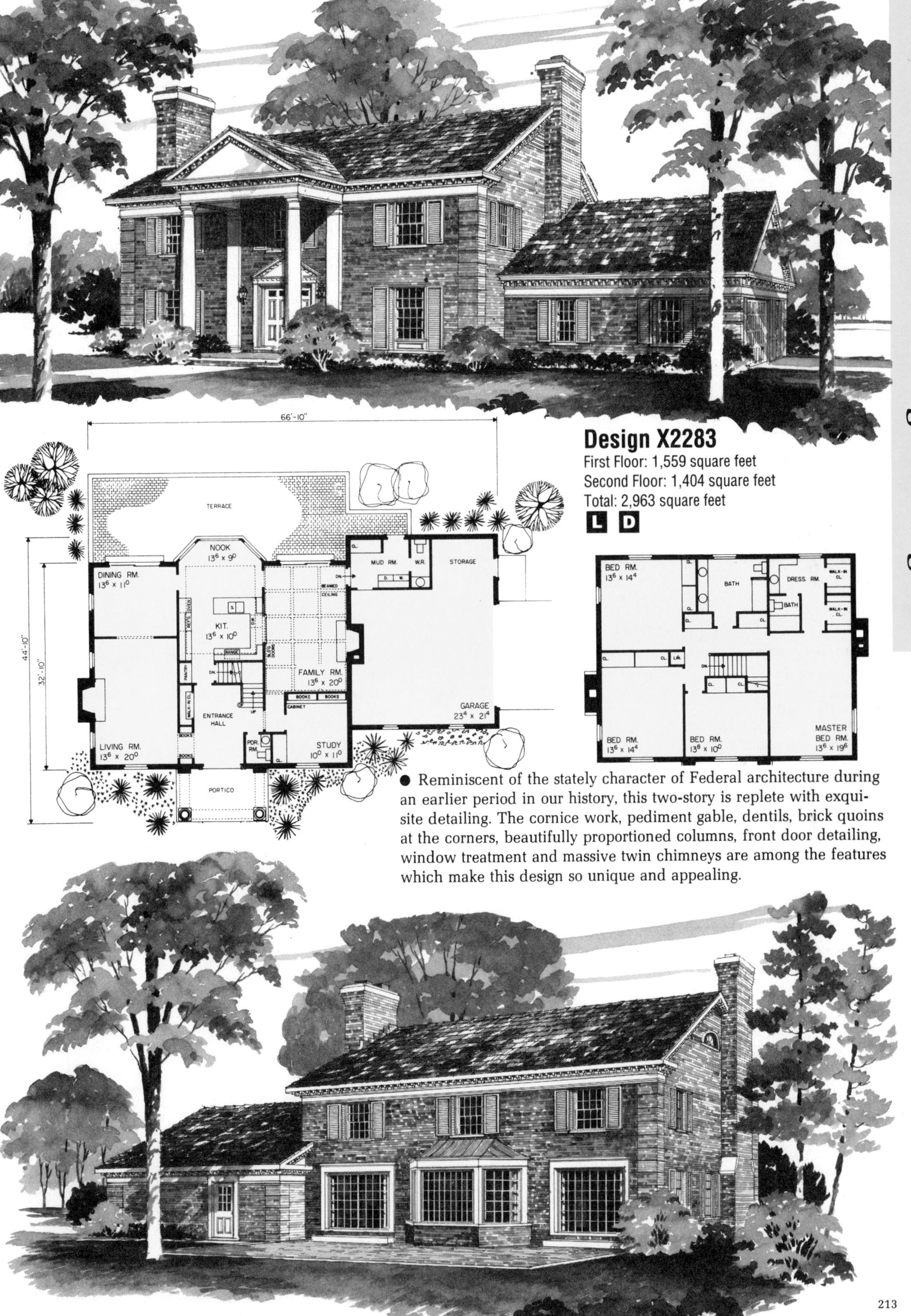

Design X2283

First Floor: 1,559 square feet
Second Floor: 1,404 square feet
Total: 2,963 square feet

L **D**

● Reminiscent of the stately character of Federal architecture during an earlier period in our history, this two-story is replete with exquisite detailing. The cornice work, pediment gable, dentils, brick quoins at the corners, beautifully proportioned columns, front door detailing, window treatment and massive twin chimneys are among the features which make this design so unique and appealing.

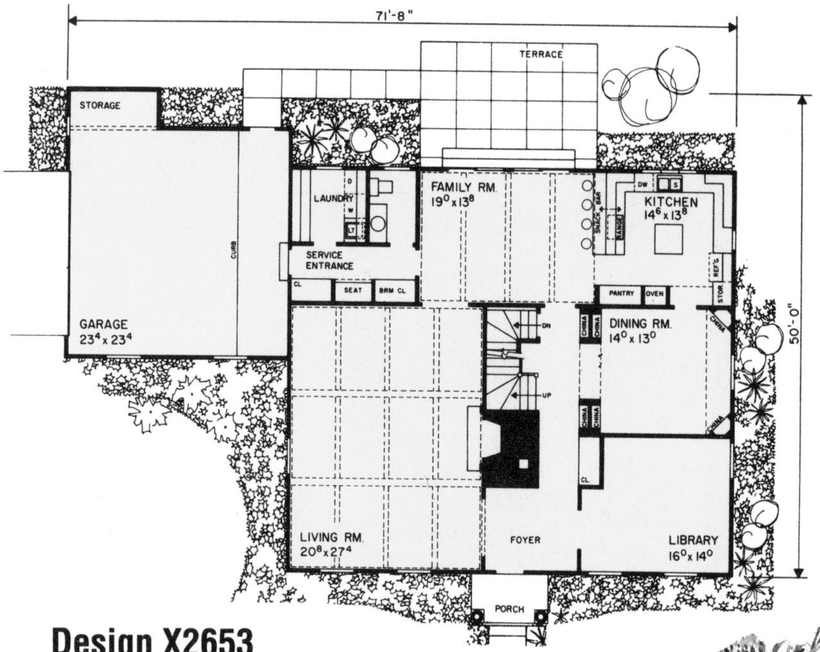

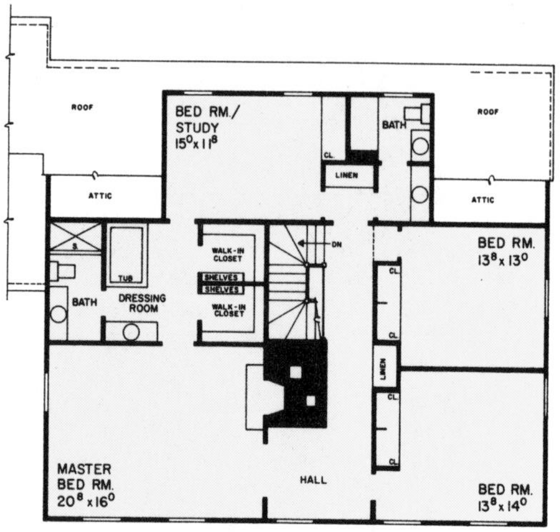

Design X2653

First Floor: 2,016 square feet
Second Floor: 1,656 square feet
Total: 3,672 square feet

- Livability and special features are absolutely outstanding in this Colonial design. Imagine a living room, with beamed ceiling and fireplace, that measures more than 20 x 27 feet. The second fireplace in the luxurious master suite makes it a very special retreat. Don't miss all the built-ins in the dining room.

Design X2188

First Floor: 1,440 square feet
Second Floor: 1,280 square feet
Total: 2,720 square feet

- This design is characteristic of early America. Along with exterior charm, the floor plan also has much to offer. The first floor contains both formal and informal living plus convenient work centers. Built-in bookshelves are the feature of both the family room and the study/bedroom. Built-ins are also featured in the garage. The second floor holds a master suite, three family bedrooms and a full bath. Folding stairs in the upstairs hall give easy access to the attic.

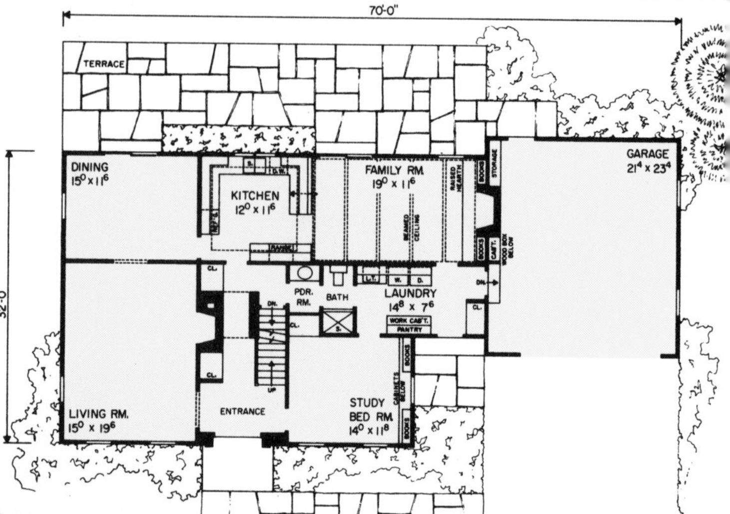

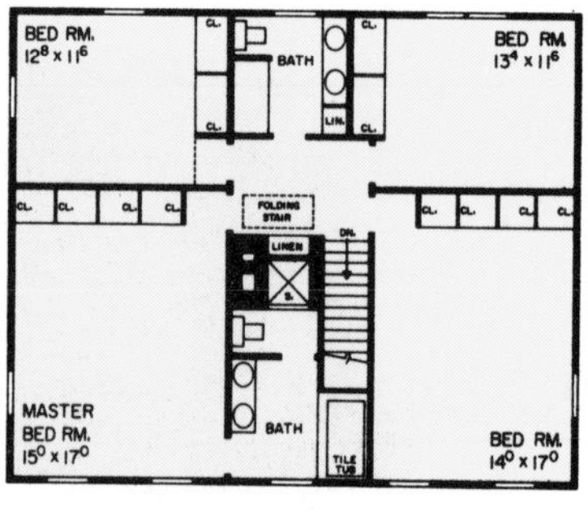

Design X2981

First Floor: 2,104 square feet
Second Floor: 2,015 square feet
Total: 4,119 square feet

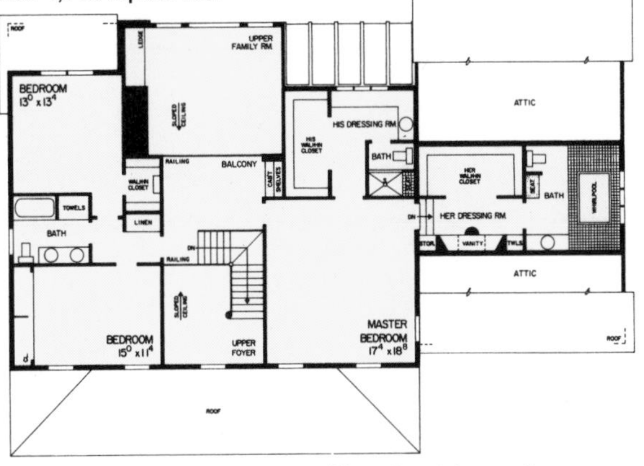

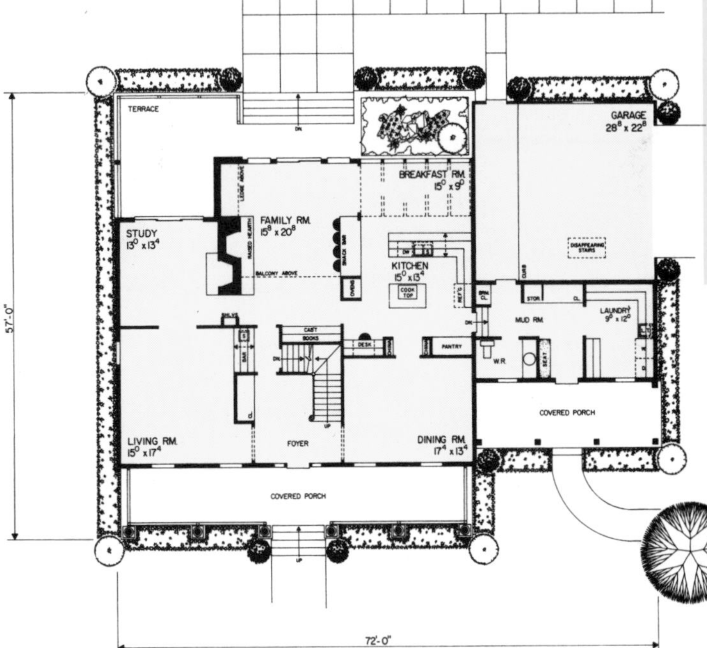

● This formal two-story recalls a Louisiana plantation house, Land's End, built in 1857. The Ionic columns of the front porch and the pediment gable echo the Greek Revival style. Highlighting the interior is the bright and cheerful spaciousness of the informal family room area. It features a wall of glass stretching to the second story sloping ceiling. Enhancing the drama of this area is the adjacent glass area of the breakfast room. Note the "His/Her" areas of the master bedroom.

Design X2899

First Floor: 1,685 square feet
Second Floor: 1,437 square feet
Total: 3,122 square feet

● This impressive Georgian home with massive twin chimneys and slender Roman doric columns is authentic in its 18th-Century detailing. Inside, the home offers comfort and elegance with living room, study, large formal dining room, breakfast room and even a butler's pantry. Upstairs is thoughtfully zoned, too, with three family bedrooms and a master suite.

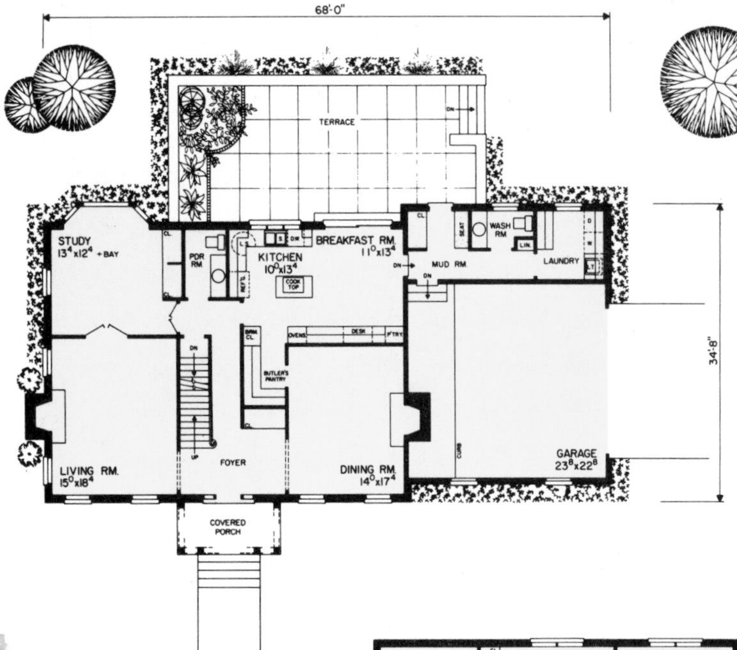

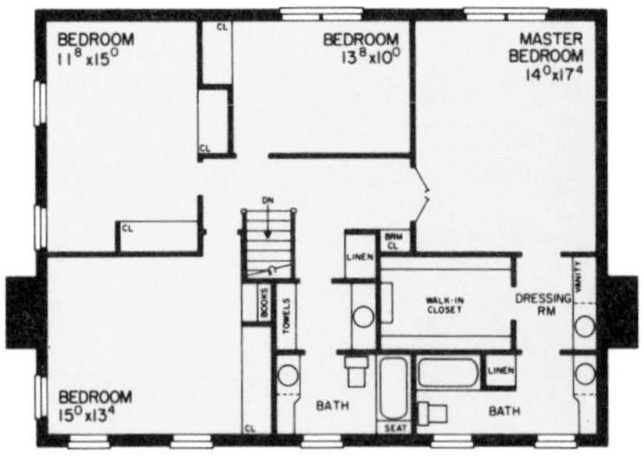

Design X2176

First Floor: 1,485 square feet
Second Floor: 1,175 square feet
Total: 2,660 square feet

L D

● A large living room featuring a fireplace and sliding glass doors is the focal point of this Georgian design. Adjacent is the formal dining room strategically located only a couple of steps from the efficient kitchen. Functioning closely with the kitchen is the family room with second fireplace.

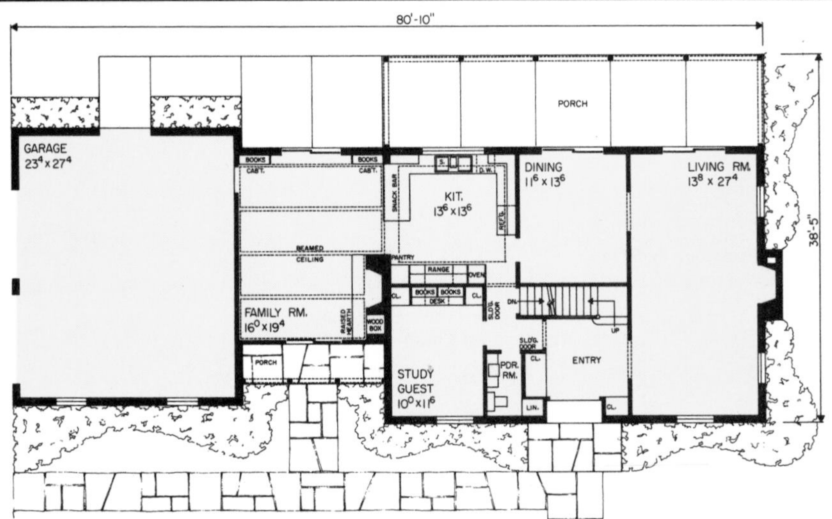

Design X2688

First Floor: 1,588 square feet
Second Floor: 1,101 square feet
Total: 2,689 square feet

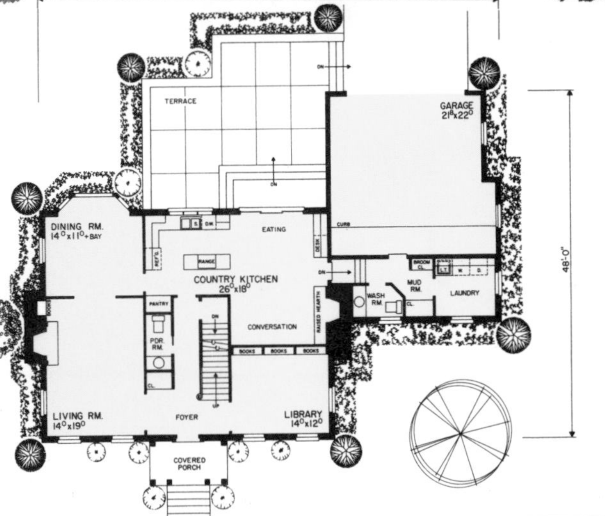

● Here are two floors of excellent livability. Start at the country kitchen. It will be the center for family activitieswith an island, desk, raised-hearth fireplace, conversation area and sliding glass doors to the terrace. Adjacent to this area is the washroom and laundry. Quieter areas are available in the living room and library. Three bedrooms are housed on the second floor.

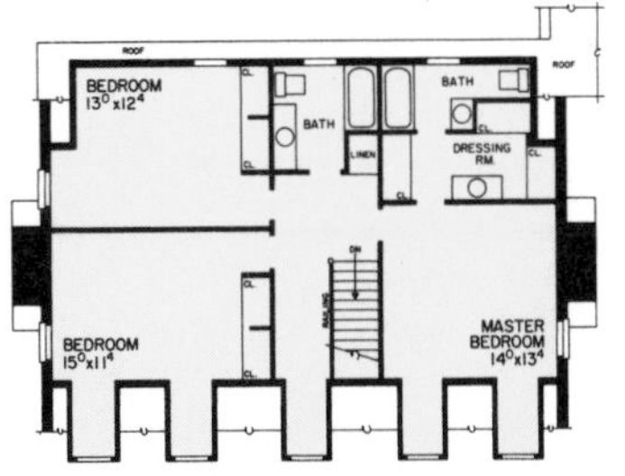

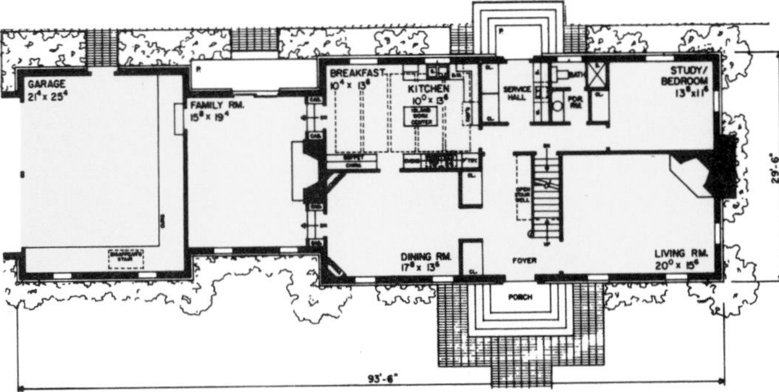

Design X2132

First Floor: 1,958 square feet
Second Floor: 1,305 square feet
Total: 3,263 square feet

● Another Georgian adaptation with a great heritage dating back to 18th-Century America. Exquisite and symmetrical detailing set the character of this impressive home. Don't overlook such features as the two fireplaces, the laundry, the beamed ceiling, the built-in china cabinets and the oversized garage.

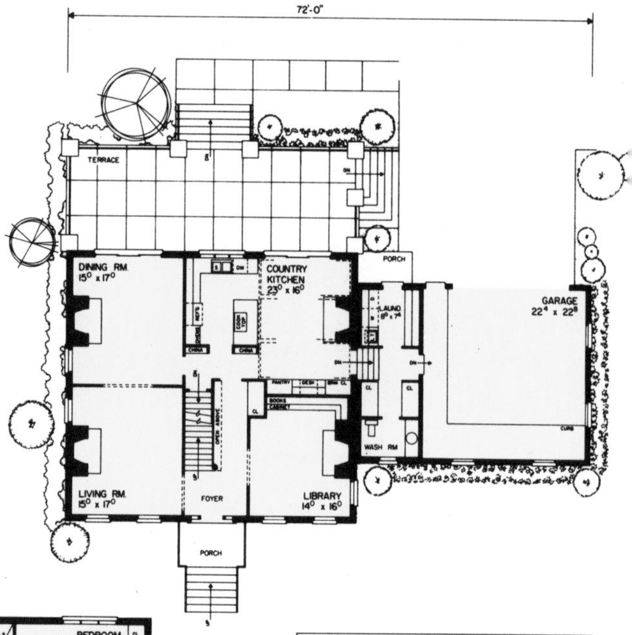

Design X2975

First Floor: 1,656 square feet
Second Floor: 1,440 square feet
Third Floor: 715 square feet
Total: 3,811 square feet

- Three wonderful floors of living space include a useful guest bedroom and study or hobbies room on the top floor. The second-floor master suite has a pampering bath. Three family bedrooms share a full bath on this floor as well. Living areas include formal living and dining rooms, country kitchen and library. Notice that this plan sports six fireplaces!

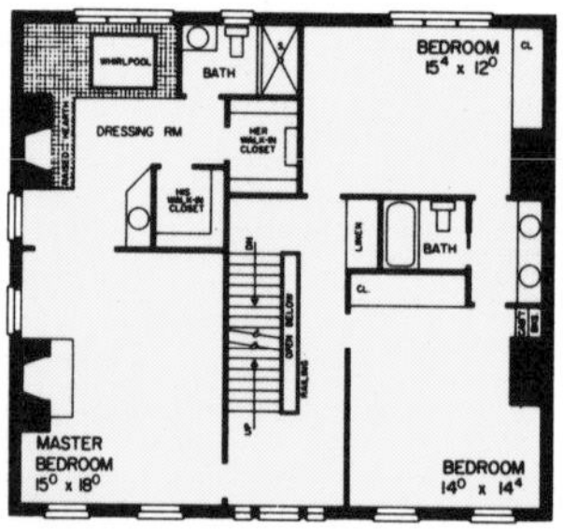

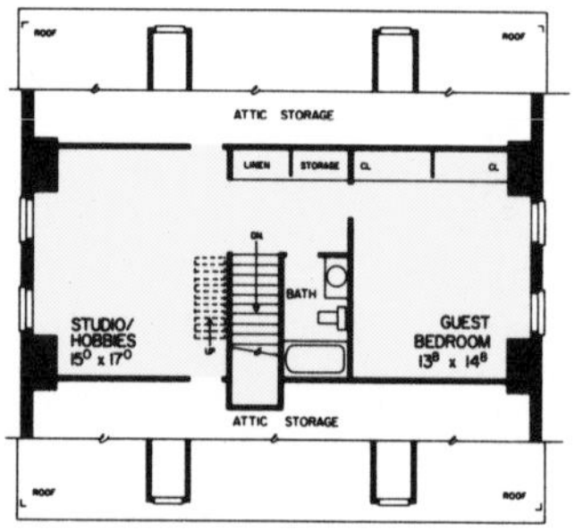

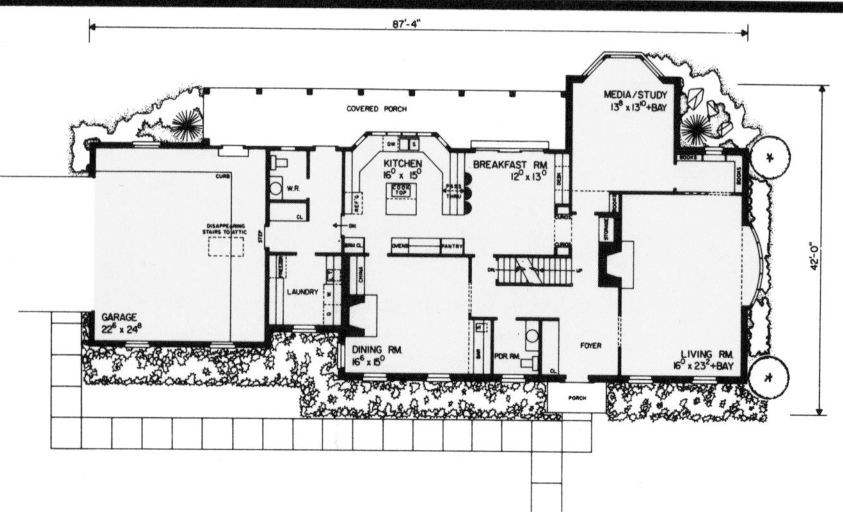

Design X2963

First Floor: 2,046 square feet
Second Floor: 1,644 square feet
Total: 3,690 square feet

- The rambling proportions of this house reflect Colonial precedents. Both the dining and living rooms boast large fireplaces. Family meals are likely to be served in the cozy breakfast room attached to the kitchen. The study is tucked away behind the living room. Upstairs, four bedrooms provide a comfortable retreat for each family member.

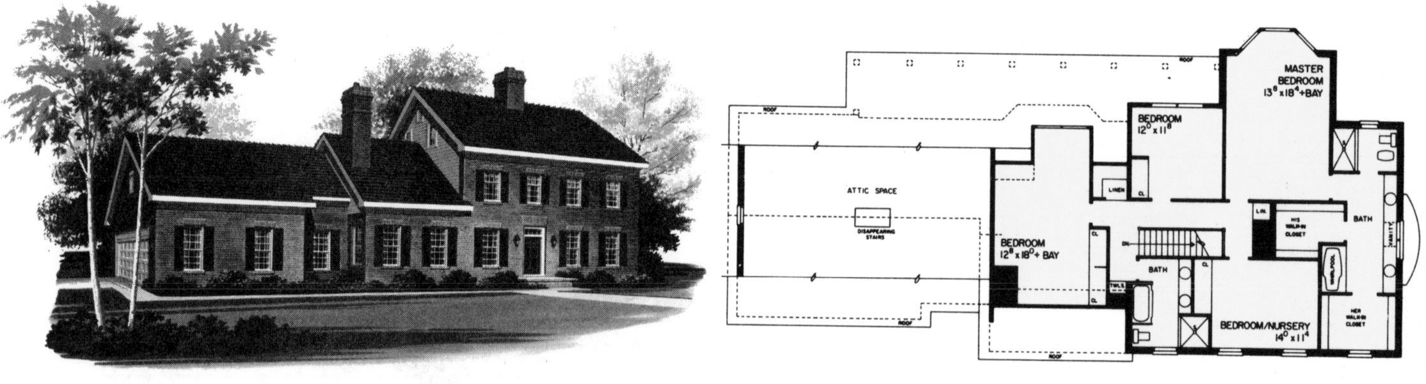

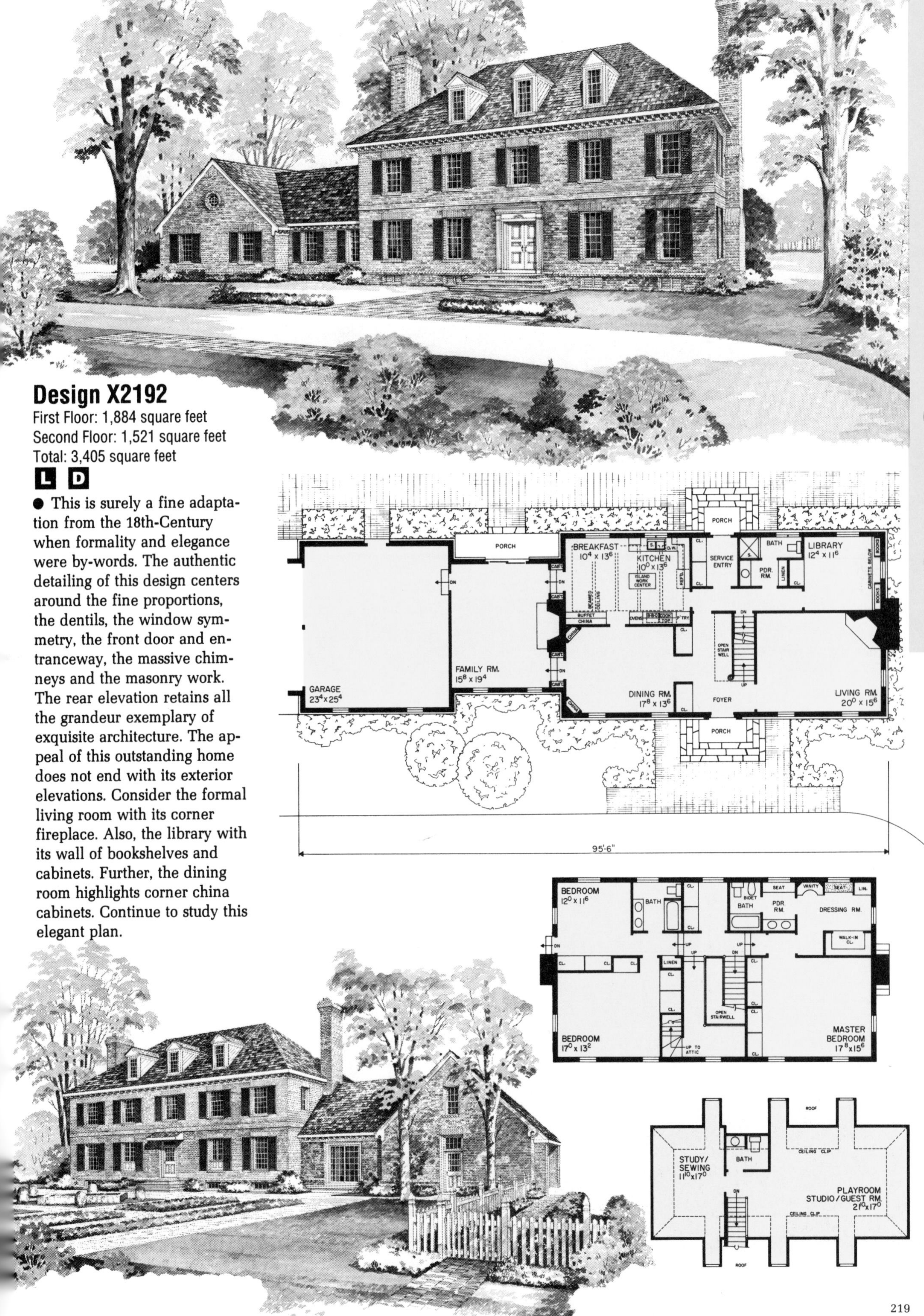

Design X2192

First Floor: 1,884 square feet
Second Floor: 1,521 square feet
Total: 3,405 square feet

L **D**

● This is surely a fine adaptation from the 18th-Century when formality and elegance were by-words. The authentic detailing of this design centers around the fine proportions, the dentils, the window symmetry, the front door and entranceway, the massive chimneys and the masonry work. The rear elevation retains all the grandeur exemplary of exquisite architecture. The appeal of this outstanding home does not end with its exterior elevations. Consider the formal living room with its corner fireplace. Also, the library with its wall of bookshelves and cabinets. Further, the dining room highlights corner china cabinets. Continue to study this elegant plan.

● Here is a New England Georgian adaptation with an elevated doorway highlighted by pilasters and a pediment. It gives way to a second-story Palladian window, capped in turn by a pediment projecting from the hipped roof. The interior is decidely up-to-date with even an upstairs lounge.

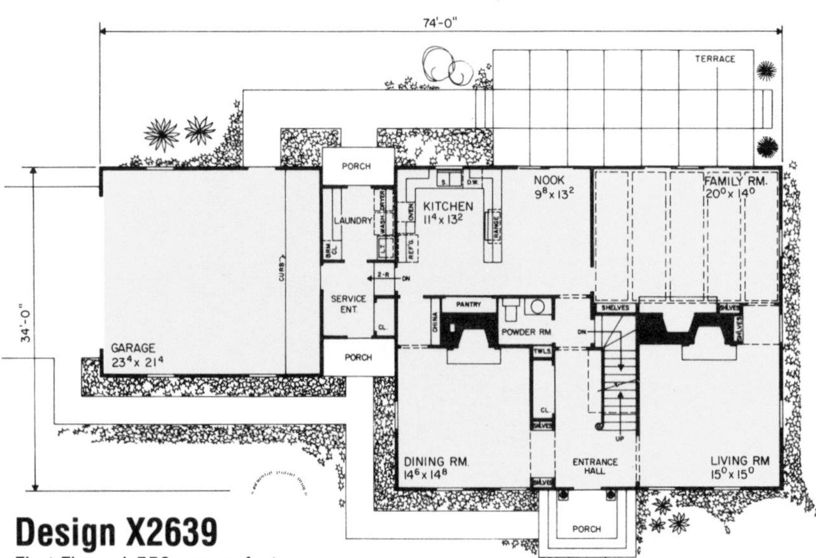

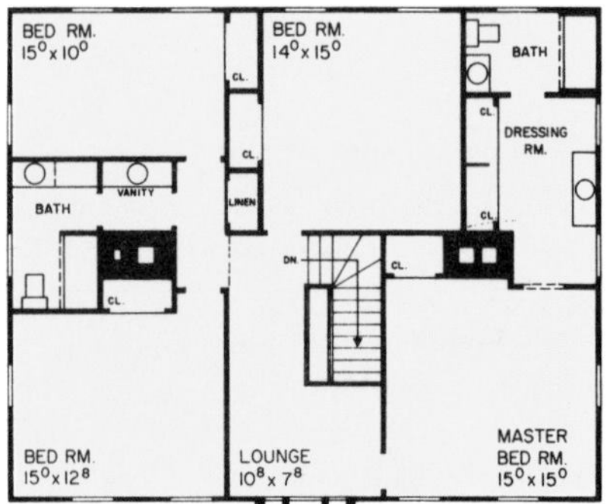

Design X2639

First Floor: 1,556 square feet
Second Floor: 1,428 square feet
Total: 2,984 square feet

L D

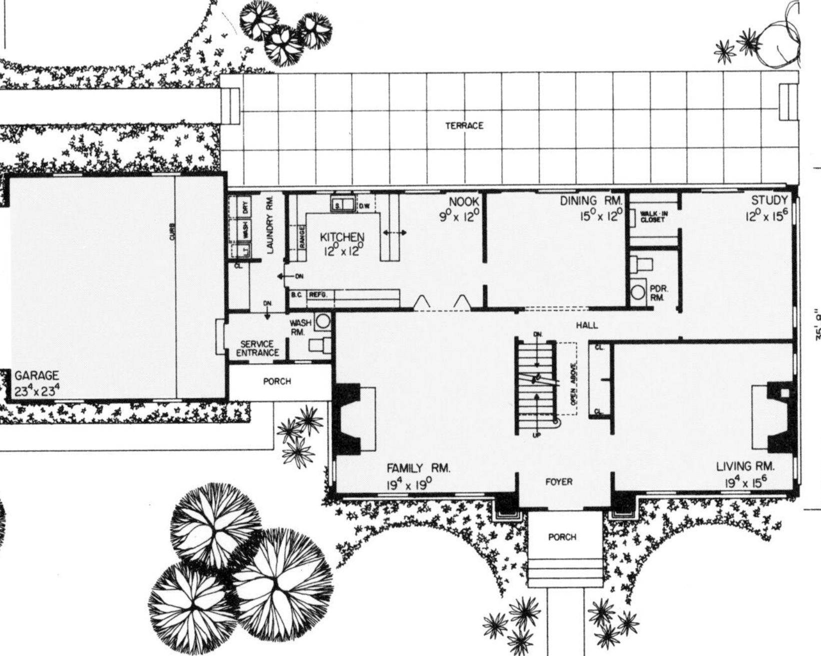

Design X2522

First Floor: 1,835 square feet
Second Floor: 1,625 square feet
Total: 3,460 square feet

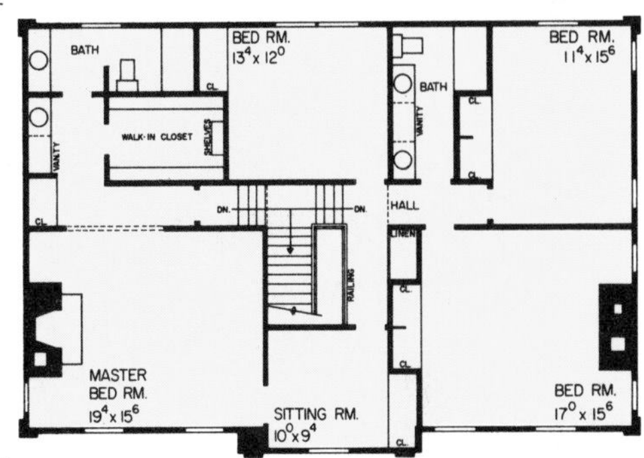

● This wood frame Georgian adaptation revives the architecture of an earlier period in New England. Its formal facade houses an abundance of spacious livability.

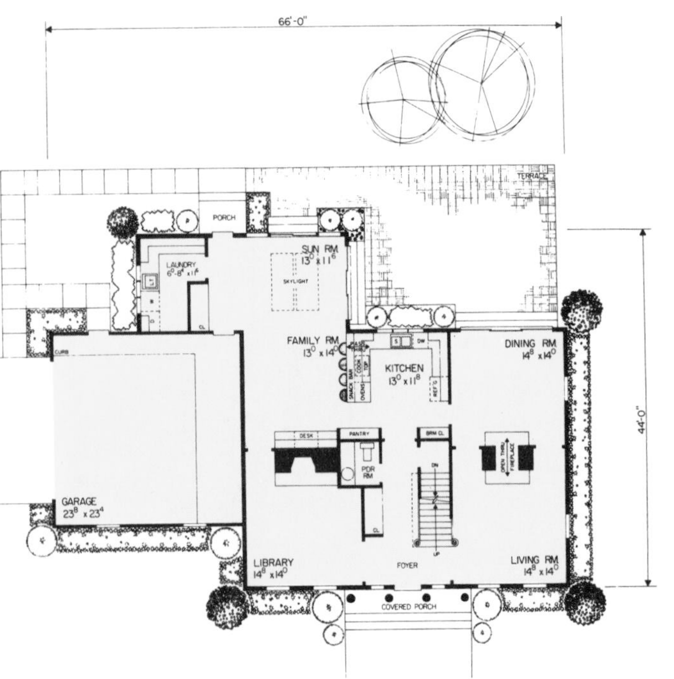

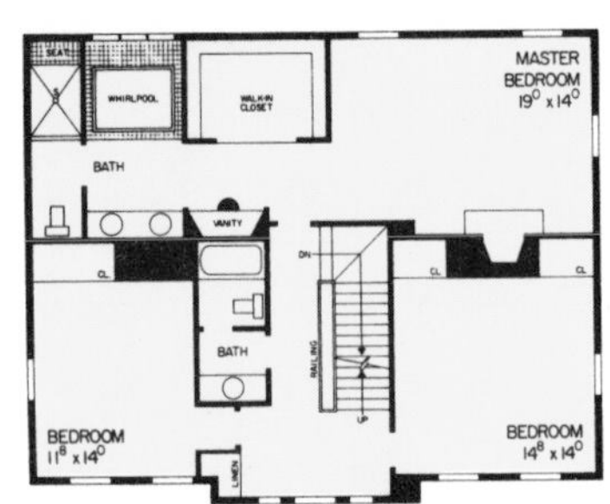

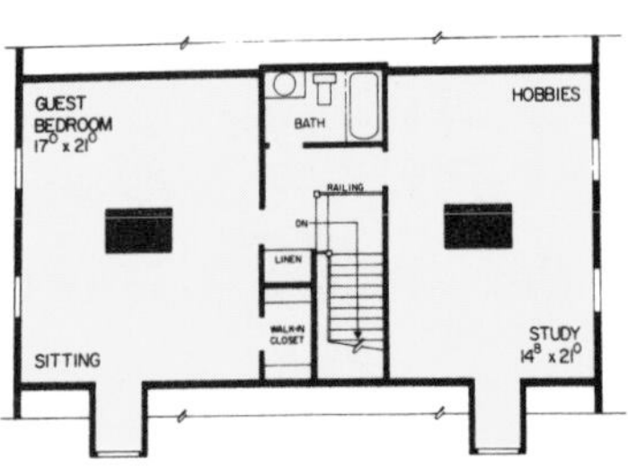

Design X2980 First Floor: 1,648 square feet
Second Floor: 1,368 square feet; Third Floor: 567 square feet
Total: 3,583 square feet

● This late Georgian adaptation is reminiscent of the Cowles house built in Farmington, Conn. around 1786. The formal symmetry and rich ornamentation were typical of houses of this period. Ionic columns, a Palladian window, and a pedimented gable are among the details that set the character of this historic house. Inside there are three floors of livability. And, of course, there is no hint of antiquity here. The centered foyer is flanked by wonderfully spacious living areas which flow around the fireplaces. Note the sun room, laundry, and bonus space of the third floor where there is all kinds of livability.

Design X2982

First Floor: 1,584 square feet
Second Floor: 1,513 square feet
Total: 3,097 square feet

● An early 18th Century Georgian so common to Williamsburg, Va. and environs. Observe the massive twin chimneys, the cornice ornamentation, and the wrought iron balcony sheltering the front panelled door. The rectangular shape of this house will lead to economical construction costs. The 30 foot, beamed-ceiling country kitchen with its commanding corner fireplace and rear yard access is outstanding. Notice the fireplaces for the country kitchen, living, dining and master bedrooms.

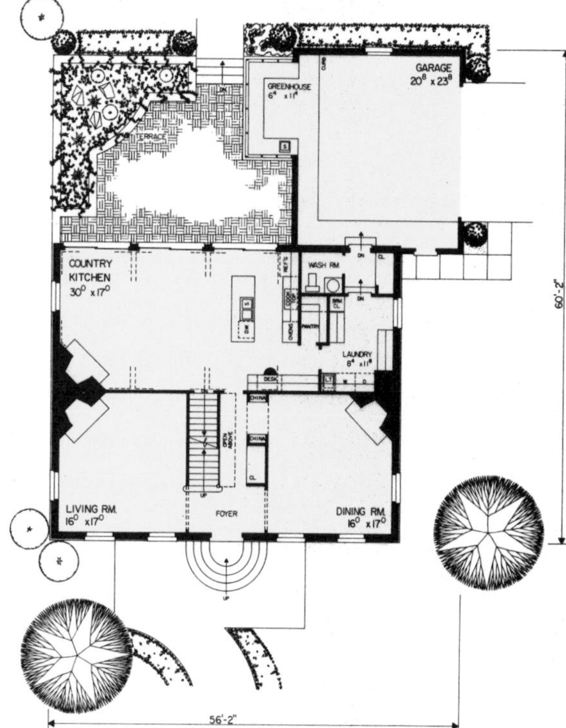

Design X2641

First Floor: 1,672 square feet
Second Floor: 1,248 square feet
Total: 2,920 square feet

● This Georgian adaptation is from the early 18th-Century and has plenty of historical background. The classical details are sedately stated. The plan promises up-to-date livability. The size of your site need not be large, either.

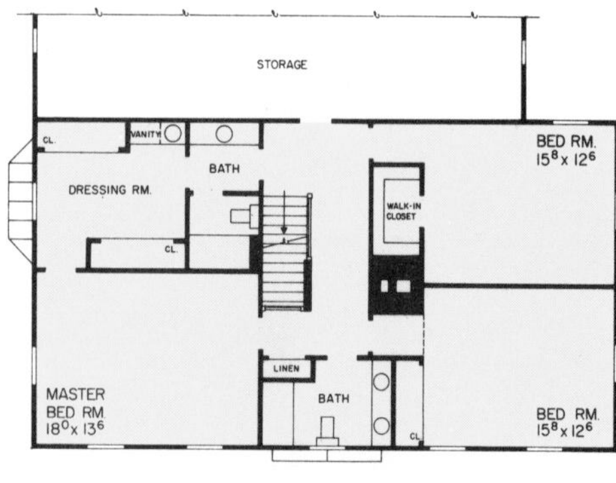

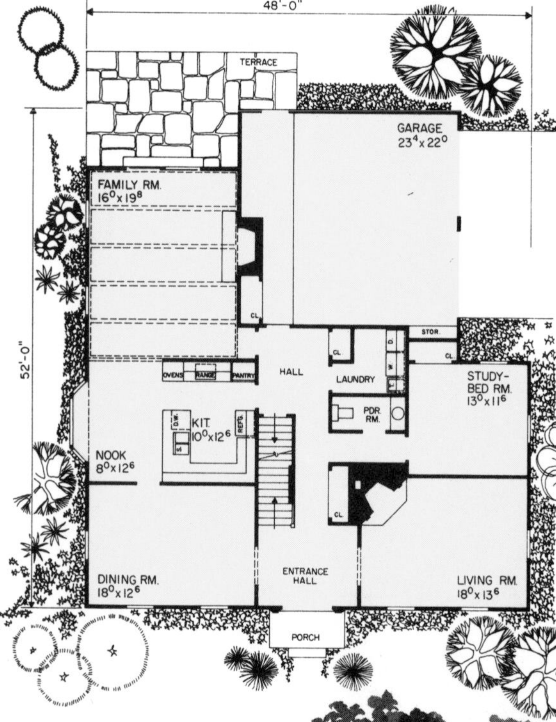

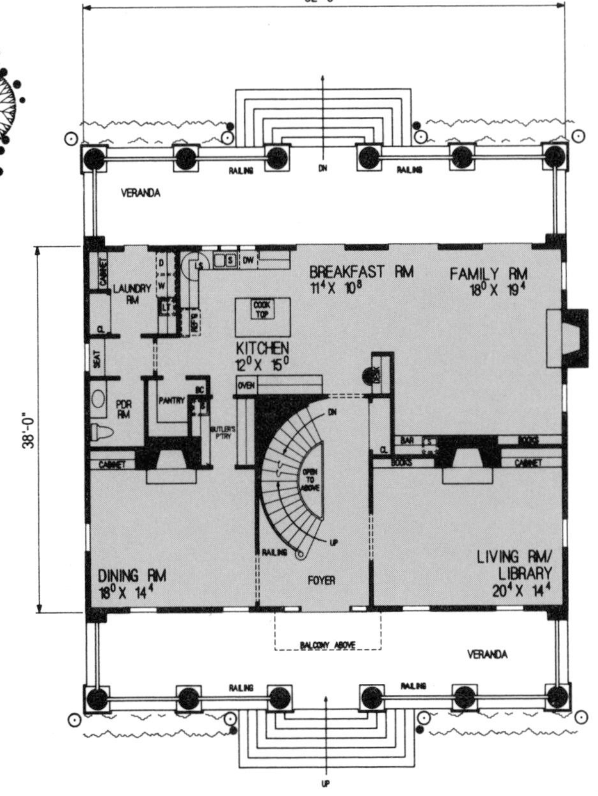

Design X3500

First Floor: 1,968 square feet
Second Floor: 1,901 square feet
Total: 3,869 square feet

● A historical facade with sweeping verandas in the front and rear conceals a livable plan. Special amenities inside include the rounded stairway, three fireplaces, two pantries, a built-in desk, built-in shelves and bookcases. Four bedrooms on the second floor have access to three full baths.

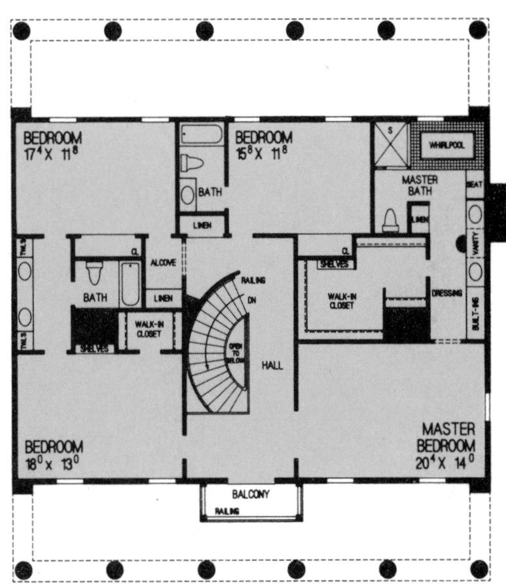

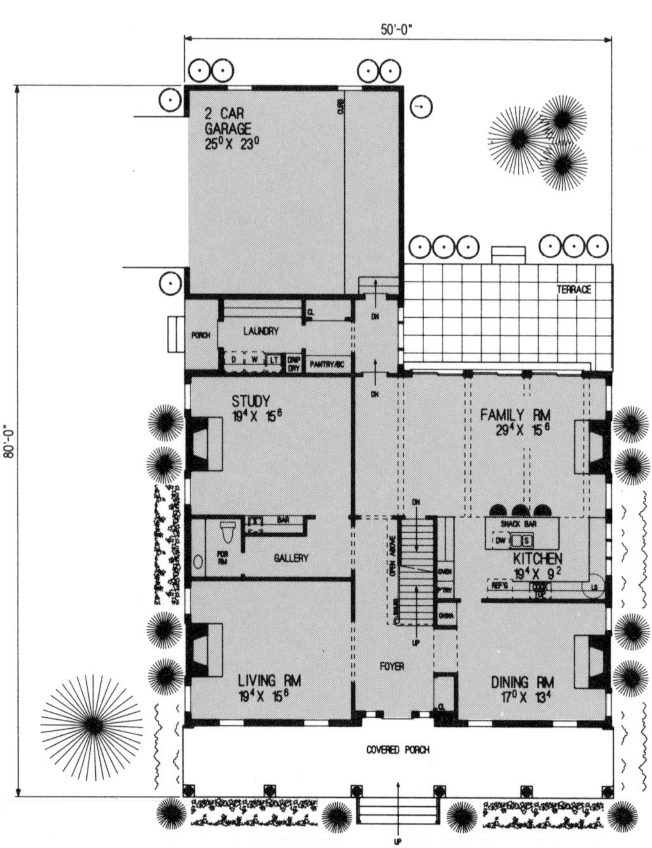

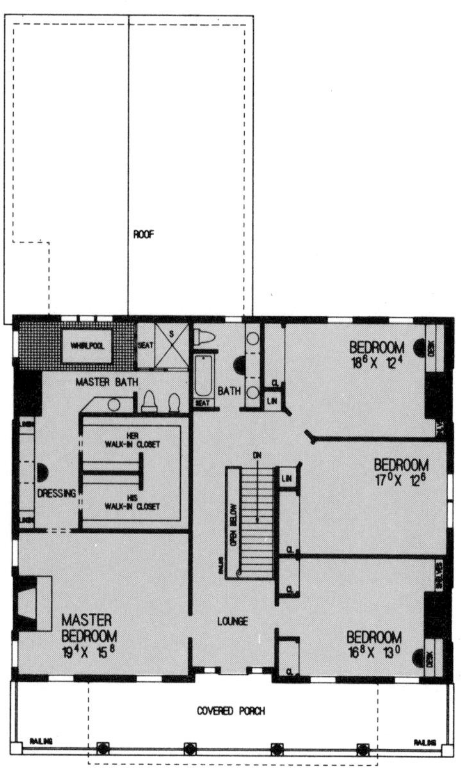

Design X2996

First Floor: 2,191 square feet
Second Floor: 1,928 square feet
Total: 4,119 square feet

L **D**

● Covered porches upstairs and down are a charming addition to the well appointed two-story. Four chimney stacks herald four hearths inside: living room, dining room, family room and study. The second floor holds four bedrooms including a master suite with its own fireplace and a huge walk-in closet.

Design X2987

First Floor: 2,822 square feet
Second Floor: 1,335 square feet
Total: 4,157 square feet

● Andrew Jackson's dream of white-pillared splendor resulted in the building of The Hermitage. The essence of that grand dream is recaptured in this modern variation. One wing of the first floor contains a luxurious master suite which accommodates everyone's needs gracefully. The opposite wing features a country kitchen, laundry, washroom and two-car garage. The family room, dining room and living room are centrally located. On the second floor are three bedrooms (one a guest room) and one and a half baths.

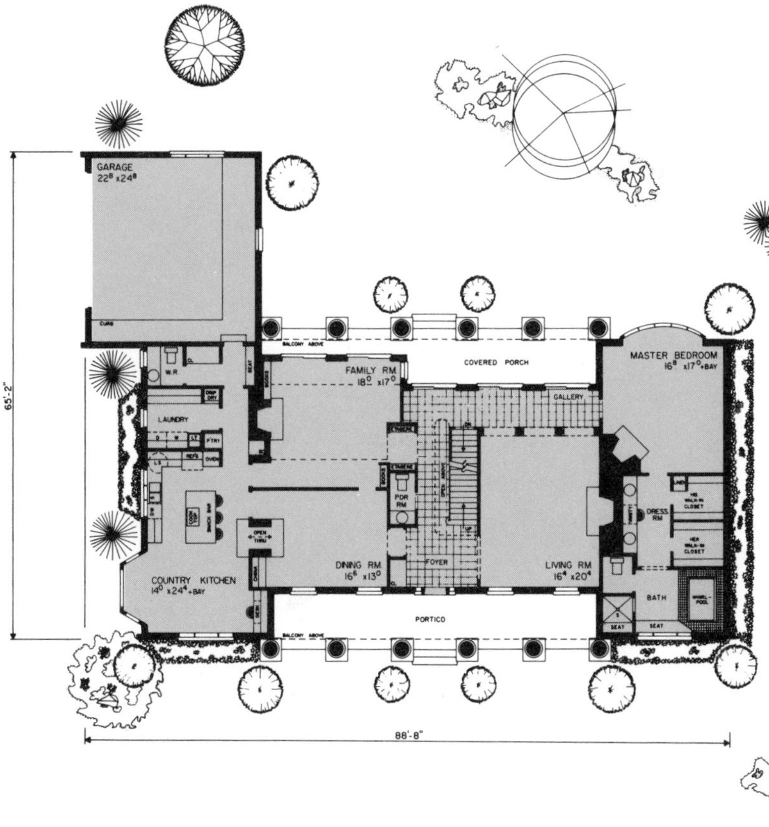

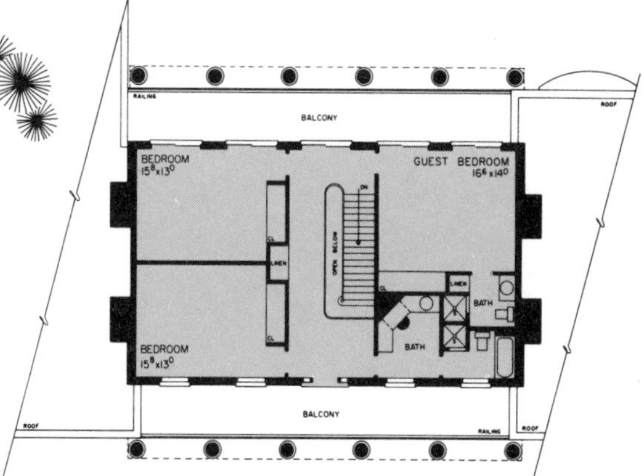

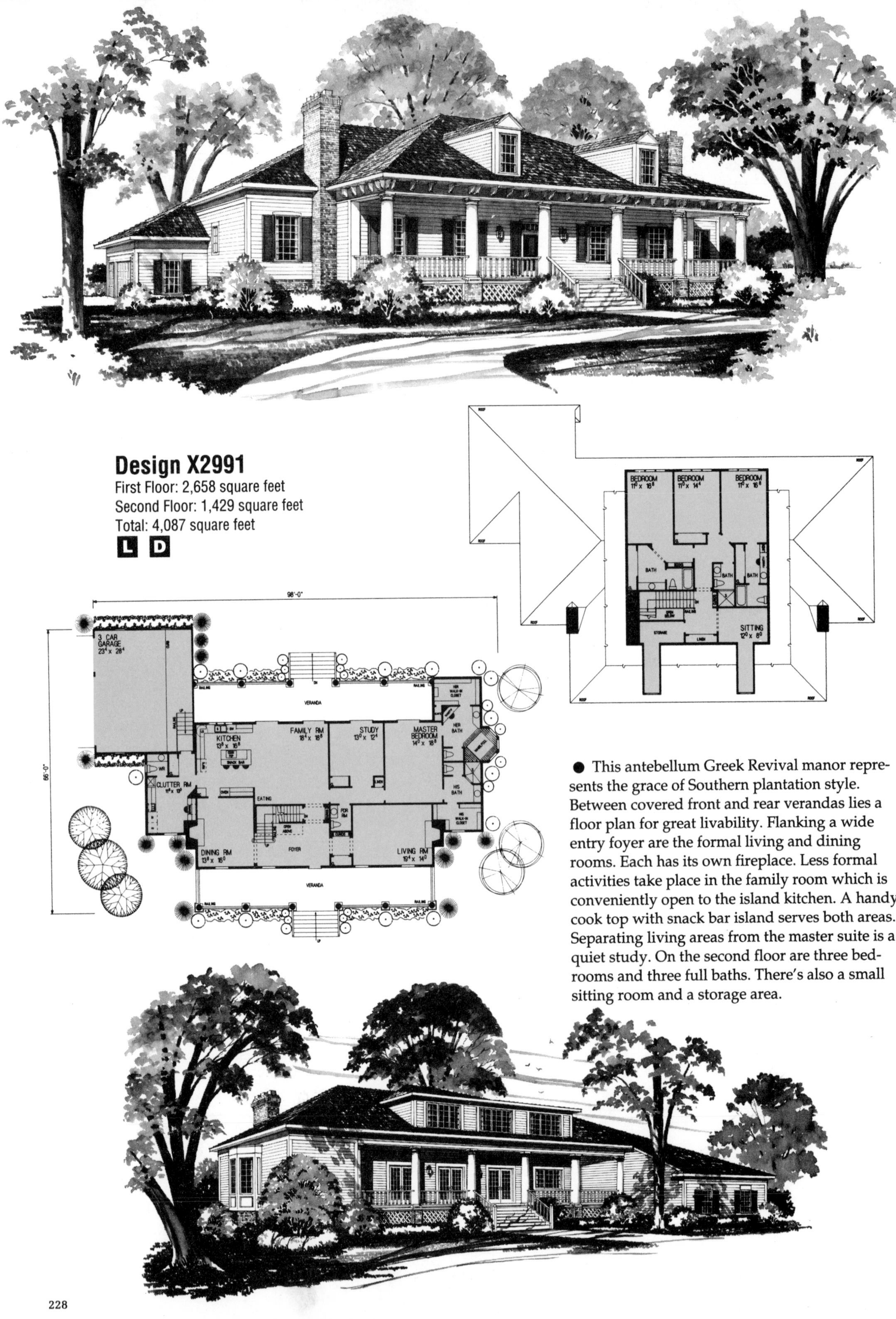

Design X2991

First Floor: 2,658 square feet
Second Floor: 1,429 square feet
Total: 4,087 square feet

L D

● This antebellum Greek Revival manor represents the grace of Southern plantation style. Between covered front and rear verandas lies a floor plan for great livability. Flanking a wide entry foyer are the formal living and dining rooms. Each has its own fireplace. Less formal activities take place in the family room which is conveniently open to the island kitchen. A handy cook top with snack bar island serves both areas. Separating living areas from the master suite is a quiet study. On the second floor are three bedrooms and three full baths. There's also a small sitting room and a storage area.

Design X2997

Square Footage: 3,442

● The fine features of this home include five fireplaces. One fireplace warms the master bedroom with expansive bath and dressing area, plus access to a private rear terrace. Two additional bedrooms each adjoin a full bath. Large living areas include the living room, dining room and family room with snack bar. A library with fireplace, sloped ceiling and built-in shelves is tucked away in the rear of the home.

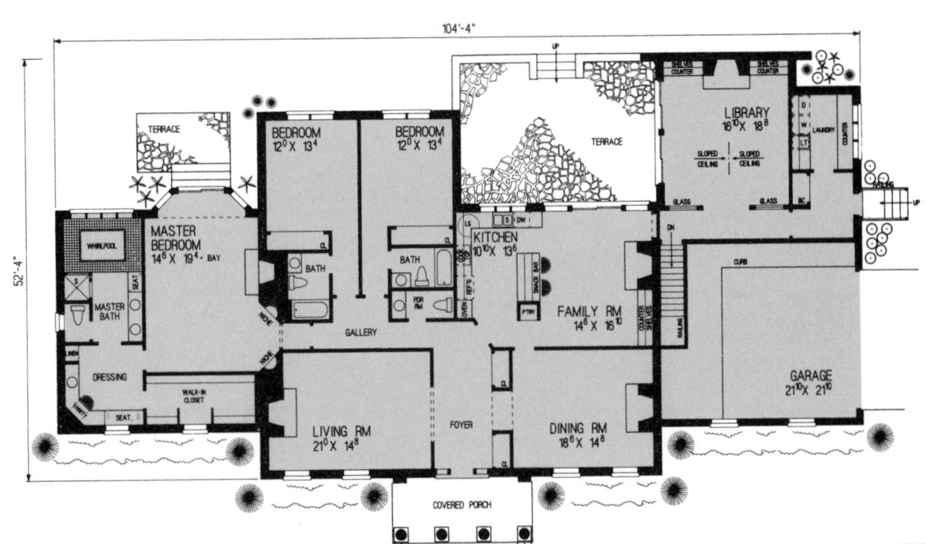

Design X2693

Square Footage: 3,462

● This elegant Georgian manor is reminiscent of historic Rose Hill, built 1818 in Lexington, Kentucky. It is typical of the classic manors with Greek Revival features built in Kentucky as the 19th Century dawned. Note the updated interior, highlighted by a large country kitchen with fireplace and an efficient work center that includes an island cooktop. The country kitchen leads directly into a formal dining room, just off the foyer. On the other side of the foyer is a living room. A large library is located in the back of the house featuring built-in bookcases plus a fireplace (one of four fireplaces).

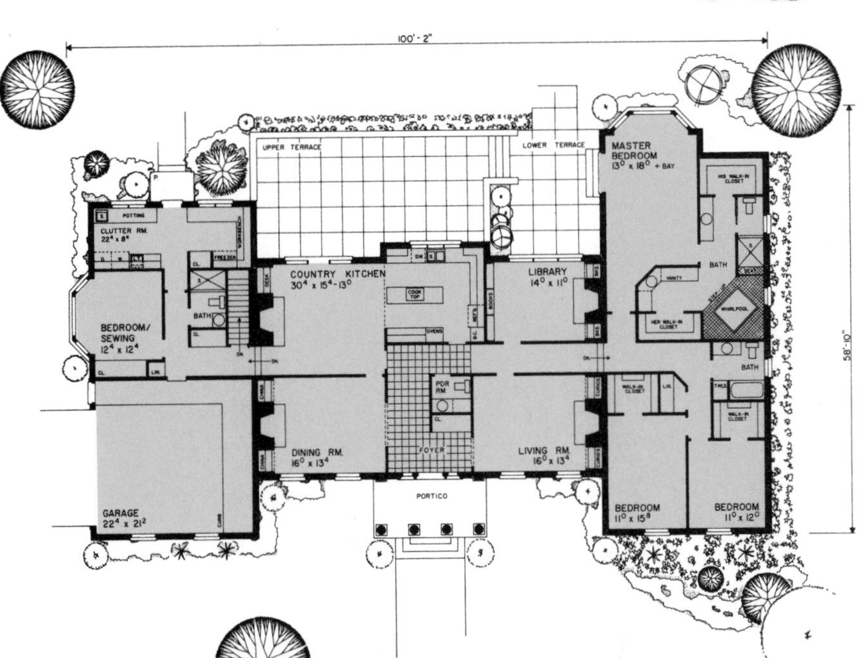

Design X2998

First Floor: 2,243 square feet
Second Floor: 1,532 square feet
Total: 3,775 square feet

● Symmetrical and simply lovely, this gambrel-roofed two-story is a fine example of historical homes. Its details will enchant the most particular enthusiast of early architecture. The floor plan is a classic as well. Note the formal dining and living rooms flanking the entry hall. The living room has a fireplace and the dining room a bay window. A media room/study also sports a fireplace and has access to a rear terrace. The family room connects to the kitchen via a through snack bar. There's also another fireplace here. On the second floor are three bedrooms and two full baths. The third floor contains unfinished space which acts as superb storage and can be developed later into more bedrooms if needed.

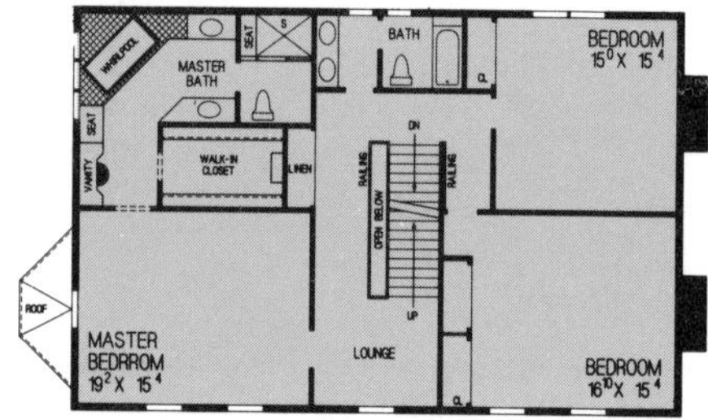

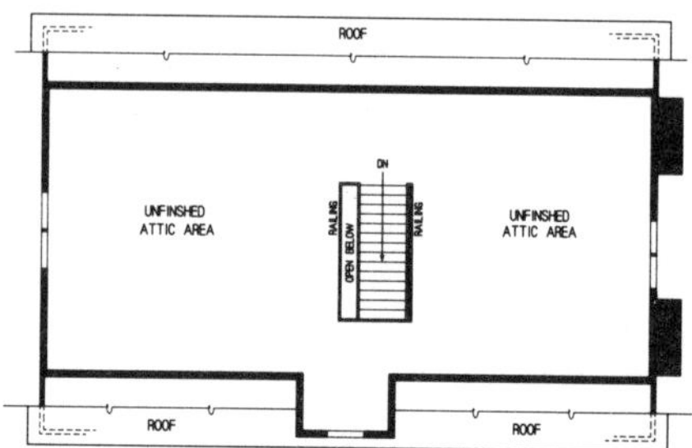

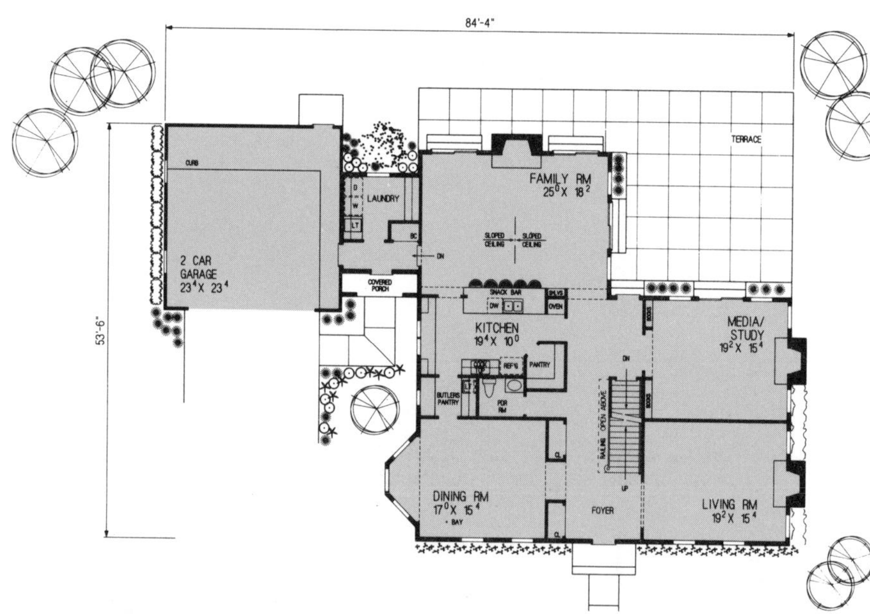

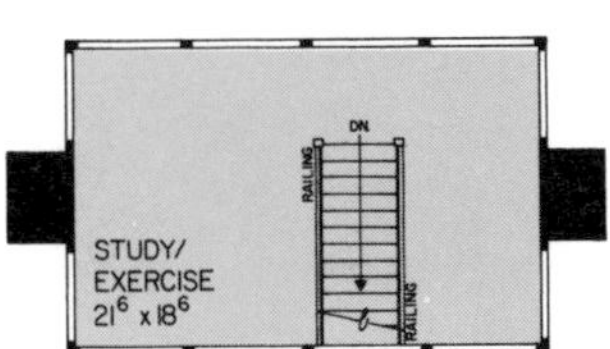

SHELVES
HER WALK-IN CLOSET
WHIRLPOOL
SEAT
BATH
BATH
LINEN
BEDROOM
12^{0} x 13^{10}
HIS WALK-IN CLOSET
VANITY
DN.
RAILING
OPEN BELOW
UP
CL.
CL.
SHELVES
MASTER
BEDROOM
24^{8} x 13^{8}
BEDROOM
16^{6} x 13^{8}

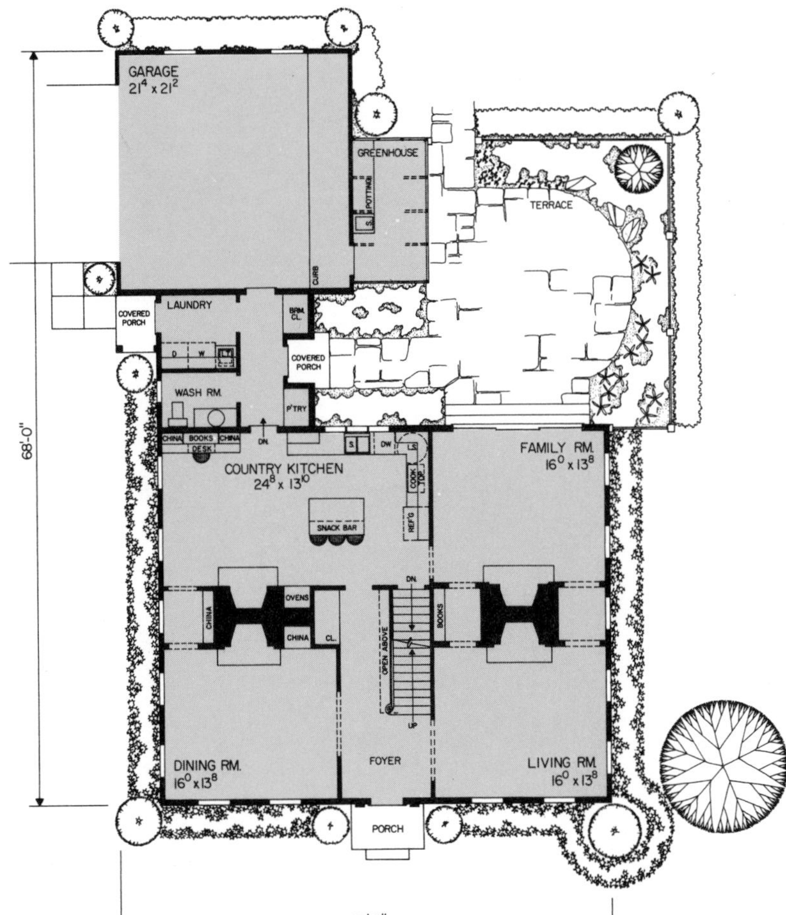

Design X2985

First Floor: 1,600 square feet
Second Floor: 1,428 square feet
Third Floor: 316 square feet
Total: 3,344 square feet

● Bonus space creates lots of livability in this three-bedroom, two-and-a-half bath design. The island kitchen, living room, family room and dining room each have their own fireplace. Built-ins abound in china cabinets, bookshelves and a desk. Outside is a huge terrace area and a lovely greenhouse extension off the garage. The second-floor bedrooms include a master suite with His and Hers closets, seated vanity and whirlpool bath. A third-floor cupola allows space for an exercise room or study, but could also accommodate guests or be used as a children's playroom.

Design X2989

First Floor: 1,972 square feet
Second Floor: 1,533 square feet
Total: 3,505 square feet

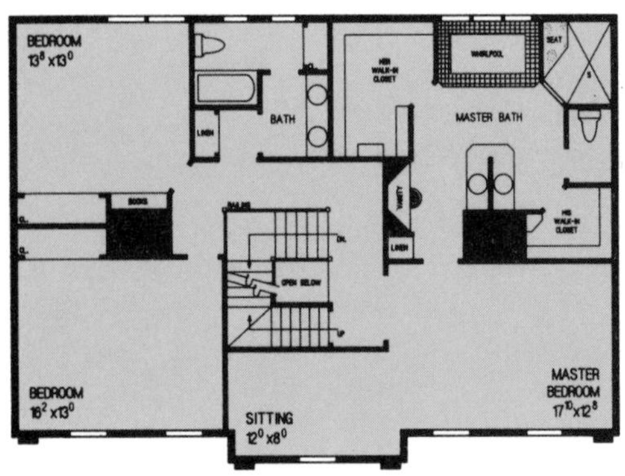

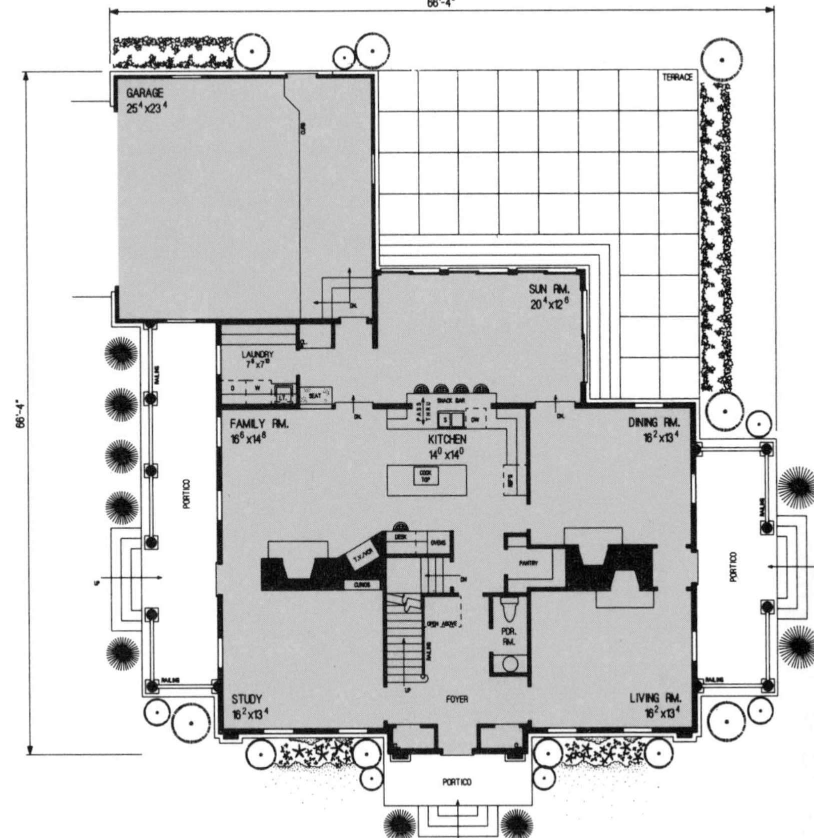

● This dramatic residence, patterned after one built in 1759 by Major John Vassall in Cambridge, offers a floor plan that is intriguing in its wealth of amenities. On the first floor are the formal living and dining rooms, each with fireplace. A front study connects to the family room with built-ins and another fireplace. Opening to the rear terrace is a most-welcome sun room with pass- through snack bar to the kitchen. Upstairs are three bedrooms. The master has a sitting room, double vanity, whirlpool tub, His and Hers closets, and built-in vanity. Two family bedrooms share a full bath.

Design X2994

First Floor: 1,736 square feet
Second Floor: 1,472 square feet
Total: 3,208 square feet

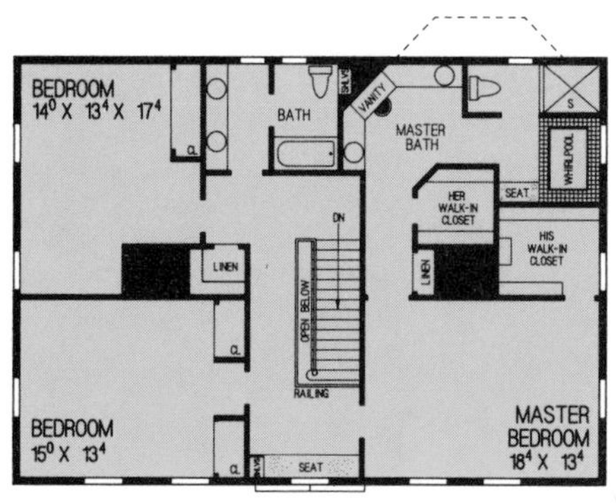

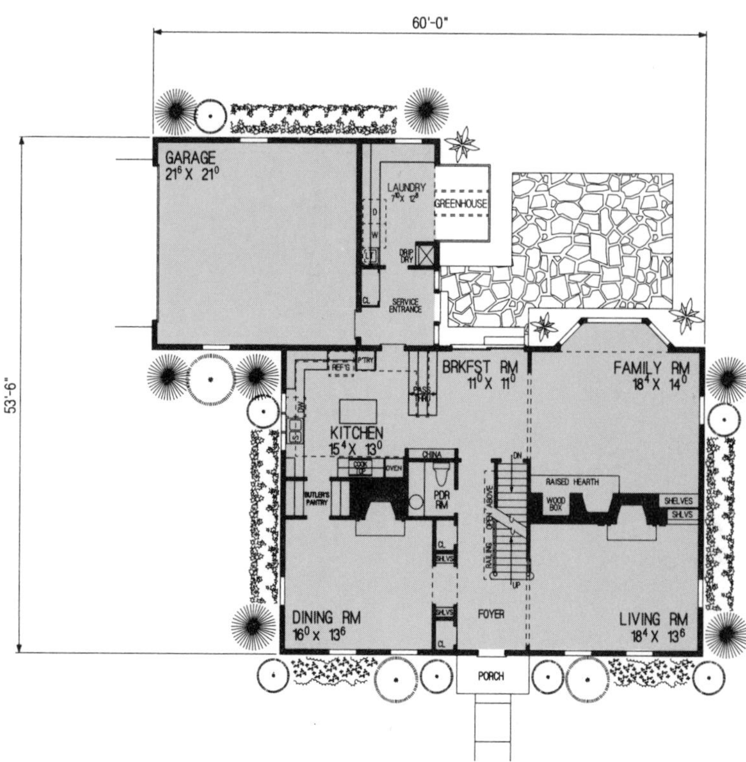

● Modeled after the homes of successful merchants in Amherst, New Hampshire, this lovely two-story plan presents an historical facade. Two chimney stacks, fluted pilasters and a bracketed pediment add their distinctive details. The floor plan is equally as classic with center hall separating living and dining rooms and leading back to the family room. All three living spaces have fireplaces. The second floor holds three bedrooms including a gracious master suite with two walk-in closets and whirlpool tub. Secondary bedrooms share a full bath with dual lavatories.

Design X2690

First Floor: 1,559 square feet
Second Floor: 1,344 square feet
Third Floor: 176 square feet
Total: 3,079 square feet

● This Cape Cod Georgian recalls the Julia Wood House built approximately 1790 in Falmouth, Mass. Such homes generally featured a balustraded roof deck or "widow's walk" where wives of captains looked to sea for signs of returning ships. Our updated floor plans include four bedrooms including master suite on the second floor and country kitchen, study, dining room, and living room on the first floor. A third floor makes a fine 15 x 10 studio, with ladder leading up to the widow's walk.

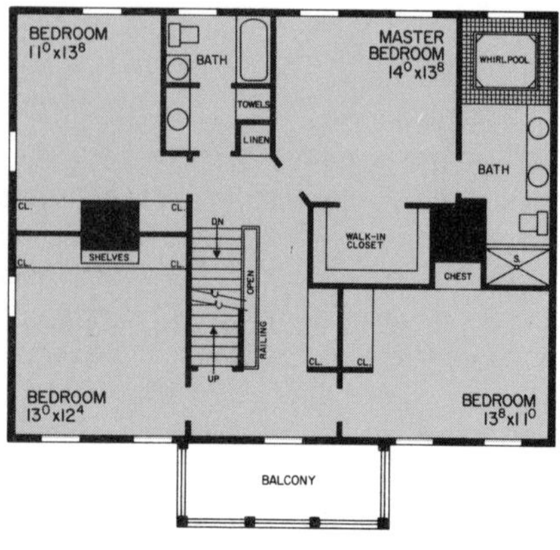

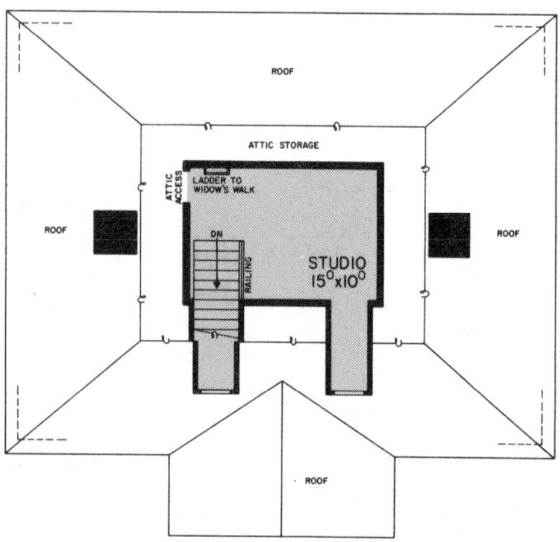

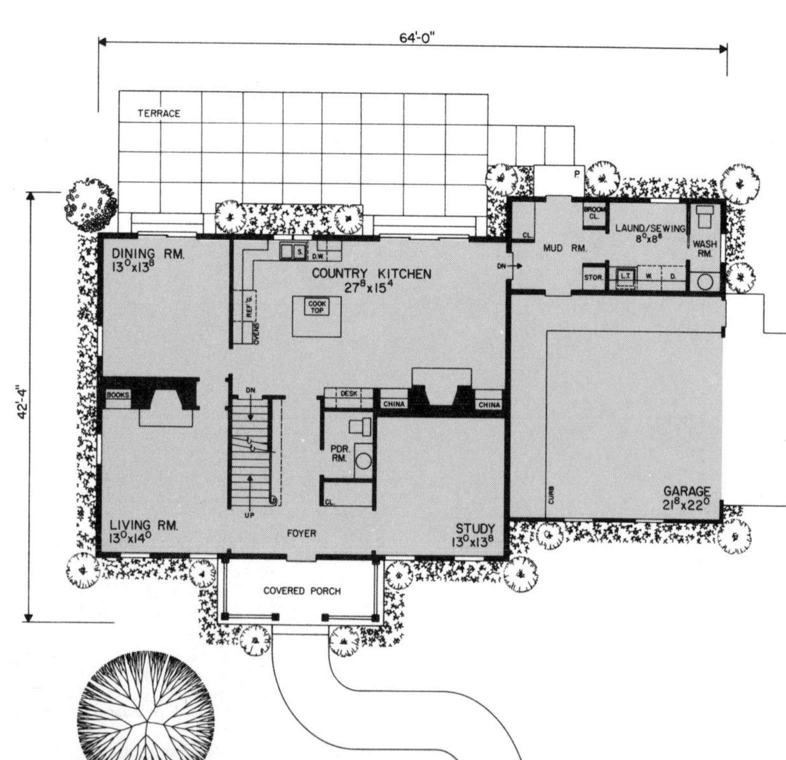

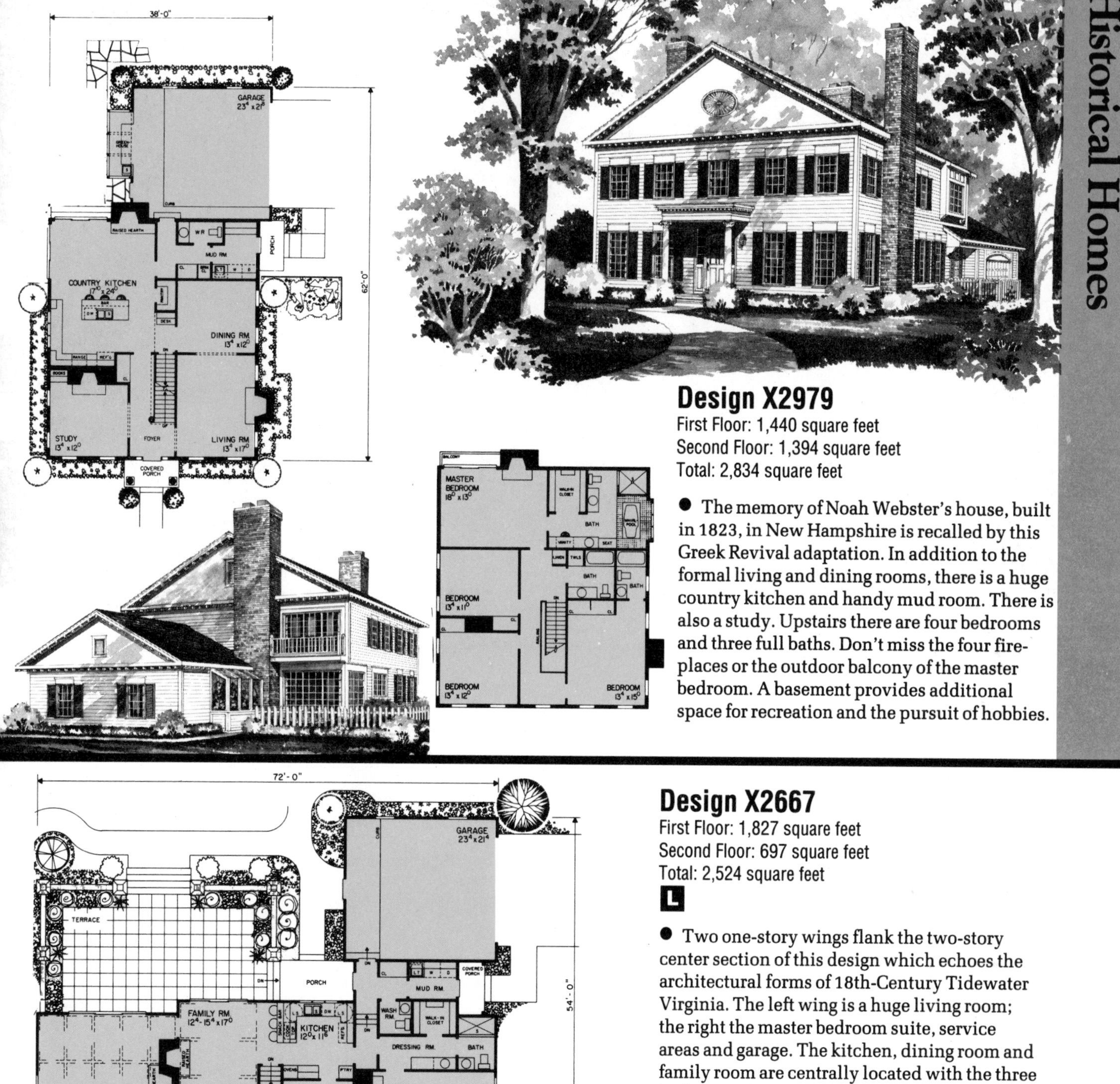

Design X2979

First Floor: 1,440 square feet
Second Floor: 1,394 square feet
Total: 2,834 square feet

● The memory of Noah Webster's house, built in 1823, in New Hampshire is recalled by this Greek Revival adaptation. In addition to the formal living and dining rooms, there is a huge country kitchen and handy mud room. There is also a study. Upstairs there are four bedrooms and three full baths. Don't miss the four fireplaces or the outdoor balcony of the master bedroom. A basement provides additional space for recreation and the pursuit of hobbies.

Design X2667

First Floor: 1,827 square feet
Second Floor: 697 square feet
Total: 2,524 square feet

L

● Two one-story wings flank the two-story center section of this design which echoes the architectural forms of 18th-Century Tidewater Virginia. The left wing is a huge living room; the right the master bedroom suite, service areas and garage. The kitchen, dining room and family room are centrally located with the three bedrooms above.

Design X2992

First Floor: 1,541 square feet
Second Floor: 1,541 square feet
Third Floor: 1,016 square feet
Total: 4,098 square feet

L D

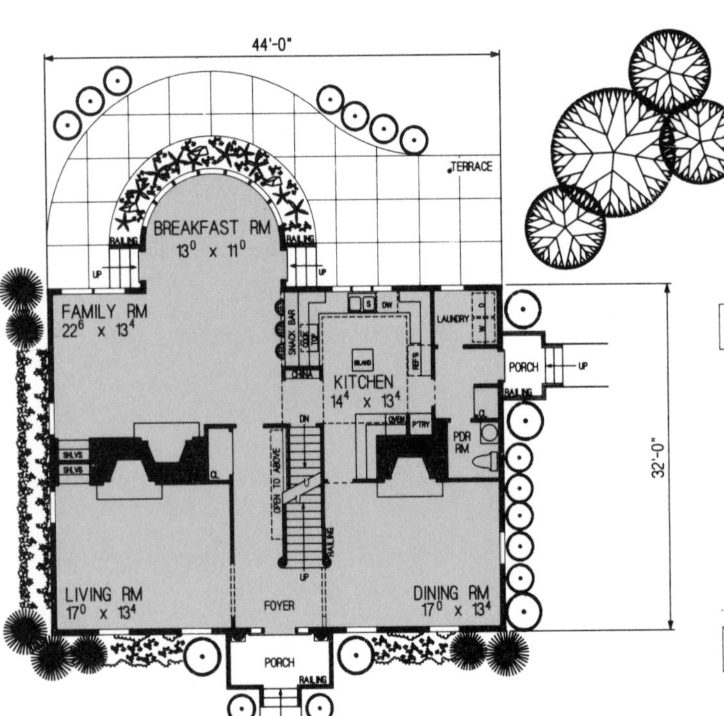

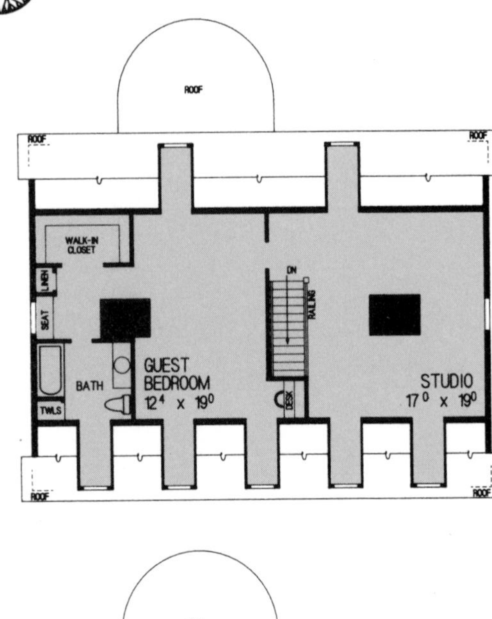

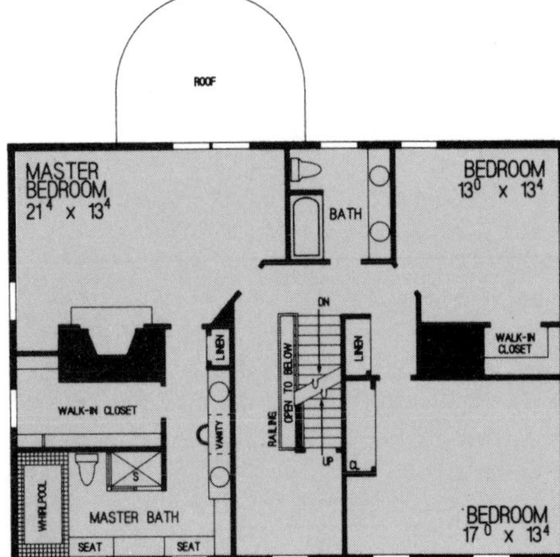

● The Dalton house, built between 1750 and 1760 in Newburyport, Massachusetts, inspired our plan shown here. Its lovely proportion and graceful exterior give way to a floor plan designed for the times. Left of the entry foyer is the formal living room; to the right formal dining. Both rooms have warming hearths. A family room to the rear of the plan connects with a unique glass-enclosed breakfast room. Nearby is the kitchen with pass-through snack bar. The second floor holds three bedrooms — the master suite and two family bedrooms. On the third floor is a guest bedroom with private bath and studio.

Design X2999

First Floor: 2,547 square feet
Second Floor: 2,128 square feet
Guest Apartment: 1,186 square feet
Total: 5,861 square feet

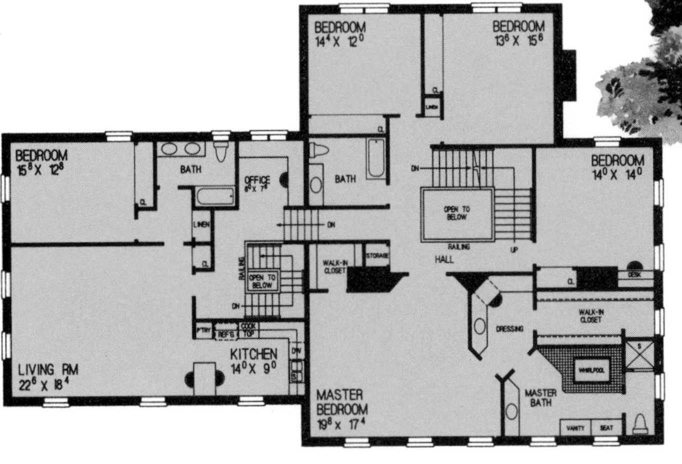

● Recalling the grandeur of its Maryland ancestors, this manor house is replete with exterior details that make it special: keystoned lintels, fluted pilasters, a dormered attic and pedimented doorway. The centerhall floor plan allows formal living and dining areas to the front of the plan. Complementing these are the cozy library and large family room/breakfast room area. A service entrance off the garage holds a laundry room and wash room. Upstairs bedrooms allow more than adequate space. Over the garage is a complete guest apartment with living area, office, bedroom, bath and kitchen.

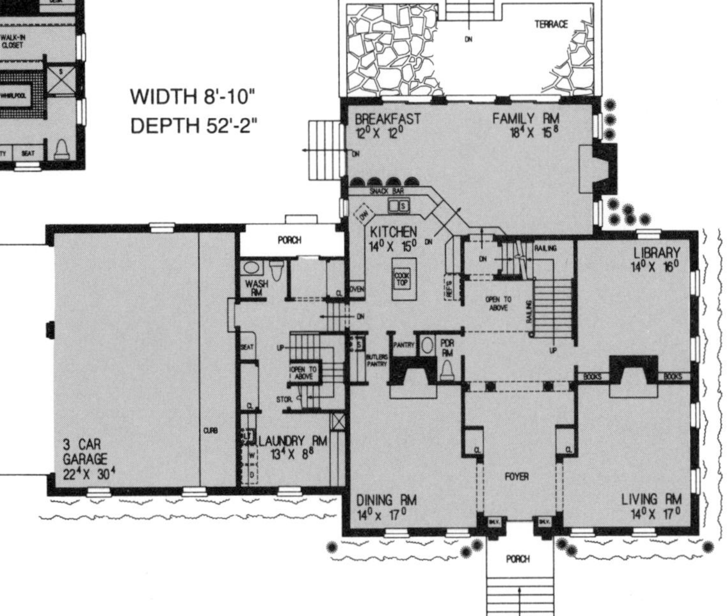

Design X2990

First Floor: 2,615 square feet
Second Floor: 1,726 square feet
Guest Bedroom: 437 square feet
Total: 4,878 square feet

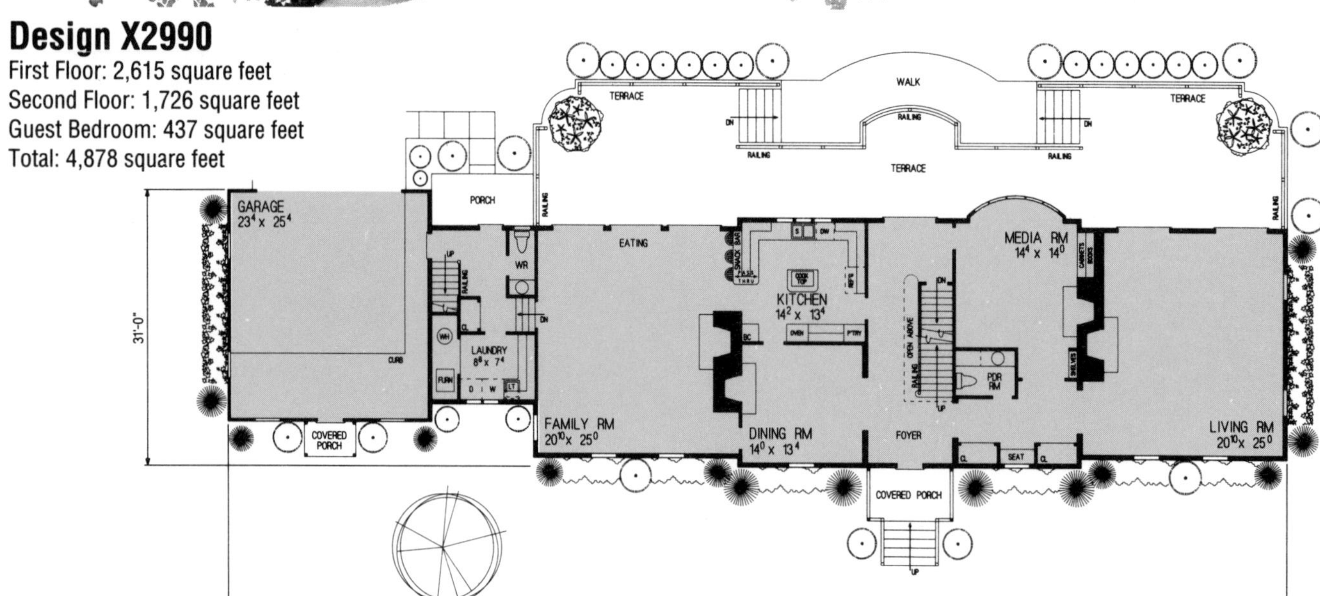

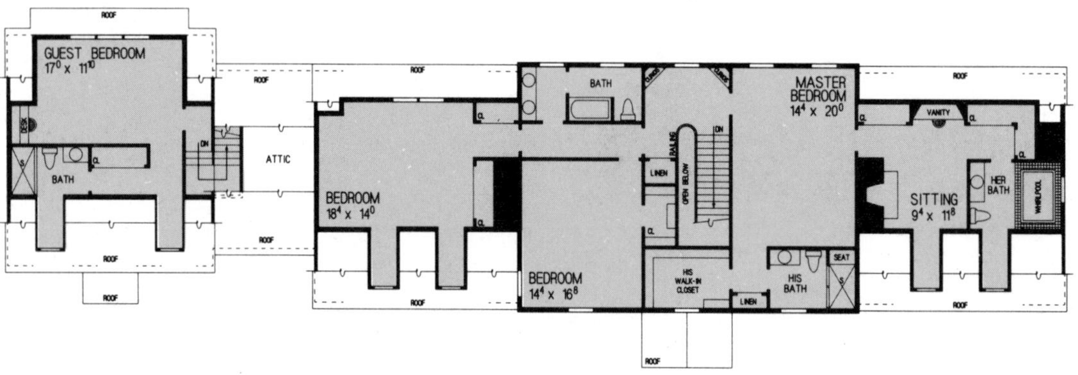

● Designed to resemble the St. George Tucker house in Williamsburg, this stately home offers a floor plan for today's family. First-floor rooms include a family room with informal dining space at one end of the plan and a formal living room at the other end. In between are the media room, guest powder room, dining room and kitchen. Three second-floor bedrooms include a luxurious master suite with sitting room. There is also a guest room with private bath over the garage.

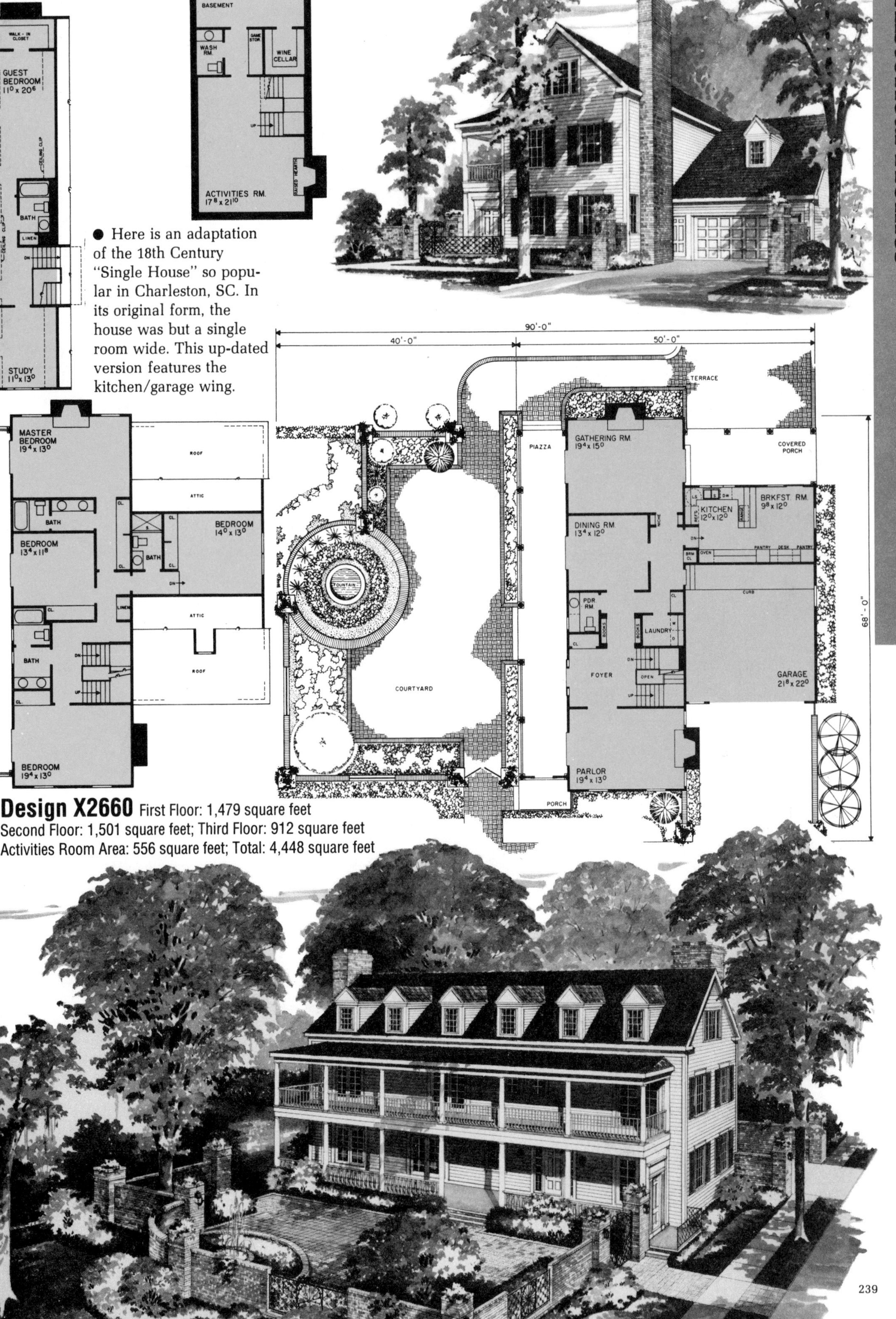

● Here is an adaptation of the 18th Century "Single House" so popular in Charleston, SC. In its original form, the house was but a single room wide. This up-dated version features the kitchen/garage wing.

Design X2660 First Floor: 1,479 square feet
Second Floor: 1,501 square feet; Third Floor: 912 square feet
Activities Room Area: 556 square feet; Total: 4,448 square feet

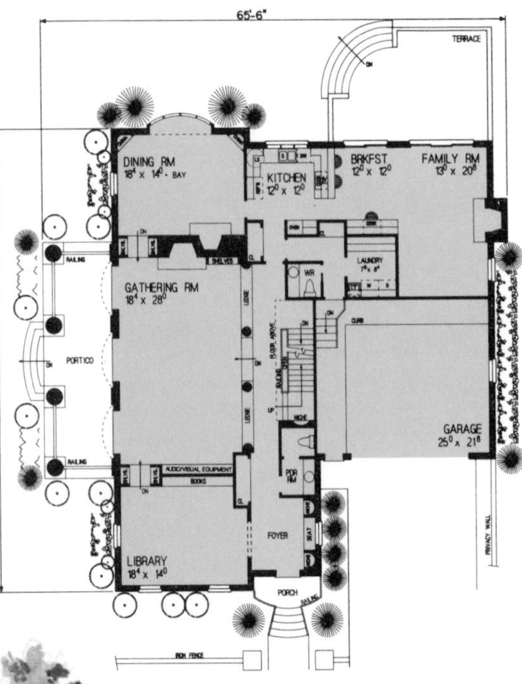

Design X2993

First Floor: 2,440 square feet
Second Floor: 2,250 square feet
Total: 4,690 square feet

L **D**

● This dramatically columned home delivers beautiful proportions and great livability on two levels. The main area of the house, the first floor, holds a gathering room, library, family room, dining room and gourmet kitchen. The master bedroom features a whirlpool tub and through fireplace. Two family bedrooms on the second floor share a full bath. A fourth bedroom is the perfect guest bedroom with its own private bath.

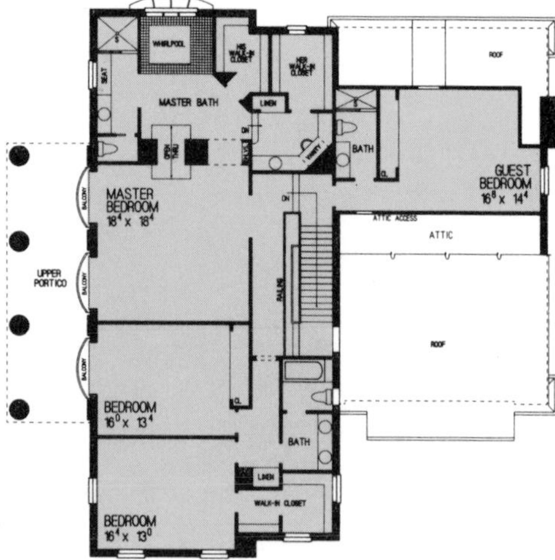

Design X3308

First Floor: 2,515 square feet
Second Floor: 1,708 square feet
Third Floor: 1,001 square feet
Total: 5,224 square feet

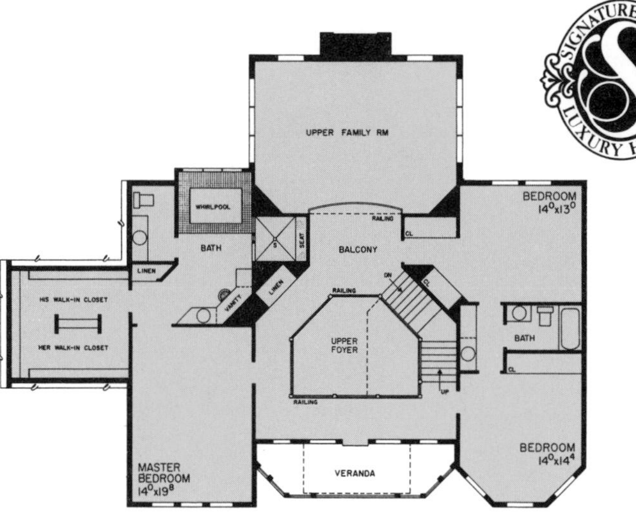

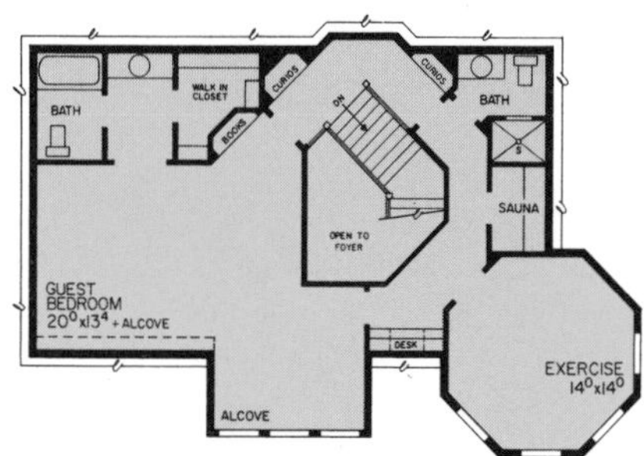

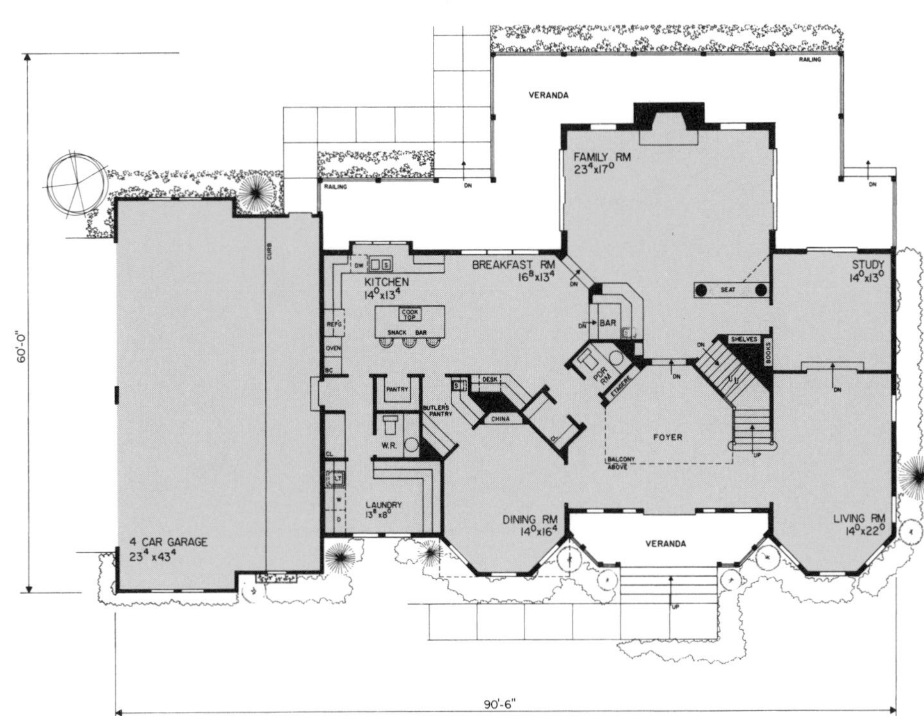

● Uniquely shaped rooms and a cache of amenities highlight this three-story beauty. Downstairs rooms accommodate both formal and informal entertaining and also provide a liberal share of work space in the kitchen and laundry. The second floor has two bedrooms and a full bath plus a master suite with His and Hers closets and whirlpool bath. An exercise room on the third floor has its own sauna and bath, while a guest room on this floor is complemented by a charming alcove and another full bath.

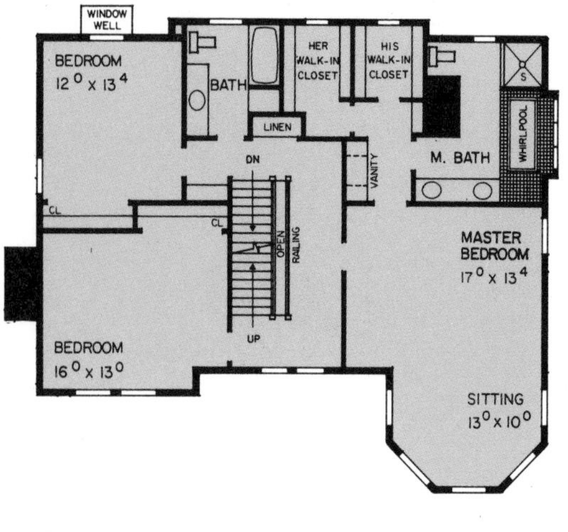

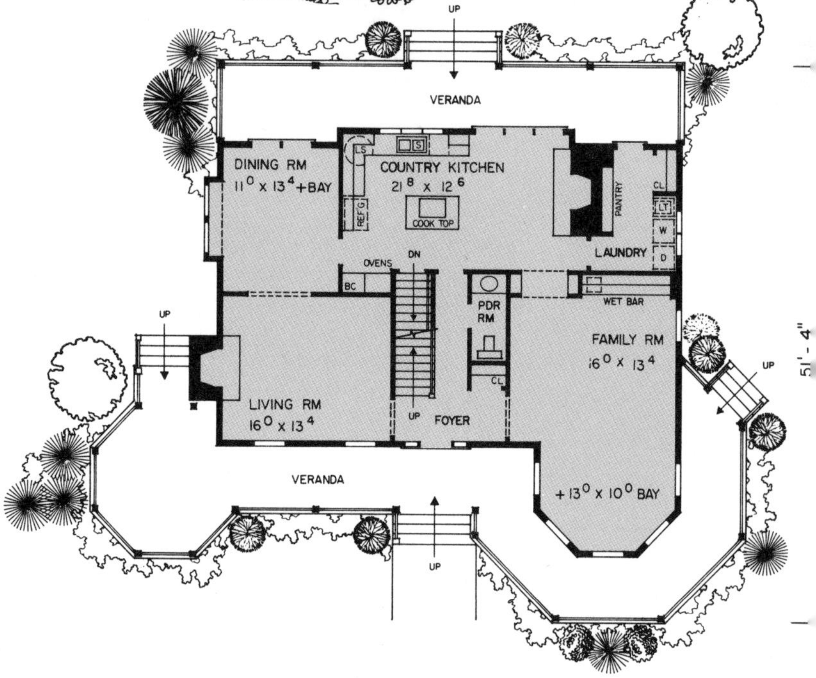

Design X3392

First Floor: 1,405 square feet
Second Floor: 1,430 square feet
Third Floor: 624 square feet
Total: 3,459 square feet

L **D**

● Named for the architect, Henry Hobson Richardson, the Richardson Romanesque is known for being ample in size. This three-story example has complementary arched turrets on the outside which give way to a convenient floor plan. Formal and informal living areas occupy the first floor in a living room, dining room, family room and grand country kitchen. Upstairs are two family bedrooms and a master suite with sitting area. The third floor contains another bedroom and private bath that could serve guests.

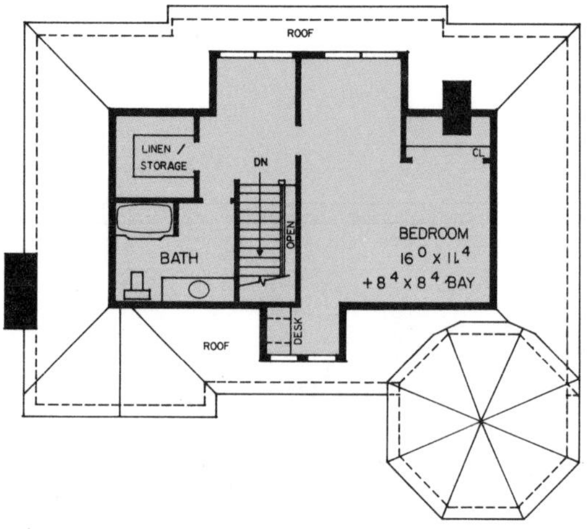

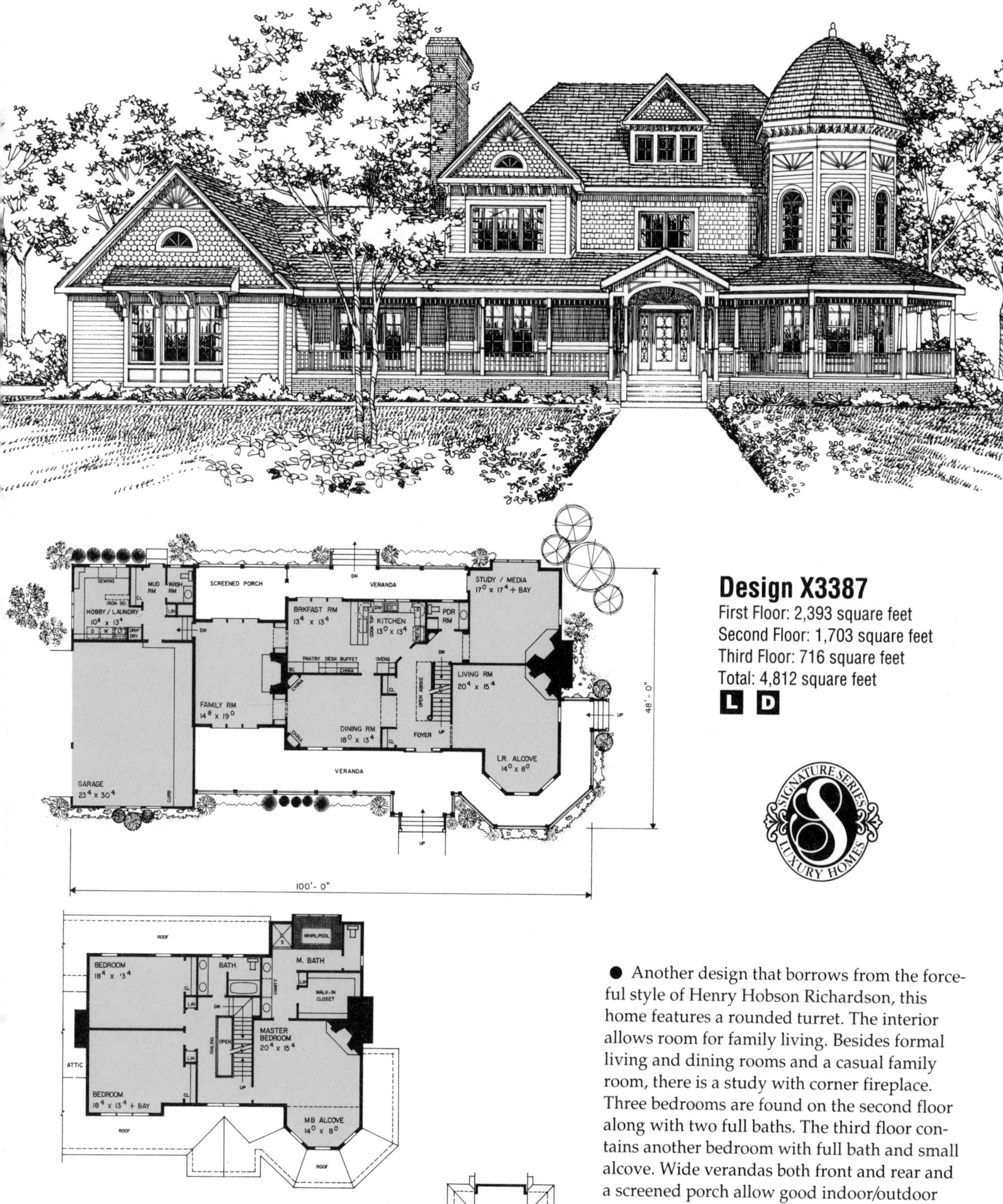

Design X3387

First Floor: 2,393 square feet
Second Floor: 1,703 square feet
Third Floor: 716 square feet
Total: 4,812 square feet

L D

SIGNATURE SERIES LUXURY HOMES

WALK-IN CLOSET
DRESSING
7⁴ x 9⁰
BATH
ATTIC
ROOF
BEDROOM
17⁴ x 13⁰
STORAGE
13⁴ x 13⁰
BR. ALCOVE
8⁰ x 5⁸

● Another design that borrows from the forceful style of Henry Hobson Richardson, this home features a rounded turret. The interior allows room for family living. Besides formal living and dining rooms and a casual family room, there is a study with corner fireplace. Three bedrooms are found on the second floor along with two full baths. The third floor contains another bedroom with full bath and small alcove. Wide verandas both front and rear and a screened porch allow good indoor/outdoor living relationships.

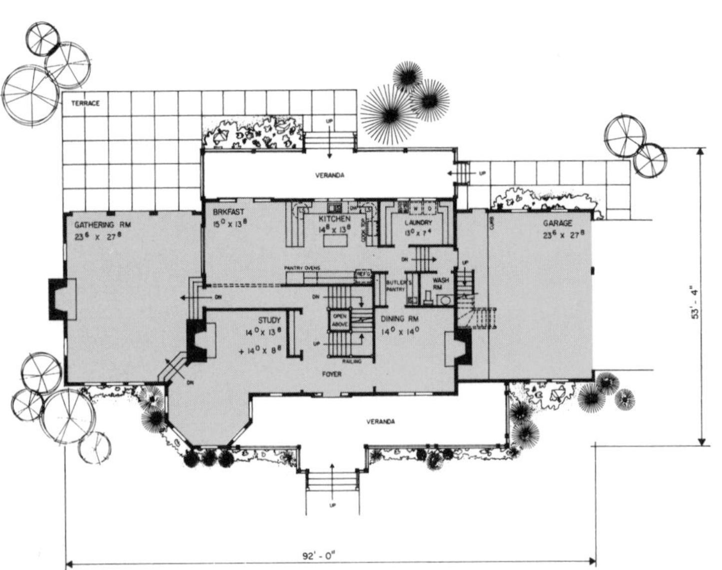

Design X3395

First Floor: 2,248 square feet
Second Floor: 2,020 square feet
Third Floor: 1,117 square feet
Total: 5,385 square feet

● This home is a lovely example of classic Queen Anne architecture. Its floor plan offers: a gathering room with fireplace, a study with an octagonal window area, a formal dining room and a kitchen with attached breakfast room. Bedrooms on the second floor include three family bedrooms and a grand master suite. On the third floor are a guest room with private bath and sitting room and a game room with attached library.

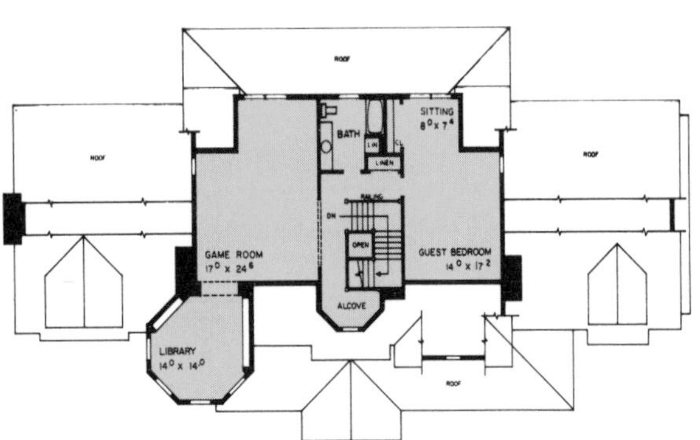

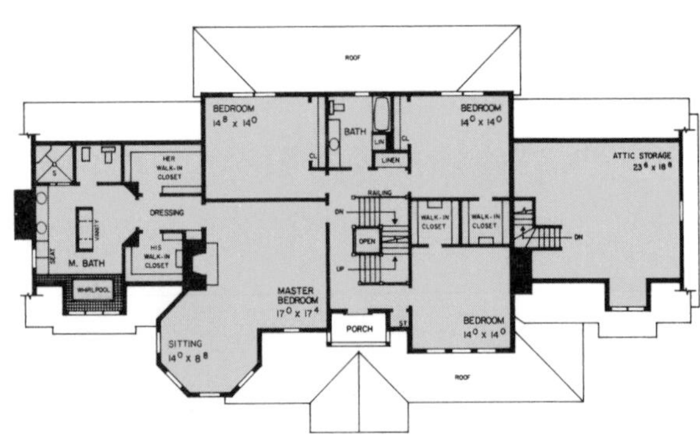

Design X3386

First Floor: 1,683 square feet
Second Floor: 1,388 square feet
Third Floor: 808 square feet
Total: 3,879 square feet

● This beautiful Folk Victorian has all the properties of others in its class. Living areas include a formal Victorian parlor, a private study and large gathering room. The formal dining room has its more casual counterpart in a bay-windowed breakfast room. Both are near the well-appointed kitchen. Five bedrooms serve family and guest needs handily. Three bedrooms on the second floor include a luxurious master suite. For outdoor entertaining, there is a covered rear porch leading to a terrace.

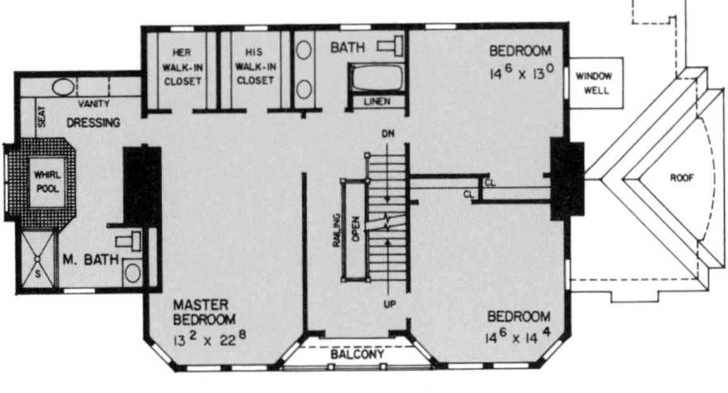

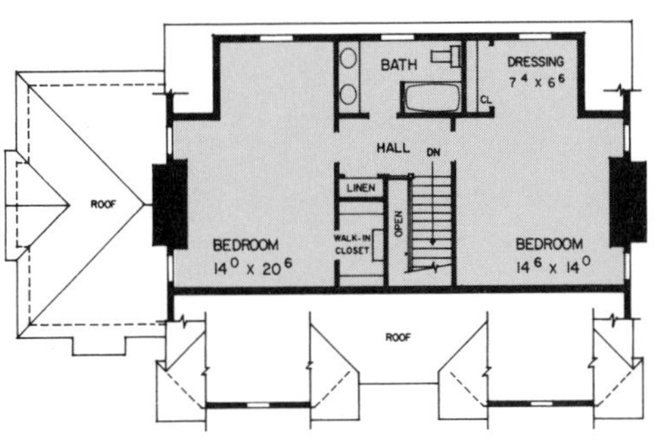

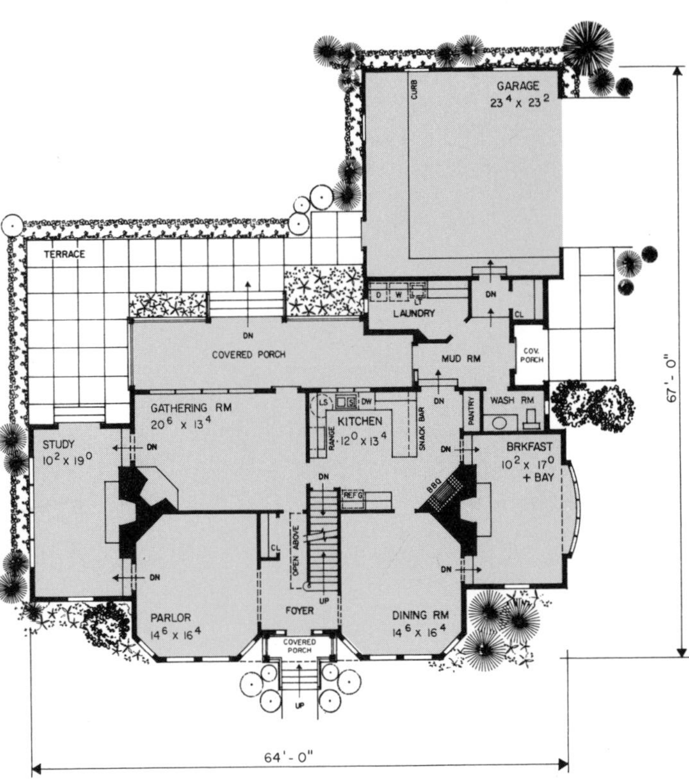

Design X3391

First Floor: 1,230 square feet
Second Floor: 991 square feet
Total: 2,221 square feet

● Detailing is one of the characteristic features of Queen Anne Victorians and this home has no lack of it. Interior rooms add special living patterns. Features include a powder room for guests in the front hallway, a through-fireplace between the ample gathering room and cozy study, an efficient U-shaped kitchen with pantry, and a full-width terrace to the rear. On the second floor are three bedrooms — one a master suite with walk-in closet and amenity-filled bath. An open balcony overlooks the gathering room.

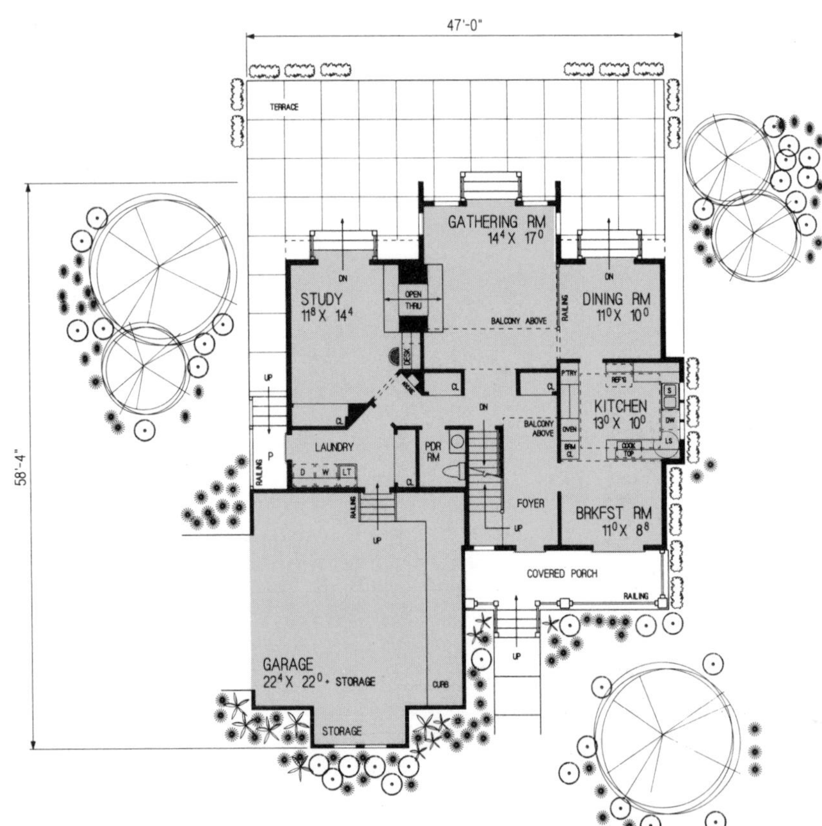

● This two-story farmhouse will be a delight for those who work at home. The second floor has a secluded master bedroom and a studio. A U-shaped kitchen with snack bar and breakfast area with bay window are only the first of the eating areas, which extend to a formal dining room and a covered rear porch for dining al fresco. The two-story living room features a cozy fireplace. A versatile room to the back could serve as a media room or a third bedroom.

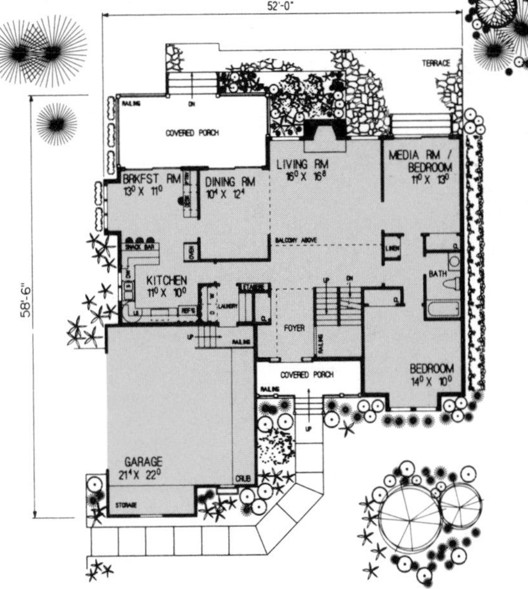

Design X3390

First Floor: 1,472 square feet
Second Floor: 1,116 square feet
Total: 2,588 square feet

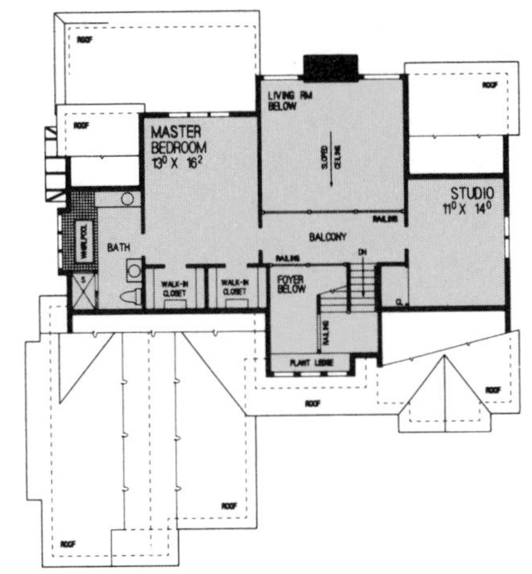

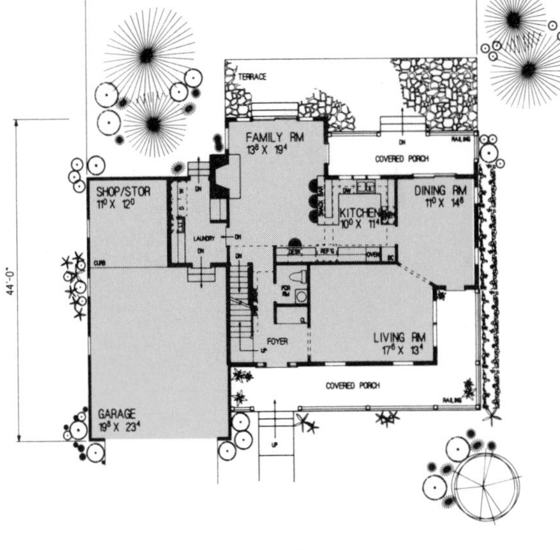

Design X3385

First Floor: 1,096 square feet
Second Floor: 900 square feet
Total: 1,996 square feet

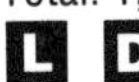
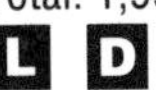

● Covered porches front and rear are complemented by a grand plan for family living. A formal living room and attached dining room provide space for entertaining guests. The large family room with fireplace is a gathering room for everyday use. Four bedrooms occupy the second floor. The master suite features two lavatories, a window seat and three closets. One of the family bedrooms has its own private balcony and could be used as a study.

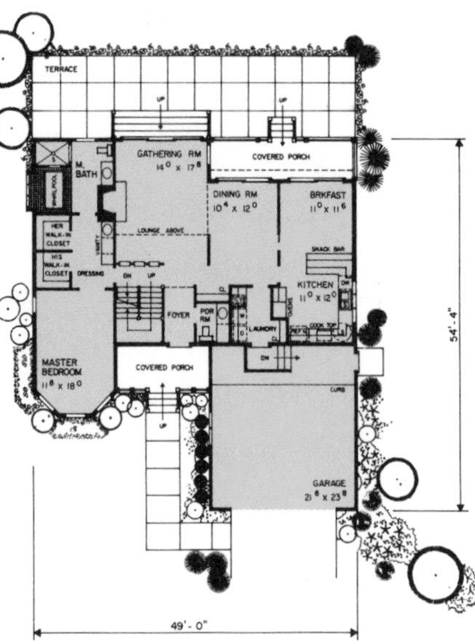

● A grand facade makes this Victorian stand out. Inside, guests and family are well accommodated: gathering room with terrace access, fireplace and attached formal dining room; split-bedroom sleeping arrangements. The master suite contains His and Hers walk-in closets, a separate shower and whirlpool tub and a delightful bay-windowed area. Upstairs there are three more bedrooms (one could serve as a study, one as a media room), a full bath and an open lounge area overlooking the gathering room.

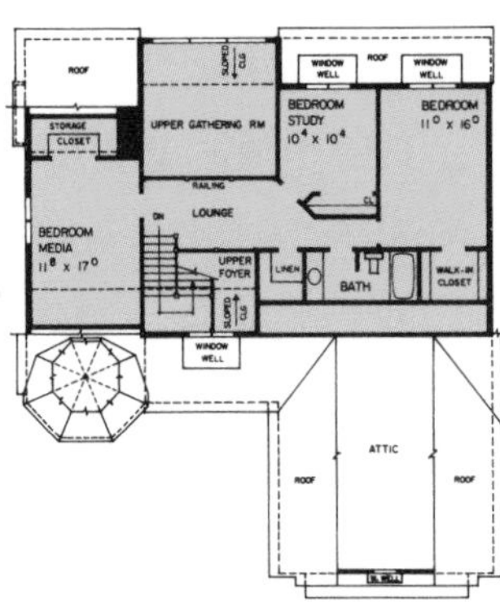

Design X3393

First Floor: 1,449 square feet
Second Floor: 902 square feet
Total: 2,351 square feet

L **D**

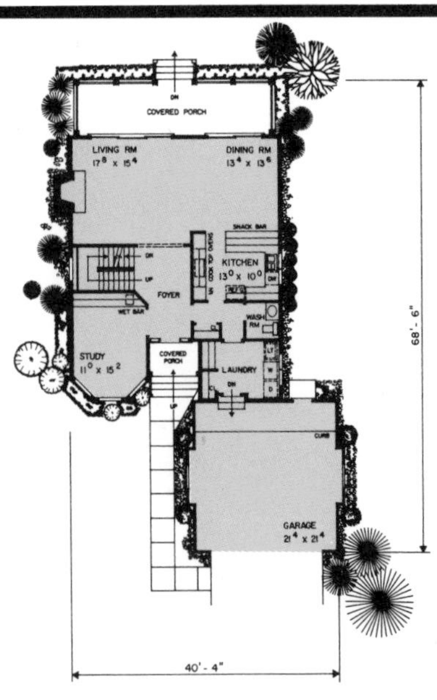

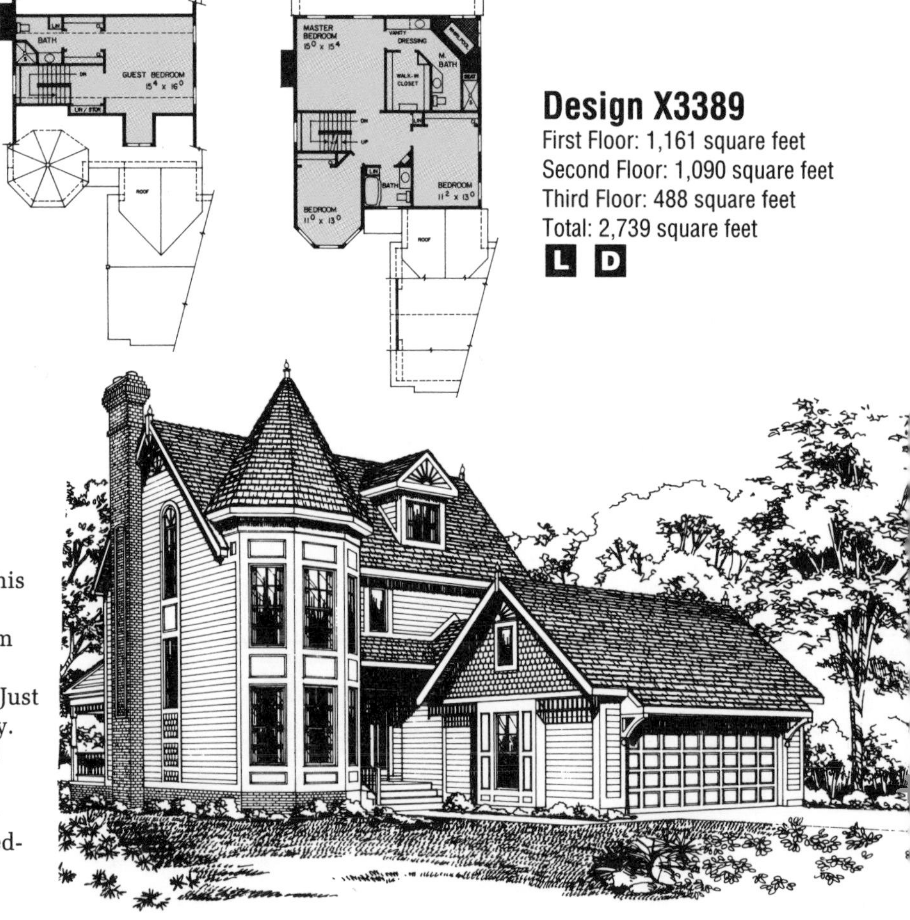

Design X3389

First Floor: 1,161 square feet
Second Floor: 1,090 square feet
Third Floor: 488 square feet
Total: 2,739 square feet

L **D**

● A Victorian turret accents the facade of this compact three- story. Downstairs rooms include a grand-sized living room/dining room combination. The U-shaped kitchen has a snack-bar pass-through to the dining room. Just to the left of the entry foyer is a private study. On the second floor are three bedrooms and two full baths. The master bedroom has a whirlpool spa and large walk-in closet. The third floor is a perfect location for a guest bedroom with private bath.

Design X2974 First Floor: 911 square feet
Second Floor: 861 square feet; Total: 1,772 square feet

L

● Victorian houses are well known for their orientation on narrow building sites. And when this occurs nothing is lost to captivating exterior styling. This house is but 38 feet wide. Its narrow width belies the tremendous amount of livability found inside. And, of course, the ubiquitous porch/veranda contributes mightily to style as well as livability. The efficient, U-shape kitchen is flanked by the informal breakfast room and formal dining room. The rear living area is spacious and functions in an exciting manner with the outdoor areas. Bonus recreational, hobby and storage space is offered by the basement and the attic.

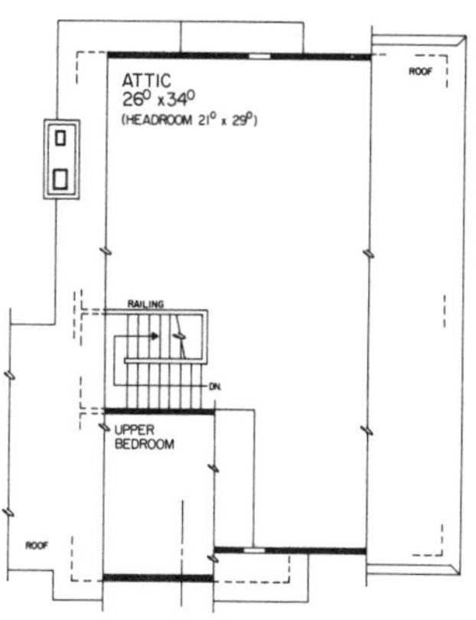

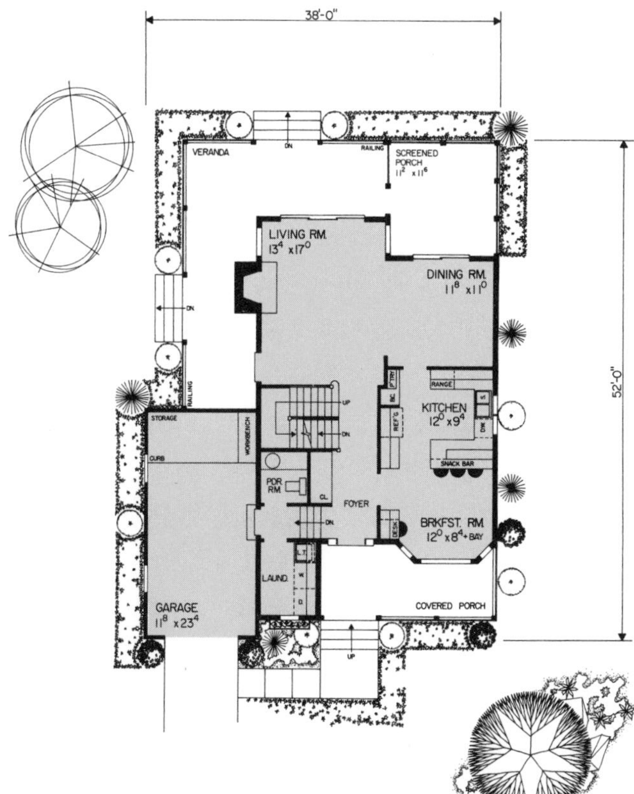

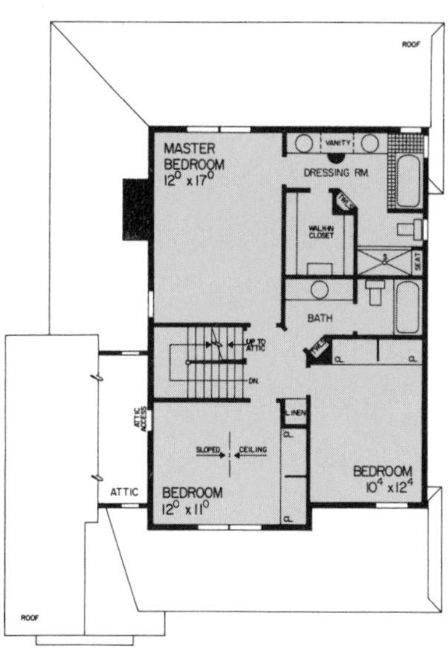

Design X3382

First Floor: 1,366 square feet
Second Floor: 837 square feet
Third Floor: 363 square feet
Total: 2,566 square feet

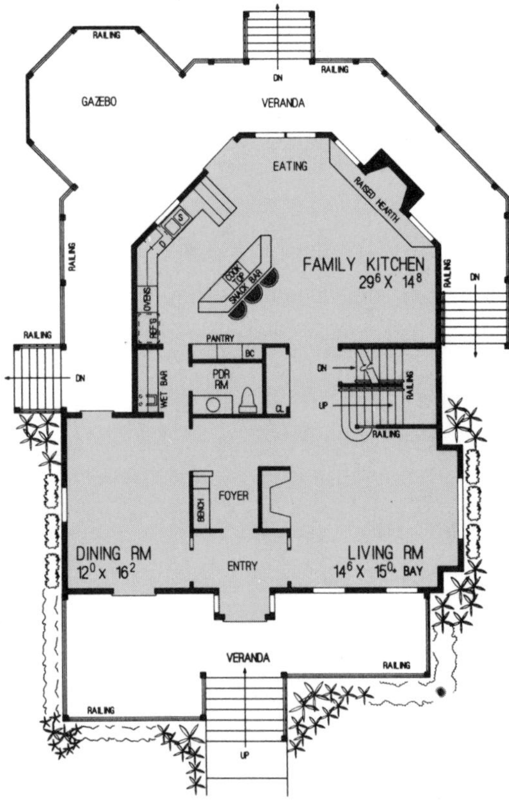

● A simple but charming Queen Anne Victorian, this enchanting three-story home boasts delicately turned rails and decorated columns on its covered front porch. Inside is a floor plan that includes a living room with fireplace and dining room that connects to the kitchen via a wet bar. The adjoining family room contains another fireplace. The second floor holds two bedrooms, one a master suite with grand bath. A tucked-away guest suite on the third floor has a private bath.

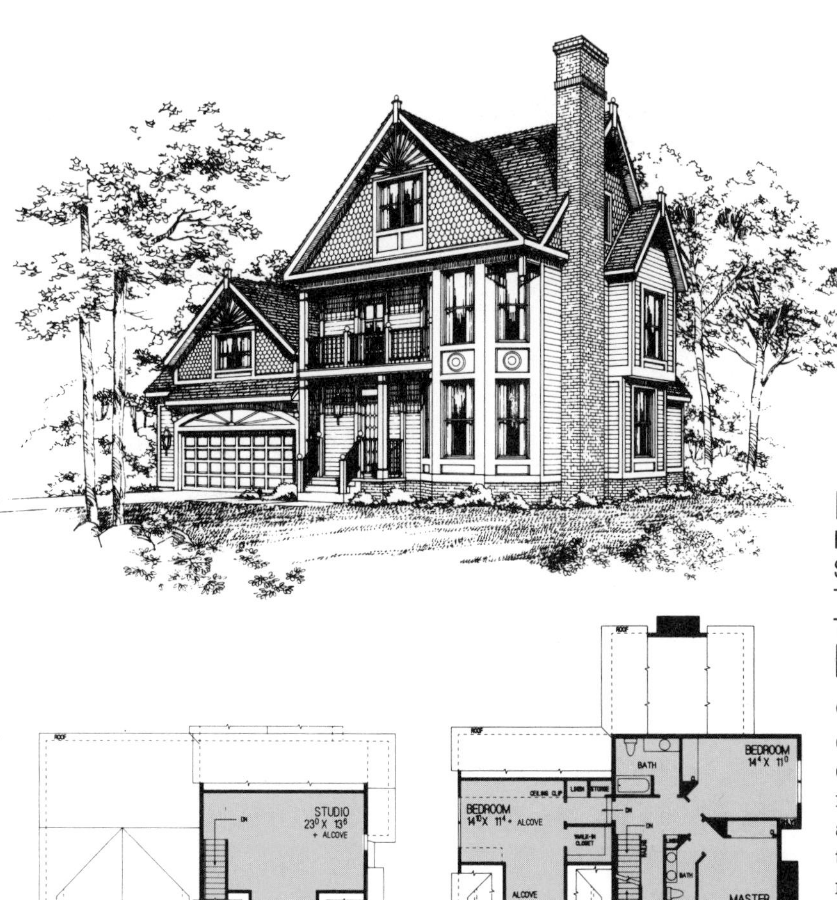

FAMILY RM 17^8 X 13^8
DINING RM 11^4 X 12^0
KITCHEN 13^4 X 10^0
GARAGE 21^8 X 23^4
FOYER
LIVING RM 11^4 X 18^8
COVERED PORCH
48'-0"
46'-0"

Design X3383

First Floor: 995 square feet
Second Floor: 1,064 square feet
Third Floor: 425 square feet
Total: 2,484 square feet

L **D**

● This delightful Victorian cottage features exterior details that perfectly complement the convenient plan inside. Note the central placement of the kitchen, near to the dining room and the family room. Two fireplaces keep things warm and cozy. Three second-floor bedrooms include a master suite with bay window and two family bedrooms, one with an alcove and walk-in closet. Use the third-floor studio as a study, office or playroom for the children.

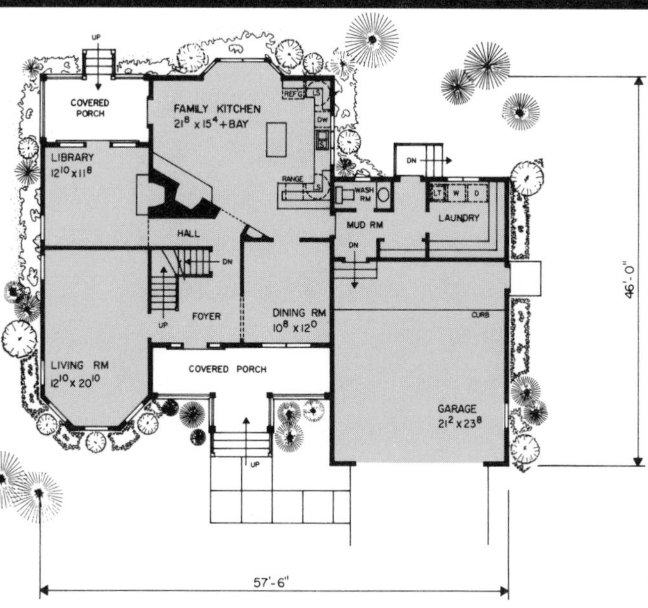

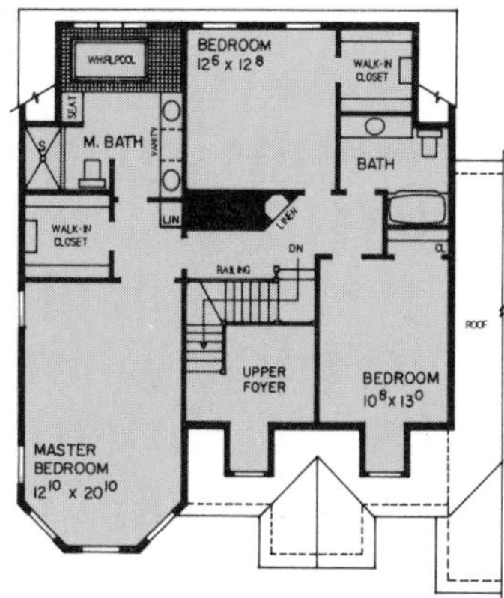

Design X3384

First Floor: 1,339 square feet
Second Floor: 1,123 square feet
Total: 2,522 square feet

L **D**

● Classic Victorian styling comes to the forefront in this Queen Anne. The interior boasts comfortable living quarters for the entire family. On opposite sides of the foyer are the formal dining and living rooms. To the rear is a country-style island kitchen with attached family room. A small library shares a covered porch with this informal gathering area and also has its own fireplace. Three bedrooms on the second floor include a master suite with grand bath. The two family bathrooms share a full bath.

Design X3388

First Floor: 1,517 square feet
Second Floor: 1,267 square feet
Third Floor: 480 square feet
Total: 3,264 square feet

L **D**

● This delightful home offers the best in thoughtful floor planning. The home opens to a well-executed entry foyer. To the left is the casual family room with fireplace. To the right is the formal living room which connects to the formal dining area. The kitchen/breakfast room combination features an island cook top and large pantry. Second-floor bedrooms include a master suite and two family bedrooms served by a full bath. A guest room dominates the third floor.

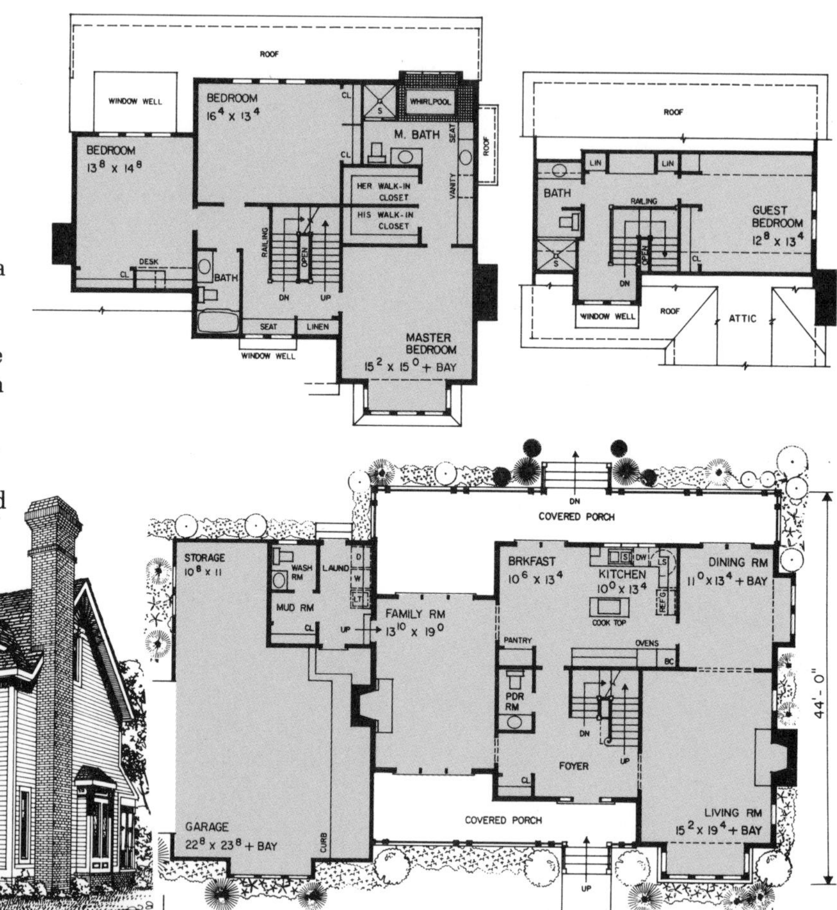

Design X3394

First Floor: 1,531 square feet
Second Floor: 1,307 square feet
Third Floor: 664 square feet
Total: 3,502 square feet

L **D**

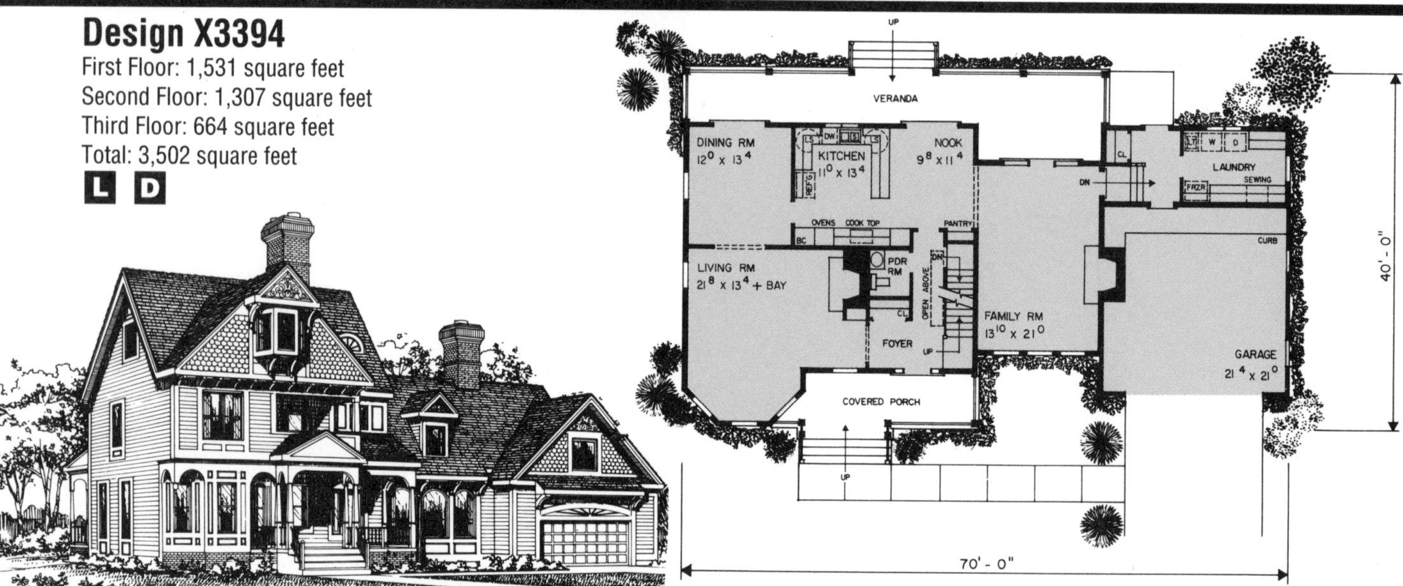

● The Folk Victorian is an important and delightful interpretation. And this version offers the finest in modern floor plans. The formal living areas are set off by a family room which connects the main house to the service areas. The second floor holds three bedrooms and two full baths. A sitting area in the master suite separates it from family bedrooms. On the third floor is a guest bedroom with gracious bath and large walk-in closet.

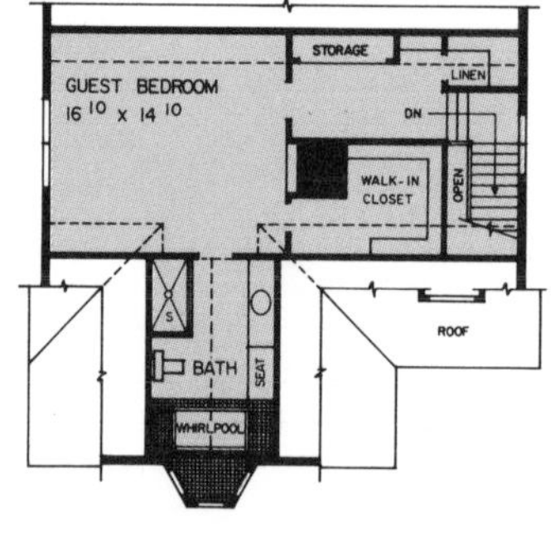

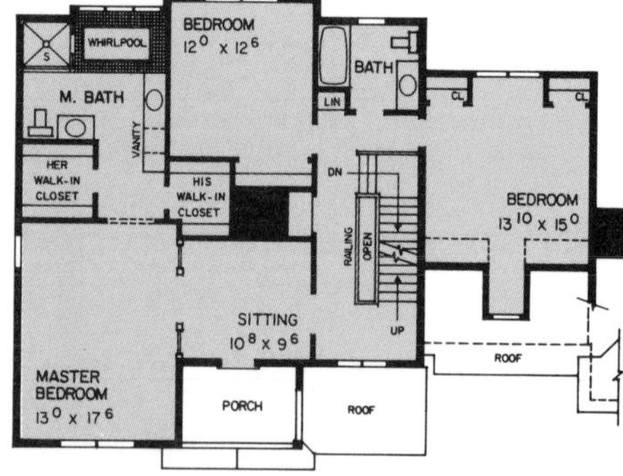

Design X2970 First Floor: 1,538 square feet

Second Floor: 1,526 square feet; Third Floor: 658 square feet
Total: 3,722 square feet

L

● A porch, is a porch, is a porch. But, when it wraps around to a side, or even two sides, of the house, we have called it a veranda. This charming Victorian features a covered outdoor living area on all four sides! It even ends at a screened porch which features a sun deck above. This interesting plan offers three floors of livability. And what livability it is! Plenty of formal and informal living facilities to go along with the potential of five bedrooms. The master suite is just that. It is adjacent to an interesting sitting room. It has a sun deck and excellent bath/personal care facilities. The third floor will make a wonderful haven for the family's student members.

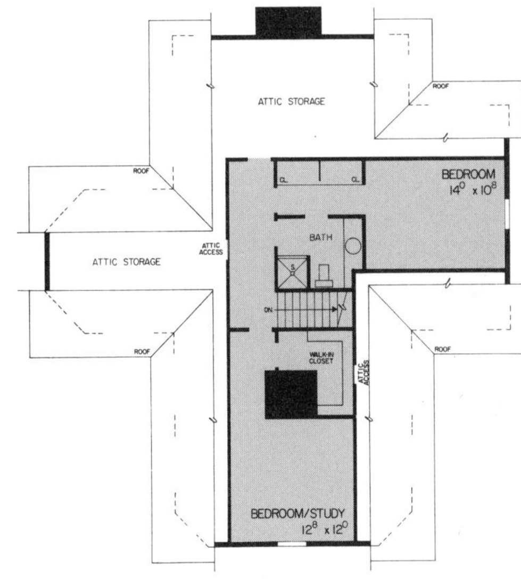

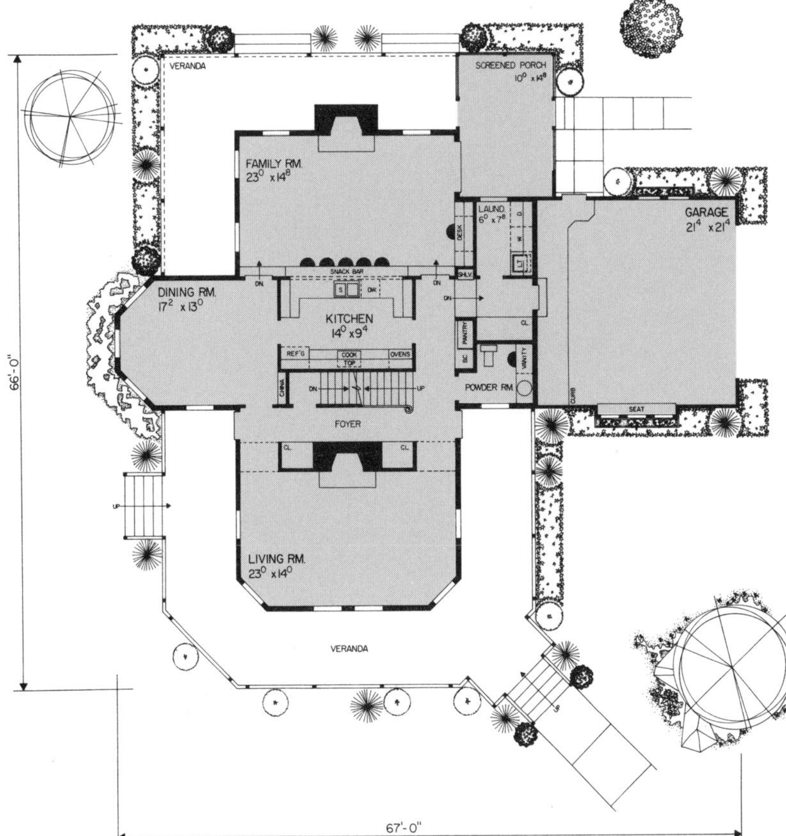

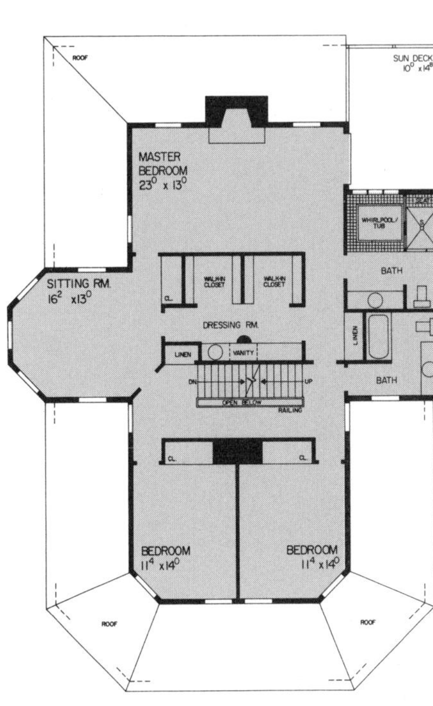

Design X2973

First Floor: 1,269 square feet
Second Floor: 1,227 square feet
Total: 2,496 square feet

L

● A most popular feature of the Victorian house has always been its covered porches. In addition to being an appealing exterior design feature, covered porches have their practical side, too. They provide wonderful indoor-outdoor living relationships. Notice sheltered outdoor living facilities for the various formal and informal living and dining areas of the plan. This home has a myriad of features to cater to the living requirements of the growing, active family.

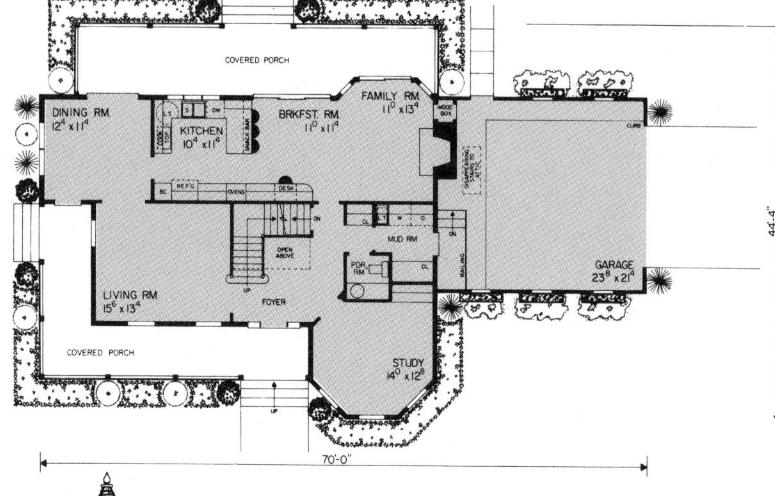

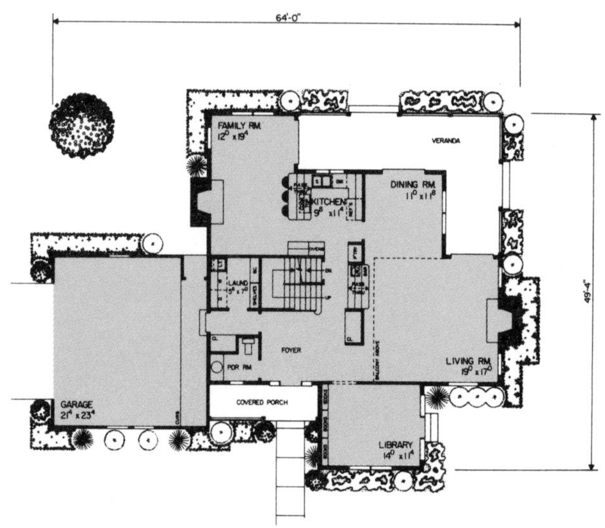

Design X2972

First Floor: 1,432 square feet
Second Floor: 1,108 square feet
Total: 2,540 square feet

L

● The spacious foyer of this Victorian is prelude to a practical and efficient interior. The formal living and dining area is located to one side of the plan. The more informal area of the plan includes the fine U-shaped kitchen which opens to the big family room. Just inside the entrance from the garage is the laundry; a closet and the powder room are a few steps away. The library will enjoy its full measure of privacy. Upstairs is the three-bedroom sleeping zone with a fireplace.

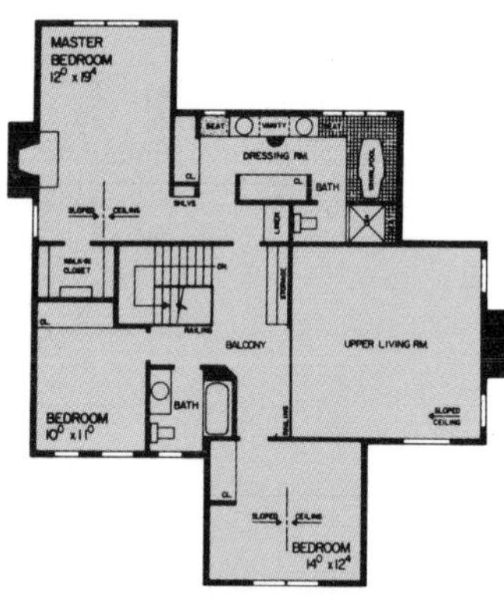

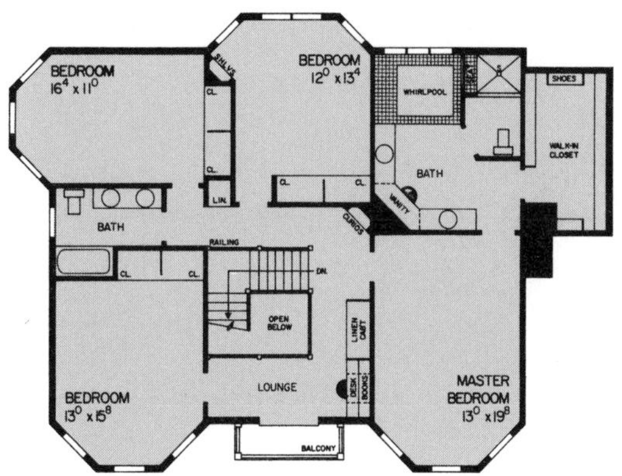

Design X2971 First Floor: 1,766 square feet

Second Floor: 1,519 square feet; Total: 3,285 square feet

L

● The stately proportions and the exquisite detailing of Victorian styling are exciting, indeed. Like so many Victorian houses, interesting roof lines set the character with this design. Observe the delightful mixture of gable roof, hip roof, and the dramatic turret. Horizontal siding, wood shingling, wide fascia, rake and corner boards make a strong statement. Of course, the delicate detailing of the windows, railings, cornices and front entry is most appealing to the eye. Inside, a great four-bedroom family living plan.

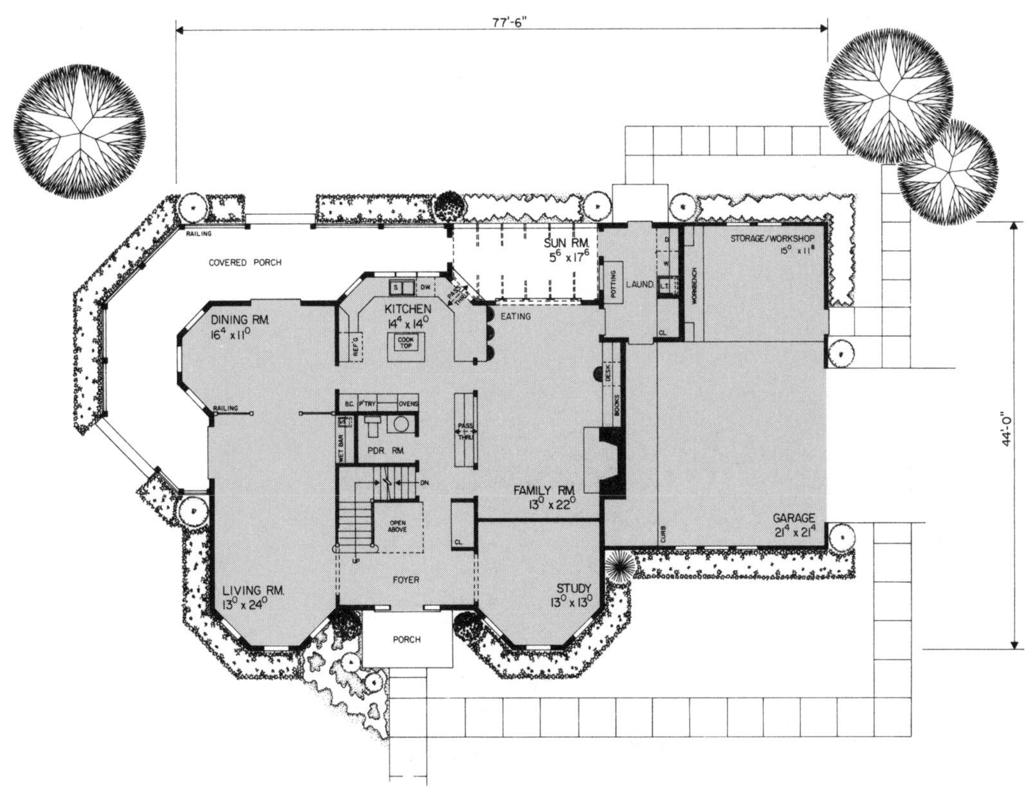

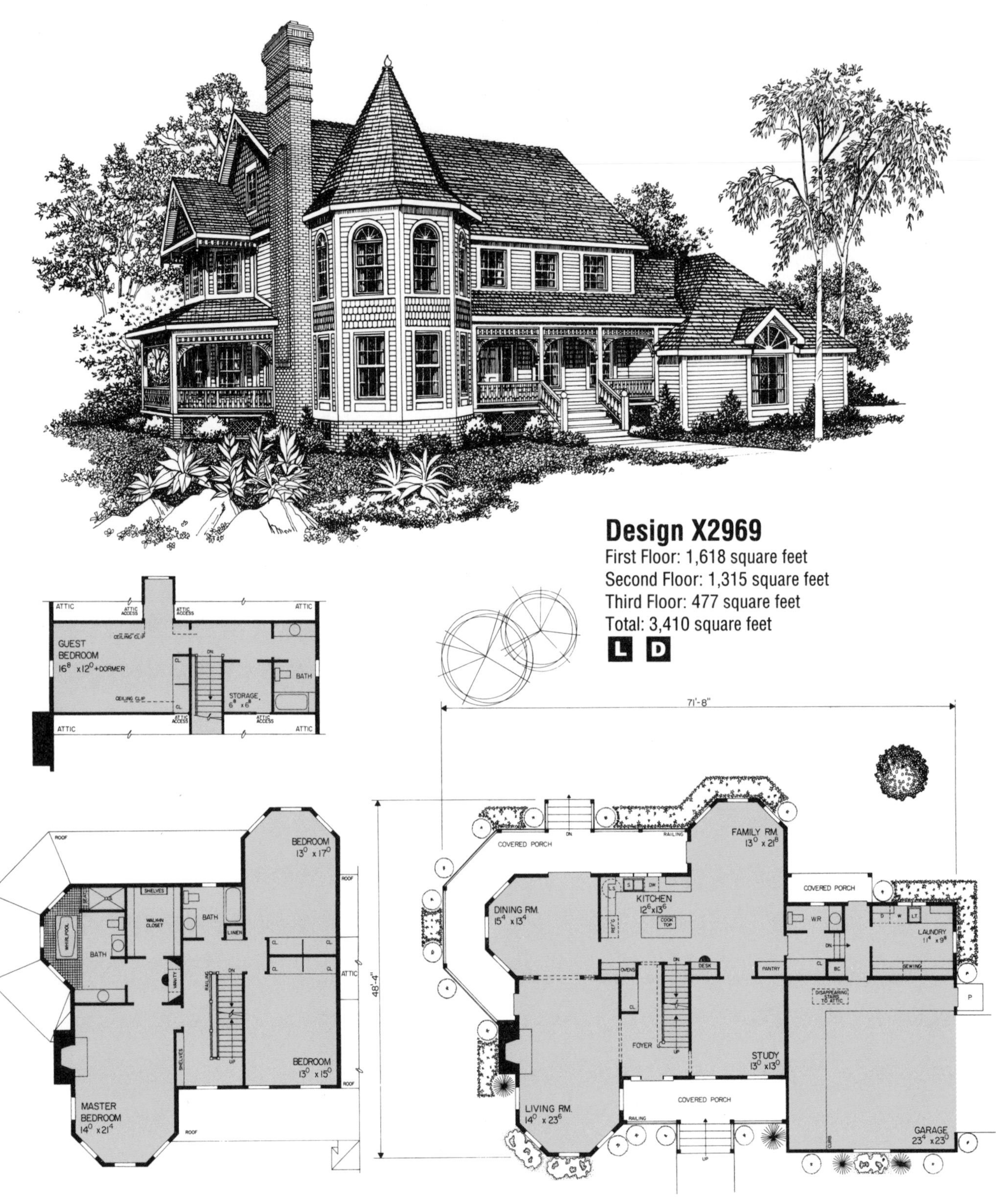

Design X2969

First Floor: 1,618 square feet
Second Floor: 1,315 square feet
Third Floor: 477 square feet
Total: 3,410 square feet

L D

● What could beat the charm of a turreted Victorian with covered porches to the front, side and rear? This delicately detailed exterior houses an outstanding family oriented floor plan. Projecting bays make their contribution to the exterior styling. In addition, they provide an extra measure of livability to the living, dining and family rooms, plus two of the bedrooms. The efficient kitchen, with its island cooking station, functions well with the dining and family rooms. A study provides a quiet first floor haven for the family's less active pursuits. Upstairs there are three big bedrooms and a fine master bath. The third floor provides a guest suite and huge bulk storage area (make it a cedar closet if you wish). This house has a basement for the development of further recreational and storage facilities. Don't miss the two fireplaces, large laundry and attached two-car garage. A great investment.

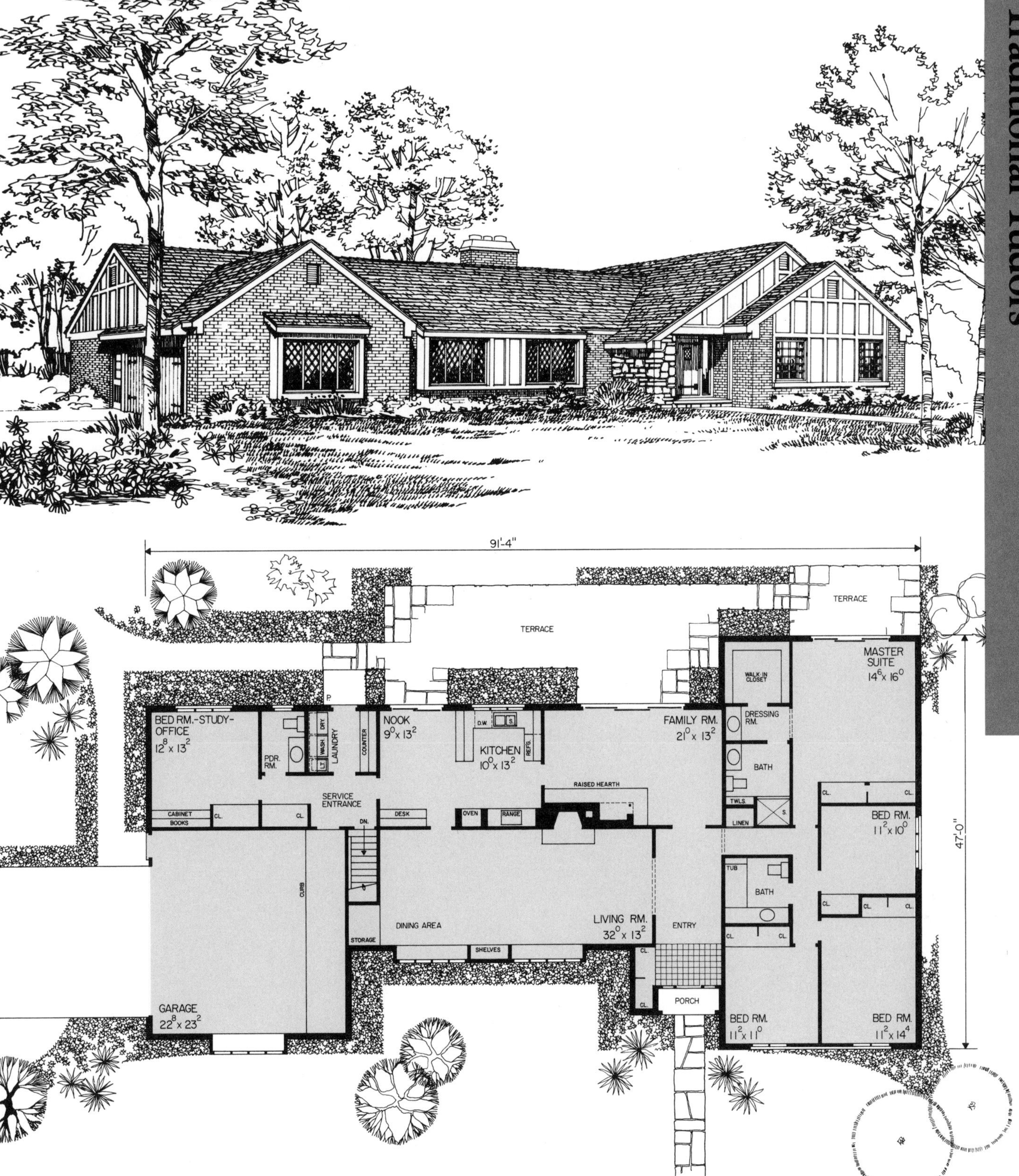

Design X2573

Square Footage: 2,747

L **D**

● A Tudor ranch! Combining brick and wood for an elegant look. It has a living/dining room measuring 32' by 13', large indeed. It is fully appointed with a traditional fireplace and built-in shelves, flanked by diagonally paned windows. There's much more! There is a family room with a raised hearth fireplace and sliding glass doors that open onto the terrace. A U-shaped kitchen has lots of built-ins . . . a range, an oven, a desk. Plus a separate breakfast nook. The sleeping facilities consist of three family bedrooms plus an elegant master bedroom suite. A conveniently located laundry with a folding counter is in the service entrance. Adjacent to the laundry is a washroom. The corner of the plan has a study or make it a fifth bedroom if you prefer.

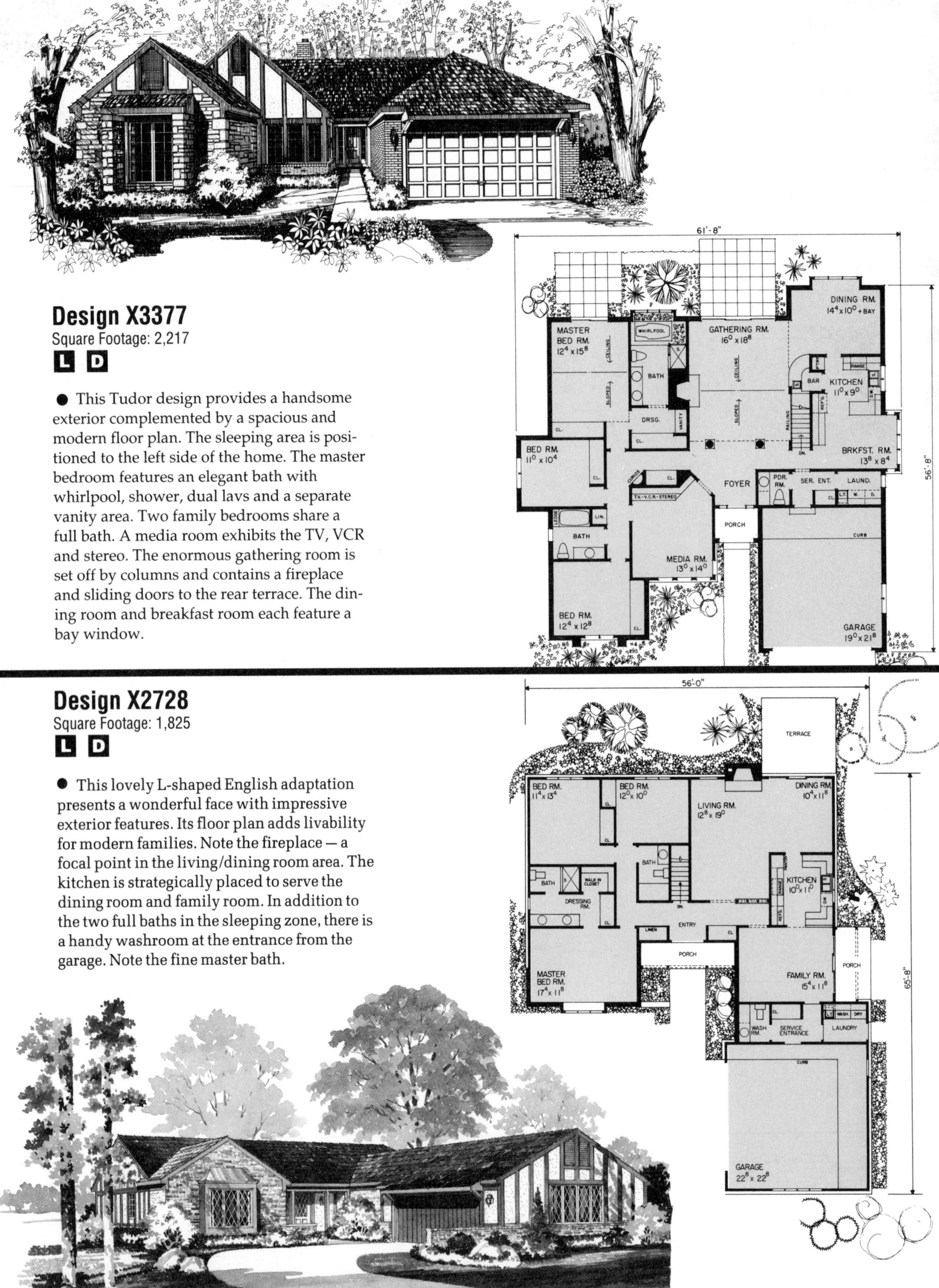

Design X3377

Square Footage: 2,217

L **D**

● This Tudor design provides a handsome exterior complemented by a spacious and modern floor plan. The sleeping area is positioned to the left side of the home. The master bedroom features an elegant bath with whirlpool, shower, dual lavs and a separate vanity area. Two family bedrooms share a full bath. A media room exhibits the TV, VCR and stereo. The enormous gathering room is set off by columns and contains a fireplace and sliding doors to the rear terrace. The dining room and breakfast room each feature a bay window.

Design X2728

Square Footage: 1,825

L **D**

● This lovely L-shaped English adaptation presents a wonderful face with impressive exterior features. Its floor plan adds livability for modern families. Note the fireplace — a focal point in the living/dining room area. The kitchen is strategically placed to serve the dining room and family room. In addition to the two full baths in the sleeping zone, there is a handy washroom at the entrance from the garage. Note the fine master bath.

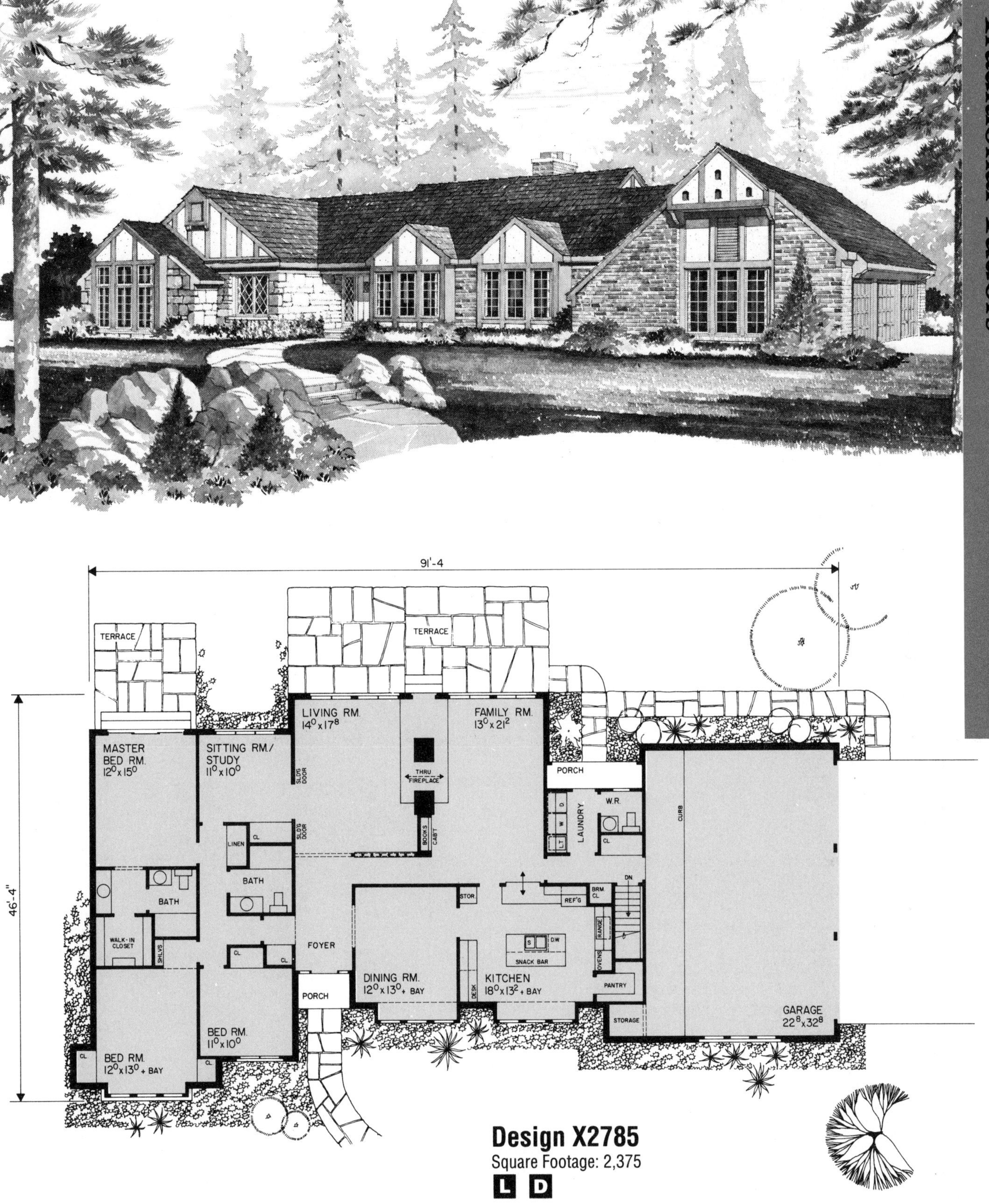

Design X2785

Square Footage: 2,375

L **D**

● Exceptional Tudor design! Passers-by will take a second glance at this fine home wherever it may be located. And the interior is just as pleasing. As one enters the foyer and looks around, the plan will speak for itself in the areas of convenience and efficiency. Cross room traffic will be avoided. There is a hall leading to each of the three bedrooms and study of the sleeping wing and another leading to the living room, family room, kitchen and laundry with washroom. The formal dining room can be entered from both the foyer and the kitchen. Efficiency will be the by-word when describing the kitchen. Note the fine features: a built-in desk, pantry, island snack bar with sink and pass-thru to the family room. The fireplace will be enjoyed in the living and family rooms.

Design X2206

Square Footage: 1,769

L **D**

● The charm of Tudor adaptations has become increasingly popular in recent years. And little wonder. Its freshness of character adds a unique touch to any neighborhood. This interesting one-story home will be a standout wherever you choose to have it built. The covered front porch leads to the formal front entry–the foyer. From this point traffic flows freely to the living and sleeping areas. The outstanding plan features a separate dining room, a beamed ceiling living room, an efficient kitchen and an informal family room.

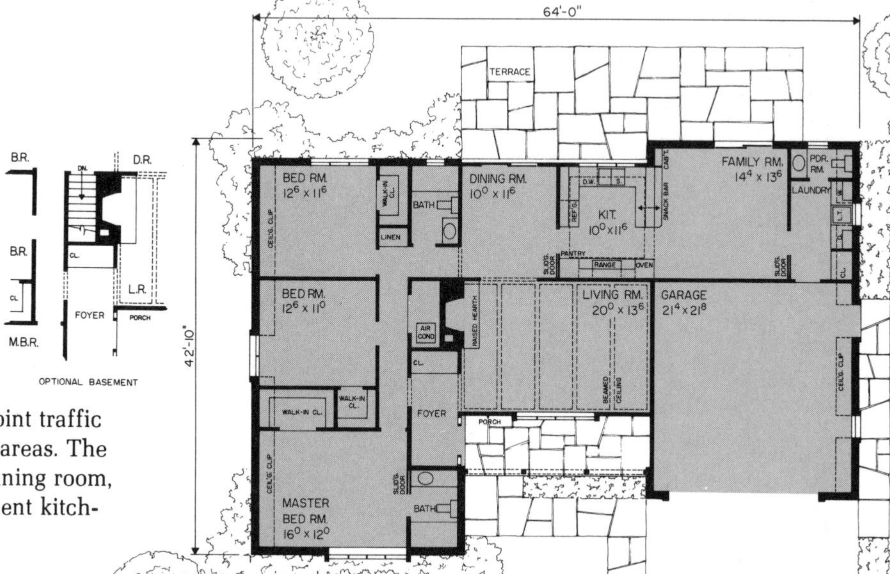

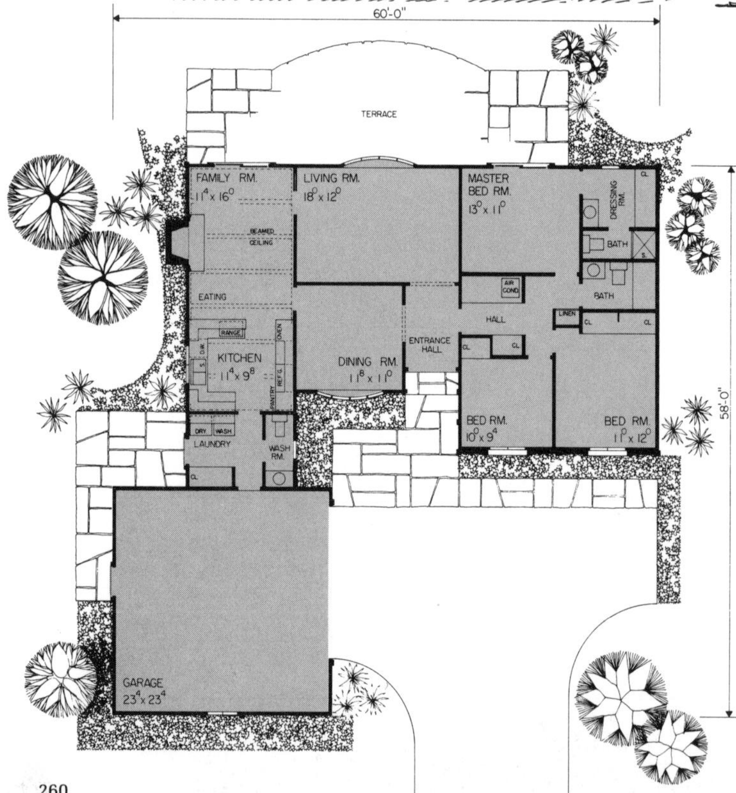

Design X2606

Square Footage: 1,499

Custom Alterations? See page 301 for customizing this plan to your specifications.

● This modest sized house with its 1,499 square feet could hardly offer more in the way of exterior charm and interior livability. Measuring only 60 feet in width means it will not require a huge, expensive piece of property. The orientation of the garage and the front drive court are features which promote an economical use of property. In addition to the formal, separate living and dining rooms, there is the informal kitchen/family room area. Note the beamed ceiling, the fireplace, the sliding glass doors and the eating area of the family room.

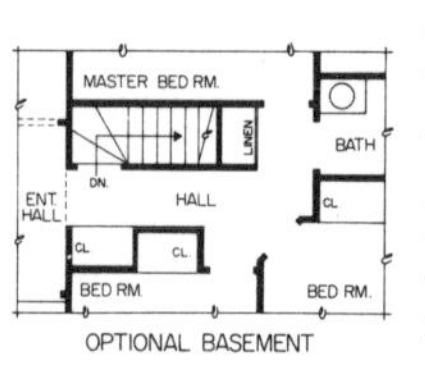

Design X2737

Square Footage: 1,796

L

● You will be able to build this distinctive, modified U-shaped one-story home on a relatively narrow site. But, then, if you so wished, with the help of your architect and builder you may want to locate the garage to the side of the house. Inside, the living potential is just great. The interior U-shaped kitchen handily services the dining and family rooms and nook. A rear covered porch functions ideally with the family room while the formal living room has its own terrace. Three bedrooms and two baths highlight the sleeping zone (or make it two bedrooms and a study). Notice the strategic location of the washroom, laundry, two storage closets and the basement stairs.

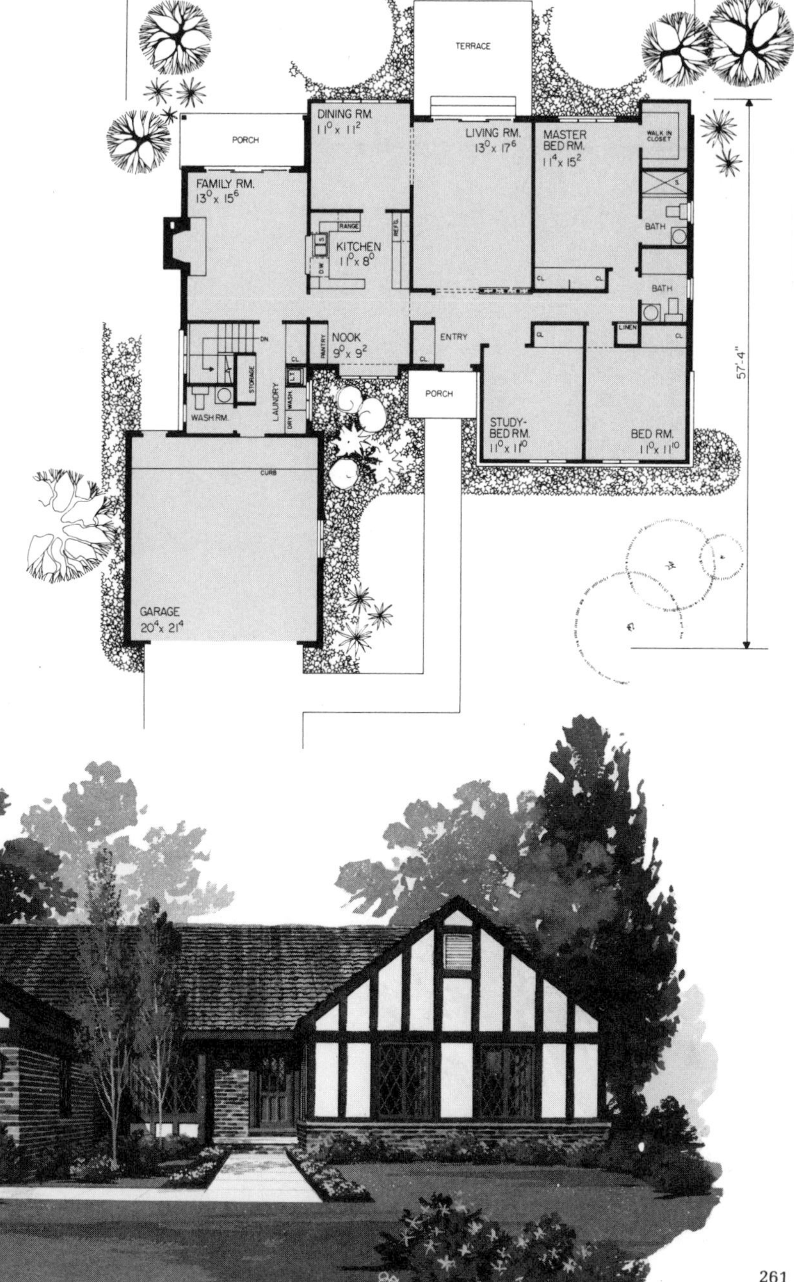

Design X3373
Square Footage: 1,378

L D

Design X3374
Square Footage: 1,378

L D

Design X3375
Square Footage: 1,378

L D

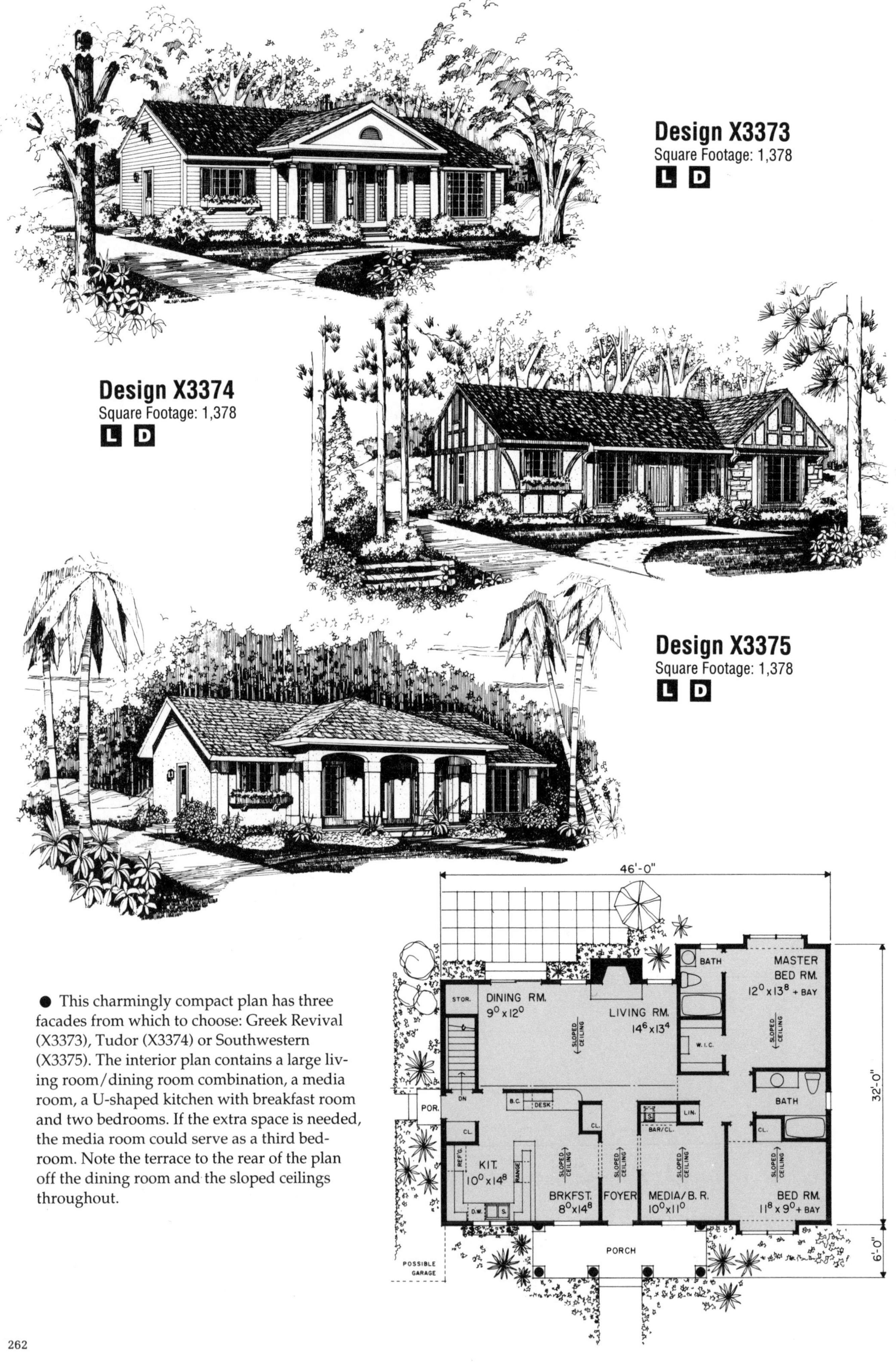

● This charmingly compact plan has three facades from which to choose: Greek Revival (X3373), Tudor (X3374) or Southwestern (X3375). The interior plan contains a large living room/dining room combination, a media room, a U-shaped kitchen with breakfast room and two bedrooms. If the extra space is needed, the media room could serve as a third bedroom. Note the terrace to the rear of the plan off the dining room and the sloped ceilings throughout.

Design X2565

Square Footage: 1,540

L D

● This modest sized floor plan has much to offer in the way of livability. It may function as either a two or three bedroom home. The living room is huge and features a fine, raised hearth fireplace. The open stairway to the basement is handy and will lead to what may be developed as the recreation area. In addition to the two full baths, there is an extra wash room. Adjacent is the laundry room and the service entrance from the garage. The blueprints you order for this design will show details for each of the three delightful elevations above. Which is your favorite? The Tudor, the Colonial or the Contemporary?

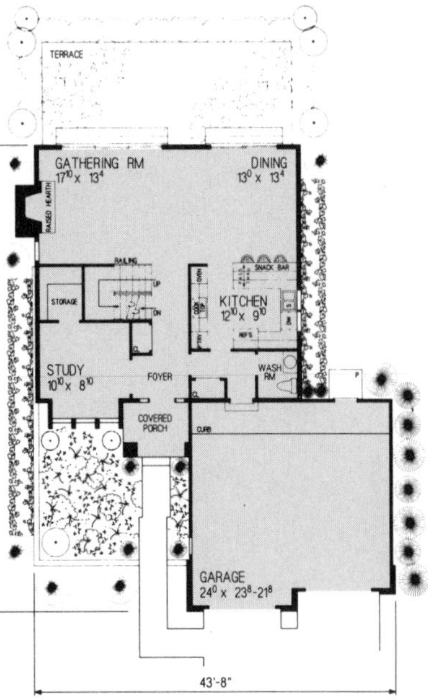

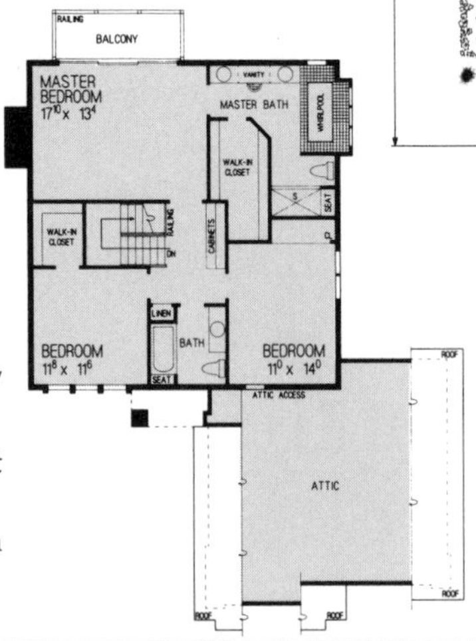

Design X3341 First Floor: 1,055 square feet
Second Floor: 981 square feet; Total: 2,036 square feet

● Designed for the empty-nester, small family, or as a second home, this appealing Tudor adaptation holds a most livable floor plan. Besides the 31′ gathering room/ dining room area and U-shaped kitchen with nearby washroom, there is front study with large storage closet on the first floor. Three bedrooms on the second floor meet sleeping needs without a hitch. Notice the walk-in closets and the master-bedroom balcony.

Design X3302
First Floor: 1,326 square feet
Second Floor: 542 square feet
Total: 1,868 square feet

● A cottage fit for a king! Appreciate the highlights: a two-story foyer, a rear living zone (gathering room, terrace, and dining room), pass-through snack bar in kitchen, a two-story master bedroom. Two upstairs bedrooms share a full bath.

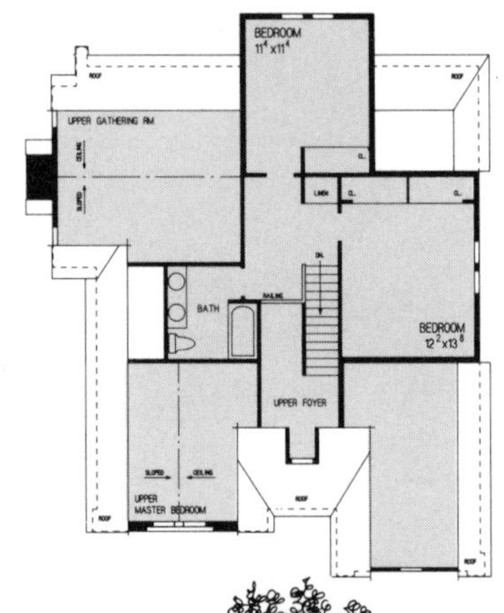

Custom Alterations? See page 301 for customizing this plan to your specifications.

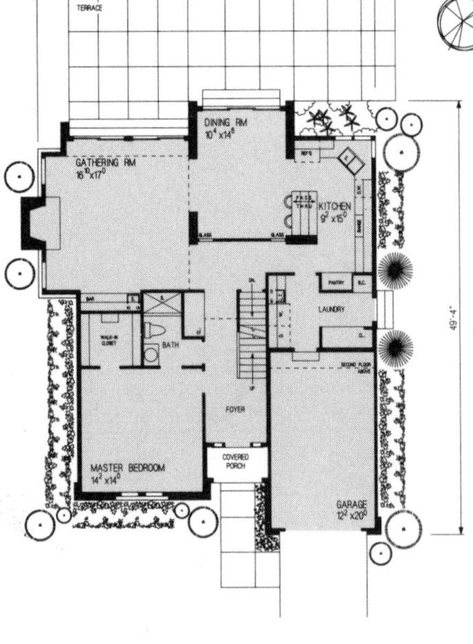

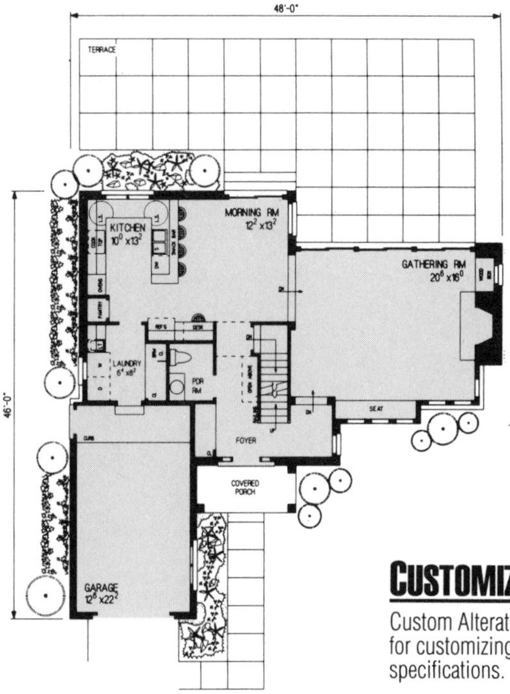

CUSTOMIZABLE

Custom Alterations? See page 301 for customizing this plan to your specifications.

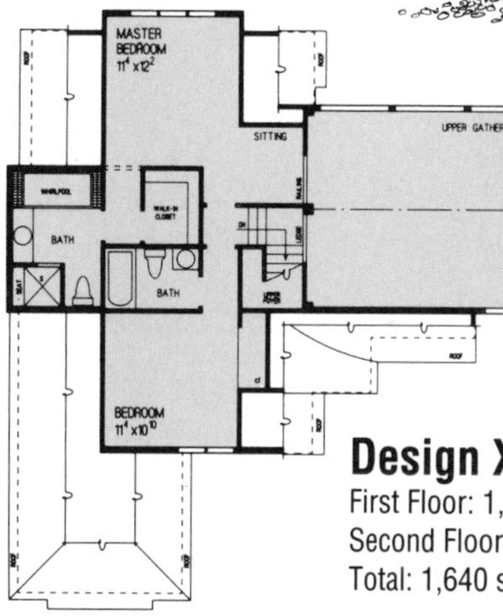

● This modest-looking plan surprises everyone with its wealth of amenities inside. Look for a U-shaped kitchen with snack bar, morning room, sunken gathering room (note fireplace with wood box), and abundant built-ins. The master suite on the second floor is a true eye-catcher.

Design X2491

First Floor: 1,060 square feet
Second Floor: 580 square feet
Total: 1,640 square feet

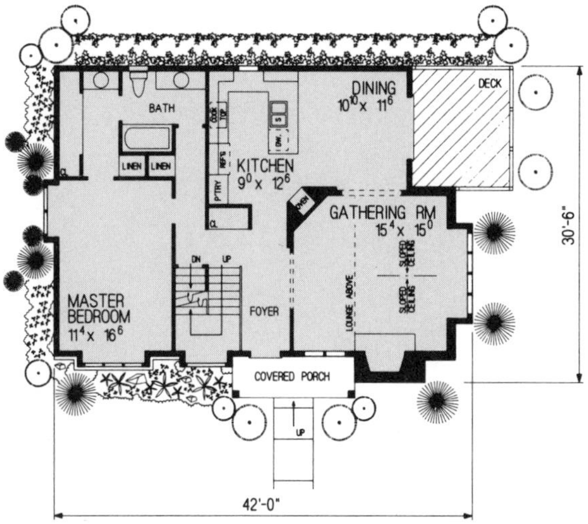

Design X3331

First Floor: 1,115 square feet
Second Floor: 690 square feet
Total: 1,805 square feet

● Who could guess that this compact design contains three bedrooms and two full baths? The kitchen is close to indoor eating space in the dining room and outdoor eating space in an attached deck. A fireplace in the two-story gathering room welcomes company.

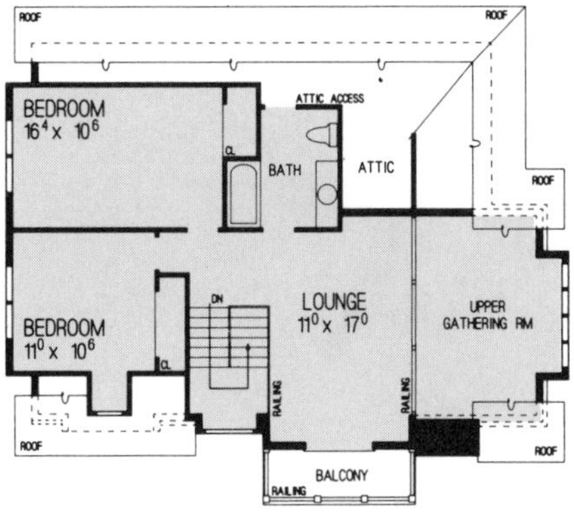

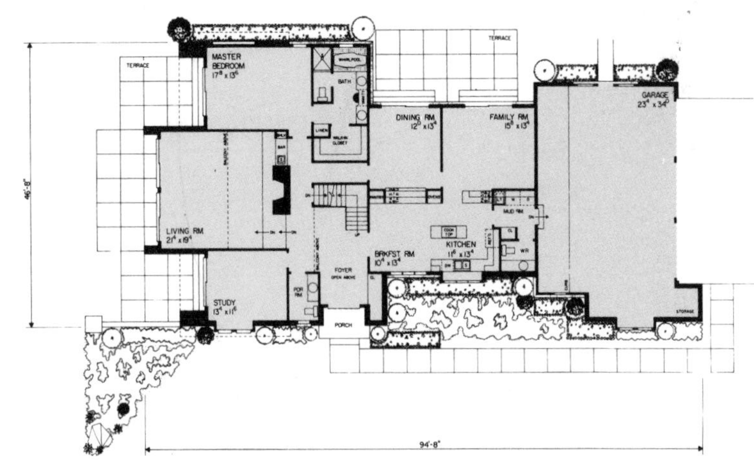

Design X2965

First Floor: 2,313 square feet
Second Floor: 1,314 square feet
Total: 3,627 square feet

● An appealing mix of contrasting exterior materials helps make this Tudor distinctive. Inside, the delightful foyer welcomes all. To the right of the foyer is a functional kitchen which opens conveniently to the breakfast room. It also serves both the formal dining room and informal family room. The sunken living room has a high sloping ceiling, a wall of windows and a fireplace and wet bar. There are also four baths serving four bedrooms.

Design X2964

First Floor: 1,441 square feet
Second Floor: 621 square feet
Total: 2,062 square feet

● Tudor houses have their own unique exterior features. This outstanding two-story has a first-floor master bedroom plus two bedrooms with a lounge upstairs. The living room is dramatically spacious. It has a two-story sloping ceiling and large glass areas across the back. The open staircase to the upstairs has plenty of natural light as does the stairway to the basement recreation area.

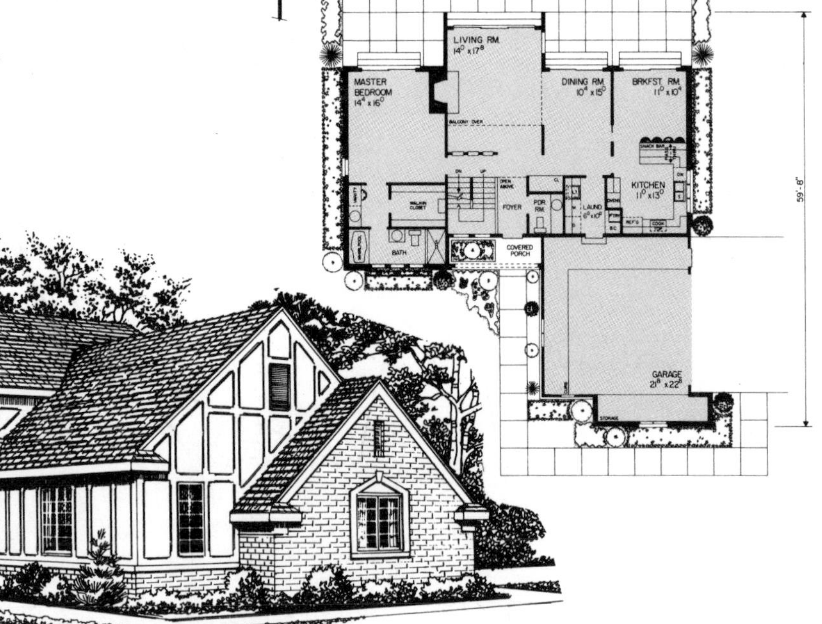

● This Tudor design has many fine features. The exterior is enhanced by front and side bay windows in the family and dining rooms. Along with an outstanding exterior, it also contains a modern and efficient floor plan within its modest proportions. Flanking the entrance foyer is a comfortable living room. The U-shaped kitchen is conveniently located between the dining and breakfast rooms.

Design X2800

First Floor: 999 square feet
Second Floor: 997 square feet; Total: 1,996 square feet

L D

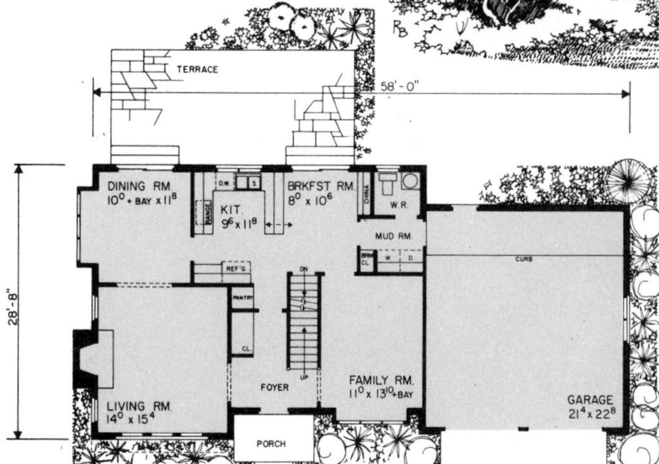

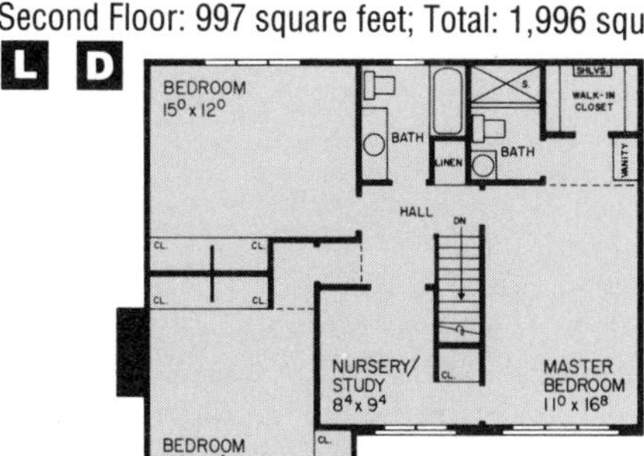

● The charm of old England has been captured in this outstanding two-story design. Interior livability will efficiently serve the various needs of all family members. The first floor offers both formal and informal areas along with the work centers. Features include: a wet bar in the dining room, the kitchen's snack bar, first-floor laundry and a rear covered porch.

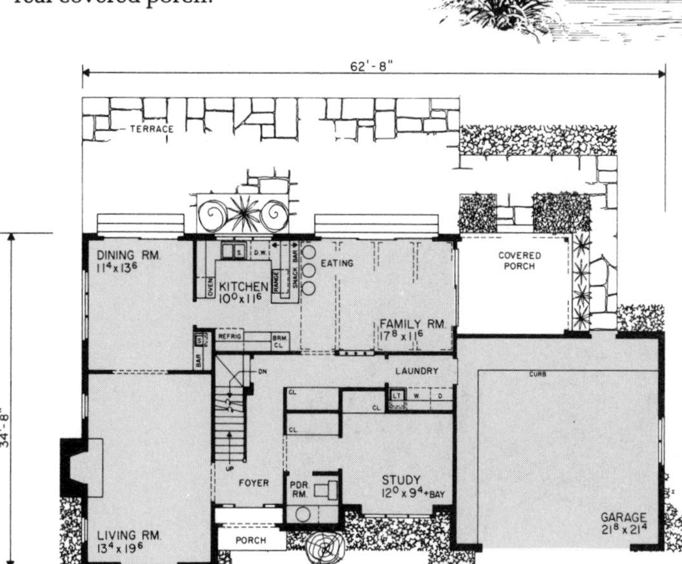

Design X2854

First Floor: 1,261 square feet
Second Floor: 950 square feet; Total: 2,211 square feet

L D

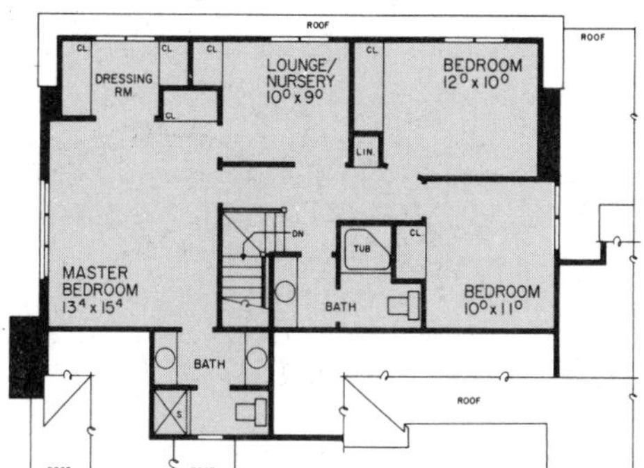

Design X2967

First Floor: 1,877 square feet
Second Floor: 467 square feet
Total: 2,344 square feet

● Special interior amenities abound in this unique 1½-story Tudor. Living areas include an open gathering room/dining room area with fireplace and pass-through to the breakfast room. Quiet time can be spent in a sloped-ceiling study. Look for plenty of workspace in the island kitchen and workshop/storage area. Sleeping areas are separated for utmost privacy: an elegant master suite on the first floor, two bedrooms and a full bath on the second.

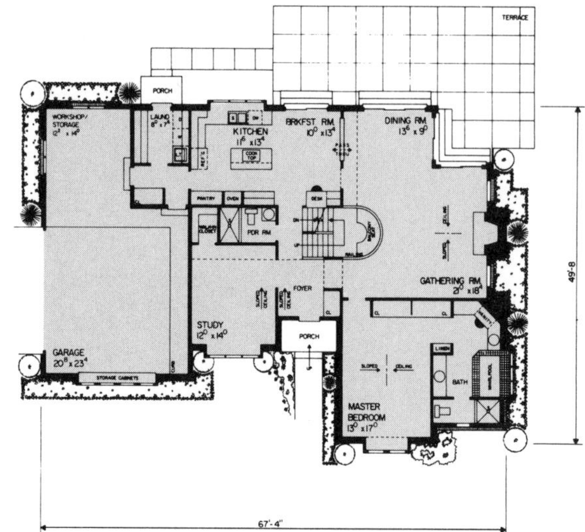

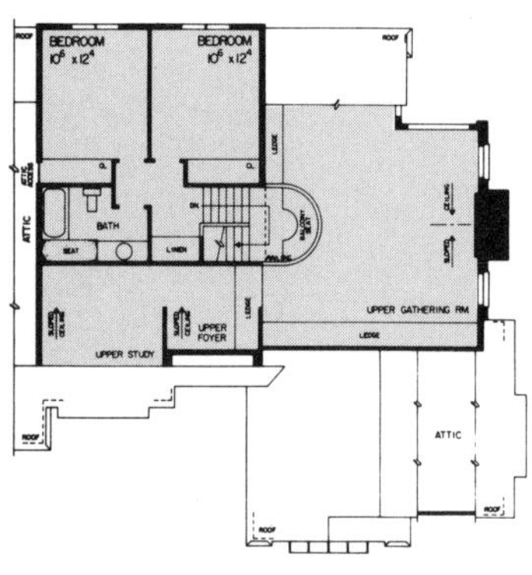

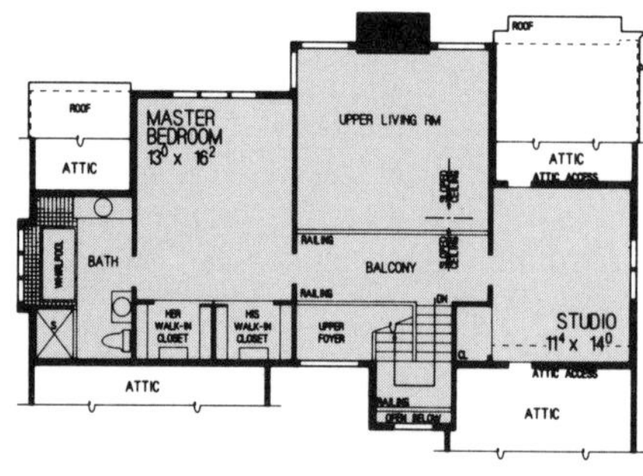

Design X3342

First Floor: 1,467 square feet
Second Floor: 715 square feet
Total: 2,182 square feet

● Just the right amount of living space is contained in this charming traditional house and it's arranged in a great floor plan. The split-bedroom configuration, with two bedrooms (or optional study) on the first floor and the master suite on the second floor with its own studio, assures complete privacy. The living room has a second-floor balcony overlook and a warming fireplace. The full-width terrace in back is counterbalanced nicely by the entry garden court.

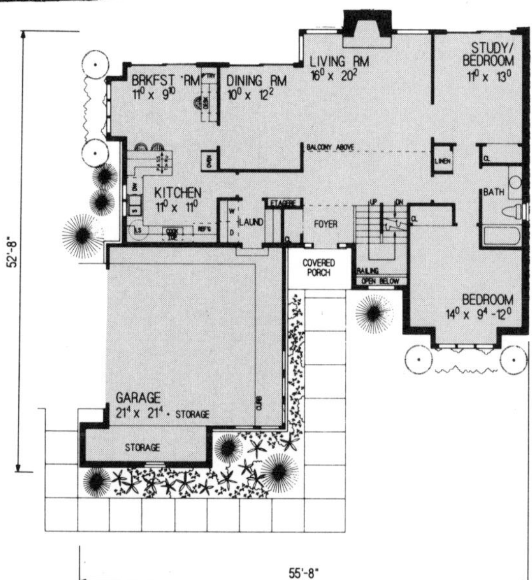

CUSTOMIZABLE

Custom Alterations? See page 301 for customizing this plan to your specifications.

Design X3346

Square Footage: 2,032

● This home boasts a delightful Tudor exterior with a terrific interior floor plan. Though compact, there's plenty of living space: large study with fireplace, gathering room, dining room, and breakfast room. The master bedroom has an attached bath with whirlpool tub. Note the double walk-in closets.

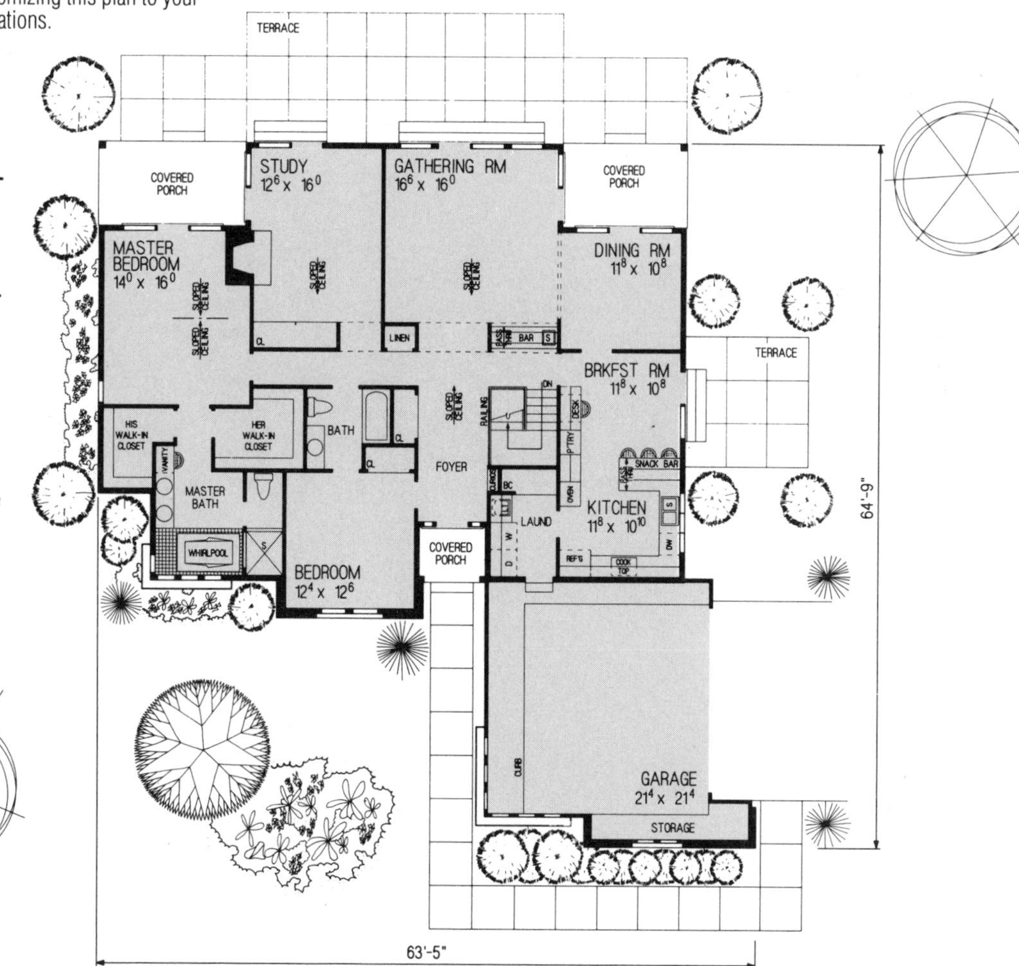

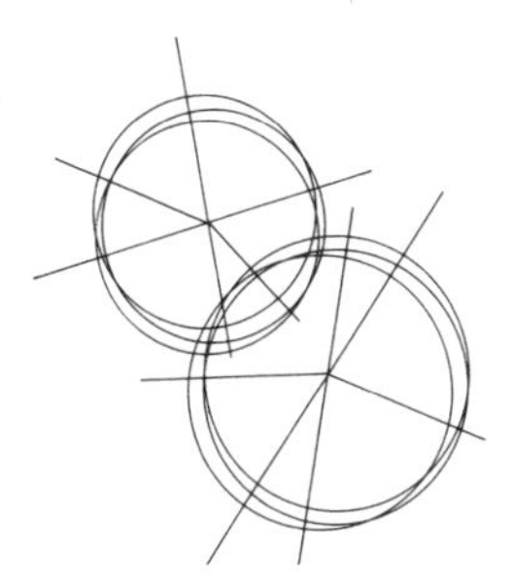

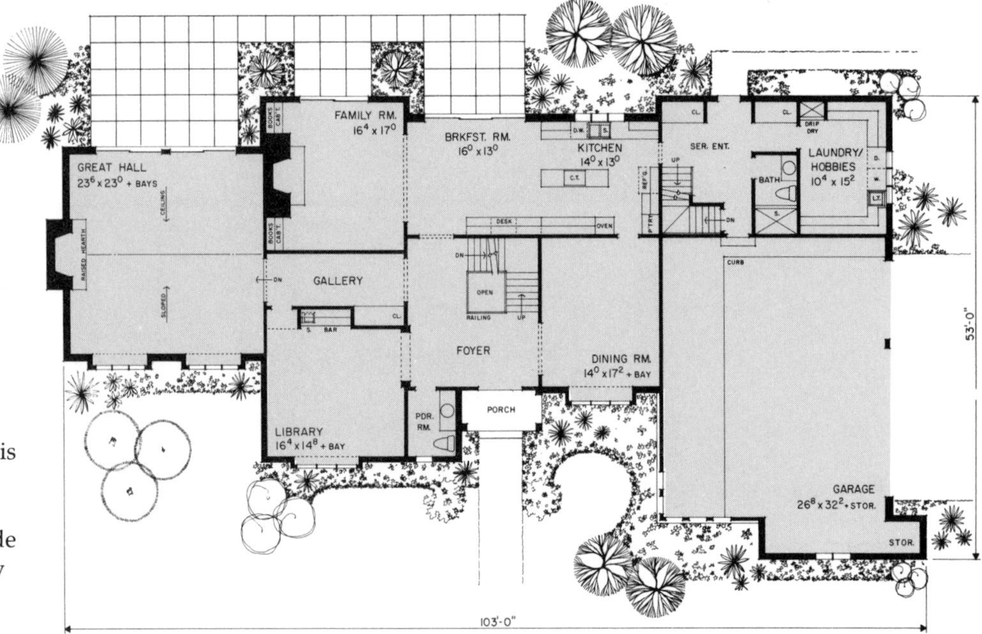

Design X3369

First Floor: 2,740 square feet
Second Floor: 2,257 square feet
Total: 4,997 square feet

● In magnificent Tudor style, this home delivers a stunning facade complemented by a most livable floor plan. The living areas include a library, a great hall and a family room (both with fireplaces) and a formal dining room. The island kitchen has an attached breakfast room. Connecting the main body of the house to the garage is a service area with full bath and laundry/hobby room. Upstairs, there are four bedrooms with walk-in closets and four full baths. The master has a fireplace and His and Hers walk-ins.

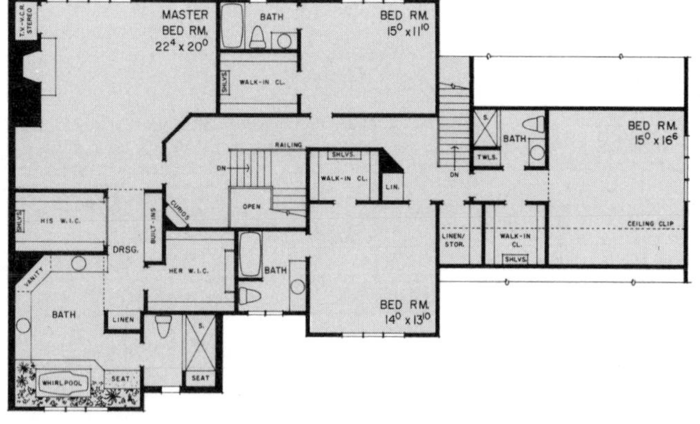

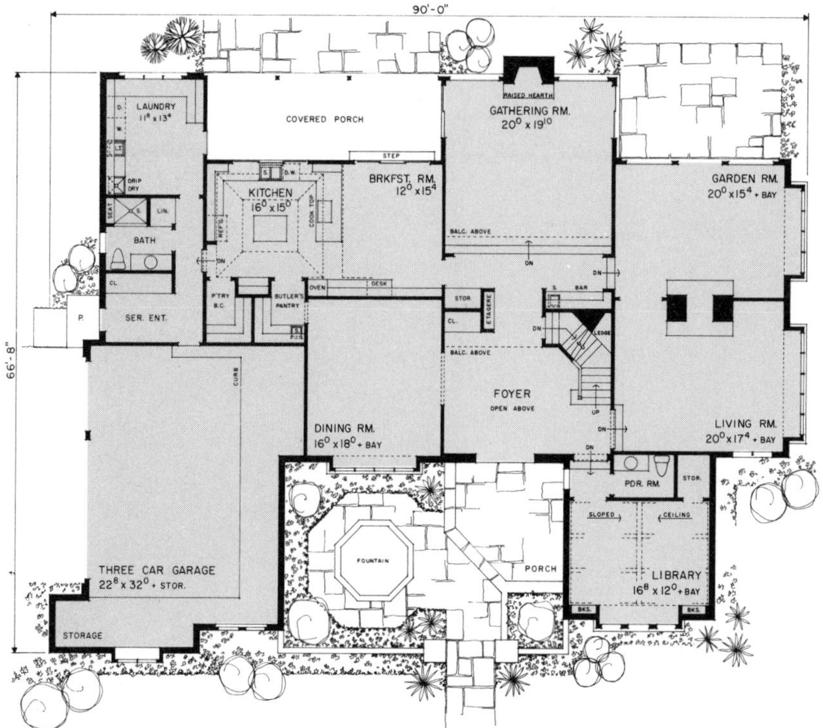

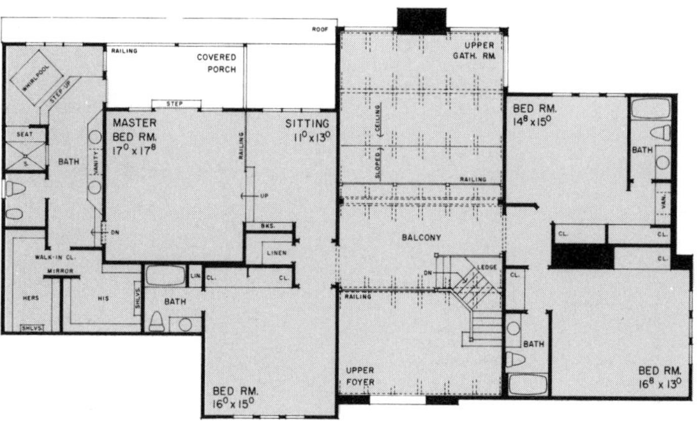

Design X3554

First Floor: 3,275 square feet
Second Floor: 2,363 square feet
Total: 5,638 square feet

L **D**

● A splendid garden entry greets visitors to this regal Tudor home. Past the double doors is a two-story foyer that leads to the various living areas of the home. A quiet library is secluded directly off the foyer and has a box bay window, private powder room and sloped ceiling. Formal living takes place to the right of the foyer—an attached garden room shares a through fireplace with this area. Formal dining is found to the left of the foyer, accessed from the kitchen via a butler's pantry. The gathering room handles casual occasions and is just across the hall from the wet bar. Upstairs there is a grand master suite with lavish bath and sitting room and three secondary bedroom, each with private bath.

Design X2847

Main Level: 1,874 square feet
Lower Level: 1,131 square feet
Total: 3,005 square feet

L **D**

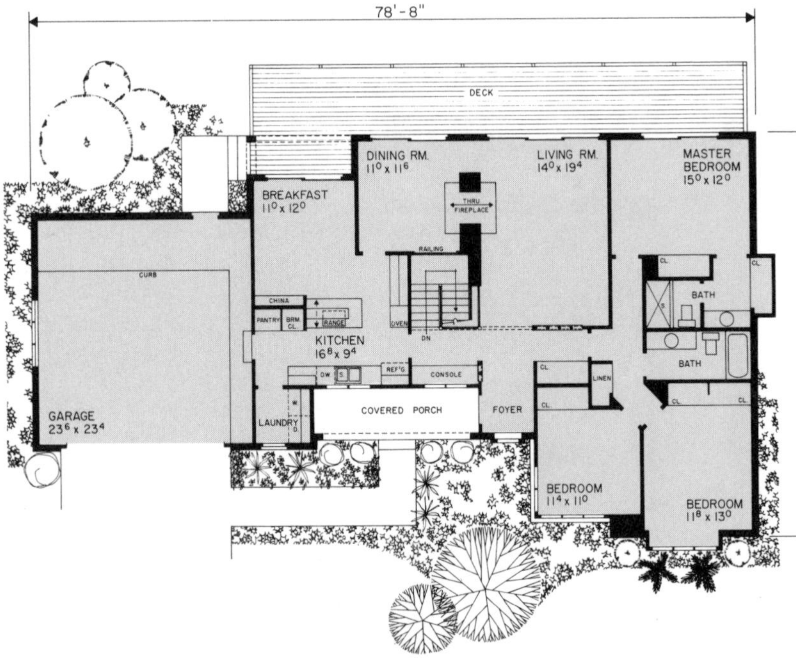

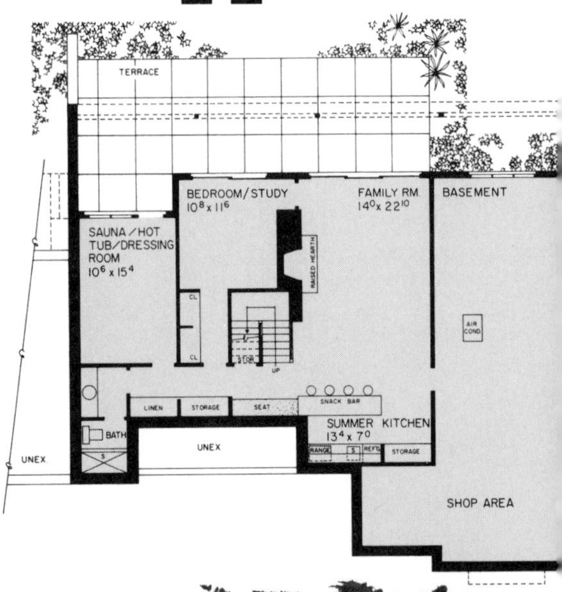

● This is an exquisitely styled Tudor tri-level designed to serve its happy occupants for many years. The contrasting use of material surely makes the exterior eye-catching.

Design X3366

Main Level: 1,638 square feet
Upper Level: 650 square feet
Lower Level: 934 square feet
Total: 3,222 square feet

L

● There is much more to this design than meets the eye. While it may look like a 1½-story plan, bonus recreation and hobby space in the walk-out basement adds almost 1,000 square feet. The first floor holds living and dining areas as well as the master bedroom suite. Two family bedrooms on the second floor are connected by a balcony area that overlooks the gathering room below. Notice the covered porch beyond the breakfast and dining rooms.

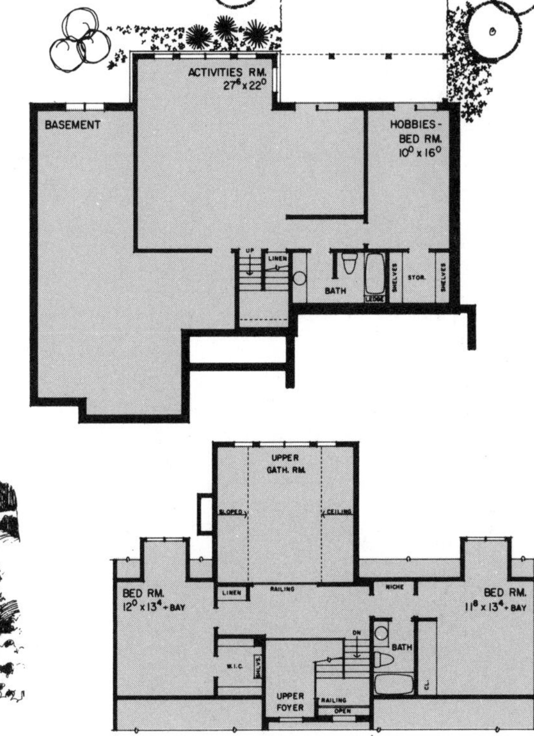

Design X2171

Main Level: 795 square feet; Upper Level: 912 square feet
Lower Level: 335 square feet; Total: 2,042 square feet

L **D**

● This English Tudor, split-level adaptation has much to recommend it. Perhaps, its most significant feature is that it can be built economically on a relatively small site. The width of the house is just over 52 feet. But its size does not inhibit its livability. There are many fine qualities. Observe the living room fireplace in addition to the one in the family room with a wood box. The breakfast room overlooks the lower level family room. It also has a pass-thru to the kitchen. Don't miss the balcony off the master bedroom. Also worthy of note, a short flight of stairs leads to the huge attic storage area.

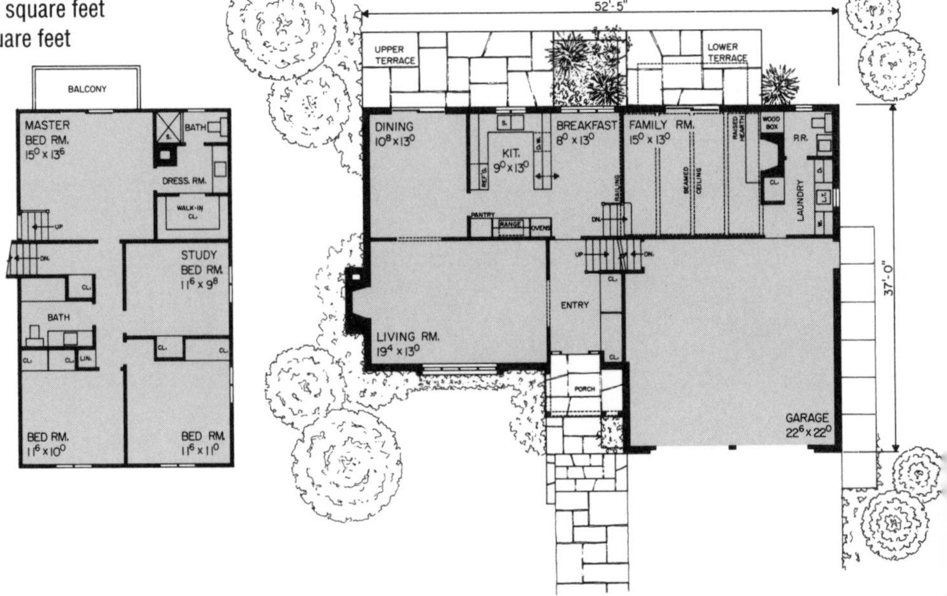

Design X2624

Main Level: 904 square feet; Upper Level: 1,120 square feet
Lower Level: 404 square feet; Total: 2,428 square feet

L **D**

WIDTH 60'-6"
DEPTH 39'-6"

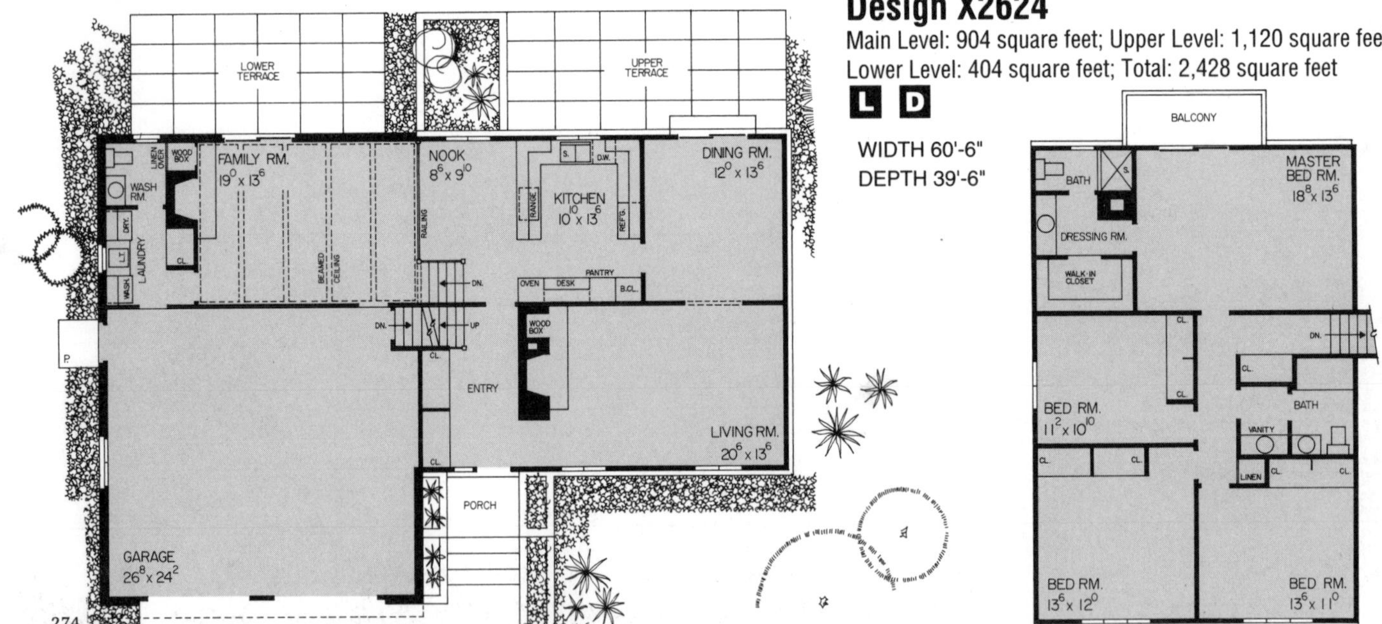

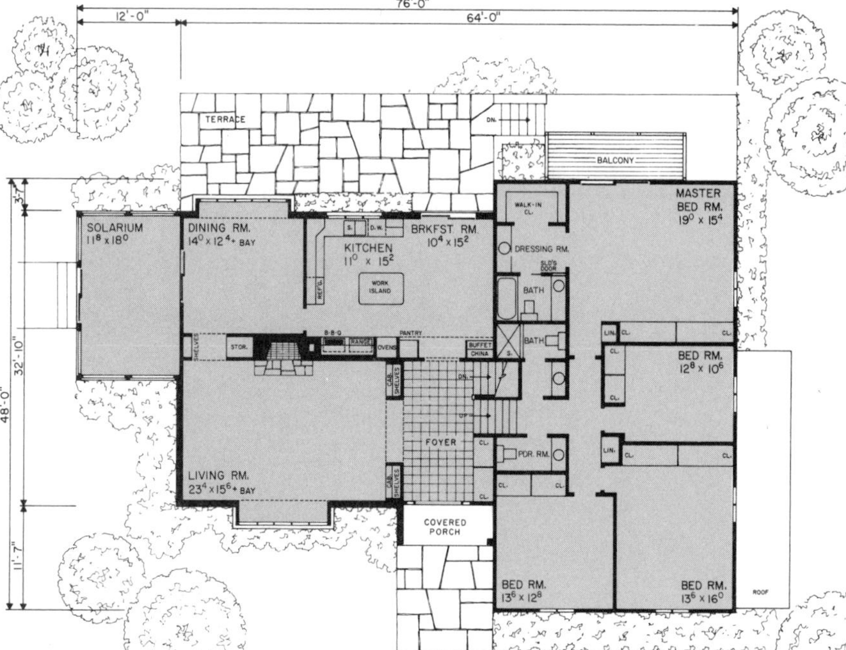

Design X2254

Main Level: 1,220 square feet
Upper Level: 1,344 square feet
Lower Level: 659 square feet
Total: 3,223 square feet

● Tudor charm is deftly exemplified by this outstanding four level design. The window treatment, the heavy timber work and the chimney pots help set the character of this home. Contributing an extra measure of appeal is the detailing of the delightful porch. The garden view of this home is equally appealing. The upper level balcony looks down onto the two terraces. The covered front entry leads to the spacious formal entrance hall with its slate floor.

Design X2842

Entrance Level: 156 square feet; Upper Level: 1,038 square feet
Lower Level: 1,022 square feet; Total: 2,216 square feet

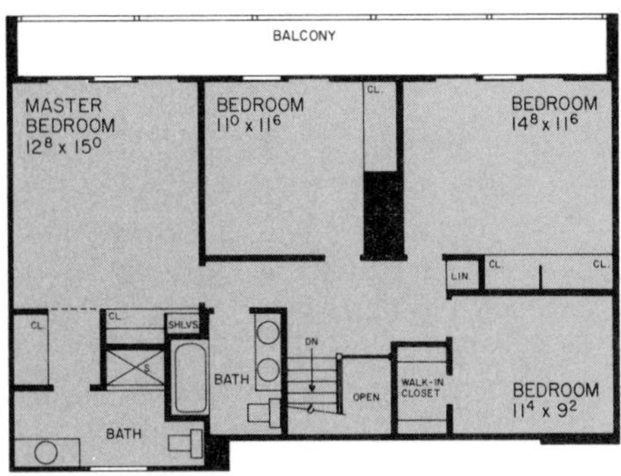

● This narrow, 42 foot width, house can be built on a narrow lot to cut down overall costs. Yet its dramatic appeal surely is worth a million. The projecting front garage creates a pleasing curved drive. One enters this house through the covered porch to the entrance level foyer. At this point the stairs lead down to the living area consisting of formal living room, family room, kitchen and dining area then up the stairs to the four bedroom-two bath sleeping area. The indoor-outdoor living relationship at the rear is outstanding.

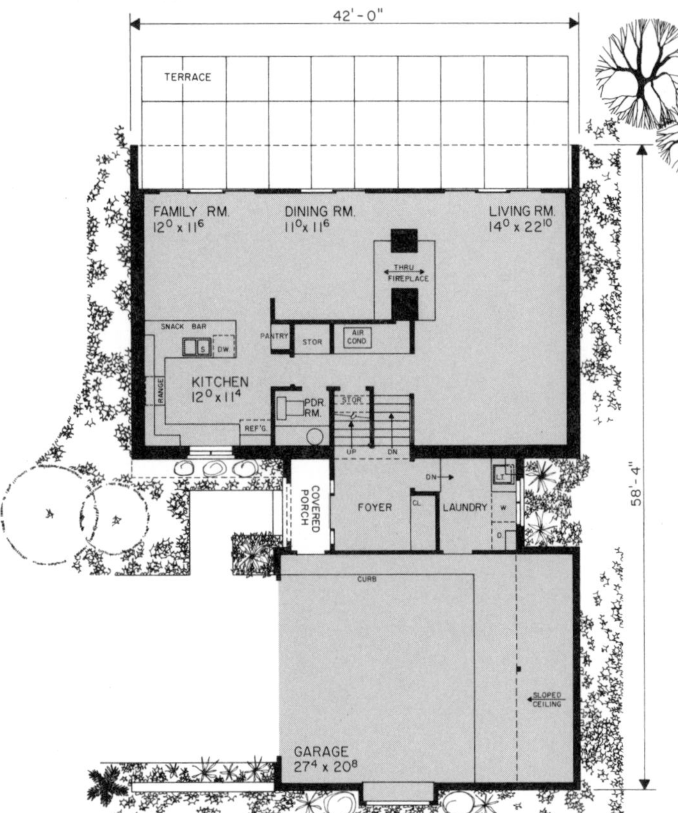

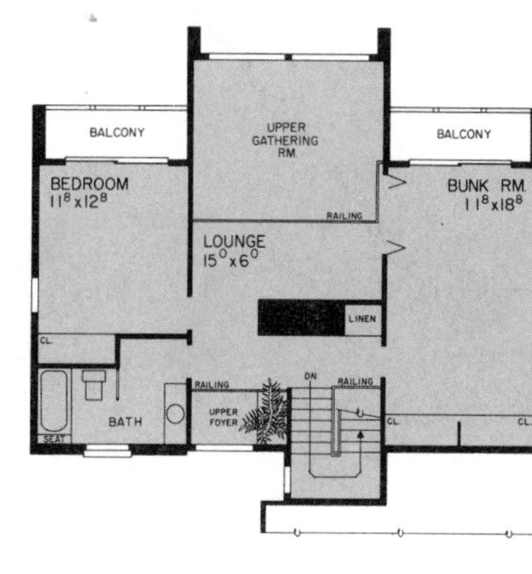

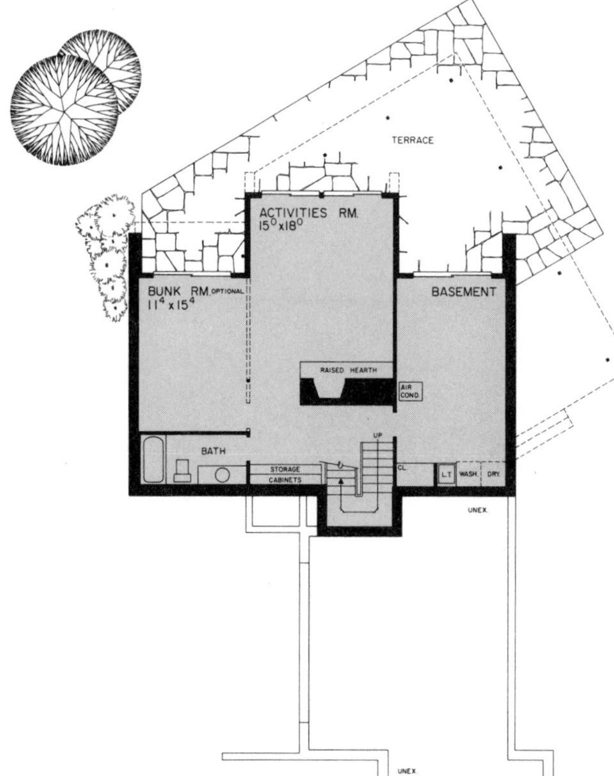

44'-0"
DECK
GATHERING RM.
15⁰x18⁰
BALCONY
STUDY/ BEDROOM
11⁸x12⁸
BALCONY ABOVE
DINING RM.
11⁸x10⁰
SNACK BAR
RANGE
KITCHEN
11⁸x11⁰
REF'G.
D.W.
BRM CL.
CL.
SEAT
BATH
DN
UP
FOYER
CL.
PORCH
62'-4"
CURB
GARAGE
21⁰x22⁰+ STORAGE
STORAGE

Design X2841

Main Level: 1,044 square feet; Upper Level: 851 square feet
Lower Level: 753 square feet; Total: 2,648 square feet

D

● This spacious tri-level with traditional stone exterior offers excellent comfort and zoning for the modern family. The rear opens to balconies and a deck that creates a covered patio below. A main floor gathering room is continued above with an upper gathering room. The lower level offers an activities room with raised hearth, in addition to an optional bunk room with bath. A modern kitchen on main level features a handy snack bar, in addition to a dining room. A study on main level could become an optional bedroom. The master bedroom is located on the upper level, along with a rectangular bunk room with its own balcony.

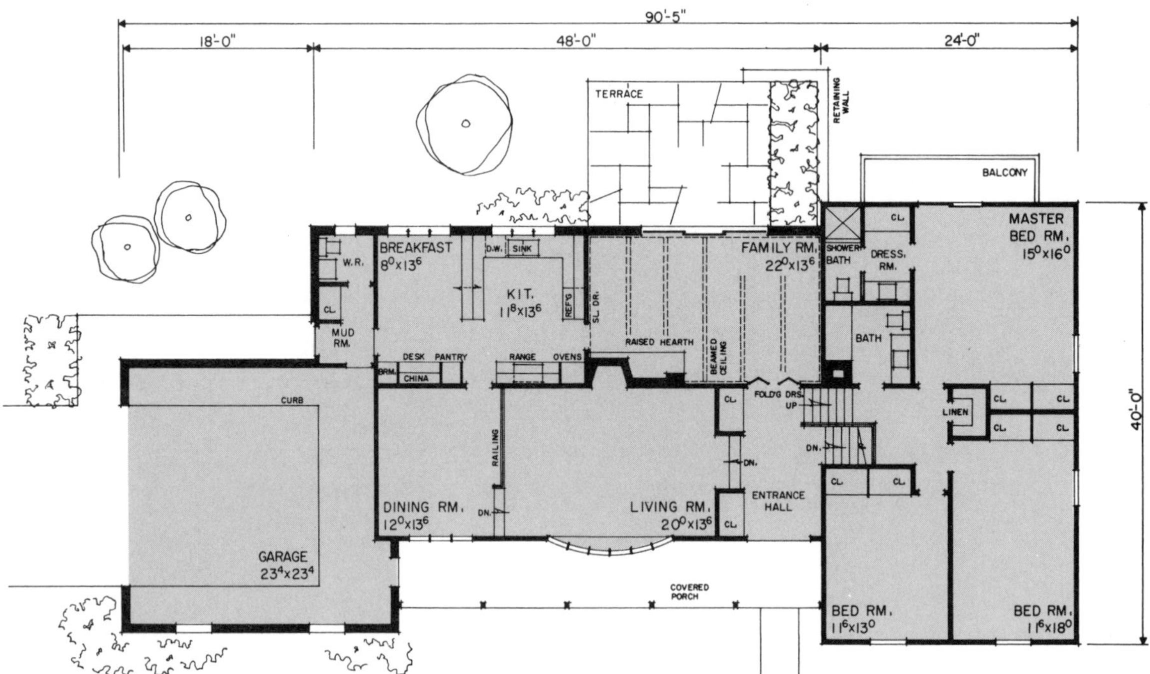

Design X1927

Main Level: 1,272 square feet; Upper Level: 960 square feet
Lower Level: 936 square feet; Total: 3,168 square feet

● Living in this traditional split level home will be a great experience. For here is a design that has everything. It has good looks and an abundance of livability features. The long, low appearance is accentuated by the large covered porch which shelters the bowed window and the inviting double front doors. Whatever your preference for exterior materials they will show well on this finely proportioned home. They start with four bedrooms and three full baths and continue with: beamed ceiling family room, sunken living room, formal dining room, informal breakfast room, extra wash room, outstanding kitchen and two attractive fireplaces.

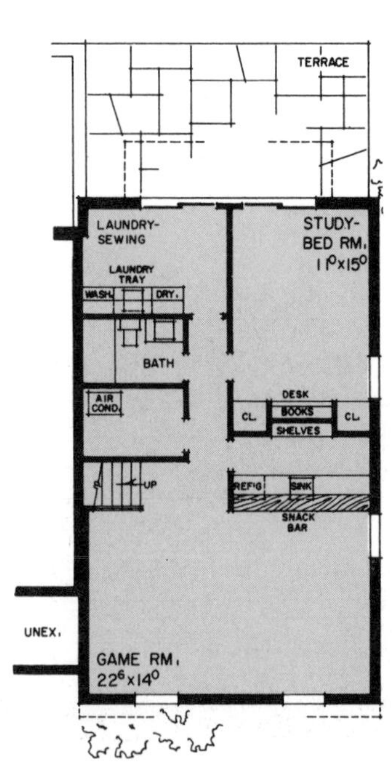

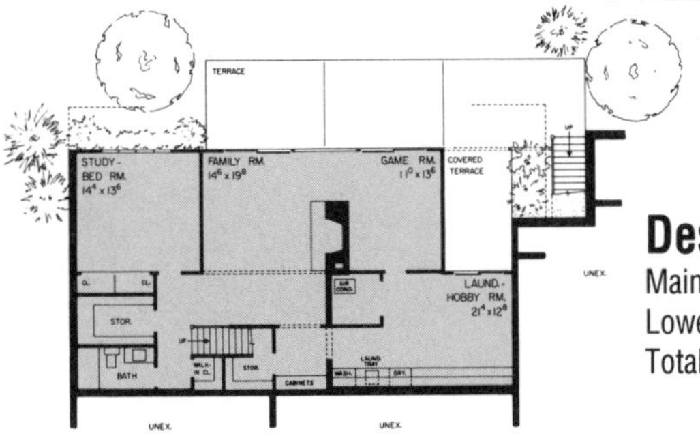

Design X1974

Main Level: 1,680 square feet
Lower Level: 1,344 square feet
Total: 3,024 square feet

● You would never guess from looking at the front of this traditional design that it possessed such a strikingly different exterior to the back. Yet its configuration means great hillside living. The most popular outdoor area will be the balcony. Inside, the formal living and dining room will serve formal functions while the informal family room on the lower level meets everyday needs.

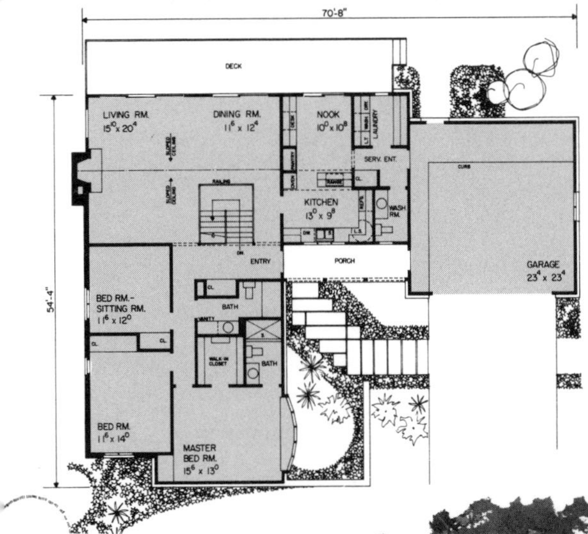

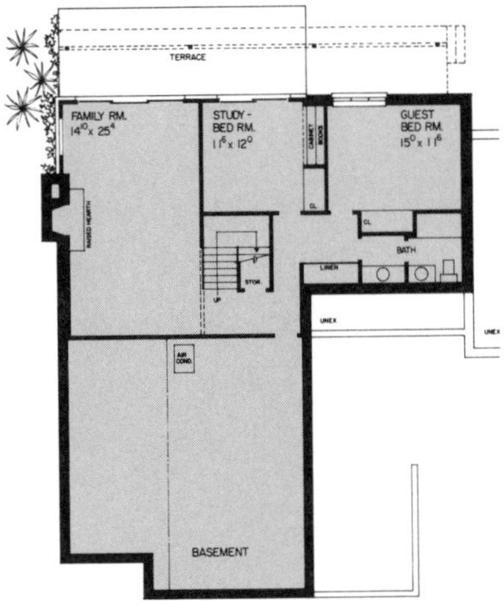

Design X2769

Main Level: 1,898 square feet
Lower Level: 1,134 square feet
Total: 3,032 square feet

● This traditional hillside design has fine architectural styling. Its floor plan allows for split sleeping areas and a separation of formal and informal living areas.

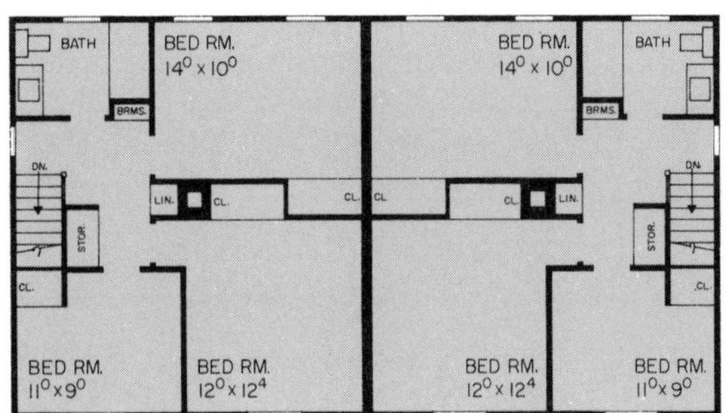

Design X2014

First Floor: 725 square feet
Second Floor: 624 square feet
Total: 1,349 square feet (each side)

● This two-story traditional duplex has all the livability of a fine single family home. The exterior is very appealing with the use of horizontal siding, shuttered windows and covered front porch. Inside is a fine living space. The L-shaped living/dining area has a sliding door to shut off the kitchen noise. A powder room and laundry are also found on the first floor. Upstairs are two bedrooms and a full bath with dual vanities. The basement may be developed as an informal recreation area.

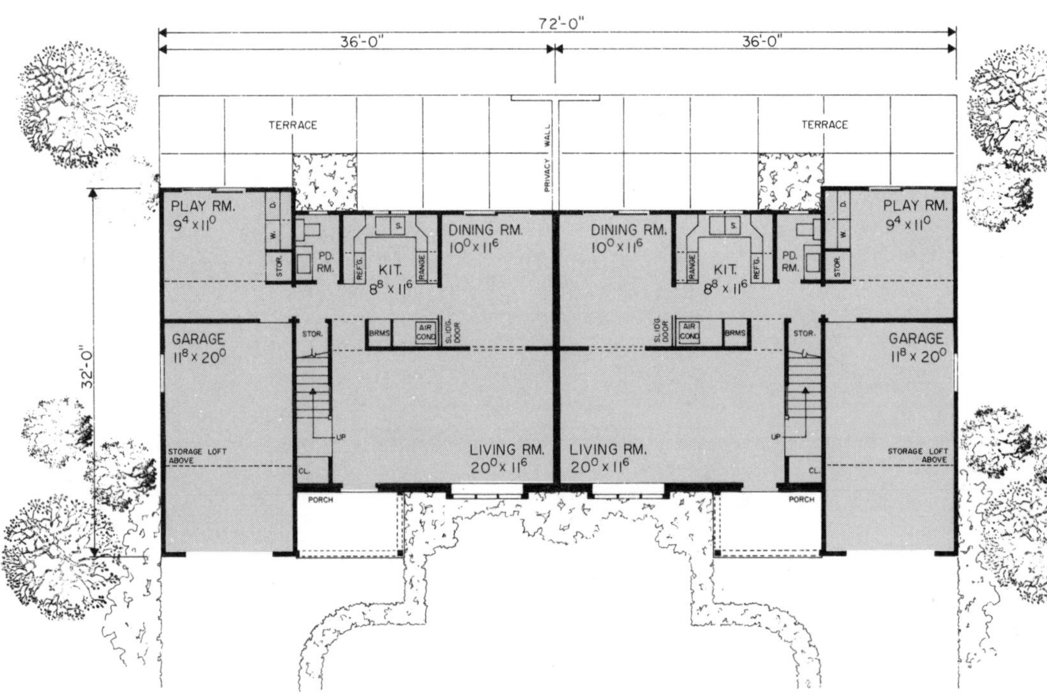

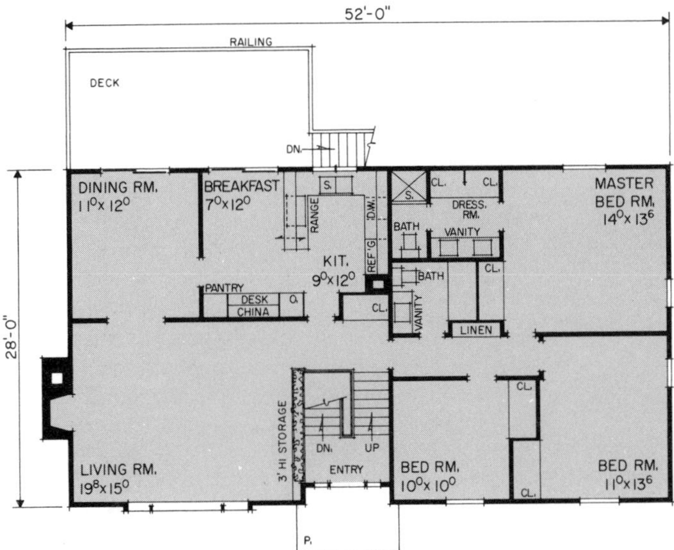

Design X1850

Main Level: 1,456 square feet
Lower Level: 728 square feet
Total: 2,184 square feet

● A perfect rectangle, this split-level is comparatively inexpensive to build and very appealing to live in. It features a large upper-level living room with fireplace, formal dining room, three bedrooms (with two full baths nearby), and an outdoor deck. Another fireplace warms the family room on the lower level, which also has a full bath and room for a study or fourth bedroom.

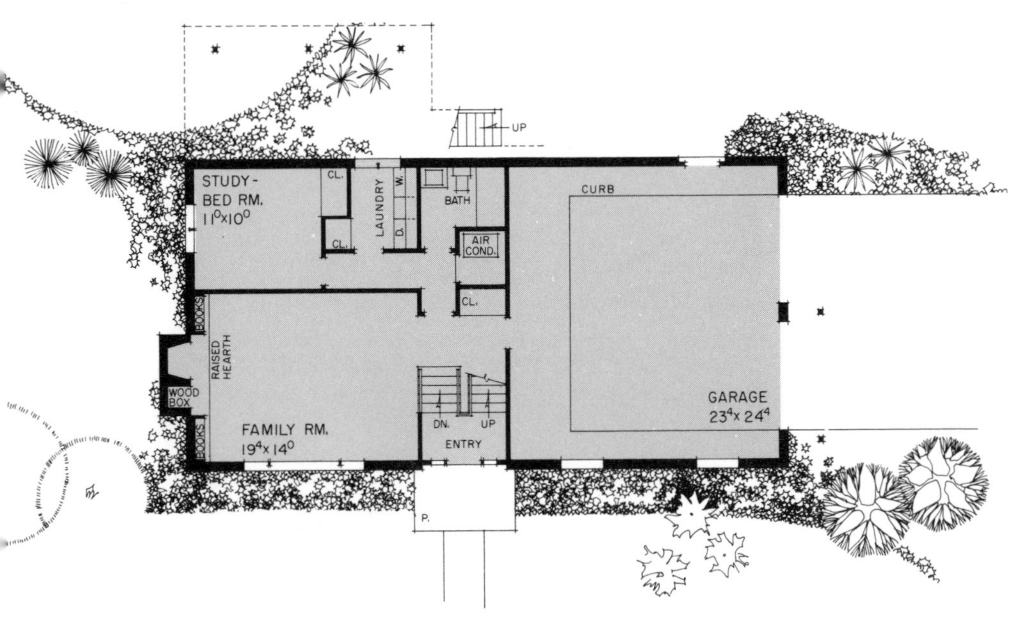

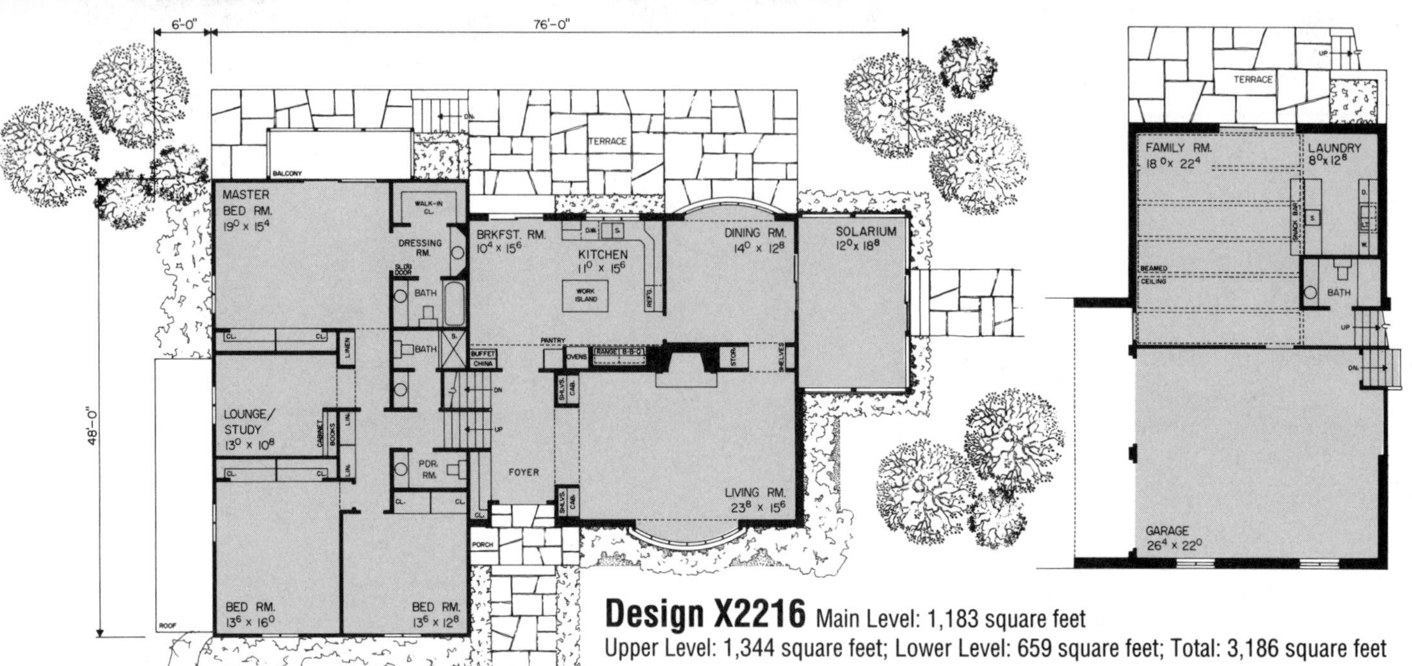

Design X2216 Main Level: 1,183 square feet
Upper Level: 1,344 square feet; Lower Level: 659 square feet; Total: 3,186 square feet

● Here are four levels just waiting for the opportunity to serve the living requirements of the active family. The traditional appeal of the exterior will be difficult to beat. Observe the window treatment, the double front doors, the covered front porch and the wrought iron work.

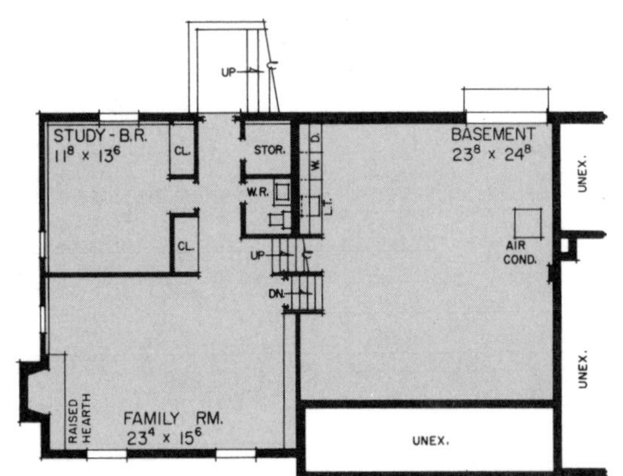

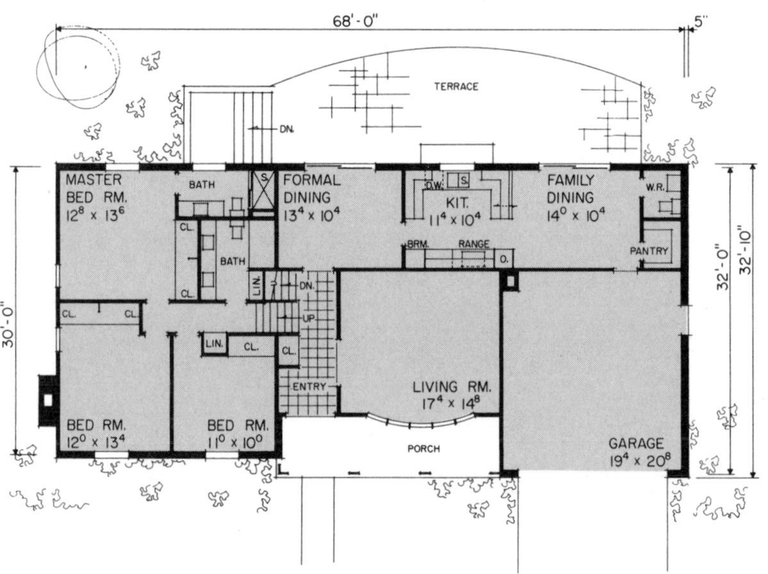

Design X1981

Main Level: 784 square feet; Upper Level: 912 square feet
Lower Level: 336 square feet; Total: 2,032 square feet

L **D**

● Here are three multi-level designs which are ideal for those who wish to build on a relatively narrow site. These split-levels have delightful exteriors and each offers exceptional family livability. Formal and informal areas are in each along with efficiently planned work centers. Outdoor areas are easily accessible from various rooms in these plans. Note that two of the upper level plans even have balconies.

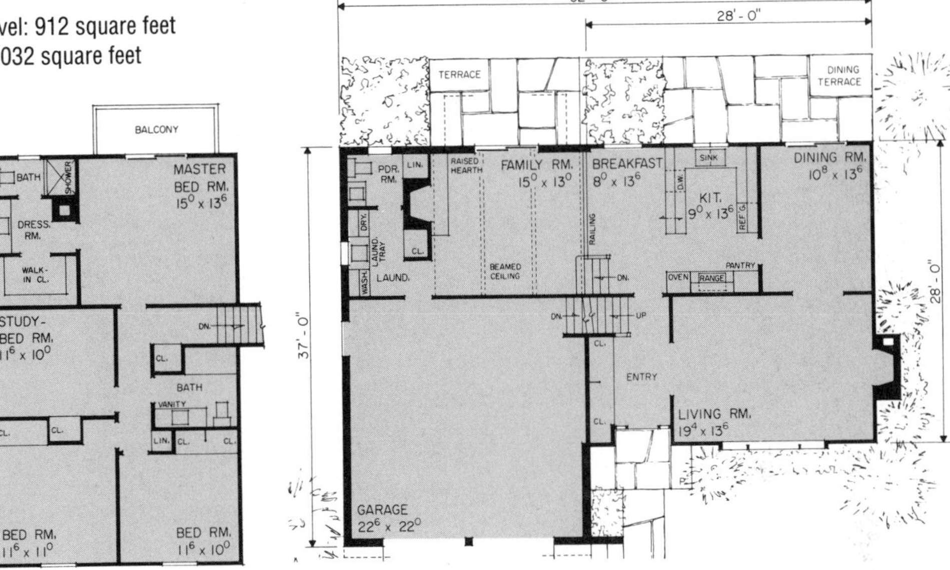

Design X1768 Main Level: 844 square feet; Upper Level: 740 square feet; Lower Level: 740 square feet; Total: 2,324 square feet

Design X2608

Main Level: 728 square feet; Upper Level: 874 square feet
Lower Level: 310 square feet; Total: 1,912 square feet

L **D**

● Here is tri-level livability with a fourth basement level for bulk storage and, perhaps, a shop area. There are four bedrooms, a handy laundry, two eating areas, formal and informal living areas and two fireplaces. Sliding glass doors in the formal dining room and the family room open to a terrace. The U-shaped kitchen has a built-in range/oven and storage pantry. The breakfast nook overlooks the family room.

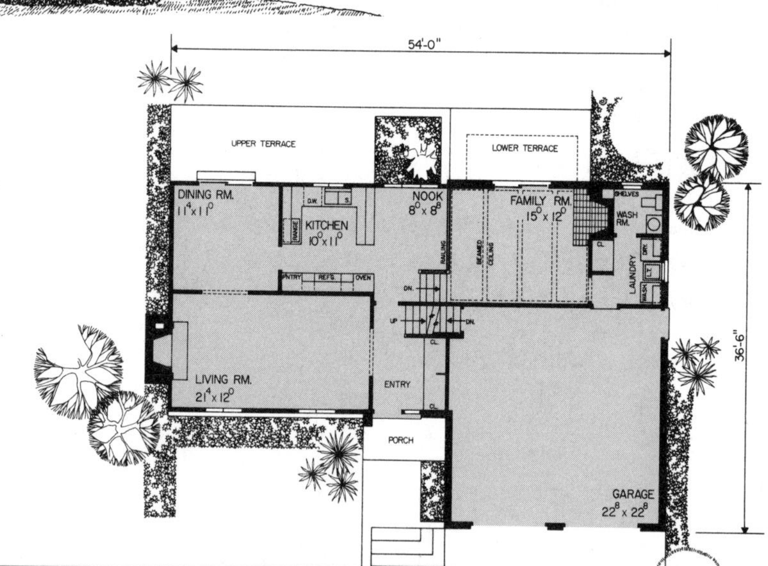

Design X2628

Main Level: 649 square feet; Upper Level: 672 square feet
Lower Level: 624 square feet; Total: 1,945 square feet

D

● Traditional, yet contemporary! With lots of extras, too. Like a wet bar and game storage in the family room. A beamed ceiling, too, and a sliding glass door onto the terrace. In short, a family room designed to make your life easy and enjoyable. There's more. A living room with a traditionally styled fireplace and built-in bookshelves. And a dining room with a sliding glass door that opens to a second terrace. Here's the appropriate setting for those times when you want a touch of elegance.

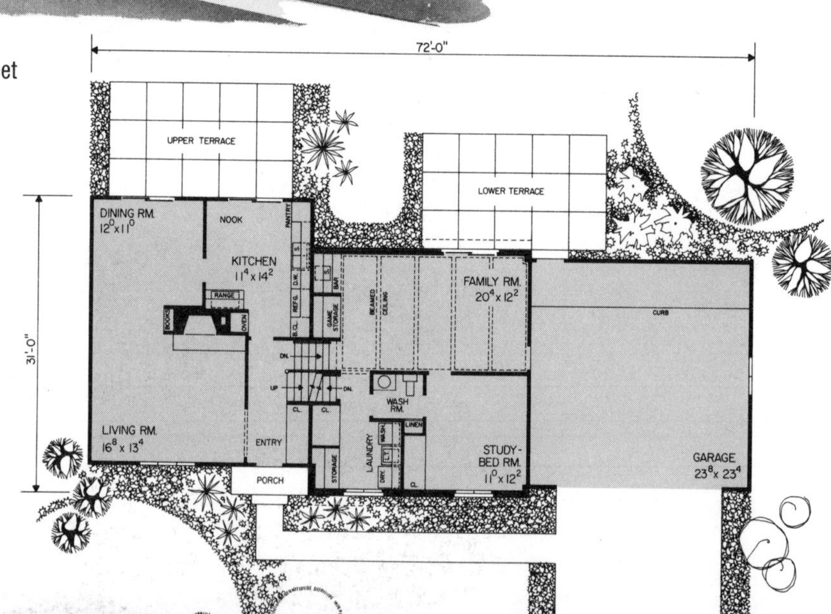

Design X2786

Main Level: 871 square feet
Upper Level: 1,132 square feet
Lower Level: 528 square feet
Total: 2,531 square feet

● Bay windows in both the formal living room and formal dining room add much appeal to this traditional tri-level. The interior livability is outstanding. An abundance of built-ins in the kitchen create an efficient work center. Features include an island range, pantry, broom closet, desk and breakfast room with sliding glass doors to the rear terrace. The lower level houses an informal family room, wash room and laundry. Note the walk-in closet in the master bedroom suite.

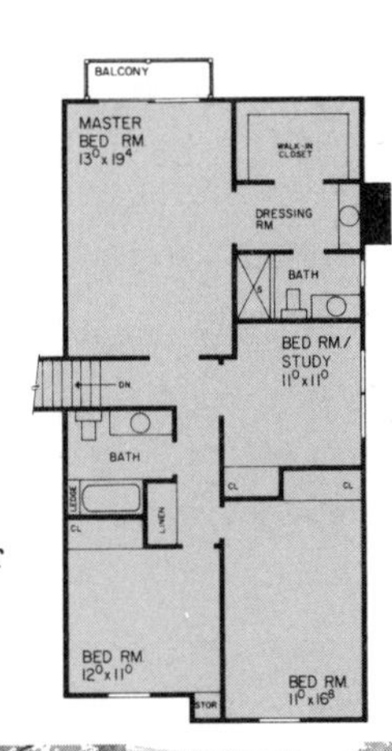

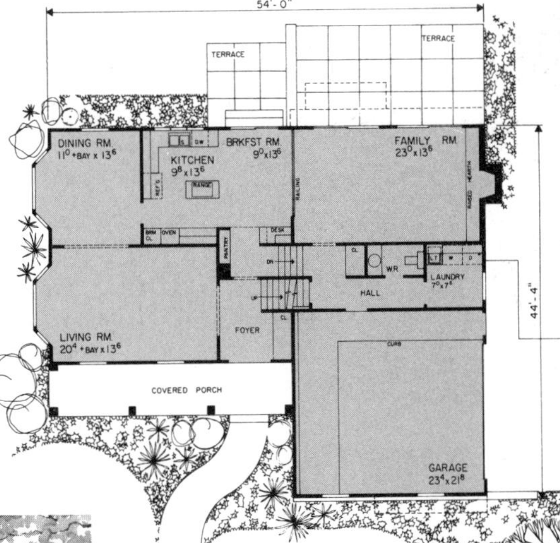

Design X2787

Main Level: 976 square feet
Upper Level: 1,118 square feet
Lower Level: 524 square feet
Total: 2,618 square feet

L **D**

● Main, upper and lower levels serve the residents of this home. The family room with raised-hearth fireplace, laundry and wash room are on the lower level. Formal living and dining rooms, a kitchen and breakfast room are on the main level. The upper level holds three bedrooms and a study (or four bedrooms, if desired) and two baths.

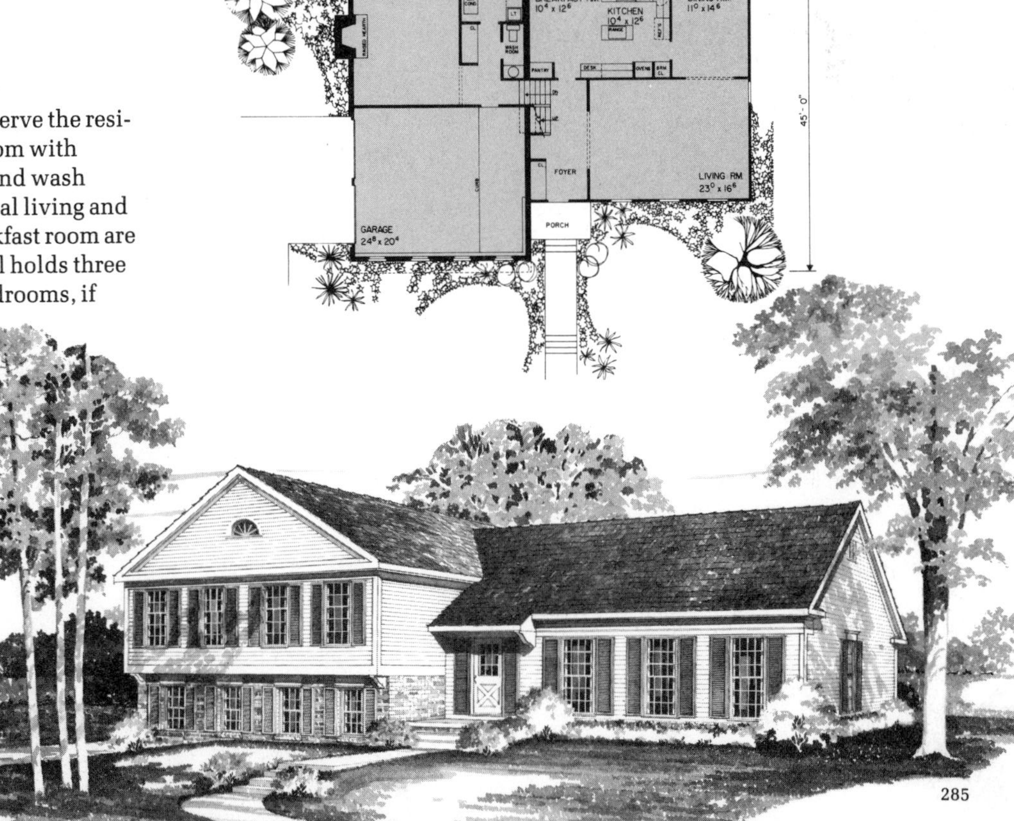

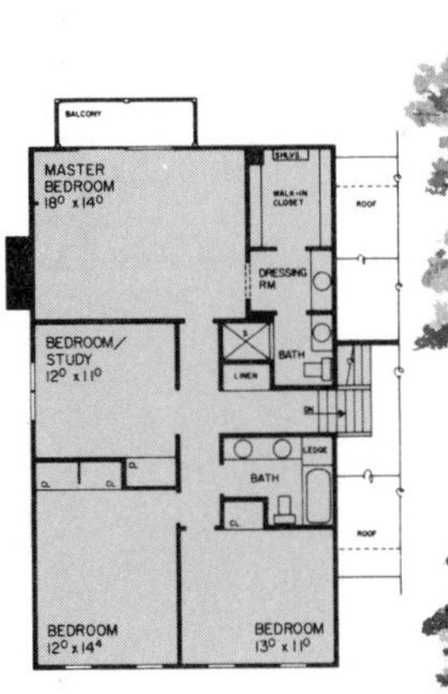

When You're Ready To Order . . .

Let Us Show You Our Home Blueprint Package.

Building a home? Planning a home? Our Blueprint Package contains nearly everything you need to get the job done right, whether you're working on your own or with help from an architect, designer, builder or subcontractors. Each Blueprint Package is the result of many hours of work by licensed architects or professional designers.

QUALITY

Hundreds of hours of painstaking effort have gone into the development of your blueprint set. Each home has been quality-checked by professionals to insure accuracy and buildability.

VALUE

Because we sell in volume, you can buy professional-quality blueprints at a fraction of their development cost. With our plans, your dream home design costs only a few hundred dollars, not the thousands of dollars that custom architects charge.

SERVICE

Once you've chosen your favorite home plan, you'll receive fast efficient service whether you choose to mail your order to us or call us toll free at 1-800-521-6797.

SATISFACTION

Our years of service to satisfied home plan buyers provide us the experience and knowledge that guarantee your satisfaction with our product and performance.

ORDER TOLL FREE 1-800-521-6797

After you've studied our Blueprint Package and Important Extras on the following pages, simply mail the accompanying order form on page 301 or call toll free on our Blueprint Hotline: 1-800-521-6797. We're ready and eager to serve you.

Each set of blueprints is an interrelated collection of floor plans, interior and exterior elevations, dimensions, cross-sections, diagrams and notations showing precisely how your house is to be constructed.

Here's what you get:

Frontal Sheet
This artist's sketch of the exterior of the house, done in realistic perspective, gives you an idea of how the house will look when built and landscaped. Large ink-line floor plans show all levels of the house and provide a quick overview of your new home's livability, as well as a handy reference for studying furniture placement.

Foundation Plan
Drawn to 1/4-inch scale, this sheet shows the complete foundation layout including support

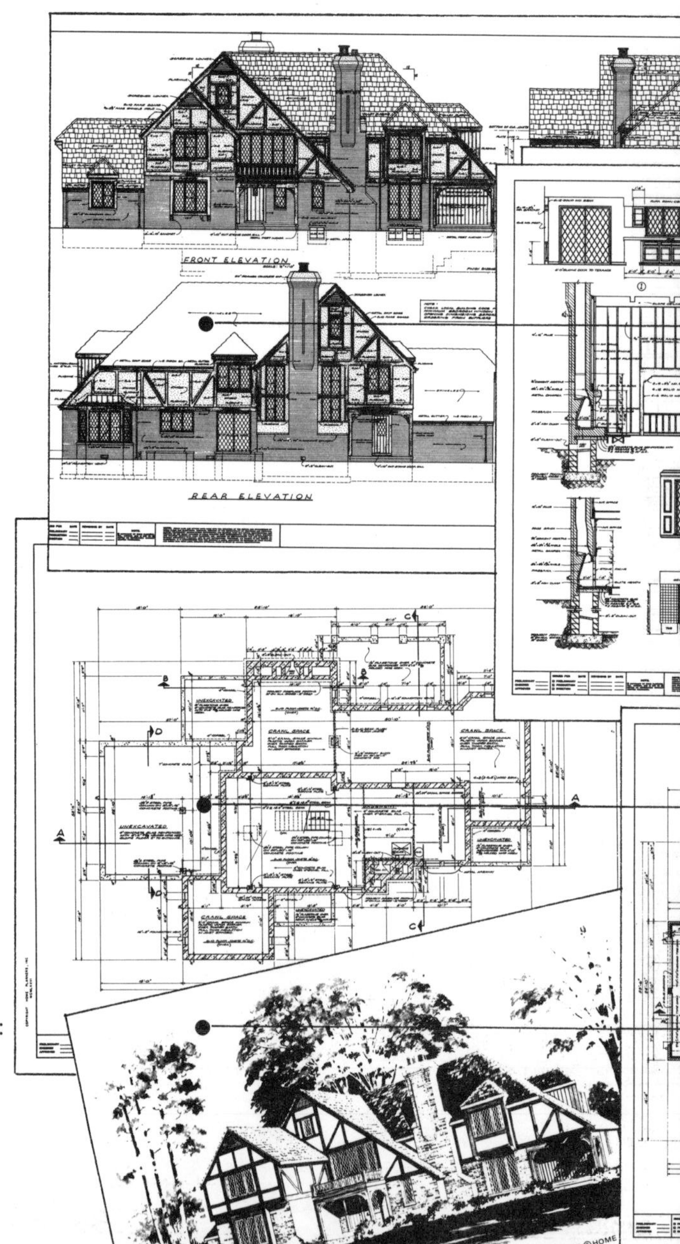

walls, excavated and unexcavated areas, if any, and foundation notes. If slab construction rather than basement, the plan shows footings and details for a monolithic slab. This page, or another in the set, also includes a sample plot plan for locating your house on a building site.

Detailed Floor Plans
Complete in 1/4-inch scale, these plans show the layout of each floor of the house. All rooms and interior spaces are carefully dimensioned and keys are provided for cross-section details given later in the plans. The positions of all electrical outlets and switches are clearly shown.

House Cross-Sections
Large-scale views, normally drawn at 3/8-inch equals 1 foot, show sections or cut-aways of the foundation, interior walls, exterior walls, floors, stairways and roof details. Additional cross-sections are given to show important changes in floor, ceiling or roof heights or the relationship of one level to another. Extremely valuable for construction, these sections show exactly how the various parts of the house fit together.

Interior Elevations
These large-scale drawings show the design and placement of kitchen and bathroom cabinets, laundry areas, fireplaces, bookcases and other built-ins. Little "extras," such as mantelpiece and wainscoting drawings, plus moulding sections, provide details that give your home that custom touch.

Exterior Elevations
Drawings in 1/4-inch scale show the front, rear and sides of your house and give necessary notes on exterior materials and finishes. Particular attention is given to cornice detail, brick and stone accents or other finish items that make your home distinctive.

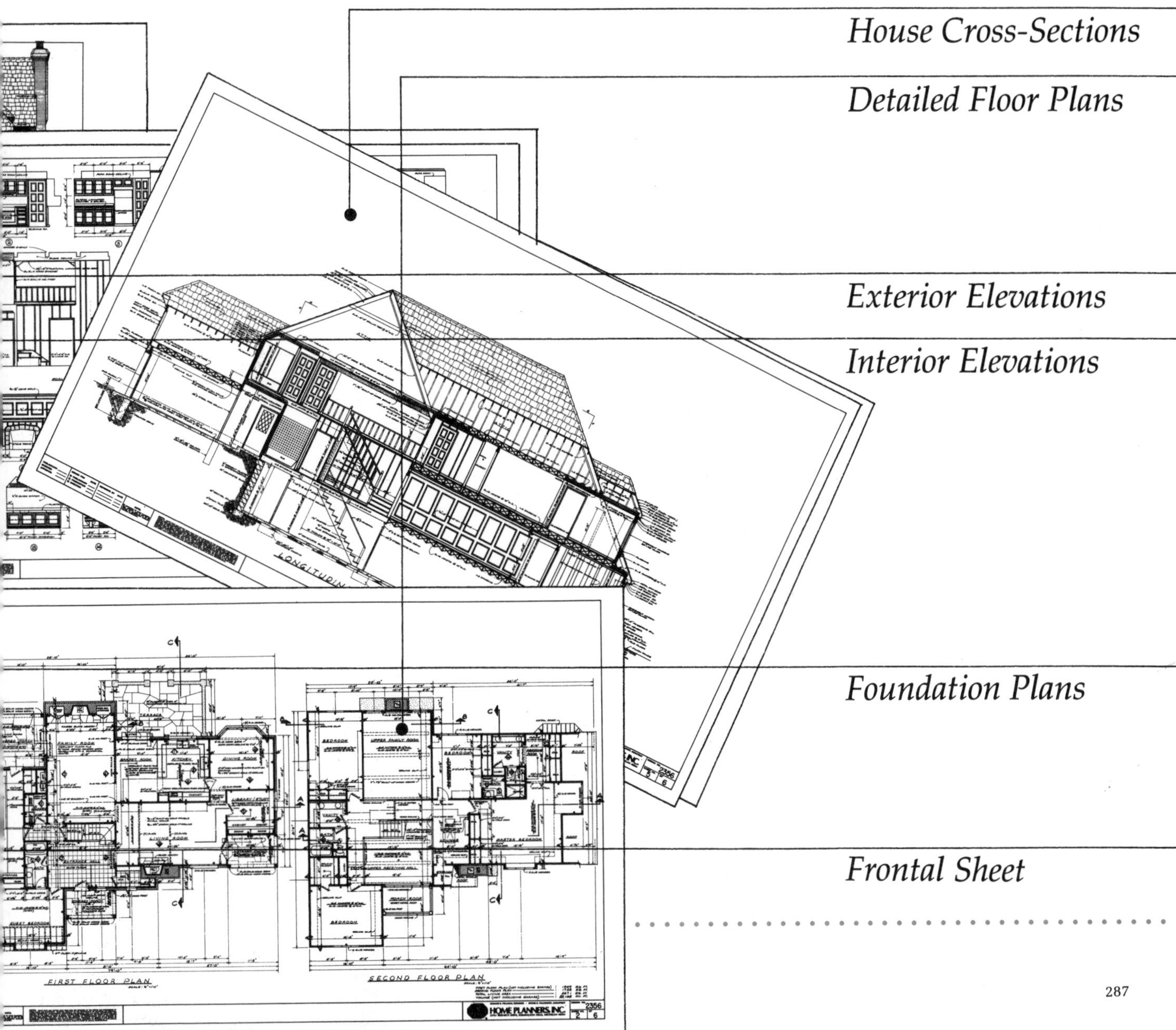

Important Extras To Do The Job Right!

Introducing six important planning and construction aids developed by our professionals to help you succeed in your home-building project.

To Order, Call Toll Free 1-800-521-6797

To add these important extras to your Blueprint Package, simply indicate your choices on the order form on page 301 or call us Toll Free 1-800-521-6797 and we'll tell you more about these exciting products.

MATERIALS LIST

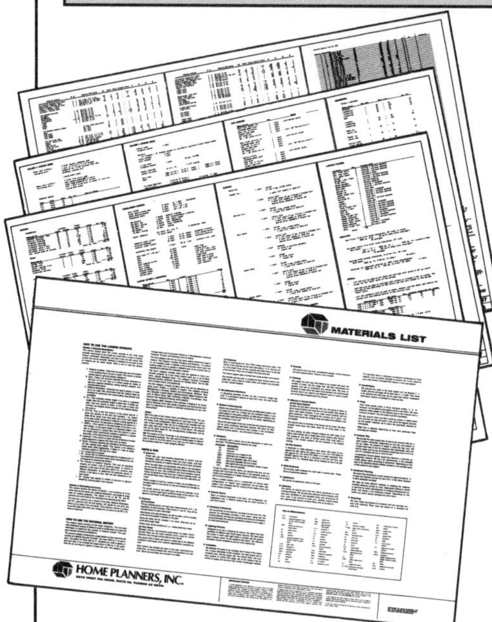

For many of the designs in our portfolio, we offer a customized materials take-off that is invaluable in planning and estimating the cost of your new home. This comprehensive list outlines the quantity, type and size of material needed to build your house (with the exception of mechanical system items). Included are:

- framing lumber
- roofing and sheet metal
- windows and doors
- exterior sheathing material and trim
- masonry, veneer and fireplace materials
- tile and flooring materials
- kitchen and bath cabinetry
- interior sheathing and trim
- rough and finish hardware
- many more items

This handy list helps you or your builder cost out materials and serves as a ready reference sheet when you're compiling bids. It also provides a cross-check against the materials specified by your builder and helps coordinate the substitution of items you may need to meet local codes.

(Note: Because of differing local codes, building methods, and availability of materials, our Materials Lists do not include mechanical materials. To obtain necessary take-offs and recommendations, consult heating, plumbing and electrical contractors. Materials Lists are not sold separately from the Blueprint Package.)

SPECIFICATION OUTLINE

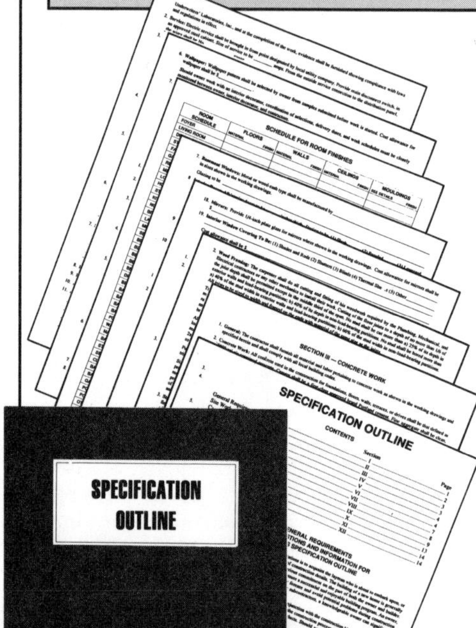

This valuable 16-page document is critical to building your house correctly. Designed to be filled in by you or your builder, this booklet lists 166 stages or items crucial to the building process.

For the layman, it provides a comprehensive review of the construction process and helps in making the specific choices of materials, models and processes. For the builder, it serves as a guide to preparing a building quotation and forms the basis for the construction program.

Designed primarily as a reference for the homeowner, this Specification Outline can become a legally binding document. Once it is filled out and agreed upon by owner and builder, it becomes a complete Project Specification.

When combined with the blueprints, a signed contract and schedule, the Specification Outline becomes a legal document and record for the building of your home. Many home builders find it useful to order two of these outlines–one as a worksheet in formulating the specifications and another to be carefully completed as a legal document.

Detail Sheets

If you want to know more about techniques—and deal more confidently with subcontractors—we offer these remarkably useful detail sheets. Each is an excellent tool that will enhance your understanding of these technical subjects.

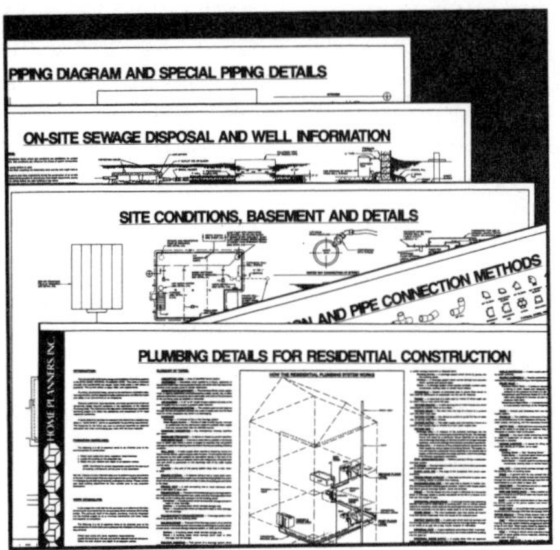

Plumbing

The Blueprint Package includes locations for all the plumbing fixtures in your new house, including sinks, lavatories, tubs, showers, toilets, laundry trays and water heaters. However, if you want to know more about the complete plumbing system, these 24x36-inch detail sheets will prove very useful. Prepared to meet requirements of the National Plumbing Code, these six fact-filled sheets give general information on pipe schedules, fittings, sump-pump details, water-softener hookups, septic system details and much more. Color-coded sheets include a glossary of terms.

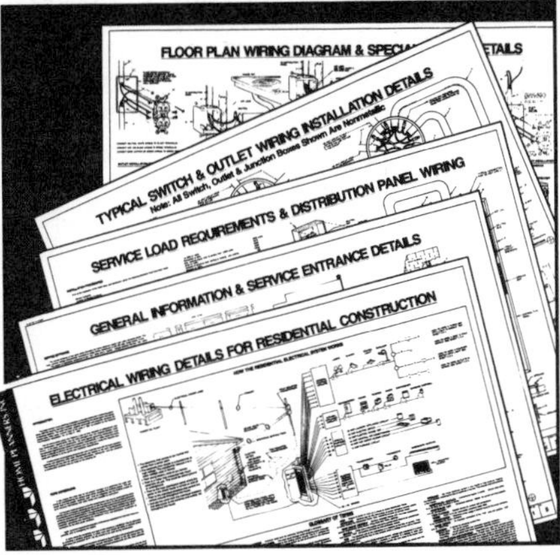

Electrical

The locations for every electrical switch, plug and outlet are shown in your Blueprint Package. However, these Electrical Details go further to take the mystery out of household electrical systems. Prepared to meet requirements of the National Electrical Code, these comprehensive 24x36-inch drawings come packed with helpful information, including wire sizing, switch-installation schematics, cable-routing details, appliance wattage, door-bell hookups, typical service panel circuitry and much more. Six sheets are bound together and color-coded for easy reference. A glossary of terms is also included.

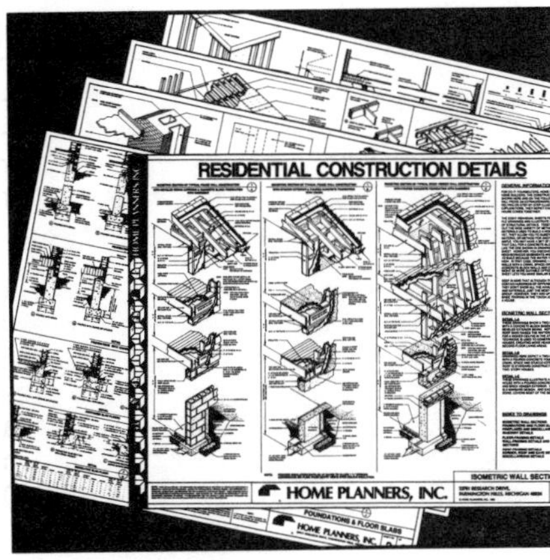

Construction

The Blueprint Package contains everything an experienced builder needs to construct a particular house. However, it doesn't show all the ways that houses can be built, nor does it explain alternate construction methods. To help you understand how your house will be built–and offer additional techniques–this set of drawings depicts the materials and methods used to build foundations, fireplaces, walls, floors and roofs. Where appropriate, the drawings show acceptable alternatives. These six sheets will answer questions for the advanced do-it-yourselfer or home planner.

Mechanical

This package contains fundamental principles and useful data that will help you make informed decisions and communicate with subcontractors about heating and cooling systems. The 24 x 36-inch drawings contain instructions and samples that allow you to make simple load calculations and preliminary sizing and costing analysis. Covered are today's most commonly used systems from heat pumps to solar fuel systems. The package is packed full of illustrations and diagrams to help you visualize components and how they relate to one another.

Plan-A-Home®

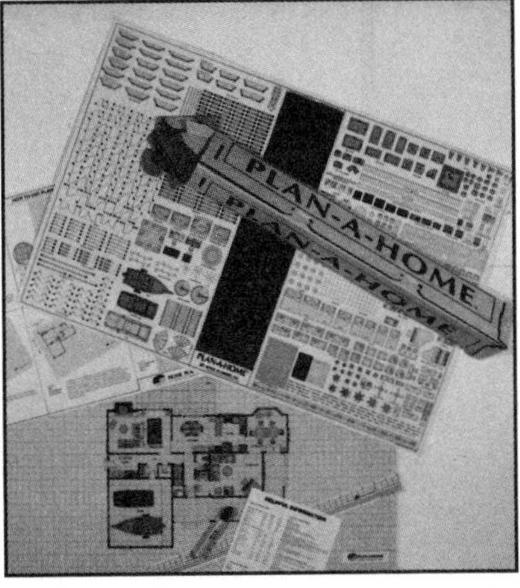

Plan-A-Home® is an easy-to-use tool that helps you design a new home, arrange furniture in a new or existing home, or plan a remodeling project. Each package contains:

- More than *700 peel-off planning symbols* on a self-stick vinyl sheet, including walls, windows, doors, all types of furniture, kitchen components, bath fixtures and many more. All are made of durable, peel-and-stick vinyl you can use over and over.
- A reusable, transparent, *1/4-inch scale planning grid* made of tough mylar that matches the scale of actual working drawings (1/4 -inch equals 1 foot). This grid provides the basis for house layouts of up to 140x92 feet.
- *Tracing paper* and a protective sheet for copying or transferring your completed plan.
- A *felt-tip pen*, with water-soluble ink that wipes away quickly.

With Plan-A-Home®, you can make basic planning decisions for a new house or make modifications to an existing house. Use with your Blueprint Package to test modifications to rooms or to plan furniture arrangements before you build. Plan-A-Home® lets you lay out areas as large as a 7,500 square foot, six-bedroom, seven-bath house.

The Landscape Blueprint Package

For the homes marked with an L in this book, Home Planners has created a front-yard landscape plan that matches or is complementary in design to the house plan. These comprehensive blueprint packages include a Frontal Sheet, Plan View, Regionalized Plant & Materials List, a sheet on Planting and Maintaining Your Landscape, Zone Maps and Plant Size and Description Guide. These plans will help you achieve professional results, adding value and enjoyment to your property for years to come. Each set of blueprints is a full 18" x 24" in size with clear, complete instructions and easy-to-read type. See the following pages for 40-different front-yard Landscape Plans to match your favorite house.

Regional Order Map

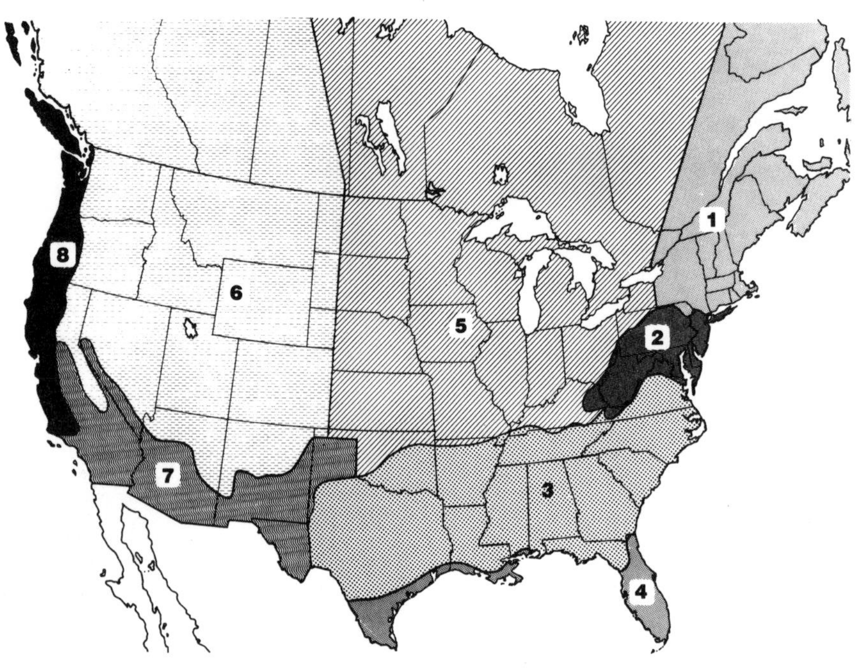

Most of the Landscape Plans shown on these pages are available with a Plant & Materials List adapted by horticultural experts to 8 different regions of the country. Please specify Geographic Region when ordering your plan. See pages 296-301 for prices, ordering information and regional availability.

Region	1	Northeast
Region	2	Mid-Atlantic
Region	3	Deep South
Region	4	Florida & Gulf Coast
Region	5	Midwest
Region	6	Rocky Mountains
Region	7	Southern California & Desert Southwest
Region	8	Northern California & Pacific Northwest

CAPE COD TRADITIONAL
Landscape Plan L200

WILLIAMSBURG CAPE
Landscape Plan L201

CAPE COD COTTAGE
Landscape Plan L202

GAMBREL–ROOF COLONIAL
Landscape Plan L203

CENTER–HALL COLONIAL
Landscape Plan L204

CLASSIC NEW ENGLAND COLONIAL
Landscape Plan L205

SOUTHERN COLONIAL
Landscape Plan L206

COUNTRY-STYLE FARMHOUSE
Landscape Plan L207

PENNSYLVANIA STONE FARMHOUSE
Landscape Plan L208

RAISED-PORCH FARMHOUSE
Landscape Plan L209

NEW ENGLAND BARN-STYLE HOUSE
Landscape Plan L210

NEW ENGLAND COUNTRY HOUSE
Landscape Plan L211

TRADITIONAL COUNTRY ESTATE
Landscape Plan L212

FRENCH PROVINCIAL ESTATE
Landscape Plan L213

GEORGIAN MANOR
Landscape Plan L214

GRAND-PORTICO GEORGIAN
Landscape Plan L215

BRICK FEDERAL
Landscape Plan L216

COUNTRY FRENCH RAMBLER
Landscape Plan L217

FRENCH MANOR HOUSE
Landscape Plan L218

ELIZABETHAN TUDOR
Landscape Plan L219

TUDOR ONE-STORY
Landscape Plan L220

ENGLISH-STYLE COTTAGE
Landscape Plan L221

MEDIEVAL GARRISON
Landscape Plan L222

QUEEN ANNE VICTORIAN
Landscape Plan L223

GOTHIC VICTORIAN
Landscape Plan L224

BASIC RANCH
Landscape Plan L225

L-SHAPED RANCH
Landscape Plan L226

SPRAWLING RANCH
Landscape Plan L227

TRADITIONAL SPLIT-LEVEL
Landscape Plan L228

SHED-ROOF CONTEMPORARY
Landscape Plan L229

WOOD–SIDED CONTEMPORARY
Landscape Plan L230

HILLSIDE CONTEMPORARY
Landscape Plan L231

FLORIDA RAMBLER
Landscape Plan L232

CALIFORNIA STUCCO
Landscape Plan L233

LOW–GABLE CONTEMPORARY
Landscape Plan L234

NORTHERN BRICK CHATEAU
Landscape Plan L235

MISSION–TILE RANCH
Landscape Plan L236

ADOBE–BLOCK HACIENDA
Landscape Plan L237

COURTYARD PATIO HOME
Landscape Plan L238

CENTER–COURT CONTEMPORARY
Landscape Plan L239

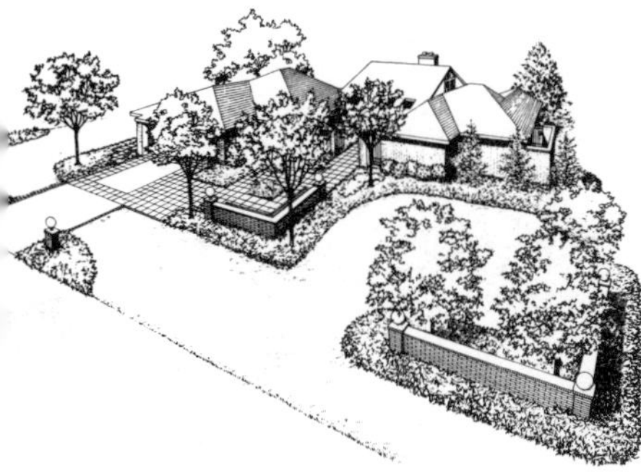

For Landscape Plan prices and ordering information, see pages 296-301.
Or call **Toll Free, 1-800-521-6797**.

D The Deck Blueprint Package

Many of the homes in this book can be enhanced with a professionally designed Deck Plan. Those home plans highlighted with a D have a matching or corresponding deck plan available which includes a Deck Plan Frontal Sheet, Deck Framing and Floor Plans, Deck Elevations and a Deck Materials List. A Standard Deck Details Package, also available, provides all the how-to information necessary for building *any* deck. Our Complete Deck Building Package contains 1 set of Custom Deck Plans of your choice, plus 1 set of Standard Deck Building Details all for one low price. Our plans and details are carefully prepared in an easy-to-understand format that will guide you through every stage of your deck-building project. See these pages for 25 different Deck layouts to match your favorite house.

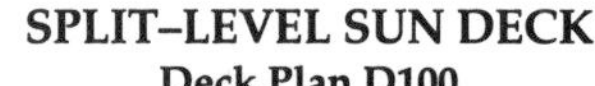

SPLIT–LEVEL SUN DECK
Deck Plan D100

BI–LEVEL DECK WITH COVERED DINING
Deck Plan D101

FRESH–AIR CORNER DECK
Deck Plan D102

BACK–YARD EXTENDER DECK
Deck Plan D103

WRAP–AROUND FAMILY DECK
Deck Plan D104

DRAMATIC DECK WITH BARBECUE
Deck Plan D105

SPLIT–PLAN COUNTRY DECK
Deck Plan D106

DECK FOR DINING AND VIEWS
Deck Plan D107

BOLD, ANGLED CORNER DECK
Deck Plan D108

SPECTACULAR "RESORT–STYLE" DECK
Deck Plan D109

TREND–SETTER DECK
Deck Plan D110

TURN–OF–THE–CENTURY DECK
Deck Plan D111

WEEKEND ENTERTAINER DECK
Deck Plan D112

STRIKING "DELTA" DECK
Deck Plan D113

CENTER–VIEW DECK
Deck Plan D114

KITCHEN–EXTENDER DECK
Deck Plan D115

BI–LEVEL RETREAT DECK
Deck Plan D116

SPLIT–LEVEL ACTIVITY DECK
Deck Plan D117

OUTDOOR LIFESTYLE DECK
Deck Plan D118

TRI–LEVEL DECK WITH GRILL
Deck Plan D119

CONTEMPORARY LEISURE DECK
Deck Plan D120

ANGULAR WINGED DECK
Deck Plan D121

DECK FOR A SPLIT–LEVEL HOME
Deck Plan D122

GRACIOUS GARDEN DECK
Deck Plan D123

TERRACED DECK FOR ENTERTAINING
Deck Plan D124

For Deck Plan prices and ordering information, see pages 296-301.

 Or call **Toll Free, 1-800-521-6797**.

Price Schedule & Plans Index

House Blueprint Price Schedule

(Prices guaranteed through December 31, 1993)

	1-set Study Package	4-set Building Package	8-set Building Package	1-set Reproducible Sepias
Schedule A	$210	$270	$330	$420
Schedule B	$240	$300	$360	$480
Schedule C	$270	$330	$390	$540
Schedule D	$300	$360	$420	$600
Schedule E	$390	$450	$510	$660

Additional Identical Blueprints in same order................$50 per set
Reverse Blueprints (mirror image)...................................$50 per set
Specification Outlines ....$7 each
Materials Lists:
Schedule A-D $40
Schedule E $50
Exchanges ....$40 exchange fee for the first set; $10 for each additional set
$60 total exchange fee for 4 sets
$90 total exchange fee for 8 sets

Deck Plans Price Schedule

CUSTOM DECK PLANS

Price Group	Q	R	S
1 Set Custom Plans	$15.00	$20.00	$25.00
Additional identical sets:	$5.00 each		
Reverse sets (mirror image):	$5.00 each		

STANDARD DECK DETAILS

1 Set Generic Construction Details $14.95 each

COMPLETE DECK BUILDING PACKAGE

Price Group	Q	R	S
1 Set Custom Plans 1 Set Standard Deck Details	$25.00	$30.00	$35.00

Landscape Plans Price Schedule

Price Group	X	Y	Z
1 set	$35	$45	$55
3 sets	$50	$60	$70
6 sets	$65	$75	$85

Additional Identical Sets ....$10 each
Reverse Sets (Mirror Image)...$10 each

These pages contain all the information you need to price your blueprints. In general the larger and more complicated the house, the more it costs to design and thus the higher the price we must charge for the blueprints. Remember, however, that these prices are far less than you would normally pay for the services of a licensed architect or professional designer.

Custom home designs and related architectural services often cost thousands of dollars, ranging from 5% to 15% of the cost of construction. By ordering our blueprints you are potentially saving enough money to afford a larger house, or to add those "extra" amenities such as a patio, deck, swimming pool or even an upgraded kitchen or luxurious master suite.

Index

To use the Index below, refer to the design number listed in numerical order (a helpful page reference is also given). Note the price index letter and refer to the House Blueprint Price Schedule above for the cost of one, four or eight sets of blueprints or the cost of a reproducible sepia. Additional prices are shown for identical and reverse blueprint sets, as well as a very useful Materials List for some of the plans. Also note in the Index below those plans that have matching or complementary Deck Plans or Landscape Plans. Refer to the schedules above for prices of these plans. Some of our plans can be customized through Home Planners' Home Customizer® Service. These plans are indicated below with this symbol: . See page 301 for more information.

To Order: Fill in and send the order form on page 301—or call toll free 1-800-521-6797.

Design	Price	Page	Customizable	Deck	Deck Price	Landscape	Landscape Price	Regions
X1075	A	152		D114	R	L225	X	1-3,5,6,8
X1100	B	168						
X1113	A	157		D113	R	L202	X	1-3,5,6,8
X1115	B	120						
X1147	A	150						
X1191	A	153		D114	R	L225	X	1-3,5,6,8
X1208	A	195						
X1239	C	142						
X1241	A	60		D117	S	L225	X	1-3,5,6,8
X1285	B	140		D117	S	L205	Y	1-3,5,6,8
X1300	A	150						
X1305	A	154		D106	S			
X1311	A	146		D114	R	L225	X	1-3,5,6,8
X1323	A	159		D117	S	L225	X	1-3,5,6,8
X1325	B	157		D106	S	L225	X	1-3,5,6,8
X1327	A	151						
X1346	B	182						
X1354	A	112		D105	R	L200	X	1-3,5,6,8
X1361	A	113		D117	S	L225	X	1-3,5,6,8
X1366	A	153						
X1371	B	116		D101	R	L207	Z	1-6,8
X1382	A	154		D106	S			
X1383	A	154		D106	S			
X1387	A	155		D101	R			
X1388	A	155		D101	R			
X1389	A	155		D101	R			
X1394	A	53		D105	R	L202	X	1-3,5,6,8
X1701	B	41		D117	S			
X1715	B	114		D100	Q	L204	Y	1-3,5,6,8
X1718	B	42		D114	R	L210	Y	1-3,5,6,8
X1719	A	67		D105	R	L203	Y	1-3,5,6,8
X1723	A	113						
X1728	C	142						
X1736	B	63						
X1761	C	186		D117	S	L217	Y	1-8
X1766	B	40		D100	Q			
X1768	B	283						
X1777	B	132						

DESIGN	PRICE	PAGE	CUSTOMIZABLE	DECK	DECK PRICE	LANDSCAPE	LANDSCAPE PRICE	REGIONS
X1788	C	187		D101	R	L206	Z	1-6,8
X1791	B	46		D114	R	L205	Y	1-3,5,6,8
X1793	C	41		D100	Q			
X1814	B	93						
X1829	B	169		D113	R	L226	X	1-8
X1850	B	281						
X1856	A	135		D117	S			
X1856	C	212		D101	R			
X1868	B	30						
X1870	B	46						
X1887	B	128						
X1892	B	183		D106	S	L225	X	1-3,5,6,8
X1896	B	147						
X1900	C	92						
X1902	B	60						
X1903	B	61						
X1911	D	189						
X1920	B	166		D103	R	L225	X	1-3,5,6,8
X1927	C	278						
X1933	B	134		D117	S	L205	Y	1-3,5,6,8
X1938	A	158						
X1939	A	146		D117	S	L225	X	1-3,5,6,8
X1947	B	156						
X1948	B	156						
X1949	B	171		D117	S			
X1950	B	180		D110	Q			
X1955	B	142						
X1956	A	140	■	D117	S			
X1957	A	115		D100	Q	L228	Y	1-8
X1964	C	120						
X1967	B	121						
X1970	C	39		D100	Q			
X1974	C	279						
X1981	B	283		D117	S	L228	Y	1-8
X1986	B	132				L203	Y	1-3,5,6,8
X1987	B	43		D101	R	L203	Y	1-3,5,6,8
X1989	C	172		D100	Q	L220	Y	1-3,5,6,8
X1993	D	192				L213	Z	1-8
X1996	B	112		D114	R	L205	Y	1-3,5,6,8
X2014	C	280						
X2101	B	73						
X2103	B	70		D124	S			
X2107	A	194						
X2124	B	40		D114	R	L203	Y	1-3,5,6,8
X2131	B	43		D117	S	L203	Y	1-3,5,6,8
X2132	C	217				L201	Y	1-3,5,6,8
X2133	D	208		D106	S	L214	Z	1-3,5,6,8
X2139	B	136						
X2142	C	176		D106	S			
X2145	A	62				L209	Y	1-6,8
X2146	A	52		D114	R	L203	Y	1-3,5,6,8
X2162	A	52		D103	R	L202	X	1-3,5,6,8
X2171	B	274		D112	R	L228	Y	1-8
X2172	C	137						
X2174	B	118		D117	S	L220	Y	1-3,5,6,8
X2176	B	216		D112	R	L206	Z	1-6,8
X2181	C	185		D100	Q	L226	X	1-8
X2188	C	214						
X2189	B	130						
X2192	D	219		D117	S	L218	Z	1-6,8
X2206	B	260		D100	Q	L220	Y	1-3,5,6,8
X2209	C	187						
X2211	B	70		D117	S	L201	Y	1-3,5,6,8
X2212	D	191				L217	Y	1-8
X2216	C	282						
X2220	C	190		D114	R	L217	Y	1-8
X2221	C	74						
X2223	B	117		D112	R	L205	Y	1-3,5,6,8
X2225	D	38						
X2230	D	200						
X2250	C	75						
X2253	C	74						
X2254	C	275						
X2261	B	173						
X2283	C	213		D114	R	L206	Z	1-6,8
X2285	A	110						
X2301	D	138						
X2320	C	83						
X2322	B	80		D100	Q			
X2356	D	8		D119	S	L219	Z	1-3,5,6,8
X2360	B	169						
X2367	B	144						
X2395	B	56						
X2396	B	46		D100	Q			
X2399	B	72						
X2488	A	111	■	D102	Q			
X2491	A	265	■					
X2500	B	106		D100	Q	L204	Y	1-3,5,6,8
X2505	A	149	■	D113	R	L226	X	1-8
X2510	A	53		D105	R	L200	X	1-3,5,6,8
X2520	B	12		D105	R	L201	Y	1-3,5,6,8
X2521	B	64						
X2522	C	221						
X2524	A	196		D105	R			
X2527	C	174		D107	S			
X2531	B	132						
X2538	B	69		D113	R	L201	Y	1-3,5,6,8
X2540	B	141		D113	R	L205	Y	1-3,5,6,8
X2542	D	26				L208	Z	1,2,5,6,8
X2543	B	98		D107	S	L218	Z	1-6,8
X2544	C	184		D124	S			
X2553	C	209						
X2556	C	78		D103	R			
X2558	A	124						
X2559	B	119		D112	R			
X2563	B	13	■	D114	R	L201	Y	1-3,5,6,8
X2565	B	263		D101	R	L225	X	1-3,5,6,8
X2569	A	56		D112	R	L200	X	1-3,5,6,8
X2571	A	50		D114	R	L202	X	1-3,5,6,8
X2573	C	257		D114	R	L220	Y	1-3,5,6,8
X2585	B	125		D113	R	L205	Y	1-3,5,6,8
X2596	B	63		D114	R	L201	Y	1-3,5,6,8
X2597	B	145		D114	R	L226	X	1-8
X2599	C	106		D100	Q			
X2600	C	77						
X2603	B	172		D106	S	L220	Y	1-3,5,6,8
X2606	A	260	■	D112	R	L221	X	1-3,5,6,8
X2608	A	284		D112	R	L228	Y	1-8
X2610	C	85		D114	R	L204	Y	1-3,5,6,8
X2611	B	163		D112	R	L225	X	1-3,5,6,8
X2612	B	163		D112	R	L226	X	1-8
X2614	C	37		D114	R			
X2615	D	35		D106	S	L211	Y	1-8
X2616	B	91						

DESIGN	PRICE	PAGE	CUSTOMIZABLE	DECK	DECK PRICE	LANDSCAPE	LANDSCAPE PRICE	REGIONS
X2617	B	82						
X2621	C	94						
X2622	A	69	■	D103	R	L200	X	1-3,5,6,8
X2623	B	93		D100	Q	L205	Y	1-3,5,6,8
X2624	B	274		D112	R	L228	Y	1-8
X2625	C	28						
X2627	A	197						
X2628	A	284		D105	R			
X2631	B	58		D112	R	L201	Y	1-3,5,6,8
X2632	B	129						
X2633	C	212						
X2639	C	220		D114	R	L215	Z	1-6,8
X2640	B	72		D114	R			
X2641	C	224						
X2644	B	131						
X2649	C	90						
X2650	A	19		D117	S	L201	Y	1-3,5,6,8
X2653	C	214						
X2654	A	89						
X2655	A	54				L200	X	1-3,5,6,8
X2656	B	55		D105	R	L203	Y	1-3,5,6,8
X2657	B	54				L200	X	1-3,5,6,8
X2658	A	62						
X2659	B	79		D113	R	L205	Y	1-3,5,6,8
X2660	D	239						
X2661	A	55	■	D113	R	L202	X	1-3,5,6,8
X2662	C	11				L216	Y	1-3,5,6,8
X2663	B	198						
X2664	B	203		D113	R			
X2665	D	205						
X2666	B	65						
X2667	B	235				L216	Y	1-3,5,6,8
X2668	B	193				L214	Z	1-3,5,6,8
X2672	B	167		D112	R	L226	X	1-8
X2673	C	201						
X2675	C	185		D106	S			
X2676	C	136						
X2680	C	23		D114	R			
X2681	B	31						
X2682	A	48	■	D115	Q	L200	X	1-3,5,6,8
X2683	D	6		D101	R	L214	Z	1-3,5,6,8
X2684	C	84		D114	R	L204	Y	1-3,5,6,8
X2685	C	96						
X2686	C	198		D112	R	L209	Y	1-6,8
X2687	C	76		D117	S	L204	Y	1-3,5,6,8
X2688	B	217						
X2689	B	127						
X2690	C	234						
X2693	D	229						
X2694	C	29				L209	Y	1-6,8
X2697	C	23						
X2699	C	34				L211	Y	1-8
X2700	C	195						
X2704	B	162		D107	S	L225	X	1-3,5,6,8
X2705	B	162		D107	S	L217	Y	1-8
X2706	B	162		D107	S	L225	X	1-3,5,6,8
X2707	A	148	■	D117	S	L226	X	1-8
X2713	C	126						
X2710	C	108		D105	R			
X2722	C	104						
X2728	B	258		D112	R	L221	X	1-3,5,6,8
X2731	B	71		D114	R	L205	Y	1-3,5,6,8
X2733	B	68		D100	Q	L205	Y	1-3,5,6,8
X2737	B	261				L220	Y	1-3,5,6,8
X2739	D	188						
X2768	D	188						
X2769	C	279						
X2774	B	5	■	D100	Q	L207	Z	1-6,8
X2775	B	28				L207	Z	1-6,8
X2776	B	18	■	D113	R	L207	Z	1-6,8
X2777	B	180		D101	R	L221	X	1-3,5,6,8
X2778	C	182		D120	R			
X2779	D	191		D100	Q	L217	Y	1-8
X2784	C	184						
X2785	C	259		D100	Q	L220	Y	1-3,5,6,8
X2786	B	285						
X2787	B	285		D105	R	L228	Y	1-8
X2798	A	98		D100	Q	L200	X	1-3,5,6,8
X2799	A	66						
X2800	B	267		D113	R	L220	Y	1-3,5,6,8
X2802	B	160	■	D118	R	L220	Y	1-3,5,6,8
X2803	B	160	■	D118	R	L225	X	1-3,5,6,8
X2804	B	160	■	D118	R	L232	Y	4,7
X2805	B	161		D113	R	L220	Y	1-3,5,6,8
X2806	B	161		D113	R	L220	Y	1-3,5,6,8
X2807	B	161		D113	R	L220	Y	1-3,5,6,8
X2826	B	123	■	D116	R			
X2839	C	88						
X2840	C	139						
X2841	B	277		D108	R			
X2842	B	276		D114	R			
X2847	C	272		D112	R	L220	Y	1-3,5,6,8
X2852	A	50		D105	R	L202	X	1-3,5,6,8
X2853	A	111						
X2854	B	267	■	D112	R	L220	Y	1-3,5,6,8
X2855	B	9	■	D103	R	L219	Z	1-3,5,6,8
X2864	A	151	■	D100	Q	L225	X	1-3,5,6,8
X2865	C	18		D114	R			
X2867	C	175						
X2870	A	67						
X2878	B	14	■	D112	R	L200	X	1-3,5,6,8
X2880	C	181	■	D114	R	K212	Z	1-8
X2883	C	59						
X2888	D	33				L211	Y	1-8
X2889	D	7		D107	S	L215	Z	1-6,8
X2890	C	19		D114	R			
X2898	C	199		D118	R			
X2899	C	216						
X2907	B	31						
X2908	B	30	■	D117	S	L205	Y	1-3,5,6,8
X2909	B	125		D103	R			
X2916	B	181						
X2921	D	10		D104	S	L212	Z	1-8
X2924	B	202	■					
X2927	B	122	■	D100	Q			
X2931	B	171	■					
X2945	B	17	■					
X2946	C	32	■	D114	R	L207	Z	1-6,8
X2947	B	16	■					
X2963	D	218						
X2964	B	266						
X2965	D	266						
X2967	B	268						
X2969	C	256		D110	R	L223	Z	1-3,5,6,8

DESIGN	PRICE	PAGE	CUSTOMIZABLE	DECK	DECK PRICE	LANDSCAPE	LANDSCAPE PRICE	REGIONS
X2970	D	253				L223	Z	1-3,5,6,8
X2971	C	255				L223	Z	1-3,5,6,8
X2972	B	254				L223	Z	1-3,5,6,8
X2973	B	254	■			L223	Z	1-3,5,6,8
X2974	A	249				L223	Z	1-3,5,6,8
X2975	D	219						
X2977	D	211				L214	Z	1-3,5,6,8
X2979	C	235						
X2980	C	222						
X2981	D	215						
X2982	C	223						
X2983	A	44						
X2984	E	210						
X2985	C	231						
X2986	B	95						
X2987	D	227						
X2988	B	22		D120	R	L201	Y	1-3,5,6,8
X2989	D	232				L215	Z	1-6,8
X2990	D	238						
X2991	D	228		D111	S	L215	Z	1-6,8
X2992	E	236		D103	R	L203	Y	1-3,5,6,8
X2993	D	240		D115	Q	L214	Z	1-3,5,6,8
X2994	E	233		D105	R	L216	Y	1-3,5,6,8
X2995	E	36		D106	S	L217	Y	1-8
X2996	E	226		D111	S	L235	Z	1-3,5,6,8
X2997	D	229		D106	S	L214	Z	1-3,5,6,8
X2998	D	230		D103	R	L210	Y	1-3,5,6,8
X2999	E	237		D105	R	L218	Z	1-6,8
X3126	A	57		D114	R	L203	Y	1-3,5,6,8
X3189	A	50		D113	R			
X3302	A	264	■					
X3303	D	207						
X3308	E	241						
X3309	B	4						
X3320	D	208						
X3330	A	124						
X3331	A	265						
X3332	B	179						
X3333	C	202						
X3334	C	104						
X3336	B	164						
X3337	D	206						
X3339	B	196						
X3340	B	165						
X3341	B	264						
X3342	B	268						
X3343	C	109						
X3345	B	170	■					
X3346	B	269	■					

DESIGN	PRICE	PAGE	CUSTOMIZABLE	DECK	DECK PRICE	LANDSCAPE	LANDSCAPE PRICE	REGIONS
X3348	C	178						
X3349	E	97		D107	S	L216	Y	1-3,5,6,8
X3351	C	119		D115	Q	L209	Y	1-6,8
X3353	C	108		D113	R	L206	Z	1-6,8
X3355	A	15	■	D117	S	L220	Y	1-3,5,6,8
X3356	C	103		D103	R	L217	Y	1-8
X3363	C	105						
X3365	C	107						
X3366	D	273				L220	Y	1-3,5,6,8
X3369	E	270		D121	S	L206	Z	1-6,8
X3370	D	103		D119	S	L235	Z	1-3,5,6,8
X3372	C	58		D102	Q	L200	X	1-3,5,6,8
X3373	A	262		D110	R	L202	X	1-3,5,6,8
X3374	A	262		D115	Q	L202	X	1-3,5,6,8
X3375	A	262		D115	Q	L202	X	1-3,5,6,8
X3376	B	177		D114	R	L205	Y	1-3,5,6,8
X3377	C	258		D110	R	L203	Y	1-3,5,6,8
X3378	E	101						
X3379	B	86		D102	Q	L200	X	1-3,5,6,8
X3380	E	99						
X3381	E	100		D106	S	L204	Y	1-3,5,6,8
X3382	C	250		D110	R	L202	X	1-3,5,6,8
X3383	C	251		D111	S	L205	Y	1-3,5,6,8
X3384	C	251		D115	Q	L207	Z	1-6,8
X3385	C	247		D100	Q	L207	Z	1-6,8
X3386	E	245		D111	S	L216	Y	1-3,5,6,8
X3387	E	243		D110	R	L224	Y	1-3,5,6,8
X3388	D	252		D111	S	L207	Z	1-6,8
X3389	C	248		D115	Q	L205	Y	1-3,5,6,8
X3390	C	247		D106	S	L207	Z	1-6,8
X3391	C	246		D116	R	L207	Z	1-6,8
X3392	D	242		D11O	R	L223	Z	1-3,5,6,8
X3393	C	248		D115	Q	L207	Z	1-6,8
X3394	D	252		D111	S	L207	Z	1-6,8
X3395	E	244		D111	S	L223	Z	1-3,5,6,8
X3396	C	20		D111	S	L207	Z	1-6,8
X3397	D	24		D110	R	L209	Y	1-6,8
X3398	C	21		D111	S	L224	Y	1-3,5,6,8
X3399	D	25		D110	R	L224	Y	1-3,5,6,8
X3500	D	225						
X3501	B	87						
X3502	E	27						
X3550	D	122		D106	S	L220	Y	1-3,5,6,8
X3552	C	81		D100	Q	L224	Y	1-3,5,6,8
X3553	D	80		D111	S	L209	Y	1-6,8
X3554	E	271		D124	S	L219	Z	1-3,5,6,8
X3555	D	102		D101	R	L235	Z	1-3,5,6,8
X3564	B	111						

Toll Free 1-800-521-6797

Normal Office Hours:
8:00 a.m. to 8:00 p.m.
Eastern Time
Monday through Friday
Our staff will gladly answer any questions during normal office hours. Our answering service can place orders after hours or on weekends.

If we receive your order by 5:00 p.m. Eastern Time, Monday through Friday, we'll process it the same day and ship it the following business day.

When ordering by phone, please have your charge card ready. We'll also ask you for the Order Form Key Number at the bottom of the coupon on page 301. Please use our Toll-Free number for blueprint and book orders only. For Customization orders call 1-800-322-6797, ext. 134.

By FAX: Copy the Order Form on page 301 and send it on our International FAX line: 1-602-297-6219.

For Customization: 1-800-322-6797, ext. 134

Canadian Customers Order Toll-Free 1-800-848-2550

For faster, more economical service, Canadian customers may now call in orders on our Toll-Free line. Or, complete the order form on page 301, and mail with your check indicating U.S. funds to:

Home Planners, Inc.
3275 W. Ina Road, Suite 110
Tucson, AZ 85741

By FAX: Copy the Order Form on page 301 and send it on our International FAX line: 1-602-297-6219.

Before You Order . . .

Before completing the coupon at right or calling us on our Toll-Free Blueprint Hotline, you may be interested to learn more about our service and products. Here's some information you will find helpful.

Quick Turnaround

We process and ship every blueprint order from our office within 48 hours. On most orders, we do even better. Normally, if we receive your order by 5 p.m. Eastern Time, we'll process it the same day and ship it the following day. Because of this quick turnaround, we won't send a formal notice acknowledging receipt of your order.

Our Exchange Policy

Since blueprints are printed in response to your order, we cannot honor requests for refunds. However, we will exchange your entire first order for an equal number of blueprints plus the following exchange fees: $40 for the first set, $10 for each additional set; $60 total exchange fee for 4 sets; $90 total exchange fee for 8 sets.... *plus* the difference in cost if exchanging for a design in a higher price bracket, or *less* the difference in cost if exchanging for a design in a lower price bracket. (Sepias are not exchangeable.) All sets from the first order must be returned before the exchange can take place. Please add $8 for postage and handling via ground service; $20 via 2nd Day Air.

About Reverse Blueprints

If you want to build in reverse of the plan as shown, we will include an extra set of reversed blueprints (mirror image) for an additional fee of $50. Although lettering and dimensions appear backward, reverses will be a useful visual aid if you decide to flop the plan. Right-reading reverses of Customizable Plans are available through our Customization Service. Call for more details.

Modifying or Customizing Our Plans

With such a great selection of homes, you are bound to find the one that suits you. However, if you need to make alterations to a design that is customizable, you need only order our Customizer® kit or call our Customization representative at 1-800-322-6797, ext. 134, to get you started (see additional information on next page). It is possible to customize many of our plans that are not part of our Home Customizer® Service.

If you decide to revise plans significantly that are not customizable through our service, we strongly suggest that you order reproducible sepias and consult a licensed architect or professional designer to help you redraw the plans.

Architectural and Engineering Seals

Some cities and states are now requiring that a licensed architect or engineer review and "seal" your blueprints prior to construction. This is often due to local or regional concerns over energy consumption, safety codes, seismic ratings, etc. For this reason, you may find it necessary to consult with a local professional to have your plans reviewed. This can normally be accomplished with minimum delays, for a nominal fee. In some cases, Home Planners can seal your plans through our Customization Service. Call for more details.

Compliance with Local Codes and Regulations

At the time of creation, our plans are drawn to specifications published by Building Officials Code Administrators (BOCA), the Southern Standard Building Code, or the Uniform Building Code and are designed to meet or exceed national building standards. Some states, counties and municipalities have their own codes, zoning requirements and building regulations. Before starting construction, consult with local building authorities and make sure you comply with local ordinances and codes, including obtaining any necessary permits or inspections as building progresses. In some cases, minor modifications to your plans by your builder, local architect or designer may be required to meet local conditions and requirements. Home Planners may be able to make these changes to Customizable Plans providing you supply all pertinent information from your local building authorities.

Foundation and Exterior Wall Changes

Most of our plans are drawn with either a full or partial basement foundation. Depending upon your specific climate or regional building practices, you may wish to convert this basement to a slab or crawlspace. Most professional contractors and builders can easily adapt your plans to alternate foundation types. Likewise, most can easily convert 2x4 wall construction to 2x6, or vice versa. If you need more guidance on these conversions, our handy Construction Detail Sheets, shown on page 289, describe how such conversions can be made. For Customizable Plans, Home Planners can easily provide the necessary changes for you.

How Many Blueprints Do You Need?

A single set of blueprints is sufficient to study a home in greater detail. However, if you are planning to obtain cost estimates from a contractor or subcontractors—or if you are planning to build immediately—you will need more sets. Because additional sets are cheaper when ordered in quantity with the original order, make sure you order enough blueprints to satisfy all requirements. The following checklist will help you determine how many you need:

_____Owner

_____Builder (generally requires at least three sets; one as a legal document, one to use during inspections, and at least one to give to subcontractors)

_____Local Building Department (often requires two sets)

_____Mortgage Lender (usually one set for a conventional loan; three sets for FHA or VA loans)

_____TOTAL NUMBER OF SETS

Toll Free 1-800-521-6797

Normal Office Hours:
8:00 a.m. to 8:00 p.m. Eastern Time
Monday through Friday
Our staff will gladly answer any questions during normal office hours. Our answering service can place orders after hours or on weekends.

If we receive your order by 5:00 p.m. Eastern, Time, Monday through Friday, we'll process it the same day and ship it the following business day. When ordering by phone, please have your charge card ready. We'll also ask you for the Order Form Key Number at the bottom of the coupon. Please use our Toll-Free number for blueprint and book orders only.

For Customization orders call 1-800-322-6797, ext. 134.

By FAX: Copy the Order Form on the next page and send it on our International FAX line: 1-602-297-6219.

Canadian Customers
Order Toll-Free 1-800-848-2550

For faster, more economical service, Canadian customers may now call in orders on our Toll-Free line. Or, complete the order form at right, and mail with your check indicating U.S. funds to:

Home Planners, Inc.
3275 W. Ina Road, Suite 110
Tucson, AZ 85741

By FAX: Copy the Order Form on the next page and send it on our International FAX line: 1-602-297-6219.

The Home Customizer® 

Many of the plans in this book are customizable through our Home Customizer® service. Look for this symbol on the pages of home designs. It indicates that the plan on that page is part of The Home Customizer® service.

Some changes to customizable plans that can be made include:

- exterior elevation changes
- kitchen and bath modifications
- roof, wall and foundation changes
- room additions
- and much more!

If the plan you have chosen to build is one of our customizable homes, you can easily order the Home Customizer® kit to start on the path to making your alterations. The kit, priced at only $19.95, may be ordered at the same time you order your blueprint package by calling on our toll-free number or using the order blank at right. Or you can wait until you receive your blueprints, spend some time studying them and then order the kit by phone, FAX or mail. If you then decide to proceed with the customizing service, the $19.95 price of the kit will be refunded to you after your customization order is received. The Home Customizer® kit includes:

- instruction book with examples
- architectural scale
- clear acetate work film
- erasable red marker
- removable correction tape
- ¼" scale furniture cutouts
- 1 set of Customizable Drawings with floor plans and elevations

The service is easy, fast and *affordable*. Because we know and work with our plans and have them available on state-of-the-art computer systems, we can make the changes efficiently at prices much lower than those charged by normal architectural or drafting services. In addition, you'll be getting custom changes directly from Home Planners—the company whose dedication to excellence and long-standing professional experience are well recognized in the industry.

Call now to learn more about how simple it can be to have the *custom home* you've always wanted.

ORDER FORM

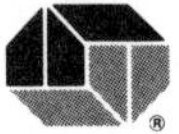

HOME PLANNERS, INC., 3275 WEST INA ROAD
SUITE 110, TUCSON, ARIZONA 85741

THE BASIC BLUEPRINT PACKAGE

Rush me the following (please refer to the Plans Index and Price Schedule in this section):

_____ Set(s) of blueprints for plan number(s) __________. $________
_____ Set(s) of sepias for plan number(s) __________. $________
_____ Additional identical blueprints in same order @ $50.00 per set. $________
_____ Reverse blueprints @ $50.00 per set. $________
_____ Home Customizer® Kit(s) for Plan(s)__________ @ $19.95 per kit. $________

IMPORTANT EXTRAS

Rush me the following:

_____ Materials List @ $40 Schedules A-D; $50 Schedule E $________
_____ Specification Outlines @ $7.00 each. $________
_____ Detail Sets @ $14.95 each; two for $22.95; three for $29.95; any four for $39.95 (Save $19.85). $________
❑ Plumbing ❑ Electrical ❑ Construction ❑ Mechanical
(These helpful details provide general construction advice and are not specific to any single plan.)
_____ Plan-A-Home® Kit @ $29.95 each. $________

DECK BLUEPRINTS

_____ Set(s) of Deck Plan __________. $________
_____ Additional identical blueprints in same order @ $5.00 per set. $________
_____ Reverse blueprints @ $5.00 per set. $________
_____ Set of Standard Deck Details @ $14.95 per set. $________
_____ Complete Deck Building Package (Best Buy!) Includes Custom Deck Plan __________ (see Index and Price Schedule) Plus Standard Deck Details. $________

LANDSCAPE BLUEPRINTS

_____ Set(s) of Landscape Plan __________. $________
_____ Additional identical blueprints in same order @ $10.00 per set. $________
_____ Reverse blueprints @ $10.00 per set. $________

Please indicate the appropriate region of the country for Plant & Material List. (See Map on page 290): Region __________

SUB-TOTAL $________

SALES TAX (Arizona residents add 5% sales tax; Michigan residents add 4% sales tax.) $________

POSTAGE AND HANDLING	1-3 sets	4 or more sets	
COMMERCIAL SERVICE (Requires street address - No P.O. Boxes)			
•Ground Service Allow 4-6 days delivery	❑ $6.00	❑ $8.00	$________
•2nd Day Air Service Allow 2-3 days delivery	❑ $12.00	❑ $20.00	$________
•Next Day Air Service Allow 1 day delivery	❑ $22.00	❑ $30.00	$________
POST OFFICE DELIVERY If no street address available. Allow 4-6 days delivery	❑ $8.00	❑ $12.00	$________
OVERSEAS AIR MAIL DELIVERY	❑ $30.00	❑ $50.00	$________
Note: All delivery times are from date Blueprint Package is shipped.	❑ Send COD		

TOTAL (Sub-total, tax, and postage) $________

YOUR ADDRESS (please print)

Name ______________________________

Street ______________________________

City ______________ State __________ Zip __________

Daytime telephone number (______) ______________

FOR CREDIT CARD ORDERS ONLY

Please fill in the information below:

Credit card number ______________________________

Exp. Date: Month/Year ______________________________

Check one ❑ Visa ❑ MasterCard ❑ Discover Card

Signature ______________________________

Please check appropriate box:

❑ Licensed Builder-Contractor
❑ Home Owner

Order Form Key: TB29

ORDER TOLL FREE
1-800-521-6797

Additional Plans Books

THE DESIGN CATEGORY SERIES

1\.

ONE-STORY HOMES
A collection of 470 homes to suit a range of budgets in one-story living. All popular styles, including Cape Cod, Southwestern, Tudor and French. **384 pages. $8.95 ($10.95 Canada)**

2\.

TWO-STORY HOMES
478 plans for all budgets in a wealth of styles: Tudors, Saltboxes, Farmhouses, Victorians, Georgians, Contemporaries and more. **416 pages. $8.95 ($10.95 Canada)**

3\.

MULTI-LEVEL AND HILLSIDE HOMES 312 distinctive styles for both flat and sloping sites. Includes exposed lower levels, open staircases, balconies, decks and terraces. **320 pages. $6.95 ($8.95 Canada)**

4\.

VACATION AND SECOND HOMES 258 ideal plans for a favorite vacation spot or perfect retirement or starter home. Includes cottages, chalets, and 1-, 1½-, 2-, and multi-levels. **256 pages. $5.95 ($7.50 Canada)**

THE EXTERIOR STYLE SERIES

9\.

THE ESSENTIAL GUIDE TO TRADITIONAL HOMES
Over 400 traditional homes in one special volume. American and European styles from Farmhouses to Norman French. "Readers' Choice" highlights best sellers in four-color photographs and renderings. **304 pages. $9.95 U.S. ($11.95 Canada)**

10\.

THE ESSENTIAL GUIDE TO CONTEMPORARY HOMES More than 340 contemporary designs from Northwest Contemporary to Post-Modern Victorian. Four-color section of best sellers; two-color illustrations and line drawings throughout the remainder. **304 pages. $9.95 U.S. ($11.95 Canada)**

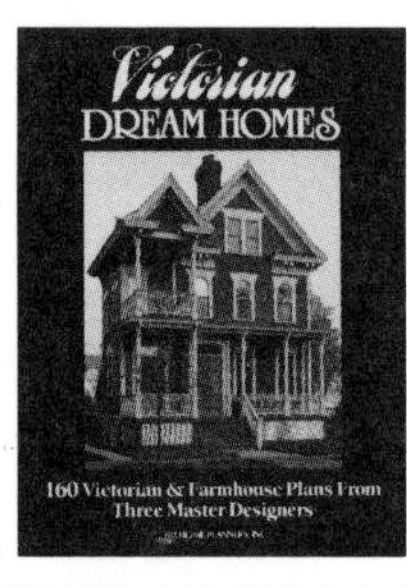

11\.

VICTORIAN DREAM HOMES 160 Victorian and Farmhouse designs by three master designers. Victorian style from Second Empire homes through the Queen Anne and Folk Victorian era. Beautifully drawn renderings accompany the modern floor plans. **192 pages. $12.95 ($15.95 Canada)**

12\.

WESTERN HOME PLANS
Over 215 home plans from Spanish Mission and Monte to Northwest Chateau and S Francisco Victorian. Historic notes trace the background and geographical incidence each style. **208 pages. $8.95 ($10.95 Canada)**

OUR BEST PLAN PORTFOLIOS

NEW ENCYCLOPEDIA OF HOME DESIGNS
Our best collection of plans is now bigger and better than ever! Over 500 plans organized by architectural category including all types and styles and 269 brand-new plans. The most comprehensive plan book ever.

15. **352 pages. $9.95 ($11.95 Canada)**

AFFORDABLE HOME PLANS For the prospective home builder with a modest or medium budget. Features 430 one-, 1½-, two-story and multi-level homes in a wealth of styles. Included are cost saving ideas for the budget-conscious.

16. **320 pages. $8.95 ($10.95 Canada)**

LUXURY DREAM HOMES At last, the home you've waited A collection of 150 of best luxury home pla from seven of the mo highly regarded desi ers and architects in United States. A drea come true for anyone interested in designi building or remodeli luxury home.

17. **192 pages. $14.95 ($17.95 Canada)**

HOME IMPROVEMENT AND LANDSCAPE BOOKS

5.

'HE HOME REMODELER revolutionary book of 31 emodeling plans backed by omplete construction-ready lueprints and materials lists. ections on kitchens, baths, naster bedrooms and much nore. Ideas galore; helpful dvice and valuable sugges- ions. **112 pages. $7.95 U.S. $9.95 Canada)**

6.

DECK PLANNER 25 practical plans and details for decks the do-it-yourselfer can actually build. How-to data and project starters for a variety of decks. Construction details available separately. **112 pages. $7.95 ($9.95 Canada)**

7.

THE HOME LANDSCAPER 55 fabulous front and back-yard plans that even the do-it-youselfer can master. Complete construction blueprints and regionalized plant lists available for each design. **208 pages. $12.95 ($15.95 Canada)**

8.

BACKYARD LANDSCAPER Sequel to the popular *Home Landscaper*, contains 40 professionally designed plans for backyards to do yourself or contract out. Complete construction blueprints and regionalized plant lists available. **160 pages. $12.95 ($15.95 Canada)**

INTRODUCING THE NEW BLUE RIBBON DESIGNER SERIES

13.

200 FARMHOUSES & COUNTRY HOME PLANS Styles and sizes to match every taste and budget. Grouped by type, the homes represent a variety from Classic Farmhouses to Country Capes & Cottages. Introductions and expertly drawn floor plans and renderings enhance the sections. **224 pages. $6.95 ($8.95 Canada)**

14.

200 BUDGET-SMART HOME PLANS The definitive source for the home builder with a limited budget, this volume shows that you can have your home and enjoy it, too! Amenity-laden homes, in many sizes and styles, can all be built from our plans. **224 pages. $6.95 ($8.95 Canada)**

Please fill out the coupon below. We will process your order and ship it from our office within 48 hours. Send coupon and check for the total to:

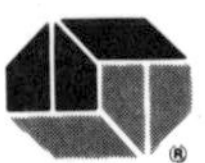

HOME PLANNERS, INC.
3275 West Ina Road, Suite 110, Dept. BK
Tucson, Arizona 85741

THE DESIGN CATEGORY SERIES—A great series of books edited by design type. Complete collection features 1376 pages and 1273 home plans.

1. _____One-Story Homes @ $8.95 ($10.95 Canada) $ _____
2. _____Two-Story Homes @ $8.95 ($10.95 Canada) $ _____
3. _____Multi-Level & Hillside Homes @ $6.95 ($8.95 Canada) $ _____
4. _____Vacation & Second Homes @ $5.95 ($7.50 Canada) $ _____

HOME IMPROVEMENT AND LANDSCAPE BOOKS

5. _____The Home Remodeler @ $7.95 ($11.95 Canada) $ _____
6. _____Deck Planner @ $7.95 ($9.95 Canada) $ _____
7. _____The Home Landscaper @ $12.95 ($15.95 Canada) $ _____
8. _____The Backyard Landscaper @ $12.95 ($15.95 Canada) $ _____

THE EXTERIOR STYLE SERIES

9. _____Traditional Homes @ $9.95 ($11.95 Canada) $ _____
10. _____Contemporary Homes @ $9.95 ($11.95 Canada) $ _____
11. _____Victorian Dream Homes @ $12.95 ($15.95 Canada) $ _____
12. _____Western Home Plans @ $8.95 ($10.95 Canada) $ _____

THE BLUE RIBBON DESIGNER SERIES

13. _____200 Farmhouse & Country Home Plans @ $6.95 ($8.95 Canada) $ _____
14. _____200 Budget-Smart Home Plans @ $6.95 ($8.95 Canada) $ _____

OUR BEST PLAN PORTFOLIOS

15. _____New Encyclopedia of Home Designs @ $9.95 ($11.95 Canada) $ _____
16. _____Affordable Home Plans @ $8.95 ($10.95 Canada) $ _____
17. _____Luxury Dream Homes @ $14.95 ($17.95 Canada) $ _____

Sub-Total $ _____
Arizona residents add 5% sales tax; Michigan residents add 4% sales tax $ _____
ADD Postage and Handling $ 3.00
TOTAL (Please enclose check) $ _____

Name (please print) _____
Address _____
City _____ State _____ Zip _____

CANADIAN CUSTOMERS: Order books Toll-Free 1-800-848-2550. Or, complete the order form above, and mail with your check indicating U.S. funds to: Home Planners, Inc. 3275 W. Ina Road, Suite 110, Tucson, AZ 85741.

TO ORDER BOOKS BY PHONE CALL TOLL FREE 1-800-322-6797

TB29BK

Where The Heart Is

Home Planners' Featured Home Design

Kathy and Mike Kalustian modeled their own home design after a house they had seen being constructed in Ohio. They inquired with the builder to discover that it was a Home Planners' design. After completing their own grand home, the Kalustians decided to build a home next door for Kathy's parents, so that they could be close to their grandchildren, Mike Jr. and Dallas.

Kathy and Mike chose this Home Planners design to remind her parents of their farm in West Virginia. They liked the look of the design—formal but with a touch of country. The porches add a welcoming look. In their quiet community of 14,000, this Victorian design has attracted a lot of attention. "Dozens and dozens of people stop by," says Kathy. "They say it is the prettiest house in Meadville, and have even given it a nickname—the gingerbread house."

Congratulations to Kathy, Mike and the rest of the family on a successful home-building experience.

Design X3309

First Floor: 1,375 square feet
Second Floor: 1,016 square feet
Total: 2,391 square feet
(also shown on the cover)

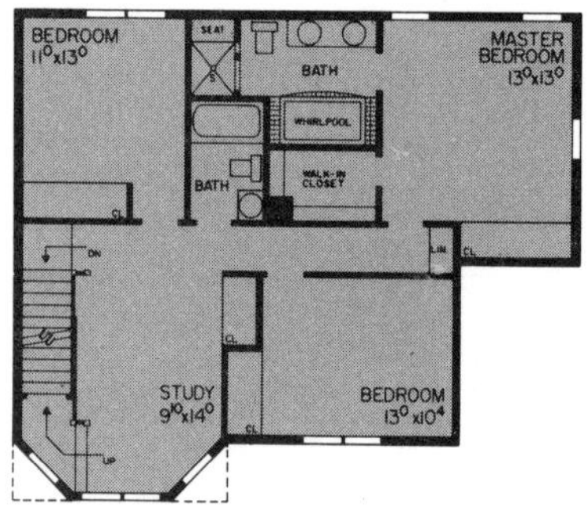

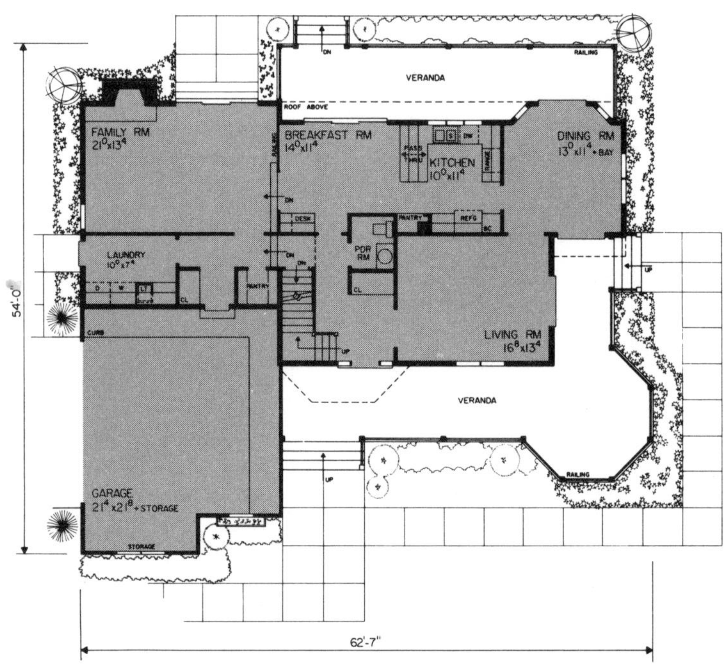

Plan as shown is built in reverse of above floor plans.

Andrew D. Lautman